ENDORSEMENTS

"If you have heard me speak, you already know I often talk about my dear friends on death row at Riverbend Maximum Security Institution in Nashville, Tennessee. KB (Kevin Burns) is one of these friends. This book is about KB and includes his close relationship with KR (Kevin Riggs), a Franklin pastor. If you are curious and want to hear a story of how an innocent man wound up on death row, read this book. If you want to know what day-to-day life is like on death row, read this book. If you want to hear a story of redemption that will surprise you, well, you know what to do. You can thank me later."

— **Paul Young**, author, *The Shack*

"Kevin Burns and Kevin Riggs are two of the most interesting and inspiring people I know. And I am elated that they have captured their story in writing. I've had the privilege of being on their journey with them for the past decade or so. KB is one of the first people I met on Tennessee's death row, and he has been firing me up ever since. I was present when KB was officially ordained by Kevin Riggs, and being served communion there on death row is one of the most powerful experiences of my life. This book is about grace, redemption, faith, and friendship. It is also a story about how broken our criminal justice system is and the lives that are on the line. Let this book move you, change you, and shape you into a revolutionary for love."

— **Shane Claiborne**, author and cofounder of Red Letter Christians

"I have known Kevin Burns (KB) for more than twenty years. I have been inspired by his faith and Christian example. I usually met KB when I went to Unit 2, RMSI, to serve communion to the Christians there on Sunday mornings. I have seen and admired his very positive relationships with the men housed there as well as the officers. He is deeply respected by all who know him. This book tells KB's story and is a strong statement of the failures and shortcomings in the justice and prison systems in the United States. I highly recommend this book to anyone who is concerned about justice and redemption."

— **Michael Duncan**

"Heartbreaking and hopeful, this book is a testament to the life-giving power of God's love as it confronts the death-dealing power of the state.

Pastors Kevin Burns and Kevin Riggs give us a rare glimpse into the machinations of the death penalty system from both an insider and outsider perspective, while demonstrating how their faith and friendship give them hope in the face of a system that often seems hopeless."

— **Stacy Rector**, executive director, Tennesseans for Alternatives to the Death Penalty

"Kevin Burns's (KB's) book (coauthored with Pastor Kevin Riggs), *Today Is the Best Day of My Life*, is essential reading for anyone wanting to understand prisoners and the role of faith in their lives. It is also, and relatedly, a priceless account of the relationship between a faith mentor and his prisoner friend. For those on the outside of prisons, the image of inmates is often shaped by reality TV documentaries, YouTube videos, and the nightly news. Through those lenses, prisoners appear as irredeemably evil and best locked up forever in their concrete cells. Understanding prisoners and the prison universe they inhabit requires seeing them from a different perspective. *Today Is the Best Day of My Life* provides that perspective. In its pages we read of crime, the streets of Memphis, arrest, and the criminal justice system. We learn of life in prison and the death penalty: all told from the vantage point of a person who is and has been there. Above all, we read the words of a man who has found God, and with the guidance and friendship of Pastor Riggs, committed to Him, studied, and lived His Word, and who has been called to become himself an ordained pastor serving the Lord. The title KB gave this book, *Today Is the Best Day of My Life*, is no mere throwaway line, no cliché ("have a nice day . . . ," "I appreciate you . . ."), but rather expresses the presence of a deep faith, the lived heart of the journey this book recounts. Despite what might appear to be terribly miserable years in prison, always in the shadow of the execution chamber, KB has found the best day of his life: a day, a life, of God's gifts, His comfort and the hope He gives each of us, whether in prison or outside. For the better part of the past ten years, I have been a faith volunteer at Riverbend prison's death row, where KB lives. Just about every Saturday, as I enter death row to meet with my group, I come across KB, and ask him, "How are things going, KB?" And every time, with a wide smile, he answers, "Today is the best day of my life!" He means it, and should you ask him how that can be so, he'll tell you that it is through his relationship with the Lord, with the One who consoles, encourages, and gives hope. There is much for all of us to learn from this faith-filled book."

— **Deacon James Booth**

TODAY!

###

THE BEST DAY OF MY LIFE

TODAY!

THE BEST DAY OF MY LIFE

KEVIN BURNS & KEVIN RIGGS

FLOODS OF JUSTICE
WORLDWIDE

TODAY!
THE BEST DAY OF MY LIFE

Copyright © 2024 Floods of Justice, Franklin, Tennessee
All rights reserved.

No part of this publication may be reproduced or transmitted in any form or by any means electronic or mechanical, including photocopy, recording, or any information storage and retrieval system now known or to be invented, without permission in writing from the publisher, except by a reviewer who wishes to quote brief passages in connection with a review written for inclusion in a magazine, newspaper, website, or broadcast. The web addresses referenced in this book were live and correct at the time of the book's publication but may be subject to change.

Scripture quotations are from the King James Version (public domain) and the Holy Bible, New International Version®, NIV® Copyright ©1973, 1978, 1984, 2011 by Biblica, Inc.® Used by permission. All rights reserved worldwide.

The Authors are represented by Ambassador Literary, Nashville, TN, www.ambassadoragency.com

Interior Layout Design and Typesetting: Lisa Parnell, lparnellbookservices.com

Book Design and Production: timmyroland.com

ISBN: 979-8-9899066-4-2 / *hardcover*
ISBN: 979-8-9899066-3-5 / *softcover*
ISBN: 979-8-9899066-5-9 / *e-book*

floodsofjustice.com

Manufactured in the United States of America
31 30 29 28 27 26 25 24 • 1 2 3 4 5

To my beloved son,
Zachary Kevin Riggs.
(1 Thessalonians 4:13)

Kevin Riggs

To my parents, Obra Carter and Leslie Burns,
and to my daughter, Briana Royston.
They have been my anchors, and the ones who have kept me
focused and centered through this entire ordeal.

Of most importance, to my Lord and Savior Jesus Christ.

Kevin Burns

This is the only picture of Kevin Burns (left) and Kevin Riggs. The picture was taken on Monday, January 29, 2018, by a prison official during the ordination service of Kevin Burns in building 2-A, Riverbend Maximum Security Institution.

CONTENTS

Introduction 1

PART ONE: FELONY MURDER

1. Captain Rutledge 11
2. Relief Denied 17
3. My Birthday 29
4. Arrested 35
5. The Trial and Sentencing 41
6. Zachary Kevin Riggs 49
7. My Journey to Death Row 57
8. The Politics Behind Capital Punishment 67
9. The Liturgy of Death 75

PART TWO: LIFE ON DEATH ROW

10. Ordination 85
11. Life on Death Row 97
12. Church of Life 105
13. Cell by Cell 113
14. Suicide 125
15. COVID 133
16. Four-Leaf Clovers 141
17. Come Pray with Us 145

CONTENTS

PART THREE: FRIENDSHIP AND REDEMPTION

18. Growing Up 155
19. Arson 161
20. A New Car 167
21. A Familiar Story 175
22. A Sermon 183
23. Encourage Yourself 193
24. Dreams and Visions 201
25. What Now? 217

Afterword 225
Acknowledgments 227
Endnotes 229
About the Authors 231

INTRODUCTION

REV. KEVIN BURNS (KB)

Growing up in a large family meant there was always something to do and always someone to play with. But sometimes I wanted to be left alone. During those times, I went to my bedroom and lay on the bed and thought about life. I thought about decisions people make, why people do what they do, and why bad things happen to good people. You know, things that a lot of people think about.

Once while I was laying on my bed, my mom walked in. It was about six o'clock in the evening. She asked, "Son, are you all right?" I responded, "Yeah, Mom. I'm just thinking." I remember my mom saying, "That's good. Thinking makes a man out of you."

When I first went to prison, I remember thinking, *It seems like some people always have it good, while other people always have it bad*, and I wondered why it was that way. But now as a pastor, I understand more. The Bible says God "sendeth rain on the just and on the unjust" (Matthew 5:45). Through it all, I have learned that life is the sum total of your experiences. Now my thoughts are different. Life is not about what happens to you but about how you respond to what happens to you. How you respond to tragedies. How you respond to circumstances, be they good or bad. I have chosen to respond in faith and hope. God's Word promises, "And we know that all things work together for good to them that love God" (Romans 8:28). We live in a broken world. When Adam and Eve ate the forbidden fruit, sin entered the world. One day Jesus will make everything right again, but until then, good things and bad things happen to all of us.

I think, in part, this book is how I have responded to what has happened in my life. My prayer is that your perspective on life will change because you hear and read my story. I pray you will learn to respond in faith and hope, regardless of what circumstance you find yourself in.

Years ago I adopted a phrase that I have made an integral part of my life. When people ask me how I am doing, I respond, "Today is the best day of my life." That is my motto—regardless of how I am feeling and regardless of what I am going through. By faith I say, "Today is the best day of my life." For me this has become more than a slogan; it has become a way of life.

But that statement is not original with me. My childhood pastor was Rev. George Moore. He pastored Old St. Paul's Missionary Baptist Church for as long as I can remember. Several years ago, my sister called me and said, "I need to tell you some bad news. Pastor Moore has passed away."

I could not believe my ears. He was such a kind and compassionate man. I asked, "What happened?"

"He was preaching last Sunday," my sister said, "and at the end of his sermon, he had a heart attack and fell behind the pulpit. The deacons of the church ran to help him. One deacon cradled Pastor Moore in his arms. Then Pastor Moore took one big breath and said loud enough for everyone to hear, 'Today is the best day of my life,' and then he died.

INTRODUCTION

I said to my sister, "Wow! What an incredible testimony. I want that to be my testimony." That's when I decided to adopt that phrase, "Today is the best day of my life."

Before you start reading this book, I want to pray for you.

Father, in the name of Jesus, I pray over every reader of this book.
I thank You for Pastor Kevin Riggs.
I thank You for moving on his heart the desire to get my story out.
I thank You for the grace You have bestowed upon us
and all You have blessed us with
and given us the ability to dig deep into my story and write these words.
I pray these words will have an effect on those who read it.
I pray they will see and understand how a relationship with You changes everything.
Not just somethings but everything.
I pray we all put our hope in You.
You are that faithful God who is able, according to Your Word,
to do exceedingly and abundantly and above all we can ask and think,
according to the power that already resides in us (Ephesians 3:20-21).

And so, Father I pray Your grace and Your mercy
over Your people, that their perception of the things that happen in their life,
whether good or bad, may change
and that they may learn, as Your people, the value You place on our lives
and Your desire to have us all working together with You,
as co-workers, reaching out to save Your people.

*Thank You for calling us to participate with You,
redeeming Your people and calling Your people back,
and healing the hurts we have experienced in our lives.*

*Father, I just thank You so much for all You have done in my life
and all You are doing and all You are yet to do.*

*Father, I thank You for Your love.
I thank You for all Your provisions.
I thank You for all the people You have strategically placed in my life
to help me now, O God, and the hearts You are moving in people.
I see Your hand at work, moving the hearts of people to have compassion
and to help lead in my situation.*

*I pray, Lord God, that Your grace may be extended
and the same mercy You have shown me
be shown to all who read this book.
I pray they will grab hold of the lessons You have taught me,
that they may grab them and hold on to them by faith,
Lord God.
And that they may exercise them and try them
and put them to good use in their lives
to grow stronger in their faith as they see You working in their lives
and in their circumstances.*

*Lord, I honor and praise You for all these wonderful blessings.
In Christ Jesus's name I pray.
Amen.*

REV. DR. KEVIN RIGGS (KR)

It all started with an article in my local newspaper. The article stated that over the next thirteen months Tennessee would carry out ten executions! It had been more than a decade since an execution. Now, in a relatively short time, Tennessee would murder 13 percent of the total population of men and women on death row. Not long after I read the article, I heard the Spirit say, "Go to death row." At the time I did not know where death row was in Tennessee. Knowing I heard God speak, I did some research, made some phone calls, and by the end of that summer, made my first visit to Unit Two at Riverbend Maximum Security Institution, the home of Tennessee's death row. That was over ten years ago. While ten executions over thirteen months never happened, during the past five years, there have been seven executions. I've said goodbye to seven friends, all of which were image bearers of the Divine.

I remember my first visit to death row. It was a Friday, and I was to meet with several of the men in Unit 2 who gathered for prayer at noon. While I had been involved in prison ministry off and on since I was a teenager, I knew visiting death row would be different. I was nervous. I didn't know what to expect. What was it like sitting in prison waiting to die? What would we talk about?

After clearing a metal detector, an x-ray machine, several secured gates, and metal doors, I walked into a room where several guys in prison uniforms sat around a table. The prison's chaplain introduced me, and before she could finish the introduction, one of the men got up from his chair, approached me with a huge smile, hugged me tight, and said, "I have been praying for you." I was speechless. I stood there and wept. It was a holy moment. With that single embrace, I knew I was accepted and loved. I went to death row expecting to take Jesus with me. Instead, I met Jesus there.

The name of the man who said he had been praying for me was Kevin Burns, TDOC# 254315. (TDOC stands for Tennessee Department of Corrections.) Someone once told me when God gives a gift, God usually wraps it in a person. One of the greatest gifts God has given me is Kevin Burns, also known as KB.

KB has been on death row (also known as Unit 2) since 1995. During much of that time, he has served as the chaplain's assistant to the men in Unit 2. It's a job in which he gets paid 50 cents an hour. KB and I quickly became friends and co-workers. At least once a week, KB made his rounds, going cell to cell talking, praying, and encouraging each man on Unit 2. I started joining him on these rounds. Over time, through KB, I met all the men on death row. I consider them my friends. The conversations I have had with each man has been priceless. But the times I have spent talking and praying with KB are treasures I will hide in my heart as long as I live.

HOW TO READ THIS BOOK

First and foremost, keep in mind that this book is not a biography. It is a story about an innocent man on death row and his friendship with a local church pastor. The stories are not necessarily chronological. Instead, they are divided into three parts: Part 1 is titled "Felony Murder" and describes what happened, from a crime to the trial and through the appeals process, which resulted in an innocent man being condemned to die. Part 2 is titled "Life on Death Row," and it's exactly what the title suggests. Part 3 is titled "Friendship and Redemption." This part consists of various stories of how the friendship between Kevin Burns and Kevin Riggs has changed each of them and some of the experiences they have had doing ministry together.

Also in this book, sometimes you will read "death row," and other times you will read "Unit 2." These refer to the same place and are used interchangeably. Death row is housed in Unit 2 at Riverbend Maximum Security Institution in Nashville, Tennessee.

Another important thing in reading this book is to pay attention to the designations "(KR)" and "(KB)." This explains who is talking. (KR) stands for Kevin Riggs. (KB) stands for Kevin Burns. Because both KR and KB share the first name "Kevin," the guys on Unit 2 often differentiate them by saying "KB," Kevin Burns' long-standing nickname, and "BK," meaning "Big Kevin." KR is 6'4" tall and weighs far more than he wishes he did.

Something else to keep in mind, with few exceptions, when I am talking about other men who are in prison, I have changed their names to protect identities. Also all the names surrounding the events on April 20, 1992, with the exception of KB's, have been changed as well. Even when using real names, with rare exceptions, I only use first names. Again, all of this is in an attempt to protect identities.

Finally, a lot of scripture verses are in this book. As you read those verses, keep the following in mind: KB prefers the King James Version (KJV) of the Bible. KR prefers the New International Version (NIV) of the Bible. So, if KB is referring to scripture, that scripture, with a few exceptions, comes from the KJV. If KR is referring to scripture, unless otherwise noted, that scripture comes from the NIV.

■ ■ ■

"May the groans of the prisoners come before you;
with your strong arm preserve those condemned to die."
(Psalm 79:11)

Part One
FELONY MURDER
■ ■ ■

*"God, if the State kills me, it's on You! I'm done.
I can't do this anymore. I'm through with it."*
KEVIN BURNS

*"Capital Punishment is a liturgy to the god
of punitive justice that ends with a human sacrifice."*
KEVIN RIGGS

CHAPTER 1
CAPTAIN RUTLEDGE

*"A savage person goes into the 201 and comes out humbled.
A humble man goes into the 201 and comes out a savage."*

■ ■ ■

(KB) The Shelby County (Memphis, Tennessee) Jail can be an intimidating place. At one time it had the reputation as one of the most dangerous jails in the United States. No one calls it the Shelby County Jail. Everyone I know refers to it by its address, 201 Poplar, or more simply as "the 201." I arrived at the 201 in July of 1992. In 1991, there was a riot inside, on the fourth floor, where violent offenders were housed. The riot was caused by overcrowding and did more than $3 million in damage. No one wanted to go to 201 Poplar. Its violent reputation was well earned.

(KR) Let me interrupt here. As KB and I sat at a table inside his pod (B-pod, also known as Baltimore Pod) and started talking about the Shelby County Jail, several other guys in the pod, when they heard us say, "201 Poplar," wanted to get in on the conversation. Everyone had their own experience inside this notorious county jail. Over the next thirty minutes, I experienced the most animated, energetic conversation I have ever had with the guys in Unit 2. They described the 201 as "chaos within chaos." One man, who goes by the nickname "Batman," said, "That jail will center-you-up real quick and make you call on God." He then continued, "A savage person goes into the 201 and comes out humbled. A humble man goes into the 201 and comes out a savage."

(KB) 201 Poplar is a long skinny building that has a basement, called Lower Level, and six floors. It was built to hold 2,500 men, but in the late 1980s and early 1990s, far more were housed there. Many inmates slept on the floor in the middle of the pods. The jail was made up of multiple pods. Each pod had twenty-four six-by-eight cells. Two men were in each cell for a total of forty-eight men in each pod.

The floors were colored coded with the exception of the first floor, which was for juveniles who had been charged and convicted as adults. The second floor was yellow. The walls were painted white with a yellow stripe across the wall, and the men wore yellow uniforms. The second floor was for those in protective custody. The third floor had a blue stripe across the white walls, and the men wore blue uniforms. The fourth floor was green, with a green stripe and green uniforms. The men on the fourth floor had been charged with the most violent charges, and as a result, the fourth floor was the most violent floor. At the far end of the fourth floor was a separate pod. Once a juvenile, who had been charged as an adult, turned eighteen, he was sent to this pod. The fifth floor was made up of the men who worked in the kitchen for the entire jail. They wore white uniforms. The sixth floor was brown. The walls were painted white with a brown stripe across the wall, and the men wore brown uniforms. This floor was the education floor and was the best floor to be on.

The Lower Level, the basement, was the first place a person went to once they were sent to 201 Poplar. The Lower Level also

CAPTAIN RUTLEDGE

housed the visitation rooms. I spent the first ten days inside 201 on the Lower Level. I was traumatized to be in this horrible place. While I was in jail in Chicago, waiting to be brought to Memphis, a man gave to me a green and white paperback Bible. I spent those first ten days laying on my bunk, reading that Bible, praying, and trying to block out all the noise of the men around me. The other men talked, fearful about what floor they would end up on. No one wanted to go to the fourth floor. After ten days I received my classification. Because of the seriousness of my charge, I went to the fourth floor, and remained there for about thirty months. Eventually I was moved to sixth floor where I worked as a teacher's aide for several months.

From the fourth floor, I started leading Bible studies and prayer groups. It started with me doing personal Bible study and prayer in my cell. Not long after I arrived on the fourth floor, my cellmate started joining me for prayer and Bible study. Then, one by one, others guys started showing up to my cell at 8:00 p.m. They asked if I would teach them the Bible. I simply shared with them what I was learning. We studied the Bible from 8:00 to 10:00 each night. My cell was usually crowded, and the guys asked me lots of questions. I relied on the Holy Spirit to give me answers. Then around 10:00 p.m., I went out into the pod and called the entire pod to prayer. We stood in a big circle and prayed until 10:30 p.m. That's when we were locked in our cells for the night. Every night, this thirty minutes was the most powerful and impactful part of our day.

Inside 201 Poplar one officer helped me more than any other. Her name was Captain Rutledge. She was a stout woman, stood six feet tall, and had paper sack brown skin. Captain Rutledge was in her late forties and wore her black hair up in a bun. She had a very stern but also very calming voice. She was a powerful woman. Above all, Captain Rutledge was a great woman of faith. She encouraged me in my own faith, and even said to me once, "KB, your faith inspires me. I think it was your faith that drew me to you when you first got here. Your faith will see you through whatever it is you have to go through."

Captain Rutledge started a choir inside 201 Poplar. I loved being a part of that choir. We practiced every day. Which meant we got to go to the chapel every day and sing and rehearse and, most importantly, pray. Being a part of this choir helped me stay strong and grow in my faith. On one occasion, we were able to have a concert inside the jail. It was great! My mom and dad were there and got to hear me sing. My favorite song was Kirk Franklin's, "He's Able." I loved the lyrics: "He's able. . . . I know that He can do it. He said He'd help me through it. . . . Hold on, my brother, your change is gonna come."[1] I would not be the person I am today without the influence of this choir and Captain Rutledge. It was during this time that God promised me He would, one day, deliver me from prison. It's a promise I have held onto every day since.

THE WATERFALL VISION

I will never forget the day I was sentenced to death. I was in shock! I never expected to be found guilty, much less be given capital punishment. After the sentencing, the officers led me back to a holding cell inside the Shelby County Courthouse to await transportation back to the Shelby County Jail. In the hallway leading to the holding cell was Captain Rutledge. As soon as she saw me, with tears in her eyes, she said, "Come here, child." I began sobbing, went to her, and planted my face on her right shoulder. She embraced me and lovingly said, "Burns, do not be discouraged. God knows what He is doing. He has not abandoned you, and neither is He finished with you." She held me for what seemed like an eternity. I cried until there were no more tears, and then I cried some more.

After several moments of uncontrolled emotions, I heard the Holy Spirit say to me, "All right, my son, that is enough. Refrain from this embrace." I pulled away from Captain Rutledge. She continued to speak encouragement over me, but I could no longer hear her because, at that moment, I received a vision. It is hard to describe what happened next. Like the apostle Paul, I can say, "I knew a man in Christ above fourteen years ago, (whether in the body, I cannot tell; or whether out of the body, I cannot tell: God knoweth;) such an one caught up to the third heaven. And I knew such a man, (whether in the body, or out of the body, I cannot tell: God knoweth;) How that he was caught up into paradise, and heard unspeakable words, which it is not lawful for a man to utter" (2 Corinthians 12:2–4 KJV).

In this vision I looked down and saw two feet standing in water. As I began looking up, past the knees, to the chest, and finally to the face, I realized I was looking into the eyes of my Lord, Jesus Christ. Jesus was standing right in front of me but also behind a waterfall. Yet He was not wet, and neither was I. The source of the waterfall was high above him and beyond my ability to see. But from His eyes, Jesus was crying tears that added to the rush of the falls. I knew His tears were for me. Jesus then asked me, "Why are you crying?" I could not answer, so Jesus asked me again, "Why are you crying?" Once again, I could not answer. All I could do was look at His face and into His eyes.

Then Jesus said, "Didn't I tell you I was going to deliver you? Go on the way they are going to send you. I have need of you there. I have a work for you to do in that place, and I am not finished with my work in you. When I finish my work in you and you finish my work in that place, then I am going to deliver you like I told you."

As I was looking into His eyes, Jesus began ascending up the waterfall and through the ceiling. As He ascended, I felt a shadow of warmth and love envelope me and a wind fall upon me. I thought to myself, *This is like Elijah's mantle falling on Elisha in 2 Kings 2:13–14.* Jesus's departing words to me were, "Peace I leave with you; my peace I give you. I do not give to you as the world gives. Do not let your hearts be troubled and do not be afraid" (John 14:27).

When Jesus left the room, strength, life, and faith returned to me. When my focus returned to the present, Captain Rutledge was still standing there talking. She had never stopped talking. She looked at my countenance and knew something miraculous had happened. In reality, she had no idea how miraculous it really was. Captain Rutledge broke into a big smile. I was smiling as well. Then we both started laughing, right there in the hallways in front of a holding cell at the Shelby County Courthouse; right after receiving the death penalty, we both stood there laughing. We then gave each other the biggest bear hug I had ever given, or received, in my entire life. The power in that place, meant for death, was palatable. Years later, I wrote a letter to Captain Rutledge, telling her thank you and telling her about my vision. I never heard back. I will never know if she received it. I hope and pray she did. She was God's angel, sent to me during my darkest night.

(KR) Over the years KB has told me about several visions he has had. The "Waterfall Vision," as I call it, is one of the more powerful ones. Once I asked KB how he knew these visions were real. He just laughed and said, "They are as real as you and I sitting here talking." And I believed him. KB continued to tell me, "The voice of God is tangible. You hear God's voice in the inside of your soul, not outside your body. God's voice is like no other. There is no mistake in who He is and what He says." Again, I believe him.

CHAPTER 2
RELIEF DENIED

*"OK, God. Here it is; this is Yours.
My trust is in You, not in the courts."*

■ ■ ■

"The United States Supreme Court has denied you relief."

That's the news I (KB) received from my lawyers on Monday, April 24, 2023. Four days after my fifty-fourth birthday. A week earlier, on April 17, Joey, my charge-mate, convicted of the same crime as me, walked out of prison on parole. A few years earlier, my other charge-mate, Thomas, convicted of the same crime, walked out of prison on parole. I didn't shoot anyone. I didn't kill anyone. I am innocent. Why am I still in prison and they are free? Why am I on death row?

After hearing the bad news, I sat in silence for several minutes. My lawyer finally asked me, "How are you feeling? What's going on in your mind?" I pondered his questions, then through faith, with a little bit of doubt, I said, "Today is still the best day of my life." I thought of the story in the Gospels when a man asked Jesus to heal his sick child. Jesus asked him, "Do you really believe I can heal your daughter?" The man answered, "I believe; help thou mine unbelief" (Mark 9:24). That's how I felt at the moment. I believed, but I needed Jesus to help me with my doubts. I immediately found comfort in the fact God has granted me relief, even while the government has not.

(KR) My faith is not as strong as KB's. When I heard he had been denied relief, my heart sank. Even though I was told the United States Supreme Court ruling in favor of KB was a long shot, I held out hope. Like KB, I wanted to believe, but I struggled with my own unbelief. I tried to hold tightly to the following promise from Scripture: "The LORD looked down from his sanctuary on high, from heaven he viewed the earth, to hear the groans of the prisoners and release those condemned to death" (Psalm 102:19–20). The writer of Proverbs accurately confessed, "Hope deferred makes the heart sick" (Proverbs 13:12). My heart was sick. One week earlier, my son was killed in a car wreck. For me, KB's news was grief upon grief.

APPEALS

Not long after a person is sentenced to death, the appeals process begins. Sometimes, within the first year of being on death row, a person receives their first execution date from a state's supreme court. This first execution date never ends in death, but it is haunting nonetheless. The first round of appeals, examining errors that happened during the trial, is referred to as "direct appeals." For KB, this process, which can take years, started at the Tennessee Court of Criminal Appeals and ended with the Tennessee Supreme Court reviewing all motions filed by KB's lawyers and reviewing the transcripts of the trial to see whether it was conducted in a constitutionally fair manner. Arguing on behalf of KB before both courts were the very same court-appointed lawyers who represented him at trial. While it is possible to win on appeal, it is difficult, especially if the court-appointed lawyers did an inadequate job at trial. KB's trial was full of ineffective representation, but because it was the same trial lawyers, this argument was not raised in this first round of appeals. In fact, ineffective representation is rarely raised on direct appeal. When it is raised, the court of criminal appeals almost always says the issue is not properly developed and should be addressed at the post-conviction phase. Unfortunately, on direct appeal no meritorious issues were raised. In some ways, this first appeal is nothing more than a formality. In fact, KB told me he doesn't know when his direct appeal was filed, and he has never seen what was filed. But he is also quick to admit his approach to all the appeals has been different from other people on death row.

Most people on death row are heavily involved with their lawyers during the entire appeals process. They become consumed by the whole process. It's all they talk about, and they dwell on it day and night. At times, they argue with their lawyers and fire their lawyers, only to fight with their new lawyers. I've often told KB that is how I would be, especially if I were innocent. KB has had his differences with his lawyers. But for the most part, he has decided to let the process play out, and in his own words, "Leave it to God to defend him." Two significant things occurred to KB that caused him to take this approach.

The first came from an experience that happened to him while awaiting trial in the Shelby County Jail in Memphis, Tennessee. Not long after being extradited from Cook County Jail in Chicago, a minister, Bishop Coppinger, came to the Shelby County Jail and visited KB regularly, mentoring him. One evening before he left, Bishop Coppinger gave KB his large, worn-out study Bible. At the time, the only Bible KB had was the one he received while in jail in Chicago. All throughout the bishop's Bible were his handwritten notes. KB read that Bible and studied all the notes. As a result, his faith grew by leaps and bounds.

Bishop Coppinger was an old man who still wore 1970s style clothing. He held services every Wednesday evening in the jail. An older white lady came with him and played the piano. An older white man, who always wore checkered pants, played the guitar. Regularly, they all sang "His Eye Is on the Sparrow." Describing Bishop Coppinger and his team, KB says, "While they would sing, Bishop Coppinger would cry, but their voices were like angels from heaven. Most of the other guys in prison would make fun of them. It was obvious how much they loved us. When I would see them start to cry, I would start to cry."

(KB) The very first time I met Bishop Coppinger he prophesied over me. He came up to me after the Wednesday night service, his eyes still red from crying, and said to me, "What is your name, baby?" I told him my name, and then he said, "I can see the Spirit of God all over you. God speaks to you through dreams and visions, doesn't He?" I said, "Yes." Then he said, "God has called you to preach. God is saying to you, 'You are my prophet and my preacher.'" I didn't tell anyone about this.

Two weeks later, Bishop Coppinger said to me, "You have not told anyone you have been called to preach, have you?" I said, "No sir." He said, "You call your mom and dad right now and tell them. Then when you get off the phone, you tell everyone in your pod." So that's what I did.

(KR) The second experience was after a heated exchange with his lawyer, early in the appeals process. The lawyer wanted to argue KB's appeal in a way he disagreed with. After several minutes of intense conversation, in frustration, KB got quiet and angrily prayed, "God, if the State kills me, it's on You! I'm done. I can't do this anymore. I'm through with it." Instantly, he heard God respond in his spirit,

"Good! That's exactly what I want you to do. Give it to Me. I will defend you." Immediately God began filling him with joy and peace and comfort. KB had to put his hand over his mouth to keep from laughing in the presence of his lawyer. Since that day, when KB receives any paperwork from his lawyers, he places the paperwork on the Bible the man gave him and prays, "OK, God. Here it is; this is Yours. My trust is in You, not in the courts."

KB told me laying the papers on top of the Bible and praying to God over them comes from a story in the Bible that I had never noticed. In the book of Isaiah, the Assyrian army captured Judah. Sennacherib, the king of Assyria, sent his messenger, Rabshakeh, to Hezekiah, the king of Judah. Rabshakeh's message was full of threats, lies, boasts, and blasphemies. Upon receiving the intimidating letter, Hezekiah took the letter to the temple "and spread it out before the Lord" and prayed (Isaiah 37). At the end of the prayer, Hezekiah said, "Lord our God, deliver us" (v. 20). That is KB's prayer, and he knows it is only God who can deliver him. God has given KB the assurance that everything is in His hands and He isn't bound by the courts of law and their man-made procedures. Knowing God is in control is what enables KB to every day say, "Today is the best day of my life."

Following direct appeal comes post-conviction. KB was sentenced in 1995. His post-conviction began in September of 2002. Post-conviction is different from direct appeal in that new evidence can be presented. The most common argument at post-conviction, and the one that has the best chance of success, is "ineffective assistance of counsel." At this stage, KB's lawyers (different lawyers from direct appeal) presented proof that should have been heard at trial that was not heard because of ineffective trial lawyers. One key example is that an eyewitness identified the shooter as "a big man in glasses with a Jheri curl." KB is five feet seven, has never worn glasses, and at the time of the shooting, his hair was closely shaved. Post-conviction is the first opportunity a condemned person gets to show how his trial lawyers misrepresented him and how that misrepresentation shaped the outcome of the trial. However, it is not enough to show the trial lawyers did a terrible job. You have to prove it would have made a difference in the outcome if they did a better job. At post-conviction, the court concluded that KB did not suffer prejudice because of ineffective assistance of counsel.

The next step was before the United States District Court for the Western District of Tennessee (Memphis, Tennessee). Many issues were raised before this court, including ineffective assistance of counsel at guilt stage, arguing that they were deficient and that KB suffered prejudice. It was argued that a competent attorney would have proven his innocence. The problem is, at this phase, you cannot appeal all things; you can only appeal issues that the district court (or the court of appeals) decides are worth appealing by giving to you a "Certificate of Appealability" (COA). In KB's case he received a COA on ineffective assistance at penalty phase but not at guilt phase. Thus, from this point forward, the only thing KB's lawyers can argue is that his death sentence is unfair. They cannot argue his innocence.

After the district court phase, a person's case is turned over to the Federal Public Defenders office. Now things move from state courts to federal courts. For KB, the next stop in this long process was the Sixth Circuit Court, which represents Tennessee, Ohio, and Michigan. The Sixth Circuit Court is located in Cincinnati, Ohio. KB's case went before a three-judge panel in Cincinnati in February of 2020. One month before the COVID pandemic, and I was there.

It was a cold, rainy February morning when KB's lawyers argued before the Sixth Circuit Court. Their main argument was that the Tennessee Court of Criminal Appeals had ruled contrary to clearly established law in concluding that it did not matter whether KB had killed anyone, and the fact KB's lawyers did not talk to any possible mitigation witnesses until an hour or so before putting them on the witness stand, was not evidence of ineffective assistance of counsel. More than two years later, the court ruled the fact KB did not kill anyone was "residual doubt," and his lawyers, who appeared before the Sixth Circuit Court, had no constitutional right to present that argument. The court also concluded KB's original lawyers had done an adequate job.

PETITION FOR CERTIORARI

The average time between a person's death sentence and execution, across the United States, is almost twenty years.[2] The final stop is the United States Supreme Court. On October 20, 2022, KB's lawyers filed a "petition for certiorari" in the Supreme Court. Once again, KB's appeal was based on "inadequate assistance of counsel at the penalty phase of his trial." All KB was asking for was a new sentencing trial. KB's lawyers were asking the United States Supreme Court to reverse the decision of the Sixth Circuit Court, something the Supreme Court almost never does. When KB was denied relief, he had been on death row twenty-eight years. He spent over three years in the Shelby County Jail awaiting trial. All total, at the time of this writing, he had spent thirty-one years incarcerated for a crime he did not commit!

Along with the petition for certiorari filed to the United States Supreme Court, five other friends of KB and I filed an "Amicus Brief" ("friends of the court") on KB's behalf. In this brief we stated, "The record in this case shows that Petitioner Kevin Burns did not take a life. Under the tenets of our faith and the law of the land, if the death penalty is ever to be applied, it must be reserved for the worst offenders. Because Burns did not take a life, it is unjust for the state to put him to death. Due to the ineffective assistance of counsel, the jury that passed Burns's sentence was not given the opportunity to take his lack of moral culpability into account in making its decision. This error cannot be allowed to stand."

The Amicus Brief summarized the arguments in the lawyers' petition for certiorari but also emphasized KB's Christian character and ministry. Below is an example of what we wrote:

> *Amicus curiae* are fortunate to be in a position to inform the Court that Kevin Burns leads an exceptional life despite his confinement in prison. When people ask how he is doing, Burns is known to respond, "Today is the best day of my life." His accomplishments are exemplified by the fact Burns became an ordained minister five years ago through the Franklin Community Church in Franklin, Tennessee. This was no small feat. Burns's ordination was the culmination of a multi-year process that required Burns to prove his active ministry by tracking and recording his ministries over time and to answer questions about Christian doctrine. Burns's accomplishment is all the more impressive because he is self-taught in prison, relying on little more than his well-worn copy of the Bible.
>
> But Burns is committed to his ministry. "Pastor Kevin," as he is known even by the prison guards, draws inspiration from a passage from the Book of Esther: "And who knows but that you have come to royal position for such a time as this" (Esther 4:14). Burns embodies the moral of this passage to turn one's circumstances into a calling to act for the benefit of others.
>
> Burns believes that he was placed on death row to be of service to fellow inmates, especially those facing

execution. He established a church—the Church of Life—through which he ministers to fellow inmates. Burns gave particular comfort to inmates during the COVID-19 pandemic. Outside ministries were prohibited from entering the prison, but every week there was a church service on death row because Pastor Kevin could lead it. Burns is often one of the last people inmates speak with before their execution.

Burns's ministry extends well beyond prison, though. Burns is employed as a minister at Franklin Community Church and regularly preaches to members of the church by telephone. This year, for instance, he will deliver sermons to the church during Thanksgiving and Christmas. Burns also teaches a weekly Bible study for Franklin Community Church families. Internationally, he corresponds with a fellow pastor ministering from prison in Honduras.

These stories are relevant not just because of what they reveal about Burns's character now. They are relevant because if Burns's trial counsel had performed a constitutionally adequate job, the sentencing jury would have seen that Burns has overcome difficult circumstances his entire life.

In denying relief, the United States Supreme Court simply said, "The petition for a writ of certiorari is denied." Straight forward and brutal, without explanation. The vote was six to three. Justices Sonia Sotomayor, Elena Kagan, and Ketanji Brown Jackson dissented, with Justice Sotomayor writing the dissent. In her dissent, Justice Sotomayor wrote,

Burns asserts that counsel failed to present mitigating evidence tending to show that he did not shoot either of the two victims killed…Evidence that Burns did not pull the trigger…was plainly relevant to the jury's determination whether to sentence him to death…Burns asks this Court to take summary action to correct these fundamental legal errors so that his claim may be fairly considered before the State executes him.[3]

Justice Sotomayor concluded her dissent by writing,

The Court's decision to deny certiorari means that Burns now faces execution despite a very robust possibility that he did not shoot (the victim, Scott) but that the jurors, acting on incomplete information, sentenced him to death because they thought he had. The Court's failure to act is disheartening because this case reflects the kind of situation where the Court has previously found summary action appropriate…The need for action is great because Burns faces the ultimate and irrevocable penalty of death. With so much at stake, I would vacate the decision below and remand. Because the Court refuses to do so, the indefensible decision below will be the last for Burns. I respectfully dissent.[4]

Upon hearing this news from KB's lawyers on April 24, 2023, I immediately wrote the following press release:

On behalf of the family of Kevin Burns, I would like to say that while we are discouraged by the Supreme Court's decision to not grant Mr. Burns relief, we are not defeated.

Even though we are *"hard pressed on every side,"* we are *"not crushed."* While we may be *"perplexed"* by this decision, we are *"not in despair"* and we are *"not abandoned; struck down, but not destroyed"* (2 Corinthians 4:8–9).

We will continue to fight, not just for relief for Mr. Burns, but for his total exoneration. We believe Mr. Burns to be innocent of the charges that placed him on death row. We ask for prayers from God's people and mercy for Kevin Burns. *"But let justice roll on like a river, righteousness like a never-failing stream"* (Amos 5:24).

Lastly, we would like to offer thanks to Kevin Burns' legal team for all their hard work.

Below is a prayer Kevin Burns recently wrote,

O Lord God Almighty, Everlasting Father,
Prince of Peace, and Wonderful Savior.
Lord You are Holy, and I lift You up and magnify Your name.
I love You my God because You first loved me.
Yes, You loved me wonderfully.
And reverently created me in Your own image.
Then You gave me power to be called, "A son of God."
O Lord God I will praise Your name forevermore.
For Your faithfulness is ever lasting,
and to Your mercy there is no end.

And now my Lord, I thank You that Your ears are open to the
    cries of the prisoners.
For upon You have we laid all our hope.
Neither will we look to any other.
For there is none other who is able to deliver like You can.
Deliver us therefore O Lord our God I pray.

Yea, deliver us swiftly.
Deliver us from bondage and shame.
Deliver us from sickness and disease.
Deliver us from the expectations of those that seek our harm.
And we will praise Your holy name.
Bring us out healthy and strong, and please don't leave us alone.
Give us those of Your people that will help us and restore us to our place in society.

And Lord we will live out the rest of our days in Your service.
In the name of Your holy Son, Jesus, I pray.
Amen.

We now anxiously wait for the Tennessee Supreme Court to issue a date for execution. At that point, the only person who can stop the sentence of death is the governor of Tennessee.

CHAPTER 3
MY BIRTHDAY

"Everything happened so fast. Yet, at the same time, it seemed everything slowed down."

■ ■ ■

(KB) Monday, April 20, 1992, changed my life forever.

It was my twenty-third birthday.

Thirteen days earlier, April 7, was one of the best days of my life.

The greatest decade for hip-hop music was the 1990s. It was the decade of Dr. Dre, Notorious B.I.G., and Ice Cube, just to name a few. My favorite hip-hop artist was Tupac Shakur, and my favorite song was "Dear Mama." I can still hear the lyrics: "Ain't a woman alive that could take my mama's place."[5] I believe that to be true of my mom.

Like many young people in West Memphis, Arkansas, in the 1990s, I had a dream of being a famous rapper. In the late winter of 1991, I joined a rap group called H.O.H. (Hall Of Hell). I joined HOH as they were finishing their first album. Rap music tells a story in a unique way. I love the lyrics, the rhymes, and the beat of rap songs. On April 7, 1992, HOH played a showcase in Memphis, Tennessee, on world famous Beale Street at the New Daisy Theater. Not long after the showcase, HOH signed with a record label. My dreams were coming true. But on April 20, my dreams turned into a nightmare.

Monday morning April 20 started off like any other day. I was excited about it being my birthday and could not wait to see what my friends had planned for me. My girlfriend wanted me to spend the day with her, but I said I would be with the guys until later that evening. I told her I would be back by 8:00 p.m., and we could celebrate then. Looking back, I wish I had spent the day with her.

Around noon, my good friend, Joey, picked me up. From my house, we drove to Tyus's house, not far away. We stayed at Tyus's house until 3:00 p.m. The only thing I remember about being at his house is that Joey and Tyus were whispering, as if they were hiding something. I figured they were talking about how they were going to surprise me on my birthday. Finally, a little after 3:00 p.m., Joey said, "Let's roll!" And off we went.

THE FIGHT

We drove from West Memphis across the Mississippi River to Memphis, Tennessee, to pick up Bobby, another friend and member of HOH. As we were driving to his house, I learned we had a scheduled 4:00 p.m. time at a local recording studio. I thought, *This was great!* There was nothing I would rather do on my birthday than record music! At Bobby's apartment, we also picked up two more people: Rico, a dancer for HOH, and Bobby's first cousin, Thomas, who was the only one of us still in high school. This was the first time I had ever met Rico or Thomas.

A few days earlier, Thomas was involved in a fight at the local high school. He was still agitated about the fight and wanted to confront the guy he had fought. He wanted us to go with him back to school, but we talked him out of it because the school was already closed for the day. Thomas then asked us to come back tomorrow and back him up as he confronted the guy. The others agreed, but I thought to myself, *I don't know this guy. I don't know what kind of trouble he is in. There is no way I'm coming back tomorrow. This is not my fight.* Besides today was my birthday. I was in a celebratory mood and had no desire to be involved in a conflict.

We left Bobby's apartment in two cars. In Rico's sky-blue Cutlass Supreme were Rico, Bobby, and Thomas. Tyus and I rode with Joey, who followed them in his black Nissan 300ZX. We drove to Thomas's house. When we got there, before we could get out of the car, from the front porch, Thomas's younger brother told us that Scott, one of the guys Thomas had been fighting, was just at the house with three other people, looking for Thomas. The other three guys in the car were Kenny, Davis, and Luis. Thomas's younger brother then pointed down the street to a car parked in a driveway, signifying that was them.

Bobby got out of his car and came back to us and said we should all go down the street and talk to the people in that car. When I got out of the car, everyone started pulling out guns. Up until that moment I was unaware anyone had a gun on them. Startled, I said, "What are the guns for?" Bobby said, "To make sure it's a fair fight." He then pulled out another gun and handed it to me. At that moment, I wanted to leave. A voice inside me said, *Get out of here. This is none of your business.* But I didn't leave. The decision to stay is the worst decision I have ever made in my life. That one bad decision changed my life forever. If I had had the courage to leave, I know Joey would have left with me. Instead of leaving, without thinking, I took the gun, and it's a decision I regret until this day.

I don't know why I took the gun. I never liked guns and had no intentions of using it. Maybe it was fear of not knowing what was about to happen. Maybe it was pressure because everyone else had a gun. It's as if time stood still. All I wanted to do was celebrate my birthday. All I wanted to do was record music. All I wanted to do was be with my girlfriend. I didn't want to fight anyone, much less shoot anyone. Everything happened so fast. Yet, at the same time, it seemed everything slowed down. It was like I was in a dream. It was like I was frozen and could not move, yet at the same time, I moved and went along.

As we were walking toward the other car, Bobby and Thomas separated from the rest of us. I stopped on the sidewalk, about twenty yards from the car. The car was a burnt orange Chevy Caprice Classic. Bobby and Thomas rushed toward the car with guns drawn, yelling at the guys in the car. Next thing I know, I heard gun shots and I hit the ground. I was disoriented, not sure where the shots were coming from—not even sure where I was. I was afraid I would be hit because bullets don't have eyes. Years earlier a friend who was riding his bike was hit by a stray bullet and died. Tyus, close by me, also hit the ground. There were several shots fired. Eventually the shooting stopped, and we all start running back toward our cars. I threw the gun I had into Rico's Cutlass Supreme. I remember the gun landing in the front seat, bouncing into the door before landing onto the floor. I got in Joey's 300ZX, and the three of us—myself, Tyus, and Joey—headed back to West Memphis.

I'm terrified and still unclear on what had just happened. After dropping Tyus off at his house, Joey and I went to a friend's house in a very rural part of West Memphis. While at our friend's house, our friend received a phone call from a mutual friend. It was from that phone call I learned two people, Scott and Kenny (two people I did not know and had never met) had been killed in the shooting. After a few hours there, I went to Mom's house.

As I was walking to my mom's house, I saw my younger sister in the window telling me to leave and not come in. I found out later the police had already been to my mom's house searching for

MY BIRTHDAY

me. I ran to my other sister's house on another side of town. I was scared and confused. I didn't know what to do. How could this have happened? It was like I was living in someone else's dream. It was a nightmare.

While at my sister's house, I remembered I had a friend who was a truck driver. His route was Chicago. I called him and asked when he was going to Chicago. He said he was leaving in a few minutes. I asked if he would take me to Chicago. He said yes, and before the day was over, I was headed to Chicago. I had family in Chicago, so I went and stayed with them. I remained in Chicago until I was arrested by the FBI in July. While in Chicago I did a lot of praying and self-reflecting. It was during this time I rededicated my life to Jesus.

While today I can confidently say, "Today is the best day of my life," April 20, 1992, my twenty-third birthday, was the worst day of my life.

CHAPTER 4
ARRESTED

"In my mind, going to Chicago was not about escaping justice. It was about survival."

■ ■ ■

(KB) When I heard what the police did to my mom's house looking for me, and when I heard that two people had been killed, I panicked. I knew I had not done anything, but I also knew what it looked like. My only thought was to get out of West Memphis and buy myself some time to get myself together. I did not trust the Memphis police or the West Memphis police. I had been wronged by the police before. I was afraid they would be trigger happy and shoot me on sight.

Between the ages of eighteen and twenty, I had a few negative interactions with the police. On one occasion, the home of a Highway Patrol officer, who lived near me, was broken into and guns were stolen. Around 2:00 in the afternoon, as I was walking home from my girlfriend's house, wearing my father's trench coat, the police stopped me and aggressively started harassing me. They arrested me and took me in because, they said, "The coat matched the description worn by the suspect." Additionally, a coat button was found inside the burglarized home they assumed belonged to the thief, and the coat I was wearing, which belonged to my dad, had a button missing. When I got to the police station, I called my dad. He came and brought the missing button. Since my dad's button did not match the button found at the scene, and there was no other evidence, they let me go.

On another occasion, the house of a different police officer, who also lived in my neighborhood, was broken into and a radio scanner was stolen, along with some money. His scanner was not an official police device but a scanner anyone could buy at Auto Zone. A few days later, a friend of mine said he had a police scanner for sale, like the one from Auto Zone, and so I bought it from him. As I was walking home, the police officer whose house was broken into, saw me walking with the device under my arm. He stopped and asked me where I got that scanner. I said, "From a friend." He didn't believe me and took me to the police station. I called my friend, who was seventeen years old at the time. He came to the station and admitted he was the one who stole it. They arrested him and sent him to juvenile detention. Once again I was let go, but the police still believed I was somehow involved.

At one time in my life, I was a pretty good barber. I was self-taught and had no formal training. I mainly cut the hair of family and friends. I owned a black bag in which I carried my clippers and other tools I needed to cut hair. One day while I was at my dad's house cutting hair, my brother, Phillip, came in. At the time, Phillip was a parole officer and licensed to carry a handgun. He is now a police officer. Phillip came into my dad's house after being in an open field, target practicing. He wanted a haircut and mistakenly placed his gun in my bag. He had a black bag, similar to mine, that he kept his gun in.

Driving home, later that night, I was pulled over for a "traffic violation." To this day, I still don't know what the traffic violation was. For some reason, the police officer decided to search my car. When he opened my bag, with my clippers in it, he pulled out the gun. I tried to explain to him that it was my brother's and he placed it in my bag by mistake. The police officer did not believe me, and since I did not have a license to carry, he arrested me. I had to spend the weekend in jail. On Monday, Phillip came to court and explained what had happened to the judge. Once again, they let me go, but they destroyed Phillip's gun.

There was only one time I was arrested for something I actually did, and I regret that I did it. One day my cousin came to me and asked if I wanted to make $500. Without knowing what he had in mind, I said, "Yes," and got in his truck. He told me he was stealing a heating and air unit from a house. I should have stopped him right there, but I didn't. I don't know why. He said he had the unit disconnected, but it was too heavy for him to lift into his truck. He needed my help. As we were loading the unit into his truck, the police came and arrested us.

During the interview, they brought up the other three incidences, especially the one involving my brother's gun, and said they were going to use those incidences, even though I was let go, along with the attempted theft of the heating/air unit, to seek the highest penalty possible and send me to prison for a long time. But if I were to plead guilty to this charge, my sentence would be lighter, and I would serve time in the county jail instead of the state prison. My mom was worried about me going to prison, so I pled guilty. I ended up serving seven months in the county jail.

While in jail, I was made a trustee, which meant I lived in a trailer behind the prison and worked each day, pumping gas into state troopers' vehicles and other "official vehicles." It was more like being in a work camp instead of in jail. I know it sounds strange, but I enjoyed my work during those seven months. I matured a lot during this time and never had any more trouble with the police until my birthday in 1992.

I know some people will not believe me when I tell them how many times I have been falsely accused and harassed by the police. But it is the truth, and my story is not unique to me. Such was the plight of many young African-American males in Memphis, Tennessee, and West Memphis, Arkansas, in the 1980s and 1990s. I can tell you this, leading up to the time of my arrest for this charge, I had started to get my life together.

At the time of my arrest, I was twenty-three years old and working full-time as an assistant manager at Shoney's, a family restaurant in my hometown. I excelled at this job and quickly earned the trust of my co-workers. In fact, I started filling in as a manager at other Shoney's restaurants in Memphis and West Memphis. On one occasion, I helped open a new Shoney's restaurant in Memphis. I helped train the new staff in all aspects of the restaurant. My manager told me I had a bright future ahead of me in the restaurant industry. This time of my life was the happiest I had ever been. My life was good. My manager wanted to testify on my behalf, but for some reason, my lawyers never asked him.

SURVIVAL

In my mind, going to Chicago was not about escaping justice. It was about survival. While in Chicago I did not try to hide, and I did not change my identity. I simply hung out with my family, played basketball at a local park, and waited for the authorities to come and get me. In my mind, it would be better for the FBI to pick me up than the local police back in Memphis and West Memphis. Looking back, I know it wasn't the best decision I could have made. But at the time, I did not think I had any other options. I knew I would eventually be caught, and about a week before I was picked up, I saw the FBI watching me and following me.

The day I was arrested was a warm July day. It had been three months since the shootings. That morning, when I walked out to the street from where I was staying, two cars with five FBI agents were waiting for me. I had seen them watching me the day before. They got out of their cars, identified themselves, and approached me. I went with them without incident. One of the agents, Eric, quickly befriended me and allowed me to sit in the front seat with him. Eric told me they had to pick up another fugitive on the other side of town. Wherever we went was a long drive, and Eric engaged me in conversation. He came across as someone I could trust. Only later did I learn my trust was misplaced.

After picking up the other guy, we went to the Cook County Jail in downtown Chicago. While there I told Eric everything that happened on my birthday. I made it clear to him that I did not shoot anyone. He wrote everything down on a yellow legal pad. I read what he wrote and signed my name on the bottom. To this day, I have never seen that yellow legal pad again. I have never seen my original confession. No one has, including my lawyers. Eric never testified at my trial, but he did submit a typed statement. Years later, after my conviction, after my sentencing, and after serving several years on death row, I saw the typed statement Eric put together and submitted. My name was typed at the bottom, but I never signed it, and would have never signed it, because there was nothing in that statement that I actually said. Eric had changed my confession and put it in a narrative that made me look guilty.

Over the years I have wanted to write the families of Scott and Kenny to express my regret for what happened, but prison policy prohibits me from doing so. All I can do is hope they read this book and realize how sorry I am for what happened. I was there. I heard the gunshots. But I did not shoot or kill anyone.

CHAPTER 5
THE TRIAL AND SENTENCING

"Where was your God while you were killing those people?"

■ ■ ■

(KR) KB was arrested in Chicago and extradited to Memphis in July of 1992. His trial was in September of 1995 and lasted for six days. In the end, he was convicted on two counts of felony murder and two counts of attempted felony murder. On the day following the trial, in a matter of a few hours, he was sentenced to death for one of the felony murder convictions and sentenced to life on the other felony murder. On direct appeal, the court of Criminal Appeals upheld the felony murder convictions but reversed the attempted felony murders. All throughout, KB has claimed his innocence. He has never robbed, shot, or killed anyone. On November 29, 1995, KB was moved from the Shelby County Jail to Unit 2, death row, at Riverbend Maximum Security Institution in Nashville, Tennessee. He has been incarcerated for thirty-plus years and on death row for more than twenty-eight of those years.

The key issue at KB's trial was who killed Scott. On that fateful day of Monday April 20, 1992, as Scott, Kenny, David, and Tracy sat in a car drinking and smoking marijuana, they were confronted by six men: KB, Joey, Tyus, Bobby, Rico, and Thomas. Shots were fired. Scott and Kenny were killed. Tracy was seriously injured. David escaped with a graze to his arm.

The confrontation on April 20 was a continuation of a confrontation that took place two days earlier between Thomas and David over a traveling call during a pick-up basketball game. KB was not present at the game and had never met Thomas, or any of the four guys in the car, before April 20. Thomas's cousin, Bobby, was the one who gathered KB and the others to go to David's house to confront him about the altercation over the basketball game.

Evidence from the scene of the crime suggested two gunmen fired the lethal shots. Scott was killed with a .32 semi-automatic pistol that also hit Tracy as he was running away. Kenny was also killed with a .32 semi-automatic pistol. Of the six men who were present that day, only KB, Joey, and Thomas were charged with capital felony murder. Two people were killed. Six people had guns, and only three people were charged with anything.

Things do not add up.

There were three separate trials. KB's trial was last. Both Joey and Thomas were convicted and sentenced to life in prison. Both Joey and Thomas are now out on parole. Only KB remains in prison. Only KB was given the death sentence.

Again, things do not add up.

At trial, two witnesses, Tracy and his mother, Ruth, implicated KB as Scott's killer. However, on the day of the shooting, Tracy told detectives that Thomas was the one who shot him. Furthermore, over the course of three trials, Tracy changed his story three times. Ruth testified that she saw two gunmen, both with Jheri curls. At the time of the crime, KB's hair was shaved close to his head. At least six witnesses, including a senior vice president of Shoney's Corporation, where KB worked at the time of the crime, were

THE TRIAL AND SENTENCING

willing to testify KB had short hair and did not have a Jheri curl. KB's lawyers did not call on any of them to testify. Although KB had longer hair with a Jheri curl by the time of the trial, on direct examination, Ruth did not identify KB as the shooter. But on cross-examination, by KB's lawyers, she pointed at KB and said, "Bobby, that man right there, is the shooter." Thus, she misidentified KB. Both Ruth and Tracy testified that the gunman who shot Scott was a big man who wore glasses. Joey was six feet four, had a Jheri curl, and wore glasses. KB was five seven, with a close-shaven haircut, and has never worn glasses.

At 4:30 in the afternoon, after six days of trial, the jury returned guilty verdicts on KB. Recess was then called for a short time before sentencing later that evening. During the recess, for the very first time, KB's lawyers met with about a dozen possible character witnesses, to determine who would be best to testify at sentencing. KB's lawyers called six witnesses whose entire testimony took less than an hour and occupies a mere fourteen transcript pages of court records. The entire sentencing hearing was completed by 9:20 p.m. The next day, during deliberations, the jury asked the judge, "Can we ask for life without parole?" and "Can we ask for consecutive life sentences?" For some reason, the judge declined to answer those questions. As a result, KB was sentenced to death, the only choice the jury had.

Throughout all his appeals, KB has argued he had inadequate counsel at trial. His court-appointed attorneys were ill prepared. Over the three years KB was in the Shelby County Jail, awaiting trial, he rarely saw his lawyers. Instead of fighting for KB, they blamed him for their failure and accused him, and members of his family, of being uncooperative. KB did not get along with his trial lawyers, but he did not know he could have them removed and receive new lawyers.

DISAGREEMENTS

Two stories, among many, stand out to me about KB's disagreements with his trial lawyers. First, remember, on April 20, 1992, KB had short hair and did not have a Jheri curl. There were plenty of people willing to testify to this fact. After his arrest, while in jail awaiting trial, KB recommitted his life to Jesus. Part of his commitment was promising God he would grow his hair out as a sign of his commitment to Jesus. KB told me, "For me, my hair growing long would symbolize my growing faith in God. I did not cut my hair for three years. It wasn't a Nazarite vow—I knew I would eventually cut it—but I kept it long to remind me of my promise to God."

The day before trial, KB's lawyers told him he needed to cut his hair, in order to make himself more "presentable." KB told his lawyers, who are supposed to represent him, about his promise to God and how he could not cut his hair. In anger, one of his lawyer's shouted at him, screaming, "Where was your God while you were killing those people?"

The second story concerns a deal KB's lawyers made with the prosecuting attorney without KB's approval. Between the ages of eighteen and twenty, KB had a few negative experiences with the police. One experience was about his brother's gun that ended up in KB's barber's bag (see chapter 4). According to KB, the prosecuting attorney approached KB's attorneys and said, "If you guys don't bring it up that there is no evidence KB fired any guns, I will not bring up his past run-ins with the police, especially the one that involved a gun." KB's lawyers agreed. Thus, at KB's trial, the murder weapons were never presented as evidence. KB's jurors never knew that both murder weapons had been recovered at Bobby's house and KB's fingerprints were not on either of the two murder weapons.

THE TRIAL AND SENTENCING

RECAP

KB's trail is complex and at times hard to follow. So here is recap of the key aspects of KB's case that demonstrate his innocence. Much of the below was provided by KB's current lawyer, Richard Tennent.

April 20, 1992, was Kevin Burn's twenty-third birthday. He wanted to celebrate by going to a music studio with his friends, Joey, Tyus, and Bobby. On the way to the studio, Bobby asked them to "back up" his cousin Thomas, who needed to squash a problem he had with another guy named David. Bobby provided guns, "just in case," though he said nothing worse than a fist fight was planned. KB had no intent to use a gun or to hurt anyone; he just wanted to go to celebrate his birthday by recording some music.

Thomas and Bobby found David sitting in the back seat of a parked car with three of his friends. Thomas and Bobby pulled their guns and demanded David exit from the car. Instead, David slammed his car door into Thomas and ran. Shots were fired, likely by Thomas and Bobby. In response, after hitting the ground until the shooting was over, KB fled, first to a friend's house, then to his sister's house, and finally to Chicago.

Eyewitnesses watched as "a big man in glasses" went to the driver's side of the car, pulled a .32 automatic pistol, and repeatedly shot the driver, Scott, and back-seat passenger, Tracy. Another man with a Jheri curl in his hair fired a .32 revolver and killed the front-seat passenger, Kenny. Two men and only two men fired all the fatal shots. We know beyond a shadow of doubt that KB was not one of the two killers. On April 20, 1992, KB wore his hair cut close to his scalp and stood all of five feet seven.

Furthermore, Luis, a survivor and an eyewitness, testified at Joey's trial that he and Scott were repeatedly shot by the same "big man in glasses." Joey is six feet four in height and wears glasses. The .32 automatic pistol that killed Scott and wounded David and the .32 revolver that killed Kenny were found at Bobby's home.

Despite KB's innocence, he, like too many men in Memphis, Tennessee, was misrepresented by unprepared, less-then-competent defense attorneys. At KB's trial, Tracy changed his story and implicated KB as the man who shot him and Scott. KB's lawyers had a transcript of Tracy's earlier testimony that could have exonerated KB, but they failed to use it.

KB's lawyers could have rebutted Ruth's identification by calling any number of witnesses, including KB's supervisor at a Shoney's restaurant where KB worked at the time of the shootings. All would have testified that KB's hair was cut to the scalp in 1992. But defense counsel did nothing at all. At sentencing, based on the conclusion that KB had killed Scott, the jury sentenced him to death. For the murder of Kenny, which the prosecution contended was committed by someone else, they sentenced KB to life. KB's life conviction and death sentence are a travesty of justice.

KB, Joey, and Thomas were all tried independently of each other. Since the trials, the following events have occurred. Once again, the information below was provided by KB's lawyer, Richard Tennent:

- Joey, the big man in glasses, made parole in April of 2023, a week after KB was denied relief by the United States Supreme Court.
- Thomas, whose altercation with Scott started this whole tragedy, made parole in 2017.
- Bobby, who provided guns for a fist fight was never prosecuted.
- Despite it all, KB has become an ordained minister. He preaches, via telephone, on a regular basis at Franklin

Community Church in Franklin, Tennessee, where KB's friend and mentor, Rev. Dr. Kevin Riggs, pastors. Pastor Riggs regularly calls KB is own personal pastor.
- With the help of Pastor Riggs and Franklin Community Church, KB started a church on death row called "The Church of Life," where he holds regular services on death row.
- KB is not discouraged and continues to testify, "today is the best day of my life."

There is one thing I want to add to all this. During KB's ordination process, he and I had several serious conversations. During one of those conversations, I asked, "KB, I have to know and you have to be honest with me. Did you kill Scott or fire your gun at anyone?" I then said, "Before you answer, we are going to ordain you anyway. We believe in forgiveness and redemption. Your answer doesn't matter to me. I just need you to be honest." Without hesitation, KB replied, "Pastor, I promise you I am innocent. I didn't shoot at anyone and I didn't kill anyone." I believe KB is innocent.

CHAPTER 6
ZACHARY KEVIN RIGGS

"Heavenly Father, please be with my sister Misty. Envelope her with Your presence, love, and mercy."

■ ■ ■

KB's lawyer told me (KR) the only time KB cried after hearing the news he had been denied relief from the United States Supreme Court was when he was told that I was writing a press statement. Why did he cry? Because nine days earlier, on April 15, 2023, my son, Zachary, was killed in a car accident. He was twenty-eight years old.

KB was heartbroken for me, not himself! He said to his lawyer, "Pastor Kevin doesn't need to do that. He and Misty [my wife] are grieving. He doesn't need to worry about me." Only a friend, a true friend, someone who loves me like few others, would say such a thing. And it's not just KB. It's all the men on death row. They were some of the first people to send Misty and me a sympathy card. To this day, when I visit death row, the men come up to me and ask how Misty and I are doing and let me know they continue to pray for me. And I desire their prayers more than any others. Why? Because God hears and listens to the prayers of prisoners. The writer of Psalm said, "The LORD hears the needy and does not despise his captive people" (Psalm 69:33). To say visiting death row has forever changed my life is an understatement. The day after my son's death, both of KB's parents called me to express their condolences. A week later, I called KB's parents to talk with them and pray with them about the Supreme Court's decision.

(KB) Pastor Kevin and his wife Misty are part of my family. The apostle Paul told us to "Rejoice with them that do rejoice, and weep with them that weep" (Romans 12:15). I was grieving with them and praying for them over the loss of their beloved son, Zach. I was still grieving with them, and for them, when I received word that I had been denied relief from the United States Supreme Court. As disappointed as I was, I felt my circumstance was secondary to what my pastor and his wife were going through.

After I read through the Supreme Court's decision, especially the dissent written by Justice Sotomayor, I read my lawyers' press release. Then Richard Tennent handed me another sheet of paper and said, "And here is a press release written by your pastor." I was shocked and said, "What? He should not have done that." As I read Pastor Kevin's statement, I started crying. His press release hit me in a way I was not expecting.

By the time of my trial, my faith had become strong, and I saw all the injustice I was enduring, and would endure over the following decades, as spiritual warfare. The brief my lawyers prepared for the Supreme Court was good. The amicus brief prepared by my friends was greatly appreciated, and while I hoped for relief, I knew it was a long shot. After all, I had been denied again and again through the entire appeals process. So while I was hopeful, I was also realistic. When the Supreme Court denied me relief, I was disappointed but not surprised. I have known all along that only God can release me. My trust is completely in Him. I know what God promised me, and I hold on to that promise. My only recourse is to move forward to the next stage and see what God will do. My faith is still strong, but at that moment, reading Pastor Kevin's press release, I started crying because what I was going through did not compare to what he and Misty were going through.

Every day, following the admonition to put on the full armor of God (Ephesians 6:10–17), I dress myself, spiritually speaking, in God's armor. The enemy used that press release to shoot an arrow through my armor, piercing my heart. My thought was, *Pastor Kevin, writing a press release on my behalf is so unfair to him and his family.* I felt like the enemy had dealt me a serious blow. The Supreme Court did not hurt me. Pastor Kevin having to write a press release on my behalf hurt me. I love Pastor Kevin and Misty more than words can express, and I greatly appreciate his unwavering love and support. But it was unfair for him to have written that press release. My appeal is before God Almighty. My case depends on God, not man. Again, I love Pastor Kevin with all my heart, but at that moment, my heart was broken that he felt like he needed to write that press release.

(KR) A few months before my son's accident, my wife and I began making plans to host a leadership cohort I was involved in with Christian Community Development Association (CCDA). These were leaders, colleagues, and friends from around the country. Our plans involved taking them to Riverbend Maximum Security Institution to visit KB and the other men on death row. My son died on April 15. We hosted the cohort April 26–29. We visited death row (eleven of us total) on Friday, April 28. This was the first time I saw KB since my son's death. (Remember, on Monday, April 24, KB found out he was denied relief by the United States Supreme Court.) I was looking forward to seeing my pastor, KB. I was not prepared for what happened on our visit.

We first went on a tour of the entire prison. Our last stop was Unit 2, death row. KB knew we were coming, but it was late in the afternoon before we got to Unit 2. KB had given up, assuming we were not going to come.

As we walked toward Unit 2, KB was outside in an oversized, enclosed pen, much like a dog run, playing handball. (KB will tell you he is the best handball player on the row. A few of the other guys disagree.) KB saw us before we saw him. He immediately spotted my wife and called out to her by name. He then took off running inside to change clothes. Everyone in my cohort started crying. As soon as we walked into Unit 2, KB ran to Misty and embraced her. She, along with others in my cohort, started sobbing. The guards starred in stunned amazement. Embracing my wife, KB started praying, "Heavenly Father, please be with my sister Misty. Envelope her with Your presence, love, and mercy." Misty sobbed with the grief only a mother can feel. Crying myself, I stood to the side, watching in holy wonder. What took place next was supernatural. I looked at the unit manager, who had tears streaming down his face.

Over the next several minutes, holding tightly to Misty, KB whispered over and over in her ear, "Peace be upon you. I love you. Peace be upon you. I love you." The next day I wrote a letter to the governor, asking him to show KB mercy. I described this scene to him and wrote, "Pastor Burns has a powerfully unique gift. I now feel as if I owe him my life. I would gladly trade places with him if the courts would allow."

During the next hour, as KB talked to my cohort about life on death row, he never let go of Misty, and Misty never let go of him. Before leaving Unit 2, KB wrote down the names of everyone in my cohort, promising to pray for them daily. Every member of my cohort commented later that their visit with KB was life changing. They were astonished by the love KB and the other men showed

Misty and me, and they were amazed by the love I had for KB and the other men as well. The unit manager said we could come back anytime.

Later that evening, Misty told me, "When KB hugged me it was as if Jesus was hugging me. When KB whispered in my ear, it was as if Jesus was whispering in my ear. At that moment, KB was Jesus in the flesh for me. For the first time since Zach's death, I felt peace and hope. He brought light back into my life where there had only been darkness." KB, a man condemned to die for something he did not do, ministered to my wife and did more for her in a few moments than myself or any grief counselor could do in years. My wife has since told me several times she doesn't know what she will do if KB is executed.

(KB) When Pastor Kevin shared with me how Misty was feeling, my only thought was, *Wow! That's heavy right there. How do I respond to that?* I think, the first thing I would say to Misty is that I love her dearly. She means the world to me. A reporter once asked me if I had thought about being executed. My response was, "No! I never consider the possibility that I will be executed. I do not allow that thought to enter my mind. My life is completely in God's hands. I believe God's promise to me that my life will be spared. But like the apostle Paul said, while facing his own execution, 'For me to live is Christ, and to die is gain'" (Philippians 1:21). I would also add, "For me, dying for a crime I did not commit; dying for a man I did not murder, would be a dishonorable death, and I want to honor God in life and death."

I would tell Misty, and everyone else, "To every thing there is a season, and a time to every purpose under heaven: A time to be born, and a time to die" (Ecclesiastes 3:1–2). The writer of Hebrews wrote, "And as it is appointed unto men once to die"

(Hebrews 9:27). We all have an appointment, and we must be ready for that day. Until then, we must continue on. We have to continue to trust and believe God. We must continue to lean into God and His promises. There is no other alternative. "Trust in the LORD with all thine heart; and lean not unto thine own understanding. In all thy ways acknowledge him, and he shall direct thy paths" (Proverbs 3:5–6). To Misty, I would say, "You have to continue on. Don't be discouraged. I love you."

(KR) The next week, Misty sent KB a card. In the card she wrote,

> KB. Words can't describe how grateful I am to you. Getting to see you was the most incredible spiritual moment I have ever experienced. When you hugged me, you were Jesus in the flesh to me. When you whispered, "Peace be upon you" in my ear, it was Jesus saying that to me. For the first time since my precious son took his last breath, I felt peace. You calmed my soul and shined a light in me that had been dimmed. Thank you is not enough. But thank you for that holy moment you gave me. Thank you for praying for me and my family. I love you! I pray for you every day and will continue to do so.

Without a doubt, this has been the hardest chapter for me to write. The emotions are real, and the emotions are raw. It is believed that somewhere between 3 and 7 percent of people on death row are innocent of the crime that sent them to death row. This has got to stop! There are 195 countries in the world and only 55 of them have the death penalty. In other words, 72 percent of the world has demolished the death penalty. As a country we must do better. We can do better. As a follower of Jesus, I believe to the core of my being, Jesus's execution should have been the last, and final, execution. There is no justice in capital punishment. There is only more heartache and more trauma. There is a better way, a way that honors God and honors victims and their families. That way is restorative justice.

CHAPTER 7
MY JOURNEY TO DEATH ROW

"I believe the totality of Scripture, and especially the words of Jesus, teaches against capital punishment. For me, capital punishment is a pro-life issue."

■ ■ ■

(KR) In the winter of 2014, during a time of prayer and meditation, I heard the voice of God clearly say to me, "Go to death row." I had been involved in prison ministry, both in my home state and in Honduras. One of the first places I preached as a teenager was a low-security prison in my hometown. But in 2013, I did not know where death row was in Tennessee, much less how to get involved.

A few days earlier, February 5 to be exact, my local newspaper, *The Tennessean*, published an article titled "State sets execution dates for 10 men." At that time there were seventy-eight men and one woman on death row in the state. That's almost 13 percent of the total population of men and women on death row scheduled to be killed in a matter of months! My spirit was grieved by this even though, at that time, I would not have considered myself a capital punishment abolitionist. Knowing I heard God speak, I did some research, made some phone calls, and by the summer of 2014 made my first visit to Unit Two at Riverbend Maximum Security Institution, the home of death row in Tennessee. My life has never been the same. I am now an active abolitionist, doing everything I can to stop the violence.

I grew up in a conservative denomination. I started preaching when I was fifteen and started pastoring when I was twenty-three. I have now been a pastor for more than thirty years. Today I believe the totality of Scripture, and especially the words of Jesus, teaches against capital punishment. For me, capital punishment is a pro-life issue.

What brought me to this conclusion?

Proximity to the condemned has brought me the farthest. My evolving understanding of biblical justice has further convinced me. Looking into the eyes of my friends, hearing their stories, and seeing the image of God in each of them have impacted me. God's desire that no one perish and all be redeemed has also encouraged me. So if you were to ask me why I am a capital punishment abolitionist, I would say, "Because of proximity, justice, *Imago Dei*, and redemption."

God's plan to reconcile the world to Himself was for His Son to take on human flesh and become one of us. We call this the Incarnation. "For God so loved the world that he gave his one and only Son, that whoever believes in him shall not perish but have eternal life" (John 3:16). God's plan was first revealed in Genesis 3:15 when God said to the tempter, "And I will put enmity between you and woman, and between your offspring and hers; he will crush your head, and you will strike his heel." The angel said to Joseph, "The virgin will conceive and give birth to a son, and they will call him Immanuel (which means, 'God with us')" (Matthew 1:23). Concerning Jesus, the early church sang, "Who, being in very nature God, did not consider equality with God something to be used to his own advantage; rather, he made himself nothing by taking the very nature of a servant, being made in human likeness. And being found in appearance as a man, he humbled himself by becoming obedient to death—even death on a cross!" (Philippians 2:6–8).

Through Jesus Christ, God moved into our neighborhood and lived in close proximity to us so He could live with us, know us, and redeem us. Likewise, He has now called us to go into prisons with His love, grace, and mercy; and that includes death row. Jesus said He came "to proclaim freedom for the prisoners" (Luke 4:18). In His parable of the sheep and goats, He said, "I was in prison and you came to visit me" (Matthew 25:36). Jesus's last conversation, before He was executed, was with two fellow death row inmates (Luke 23:39–43). The writer of Hebrews tells us, "Continue to remember those in prison as if you were together with them in prison, and those who are mistreated as if you yourselves were suffering" (Hebrews 13:3). When people ask me why I go to death row, I tell them I go because that is where Jesus is. From the beginning to the middle and to the very end of His ministry, Jesus placed priority on living in proximity with prisoners, including those condemned to die. We can do no less.

Our God is a holy, loving, merciful, and just God. It is because of the nature and character of God that I am a capital punishment abolitionist. The justice of God cannot be separated from the holiness of God, the love of God, and the mercy of God. Thus, taken as a whole, God's justice is restorative justice. The Hebrew word most often translated "justice" is *mishpat*. The simplest meaning of *mishpat* is to treat people fairly and equitably. This is the basic idea behind our understandings of distributive justice and retributive justice. This meaning of justice is in Old Testament verses that talk about treating the rich and poor equally in the marketplace and in the courts of law. One example of distributive justice is Leviticus 19:15: "Do not pervert justice; do not show partiality to the poor or favoritism to the great, but judge your neighbor fairly." An example of retributive justice is Psalm 105:7: "He is the LORD our God; his judgments are in all the earth."

However, often times, when the Old Testament speaks of God's justice, it is followed closely by the words *righteousness* and/or *mercy*. It is this relationship between justice, righteousness, and mercy that convinces me God's justice is primarily restorative.

While God's justice most definitely includes fairness and equality, it goes far beyond that. Intrinsic in God's justice is the desire to make things right—to reconcile all things to Himself. Thus, all of God's justice, be it distributive or retributive, is, at its heart, restorative. A great mystery of God is even God's punitive justice is somehow meant to be restorative in nature.

A favorite verse for proponents of capital punishment is Genesis 9:6: "Whoever sheds human blood, by humans shall their blood be shed, for in the image of God has God made mankind." They like to point out that this is part of the Noahic covenant and separate from the law of Moses. Even if that is true, nowhere was death meant to be an absolute law—meaning it must take place at all times, in all places, under all circumstances. I say this because, in the preceding book of Exodus, Moses killed a man and God did not demand he pay with his life. God cannot violate an absolute law. Thus, the bigger picture behind Genesis 9:6 is justice, not the need for additional killings. If there is another way for justice to be fulfilled without the taking of another life, that is what God's people should fight for. Capital punishment, even in the best of circumstances, is not carried out in a just manner. There are too many variables that go into who gets death and who doesn't get death when the same crime is committed. The arbitrary nature of our capital justice system has caused me to conclude, even if one thinks capital punishment is just, it is impossible for us to do it justly so we should not do it at all—especially when there is another way for justice to be done, a better way for justice to be done.

A BETTER WAY

I am convinced that better way is restorative justice. Restorative justice more accurately reflects the nature of God and protects the image of God in every person. Restorative justice is seen in Jesus's words in the Sermon on the Mount, where He said, "You have heard that it was said, 'Eye for eye, and tooth for tooth' [distributive, retributive, and punitive justice]. But I tell you, do not resist an evil person. If someone slaps you on the right cheek, turn to them the other cheek also. And if anyone wants to sue you and take your shirt, hand over your coat as well. If anyone forces you to go one mile, go with them two miles. Give to the one who asks you, and do not turn away from the one who wants to borrow from you" (Matthew 5:38-42). This is restorative justice! This is the heart of God! Then Jesus added, "You have heard that it was said, 'Love your neighbor and hate your enemy.' But I tell you, love your enemies and pray for those who persecute you" (Matthew 5:43-44). Once again, restorative justice.

Donnie was a friend of mine. He was executed by the state of Tennessee for the murder of his wife. The Donnie I knew loved to read and teach the Bible. For a while, he even taught the Bible on the radio from his prison cell. He was an elder in his local Seventh Day Adventist Church. None of that excuses his crime, but it does show the grace and mercy of God.

At the time of his crime, his stepdaughter, Susan, was seven years old. By her own admission, she grew up with a lot of anger toward her stepdad. Who could blame her? As a young adult, Susan decided to reach out to her stepdad. She wanted him to know how angry and hurt she was. She did not have the desire to reconcile with him. But something miraculous happened. After expressing her anger toward her stepfather, she decided the best way to heal was through forgiveness and reconciliation. I will never forget the day Donnie showed me a letter she had written to him, expressing how much she loved him. Susan became his biggest advocate, asking the State to show him mercy. In an editorial Susan wrote in our local newspaper, she said, "After being trapped in the death penalty process for most of my life and finally receiving some peace, I now face more trauma and loss. Over these past few years, Don has become one of my last connections to my mother, and his execution will not feel like justice to me. It will feel like losing my mother all over again. I want to save his life."

That's restorative justice! That is the heart of Jesus. Sadly, Susan's request for mercy was denied.

As her stepfather, and my friend, was being killed, he sang, "Soon and very soon, we're going to see the king." God is a restorative, reconciling God, and God has called us to be the same way. I am a capital punishment abolitionist because of the nature of God's justice.

Genesis 1:27 tells us, "So God created mankind in his own image, in the image of God he created them." Every person on earth bears the image of God, the Imago Dei, in them. Regardless of what a person has done or not done, regardless of guilt or innocence, the Imago Dei is still there. You can see the image of God in people by looking into their eyes. The eyes truly are the windows to the soul. Jesus said, "The eye is the lamp of the body" (Matthew 6:22). No matter what condition a person is in, look into their eyes and you will see their souls. Matthew tells us, "When [Jesus] saw the crowds, he had compassion on them, because they were harassed and helpless, like sheep without a shepherd" (Matthew 9:36).

One of my friends on death row has a severe mental disability. He should have never been sentenced to death. He is in his fifties, but in reality, he is a child. When I see him and when I pray with him, I see the Imago Dei in him, and I hear the words of Jesus, "Truly I tell you, unless you change and become like little children, you will never enter the kingdom of heaven. Therefore, whoever takes the lowly position of this child is the greatest in the kingdom of heaven. And whoever welcomes one such child in my name welcomes me. If anyone causes one of these little ones—those who believe in me—to stumble, it would be better for them to have a large millstone hung around their neck and to be drowned in the depths of the sea" (Matthew 18:3–6).

It is because of the Imago Dei that no one should be defined by the worst day of their lives or the worst thing they have done. Pope Francis has said, "The death penalty is inadmissible because it is an attack on the inviolability and dignity of the person." He further added that capital punishment is a "serious violation of the right to life"[6] belonging to every person.

All the men and women on all the death rows in our country were created in the image of God. The crimes for which they have been accused did not destroy God's image within them. I am a capital punishment abolitionist because taking the life of another person, by an individual or by the government, is an attack on the Imago Dei.

The Bible says, "The Lord is not slow in keeping his promise, as some understand slowness. Instead he is patient with you, not wanting anyone to perish, but everyone to come to repentance" (2 Peter 3:9). The apostle Paul wrote, "Everyone who calls on the name of the Lord will be saved" (Romans 10:13). Again, the apostle Paul said, "For he has rescued us from the dominion of darkness and brought us into the kingdom of the Son he loves, in whom we have redemption, the forgiveness of sins" (Colossians 1:13–14).

FINALITY

A major problem with the death penalty is that it is final. There is no taking it back. There are no second chances. Through executions, we are saying that some people are so bad they are beyond hope and beyond redemption. That is blasphemy! No one is so far gone God's grace cannot reach them. No one is so bad God no longer loves them. As long as there is life there is hope through the power of redemption. Psalm 111:9 reads, "He provided redemption for his people . . . holy and awesome is his name."

Abu is another friend of mine. I met him on death row, but a few years ago his sentence was commuted to life without parole. Abu is one of the kindest, most gentle, intelligent men I have ever met. His story of abuse growing up is horrendous. How he ended up on death row is heartbreaking. His story of redemption, however, is wonderful. For a long while, on death row, Abu was not a Christian. He was a man of faith. He loved and respected Jesus. He simply did not identify himself as a Christian. He chose another path. However, once a week for twenty-five years, a small group of people from a local church visited him. Their agenda was nothing more than love and friendship. For twenty-five years they practiced what I call the ministry of presence. They were just there . . . every week . . . year after year . . . decade after decade.

As Abu was nearing his sixty-fifth birthday, he asked his friends if he could convert to Christianity and become a member of their church. Of course, the answer was yes! And so the bishop of this church's denomination along with several friends (myself included) gathered in the law library on death row to witness Abu's conversion on his sixty-fifth birthday. On that day he placed his faith in

Christ, was baptized, and was served communion. Afterward Abu sang a soulful rendition of "Amazing Grace." It was one of the most beautiful and sacred services I have ever witnessed.

On more than one occasion, over the years of his incarceration, Abu came within hours of being executed. I am thankful he was not killed. He has been redeemed by the blood of Jesus! He is a dear brother and an even dearer friend. I am a capital punishment abolitionist because as long as there is life there is hope through the power of redemption.

The story behind this book is the story of my relationship with KB. I want to close my journey to death row with this prayer, written by KB.

> *O LORD GOD,*
> *even The GOD and FATHER of our LORD and SAVIOR JESUS, The CHRIST.*
> *LORD GOD, You are HOLY and RIGHTEOUS;*
> *GRACIOUS and altogether TRUE.*
> *YOUR Mercies are everlasting, and they are renewed every morning.*
> *O LORD GOD,*
> *unto THEE do I lift up my Soul.*
> *And unto THEE do I cry in despair.*
> *Have mercy on me, LORD, I pray, and deliver me.*
> *Deliver me from those who are too Strong for me:*
> *And deliver me from certain death.*
> *YOU said in YOUR WORD, that YOU looked down from the height of YOUR Sanctuary;*
> *From Heaven YOU beheld the earth; To hear the groaning of the prisoners;*
> *To loose those that are appointed to death.*

Behold, I am in prison, and they have appointed my soul for death.

But unto YOU, O LORD my GOD, do I make my appeal.

For YOU are that GOD that took me from my Mother's bosom,

and declared YOUR Love for me, and made YOUR covenant with me,

and told me that YOU will never leave me nor forsake me.

But that YOU will be with me always, even until the end of the World:

And caused me to hope in YOU.

And now, O LORD my GOD, in THEE do I put my Trust.

Let me not be brought to shame.

Neither let any that Trust in YOUR HOLY NAME be brought to shame.

But bring me out of this prison swiftly, I pray;

And deliver me by a strong HAND, O LOVER of my soul.

In the NAME of JESUS, I pray

AMEN, and AMEN!

CHAPTER 8
THE POLITICS BEHIND CAPITAL PUNISHMENT

"The system doesn't want to admit it made a mistake."

■ ■ ■

"Justice may be blind, but she sees what she wants to see." KB said this to me (KR) one day while we were talking about his experiences with the criminal legal system. It's a profound statement. Right or wrong, many Americans believe the United States has a two-tiered "justice" system—meaning, one for ordinary people and another for people of wealth, influence, and power. An example of this is our country's bail system. Right now, thousands and thousands of people are sitting in jail who have not been charged with a crime. They are waiting for trial, but because they could not afford bail, they are waiting from behind bars. And it's not just violent offenders! People without financial resources can be arrested for minor offenses, but because they cannot afford a bail of a few hundred dollars, they sit in jail. As a result, they lose their jobs and get further behind on their bills.

There's a saying in Unit 2: "There are no rich people on death row." Far too often, people on death row are there not because of the crime they committed or have been accused of committing, but because they could not afford their own attorney. In KB's case, he had a court-appointed attorney who spent minimal time with him before trial and seemed more interested in getting his case "off his plate" then in zealously fighting for his client. In fact, KB's court-appointed trial lawyers have lost every one of his six capital offense cases! In each instance, they were the "court-appointed" attorney. Throughout the entire appeals process, lawyers who have represented KB have said, "Any competent attorney would have had a different outcome at trial. A good attorney would have won, and KB would have never gone to jail."

There is something else about the appeals process that many people do not know. In most cases, you can only argue what is on the record. At a certain point in the appeals process, you cannot bring up new evidence. So if a key piece of evidence, which could exonerate a person, was not presented at trial or was discovered later, it is unlikely you can bring it up on appeals. The farther you go in the appeals process, the more limited you are on what you can and cannot argue. In other words, our criminal legal system is designed to protect the system. The system doesn't want to admit it made a mistake.

One day KB said to me, "I've had lawyers tell me that while our system isn't perfect, it is the best in the world. Well, from where I am sitting, that is not true. The system has failed me time and time again. It's not about guilt or innocence or even culpability. It's about wins and losses and advancing in your own professional career. Don't get me wrong. I have had some very good lawyers, and I have had some great investigators, but they are fighting an uphill battle. They are fighting with one hand tied behind their backs. My experience has not been, 'innocent until proven guilty.' My experience has been 'guilty until proven innocent.'"

Society likes to think capital punishment is reserved for the worst of the worst. Well, that just isn't true. Over the years visiting prisons, I have talked with and prayed with some notorious people, who have admitted to me some horrible and evil acts. I have talked to serial killers, rapists, hit men, and gang leaders. Some share their stories with great remorse; others seems like they are bragging. Some are serving multiple life sentences without the possibility of parole. Others have made parole or completely served their time, called "flattening out," and are back on the streets. Then I go to death row where a few of the men are innocent, and others committed a "crime of passion" or killed someone by accident. But because of bad representation, instead of a manslaughter or some other lesser charge, they receive the death penalty. It doesn't make sense! The one thing the men on Tennessee's death row have in common is they come from low-income to poverty backgrounds and could not afford their own, private attorney.

COFFEE WITH ED

Ed Miller is a friend of mine. He is an elderly man now, though he refuses to tell me his age. My guess is he is in his eighties. He has been a lawyer for more than fifty years. He now focuses his time doing research for criminal defense lawyers across the country. He is brilliant. A few years ago, in addition to practicing law, he started taking classes at Vanderbilt Divinity School for fun and for something to do. He has researched every murder conviction in Tennessee since 1976, the year the United State Supreme Court reinstated the death penalty. He has written articles for major law journals and has charts and figures about everything you may want to know about murder and the death penalty in Tennessee.

Ed and I met for lunch at a coffee shop in Nashville to talk about capital punishment in Tennessee. I asked him, "What are the politics behind capital punishment?" His answer was short: "It's all about politics." Since I was buying his lunch, I told him I needed more than that. He laughed and then went into a long explanation.

Ed explained, "The majority of men on Tennessee's death row are African American, and a disproportion of men are from Memphis. Many of them were put on death row by the same Shelby County District Attorney. KB is one of those men." (KB has told me stories about this particular district attorney and how he, and others on death row, went to trial and received the death penalty during an election year.)

Ed went on to explain how each county's district attorney decides whether to pursue the death penalty when a murder is committed. A district attorney's political leanings dictate if he will pursue capital murder charges or not. What this means, practically speaking, is if you commit murder in a Republican-led county you have a greater chance of receiving the death penalty than if you commit that same crime in a Democrat-led county.

Ed then asked me, "Do you remember the story of a fellow in a southern Tennessee town who went into Alabama and killed a person, just to see if he had the guts to do it, and then returned home to Tennessee and killed several members of his family?" I said, "Yes." He continued, "The county where he committed several murders was a Democrat-led county. The local district attorney did not believe in capital punishment. So instead of receiving the death penalty, he received several life sentences." Ed then added, "Right now, in Davidson County (Nashville) the district attorney doesn't believe in the death penalty. As a result, no one has been charged with a capital offense since he has been in office."

In April of 2023, while working on this book, the Tennessee Legislature, controlled by Republicans, passed a statute expanding the authority of the state-appointed attorney general in death-penalty cases. The purpose of this statute was to give the state attorney general power in death-penalty cases, beginning at the post-conviction stage of appeals. On July 17, 2023, a Shelby County criminal court judge, appointed by a Democratic governor, struck down the statute, stating that it unconstitutionally removed the power of the locally elected district attorney. In case you missed it, the state attorney general is appointed by the ruling party. Local district attorneys are elected by the people of each county. Those who opposed the statute believed this was an attempt to control what evidence could be presented at post-conviction to prevent death penalty cases being overturned. The Tennessee attorney general's office is appealing the decision. The politics behind capital punishment continues.

As we continued our conversation over lunch, Ed told me, "Since 1977, the year the death penalty was reinstated in Tennessee, 2,909 Tennessee adults have been convicted of first-degree murder. Only eighty-four people of the 2,909 convictions ended with a sentence of death; that's less than 3 percent of the time. To put it another way, 97 percent of all first-degree murder convictions ended in something less than a death sentence! If less than 3 percent of first-degree murder convictions end with the death penalty, why do we even have capital punishment in Tennessee? There is no rhyme or reason as to why the 3 percent received the death penalty. My only explanation is that it is political. In my opinion, if less than 3 percent of all first-degree murders results in a death sentence, and they are not the most heinous of crimes, we should not have capital punishment in Tennessee at all."

I could not agree more.

"Furthermore," Ed continued, "The Tennessee Supreme Court mandates that after every first-degree murder conviction, a Rule 12 Report must be filed with the Supreme Court. One of the primary purposes of the Rule 12 Report is to assist the appellate court judges in determining if a sentence, following a conviction, is comparatively proportional with the sentences in other cases. This is vital in determining if a sentence of death is proportional! Since 1977, of the 2,909 first-degree murder convictions across the state, only 57 percent of the cases, or 1,648, had Rule 12 Reports filed. That means 43 percent of the time, Rule 12 Reports were not filed! If 43 percent of the Rule 12 Reports are not filed, if judges are not going to follow the rules, how can we know if a sentence of death is proportional? We can't! The question is, 'Why does the Tennessee Supreme Court not enforce the requirements of Rule 12? In my opinion, if we are not going to follow the rules, we should not have the death penalty."

Again, I could not agree more.

In a follow-up email later that evening, Ed wrote,

> Based on my calculations, there are 41 inmates in Tennessee who are subject to execution. There are five others who are housed on death row, but they are awaiting new sentencing hearings or other procedures. Of the 41 men on death row, 26 were convicted of a single murder, 9 were convicted of double murders, 5 were convicted of triple murders, and 1 was convicted of 6 murders. There are NO defendants on death row for conviction of 4 or 5 victims.
>
> How about 6 victims? Since 1977, 5 defendants have been convicted, statewide, of 6 murders. Two were in Lincoln County, where they received life sentences. One was in Hardeman County, and he received a Life Without Parole sentence. One went into Madison County, Alabama and killed a man to determine if he had the guts to kill his wife. He did. He came back into Lincoln County and killed his wife and 4 others. He killed 6 people on the same day.

He ultimately received a Life Without Parole sentence. The only defendant to receive a death sentence for killing 6 people was in Shelby County (Memphis).

Based on the foregoing, the death sentence is a disproportional sentence for defendants who have been convicted of killing 1, 2, or 3 Tennessee victims. Life and Life Without Parole are comparatively proportional sentences . . . . The abolishment of the death penalty would save the citizens of Tennessee thousands of dollars, and those who have been convicted of First-Degree murder will be incarcerated, preventing them from harming other people. Furthermore, with the establishment of rehabilitation programs, we may be able to rehabilitate inmates in order for them to become productive citizens of Tennessee and the United States.

For the third time, let me say, "I could not agree more." There is a better way. A way that serves justice and honors the victims. That way is restorative justice. Politics should not be used in determining life and death.

CHAPTER 9

THE LITURGY OF DEATH

"There is no justification in killing someone to prove killing someone is wrong."

■ ■ ■

Robert Coe	Billy Irick
Sedley Adley	David Miller
Phil Workman	Ed Zagorski
Daniel Holton	Stephen West
Steve Henley	Don Johnson
Cecil Johnson	Lee Hall
	Nick Sutton

(KR) These are the names of the men who have been executed by the State of Tennessee since KB has been in prison. He was their pastor. They were his friends. For many of them, he was the last person they talked to and prayed with before being escorted from Unit 2 to the death chamber. Billy, David, Ed, Stephen, Don, Lee, and Nick were all friends of mine. In addition to those men, David McNish, Stephen Hueguely, Charles Wright, James Dillinger, Gary Cone, Robert Faulkner, and Derrick Quintero—all friends—have passed away since I began visiting death row. Fourteen deaths in ten years of visiting Unit 2.

Across the United States, twenty-four states and American Samoa practice capital punishment.[7] Three additional states have governor-imposed moratoriums, meaning capital punishment is legal in that state but not practiced.[8] The death penalty is also legal at the federal level. Only twenty-three states have abolished the death penalty.[9]

Tennessee's history with capital punishment is complicated. In her history, the state has had a moral struggle, an off-and-on-again relationship, with the death penalty. Before 1913 capital punishment was carried out by hanging, but very few people were executed. From 1913 through 1915, the state took a hiatus from the death penalty.

In 1916, electrocution became the method of execution. From 1916 till 1960, 125 men were electrocuted at the Tennessee State Penitentiary in Nashville. In 1972 the United States Supreme Court declared capital punishment unconstitutional. In 1976 once again the death penalty became legal. However, in Tennessee those sentenced to death from 1960 to 1978 had their sentences commuted to life. Since 1978 thirteen men have been executed. Their names are mentioned at the beginning of this chapter. KB knew all thirteen individuals.

Lethal injection was added as an alternative to electrocution in 1998. In March of 2000 the state legislature specified that lethal injection be the primary method of execution. From 1960 until April 19, 2000, no state deaths were administered in Tennessee. However, after nearly four decades, Robert Glen Coe was executed by lethal injection at Riverbend Maximum Security Institution.

After Mr. Coe's execution, it was six years before the next execution. Between 2006 and 2009, there were five executions, and then an almost nine-year hiatus. From August 2018 through

February 2020, Tennessee executed seven men. Thankfully, because of COVID, and because of a botched execution in April of 2022, at the time of this writing, there have been zero executions since Nick Sutton was put to death in February of 2020. But any day now, the Tennessee Supreme Court could issue a new round of executions' dates.

(KB) Words cannot describe what it is like to receive a date of execution. It is excruciating. I have witnessed the physical pain, mental anguish, and spiritual agony that takes place as men move closer to their death. I have also seen God's peace reign and comfort those condemned to die. I vividly remember each of the men who have been killed since I have been in Unit 2. I carry each of their names in my heart, and I daily endure the heavy burden on me, and the others left behind.

I am often the last person a man talks to before he is escorted by the guards to the death chamber, located in another building, not far from Unit 2. I spend those last moments praying with them and for them and encourage them to remain strong and trust in God. It is haunting to see your friends handcuffed and shackled, surrounded by guards, being led away, never to see them again. It is immoral and inhuman. There is no justification in killing someone to prove killing someone is wrong.

When KR told me he wanted to write a chapter titled "The Liturgy of Death," I gave him a confused look. I didn't understand what he meant. When I think of liturgy, I think of a religious service. I asked KR, "How is capital punishment a religious service?"

KR answered, "The word *liturgy* refers to a formula used in public religious services. Capital punishment has to do with following a routine that turns something profane into something sacred. There is a ritual around capital punishment that tries to make sense out of nonsense. There is a liturgy around state-sponsored murder that tries to justify the unjustifiable."

I'll admit I had never thought of it that way, but it makes sense. For some people, capital punishment has become part of their religion.

DEATH ROW

For those of us on death row, we follow a routine in the days leading up to an execution of one of our brothers. This is hard for me to write, but I do so hoping it will help change people's minds. Some of the things we do are private and will remain private, but one thing we all do is try our best to support the individual and let them know we love them and will not forget them. Usually, as the time draws near, the individual will give his personal belongings away to the guys in his pod. We then have our own ways of offering our thoughts and prayers. We almost never say, "good-bye," but "see you later." Sometimes we will pull our commissary together and have a "potluck" for the pod.

Usually on Monday night before the Thursday execution, while we are all locked down, the guards come for the person and take them to the death chamber where they will live out their final days. On the day of execution, we are locked down, and in the days following, we gather for a memorial service for our friend. I do not know, nor do I care to know, the type of liturgy the prison follows. I will let KR explain that.

(KR) The reason I think it is important to write about the liturgy of death is so people can see how evil, and how empty, capital punishment is. More violence, no matter how much it is sanitized, is never the solution to violence. By the time a person sentenced to death is executed (more than twenty years), they are not the same person

THE LITURGY OF DEATH

who committed the crime. Furthermore, the thought of executing an innocent person is abominable and should make everyone sick to their stomachs.

THE STATE

The liturgy in Tennessee (every state is different) begins with the state supreme court signing a "death warrant" and setting a date for execution. In Tennessee, the condemned person can choose to die by lethal injection or electrocution. If a person does not choose, the default method is lethal injection. What would you choose?

Tennessee executed Ed Zagorski in November of 2018. He chose the electric chair. The first person to do so in a long time. I asked Ed about this decision and his thought process. He said, "Pastor, the way I see it, electrocution is quicker. It can take twenty-minutes or longer to die by lethal injection. But through electrocution, you are dead within twenty seconds."

PRISON OFFICIALS

The liturgy for the prison officials begins with practicing executions monthly. These practices include a prison employee volunteer being strapped to a gurney (for lethal injection) or strapped to the electric chair (for execution). Every prison official involved in an execution—from the warden to the doctor to the prison chaplain to the guards—have a specific task to perform. They must follow the "approved protocol" to the letter, without any deviation. There is a particular way to store the drugs and a particular method to mix and administer the drugs. There is a particular way to set a person down in the electric chair and a particular order to strap down the arm and legs. The reason for monthly practices is to get the routine, the liturgy, down to perfection, and by doing so, remove the emotions and the humanity from the process. Unfortunately, most of the protocols and procedures, most of the liturgy surrounding the actual execution, is veiled in secrecy. The religion of capital punishment is like a secret society, where only the initiated know what happens, and they are sworn to secrecy.

Over the years, I have had a couple of guys ask me to be their "spiritual advisor" for their execution. Thankfully, so far, none of those guys have been executed, so I have not had to experience it with them. My friend, Rev. Joe Ingle, has been a spiritual advisor more than once. I asked him to describe the process. Here is what he said.

> About a month or so before an execution, if you are the person's spiritual advisor, you will receive a letter from the warden. The letter will outline everything you need to know and will give you access to the person for the last seventy-two hours of their life. It's all very cold and calculated. You will be told your visits the last seventy-two hours will be 'non-contact' visits—meaning you will be separated from the person by glass. However, the law of Tennessee, Code TCA40-23-116 states the spiritual advisor 'preparing the condemned person for death,' has the right to be present with the person. I have used that statute in court to win the right of contact visits during those last seventy-two hours.

In his book, *The Inferno*, Reverend Ingle has a copy of the letter he received from the warden. It is dated April 19, 2007, and, in part, reads, "Pursuant to TCA 40-23-116, a priest or minister who prepares a condemned person for death may witness the execution. As you have been selected by inmate Workman to provide spiritual guidance during confinement on Death Watch, you may be present at the carrying out of such death sentence. The Tennessee Department of Correction needs to know if you are interested in viewing the legal execution of inmate Workman."[10] In his words to me, as well as in his book, Reverend Ingle describes being with someone condemned to die over the final seventh-two hours of life as very much a "Garden of Gethsemane" experience.

ADVOCATES

For many of us who are against the death penalty, we go through a ritual as well. In Tennessee executions typically take place on Thursdays. The Sunday before, we gather in front of the entrance of Riverbend Maximum Security Institution and march from there to the state capitol, a distance of approximately eight miles. We call this "March for Mercy." We carry signs and sing. Then in front of the capitol, we have a time of prayer and reflection.

The next day, Monday, we return to the capitol and go inside to the governor's office to deliver a letter from the guys on Unit 2 asking the governor to come and pray with them. The governor is never in his office. On Thursday evenings, a couple of hours before the scheduled state murder, we gather in an open field on the property of Riverbend for a prayer vigil. We sing, pray, listen to short speeches, participate in communion, and wait to hear that the execution is over and the person is dead. Once the execution is over, the prison guards and Tennessee Highway Patrol officers on horseback tell us we have thirty minutes to vacate the premises or be subject to arrest.

Everything around an execution, including peaceful, prayerful protests, is tightly regulated and enforced. Capital punishment is a liturgy to the god of punitive justice that ends with a human sacrifice.

Part Two
LIFE ON DEATH ROW
■ ■ ■

*"The first thing the prison system tries to do
is strip you of your humanity.
You are no longer a person but a number.
You are no longer an individual but a ward of the State."*
KEVIN BURNS

*"In their own unique ways, every man in Unit 2
has impacted and changed my life for the better."*
KEVIN RIGGS

CHAPTER 10
ORDINATION

*"In my car, on the way home, thinking about
my conversation with KB and how he is Unit 2's pastor,
I heard the Spirit of God say to me, 'If you truly believe
KB is a pastor, you need to ordain him as such.'"*

■ ■ ■

The first few years of ministering beside KB on Unit 2 were exciting. Don't get me wrong, I look forward to every visit, and I enjoy every minute getting to know KB. We have had many deep conversations. Sometimes we talk about nothing. We have laughed together, prayed together, read Scripture together, and cried together. We have lived life together, and we have experienced community. But there was something special about those first few years.

Our routine was simple. Once entering Unit 2, I greeted a few of the guys in the center, administrative pod referred to as Echo Pod, or E-pod. These guys were working in the kitchen, the laundry, or the Unit 2 office. One of them was usually buffing the floor. I said hello to the guards and unit manager, then I went into Baltimore Pod (B-pod) where KB lived in a six-by-eight cell.

On most days, KB was still in his cell, having his morning devotions, getting ready for the day. A few of the guys were in the pod reading, playing dominoes, drinking coffee, or just talking. One of them yelled, "KB, Pastor Kevin is here!" And then another jokingly said, "You know KB; he's not coming out until he is perfectly dressed." I joked back, "Yeah, he's a diva." Even though he wears the same thing every day, KB takes pride in how he looks. His mom told me that, beginning in his teens, KB ironed all his clothes, making sure his shirts and pants (even his blue jeans) had a nice, clean crease in them.

While waiting on KB, the guys in B-pod fixed a cup of coffee for me, and I talked to them about the books they were reading, sports, the news of the day, their families, and periodically, their cases and where they were in their appeals process.

Eventually KB came out of cell 211 on the second floor, with a big smile on his face. As he skipped down the steps, he said, "Hey Pastor, how are you today?" We embraced as I said, "I am good. How are you?" He always responded, "Today is the best day of my life." We talked for a few moments, catching up with each other, and then we started making our rounds.

Four pods are in Unit 2: A, B, C, and D. Also known as Atlanta Pod, Baltimore Pod, Chicago Pod, and Dallas Pod. The pods Atlanta, Baltimore, and Dallas were occupied. No one was housed in C-pod. We went to each pod, first visiting B- and C-level guys who were locked in their cells twenty-three hours a day. I carried a collapsible three-legged stool with me, so I could sit in front of the cell doors and talk to the guys through the pie flap.

After visiting the B and C guys, we then gathered any of the A guys who wanted to meet. I read Scripture, made a few comments, and then we prayed together. Longer conversations happened with the guys who were locked down.

On this particular day, we visited Kyle, a huge University of Tennessee football fan. Our conversations always started off, "Go Vols." Kyle was executed in 2019.

Next, we visited Rick. Rick loved to write poetry. He shared the following poem with me. It's titled "Flower."

Like a prayer
    That God always answers.
A flower is always giving,
    Due to God's grace;
Just open your eyes,
    And your heart
        And you'll see;
The love of God
    Is all around us.

After praying with Rick, we spent some time with Mack, who was a loner. He kept to himself, and KB was one of the few persons he talked to. Because of my friendship with KB, Mack talked to me and we developed a good friendship. Like many of the guys in Unit 2, Mack had an abusive childhood. But he knew his Bible. He grew up Church of God and loved talking about God and church. Mack developed bladder cancer, but he refused all treatment. He did not trust the prison's healthcare, even though he was in tremendous pain. During our conversation, he told us his urine was black. We encouraged him to get help. Within a few days after our visit, Mack was taken to the prison hospital. Not long after that, he passed away.

Our conversations this day were more intense than usual. Before I left, KB and I reflected on our visits. KB said to me, "You know, all the men here love you and look forward to your visits. When you are not here, I make the rounds by myself, and they always ask me about you and when you are coming again. They all look to you as their pastor."

I started crying and responded, "These guys do more for me then I ever do for them. I hope they know how much I love them." KB assured me they did. Then I said, "You know, KB, I don't think these guys would talk to me if it weren't for you. They love and respect you, which is why they have embraced me like they have. I am not their pastor. You are their pastor, and Unit 2 is your church." Now KB was crying. We hugged each other, said good-bye, and told each other to tell our families hello.

DRIVING HOME

As I walked out of Unit 2 on a crisp, sunny fall day, I thought to myself how fortunate I was to be able to minister on death row, and how thankful I was to have KB in my life. With tears in my eyes, I said to myself, "Today truly is the best day of my life." In my car, on the way home, thinking about my conversation with KB and how he is Unit 2's pastor, I heard the Spirit of God say to me, "If you truly believe KB is a pastor, you need to ordain him as such." In my spirit, I responded, "The prison would never allow that." I heard back, "The prison has nothing to do with it. You pastor a church and your church can ordain him. You don't need anyone's permission."

"Well," I said, "that's not entirely true. I do need the permission of the elders at my church." Then I smiled because I knew they would say yes. On the rest of the drive home, I started planning KB's ordination.

The following week I spoke with my elders about ordaining KB, and they were as excited about the possibility as I was. One of the elders, summarizing the others, said, "If we do this, we need to do it right. We can't just give KB his ordination. He needs to earn it. It needs to be something in which he can be proud. His ordination process needs to be equal to your ordination process." As usual, my elders were right. KB's process of ordination started in December of 2016 and wasn't completed until his ordination service on January 29, 2018.

THE PROCESS

The first step was to make KB a member of our church. This was the simplest step. The following Friday after my conversation with my elders, I presented KB a certificate of church membership. The next step was to license KB for pastoral ministry. In order to be licensed, KB had to answer seven simple questions. Then over the course of a year, he had to meet with me regularly and keep a journal of all his ministry experiences over that year. Of the seven questions, the two most important ones were (1) Tell briefly of your conversion and give reasons you are saved. (2) Why do you want to be a minister? What is your view of what is termed the "call to preach"?

To the first question, KB answered:

> "In reference to my conversion, I don't recall a moment of instantaneous change. I think it has been a process. God began to change my heart when I began to seek Him at the Memphis jail. My conversion has been an overall and total change in my way of life. It has affected my thinking, acting, and responding. I think about the words of Jesus and what he said to the apostle Peter: 'When you are converted, help your brothers.' (Luke 22:32) I think about that and how over a period of time, God began to change my heart and give me a heart to minister to His people and love them. The love forces me to want to help them in any kind of way that I see they are hurting, or remaining in bondage. I am called to minister in every way. My conversion has been a total overhaul of life.

"How do I know I am saved? I know that I'm saved by faith. The Lord says in scripture, 'For if our heart condemn us, God is greater than our heart, and knoweth all things. Beloved, if our heart condemns us not, then have we confidence toward God' (1 John 3:20–21). But by faith, I believe that I'm saved because I have confidence according to the scriptures that I have lived them out and am living them out and in my heart. I have confidence towards God. Also, I know that I'm saved because God has cleansed me; cleansed my soul from guilt, condemnation, from sin and His Spirit now resides in me. His Spirit guides my life."

To the second question, KB answered:

"First of all, I don't think I ever had aspirations to be a minister. I grew up in church, always loved the ministry, always loved the preaching of the gospel, but I don't think I ever had specific aspirations to be a minister. But God spoke to me and told me that I am His minister. I want to be a minister because He said I am a minister.

"My view of the term, 'call to preach,' is this: I believe only God calls His preachers. I believe the call to preach is enacted when God Himself separates one for the purpose of preaching the gospel of Jesus Christ to all. I believe only God can make such a call because God knows the heart that He has placed in every individual. A true preacher must be converted and must have a shepherd's heart; one that is filled with the unconditional love of God, *agape*."

KB received his license for the gospel ministry on March 5, 2017.

ORDINATION

Between licensing and ordination, KB had to continue to meet with me, continue to keep a ministry journal, and answer forty-five questions, broken down in the following categories: (1) General Information; (2) Personal Life; (3) Bible, Theology, Doctrine, and Ecclesiology; and (4) Social Issues. KB answered most of the questions in written form. The other questions he answered to me orally. Below is a sampling of some of those questions, along with KB's answers.

Explain what you mean about the deity and humanity of Christ. How would you evaluate the Council of Chalcedon? *"I believe that Christ Jesus was (and is) 100% God (thus deity) and simultaneously He was 100% man (thus humanity). The Council of Chalcedon (451 A.D.) settled the critical matter of how to view the two natures of Jesus as God and man. The great legacy of the Council of Chalcedon reflects a consensus on the language that preserves both the complete deity and humanity of Jesus in His person. A complete salvation demands it. Faith in the God-man Jesus Christ procures it."*

What is repentance and is it essential to salvation? *"Repentance comes from the Greek word 'metanoia'; 'meta' meaning 'afterwards,' and 'noia,' meaning 'to consider, think, or comprehend.' It means to exercise the mind. The consideration here is with contrition. Metanoia means to think differently or afterward, that is, to reconsider. Morally, it means to feel compunction and to repent.*

"Yes, repentance is absolutely essential to salvation. John the Baptist spoke to the Pharisees and Sadducees that came to his baptisms saying unto them, 'O generation of vipers, who hath warned you to flee from the wrath to come? Bring

forth therefore fruits meet for repentance: And think not to say within yourselves, We have Abraham to our father: for I say unto you, that God is able of these stones to raise up children unto Abraham' (Matthew 3:7–9). Also, in Romans 12:2, Paul writes, 'And be not conformed to this world: but be ye transformed by the renewing of your mind, that ye may prove what is that good, and acceptable, and perfect, will of God.' Repentance is essential to salvation because there must be a changing of the way we think."

What is your passion? "My passion is the Word of God. To read it, to study it, to meditate upon it, and preach and teach it. But most importantly, to obey it."

Why are you passionate about that area of ministry? "Because I believe it's the most important part. For by the Word, God created the heavens and the earth, and the seas, and all that is in them [see Nehemiah 9:6]. And again, 'he sent his word, and healed them' (Psalm 107:20) And again, 'In him [the Word] was life; and the life was the light of men. . . . That was the true Light, which lighteth every man that cometh into the world' (John 1:4, 9). And after all, it was the Word in Sunday School that God used to capture my heart.

I will never forget the day of his ordination service. KB had a beautiful invitation card made that he mailed to all his friends and family. The outside of the card resembled his cell door with his cell number, 211, on it, a small window, like the one on his cell, and his door handle. Inside it read,

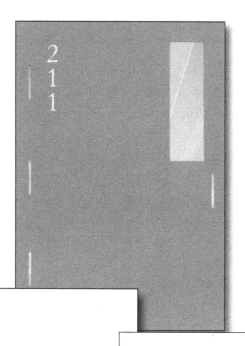

You are cordially invited
to the ordination of

KEVIN BENARD BURNS

Into the Gospel Ministry....
Please know that I would be very
honored if you could join together
with us in this celebration.

Thank you,
With the love of **CHRIST**

Kevin B. Burns
Pastor

January 29, 2018
12:00 PM
Riverbend Max. Sec. Institution
2-A Building

This shall be written for the generation to come:
And the people which hall be created shall praise **THE LORD**.
For **HE** hath looked down from the height of his sanctuary:
From heaven did **THE LORD** behold the earth;
To hear the groaning of the prisoner:
To loose those that are appointed to death...
PSALMS 102: 18-20KJ

It's hard to put into words the beauty of this service. Riverbend Maximum Security Institution bent over backward to allow us to have a wonderful experience. The library in Unit 2A was filled. KB's mom and dad were there. Hymns were sung ("Saved, Saved, Saved," "Amazing Grace," and "Doxology"), and scriptures were read (Joshua 1:6–9 and 1 Timothy 3:1–7). Prayers were prayed, I delivered the Ordination Charge, and KB preached and led us in communion. It was a day I will never forget.

My charge to KB included the following words:

> "Kevin Bernard Burns senses God's call on his life to be an ordained minister. Through my relationship with him, our church senses the need to affirm that call through ordination. Since Kevin has been faithfully serving the Lord, here at Riverbend, as a chaplain's assistance for several years, some may ask why the need for ordination? They may ask, *'Kevin doesn't need man's approval to serve, and besides, what difference is a piece of paper going to make, especially inside Riverbend.'* Ordination is not man approving a person. Rather, ordination is a public confirmation, and affirmation, of the Holy Spirit's calling on an individual's life. The difference a Certificate of Ordination makes is twofold:
>
> First, it gives authority to the position of a minister. The ultimate authority comes from God, but being recognized by the people of God as a minister gives a degree of authority. With authority, however, comes responsibility, and Kevin must always remember that the authority of a minister is the authority to serve, not be served.
>
> Second, with a Certificate of Ordination comes accountability. Kevin is not just an ordained minister. He

is an ordained *Franklin Community Church* minister. He has submitted himself to our Elders. Being accountable to others is Biblical and it keeps a person humble and in line with the gospel. With this in mind, I will now ask Kevin to respond to the following questions: (KB answered in the affirmative to all the questions.)

- Are you fully aware of the responsibilities that are about to be placed upon you by being ordained and set apart as an ambassador of Jesus Christ?
- Do you accept the Bible as the Word of God?
- Since you are being ordained to the gospel ministry by *Franklin Community Church,* will you promise to preach and uphold the doctrines and practices of *Franklin Community Church*? Will you assume the responsibility to serve God faithfully in whatever capacity God calls you to, and to give yourself sacrificially and without reserve to the building of the body of Christ?
- Will you endeavor to be diligent in the study of God's Word; instant and faithful in prayer; opened to and directed by the Holy Spirit; living as an example of Christian character and discipline before the church and the community, in order that your life may be a worthy Christian example and that upon your ministry the blessing of God may rest?

(KB) All day on the day of my ordination, and all through the service, I just kept saying, "Wow!" over and over again. My ordination service was the single most moving experience I have ever had. I was overwhelmed with emotions and gratitude. I was humbled by the work of God in my life.

Growing up in church like I did, I had several experiences with God. On several different occasions, different pastors told me they saw the call of God on my life. These pastors said the same thing about my brother, Phillip. Late in my teen years, I veered off course and backslid, but not Phillip. He remained true and was ordained around 1989. I was there to hear him preach his first sermon. Today, Phillip is a pastor. He pastors the same church my dad pastored, New Hope Baptist Church in West Memphis, Arkansas. I am so proud of my brother and his faithfulness after all these years.

Pastor Kevin (KR) asked me what it means to me to be ordained. My answer is, it means everything. I am finally the man God created me to be. God is first in my life, and I am in the center of His will. I know who I am and Whose I am. I am not a property of the state of Tennessee. I am not inmate number 254315. I am an ordained minister of the Gospel of Jesus Christ. I am exactly who God created me to be.

CHAPTER 11
LIFE ON DEATH ROW

"According to the criminal legal system, I was no longer a person. I was simply Inmate #254315."

■ ■ ■

(KB) People ask me how I am doing, and I always respond, "Today is the best day of my life," and I mean it. I am thankful for every day God has given me to serve Him, even in this desolate place called death row. Years ago I stopped saying "death row" and started saying "life row." Life in Unit 2 is much like life anywhere else. There are good days and bad days, ups and downs, victories and defeats. The only difference is our days are scheduled by the Tennessee Department of Corrections, and our movements are severely restricted. As a result, our world is small, and with every execution, it becomes smaller.

Life on Unit 2 is the same every day. It starts at 5:00 a.m. when the guards check every cell to make sure everyone is alive and well. The guards return at 6:15 a.m. to make sure everyone is up and dressed. Breakfast is served between 6:30 a.m. and 6:45 a.m. Kitchen workers are up and at work by 4:00 a.m. A-level persons can eat in groups, for all meals. Levels B and C people must eat in their cells. Even though I don't have to, I usually eat in my cell.

B- and C-level persons are locked down twenty-three hours a day. A-level people are allowed out of the cells most of the day. As an A-level person, I can be out of my cell from 6:30 a.m. until 11:15 a.m. By 11:15 a.m. each day, I must be back in my cell for count. Lunch is served at 11:30 a.m., and then A-levels can be out of their cells from 11:30 a.m. until 4:00 p.m., for another count at 4:15 p.m. Supper is served at 4:30, and then we (A-level guys) can be out of our cells until 8:30 p.m.

Beginning at 12:30 p.m., the "yard" is open. We call it the yard, but it's really an outside cage on concrete with metal roofing. It can get really hot out there, but it is still good to get out and get some fresh air. I usually stay outside from 12:30 p.m. till 4:00 p.m. A-level persons can come and go outside and can be in cages that are large enough for multiple people at a time to play basketball or handball. B- and C-level guys have to be escorted outside by guards to smaller, single-person cages. B-level guys are handcuffed and escorted by one guard. C-level guys are handcuffed and shackled and escorted by two guards. B- and C-level people only get one hour outside, and then they are escorted back to their cells. After supper, the yard is open until 7:30 p.m. I take a shower every day between 7:30 p.m. and 8:00 p.m.

There is a building adjacent to Unit 2 called 2A. It is connected to Unit 2 by a short walkway that is completely enclosed. Level-A guys can go to 2A for arts and crafts and do research for their cases in a small law library. Unit 2A is open from 8:30 a.m. till 11:00 a.m., again from 12:30 p.m. till 4:00 p.m., and a final time from 5:30 p.m. till 8:00 p.m.

Everyone has to be back in their cells by 8:30 p.m. and are locked down until the next morning. Through the night, there are counts at 9:00 p.m., 10:30 p.m., 2:00 a.m., and then the day starts all over at 5:00 a.m. At each count the guards shine a light in the cells to make sure we are there. They usually shine the light on the ceiling, and the light reflects enough for them to see inside. Sometimes, just to get on our nerves, a guard will shine the light in our eyes and wait for a response.

Tuesday is commissary day, and everyone loves commissary. By 3:30 p.m. each Tuesday, we must turn in our commissary order to be delivered the following Tuesday. Commissary is where we can order snacks like those out of a vending machine, stamps for letters and cards, instant coffee or cocoa, Gatorade, soft drinks, and a host of other things. Of course, we have to pay for these things. Unfortunately, some of the guys cannot afford to purchase anything. I do my best to make sure everyone has something. Through commissary we can also purchase toiletries like shampoo, soap, deodorant, shaving cream, toothpaste and toothbrushes. If a guy cannot afford to buy his own supplies, the prison provides an "indigent package." But that stuff is of low quality. The most desired item, of all commissary items, is stamps.

In addition to weekly commissary, we can purchase things like baseball hats (either white or gray with no writing on them), gray sweatpants and sweatshirts, watches and other types of jewelry, and shoes. Since we all have to dress the same, people express their individuality through their shoes. Most of the men purchase Nike tennis shoes (either white or black) and/or brown work boots. Then they paint them different colors, with different schemes and outlines. Quarterly is also when guys purchase their arts and crafts supplies. Books can be ordered through a few different book distributors, but they have to be softback books. Hardback books are not allowed in prison.

TODAY! ■ THE BEST DAY OF MY LIFE

RIVERBEND MAXIMUM SECURITY INSTITUTION

On November 29, 1995, I left the Shelby County Jail in Memphis, Tennessee, where I had been since July 23, 1992, and walked onto Tennessee's death row inside Riverbend Maximum Security Institution (RMSI) in Nashville, Tennessee. I had been found guilty of felony murder and attempted felony murder. To the world I was a condemned man who should be executed and shown no mercy, even though I was innocent. According to the criminal legal system, I was no longer a person. I was simply Inmate #254315.

The first thing the prison system tries to do is strip us of our humanity. We are no longer people but numbers. We are no longer individuals but wards of the state. All we have is time, but it is their time not ours. Every day is regimented. Every day is the same. We get up at the same time. We eat at the same time. We shower at the same time. We go outside at the same time, and we wear the same clothes day after day, month after month, year after year, decade after decade. We are treated as if we are nothing. We are treated as if we do not matter. Over time, if we are not careful, we will start to see ourselves the way the criminal legal system sees us.

But I am not who other people say I am. I am not who the prosecutor says I am. I am not who the jury says I am. I am not who the Department of Corrections says I am. I am not who the guards say I am. And, most importantly, I am not who I say I am.

Who am I?

I am who God says I am!

I am a reflection of God's image.

I am *Imago Dei*.

I am holy.

I am pure.

I am forgiven.

I am sanctified.

I am Holy Spirit indwelled.

I am a father, a grandfather, a son, a brother, an uncle, and an ordained minister of the Gospel of Jesus Christ.

I am Kevin Burns, a child of the King and an heir of God.

When people ask how I can be so positive and stay so joyful, I tell them it's because I see myself the way God sees me, not how others see me and not even how I see myself. For me it's quite simple. I believe the testimony of God about me more than I believe the testimony of man about me. God's word is higher than my thoughts. God's opinion of me supersedes other people's opinion of me. The words of Jesus are the most important thing to me. Ultimately, I believe, "I am crucified with Christ: nevertheless I live; yet not I, but Christ liveth in me: and the life which I now live in the flesh I live by the faith of the Son of God, who loved me, and gave himself for me." (Galatians 2:20). I hold tightly to the truth, "For me to live is Christ, and to die is gain" (Philippians 1:21). This doesn't mean I don't have challenges. This doesn't mean life is easy. There have been times that have tried my faith, but I have always found God faithful. The truth is, I have no plan B. This is it for me. God is all I've got. Either God saves me, or I am a dead man.

Right now, inside Riverbend Maximum Security Institution, I serve as the chaplain's assistant for Unit 2, otherwise known as death row. But several years ago, I worked in the kitchen, washing dishes in what we call the "Tray Room." I worked from 6:00 a.m. till 4:00 p.m. every day. When I started working in the kitchen, I got paid 17 cents an hour. Eventually I was making 42 cents an hour. Now, as the chaplain's assistant, I make 50 cents an hour.

While working in the Tray Room, there was a guard who never seemed happy and who only had negative things to say. Regularly this guard would remind us he was in charge, and we were nothing but criminals. One day the guard asked me, "How does it feel?"

This questioned surprised me. I did not know what he meant. All I could say was, "What?"

Then he said, "How does it feel to see us leave every day to go home to our families and you have to stay here?"

I knew his question wasn't sincere. Rather it was asked in a sarcastic way meant to intimidate and humiliate me. His tone was very derogatory. With a smile I replied, "I don't think about it that way. The way I see it, you leave every day only to come back the next day. This is your job. But one day I am going to leave through that same door, and I'm going to walk down that same sidewalk, and I am going to walk through that same gate you walk through. When I do, unlike you, I am never coming back. In fact, the only way I would come back is if God told me to come back and minister to my brothers. This is your job, but it's my calling!"

There is one thing that happens every three months that serves no purpose but to humiliate us. And by "us," I mean all incarcerated individuals, not just those on death row. This happens in every prison. Every three months we get a "time sheet." This is a sheet that tells you when you committed the crime for which you have been charged, when you were sentenced, what your sentence is, and how long you have been incarcerated. So, every three months, I am reminded, even though I am innocent, why I am in prison. As if, somehow, I would forget. So, I repeat, I am not what others say I am. I am who God says I am. As long as I keep that perspective in mind, every day I can say, "Today is the best day of my life."

Here is a prayer I wrote, after writing this chapter.

O Lord God Almighty, Everlasting Father,
Prince of Peace, and Wonderful Savior.
Lord, You are Holy, and I lift You up and magnify Your name.
I love You my God because You first loved me.
Yes, You loved me wonderfully.
And reverently created me in Your own image.
Then You gave me power to be called, "A son of God."
O Lord God, I will praise Your name forevermore.
For Your faithfulness is ever lasting,
and to Your mercy there is no end.

And now my Lord, I thank You that Your ears are open to the cries of the prisoners.
For upon You have we laid all our hope.
Neither will we look to any other.
For there is none other who is able to deliver like You can.
Deliver us therefore, O Lord our God, I pray.

Yea, deliver us swiftly.
Deliver us from bondage and shame.
Deliver us from sickness and disease.
Deliver us from the expectations of those that seek our harm.
And we will praise Your holy name.
Bring us out healthy and strong, and please don't leave us alone.
Give us those of Your people that will help us and restore us to our place in society.

And Lord, we will live out the rest of our days in Your service.
In the name of Your holy Son, Jesus, I pray.
Amen.

CHAPTER 12
CHURCH OF LIFE

*"What I envision is a church for the men of Unit 2,
led by the men of Unit 2."*

■ ■ ■

(KR) When I started visiting death row, a person could visit four times a year without going through any type of orientation. I knew I wanted to visit regularly, so I started the process of becoming a "badged volunteer" before my fourth and final visit. It ended up taking more than a year to get my badge! During the process, the prison's chaplain asked me why I wanted to volunteer on death row. He said, "Everyone wants to go to death row. No one wants to go to Unit 1 and Unit 3."

Riverbend Maximum Security Institution is divided into two general areas. They are known as the "high side" and the "low side." The low side is minimum security. Two large units are on the low side, Units 5 and 6. My guess is the low side houses between four hundred and five hundred men. The low side is also where the chapel is, a library, a large cafeteria, ball fields, a walking track, and a small clinic/hospital. When the men at Riverbend need more medical care than the prison can provide, they are taken to Meharry Medical Center, a part of Meharry Medical College in Nashville. Sometimes they are taken to Nashville General Hospital. The low side also houses Riverbend's nationally acclaimed braille certification program where men translate textbooks into braille for students at the Tennessee School for the Blind. This program is part of the Tennessee Rehabilitative Initiative in Correction (TRICOR).

The high side is maximum security, sometimes referred to as "Super Max." Units 1 and 3 house the most violent and most vulnerable offenders in the entire state. Usually men get sent to these units not for the crimes they committed on the outside, but for crimes and violations they have committed while being incarcerated. The men in Unit 1 and Unit 3 are locked down in their individual, small, six-by-eight cells twenty-three hours a day. They are doing "hard time." These two units are not where anyone wants to be. Unit 1 and Unit 3 are usually loud and chaotic, with a very distinctive smell of bleach, body odor, and occasionally, marijuana. One of my friends in these units once told me, "The guards like it when we smoke weed. It chills us out and makes their job easier." Unit 2 is death row. Unit 4 is a "step-down" unit. Guys from Units 1 and 3 usually go to Unit 4 for a period of time before going back to "general population." There are no rehabilitation programs in Unit 1 and Unit 3. Both are oppressive and depressive environments.

I told the chaplain if he would let me go to Unit 2 (death row), I would also go to Unit 1 and Unit 3. The chaplain asked, "Are you sure?" I said, "Yes." A short time later I finally received my volunteer badge. My experiences in Units 1 and 3 could be a book in and of themselves.

Unit 2 has plenty of volunteers. Most of the volunteers are religious volunteers. Throughout the week, there are numerous Bible studies, classes, opportunities to receive communion, and one-on-one mentoring. The chaplain was right, "Everyone wants to go to death row. No one wants to go to Unit 1 and Unit 3." In truth, most volunteers could not handle Units 1 and 3.

AN IDEA

When KB first arrived in Unit 2, a couple of volunteers led a church service on Thursday evenings. These volunteers were faithful and well respected by the guys on death row. They had a huge influence on KB and encouraged him in his faith. On a regular basis, they allowed KB to preach. KB would not be the preacher he is today without the influence of these men. KB said to me, "These volunteers were great. In fact, all our volunteers are great, but there was nothing that was 'just for us.'"

A few months after my church ordained KB, I told KB I had an idea. I said to him, "Why don't we start a church." Unbeknownst to me, KB had been thinking and praying about this for years. An actual church on death row was a dream of his. He smiled at me and said, "I think that's a great idea."

Over the years, I have seen Bible studies start in Unit 2 and eventually dissolve or turn into another group therapy session. As important as a Bible study or group therapy session may be, that is not what I had in mind. I said to KB, "What I envision is a church for the men of Unit 2 led by the men of Unit 2." I then said, "I want this to be an actual church service, not another Bible study or small group discussion." With that in mind, we worked on a liturgy that would be followed each week. The liturgy included prayers, Scripture readings, songs, communion (when available), and a sermon.

The next decision was what to call the church. We brainstormed a few ideas, but nothing seemed to stick. KB then said, "You know, for years, I have referred to this place as 'life row' and have tried to get other people to refer to it that way as well. Maybe we could call it something like that." I threw out the name "Life Church." And KB replied, "What about 'Church of Life?'" The moment he said, "Church of Life," we both knew that was the name. Then we came up with a tag line: "The 'Church of Life.' A church for the men on death row led by the men on death row." The foundational verse for the Church of Life is Jesus's words in John 5:24: "Truly I tell you, whoever hears my word and believes him who sent me has eternal life and will not be judged but has crossed over from death to life." The Church of Life even has a logo. It's two birds flying out of a cage into the sunset. The logo is a visual representation of incarcerated people being set free.

With the name, liturgy, foundational verse, and logo, the only decision remaining was the day and time each week. We decided the Church of Life would meet on Sunday evenings at five o'clock. A few weeks later, we filled out the necessary paperwork for the prison. My church, Franklin Community Church, would be the sponsoring group. In no time at all, we received approval and held our first service. About fifteen guys were present that first service. Everyone was excited about this new venture.

My plan was to attend the first month or so and then only attend once a month or whenever KB thought I needed to. I truly wanted this to be their church. I did not want volunteers (even from my own church) attending and "taking over." I'll admit, I was, and still am, very protective of the Church of Life. I didn't realize how radical this idea was. I didn't realize how hard it would be to keep volunteers away. I didn't realize how hard some prison officials would try and stop the Church of Life from flourishing. I would, however, soon learn.

A few months after starting the church, and several weeks after I stopped attending, I ask KB how the church was doing. He said, "Things are going really good. This past Sunday we had a special speaker." I asked who the guest speaker was. KB told me it was a guy from Michigan who had spent several years in prison and was now going to churches and prisons sharing his testimony. I asked how he heard about this guy. KB mentioned a well-known prison ministry that often receives special treatment at Riverbend. This prison ministry also has local celebrities who volunteer with them. KB said, "Chaplain Wiggins [a different chaplain than the one who helped me get my volunteer badge] told me about this man, and then Smitty [a leader in this famous prison ministry] reached out to me. Said he had heard about our Sunday evening group, and asked if he could bring this guy from Michigan to share in our church service." By this point, my antenna was up, but KB seemed happy, and I thought this was just a one-time thing, so I let it go.

The next Sunday evening, the same group brought in another guest speaker. The same thing happened the Sunday after that. Three weeks in a row there was no church service. Three weeks in a row, KB was not allowed to preach. My fear was being realized. The Church of Life was dissolving into another group therapy session led by volunteers. The Church of Life was being hijacked by this well-known local prison ministry.

By this time, even KB was getting concerned. Most of the guys who had been attending Church of Life were also concerned. They asked KB, "When will our church meet again? I miss our church. What happened to Sunday evenings being a church for us and led by us? Why has this other ministry taken over?"

KB said to me, "I tried to explain this to the volunteers, but they won't listen. I gave them your name and number and told them they need to call you." He then told me that one of them, the local celebrity, said he did call me and talk to me and everything was fine. KB then asked, "Did he call you?" I said, "No KB. He did not call me. No one has called me and talked to me about this."

KB and I both knew this particular prison ministry was so connected to the administration at Riverbend that pushing back against them would be the same as pushing back against the institution.

There was very little any of us could actually do. The following Sunday evenings there were no special speakers, but these volunteers had taken over and were leading the services every week. KB was never asked to preach. Each week became just another time for guys to get together and talk. What ceased to happen on Sunday evenings was a church for the men on death row led by the men on death row.

What was supposed to be a one-week special speaker turned into a takeover. I am convinced certain prison officials did not like the guys meeting on their own, and so they reached out to this prison ministry to come in and "help organize it." The unit manager at the time told KB it was against prison policy for inmates to meet without volunteers present. KB said he had never heard of that policy, and no policy had ever been shown to him. I don't know if this local prison ministry that took over knew they were taking over a church. I would like to give them the benefit of the doubt. But the end result was the same. An attempt had been made to squash the Church of Life.

After several more weeks of the Church of Life not meeting, Pervis, a man on death row who was acting as the deacon of the church, said to KB, "We've got to do something. We need to keep the Church of Life going. It's too important. Besides, I need to hear the Word preached each week." Since the volunteers who led a church service on Thursday evenings were no longer coming, the decision was made to move Church of Life to Thursday evenings.

More than five years later, the Church of Life still meets on Thursday evenings. But now, to prevent another takeover, volunteers from my church are there every week. They understand their role is to be present and participate, but KB is the pastor, and he leads the service each week. The church is thriving, and it has been fun to watch.

Church of Life is like any other church. They have their ups and downs, and every problem a church on the outside has, they have had—from disgruntled members to people coming and going to complaints about the sermons being too long. I know Church of Life is a real church because it has had the same experiences—good and bad—of a real church. KB is a great pastor. He has more patience than I have. On more than one occasion, I have said to him, "If I had to live with my church members twenty-four hours a day, seven days a week, 365 days a year, I would go crazy."

And they still follow the original liturgy we set up.

Welcome
Worship Through Songs
Opening Prayer
Old Testament Reading
New Testament Reading
Worship Through Songs
Worship Through Communion
Worship Through the Word
Closing Song
Closing Prayer and Benediction

(KB) I think the uniqueness of the Church of Life is that it is for the guys in Unit 2 and *led by the guys in unit 2*. In the outside church world, there is a lot of talk about "incarnational ministry" and relocating into marginalized communities to do ministry. What is more incarnational than God calling a man from the outside world to go into death row, as a death row inmate, to minister to the men on death row? There is no more marginalized, and hated, community like the incarcerated community. There is no farther relocation than relocating from the free world into a world where your freedom is taken away and you have been condemned to die. When God told me He needed me on death row because He had a job for me to do and a work in me to complete, I think the Church of Life is what He meant. I am in Unit 2 for such a time as this. Don't get me wrong, I'm ready to be set free, but until that time, I will continue ministering to the guys on death row as a guy on death row myself. For as long as God allows, I will continue to be the senior pastor of the Church of Life.

CHAPTER 13
CELL BY CELL

"I am grateful I have lived long enough for God to forgive me of all the horrible things I have done."

(KR) I grew up in a conservative denomination and church. During my teen years and through most of my twenties, I practiced what we called "door-to-door evangelism." That means I spent lots of Saturdays walking through neighborhoods, knocking on strangers' doors, praying with them, and telling them about Jesus. For a period of time, I enjoyed it and was quite good at it, which is odd because deep down I am an introvert. I did it, believing it was what God required of me. God never wastes an experience. When KB suggested to me that we go cell to cell and pod to pod talking and praying with anyone and everyone, I was excited about it and immediately thought about how much door-to-door evangelism I had done in my life. I was more than prepared for the challenge.

Walking around Unit 2 allowed me to meet all the men on death row and build lasting relationships with a lot of them. I consider these men my friends, and I love each of them. I believe the feelings are mutual. At least I hope they are. I want to tell about some of my friends, but first, let me describe death row. It's not what you may think.

Walking into Unit 2 can be intimidating. At the entrance, are four small cells that are used for attorney visits and "non-contact" visits. In the right corner of the entrance is a restroom. The next room is medium sized and is for "contact visits." (I'll explain "non-contact" and "contact" visits shortly.) Next a narrow hallway goes through a couple more locked doors then to the main door. Once it is unlocked, you step into Echo Pod.

Visitors have to navigate through five locked doors before actually entering the unit itself. Off of Echo Pod (the central area) are offices for the guards, the unit manager, and the unit counselor. Also, off this area is a kitchen, a couple of washrooms with washers and dryers, and another restroom. Up top, in the middle of the unit, is the "bird's nest." After more than ten years visiting Unit 2, I still do not know how to get to the bird's nest. I have never seen any stairs leading up, and I have never seen anyone coming or going from the bird's nest. From there, however, guards can monitor each pod and all the cameras in Unit 2.

At the far end of this area is another locked door that leads outside to a caged walkway that goes to the separate building called 2A. In this building is the small law library, a few really old computers (no internet access), an office for the guards, a restroom, a big meeting room, and a room for arts and crafts. It is important to point out that none of the guards inside Unit 2 are armed. In fact, none of the guards throughout the entire prison are armed.

Each pod has two levels with twelve cells on each level. It is fifteen steps up to the second level. When first walking into a pod, you walk through a locked door into a small cage. If the door of the cage is locked, a guard must unlock it. Once through the cage, you walk into a large room with the cells in a semi-circle around the outside walls. On the bottom floor, before the cells start, usually to the left, are four showers. Some of the cells have a shower in them. Also on the bottom floor is a microwave, a bulletin board, a ping-pong table, and a few tables. Off to the side are a couple of rooms used mainly for haircuts. Everything is concrete, including the floors, and all the walls are painted white. The pods are also spotless. All and all it is a very cold, very uninviting place.

THE LEVEL SYSTEM

Tennessee's death row is unique in that it operates on a level system, based on good behavior, that was won in a court case. After a prisoner rebellion in 1975, two lawsuits were filed in Tennessee. One, *Grubbs v. Bradley*, was against the entire Tennessee prison system. The other, *Gloseclose v. Dutton*, was specifically directed at Tennessee's death row. Judge Thomas Higgins presided over *Grubbs v. Bradley*, and Judge John Nixon presided over *Gloseclose v. Dutton*. Each case prevailed and were consolidated. Governor Lamar Alexander called a special session of the Tennessee Legislature in 1984 to deal with the demands of the court order because of *Grubbs v. Bradley*. Millions of dollars were appropriated, new prisons were built, including Riverbend Maximum Security Institution, and old prisons were closed. Judge Higgins appointed Pat McManus as special master to oversee all the new implementations. One of those implementations was the creation of a behavior modification model on death row, referred to as the level system.

The levels are categorized as A, B, and C. When a man arrives on death row, he is labeled as a "C-Level Inmate." Level C is the harshest level. A level-C inmate has very few privileges. He is locked in his cell twenty-three hours a day. He is allowed one hour per day to be outside. But even outside, he is in a solitary cage that's nothing more than a dog run. A level-C person is allowed zero physical contact, not even a handshake, from anyone, including other inmates. If a family, friend, or even an attorney, comes to visit a level-C person, they meet in one of the front rooms at the entrance that has Plexiglas between the inmate and whomever is visiting him. Anytime a level-C person leaves his cell for a shower or for a visit, his wrists and ankles are shackled, and he is escorted by two guards. One of the guards must be a corporal. A person stays at level C for eighteen months. If he has no "write ups" and has not caused any trouble, he moves to level B.

The main difference between level C and level B is a level-B person is allowed contact visits. In other words, his lawyers can talk to him in a room without the Plexiglas, and family and friends can visit him in the visitation room where they can hold hands. Level-B persons are still locked down twenty-three hours per day and only allowed one hour per day outside, in that dog run. Anytime a level-B person is moved from his cell, his hands are shackled but not his ankles, and only one guard is needed to escort him. If a level-B person has no disciplinary actions against him, after eighteen months, he moves to level A.

Level A is as good as it gets on death row. Level-A people can spend several hours outside of their cells. However, unless they are working, they have to remain in their pods and cannot go into other pods. Level-A persons can get a job to earn commissary money. Available jobs include working in the kitchen or in the laundry, acting as "Rockman" to the pods, working as a clerk, and in KB's case, working as the chaplain's assistant. Being Rockman is a position of responsibility and is usually given to the most respected man in the pod. The most anyone in Unit 2 can earn is 50 cents an hour. Level-A guys can also walk around their pods and stay outside for longer periods of time in a larger dog run, playing handball, basketball, and exercising. If a person gets a write-up, depending on the seriousness of the offense, they can be demoted back to a B or C level, and the process starts all over again.

Because of the level system, Unit 2 is the calmest unit inside the entire prison, with very little problems, conflicts, or disturbances. KB is level A, and in thirty years he has never had a single write-up. Because of his outstanding reputation, and because he works as the chaplain's assistant, he is one of the few people who has the freedom to walk from pod to pod, visiting all the men on Unit 2, including the B- and C-level guys.

FRIENDS

Now let me tell about a few of my friends. I have chosen to use nicknames to protect their families and the families of the victims.

Diamond Jim arrived on death row in 1984. He was executed on November 1, 2018. A few weeks before his execution, Diamond Jim told me his story. In his twenties, he started working on boats in the Houston area. These boats shuttled people out to the many oil rigs in the Gulf of Mexico. He started out as a deckhand but quickly moved up the ladder. Eventually he became a captain.

Diamond Jim gained a reputation as a hard worker and skillful captain. He was known to take people back and forth to the oil rigs in rough weather, when no other captain dared go out. He made a lot of money as a captain, and by his own admission, during this time in his life, he drank, partied, and "chased women." Afterall, he said, it was the late 1970s and 1980s. Diamond Jim worked for months at a time then had several weeks off. During his time off, he rode his Harley Davidson motorcycle all over the country. With a big smile on his face, he said he was having "the time of my life."

One day, at the end of a grueling work season, looking forward to a month off, a stranger approached him in Houston and offered him "a bundle of cash" to drive a car from Houston to Phoenix. All he had to do was drive the car and park it at an address the man gave to him. He did not ask what was in the car, but he assumed it was drugs.

He drove to Phoenix, and when he parked the car and got out, the stranger who had hired him approached him and gave him another bundle of cash. Unbeknownst to Diamond Jim, this man had been following him. The man then said, "This was a test run. I needed to know if I could trust you. There is nothing in this car. What I want to hire you to do is run your boat out into the Gulf of Mexico where you will pick up 'packages' off of other boats and deliver them back to Houston." The man then went into detail about what would be expected of him and how much money he could make.

Finally, the man handed him a file folder. Inside the folder were pictures of his mom and sisters, along with their home addresses and phone numbers. The man then said, "This is your choice. You can accept it or reject it. If you accept it, you can quit anytime you desire, no questions asked. But if you ever turn on me, or tell anyone what you are doing, I will not come after you. I will go after your family." Diamond Jim said the money was too good to turn down, so he accepted and became a "mule" for one of the Cartel families in Mexico. Again, smiling, Diamond Jim said, "I made a lot of money." When I asked him why he agreed to this, he said, "I was young and dumb. Besides, if I didn't do it, someone else would have."

Fast forward years later, and Diamond Jim was in rural Tennessee, selling marijuana to a couple of guys. The guys tried to rob him, and Diamond Jim, in self-defense, killed them both. When Diamond Jim was arrested, the district attorney (DA) offered him a deal. The DA said he knew who Diamond Jim was and who he worked for. If he offered up the name of his boss, he would be charged with manslaughter and be out of prison in a few years. Then the DA said, "If you do not give us a name, we will seek the death penalty." Diamond Jim then looked me straight in the eye and said, "Pastor, there is no way I could take that deal. If I would have, they would have killed my family. So here I am."

St. Luis is an Army veteran who did jungle training in Panama. He has survived his years on death row by keeping to himself and not "getting involved in the drama" inside prison. He is also an accomplished artist, mainly of nature scenes and landscapes. I have one of his paintings hanging in my office. It's a painting of an old white church building, surrounded by mountains, with people coming to church in horse and buggies. It's beautiful. St. Luis loves to talk about current affairs and worries about my safety in the "outside world." He spends his days painting and writing letters to his many friends in the "outside world."

Big Bro. is a gentle soul. He was scheduled to be executed in December of 2022, but because of a drug protocol violation by prison officials in the spring of 2022, the governor of Tennessee stayed all executions until an independent investigation was completed. Big Bro. is an older man in declining health. He has to use a walker to get around his small cell and his pod.

Big Bro. has a large family and loves German shepherds. Several members of his family have died since he has been incarcerated. Big Bro. loves to sit down and share pictures of his family, and he has hundreds of pictures. Every couple of years his family has a huge family reunion. By "huge," I mean hundreds of people attending. They take pictures of everything that happens during the reunion, and they write him detailed letters, explaining all they did, including what they ate. Big Bro. shows me all these pictures and explains to me, in detail, what all happened at the reunion as if he were there. He will say things like, "We got up that morning, and after breakfast several of us went fishing. You would not believe all the fish we caught. Then that night we fried them up and had a banquet of fish, corn on the cob, and turnip greens. For dessert my Aunt Betty and Aunt Carol made homemade peach cobbler. It was delicious. The best thing you've ever put in your mouth." On one occasion he told me, "In a couple of years, the reunion will be in Nashville, and we would love it if you would come." The reunion hasn't come to Nashville yet, but when it does, I will be there. I will go hungry, and I will take lots of pictures for my friend, Big Bro.

Some of the men on death row did not have the opportunity, for a variety of reasons, to obtain a quality education. But on death row, they have educated themselves and become scholars in the fields of philosophy and religion. One such man is Little Pale. On most visits with KB, I find Little Pale sitting at a table reading. The books he reads are not typical books. And he doesn't just read them; he devours them and can talk for hours about what he has read. Here is a sampling of some of his favorite books: *The Destruction of Black Civilization: Great Issues of Race from 4,500 B.C. to 2,000 A.D.* (1987, Chancellor Williams), *Black Man of the Nile and His Family* (1989, Dr. Yosef A. A. ben-Jochannan), *The African Origin of Civilization: Myth or Reality* (1967, Cheikh Anta Diop), and *I Am a Divine Being* (2008, Ra Un Nefer Amen). Little Pale is quick to point out the real title of that last book is, *Nuk au Neter,* which translates, "I am a divine being." Little Pale's mind is as sharp as anyone I have ever met.

K-Hen is an incredibly talented artist and athlete. His favorite subject to draw is Kobe Bryant, and I promise, I can't tell whether his paintings are really paintings or actual portraits. K-Hen and I have dreams of him painting pictures of Jesus's parables and me preaching a series of sermons (and maybe write a book) on those parables and showing his paintings.

As a sophomore in high school, K-Hen started getting letters from a number of big-time college basketball programs. Kentucky was one of them. Coming out of high school, K-Hen was recruited by Rick Pitino to play at the University of Kentucky. K-Hen was a three-point marksmen. After graduation, before signing a letter of intent, he was involved in a tragic accident and was pinned against a wall by a car. His right leg was seriously damaged. At one point the doctors told him his leg would have to be amputated. They were able to save his leg, but this tragedy ended his dreams of playing basketball and led him down a path that ended on death row.

Bam-Bam and Fly work in the laundry together. In Unit 2, the laundry room is right beside Baltimore Pod. I pass by the laundry room every time I visit KB. I always stop and talk with Bam-Bam and Fly. They love to talk sports. Bam-Bam is a huge Alabama football and Golden State Warriors basketball fan. Fly loves Golden State, but his favorite football team is the Oregon Ducks. I live and breathe Tennessee Vols football and Memphis Grizzlies basketball. The three of us love to give each other a hard time. During football and basketball seasons, we do a lot of smack talking. I look forward to my conversations with Bam-Bam and Fly.

I only met Skillet a couple of times. Not long after I started visiting death row, his sentenced was commuted to life, and he was transferred to a prison in West Tennessee. A few years later he passed away of natural causes. As an adult, while in prison, Skillet was diagnosed with fetal alcohol syndrome. He told me he always knew something was wrong with him, but no one knew exactly what it was. In a weird way, he found it comforting to finally know what it was. He just wished they would have diagnosed him as a child. He believed his whole life would have been different, and he would not have ended up in prison, on death row. He then said to me, "Today is my sixty-fifth birthday. I am grateful I have lived long enough for God to forgive me of all the horrible things I have done."

When my son, Zachary, died, one of the first sympathy cards my wife and I received was from the men on Unit 2. Here is just a sampling of what they wrote inside the card: "Just wanted to let you know that we feel your pain. Praying for your family." "I can't imagine what you and your family are going through. Know that you and all your family are in my thoughts and prayers." "My thoughts, love and prayers are with you, your wife Misty, and your daughter Katherine. If my family and I can do anything at all for you, we are at your disposal. May God bless, keep, comfort, and uphold you and all of your family."

I could tell stories for hours on end:

Stories of Taco, who got his nickname because he was Hispanic, and because of the many attempted escapes he made from jails and prisons. His nickname came from the Taco Bell commercial with the tagline "Make a run for the border."

And then there's Nick, another outstanding artist who loves to talk religion.

I wish I had time to tell all about Don, who had a Bible study on the radio and was an elder in his church. Don was executed on May 16, 2019. He sang the song "Soon and Very Soon" as prison officials administered the drugs that killed him. And Heck, a person whose intellectual disability should have kept him off death row. And Abu, whose life was spared from several executions. Not long ago, his sentence was commuted to life without parole. He now serves as a mentor and conflict mediator on the low-security side of Riverbend Maximum Security Institution.

In their own unique ways, every man in Unit 2 has impacted and changed my life for the better. All of these friendships have a common denominator and that is KB. It is because of his faithfulness and love and loyalty to these men that I have gotten to know them. On many occasions I have told KB, the only reason some of these men speak to me at all is because of the trust they have placed in him. These men tolerate me because they love KB.

My purpose in telling these stories is not to romanticize these men, nor is it to disregard the victims of violent crimes and their families. Quite the contrary! I know what it is to lose a family member through violence. Growing up, my wife had an uncle who was the same age as her. His name was Jimmy. The two of them were like brother and sister. Jimmy was murdered in a dispute over a girl. I preached his funeral. His killer only served fifteen years in prison and is now a free man. I know the pain and the temptation to seek revenge. I believe the victim's lives need to be honored and remembered, and the victim's families need all the love and support they can get. I just don't believe the way to honor victims is through more violence.

I tell these stories because the men on death row are not monsters. Some of the things they did, or are accused of doing, are monstrous, but they are not monsters. They are human beings created in the image of God, and they are far more than what they did (or did not do). No one's entire life should be defined by what happened on the worst day of their life. Redemption is possible. Forgiveness is possible. As a society, our goal should be reconciliation and restorative justice, not revenge and punitive justice.

CHAPTER 14
SUICIDE

"Joseph done went over there and killed himself."

■ ■ ■

(KB) I love all sports. I love Florida State football, North Carolina Tarheels basketball, and the Dallas Cowboys. Since being incarcerated, I have learned to love handball and have become quite good. I remember, from my cell, watching Andre Agassi play tennis. I took what I learned from watching him and apply it to the handball court. Not long ago, Mr. Agassi visited death row. I got to talk to him, and he autographed my white baseball hat.

At Riverbend, when we go outside, we can play handball or basketball. The basketball area is small, and with a low roof overhead, we can't take long shots, but it's perfect for three-on-three games. In my younger days, I played a lot of basketball, but now I prefer handball.

Years ago, we had a sergeant in Unit 2 who loved to watch us compete on the basketball court. Often the games were intense, and guys took great pride in winning. It was fun and a great diversion. At times I was so into the game that I forgot I was in prison.

Unit 2 has four pods. Most of the time the pods are kept separate from each other, but sometimes the officers let adjoining pods compete against each other on the basketball court. That meant

A- and B-pods played against each other, and C- and D-pods competed. My usual teammates were Ndume and CJ. We were the best team in the A- and B-pods.

There are a few days throughout the year that are called "free days." A lot of activities are on these days, plus a lot of Pepsi, potato chips, and candy bars. Sometimes the prison grills hamburgers and hotdogs for us on these days. Additionally on free days, A-level guys are given extra time outside—usually on Thanksgiving, Christmas, and July 4th.

One year as July 4th was nearing, I approached Sergeant Davis with an idea. I asked him, "Why don't we have a three-on-three basketball tournament. Pods A and B can compete, as well as pods C and D. Then the winner of the A- and B-pods can play the winner of the C- and D-pods in a championship game." I gave my word to Sergeant Davis there would be no arguments or fights and that I would even put it in writing so that the institution would not be responsible for anything negative that happened. Sergeant Davis pitched the idea to the warden and said he would take "full responsibility." To everyone's surprise, the Warden approved the tournament without putting anything in writing. Unit 2 was excited about the tournament, and for days leading up to the tournament, there was a lot of good-natured trash talking. This was an exciting time for all of us. My team was called the B-Pod Ballers. We practiced every day leading up to the tournament.

On July 4th, the day of the tournament, there was a buzz throughout the entire unit. The competition was fierce and tough. I can't say for certain, but I think the guards had bets on which team would win. I know some of the guys in the unit did—nothing major, just soft drinks and candy bars. The only thing really on the line was bragging rights. My team prevailed as the champion of A- and B-pods and were set to play the champions of C- and D-pods. The championship team from C- and D-pods was C-pod. Their players were Big Mike, Little Pale, and DT. My team played hard and gave it everything we had. But the other team was better and won the title as champions of Unit 2.

After the loss, I walked back into B-pod tired and a little upset that we did not prevail. The first person I saw was my dear friend, Joseph. Because the championship game was played on the C and D court, the guys in A and B did not get to watch it. Joseph asked, "How did you do?" I said discouragingly, "We lost man."

"Did you do your best?" Joseph asked.

"Yes sir. We did our best. It was a good game. We fought hard and never gave up. But they were better than us."

Joseph then said, "Losing ain't the end. As long as you did your best, I'm proud of you."

Joseph, who was quite a bit older than me, had become a father figure to me. Our relationship was like a father and son relationship. Hearing him say he was proud of me meant the world to me. I will never forget that moment.

THE STORY

(KR) Not long after arriving on death row, KB became friends with Joseph, a guy who had been on death row since 1988. Joseph was an ordained minister and pastor of a local church in Nashville. Joseph admitted to shooting and killing his church's handyman in a futile attempt to fake his own death, so he could start a new life. After shooting the man, Joseph dressed the body in his own clothes, beheaded the deceased, and cut off an arm to remove tattoos. This was done in an attempt to hide the man's true identity. Next, with the dead body inside, Joseph set fire to his church.

The men on death row rarely discuss the details of their cases with each other, what each other has done or been accused of doing.

On death row, everyone is in the same predicament, and everyone is accepted unconditionally. No one is judged for what they did on the outside. Friendships and trust are forged by living together in a small space for a long period of time. KB knew very little about Joseph's story. He only knew he befriended him and became an early mentor to him on how to live and survive on death row. In his own words, KB says Joseph acted like a father figure to him. KB was closer to Joseph then he was anyone else.

At this time, the Unit 2 Thursday night church service was led by two volunteers, and periodically they asked KB to preach. Joseph attended faithfully but he never preached, even though KB asked him many times. KB said, "Joseph knew of God's forgiveness and the call God had on his life. But he felt like he had failed and was unworthy to ever preach again." On one occasion, after KB asked him to preach, Joseph said, "No. You are now carrying the torch. Not me."

On one Thursday night, after the service was over, KB felt the Holy Spirit say, "KB, you need to pray for Joseph." KB felt an unusual urgency in his spirit. Once again, the Spirit impressed on him, "You need to pray for Joseph right now!" So he stopped everyone from leaving and gathered around Joseph to pray. KB placed his right hand on Joseph's head and began, "God have mercy on him. God have mercy on him." KB didn't know why he prayed those words.

KB then explained, "After I prayed, I took my hand off Joseph's head and felt impressed to extend my right hand to him and say, 'Joseph, Jesus is saying, "Take my hand. I can help you. Please take my hand."'"

"To my surprise," KB continued, "Joseph said, 'No!'" I thought to myself, *Why would he say no?* I did not understand. "Why would he say no to Jesus?"

SUICIDE

KB asked again, and again Joseph said, "No!"

KB pleaded with him, "Please take my hand."

Joseph began crying but again said, "No!" Then he added, "No, Lord, they don't understand." And he continued to weep.

KB knew Joseph had a court date the following Monday. He also knew his previous court date had not gone well. Prosecutors bullied him with difficult questions. Joseph thought the only reason for the questions was to further traumatize him. He had already admitted to his crime and had been sentenced to death. But for some reason, they were forcing him to relive everything again. At one point, Joseph shouted at the prosecutors, "What more do you want from me? You can only kill me once." Joseph told KB he was never going to court again. KB decided Joseph's strange reaction to his prayer and request was because of the stress he felt about the upcoming court appearance.

KB was upset about Joseph saying no to Jesus, but he ended the prayer. As he was hugging the volunteers good-bye, KB noticed Joseph hurriedly leave the room and return to his cell. KB followed him into B-pod and up the stairs to his cell. Joseph closed his cell door and stared at KB through the small window in the door. KB was going to say something but heard the Holy Spirit say to him, "Son, say nothing of what you intend to say. Just be at peace." After a few moments of staring at each other, Joseph said to KB, "What ever happens, just know I love you like you were my own son. Never forget that." KB replied, "I love you too," and then went to his cell and cried.

(KB) The next morning, Friday, I got up at 5:30 to go work in the kitchen. Pervis and I prepared breakfast and cleaned up. Pervis had to go back to his cell for something. I was in the kitchen by myself, with my back toward the door, cleaning the steaming tables. I heard someone walk by the door. I sensed it was Joseph, but I did not look, and he did not say anything. I knew Joseph would be walking by, going to 2A where he worked as the Rockman. The "Rockman" serves a crucial and respected role in prisons, not just death row. The term comes from the fact everything in prison is made of concrete. We live on concrete, so the person on the floor is called the Rockman. He keeps the pod clean and helps the guys who are locked down get things from forms to fill out to heating up food in the microwave. The Rockman is usually the most trusted guy in the pod. A few moments later, I sensed something else rush by the door. I turned around but did not see anyone or anything. I thought about going over to 2A but decided not to. A few moments later, David walked by on his way to 2A. He worked with Joseph. David said, "Good morning, KB," as he walked by the kitchen.

About thirty minutes later, over the intercom, I heard "Code 4," which means a medical emergency. Next thing I know officers ran by me on their way to 2A. David came back to the kitchen. He was frightened and in shock. He said to me, "Joseph done went over there and killed himself." By this time Pervis was back in the kitchen with me. We both started crying.

Joseph walked over to 2A and convinced the officer there he was going to clean the bathroom. He then went into the bathroom, locked the door, and hung himself. David told the officer on duty to unlock the bathroom, and when he walked in, he saw Joseph hanging from the ceiling. David said it was an image he will never forget. The officer, when he saw Joseph, had a heart attack and passed out, but he survived. When the medical team, and other officers, got to the bathroom, they saw the officer on the floor and did not, at first, see Joseph hanging from the ceiling. We were all put on lockdown for the rest of the day. Pervis and I went to our cells and cried and prayed. My dear friend and mentor was gone.

SUICIDE

At lunch time that same day, the officers came by my cell and asked if I felt like coming out and going back to the kitchen to prepare lunch. At first I said no, but then I decided I would go. Pervis decided he would go with me. Pervis and I prepared lunch without talking. After lunch was served, we stayed in the kitchen and talked. It was obvious to us that on Thursday evening, at church, Joseph had already decided to kill himself. My prayer, and my extending my right hand, was Jesus extending mercy to him.

Then it dawned on us, earlier in the day on that Thursday, Joseph gave a lot of his stuff away. He gave some clothes to Pervis and his art supplies to K-Hen. At the time, we didn't think much about it. Looking back, we should have recognized the signs. I told Pervis I had sensed Joseph walk by and then something else run by. We both decided what I felt was death running after Joseph. One thing I do know is that God is a God of love, mercy, and grace. I pray my dear friend, Joseph, has found peace. I miss him every day. I will continue to carry the torch in his memory.

(KR) I was in college in Nashville, studying to be a minister, when Joseph committed his heinous crime. I remember following his arrest and trial on the news. The fact he was a pastor intrigued me. I never met Joseph, but there are a few of the other guys on death row whom I remember reading about in the newspaper. It's hard to explain the feelings I have when I meet someone in person after having read the horrible things they have done or been accused of doing. It's easy to think these guys are subhuman and not deserving of mercy and compassion. But nothing could be further from the truth. At times it is difficult to reconcile the kind, gentle men I meet on death row with the public records I read about them and their crime. I have come to learn an important lesson: closeness changed my perspective; proximity changed my theology.

CHAPTER 15
COVID

"Having a church in Unit 2 means so much. To be able to hear the Word of God, to revive my soul, mind, and spirit, reminding me that God is here with me in this hell hole."

■ ■ ■

(KR) Nick Sutton was executed on February 20, 2020. The next day, I visited KB and the other guys on Unit 2. Because of some traveling coming up on my schedule, I told KB it would be at least a month before I could visit again. Little did I know it would be fifteen months before I returned to death row.

I was on a retreat in Jackson, Mississippi, with Dr. John Perkins and Christian Community Development Association, when the world shut down. I left Jackson at 5:00 a.m., on Friday, March 13, 2020, to drive back to Franklin, Tennessee, to pick my wife up after school so we could drive to New Orleans and leave on a cruise over her spring break on Saturday, March 14. There was very little traffic on the road that day. On our way to New Orleans, President Trump gave a speech, and within an hour after the speech, our cruise was cancelled. Not knowing the seriousness of what was going on, we spent the weekend in New Orleans. I left my house on Monday, March 9, 2020, and returned on Tuesday, March 17 to a brand-new world and a brand-new reality.

But what I experienced pales in comparison to the experiences of the incarcerated, especially the guys on Tennessee's death row. There's a policy at Riverbend that states a badged volunteer (like me) cannot be on an inmate's call list. In other words, while I could visit KB personally, he could not call me. I thought of KB a lot during the early days of COVID, but I had no way of contacting him. I wondered if every day he still said, "Today is the best day of my life." That thought usually made me smile because I knew that is what he would still say. Brad Davis, a member of my church and a long-time personal friend, was on KB's visitation and call list. Thankfully, after a couple of weeks of silence, KB called Brad to report he was OK. Over the next fifteen months, through Brad, I was able to keep up with KB and how things were going in Unit 2.

During the Winter of 2021, before the vaccines were available, I contracted a serious case of COVID. I was down for several days, and it took several more weeks to fully recover. One of the things that helped me through that time was knowing the guys on death row were praying for me. I'm sure my experience with COVID and through COVID was similar to yours, reader, so I won't bore you with my story. Instead, KB will share what life was like on death row during the pandemic.

(KB) For those of us on Unit 2, to say COVID changed everything is an understatement. One of the things that gives us comfort, and provides us with hope, is all the volunteers and visitors who spend time with us. It is our connection to the outside world. In an instant, that connection was taken from us. Thankfully, we could still make phone calls, but that cost money. Many of the guys have limited resources and can't afford to make calls. Others must limit themselves to one call a week or one call a month. Like everything else I have faced, I approached COVID believing in God's sovereignty over all things and tried to use that time to grow in my faith and minister to the guys on Unit 2. But it wasn't easy.

Out of "precaution," and the fear of the unknown, the first thing the prison did was lock everyone down. The first lockdown lasted for twenty-one days. So for three straight weeks, I, along with everyone else, was stuck in our six-by-eight cells. We weren't even allowed to go outside during this time. We were in our cells twenty-four hours a day, seven days a week! The only time we were out of our cells was to be escorted to the shower, which is an even smaller, three-by-six, cell. Thankfully, we were allowed to shower once a day.

During the lockdown, they tested everyone for COVID. During this first test, twelve guys tested positive; most, however, were asymptomatic. For years, only three of the four pods in Unit 2 have had anyone in them. Since no one was housed in C-pod, those who tested positive were moved to C-pod and quarantined there. Twelve guys, spread out in a pod with twenty-four cells, meant they experienced extreme isolation. They were also treated as if they had the plague. Two of the guys, Donny and Walker, got really sick. Walker had to be taken to the hospital. Thankfully, he recovered. This was the first COVID tests and the first quarantine and lockdown, but it wasn't the last. Later when guys tested positive for COVID, they were moved to C-Pod.

When guards entered C-pod, they wore white scrubs from head to toe, with masks and gloves. None of the guards wanted to go into C-pod, and when they did, they did not stay long and were usually in a foul mood. On a positive note, while under quarantine, the guys were permitted to make phone calls and take showers. I've talked with all the guys who were quarantined, and they tell me the biggest challenge of quarantine was dealing with the loneliness of it all.

In addition to the loneliness and isolation, the guys in quarantine received their meals last, which meant their food was always cold. One of the men who was quarantined, Billy, said he asked the guard if he could warm up his food in the microwave that was located in the pod. This was over Thanksgiving of 2020, and this particular meal was our special holiday meal. The guard became enraged and said, "Who do you think you are? I was in the military, and I ate cold food all the time. You guys don't even deserve cold food. How dare you ask me to warm it up for you. Who do you think you are, and who do you think you are speaking to?" Billy responded back in anger. He and the guard got into an argument. The guard could have written Billy up, but he decided not to. After all, Billy was already locked down in quarantine. There was nothing more the guard could do to make life any harder on him than it already was.

All of this affected the guys mentally. It took a long time for each of them to recover from this experience. As for myself, I spent those first three weeks in lockdown reading, meditating, watching TV, and talking on the phone with family and friends—that is, when I could afford it. Pervis Payne was in the cell beside mine, and we spent a lot of time talking through the wall.

After three weeks, the lockdown was lifted, but throughout the pandemic, if anyone tested positive, they were sent to C-pod for twenty-one days. I never tested positive, but Pervis did, and he described being quarantined as a time of deep isolation and loneliness. He told me it seemed as if no one cared. Being quarantined was discouraging but was also probably necessary. All throughout COVID, if someone tested positive, their clothes were washed in a biodegradable bag that treated the clothes with some type of chemical that killed the virus.

COVID

The only way COVID was spread in Unit 2 was through the guards. At one time or another, all the guards had COVID. Yet many of them still came to work, coughing and sneezing through their masks. As a result, to this day, a lot of the guys, myself included, wear masks when they are around guards. In addition, I wear a mask when I visit other pods, but I don't wear one when I am in my pod.

For me personally, one of the positives that came out of COVID was that my ministry through phone calls increased. During this time, I reconnected with friends and family I had not talked to in years and decades. Some of those phone calls continue to this day. I am thankful to God for allowing that to happen.

Another positive during COVID was the Church of Life. After the initial lockdown was over, the Church of Life continued its weekly Thursday night service. This was nothing short of a miracle. During COVID, for fifteen months, no volunteers were allowed inside. All volunteer-led programs and Bible studies ceased. But once a week, we had church services. The only change in our service was instead of singing songs we listened to worship songs via CDs. Plus, we all wore masks. But everything else remained the same. We had Scripture readings and prayers, and I preached each week. This brought a sense of normalcy back to our lives. In addition to preaching each Thursday, I preached, through recordings posted to their YouTube Channel, every Wednesday night for Franklin Community Church. This was a real blessing for me and a great source of encouragement. (KR here; it was also a great source of encouragement to me and my church.) God works in mysterious ways, which is another reason I can confidently say, "Today is the best day of my life."

Speaking of the Church of Life, KR recently asked me to ask the members of our church to respond to two questions: (1) What does it mean to you that we have the Church of Life? (2) How has the Church of Life helped you? A few replies follow.

> I have been incarcerated for thirty-eight years. All of which has been without family or friends. What Church of Life means to me is that while those that I called family have written me off, God has not. It means that in this place of darkness there is a light of hope. There is a way beyond the path I have walked. That way is Jesus. Our church has been an island of peace in this world of confusion. I have found a spiritual release in attending Church of Life. I have found a church that instead of judging me, encourages me. — Donny
>
> Having a church in Unit 2 means so much. To be able to hear the Word of God, to revive my soul, mind, and spirit, reminding me that God is here with me in this hell hole, is invaluable. The Church of Life encourages me and gives me assurance to stand on God through Christ Jesus. The Church of Life reminds me that I am who God says I am, not who the Department of Corrections says I am. I thank Jesus for the Church of Life. — Pervis
>
> The Church of Life means we can have hope and salvation and freedom to worship God in a meaningful way on death row. Pastor Kevin Burns is a great spiritual leader and advisor. Pastor Burns pours out his heart when he praises God and lifts our spirits, much like Jesus did when he was persecuted and died on the cross for our sins. Having a pastor, who is one of us, and knows what we go through on death row is great. The Church of Life has helped me be a better person by making me realize it's not just about me, and that we must all face our own persecution in our own

way in this world. The Church of Life has given me hope that I am more than just worm food when that inevitable days comes for all of us condemned to die. God cleanses us of our sins and forgives all of us, regardless of what we have done. Through the Church of Life, I have learned that God loves us all and has a plan for us all. God loves me, even though I am living under a sentence of death and my life is restricted to a bathroom sized home. — John

(KR) After Nick Sutton's execution in February of 2020, five more executions were scheduled through December of that year. Because of COVID, all five executions were stayed. Abu Ali Abdur Rahman was scheduled to be killed in April of 2020. Thankfully, his execution was halted. The delay allowed his lawyers more time to ask for clemency. Abu's sentence was commuted to life without parole. He is now off of death row and serving as a mentor to other prisoners in Unit 5 at Riverbend Maximum Security Institution. COVID saved Abu's life.

The same can be said about Pervis Payne. Though completely innocent of any crime, he was scheduled to be executed in December of 2020. But like Abu, because of COVID, his execution was stayed, and with the help of his lawyers and the Innocence Project, his sentence has been commuted to two life sentences, served concurrently, with the possibility of parole. The fight continues, however, for his complete exoneration.

During COVID the news regularly reported that the two places where COVID spread the fastest were nursing homes and prisons. Thus, when the vaccines were made available, it was argued the first people to receive the vaccines should be nursing home patients and people in prison. I was shocked and horrified when my local news reported that a pandemic advisory group, put together by the governor of Tennessee, advised the governor that inmates be the last people in the state to receive the vaccine. Their reasoning was, and I quote, "The board decided prioritizing inmates above other residents would result in a 'public relations nightmare.'"

A local news station contacted me and, through Zoom, interviewed me about this. Among other things, I said, "We don't make decisions based on public relations when it comes to morality and ethics. . . . You've got people who are in jail, and they haven't even been convicted of anything. . . . They couldn't afford bail, so they are sitting in jail innocent until proven guilty, and now they have a high chance of catching COVID."

In the interview, I encouraged the governor to keep his plan of vaccinating inmates sooner rather than later. Thankfully, the governor continued his plan and rejected the advice of his own committee. A few months later, I received a letter from someone incarcerated in a prison in West Tennessee. I had never met this person or even been to that prison. In the letter, this person wrote,

> Pastor Kevin, on behalf of myself and the other guys housed in the prison, I want to say "thank you" for speaking out. We watched you on the news, asking the Governor to make sure inmates get vaccinated sooner rather than later. There were plans to vaccinate us a while back, and then they decided not to vaccinate us. Not long after your interview, the prison started vaccinating us. We were nervous. We thought the state was just going to let us get sick. We know, without you speaking up, we would not have been vaccinated. So, thank you.

CHAPTER 16
FOUR-LEAF CLOVERS

"Pastor, I am tired. I am tired of living the life I have lived. I am tired of the anger and bitterness I have carried most of my life."

■ ■ ■

(KR) Joey arrived on death row in 2002. In 2019, because of inadequate representation at the sentencing phase of his trial, Joey's death sentence was commuted to life without the possibility of parole. When I first started visiting death row, Joey latched on to me for some reason. He seemed to be interested in what I had to say, and he seemed to like me. I found out later how unusual this was. Joey had developed a reputation of being hard to get along with. He had very few friends.

In 2015 Joey turned seventy years old. Around the time of his birthday, Joey made me a cross necklace that I wore every day for several years. I only retired Joey's cross when I was gifted a large, heavy cross made from a melted down AR-15 gun barrel. That is the cross I wear every day now. Joey's cross was large as well. I wore it under my shirt, and when I felt it move or when it poked me in my chest, it reminded me to continually pray for prisoners as incarcerated with them. (Remember Hebrews 13:3.)

After Joey gave that cross to me, he told me some of his story. Joey grew up poor on a farm in Mississippi. His father was a tenant farmer. Joey said his father beat him most every day, along with his mom and his brothers and sisters. His childhood was one of hard work, abuse, and scarcity. By his own admission, Joey told me he had never been to school nor stepped foot inside a church. As a result, he could neither read nor write and knew little about the Bible and Jesus.

Before Joey was a teenager, he was arrested and spent time in and out of juvenile detention. By the time he was arrested and sentenced to death, he had at least thirteen other felony charges. Joey then said to me, "I am now seventy years old, and I have spent fifty of those years incarcerated." Those words shocked me.

He then said, "Pastor, I am tired. I am tired of living the life I have lived. I am tired of the anger and bitterness I have carried around most of my life." He went on to explain how he had been watching me since I had been visiting death row. He said, "I have seen a lot of volunteers and ministers come and go. But I noticed something different about you. I can't explain it, but I was drawn to you."

He continued, "Not long after you started coming to Unit 2, right after one of your visits, I went back to my cell and prayed for the first time in my life. I prayed, 'God, I don't know if You are real. But I do know I need to change my life. I do know I can't keep living like this.'"

He then offered God a challenge: "I said, 'God, if You will teach me to read, I will put my faith and trust in You.'" He pulled a small devotional booklet out of his pocket, opened it to the day's date, and started reading it aloud to me. It wasn't perfect. He stumbled along and had to sound out a lot of the words. It took him several minutes to read a small paragraph. But he read it, and he has been reading ever since. He closed the devotional booklet, and with tears in his eyes, he pointed heavenward and said, "God taught me to read. I believe in God now, and I thank you for pointing me to God."

I asked KB about Joey. He said that he was a quiet person and kept to himself. KB said, "Joey and I have always got along, but like most of us, he can have his days where he is ornery. Joey does care about his health. He is constantly exercising and staying in shape. One thing I can say about him is that once he started coming to church, he came each week. He was very faithful, and once he started reading, he loved to read Scripture out loud."

FOUR YEARS LATER

In October of 2019, Joey moved from Unit 2 (death row) to Unit 6 (general population). I did not see him again for more than four years.

In April of 2023, I arranged for some colleagues of mine to visit and tour Riverbend Maximum Security Institution. As we were visiting Unit 6, I spotted Joey from across the room. He is now seventy-eight years old, but he is as strong as an ox. Every day he does hundreds of push-ups and hundreds of sit-ups. Joey walked across the room and gave me a big hug. My wife, Misty, was with me, and I introduced him to her as "the guy who made my cross." Joey then said, "Wait right here. I will be right back."

Joey went to his cell and a few minutes later returned to my wife and me and handed each of us a four-leaf clover. Joey had meticulously placed these four-leaf clovers on a small piece of cardboard and then covered the cardboard in a small piece of clear, plastic wrap to protect the four-leaf clover. He handed us our four-leaf clovers and said, "This is what I do now. When I am not working, I go outside and look for four-leaf clovers, and then I give them to friends to let them know I am praying for them and wish them nothing but luck." Both of our four-leaf clovers now hang proudly on our refrigerator door.

What's the big deal about a four-leaf clover? Well, let me tell what I imagine.

TODAY! ∎ THE BEST DAY OF MY LIFE

Unit 2 is nothing but solid concrete and steel. There is nothing appealing and comforting about it. The walls are concrete blocks painted white. The stairs are solid steel. The cell doors are solid steel. A bed is skinnier than a twin bed, is made of steel, and has a thin, uncomfortable mattress on top. A room is all concrete, including the floor, with one small window looking outside. The commode in a cell is steel, and a prisoner is locked behind a steel door, with one small window. When he goes outside, he is completely enclosed in a steel cage. Even the basketball goal is made of steel. The entire time on death row, he never has direct sunlight and never touches grass.

After twelve years of living on death row, Joey was moved to Unit 6. Like Unit 2, everything in Unit 6 is steel and concrete. That hasn't changed. But what has changed is now Joey has the opportunity to go outside without being put in a cage. He can now bask in the sun, the warmth on his face and shoulders, and he can now roll around in the grass.

And that is what I imagine!

After more than a decade on death row, Joey now goes outside every day and gets on his hand and knees, feeling the grass, smelling the grass, and crawls around the grass looking for four-leaf clovers. He is still incarcerated. He will spend the rest of his life in prison, but rolling around in the grass, rubbing his fingers through the grass, he looks for four-leaf clovers, and for a time, even a short time, he is free. It makes me smile, imagining him crawling across the grass. And I hope, every so often, he stops and lays on his back, looking up at the sun. I bet he also does push-ups and sit-ups, with his shirt off, feeling the grass on his face, chest, and back. If you ask him, I bet while surrounded by nature, looking for four-leaf clovers, Joey would say, "Today is the best day of my life." I will treasure my four-leaf clover for the rest of my life.

CHAPTER 17
COME PRAY WITH US

"Governor Lee, we understand you are a man of faith, and we would like to ask you to please come pray with us."

■ ■ ■

(KR) After I received my volunteer badge to go into Riverbend Maximum Security Institution, I made one phone call. It was to a person I knew by reputation but had never met. At the time, he had no idea who I was. I can't remember who gave his number to me. I dialed the number, and after several rings, the voice on the other side said, "Hello." I said, "Reverend Ingle, my name is Kevin Riggs. I pastor a church in Franklin, Tennessee, and I believe God has told me to minister on death row. If you have time, I would love to talk to you." Reverend Ingle agreed, and we spent several minutes talking about Unit 2. A few days later, we met for lunch at a hot chicken restaurant near Tennessee State University. I had catfish instead of chicken.

Reverend Joe Ingle is a legend in death row ministry and a staunch advocate for the elimination of capital punishment. Since that initial phone call, he has become a dear friend and mentor to me. His ministry to incarcerated people began while living in East Harlem, New York, and studying at Union Seminary. He has been ministering on death row throughout the United States since 1974.

Over lunch I described to Reverend Ingle what I thought God was telling me. He patiently listened and offered his unique insights and advice. I asked if I could go to death row with him and just follow him around. He once again agreed, and a few days later, we visited Unit 2 together. I watched how he interacted with the administration, the guards, and the men. I knew, if I wanted to be successful, I needed to learn as much as I could from this man as quickly as I could. Reverend Ingle showed me around, gave me some "behind the scenes" advice, and introduced me to the men in Unit 2, even though I had already met several of them.

As we were leaving, Reverend Ingle gave two pieces of advice I have tried to put into practice. First, he said, "Kevin, you need to know that your volunteer badge gives you permission to be here. So walk around confidently, even if you don't know what you are doing, and don't let anyone intimidate you. Walk around like you belong." Then he gave a second piece of advice. He said, "My approach to these men is what I call 'the ministry of presence.' The most important thing you can do for these guys is to be here. Show up over and over again. Let them know they can count on you. Don't come with an agenda. Don't worry about what you are going to say and do. Let the guys dictate what you say and do. Just be present. That's all you have to do. That's the most important thing you can do. Simply be present and love on the guys."

Being present is all I have tried to do. Only time will tell if I have been effective. I do know my life has been changed. I do know proximity changes perspective. I thought my job was to "take Jesus with me." What I have learned, through proximity and presence, is that I do not take Jesus with me onto death row. I go to death row to meet Jesus because He is already there. He has always been there, and He will always be there.

A LETTER

Frank Clement was the governor of Tennessee from 1953 until 1959 and again from 1963 until 1967. During his first term as governor, between April 1955 and May 1957, he oversaw six executions. Each execution weighed heavier and heavier on his heart and soul. During his second term, Governor Clement started visiting death row, talking and praying with the men condemned to die. During this time, he experienced the ministry of presence. As a result, on March 19, 1965, he commuted to life imprisonment the death sentences of five men—thus, abolishing the death penalty for the remainder of his term as governor. Proximity changed Governor Clement's perspective. Proximity changes everything.

Sometime around 2015, a death penalty abolitionist, Shane Claiborne, visited Tennessee's death row. Shane, originally from East Tennessee, had come to Nashville for a meeting with Gov. Bill Haslam. Governor Haslam oversaw three executions during his term. Shane reached out to Riverbend's chaplain, Jeannie Alexander, and visited a class in Unit 2 called "Learning to Live. There were about twelve guys in the class. Shane said to them, "I just left a meeting with the governor, and I want to ask you a question. If you could talk to Governor Haslam, what would you ask him?" Most of the guys said they would talk to the governor about their cases and ask the governor for clemency.

KB was the last one to speak, and after thinking about it, he said, "I would ask Governor Haslam to come and pray with us." He continued, "I would not talk about my case. I would want to build a relationship with him. Governor Haslam says he is a man of faith, and so are we. We are men of faith and prayer. So I would ask that he come and pray with us."

Shane smiled and said, "That's a great idea! I think you should write Governor Haslam a letter, asking him to come and pray with you."

Here is how KB tells the rest of the story.

(KB) After Shane left, I went back to my cell and meditated about writing a letter. I really did not know what I would say. Two days later a group of us gathered for our Friday prayer service called "Family Talk." We started this prayer service after watching the documentary, *Fambul Tok*, which means "family talk." This documentary is about reconciliation and forgiveness after the long-fought civil war in Sierra Leone, Africa. In the documentary, victims and offenders of the civil war, come together to talk and heal wounds through truth telling and forgiveness. That's what we desired, so we started our own version of Family Talk with the same objective.

On this Friday, Chaplain Jeannie Alexander brought in a man. I don't remember his name, but I do remember he was running for state office. We began to talk to this man, and after a while, he asked the same question Shane had asked two days earlier: "If you had the opportunity to talk to the governor, what would you say? We all looked at each other in amazement. The guys told him the same things they had told Shane. When it was my turn to speak, I repeated, "I would ask the governor to come and pray with us." This man running for state office responded exactly like Shane, "That's a great idea! I think you should write the governor a letter, asking him to come pray with you." We all smiled, and I told him what had happened two days earlier. This was confirmation. Now I had to write that letter.

I spent the whole weekend working on the letter. It was a handwritten letter. I started the letter by introducing myself and greeting Governor Haslam. I then told him a little bit about my case and what I have been doing since then. Next I acknowledged the governor's faith and told him we were brothers in Christ. Finally, I asked if he would come to Unit 2 and pray with us.

The following Monday, Chaplain Alexander brought in a very special guest to Unit 2: Canon Andrew Wright, also known as the Vicar of Baghdad. Canon Wright led the only Episcopal Church, St. George's Church, in Baghdad, Iraq. Like Shane, Canon Wright had come to Nashville to meet with Governor Haslam. Believe it or not, over the course of our conversation, he asked us the same thing. Once again, I repeated, "I would ask Governor Haslam to come and pray with us." And once again, his response was the same, "I think you should write Governor Haslam, asking him to come pray with you."

Three different people, over a five-day period, and the exact same conversation! This time, however, I had my letter ready. I gave the letter to Canon Wright. He read it and thought it was good. He then handed the letter to Chaplain Alexander who said she would personally get the letter to Governor Haslam. I am confident Chaplain Alexander kept her word. Sadly, I never heard from Governor Haslam, and he never came and prayed with us. I wrote Governor Haslam sometime between 2015 and 2016. In 2018, during the last five months of his administration, Governor Haslam oversaw three executions. These were the first executions since 2009.

But that's not the end of the story.

Bill Lee became the governor of Tennessee in January of 2019. Not long after he took office, the Tennessee Supreme Court set more execution dates. In anticipation of these dates, several volunteers, who knew about my letter to Governor Haslam, suggested I write Governor Lee. This time, however, it was suggested the letter only be one sentence and any death-row guys who wanted to could sign it.

Governor Lee's first execution was scheduled for August 15, 2019. Our letter was dated June 6, 2019. The letter read, "Governor Lee, we understand you are a man of faith, and we would like to ask you to please come pray with us." Thirty-two men, more than half of all the men on death row at the time, signed the letter. Three of the men who signed the letter have been executed, and one died of cancer. Once again, sadly, Governor Lee has never responded to, or even acknowledged, our request for him to come and pray with us.

(KR) A small group of us with the help of a national non-profit called Death Penalty Action (deathpenaltyaction.org) decided to mass-produce the letter and the signatures in the size of a greeting card. We made these cards available to anyone who wanted them and had people from all over the country mail them to the governor's office. Thousands have been mailed. The letter and signatures have also been published in various news articles and even shown on local news outlets.

Executions in Tennessee take place on Thursdays. (I don't know why.) As mentioned in chapter 9, every Sunday before an execution, volunteers and activists participate in our March for Mercy. We carry poster-size replicas of the letter and signatures. We are confident the governor and/or his team have received the letter and are aware of the request. But as KB said, Governor Lee has never responded to or acknowledged receipt of the request.

On one occasion, on a Monday morning after our Sunday march and before a Thursday execution, myself and my good friend, Dan Mann, went to the state capitol. Our purpose was to go to the governor's office, hand deliver the letter, and ask to speak with Governor Lee about this simple request. We had done this a couple of times before, but the governor was not in his office. Sometimes one of Governor Lee's young assistants talked with us, and we left the letter with him. Once again, if the governor was not there, we would leave the letter with the Tennessee state trooper who keeps watch over his office.

On this particular Monday, we were told the governor was not in. We handed the letter to an assistant, while the Tennessee State Trooper stood by, and started leave. As we turned to leave, we saw Governor Lee walking toward us. Dan introduced himself first. I started introducing myself, but Governor Lee stopped me and said, "I know who you are, Pastor Riggs." The governor and I had met a few times before he was governor, and I knew we had several mutual friends, but I was surprised he knew who I was. We handed the letter to Governor Lee and told him why we were there. He was very cordial. He stated how much he admired our commitment and our faith and acknowledged how thankful he was for men like us who visit the guys on death row. I then asked if we could pray with him. He agreed, and so in the hallway in front of his office at the state capitol, we prayed together. I have been told, through mutual friends, how much Governor Lee agonizes over every execution. It is my understanding he spends every execution day in prayer, surrounded by his spiritual advisors. Dan and I were thankful for this opportunity to pray with Governor Lee. We both left encouraged and hopeful that one day, like Governor Clement before him, Governor Lee will go and pray with the men on death row.

Part Three
FRIENDSHIP & REDEMPTION

∎ ∎ ∎

*"I have spent the best years of my life on death row
for a crime I did not commit. I can never get these years back.
If I let it, it can make me bitter. But instead, I think about
how much God has forgiven me for all the wrongs I have done.
When I think about God's forgiveness of me, I can forgive
others for all the wrong that has been done to me.
Instead of being bitter, I try to be better,
and become more of what God wants me to become."*
KEVIN BURNS

*"By the end of His life, Jesus became a prisoner Himself.
Jesus was arrested and beaten by the authorities.
Jesus had a criminal record. Jesus was a convicted felon.
Jesus was sentenced to death by the State.
Maybe one reason God loves prisoners so much was
because He knew His Son would be a prisoner Himself."*
KEVIN RIGGS

CHAPTER 18
GROWING UP

"From my perspective, I had a normal, happy childhood."

■ ■ ■

(**KR**) West Memphis, Arkansas, sits across the Mississippi River from Memphis, Tennessee and is considered part of the Memphis metropolitan area. In the 1990s, the population of West Memphis was around 28,000[11] and had a median household income of just over $27,000 per year.[12] By contrast the median household income in the United States in 1990 was a little over $30,000 per year.[13] By the 2020s, the population dropped to just under 25,000,[14] and the median household income had not kept up with inflation, topping out at slightly more than $40,000 per year.[15] Again, compared to the United States as a whole, the median household income was over $70,000 per year in the 2020s.[16] Change happens very slowly in West Memphis. Today it's a typical small, working-class community, just like when KB was growing up.

KB has said he did not grow up poor, or if they were poor, so was everyone else and so he didn't know he was poor. I have visited KB's mom, Leslie, in her home, the same house in which KB grew up. It's a very quaint, modest house, well kept, with family pictures all over the walls. Leslie worked, and retired, as a cafeteria employee in the public schools in West Memphis. KB's dad, Obra, in addition to pastoring a church, worked for the city of West Memphis. KB had a solid, working-class upbringing.

FAMILY

KB will tell you he has a close-knit family. Growing up, he always felt love from his parents, and as one of twenty children, he never felt alone. It is because of his love for his family that KB hates what his lawyers did to him during the post-conviction stage of his case.

At post-conviction, KB's lawyers wanted to paint a picture that KB grew up poor and was abused and deprived as a child. They wanted to paint an ugly picture of his dad as the main abuser in his family. Their plan was to bring up, and highlight, one incident that happened when KB was around ten years old.

But first you must understand that KB's mom and dad were never married to each other. They had a complicated, on-again-off-again relationship, but their love for their children never wavered. KB's aunt (his mom's sister) lived across the street from KB's dad. One afternoon Leslie pulled up in her sister's driveway. In the passenger's seat was another man. Leslie was giving this gentleman a ride home, but Obra saw it and became jealous. As a result, they got into an argument that became physical. Leslie was injured in the altercation and had to be taken to the hospital. Neither KB, nor any of his siblings, witnessed the altercation. In fact KB will tell you, "Mom and dad never argued in front of us."

A few days later, after things cooled down, KB's dad called all the children together, and with KB's mom present, through tears, apologized to the entire family, asking everyone to forgive him. KB said, "My dad admitted his mistake, asked for forgiveness, and nothing like that ever happened again. This was a one-time incident that got out of control. As for me and my siblings, my mom and dad never abused or mistreated me. Sure, like most kids of that time, I got a few spankings, but I earned every one of them. My mom and dad loved me and my brothers and sisters. I have never doubted their love. That is why it hurt so much when my lawyers wanted to introduce an 'abusive upbringing' as a mitigating factor for the crime of which I was charged. It wasn't true, and I told my lawyers it wasn't true. But they brought it up anyway. As a result, all through the appeals process, all the way to the United States Supreme Court, this false narrative of an 'abusive upbringing' has been part of the legal record. But again, it's just not true! From my perspective, I had a normal, happy childhood."

(KR) Though filled with love, and though "normal," KB's family background is unique. I will let him explain.

(KB) I have nineteen brothers and sisters! Yes, you read that right. My dad got married at the age of eighteen, right out of high school. That marriage ended in divorce two years later. My sister, Teresa, was the only child of my dad and his first wife. Teresa now lives in Washington, DC.

Eventually, after the divorce, my dad met Louise. Together they had nine children, but they did not get married until 1979, after all the children were born. My dad and Louise stayed married until she passed away in the early part of 2023.

My mom married Nathaniel Burns, and they had five children together. Not long after the fifth child was born, Nathaniel left my mom and moved to Chicago, leaving my mom alone to raise five children. My mom and dad met in 1962, and were together for seven years before I was born. I was their firstborn. After me, Mom and Dad had four more children. Counting myself, that's twenty children total.

My family is unique in that, in reality, there were two families going on at the same time. Neither family knew about the other. In a small town like West Memphis, there were rumors, and years later I found out that my dad's wife, Louise, had suspicions. But anytime Louise brought it up to my dad, he denied it, and said, "People need to mind their own business and stay out of my business."

On the first day of seventh grade, I made friends with another seventh grader named Phillip. He and I attended two different elementary schools and had never met. Phillip was six months older than me, and we became good friends real fast. We both went out for the school's football team. On the first day of tryouts, the coach talked to each of us individually, to gather information about our families and who to call in case an injury occurred at practice. The coach said to me, "What's your mom's name?" I responded, "Leslie Burns." Then he asked, "What's your dad's name?" I answered, "Obra Carter." He looked at me like he had seen a ghost. He asked me again, and I said, "Obra Carter." Phillip had already talked to the coach, and so the coach yelled, "Phillip, get back over here quick!" Phillip ran back to the coach and said, "Yes sir. Is anything wrong?" The coach asked Phillip, "What did you say your dad's name was?" Phillip answered, "Obra Carter." Then he said to Phillip, "Did you know Kevin says his dad's name is also Obra Carter? I think you guys are brothers." Phillip said, "Well, I guess we are." And that's how we all found out about the other's family.

That afternoon I told my mom what had happened and Phillip told our dad. That night, dad came clean to Louise. The following Sunday, dad brought all of us together, both families, and confessed everything to us. In one day, the size of my family doubled! To this day, believe it or not, we are all close. There has never been any animosity or jealousy between the two families. If anything, growing up with so many brothers and sisters, and even more cousins, made my life full. There was always someone to play with. We never got bored. We had fun growing up, and we were all brought up in church. My mom always made sure we were at Old St. Paul's Missionary Baptist Church every Sunday. When I was sixteen, I started attending the Church of God in Christ, under Pastor Famous Smith.

When my dad started pastoring, from time to time, we went to his church, New Hope Missionary Baptist Church. My dad still pastors there, but he has semi-retired. My brother, Dericus, is now the senior pastor, and my brother, Phillip, is the associate pastor. One day, about ten years ago, while dad was visiting me on death row, he told me that New Hope Missionary Baptist Church had been in our family for over one hundred years! He explained to me that his great-great-grandfather started the church, and he actually completed the first building in 1907. Dad went on to explain the pastorate of the church had been passed all the way down to my brothers.

The only Carter who did not pastor the church was my grandfather. He fought in World War II, and was one of the infantry soldiers who stormed Normandy Beach. He was injured and received the Purple Heart. He lived across the street from the local car wash in West Memphis. A couple of times a week, my mom had her car washed and took us with her. Every time we went, my grandfather was sitting on a bench in front of the car wash, waiting for us. For a long time, we thought he lived at the car wash! He gathered us around him, gave us coins from his pocket, and told us stories about the war. I loved listening to his stories. Some of the best times of my life as a child were at the car wash with my grandfather.

I don't know what I would do without my family. They have always supported me through my trial and incarceration. My mom and dad, now in their eighties, drive three hundred miles each way, once a month to come visit me. I am now the only person on death row who has both parents come and visit regularly. I am truly blessed. I stay in contact with my brothers and sisters through phone calls, cards, and letters. My family is my support system, and I love each and every one of them. It is a privilege to have the family I have.

When I got arrested, my daughter, Briana, was three months old. She now lives in Texas and has blessed me with two grandsons, Demere (born in 2013) and Makhi (born in 2015). I talk to my daughter and grandsons often. Demere and Makhi have three very close cousins. Most of the time, when I call Briana, the cousins are there as well. They call me PaPa. So, I guess I really have five grandchildren.

Then there is my extended family. All the men in Unit 2 are my family, and a lot of their families have become my adopted families. Over the years, God has brought all kinds of people into my life through the volunteers at Riverbend Maximum Security Institution. Many of them have become like family to me. Finally, there is my church family, Franklin Community Church. Pastor Kevin Riggs and FCC have blessed me beyond measure. They have extended my ministry farther than I would have ever thought possible. Then there is Brad and Jessica Davis, who are as close to me as brothers and sisters. Also, Eric Boucher and Tim Webb, who help keep Church of Life going. I wish I could, but it is impossible for me to name all my friends and families. God has promised that he will do exceedingly, abundantly more than we could ever ask. God has most definitely fulfilled that promise in my life.

CHAPTER 19
ARSON

"How can I sign a piece of paper allowing the State of Arkansas to kill someone when my own son is on death row in Tennessee. That would be hypocritical. I can't pray for my son to receive mercy and not show mercy to someone else."

(**KR**) Even under the best of circumstances, being incarcerated is difficult. I know many people believe, "Don't do the crime if you can't do the time." That's easy to say, and it's usually said by people who do not have a loved one serving time. For people living behind bars, there is no distinction between "easy time" and "hard time." It's all time. Time away from family. Time away from friends. Time away from birthday celebrations and holidays. It's even time away from saying good-bye to loved ones who died while someone is on the inside. A friend of mine doing hard time in a super-max facility once told me, "Pastor, can't no one do your time for you. You have to do it all by yourself." KB once said to me, "Being in prison is punishment enough." I've often thought about both those sayings.

Serving time is hard. Period. KB was offered one plea deal. The district attorney said, "Plead guilty and we will give you a life sentence with a minimum of fifty years served." What the attorney didn't tell him is very few people, regardless of age or health going into prison, survive fifty years locked up. Besides, why should KB plead guilty to a crime he did not commit? KB rejected that deal. After he was sentenced to death, his lawyers lied and told people he was offered several different deals, each with less time served, but he denied them all. But the records show he was only offered the one deal. But again, why would KB accept any deal where he had to admit guilt?

I think one of the hardest things about being incarcerated is receiving news that someone close to you in the outside world has passed away. I have prayed with and counseled my fair share of inmates who received such news. The reality that they will not be able to say good-bye and grieve *with* their family is excruciating. On one occasion, a member of my church was in our local county jail on a small charge. While locked up, his father passed away. After lots of phone calls and begging, we were able to convince the authorities to let him out for a few hours so he could attend the funeral. A sheriff's deputy had to be with him the whole time, and I had to give my word he would return to jail at the appointed time. That privilege would never be allowed for someone serving time in a maximum-security institution like death row. KB admits that his family tries to keep bad news from him, but he has convinced them to not do that anymore. KB says, "I'm a minister of life and death. I know how to pray for these things."

Several of KB's family members died since he has been on death row. During COVID he lost a brother, Steve, and two cousins, Derrick and Denise. All three were only in their forties, and all three died in the spring of 2021, within nine days of each other.

Another of KB's brothers, Nathaniel, was shot and killed in Gary, Indiana. Nathaniel was living in Chicago at the time but had gone to Gary for some reason. KB's mom, Leslie Burns, told me, "I don't know why he was in Gary, and I don't know why he was shot. I received a phone call at 1:00 a.m., and while they were telling me he had been shot, I received another phone call that said he had died." Then with a sadness in her eyes, she said, "It's very hard for me to talk about it. One day I will tell you more, but right now, it is too difficult to discuss."

TRAGEDY

A few years after KB was incarcerated, his family suffered an unimaginable tragedy. Misty and I traveled to KB's hometown in West Memphis to spend time with his family, talking about this horrible event. After all these years, the pain this family has endured is still fresh. But they wanted to share the story with me in the hopes that somehow, in some small way, it will help KB's case.

One evening in the summer of 1996, some of KB's cousins and nieces and nephews gathered in the upstairs apartment of Lakeisha, KB's cousin, for a sleepover birthday party. A few days earlier, a woman named Susan, moved into the adjoining apartment. Lakeisha had not yet met Susan. Unbeknownst to everyone, Susan was in an abusive relationship with her boyfriend, Phillip. No one in KB's family knew either Phillip or Susan. In May the relationship between Phillip and Susan had become so violent that Susan had an order of protection issued against Phillip. He had beaten Susan, and in retaliation, Susan's brother shot Phillip in the leg. Phillip vowed revenge on both of them. Again, KB's family had no idea about any of this.

Two weeks prior to the birthday party at Lakeisha's apartment, and three weeks after the restraining order was issued against Phillip and he was shot, in another building in the same apartment complex, where Susan was living at the time, a suspicious fire broke out. No one was injured in the fire, and the damage was contained to a single unit. Phillip was suspected of starting the fire but was never charged. It was as a result of that fire that Susan moved to the apartment beside Lakeisha.

On the morning following the birthday party, at approximately 4:30, as everyone was sleeping, another fire broke out, which destroyed both Lakeisha's and Susan's apartments. Susan escaped injury by jumping out of a second-story bedroom window. Patricia, KB's fourteen-year-old cousin, was in the apartment with Lakeisha and the children. After being awakened by the smell of smoke, Patricia opened the door to the apartment. The fire was coming from the stairwell and quickly spread through the open door. Patricia and Alicia, another fourteen-year-old girl, escaped the fire. Alicia, however, was badly burned. Sadly, three children did not get out in time and died from smoke and soot inhalation. Two of the children were KB's cousins, and the third child was his niece. KB's cousins who perished were Kevin, named after KB (six months old) and Ashley (three years old). His niece, Latoya, the daughter of KB's sister, Ann, was twelve years old.

MERCY

The fire and the loss of three innocent lives rocked the city of West Memphis and devastated the Burns family. Not long after Phillip was arrested, the district attorney of Crittenden County (West Memphis), Arkansas, approached KB's family with the news that he wanted to seek the death penalty for Phillip, but he needed their help to do so. To his surprise and dismay, the family said, "NO!" They would not approve of capital punishment for this crime, or any other crime. The district attorney kept pressing, but KB's family stood strong and stayed together in their opposition to the death penalty, refusing to sign any documents that stated they wanted the district attorney to pursue capital punishment. KB's mom said to me, "Don't get me wrong. We are angry and believe Phillip should be punished to the fullest extent of the law. But how can I sign a piece of paper allowing the state of Arkansas to kill someone when my own son is on death row in Tennessee? That would be hypocritical. I can't pray for my son to receive mercy and not show mercy to someone else."

The district attorney was not pleased with their decision. In fact, he was angry and extremely rude to the family. He accused them of defending Phillip and said they were lying when they said they did not know him and had never met him.

The district attorney built a strong case against Phillip. Phillip was eventually convicted of three counts of capital murder and one count of first-degree battery. He is currently serving three life sentences without parole somewhere in a state prison in Arkansas. The family does not know where and have never had any contact with him, nor do they want to.

KB describes this event on his family as completely devastating. He said he doesn't understand why, or how, someone could do such a thing. When he received news of what had happened, he felt useless and just wanted to hug his family. He will tell you that this was one of the hardest times he has ever had while incarcerated.

In my opinion, it took an incredible amount of faith, courage, and mercy to not sign the piece of paper that would have allowed the district attorney to pursue the death penalty. I don't know if I could have been that brave. Words cannot describe the anger the family must have felt, and the grief they had to endure. However, it does bring to mind the words of Jesus when He said, "Blessed are the merciful, for they will be shown mercy" (Matthew 5:7). My sincerest prayer is that KB, and KB's family, will be shown the same mercy by the governor of Tennessee that they showed Phillip. That truly will be the best day of my life. While I sit at my desk, writing these words, I am wearing a black T-shirt with white words that read, "Execute justice, not people." I think this summarizes it all.

After spending time with KB's family, crying, and discussing this horrendous event, I took the family out to eat. We enjoyed a wonderful meal together that was full of joy and laughter. As Misty and I were leaving KB's house, his mom pulled me off to the side, away from everyone else, and with tears in her eyes said, "Today is the best day of my life." I pray for better days to come.

CHAPTER 20

A NEW CAR

*"I loved that car. But I loved it too much.
Looking back, buying that car
was the beginning of my downfall."*

■ ■ ■

(**KR**) The famous philosopher Socrates once said, "An unexamined life is not worth living."[17] The prophet Jeremiah said, "Let us examine our ways and test them, and let us return to the LORD" (Lamentations 3:40). The psalmist wrote, "Search me, God, and know my heart; test me and know my anxious thoughts. See if there is any offensive way in me, and lead me in the way everlasting" (Psalm 139:23–24). We are all more than the by-product of any one decision we have made, good or bad. Yet it is healthy to take time to look back over our lives and examine some key events that have shaped who we are.

KB grew up in church, and at a young age, felt God leading him into ministry. But something happened. Like a lot of young people, in his late teens, he rebelled. Or as he says, "I backslid." I once asked KB what he thought the turning point was. Without hesitation, he told me about the first time he bought a car. Here is how he described this key event in his life:

(KB) I was nineteen years old when I purchased my first car. It was a light blue, inside and out, two-door 1978 Oldsmobile Cutlass Supreme Brougham. The top of the car was half vinyl (also light blue) and half hardtop. This car was my pride and joy. She popped when I placed Cragar rims and brand-new tires on her. After I installed a top-of-the-line Kenwood AM/FM cassette radio with Kenwood speakers, everyone knew when I was coming down the road. I loved rolling the windows down, turning the volume up, and cruising to Too $hort's "Partytime" or LL Cool J's "I'm Bad." For me, this car represented freedom, independence, and adulthood. I loved that car. But I wasn't the only one who loved my new car.

One Saturday morning, my mother asked me to wash her car. So with the help of my twelve-year-old sister, Renita, I started washing Mom's car in our driveway. Renita and I had it all soaped up, when Mom said, "No, Kevin. I want you to take my car to the car wash and clean her up real good." I thought her request was strange. Mom never let me drive her car. Renita and I quickly rinsed the car off and drove to the car wash and washed it again.

As we were drying off Mom's car, I heard loud music coming down the road. I can't remember the exact song, but it was a gospel song, and it was loud. As the music got closer to us, I stopped drying the car and said, "Renita, look who's driving down the street in *my* car?" Even though she could barely see over the steering wheel, my mom was cruising the neighborhood in my car! To this day, the memory of Mom driving it makes me smile.

I loved that car, but I loved it too much. Looking back, buying that car was the beginning of my downfall. Four years later, I was charged with felony murder. I have never recovered from purchasing that car.

A NEW CAR

(KR) I remember my first vehicle. It was a small, five-speed manual transmission, two door, mist-orange Nissan pickup. I don't remember the year, but it was in the early 1980s. I do remember on the tailgate was written "Nissan," and then in smaller letters underneath, it said "Datsun." So it was the year Datsuns became Nissans. I think it was 1984. I was nineteen, and I loved my little truck. However, in less than a week after I purchased it, with the temporary tags still on it, and my girlfriend—now my wife—in the front seat with me, I wrecked my truck. No one was hurt, and the damage was minimal, but I was embarrassed.

(KB) I was raised in the church. My childhood centered around church services, revivals, vacation Bible schools, and various other activities at Old St. Paul's Missionary Baptist Church in West Memphis. At the age of sixteen, I started attending a Church of God in Christ congregation, also in West Memphis. By the age of nineteen, when I purchased my car, I was attending church regularly and was involved in numerous ministries of the church. But all that changed three weeks after buying my car. I clearly remember the third Sunday after I had my car, walking outside and admiring how pretty she looked with new rims, tires, and tinted windows. The first two Sundays I had my car, I went to church and praised God for the blessing He had provided me. But on this particular Sunday, instead of going to church, I decided to wash and wax my car. After-all, what could missing one Sunday hurt? Only later would I realize how Satan used that car to turn me away from God.

(KR) Like KB, I also grew up in church—Sunday morning, Sunday night, Wednesday night, and any other time the church doors were open. My dad was a university professor and also an ordained minister. (I am a fourth-generation ordained minister.) My dad did not teach in the summer. Instead, growing up, we spent summers traveling across the Southeast holding revivals. My family sang and dad preached. We went to church every night during the summer! I may have been the only kid who could not wait for summer to be over and school to start.

KB said it was his car that turned him away from God. Sports was my temptation, especially football, but God got my attention early. In seventh grade I tried out for the football team at my school. Back then, junior high school and high school were the same school, and sports were divided into junior varsity (JV) and varsity (high school). Most students did not try out for school sports until they were in the ninth grade. A few eight graders tried out, but no seventh graders did. Except me. I tried out and made it, and as a seventh grader won the starting position as a JV offensive guard. During practice one week before our first game, while blocking a teammate, my teammate fell backward on the ground, and I followed him. Unfortunately, he curled his knees and I landed on his knees, rupturing my spleen. I could have easily bled to death, but I did not. Instead, my spleen was removed, and it now sits in a jar on my bookcase.

(KB) Satan only has one objective, and that is to turn our hearts away from God. He will use whatever he can to accomplish that objective in our life. For me it was a car. For KR it was sports. For you it could be a job or a house or prestige or a host of other things. The moment something becomes more important to us than our relationship with God, at that moment we have an idol in our life. The first two commandments read, "You shall have no other gods before me. You shall not make for yourself an image . . . for I, the LORD your God, am a jealous God" (Exodus 20:3–5). I learned this lesson the hard way.

A NEW CAR

It really wasn't the car, but it's what all came with the car. The car made me a somebody, or so I thought. All of a sudden, I was popular. People who previously ignored me now wanted to be my friends. Girls never gave me the time of day; now they wanted to be my girlfriend. I was young and could not handle the attention. My focus became me and was no longer God.

From the Shelby County Jail, God spoke to me and revealed where I went wrong and where my life went off-track. From that jail cell, I learned we have to let go of everything, so we can see God clearly. God desires every area of our life. God requires full commitment and complete surrender.

While reading Isaiah, I saw myself in the prophet's words: "'Woe to me!' I cried. 'I am ruined! For I am a man of unclean lips, and I live among a people of unclean lips, and my eyes have seen the King, the LORD Almighty'" (Isaiah 6:5). And just like Isaiah, "Then one of the seraphim flew to me with a live coal in his hand, which he had taken with the tongs from the alter. With it he touched my mouth and said, 'See, this has touched your lips; your guilt is taken away and your sin atoned for'" (Isaiah 6:6–7). Then just like Isiah, I heard God say, "Whom shall I send? And who will go for us?" So moved by God's grace, love, and forgiveness, I could only respond like the great prophet, and so I said, "Here am I. Send me!" (Isaiah 6:8). I now know God sent me to death row to be a light in a dark place, and when He is finished with me, He will open up the bars and I will be set free. Until then, my life is God's, not my own. Until then, I will faithfully serve Him on my mission field behind these walls.

SYNCRETISM

(KR) There is a lot to unpack in KB's story about a new car. Was God punishing KB for purchasing a car? If so, isn't that a little harsh? How does the decision to buy a car end up causing someone to be sentenced to death? Where does the love and grace and forgiveness of God fit in this story? And who is this Satan guy who is out to destroy us?

Don't let those questions keep you from the lesson KB is teaching. This story isn't really about a car. The lesson is a warning about our priorities. The truth is, most people drift slowly away from God. Very few people make a spontaneous, conscience, emotional decision to walk away from God. Most of the time we are not guilty of rejecting God. Most of the time we are guilty of syncretism. In other words, we don't replace God with other things; we add other things to our devotion to God.

Syncretism is attempting to blend, or amalgamate, different religions and beliefs systems into one. Satan's strategy is not to get us to completely reject God but to add things to our devotion to God. It could be other religions or philosophies or rules or things or anything else that can get our eyes off the one true God.

Syncretism was the downfall in the garden of Eden. Adam and Eve did not reject God. To their belief in God, they added belief in what the serpent told them and the belief they could be their own god, making up their own rules.

Syncretism was the downfall of the Israelites in the Old Testament. Nowhere in Scripture do the Israelites completely reject God. Instead, they added other beliefs and other things to their faith in God. For example, the story of the golden calf in Exodus 32 was not a rejection of God. Rather, it was an attempt to blend religious practices they learned in Egypt to their worship of God. Syncretism is the warning behind the first two commandments:

> And God spoke all these words: "I am the LORD your
> God, who brought you out of Egypt, out of the land of

slavery. You shall have no other gods before me. You shall not make for yourself an image in the form of anything in heaven above or on the earth beneath or in the waters below. You shall not bow down to them or worship them; for I, the LORD your God, am a jealous God, punishing the children for the sin of the parents to the third and fourth generation of those who hate me, but showing love to a thousand generations of those who love me and keep my commandments." (Exodus 20:1–6)

"'You shall have no other gods before me.... You shall not make for yourself an image in the form of anything.'" Neither of those commandments is a complete denial of God. Rather, both are adding things to one's belief in God. In other words, you can still believe in God and violate the first two commandments.

The apostle Paul had syncretism in mind when he wrote, "See to it that no one takes you captive through hollow and deceptive philosophy, which depends on human tradition and the elemental spiritual forces of this world rather than on Christ" (Colossians 2:8). "[H]ollow and deceptive philosophy" could include other religions and popular "isms," like humanism, hedonism, materialism, and on and on and on. Often, we add those types of things to our belief in God. The result is always a weakening of your faith. Syncretism always results in a drifting away from God. This is the lesson behind KB's story of the car.

CHAPTER 21
A FAMILIAR STORY

"I don't think God will ever forgive me for what I've done."

■ ■ ■

(KR) With tears in his eyes, Allen said to me, "Growing up, my grandma and mom took me to church every Sunday morning, Sunday evening, and Wednesday night. I loved church, especially Sunday school. As a kid, I loved reading the Bible. I really enjoyed all the stories."

When I met Allen, he had been incarcerated for more than thirty years. Most of that time was in solitary confinement. We sat on opposite sides of a metal door, speaking through the pie flap. I had been warned by prison guards not to touch Allen or shake his hands through the pie flap because, according to the guards, "Inmates have been known to pull your arms through and cut you up." I asked KB about what the guards said and if it was safe to shake Allen's hand. KB told me of one incident he knew of where someone pulled a guard's arm inside, doing serious damage to the arm, but it was not Allen, and it was a long time ago. KB was one of the few men on death row Allen liked and trusted. KB assured me it would be OK. Anytime I talked to Allen, I always shook his hand, and the few times I did pray with him, I held his hand. Allen died of natural causes, spending the last quarter of his life in solitary confinement.

By his own admission, Allen was guilty of multiple murders, plus a host of other crimes. Allen grew up in southern Middle Tennessee in a part of the state made infamous by a notorious sheriff, Buford Pusser, otherwise known as "Walking Tall." Coincidentally, Sheriff Pusser was a friend of Allen's family. Some of Allen's relatives were deputies for Sheriff Pusser.

A masterful storyteller, Allen was fun to talk with, and so KB and I talked with him frequently. On one occasion, Allen told us as early as nine years of age he preached in local churches and tent revivals all over southern Tennessee. He bragged about preaching one time on the back of a pickup truck, to a crowded parking lot, after a local high school football game.

During one of our visits, I asked Allen what he thought happened. What caused a smart kid (Allen had a photographic memory) who loved Sunday school and preaching to end up spending all his adult life incarcerated for murder? Once again with tears in his eyes and a little anger in his voice, he said, "When I was ten years old, I went to summer church camp. This was my first time ever going, and I was excited. One night, however, I was awakened in the middle of the night with a man I trusted (a deacon in my church) on top of me, fondling me. He then forced me to perform sexual acts on him. I told people at the camp what happened. I went home and told my mom, and I told people at church. But no one believed me. They assumed I was only wanting to cause trouble. I was labeled a bad kid. I was never the same after that experience. I became an angry child, an angry teenager, and an angry adult." He stopped for a second, gathered his thoughts, and then added, "I don't think God will ever forgive me for what I've done."

KB and I did the best we could explaining the full capacity of God's grace and forgiveness to Allen. He listened, but he had heard it all before. Allen was a student of the Bible. He knew it, cover to cover. In fact I have several Bible studies in my personal library Allen wrote. A few years after our conversation, Allen passed away, quietly, in the middle of the night in his cell. I pray he is finally at peace. I am thankful God's grace and forgiveness is greater than Allen's doubts, or as KB has said on numerous occasions, "You cannot out sin the grace of God."

I know Allen's story is extreme, but it is an all-too-familiar story of people who are in jails and prisons across the United States. Early childhood trauma, if not dealt with, can result in all kinds of physical, mental, and spiritual problems as an adult. Psychologists, counselors, educators, and medical doctors all agree that trauma experienced in early childhood impacts brain development, future health concerns, family dynamics, and community safety. Some experts have even suggested that as many as 97 percent of juvenile offenders have experienced some sort of early childhood trauma. When a child who has experienced prolonged stress and trauma acts up at school or at home or in the community, they get labeled a delinquent, which further adds to their trauma. Many of these children end up in the criminal legal system.

FORGIVENESS

Reflecting on our conversation with Allen, I asked KB about forgiveness. What does forgiveness mean, and how important is forgiveness? Here is what KB said:

(KB) Forgiveness is a big deal. Forgiveness is vital to our lives as followers of Jesus. When I think of forgiveness, the first thing I think of is the Lord's prayer. The Gospel writer Luke tells us Jesus's prayer came in response to the disciples' desire to learn to pray. The disciples said to Jesus, "Lord, teach us to pray" (Luke 11:1). Jesus's prayer is a model for our own prayers. The thing I've always loved about this prayer is its simplicity. Praying is not complicated. Praying is simply talking to God.

Jesus mentioned forgiveness in His model prayer. He prayed, "And forgive us our debts, as we forgive our debtors" (Matthew 6:12). The idea of forgiving debts every seven years and every fifty years is seen in the Old Testament. But I think the idea of "debts" in Jesus's prayer goes beyond financial forgiveness. I think it included any type of wrong we have done before God, any type of wrong we have done toward others, and any type of wrong others have done toward us. A debt is something we owe. I owed God a payment for my sins, but through Jesus Christ, God has forgiven me of that debt. Likewise, we may think people owe us something. Maybe they have wronged us and owe us an apology. Maybe they have hurt our feelings and owe us an explanation. Maybe we owe someone else an apology or explanation. Whatever it is, whatever we think others owe us, we are to forgive them that debt in the same way God has forgiven us.

This means a lot to me personally. I feel like I have been wronged by the court system. If I am not careful, I can feel like the whole world owes me an apology. I have spent the best years of my life on death row for a crime I did not commit. I can never get these years back. If I let it, it can make me bitter. But instead, I think about how much God has forgiven me for all the wrongs I have done. When I think about God's forgiveness of me, I can forgive others for all the wrong that has been done to me. Instead of being bitter, I try to be better, and become more of what God wants me to become. I think about Jesus hanging on the cross. That's the greatest injustice that has ever happened in the history of the world. Yet what did Jesus do? How did He respond to that horrendous wrong committed against Him? He said, "Father, forgive them; for they know not what they do" (Luke 23:34). Most of the time, when people wrong us and offend us, they truly don't know what they are doing, and how they are being used by the enemy to oppress us.

Then to emphasize the importance of forgiveness, at the end of His prayer, Jesus concluded, "For if ye forgive men their trespasses, your heavenly Father will also forgive you: But if ye forgive not men their trespasses, neither will your Father forgive your trespasses" (Matthew 6:14–15). If that doesn't challenge you, I don't know what will. Jesus said our forgiveness from God is wrapped up in our forgiving others. God's whole purpose in sending Jesus to earth was forgiveness. The only way we could be brought back into a right relationship with God is through His forgiveness offered through the death, burial, and resurrection of His Son. We cannot survive, this world or the next world, without forgiveness from God and without forgiving other people.

We must forgive! Unforgiveness poisons all our relationships. God requires me to forgive. I will forgive others, even when I don't feel like it, because I will not allow anything to mess up my relationship with God.

Forgiveness involves accepting God's forgiveness and then forgiving others. But another important aspect of forgiveness is forgiving ourselves. I think that is where Allen struggled. Deep down, I think he knew God had forgiven him. He just could not forgive himself. If I could talk to Allen again, I would tell him, "If God says you are forgiven, you are forgiven. Not to forgive yourself is saying you know more about forgiveness then God does. Deep down you know that is not true." Then I would ask him, "Allen, who are you going to believe—yourself or God?"

(KR) I miss Allen tremendously. Over the years, he became a dear friend. I greatly miss his unique ability to tell a story. He had a way of weaving together a narrative that made the most normal life experience sound exciting and humorous.

Allen also loved music, all genres of music. For some reason years ago, the administration at Riverbend Maximum Security Institution, took Allen's stereo away from him, leaving him with no music. With the help of his lawyers, Allen was able to get a new stereo, but was told he could have no more than fifteen CD albums. Always looking for a way to "one-up" the system, Allen purchased fifteen high-capacity CDs. Each could hold dozens of full-length albums. So instead of only having fifteen CDs, Allen had a couple of hundred albums.

Periodically Allen asked me to purchase a particular CD of a particular artist. I bought the CD and then got it to one of Allen's lawyers. The lawyer made a copy of the CD on one of Allen's high-capacity discs and keep the original in her office—thus, not violating any copyright laws.

One day, while talking about music, Allen asked me what my favorite style of music was and who my favorite bands or artists were. I think, to his surprise, I told him my favorite music was rock music and my favorite band was Stryper, a Christian heavy-metal band that made it big in the 1980s and 1990s. Allen laughed and then told me how much he did not like Stryper. I told him he needed to give them another chance and that I was going to buy him the album they were most known for, with the greatest song in the history of all songs, "To Hell with the Devil." Allen laughed even harder but agreed; if I purchased the album, he would listen to it. So that's what I did. I purchased the album *To Hell with the Devil* (1986) and took it to his lawyer, who placed it on one of his high-capacity CDs and gave it to him.

A few weeks went by, and to be honest, I had forgotten about it. Then one Friday, as I walked into Allen's pod, he had been waiting for me. He cranked up the song "To Hell with the Devil" as loud as he could on his CD player. All the guys in the pod started laughing and singing. That day was the best day of my life. Thinking about that day still brings a smile to my face. The friendships I have made with the men in Unit 2, and the memories I have of those friendships, are among my favorite friendships and memories of all my life.

CHAPTER 22
A SERMON

"Everything about prison is traumatic.
Nothing about being behind bars is easy.
Every day is a challenge to stay mentally and spiritually strong."

■ ■ ■

(KR) I am amazed at how vast KB's ministry has grown from behind the walls at Riverbend Maximum Security Institution. One such avenue, which stretches across the nation, is through Christian Community Development Association or CCDA. Every year CCDA sponsors a weeklong emphasis on mass incarceration called "Locked in Solidarity." It's a week where individuals, churches, and nonprofits strive to bring awareness and action on mass incarceration in the United States. I have had the privilege of working alongside CCDA to develop a sermon and study guide for the week to be used in churches and small-group discussions. KB partners with me in writing the sermons and study guides. He is now well known across the CCDA network. It amazes me how often, when I am at a CCDA event, strangers come up to me and ask how KB is doing and how much his prayers and written words have meant to them. From Unit 2 at Riverbend Maximum Security Institution, KB is changing the world.

THE DEMONIAC

One year the theme for "Locked in Solidarity" was mental health and trauma. As always, our task was to develop a sermon around the theme. As KB and I started talking about this theme and brainstorming ideas, we soon realized this was the most difficult topic we had ever addressed together. I wrote the background material and a lot of the introduction for the theme. KB wrote the main part of the sermon. His sermon was based on the story of Jesus's encounter with a man possessed by an evil spirit in Mark 5:1–20. The title of his sermon was, simply, "The Demoniac."

(KB) Everything about prison is traumatic. Nothing about being behind bars is easy. Every day is a challenge to stay mentally and spiritually strong. Maintaining physical health in prison is difficult but maintaining mental and spiritual health is even more difficult. In prison we are deprived of everything. Our names are replaced by numbers. Every moment of every day is scheduled by someone else. There are no liberties. There are only earned privileges that can be stripped from us without cause and without warning. Being arrested is traumatic. Going through a criminal trial is traumatic. Hearing the word "GUILTY!" is traumatic. Unfortunately, and for many, stress, trauma, and mental illness started long before being locked up. The prison industrial complex only adds to the trauma. I know many will read these words and say, "That's what prison is for. You are there to be punished. Don't do the crime if you can't do the time." Most people have no idea what it's like to be incarcerated. Simply put: ***Prison, by itself, is enough.*** Once a person is locked up, everything else that goes on is nothing but punishment and an attack on their mental health. The goal of prison is to break them down, making them feel like they are nothing.

Here are some examples: I have a strong and supportive family. I don't know what I would do without them, but I can only call home once a week. Why? Because a thirty-minute, long-distance phone call costs me $30. I have a full-time job in prison. I am the chaplain's assistant for my entire unit. I get paid 50 cents an hour. I started out working in the kitchen making 17 cents an hour. Fifty cents an hour is the most anyone can make in Unit 2. I use that money to pay for phone calls home, to pay for commissary, and to purchase all my hygiene products. Contrary to what many people on the outside think, the prison provides none of these things. I must buy my own soap, my own deodorant, my own toothpaste, and my own toothbrush. More than a few inmates go without because they cannot afford these things. The prison does provide "indigent packages" upon request. But I cannot describe to you how horrible those packages are.

One time, the families of the guys in my unit petitioned the prison for us to get cable television. By cable I mean two channels: one movie channel and one sports channel. Our families agreed to pay for everything, so it would not cost the prison anything. The prison administration agreed and cable was installed. This did wonders for our morale. Several months later the cable was disconnected because someone in the outside world found out about it and complained. It seems people on the outside think we should all just sit and rot away, as if we are human garbage instead of human beings.

We once had a guard in our unit who liked to start rumors among the guys. This guard said something that was not true to one of the guys and then laughed after seeing how far the rumor went and how much it changed over the course of his shift. The only reason for these rumors was to keep the guys upset and to make fun. It was nothing more than mental torture. No matter what a guard says or does, we cannot retaliate. If we do, we will be accused of "defiance" and locked down for however long they want to lock us down.

Everything in prison is a mental struggle. Like a virus, it will eat us alive if we let it. I have seen people literally go crazy inside these walls. I have watched people's mental illness exponentially increase over time. It's not the big things that break people's emotional state. It's the accumulation of small things over time. The only way to survive prison is to have a solid foundation. If you don't, you will break. My foundation is my family, time spent in prayer and fasting, and studying God's Word. But it's a daily struggle. It's non-stop stress and trauma. I repeat, prison is enough punishment by itself.

There is a story in Mark's Gospel that I think can be applied to the trauma we face being incarcerated. It begins, "They went across the lake to the region of the Gerasenes. When Jesus got out of the boat, a man with an impure spirit came from the tombs to meet him" (Mark 5:1–2, NIV). This man had been traumatized his entire life, and now he was ostracized from his community and forced to live in the local graveyard. We are not told exactly what had happened to this man, but I imagine he lived a tortured life, both mentally and physically. As some point, taking advantage of his weakness, evil spirits possessed and controlled him. Being incarcerated as long as I have, I have witnessed this happening to people and have battled against demonic spirits myself. I am convinced evil spirits latch on to a person's weakness and use that weakness to oppress them.

Mark continues, "This man lived in the tombs" (v. 3a, NIV), a reference not only to his exact location but also to the continued torture and trauma of his existence. Mark then adds, "Night and day among the tombs and in the hills he would cry out and cut himself with stones" (v. 5, NIV). Living in prison is like living in a tomb where we are tormented daily. We are forgotten about by the outside world. No one hears or sees us. Some people inside prison, out of despair and hopelessness, cut themselves and practice other types of self-harm. I and many others like me relate to this man who has been abandoned by society and left for dead.

The story continues, "When he saw Jesus from a distance, he ran and fell on his knees in front of him. He shouted at the top of his voice, 'What do you want with me, Jesus, Son of the Most High God? In God's name don't torture me!" (vv. 6–7, NIV). I imagine this man ran to Jesus out of fear and desperation. Fear because he knew who Jesus was, the Son of God, and desperation because he had no other choice and no other person to run to.

Jesus, knowing the trauma and turmoil of this individual, looked past the person and spoke to the evil spirit, saying, "Come out of this man, . . . What is your name?" (vv. 8–9, NIV). The evil spirit replied, "My name is Legion . . . for we are many" (v. 9, NIV). A "legion" was a contingent of Roman soldiers numbering between three thousand and six thousand. This legion of evil spirits knew who Jesus was. They knew what type of power and what type of authority Jesus had. They knew Jesus could destroy them, so they asked for mercy. They begged Jesus, crying, "Send us among the pigs; allow us to go into them" (v. 12, NIV). Jesus "gave them permission, and the evil spirits came out and went into the pigs. The herd, about two thousand in number, rushed down the steep bank into the lake and were drowned" (v. 13, NIV). There is an important lesson here that cannot be overlooked. Jesus showed mercy to demons! In the end, the demons chose to destroy themselves, but still, Jesus showed them mercy. If evil spirits are shown mercy, surely all human beings, regardless of what they have done or not done, can be shown mercy as well. Everyone deserves a second chance. No one deserves to live the rest of their lives in the tombs tortured by evil spirits.

I know not everyone agrees with me. I know some people believe when a person is arrested they should be locked up and the key thrown away. Some people get angry when others are shown mercy. They are like the people who lived in the village surrounding the cemetery where the man in our story lived. They knew how tortured he was. They were afraid of him. But now they saw him "sitting there, dressed and in his right mind" (v. 15, NIV). You might think they were happy and rejoicing that this man had been healed. But you are wrong! Instead of joy, "they were afraid. . . . Then the people began to plead with Jesus to leave their region" (Mark 5:15b, 17, NIV). Can you imagine that? Instead of being happy for the man, they were upset that he had been shown mercy.

Let me make an application here. This man, who was possessed—practicing self-harm and cut off from society—in a lot of ways resembles a person living in prison. There are a lot of people behind bars who struggle with a host of mental issues. Yet when they are shown mercy by the courts, some people get upset. When a death sentence is commuted, many people get upset.

Then when Jesus cast the spirit into a herd of pigs, the pigs ran off a cliff, into the water, and drowned. This meant that the people of the village lost their main source of income. And that is what made them angry!

Likewise, the prison industrial complex is tied to our economic system. When people are released from prison, other people lose money. There was profit in the pigs, just like there is profit in the prisoner. The drowning pigs disrupted their economic system. Likewise, prisons are not about justice and rehabilitation but about big money, especially private prisons. But even state-run prisons are paid from the federal government based on how many prisoners they house. If everyone was released from jails and prisons tomorrow, lots of people would lose lots of money, and lots of people would lose their jobs. There are financial incentives to keep prison beds full. In a capitalistic system, where prisons make profits, people don't want people released. It is in their financial interest to keep people locked up. That is what I see when I read that people were upset that the demoniac had been set free.

Instead of focusing on the people, I want to focus on the tortured individual who experienced peace. At one time he was tormented, chained, naked, and suicidal. But then he met Jesus, and the next moment he was at peace, freed, clothed, and full of life. Mentally he went from chaos and oppression to calmness and liberation. Spiritually he went from despair and despondency to healing and wholeness. Jesus reached him in his prison of death and set him free! Jesus fulfilled His word where He said He came to "proclaim freedom for the prisoners" (Luke 4:18, NIV).

Here is the big lesson behind this story: One encounter with Jesus changes everything! This is what has happened to me and many other men and women behind bars. But it is also what happened to you the moment you professed faith in Jesus Christ. This means, regardless of the situation you are in, there is hope. Regardless of your past trauma, there is a bright future. A future full of healing, grace, and mercy. Yes, talking about your childhood and past trauma is important. Seeking professional help is vital. Developing habits that strengthen your mental health is a must. But above all, seek Jesus. Place your faith in Him. Allow the Holy Spirit to indwell you and clothe you in righteousness and bring peace to your troubled mind.

In conclusion, here's one last thing from the end of the story. Remember, part of the man's trauma was being ostracized from his community. The graveyard had become his prison yard. After being healed, the man wanted to go with Jesus. Instead Jesus told him, "'Go home to your own people and tell them how much the Lord has done for you, and how he has had mercy on you.' So the man went away and began to tell in the Decapolis how much Jesus had done for him. And all the people were amazed" (vv. 19–20, NIV). This man's healing was not complete until he was reunited with his family and with the community. For people like me, who are behind bars but have been changed by an encounter with Jesus and healed by His grace and mercy, we wait for our complete healing when we are reunited with our family and with our community. This is why restorative justice should be the goal. Restorative justice is the way of Jesus. Restorative justice should be our cry as well.

> *Let me finish with a prayer.*
> *Gracious and Eternal God:*
> *You are the God and Father of our Lord and Savior,*
> *Jesus, the Christ.*
> *Lord God, I thank You for Your grace and Your mercies;*
> *And I thank You that Your faithfulness is everlasting;*
> *enduring the tests of trials and tribulations that*
> *we must endure because of life's challenges,*
> *and the subtle oppositions that we face throughout our lifetimes.*
> *Lord God, and I thank You, that Your love does not vacillate.*
> *Your love remains steadfast, unmovable,*
> *and always abounding,*
> *unchanged by the multitude of our faults.*
> *Father-God, I lift up those among us that are afflicted with mental illness,*
> *and even demonic possession.*
> *Though we ourselves may not be able to discern the difference,*
> *Your Spirit can!*
> *I pray for these, O Lord God,*

A SERMON

that You will loose them from these binding and tormenting oppressions,
and that You will deliver them back unto their families and communities,
free and clothed in their right minds.
Father-God, and I pray for men and women, boys and girls,
that are incarcerated everywhere.
That there will be reformations and restorations
and that this mass incarceration machine may be brought down!
And that this wicked industry, and this vile business,
will be stopped!
I pray also, Father, for those of us that are on death row,
the most crucial of this vile business because of politics.
I pray that You will make a full end of it, O God, and bring to pass your own Word,
"...preserve thou those that are appointed to die" (Psalm 79:11).
Finally, Father,
I pray for Your people (the Church)
that You will stir up in us, O God,
a fire and a compassion for the incarcerated,
and those of us on death-row.
That being led by Your Spirit,
the Church and the Pastors,
may take their place, "the lead,"
in the charge for reforms and restorations.
For so have You ordained for us to do.
That Your compassion and Your mercy and Your glory
may fill the whole earth.
In the name of Your Holy Son, Jesus,
I pray and I thank You Father,
Amen and Amen.

CHAPTER 23
ENCOURAGE YOURSELF

"My flood will not rise above my standing in Christ Jesus."

■ ■ ■

(KR) KB is the most optimistic person I have ever met in my entire life. He absolutely refuses to be discouraged, and he will not allow those around him to be discouraged either. One of his favorite verses in the Bible, which he has repeated to me several times, is, "But David encouraged himself in the LORD his God" (1 Samuel 30:6). Somehow, in spite of his situation, KB has figured out how to keep himself encouraged. I don't know how he does it. Early on in our relationship, I wondered to myself if he was living in denial. But I can confidently tell you he is not! KB simply has incredible faith. In fact I unashamedly tell you his faith is stronger than my faith.

Over the years, KB has become my pastor. There have been numerous times, during our visits, that I have told him about my struggles and my discouragements. Every time he patiently listens, takes me to the Scriptures, prays for me, and encourages me. There have been times over the years, because of my own ministry and my own pressures, that I have gone weeks without visiting KB. During those times, my wife eventually says to me, "Are you going to see KB this week?" I will reply, "I don't know; I have a lot going on right now." She then scolds me, saying, "I don't care what's going on. You better go visit KB. You need him to encourage you." She is always right.

On one occasion, I was in the middle of several weeks of personal discouragement. The impetus for my discouragement was broken relationships with people I had known, and done ministries with, for years. These "friends" started rumors in the community about me, attacking my integrity, and were actively trying to sabotage my ministries! They even attempted to petition the elders of my church to remove me as pastor! The personal attacks were vicious. The pain and the hurt of these attacks go deep. It was one of the few times in my over thirty years of pastoral ministry that I seriously thought of quitting. I was under enormous stress and pressure. There are days when I am still not sure I have fully recovered from this time in my ministry.

During this time, as KB and I were talking, he sensed I was discouraged and ask me, "Pastor, what's wrong?" I told him the whole story. He listened and then said to me, "Do you remember what you told me as you were preparing me for ordination?"

"Can you be more specific?" I asked.

"You told me that once I was ordained people, especially the other men in Unit 2, would start to watch me closely."

I said, "Yes, I remember."

"You told me that because I would be given more responsibilities, and possibly more privileges, that the other guys might become jealous and try to knock me down or say things about me that were not true. You told me that while I could not control what other people say and do, I can control how I respond, and that I need to always remain humble and recognize that the attacks are not really from the people attacking me but from the enemy."

"Yes, I remember."

CHAPTER 23
ENCOURAGE YOURSELF

"My flood will not rise above my standing in Christ Jesus."

■ ■ ■

(KR) KB is the most optimistic person I have ever met in my entire life. He absolutely refuses to be discouraged, and he will not allow those around him to be discouraged either. One of his favorite verses in the Bible, which he has repeated to me several times, is, "But David encouraged himself in the Lord his God" (1 Samuel 30:6). Somehow, in spite of his situation, KB has figured out how to keep himself encouraged. I don't know how he does it. Early on in our relationship, I wondered to myself if he was living in denial. But I can confidently tell you he is not! KB simply has incredible faith. In fact I unashamedly tell you his faith is stronger than my faith.

Over the years, KB has become my pastor. There have been numerous times, during our visits, that I have told him about my struggles and my discouragements. Every time he patiently listens, takes me to the Scriptures, prays for me, and encourages me. There have been times over the years, because of my own ministry and my own pressures, that I have gone weeks without visiting KB. During those times, my wife eventually says to me, "Are you going to see KB this week?" I will reply, "I don't know; I have a lot going on right now." She then scolds me, saying, "I don't care what's going on. You better go visit KB. You need him to encourage you." She is always right.

On one occasion, I was in the middle of several weeks of personal discouragement. The impetus for my discouragement was broken relationships with people I had known, and done ministries with, for years. These "friends" started rumors in the community about me, attacking my integrity, and were actively trying to sabotage my ministries! They even attempted to petition the elders of my church to remove me as pastor! The personal attacks were vicious. The pain and the hurt of these attacks go deep. It was one of the few times in my over thirty years of pastoral ministry that I seriously thought of quitting. I was under enormous stress and pressure. There are days when I am still not sure I have fully recovered from this time in my ministry.

During this time, as KB and I were talking, he sensed I was discouraged and ask me, "Pastor, what's wrong?" I told him the whole story. He listened and then said to me, "Do you remember what you told me as you were preparing me for ordination?"

"Can you be more specific?" I asked.

"You told me that once I was ordained people, especially the other men in Unit 2, would start to watch me closely."

I said, "Yes, I remember."

"You told me that because I would be given more responsibilities, and possibly more privileges, that the other guys might become jealous and try to knock me down or say things about me that were not true. You told me that while I could not control what other people say and do, I can control how I respond, and that I need to always remain humble and recognize that the attacks are not really from the people attacking me but from the enemy."

"Yes, I remember."

"Well now," KB lovingly but sternly said, "I am telling you the same thing. Be mindful, and know the attacks on you are because of the labor and work you put in for the kingdom of God." He then continued, "You, being on the level of ministry you are, and the instrument you are for God, you are a powerful weapon of spiritual warfare, doing damage to the kingdom of darkness. Satan is not going to sit back and do nothing. The enemy will strike at you by any means necessary. Those attacking you are instruments Satan has used to get to you. You know that Satan doesn't mind using those who are closest to us, those who can strike right to the heart of who you are, to get to you and discourage you. Remember, Jesus chose Judas Iscariot and had to look him in the eye on the night He was betrayed, saying to him, 'Friend, do you betray me with a kiss?' [see Luke 22]. Be mindful and watchful and remember that your labor will not be in vain."

Those words spoke life to me, and I will be forever grateful for KB speaking the truth in love to me.

DISCOURAGEMENT

There has been only one occasion when I have seen KB discouraged. In a span of a year or so, Tennessee executed seven people. Not long after the seventh execution, the Tennessee State Supreme Court released execution dates of several more people. One day as we were talking about this, KB started crying but quickly stopped. He said the stress of so many friends being killed in a relatively short period of time was beginning to take its toll on everyone left behind. I remember all too well this dark period. Things were quiet in Unit 2. The discouragement in the air was thick. As pastor to all the men on death row, each execution weighed heavy on him. KB has the respect of everyone on death row. Often he is the last person the condemned talk to before being led out of the unit to the death chamber. KB will tell you the hardest thing he does is speak to guys before they leave to be executed, and then leading the unit in memorial services after each person is killed.

KB believes he is called to be an instrument of peace and encouragement. He tries hard to always be upbeat and to not let others see his own discouragement. But often, he told me, at night alone in his cell, with just himself and God, he cries. At one time, he thought this was a sign of weak faith. But now he finds strength in his tears. On one occasion, as he cried in the darkness, he started feeling sorry for himself and prayed, "God, I am so sorry. I know my faith needs to be stronger." He heard God say back to him, "Don't ever apologize for crying. None of your tears are in vain. They will be stored in a bottle of remembrance. Every tear you cry and every pain and hurt you experience, you will be rewarded for them."

KB then looked me straight in the eye and said, "You know, I often ask God why I am here, and why doesn't He deliver me. In the middle of this new round of executions, I now know why I am here. I am here to bring hope and comfort to all of us who have been condemned to die. I am God's missionary in this place. I feel like Esther. I am here for such a time as this."

On my way home after this conversation, in the quietness of my vehicle, I cried and asked God to give me just a portion of KB's faith. That is still my prayer. Not long after this conversation, COVID hit, and all scheduled executions were stopped. Two years later, several more executions were scheduled. But the first one, scheduled the week after Easter, was stopped at the last minute because of a violation of execution protocol concerning the drug cocktail. The remaining scheduled executions were halted, so an independent investigation could be done. There has not been an execution in Tennessee since February of 2020. I pray Tennessee never executes another person.

ENCOURAGEMENT

KB likes to say, "Today is the best day of my life." He likes to quote 1 Samuel 30:6, "but David encouraged himself in the LORD his God." Surrounded by death, he pushes against the darkness with hope. On more than one occasion, I have asked KB what he does to encourage himself. He always replies, "I do exactly what David did."

He then recites how many of the psalms David wrote that go over the history of God delivering the Israelites from bondage and caring for them in the wilderness. He will quote other psalms where David talks about God being his stronghold and giving him the victory over his enemies. KB then testifies, "I think about all the past victories God has won on my behalf. How He has healed my heartbreak and turned around my disappointments. God has brought good out of my horrible circumstance, and He has forgiven my sins, shortcomings, and failures. I remember how God has brought me through time after time after time. When I realize all God has brought me through, I am confident He will do it again. I am reminded of the apostle Paul's admonition, 'If God be for us, who can be against us?' (Romans 8:31). I am reminded of the promise of Jesus, '[A]nd, lo, I am with you always, even unto the end of the world" (Matthew 28:20. I encourage myself by reminding myself of God's goodness to me and by immersing myself in Scripture."

As KB and I were talking about all this, Pervis Payne sat down and joined us. Pervis is KB's best friend and a deacon in the Church of Life. Pervis has been on death row since July of 1987. Recently his death sentence was commuted to two life sentences, running concurrently, with the possibility of parole. Through the work of the Innocence Project, his case received national attention. The prosecutors have appealed commutation. Pervis waits on death row until the appeal is over. Then he will be moved to general population. If all goes well, he will be out on parole shortly. If all goes extremely well, he will be exonerated. I asked Pervis how he keeps himself encouraged while he waits for a new beginning. Here is what he said.

"I begin every day with the following prayer: 'Father God, I thank You for another day of life. I ask You to forgive me of my sins. I struggle with the lust of the flesh, lust of the eyes, and the pride of life. Help me overcome the many temptations I encounter every day. I confess with my mind, heart, and body that Jesus died for my sins and rose from dead. I am Yours. You are my Lord and Savior.'"

Pervis then continued, "In prison your identity is taken away. So every day I have to remind myself who I am. Who am I? I am the breath of God, through faith in Jesus Christ. I am the resurrection of God, through faith in Jesus Christ. I am for God and by God, through faith in Jesus Christ. I am more than a conqueror, through faith in Jesus Christ. I am who God says I am, not who others say I am, through faith in Jesus Christ."

He then concluded, "During the day, when I get down, I channel myself into my mind and spirit. I know I have to die to self. Sometimes it hurts to give things to God because it causes me to relive my situation. That is why I am thankful for God's grace and mercy. Then I remind myself that my flood will not rise above my standing in Christ Jesus."

(KR) That last phrase, "my flood will not rise above my standing in Christ Jesus," got to me. I desire that kind of faith for myself. Once again, I was reminded that I did not take Jesus with me to death row. I met Jesus on death row. He was there waiting for me, and people like KB and Pervis introduced me to Him.

I have been involved in ministry for more than forty years, over thirty of those years as a pastor. During the past four decades, I have been visited by a dark spirit on at least three occasions. This spirit hovers over me like a dark cloud and breathes on me with the smell of hot burning sulfur. A few nights before I started visiting death row, this dark spirit came to me while I was sleeping and pushed me down into my mattress. I was paralyzed. The spirit hovered above me, breathing heavily, and said, "If you go to death row, I will cause you great harm." I prayed like I had never prayed before. While I was praying, the spirit released me and vanished, leaving me in a cold sweat.

The next day was a Sunday. I told one of my elders and his wife about my experience and had them pray over me. In my mind, I took this encounter as a warning because death row was a dark and dangerous place. I now know this was meant to discourage me because the place I was about to go to was not dark and dangerous. Rather, it was, and is, a place of light and love. It was going to be a place where I met Jesus like never before. It was going to be a place that would have a profound influence on me for the rest of my life.

CHAPTER 24
DREAMS AND VISIONS

*"God spoke to me thirty years ago and told me
He needed me on death row, and when I finished
what He had for me to do, I would be released."*

◼ ◼ ◼

(KR) Mother Teresa once said, "You will never know Jesus is all you need until Jesus is all you've got."[18] I love that quote. It's one thing to live out your faith when things are going splendidly. It's another thing to keep your faith, and even grow your faith, when life is bleak and when life seems hopeless. This is what makes KB's faith astounding! In the darkest of times and in the most dire circumstance imaginable, he is a bright light and a beacon of inspiration. KB has experienced what a legendary Spanish priest, John of the Cross (d. 1591), described as the "dark night of the soul" and has come out stronger on the other end. He is the epitome of these words: "Consider it pure joy, my brothers and sisters, whenever you face trials of many kinds, because you know that the testing of your faith produces perseverance. Let perseverance finish its work so that you may be mature and complete, not lacking anything" (James 1:2–3).

In prison, especially on death row, KB lacks access to the internet and even the simplest of Bible commentaries and other biblical tools that overflow my personal library. I am amazed at the depth of his biblical knowledge. He has much of the Bible memorized and can tie passages from both the Old and New Testaments together in ways that continually astonish me. He will tell you he relies completely on Jesus's promise that the Holy Spirit "will teach you all things and will remind you of everything I have said to you" (John 14:26).

One way the Holy Spirit teaches KB is through dreams and visions. He lives out the prophet Joel's words, "I will pour out my Spirit on all people. Your sons and daughters will prophesy, your old men will dream dreams, your young men will see visions" (Joel 2:28). The dreams and visions KB has are real, and they are beautiful. In writing this book, KB was insistent that some of his visions be included. Often, after having a dream or receiving a vision, KB writes them down in the old King James fashion. So here are three of those visions, as written by KB himself. KB doesn't give his visions a title. I have taken the liberty to title them. This first one I call "A Declaration of War."

> In the nineteenth hundred and ninety ninth year of the reign of JESUS as SAVIOR of all mankind is the LORD highly exalted above all. In the seventh month, on the sixth day of the month, even the selfsame day, came a vision from the LORD; THE MOST HIGH GOD unto the prophet.
>
> I saw in a vision Satan galloping upon a horse over the whole world. And as I beheld, he came to the end of his gallop and circled, like a warrior, and thrust his spear into the ground; to proclaim his territory and declare war on his enemies, even so did Satan thrust in his rod into the

earth declaring war on the Sons of GOD, the Saints...And his rod was his flag in the earth.

As I beheld, lo, there went forth a spirit from before Satan, even the spirit of pride. And as I looked, the spirit of pride from Satan spoke, saying, "the whole earth is mine! I have conquered, and who can undo what I have done?"

I continued to look, and Satan withdrew himself and stood as a dark cloud over the top of the whole earth. Then there went forth from Satan all manner of evil spirits like lightnings into the earth: Demons of all manner of lies, hatreds, anger, violence, murders, envies, jealousies, wrath, clamor, lusts, fornications, evil concupiscence, all manner of uncleanness, effemination, unnatural affections, disobedience to parents, the spirit of despite, pride, all manner of boastings and blasphemies, the spirit of hatred for GOD, covetousness (which is idolatry and idol worship). All these filthy spirits, and more, went forth into all the cities of the earth, and they went to deceive and to seduce whosoever they can, even the elect of God...And after I saw all this, then THE LORD GOD kindled a fire in my belly, and a righteous indignation was inflamed in me. And I thought in my mind; I thought to take a sword and begin to slay, because Satan had mocked all the Sons of GOD.

As I meditated upon this vision (I slew for about forty-five minutes). And it came to pass that THE SPIRIT of THE LORD spoke: "FOR WHATEVER IS BORN OF GOD OVERCOMETH THE WORLD AND THIS IS THE VICTORY THAT OVERCOMETH THE WORLD, EVEN OUR FAITH. WHO IS HE THAT OVERCOMETH THE WORLD, BUT HE THAT BELIEVETH THAT JESUS IS THE SON OF GOD" This is the end of the vision.

But it came to pass, as I meditated from day to day upon this vision, that the understanding of it was imparted unto me in full.

Now, in this thirteenth day of the seventh month of the nineteenth hundred and ninety ninth year of the reign of CHRIST JESUS, THE LORD, THE SAVIOR; in this selfsame day was my hand directed again of THE SPIRIT OF THE LORD to write:

This is that which was spoken of by our LORD, saying, "TAKE HEED THAT NO MAN DECEIVE YOU. FOR MANY SHALL COME IN MY NAME, SAYING, 'I AM CHRIST;' AND SHALL DECEIVE MANY." And again, "WHEN YE, THEREFORE, SHALL SEE THE ABOMINATION OF DESOLATION, SPOKEN OF BY DANIEL THE PROPHET, STAND IN THE HOLY PLACE AND WEAR IT OUT NOT (WHOSOEVER READETH LET HIM UNDERSTAND)."

This is that son of perdition: that man of sin spoken of, that shall be revealed in the last days, who opposeth and exalteth himself above all that is called GOD, or that is worshipped, so that he, as GOD, sitteth in the temple of GOD, showing himself that he is GOD.

This is the mystery of iniquity at work; only he who now letteth will let, until HE be taken out of the way. And then shall that wicked be revealed, whom THE LORD shall consume with THE SPIRIT OF HIS MOUTH, and shall destroy with the brightness of HIS coming: Even him, whose coming is after the working of Satan with all power and signs and lying wonders, and with all deceivableness of unrighteousness in them that perish; because they receive not the love of the truth, that they might be saved. And for this cause GOD shall send them strong delusion, that they should believe a lie: That they all might be damned who believed not the truth, but had pleasure in unrighteousness.

Now Satan by pride has set his claim on this earth saying that the whole earth is his. And has mocked all the Sons of GOD saying, "Who can undo what I've done?" But Satan is a liar, he is the father of lies. For the earth is THE LORD'S, and the fullness thereof; the world, and they who dwell therein. For THE LORD GOD has founded the earth and all things by the power of HIS MIGHTY WORD.

This is THE WORD that THE LORD began to speak unto me, and caused me to understand the revelation thereof: Thus saith THE LORD GOD unto me; even JESUS OUR KING said unto me, "MY SON, IT IS NOT SO MUCH AS IN YOUR ABILITY IN THE SLAYING OF DEMONS…YES, I HAVE GIVEN YOU POWER TO TREAD UPON SERPENTS, REJOICE NOT IN THIS. FOR LOOK YE HOW SATAN YET PREVAILETH: BUT RATHER, PLANT MY WORD IN THE HEARTS OF MY PEOPLE AND TEACH THEM THAT JESUS IS THE CHRIST: THE SON OF GOD; EVEN GOD HIMSELF, AND TO BELIEVE ON HIM, AND THAT THEY MUST BE BORN AGAIN. BORN OF WATER, AND OF THE SPIRIT. THEN SHALT THOU PROSPER THE MORE, AND PREVAIL ALSO."

This second vision I call, "The Storm and the Call."

The vision which the LORD GOD gave unto His servant, Kevin: And the vision is certain, and must be so!

For by HIS SPIRIT has the LORD spoken it. Who can but prophesy?

Unto the SAINTS; my brethren in the faith and fellow believers in Christ Jesus: I bring thee greetings in HIS HOLY NAME.

I was in the SPIRIT on the LORD'S Day, and listened as the prophet of the LORD prophesied, and when he was come to the end of the prophecy, I heard him say, "I can hear the sound of an abundance of rain…" And immediately I was caught away in the SPIRIT and heard the sound of an abundance of rain. A storm is brewing, Yea, and the thunder roared. And when I looked, I saw from afar all the blackness of the thick clouds and the lightning flashing. As I beheld, the storm grew violently. And as I wondered, the thick black clouds funneled and became a whirlwind. Then it began to move directly towards me, and as it approached, it moved with great speed and destruction: And in destroying, behold, it destroyed everything in its path and left nothing standing. I could see nothing above it nor anything beneath it. I looked to the left and the right, and behold, nothing but destruction. Then was I caught away in the SPIRIT afar off to the side, and I could see before the Vision and behind the Vision. I looked before the Vision; And the violence of the whirlwind raged with destruction. I looked behind the Vision and there was great calm, and peace, and the sun shined; and when I looked, there appeared houses as if they were mansions, and they were all alike, they only differed in sizes, and they were all on one straight street.

And again, I looked before: And behold, the thick blackness and the lightning and the thundering and the violence of the whirlwind, destroyed. And when I looked behind; again, there was great calm and peace and the sun shined and houses that were all alike, that differed only in sizes.

Again, I looked, for the third time, before the Vision and behind the Vision: And behold, I saw the same things as before.

Then I set my heart to know the meaning of the matter: So I questioned the LORD, and said, "LORD, what means this?" And the LORD said unto me, "THIS IS THE MINISTRY OF THE SPIRIT THAT I HAVE PLACED WITHIN YOU: YEA, AND I HAVE SET YOU TO PLUCK UP AND TO PULL DOWN, TO DEVOUR AND TO BREAK IN PIECES: TO TOTALLY DESTROY AND TO STOMP THE RESIDUE WITH THE FEET."

Then I considered, in my heart, behind the storm and said unto the LORD, "LORD, what means this?" And the LORD said unto me, "AFTER YOU WILL HAVE MINISTERED, THIS SHALL BE THE RESULTS: YOU SHALL PLANT AND LAY AND BUILD UPON." (And all shall believe alike, according to the truth, as it is in CHRIST JESUS.)

And the LORD said unto me, "THE DIFFERENCES IN THE SIZES OF THE HOUSES IS ACCORDING TO THE MEASURE OF THEIR OWN FAITH." (As they believe, so shall it be LORD!)

Then was scripture revealed unto me that saith, "And from the days of JOHN the BAPTIST until now the Kingdom of heaven suffereth violence, and the violent take it by force."

Then I began to weep sore, but joyously, because the word of the LORD. Yet I doubted within myself as I stood in amazement meditating on the Vision and the Words of the LORD, saying within myself, "has the LORD of a surety called me unto such a calling as this? And what am I that the LORD has looked on me so?"

Nevertheless, I know that the gifts and calling of the LORD GOD are without repentance, and sure! Amen.

The final vision I call, "The Man in the Brim Hat."

Kevin, a servant of the MOST HIGH: Called by GOD and chosen before the foundation of the world. Sanctified, and ordained a prophet unto the nations, according to the grace of GOD which HE bestowed upon me through CHRIST JESUS, our LORD:

Unto the Saints of GOD that are scattered abroad; elect according unto the same grace of GOD which is in CHRIST JESUS, our LORD and SAVIOR.

My brethren, I bring you greetings in the name of JESUS, the CHRIST of GOD.

I have dreamed a dream, and in the night has the ALMIGHTY given me a vision. I will speak the dream and the interpretation of it. For the LORD, the Great and Faithful GOD, has provided me a way to know the dream and the understanding thereof.

This is the dream: I met a man, a strange man, and different from all other men of this particular time. The man wore a brim hat, like a hat that a preacher would wear, only bigger. And with the brim was his face covered that I could not see him. For I desired to see him and could not, and wanted to reach out and lift up the brim, but was hindered. And he wore a trench coat that came down to the feet.

Such a one spoke with me, and I received him even as CHRIST; whom I thought him to be. And I bowed myself down before him, as if to worship him, but he removed himself from before me. Then I looked up for him, and as I beheld, there appeared as it were a right arm out of the atmosphere, that went forth, and with the fist clinched, hit the man in the stomach. And behold, the whole arm went into the man's stomach. Then after being hit, the strange man folded his arms across his body to hold his trench coat closed, and he began to walk. Then, was I caught away in the SPIRIT afar off to the side, and I watched the man as he walked. And as he walked, many followed after him; he did not run, but he walked with speed, as in a hurry.

Finally, he eluded the people and came and stood beside me. Then came the people, and began to question me, saying, "Where is he? Where is the man?" And I turned to see, but he was not there. So I said to the people, "I don't know where he is." But the people were persistent, so I turned the second time, and behold, the man reappeared. Then he came forth and opened his trench coat and showed his stomach, and to my surprise, there was no bruise there (for I thought there should be a bruise left after he received the punch, but there was none). Then were the people caught away, and I was left with the man. And he turned from me and entered into a door and closed the door behind him. So I followed him, and when I had entered and closed the door, I fell down behind him to worship (because he stood with his back to me and the door). And I desired to speak with him, but when I looked up for him, he was gone, and when I looked around for him, he was not there. So I got up and into my bed (for the room we entered was my room), and the head of my bed was closest to the door. And I waited for his return and did not leave the room until he returned. Finally, the time came that he did return, and as the light of his presence approached, I was awakening simultaneously out of my sleep. Then he entered the room, the door being shut (for he walked through the door), and immediately, when he entered the room, my eyes were opened. And he came and stood half-ways to the bed, with his back towards the door and the head of my bed.

Then was my heart glad, and my spirit rejoiced within me. I cried after him, for I longed to see him, and to speak with him. I cried after him and he answered not, but spoke with one that stood at the foot of my bed, whom I did not know was there. So, after I cried the second time, he turned unto me having some papers in his hand rolled together, like a scroll, which I knew was the WORD of GOD; and he put them in the back of my head (in my mind). Then he turned back to the fellow with whom he spoke and gave him some papers as well, which also was the WORD of GOD. But the papers that he gave him was straight, not rolled, and they were brand new papers, white and clean, not having a blemish nor wrinkle.

After he had given us the WORD, the strange man stepped across the bed to the other side of the room. Then I got out of the bed, and the fellow and I stood and watched. And as we beheld, the man ascended up out of the room, through the ceiling. Then was I awakened out from the dream, and knew that it was a dream from GOD, but I wondered greatly at it and did not understand the dream.

But the GREAT and MIGHTY GOD, the Faithful, the LORD my GOD provided me a way to know the dream, yea and the interpretation thereof. For I called my brother, Calvin Mason, and told him the dream. But neither could he understand or interpret the dream. But he said unto me, "I go to church with a woman who is an interpreter of dreams. She can interpret it! Do you want me to call her?" I said, "Yes. Call her." So we called the woman of God, who after she heard, did give me the interpretation of the dream.

Now will I communicate unto you the understanding thereof. And she said unto me, "Yes, my brother, the LORD has shown me the vision, and I will tell it to you." . . .

"Now, the man is you! For the LORD has allowed you to see yourself as HE does, in holiness and righteousness; and I want to say, it's you that is to come, but it's you right now. That's why you couldn't worship him like you wanted to, or were trying to, because you can't worship yourself. No, the punch that you received in the stomach, it was the impartation of the HOLY SPIRIT (for out of your belly shall flow rivers of living waters). And the people that followed, they followed not to do harm, but they wanted what you had, which was the WORD of GOD. For the LORD is going to cause you to minister unto many. And what the LORD is doing with you is a swift work: That's why, when you walked, you walked with speed."

Then she said unto me, "Get all the WORD in you that you can right now; that's what it was when 'He' put the Word/Scroll in the back of your head. (For the WORD must be in your mind and in your heart.) And when you preach, you are not going to preach any junk (that is, of my own understanding, or of man's understanding); but when you preach, you are going to preach the pure WORD of GOD. That's why you gave the fellow brand-new papers, straight and clean and without blemish. For the WORD of GOD is pure, not having a spot or wrinkle (Psalm 12:6)."

And with other words also did my sister, the Prophetess, speak unto me; edifying and exhorting me, saying, "Fear not, my brother, but be of good courage, for the LORD is going to do all that HE has shown you."

And she said unto me, "Write the dream down my brother" (the same thing the HOLY SPIRIT said unto me before she began speaking), "For I can see you in the spirit, after all has come to pass; I can see you reading over the dream. Then shall you know that the LORD has done it. And it shall be a testimony unto you."

The GREAT GOD has made known unto me, HIS servant, what shall come to pass hereafter; and the dream is certain, and the interpretation of it sure.

And blessed is he that believed; for there shall be a performance of those things which were told him from the Lord. And it is so!

My soul doth magnify the LORD, and my spirit hath rejoiced in GOD my SAVIOR. For HE has regarded the low estate of his servant; for, behold, from henceforth all generations shall call me blessed.

For He that is mighty has done to me great things; and holy is his name.

And his mercy is on them that fear him from generation to generation.

He has shown strength with His arm; He has scattered the proud in the imagination of their hearts.

He has put down the mighty from their seats, and exalted them of low degree.

He has filled the hungry with good things; and the rich he has sent away.

He has helped His servant, Kevin, in remembrance of His mercy; as he spoke to our fathers, to Abraham, and to His seed forever. Hallelujah: Thank You, Lord Jesus! Amen.

(KR) After copying down these visions, I asked KB, "What would you say to those who read these visions but doubt the authenticity of them? What would you say to the skeptics who will read this? I know not everyone understands, or believes, in dreams and visions."

KB replied, "I would tell them like God told Moses, 'If I call a Prophet, and they prophesy anything concerning God, notice if it happens or not. Wait and see the outcome. Don't judge it as real or not real, right or wrong, or good or bad. Wait to see what happens. That's the test.'"

He then added, "God spoke to me thirty years ago and told me He needed me on death row, and when I finished what He had for me to do, I would be released. I am still waiting for that fulfillment, but I know that is what God said to me. When God speaks, He also affirms His Word, and often He affirms it through the words of others.

"Another example," he continued, "is God gave me a vision, years ago, of a church on death row. In that vision I saw birds being released from a cage. I did not tell you about that vision. Then one day you told me of your idea to start a church on death row, and you showed me a picture of two birds flying out of a bird cage. You said you thought that picture captured the idea of what the church should be. The moment I saw that picture, I remembered the vision God had given me. God's Word was confirmed by your idea."

A third example comes from KB's sister, Robin. KB has said for decades that God told him, "I need you on death row. I have a work for you to do there, and when you have completed that work, I will get you out." A few years ago, Robin was at her home church in West Memphis, Arkansas, attending a special service. A lady minister was speaking. This lady did not know Robin or the story about KB. At the end of the service, the lady called Robin up front and said to her, "You have a loved one who is in prison for a crime he did not do." Robin replied, "Yes, my brother." Then the lady said to her, "You need to know your brother is not there to serve time; he is there because God wants him there, and when he has finished the task God has for him, God will release him."

I then asked KB why he thought God spoke to him through dreams and visions. He replied, "God called me to be a prophet and that is how He speaks. Everything He says to me, I check it with what He has already revealed in the Bible. I believe God speaks to me in my spirit, so I can translate it so people will understand. He gives me insights into the spirit realm, where He resides, and His Word plays out in the physical world through other people. It's like the parables of Jesus. Jesus's parables were spiritual principles in the natural world. When I don't understand things, I pray, and through the Holy Spirit, God gives me understanding. Years ago from the Shelby County Jail, you know, 201 Poplar, Bishop Coppinger said to me, 'God is going to show you all the mysteries of the Kingdom.' And that is what happens through my dreams and visions."

KB concluded this conversation by saying, "I understand people's cynicism. Like Paul, I am the chief of sinners (see 1 Timothy 1:15). What can I do from the position I am in? I don't take their cynicism personally. I know when God marks you as a prophet, Satan will try to discourage you. But God's Word to me is so clear, and His calling on my life is so strong, all I can do is trust Him and keep moving forward. But I will repeat what I said earlier. Wait and see what happens. That is the test."

(KR) You can believe KB or not believe KB. But one thing you can't do is deny the genuineness of his faith. It is his deep faith in the Word of God that enables him to say, "Today is the best day of my life."

CHAPTER 25
WHAT NOW?

"There are lots of innocent people behind bars. And even if a person is guilty, that doesn't mean they are no longer human."

■ ■ ■

(KR) I know many people find it hard to believe that an innocent person could be executed. Unfortunately, it happens far too often. Since 1973, across the United States, more than 190 former death-row prisoners have been exonerated of all charges that placed them on death row.[19] There is no way of knowing how many innocent persons have been executed. Once a person is killed, it is impossible to go back. As late as January of 2019, the state of Florida granted posthumous pardons to four individuals who were arrested for a crime they did not commit in 1949! Two of the innocent men were executed for those crimes.[20] I believe, even if you think capital punishment is just, we cannot do it justly. Thus, we should not do it all.

So, what now? If you have made it to the end of this book, what can you do about KB and others like him on death rows across the United States?

The most important thing you can do is get involved and stay informed. Contact your governor and your state officials and ask them to repeal capital punishment in your state. If you live in Tennessee and are concerned about KB, contact the governor of Tennessee and ask him to grant KB clemency. The governor's address is State Capitol, First Floor, 600 Dr. Martin L. King Jr. Blvd., Nashville, TN 37243.

You can also send KB cards and letters of encouragement at Pastor Kevin Burns (#254315), RMSI, 7475 Cockrill Bend Blvd., Nashville, TN 37209. I know he will appreciate all the prayers, cards, and letters you send. We have also created a website for KB: savepastorkb.com. You can continue to follow his story there.

Another thing you can do is get involved in any anti-death penalty coalition in your community. Most states have them. A quick google search will help you out. In Tennessee I suggest Tennesseans for Alternatives to the Death Penalty (tennessee deathpenatly.org). Nationally I suggest Death Penalty Action (deathpenaltyaction.org).

(KB) Writing this book has been like going on a journey back in time. I have thought and talked about things I have not thought and talked about in decades. Some of the things I have written about, I have intentionally avoided thinking and talking about. At times, reflecting on my memories has been painful, but I have grown personally through the process of writing this book.

One of the things I pray happens through reading this book is that people learn not to make knee-jerk judgments about people who are in prison. When you see people, on the news, getting arrested, that doesn't mean they are guilty. Likewise, just because a person is convicted of a crime and sent to jail or prison doesn't mean they are guilty. There are lots of innocent people behind bars. And even if a person is guilty, that doesn't mean they are no longer human. Every incarcerated person—guilty or innocent—is still a child of God, created in the image of God. No one is beyond the reach of God's love and grace. Everyone can be redeemed. All of us, including the reader, deserve a second chance and a third chance and more.

Police, lawyers, judges, and everyone associated with the criminal legal system are human beings and make mistakes. Yes, there are some people who do lie and put charges on people, but those people are few and far between. I think most people want to do the right thing, but the system, at times, will not allow them. The problem is with our criminal legal system. I used to think the system was corrupt, but I no longer believe that. I used to think the system was broken, but I don't believe that either. After decades of interacting within the system, I believe our system is neither corrupt nor broken. Our system is doing exactly what it was designed to do. Our system of justice is designed to perpetuate injustices on some people. Then it's designed to protect itself against pushback and critique.

What now? I would like to see more people visit jails and prisons after reading this book. Proximity changes things. I challenge everyone who has read this book to contact the chaplain at your local jail or prison and see how you can get involved. Come and talk to us and listen to our stories. We will gladly share with you and listen to your stories. Through building relationships with each other, we will both be changed for the better.

Several years ago, we had a chaplain who loved to bring people into Unit 2. One time during a three-month period, she brought in more than two hundred people. Most of the time, the people came in groups and met with a group of us. These group meetings usually had lots of tears and lots of hugs. Everyone left different than when they came. Meeting with people like this is our way of giving back and contributing something positive to society.

Of all the people I met during that three-month period, one lady stands out. This lady was in her mid-fifties and had recently moved to Tennessee from Texas. She was in a large group of twenty-five people. Twenty of us on death row met with them. After a brief introduction from the chaplain, we separated into four groups. In each group were five of us from death row, and anywhere from five to seven from the group. We talked to a group for fifteen minutes, and then another group came. We continued this until we had talked with everyone, and everyone in the group had a chance to talk to all of us.

The lady from Texas was in our last group and sat down beside me. As she began to talk, she shared with us about her life in Texas. She lived there during the time George Bush was governor. She talked about how much she loved and admired Governor Bush. My thought immediately went to the more than 150 executions that took place during his governorship. More than any governor in modern history!

As she continued her story, she began to cry. She said she was a proponent of the death penalty and had only come to visit us to see "what all the fuss was about" and because a friend from church invited her. She confessed she came with a certain attitude and perception about us. Then through her tears, she said, "I want to apologize and tell you how sorry I am. I want you to know I have changed. You guys have changed me. You guys have won me over. From this moment forward, I can no longer support the death penalty." Everyone clapped. She and I stood and gave each other a big hug.

She then asked, "What can I do to help you guys?" We said to her, "Get involved. Tell other people to come visit us. Tell others about your own experience. Tell other people what you thought coming in and what you now think. Ask them to come and experience it for themselves."

WHAT NOW?

After that group left, I went to the chaplain and said, "Chaplain Jeannie, we only want to talk to people who are for the death penalty. Bring us more people like that, so we can change their minds."

A FINAL THOUGHT

(KR) I want to leave you with one final thought to be considered. Often I am asked to speak to groups about prison ministry. I have also had opportunities to speak to men and women incarcerated here and throughout Honduras. In fact KB has a relationship with a pastor serving time in a Honduran prison. Like KB this pastor has started a church inside his prison. When I go to Honduras, I usually take a letter written by KB to him and then return with a letter written by him to KB. People in prison and outside of prison all across Honduras pray for KB on a regular basis. When I speak about prison ministry, I look to Scripture to show there is a special place in God's heart for those who are incarcerated.

I think most people would be surprised how often the Bible talks about prisoners. It's as if those who are incarcerated are in a privileged position. The psalmist wrote, "The LORD hears the needy and does not despise his captive people" (Psalm 69:33). Again, "May the groans of the prisoners come before you; with your strong arm preserve those condemned to die" (Psalm 79:11). And once more, "The LORD sets prisoners free" (Psalm 146:7). No one wants to serve time, but there is comfort in knowing that God has not forgotten those behind bars. Even if society has forgotten them, God has not.

Consider the life of Jesus. Not long after He was born, Caesar put Him on Rome's "Most Wanted" list. From the beginning of His life, the authorities wanted to execute Him! (See Matthew 2:16.) Early in His ministry and not long after He was baptized, His cousin, John the Baptist, was arrested and executed by beheading (see Mark 1:9–14 and 6:27–29). In His very first sermon, Jesus had the incarcerated on His mind, quoting from the prophet Isaiah: "'The Spirit of the Lord is on me, because he has anointed me to proclaim good news to the poor. He has sent me to proclaim freedom for the prisoners" (Luke 4:18). Are you getting this? Jesus specifically said He came for prisoners! We understand Jesus came for everyone, but nowhere does He specifically say He came for the rich and powerful, but He does say He came for the poor and for the prisoners. Don't you think Jesus's target audience should be our target audience?

Then in Jesus's parable, of the sheep and the goats (see Matthew 25:31–46), He identified Himself with prisoners by stating His followers (the "sheep") visited Him in prison (v. 36). He then concluded, "Truly I tell you, whatever you did for one of the least of these brothers and sisters of mine, you did for me" (v. 40).

By the end of His life, Jesus became a prisoner Himself. He was arrested and beaten by the authorities (Matthew 26:47–68; Mark 15:1–20; Luke 22:47–53; John 18:1–14). Jesus had a criminal record. Jesus was a convicted felon. Jesus was sentenced to death by the state! Then right before He died by crucifixion, the very last person He talked to was a fellow death-row inmate. In love and compassion, He said to this condemned man, "Truly I tell you, today you will be with me in paradise" (Luke 23:43).

Maybe one reason God loves prisoners so much is because His Son was a prisoner Himself. From the beginning, in the middle, and at the end of His life, Jesus held the incarcerated close to His heart. But it doesn't end there. I don't understand it all, but the apostle Peter said, "After being made alive, he went and made proclamation to the imprisoned spirits" (1 Peter 3:19).

So what now? Now is the time for you to get involved and stay informed. The writer of Hebrews said, "Continue to remember those in prison as if you were together with them in prison, and those who are mistreated [like those who are condemned to die] as if you yourselves were suffering" (Hebrews 13:3). I added the brackets for emphasis.

May God richly bless you for taking the time to read this book. And remember, "Today is the best day of my life."

AFTERWORD

(KB) Writing this book and working with KR have been some of the greatest joys of my life. For so long, I have felt like no one had heard my voice or listened to my story. Now I feel like I have been heard. I want to personally thank KR for his dedication and research. This book was his idea, and he pushed me through to see it complete.

I told KR writing this book was like going fishing. KR threw something out there, like casting bait, and I took the hook. KR pulled things out of me I had long forgotten. One thing I have been reminded of again and again is how God has brought me through all things. Watching this book unfold has been like watching the story of my life on the big screen. It has been an incredible journey and a great joy.

My life has not been easy, but I have learned like King David, "It is good for me that I have been afflicted; that I might learn thy statutes" (Psalm 119:71). And the apostle Paul: "we glory in tribulations also: knowing that tribulation worketh patience" (Romans 5:3). And the words of Jesus's brother, James: "My brethren, count it all joy when ye fall into divers temptations; Knowing this, that the trying of your faith worketh patience" (James 1:2–3). The Bible even tells us that Jesus learned obedience through the things He suffered (Hebrews 5:8).

That is the prayer for my life. I have learned obedience through suffering. All my afflictions have worked out for the good. Through it all, my relationship with God has grown stronger and stronger. I am not being arrogant. Trust me, God has humbled me, and He has a way of keeping me humble. I simply believe God's Word. His Word is the foundation of my life. I am not saying I am glad what happened to me happened. I wish things had been different. But I am happy with where I am in Christ Jesus. He has taught me to make the best out of a bad situation, and He has allowed me to participate in His work far beyond my wildest imagination.

The key to walking with God is your ability to wait on God and to trust Him to bring His Word to pass. God has never forgotten a word He has spoken. In fact the Bible tells us He is the Word (John 1:1). My prayer is that you will learn to be patient and wait on God.

Finally, always remember that no matter what happens, "Today is the best day of my life," and it can be the best day of your life as well. May God richly bless you.

— *Rev. Kevin Burns*

ACKNOWLEDGMENTS

■ ■ ■

(KR) This book has been a work of love. The day I first walked into Unit 2 changed my life forever. KB is part of my family and one of my closest friends. Thank you for opening your life to me and thank you for being my pastor. A huge thanks to my wife, Misty. I am who I am because of you.

(KB) Words cannot express what writing this book has meant for me. For the first time in a long time, I feel like my story will now be heard. To God be all the glory. God told me he had a job for me to do on death row and when I complete that task He will deliver me from this place. Thank you, KR, for believing in me and for being my friend and pastor. I especially want to thank Franklin Community Church and Brad and Jessica Davis. I love you all. Today truly is the best day of my life. I also want to thank my mom, dad, daughter, and all my brothers and sisters for standing with me and praying for me. I love you all.

Both KB and KR would like to thank the following people who helped make this book possible:
- Wes Yoder. Your commitment and encouragement throughout this process has been invaluable.

- Lisa Parnell. You are the best. Thank you for your professionalism in the final edit and interior design.
- Tim Gilman. Thank you for believing in this project and guiding us through the final steps to publication. Who knew a trip to England would bring us together in this way.
- Mike Duncan. We don't know what we would have done without you and your attention to details.
- To all the men in Unit 2 at Riverbend Maximum Security Institution. Thank you for your friendships and for sharing your stories with us.
- To all the volunteers who visit Unit 2. You are invaluable.
- To Eric Boucher and Tim Webb for being a big part of the Church of Life.

We are sure we have missed some people. Please accept our apologies. We are thankful for you all.

Most importantly, we thank our Lord and Savior Jesus Christ. Thank You for Your love, grace, and mercy.

ENDNOTES

■ ■ ■

1. Kirk Franklin, "He's Able," track 2, *Kirk Franklin & the Family*, producers Arthur Dyer and Rodney Frazier (1993).
2. https://www.statista.com/statistics/199026/average-time-between-sentencing-and-execution-of-inmates-on-death-row-in-the-us/
3. Supreme Court of the United States: *Kevin B. Burns v. Tony Mays, Warden*; No. 22-5891.
4. Supreme Court of the United States: *Kevin B. Burns v. Tony Mays, Warden*; No. 22-5891.
5. Tupac Shakur, "Dear Mama," *Me Against the World* (1995), producer Tony Pizarro.
6. Junno Arocho Esteves, "Death penalty a 'grave' violation of human right to life, pope says," National Catholic Reporter, February 27, 2019, https://www.ncronline.org/news/francis-comic-strip/francis-chronicles/death-penalty-grave-violation-human-right-life-pope.
7. World Population Review, https://worldpopulationreview.com/state-rankings/death-penalty-states; Death Penalty Information Center, https://deathpenaltyinfo.org/news/samoa-to-abandon-death-penalty.
8. https://worldpopulationreview.com/state-rankings/death-penalty-states. The three states with governor-imposed moratoriums are California, Oregon, and Pennsylvania.
9. https://worldpopulationreview.com/state-rankings/death-penalty-states
10. Joseph B. Ingle, *The Inferno: A Southern Morality Tale* (Westview, Inc., 2012).

11. https://www.biggestuscities.com/ar/1990#:~:text=West,Memphis%2028%2C463
12. From author's notes.
13. https://www.multpl.com/us-median-income/table/by-year
14. https://www.census.gov/quickfacts/fact/table/westmemphiscityarkansas/PST045222
15. https://datausa.io/profile/geo/west-memphis-ar?redirect=true
16. https://www.multpl.com/us-median-income/table/by-year
17. Author's notes.
18. Author's notes.
19. https://deathpenaltyinfo.org/policy-issues/innocence/innocence-by-the-numbers
20. https://deathpenaltyinfo.org/policy-issues/innocence/posthumous-declarations-of-innocence

ABOUT THE AUTHORS

KEVIN BURNS

Rev. Kevin Burns was born on April 20, 1969, at the John Gaston Hospital (now Regional One Health) in Memphis, Tennessee. At the age of six, KB's family moved to West Memphis, Arkansas, where KB grew up.

KB graduated from Memphis Senior High School, home of the Blue Devils, in 1987. Not long after high school, KB started working at Shoney's Restaurant. He was on track to be a manager at Shoney's before his arrest. While incarcerated, KB has been a model inmate and has gained the respect of fellow inmates, guards, and prison administrators. Since 2015, KB has served on Tennessee's death row as the "chaplain's assistant." On January 29, 2018, inside Riverbend Maximum Security Institution's death row, KB was ordained into the gospel ministry by Rev. Dr. Kevin Riggs and Franklin Community Church.

KB has one adult daughter, Brianna, and two grandsons, Demere and Makhi. KB is an outstanding athlete and especially excels at basketball and handball. He claims to be the best handball player in Unit 2.

KEVIN RIGGS

Rev. Dr. Kevin Riggs (Pastor Kevin) has been the senior pastor of Franklin Community Church for more than thirty years (www.franklincommunitychurch.org). He is also the founder and executive director of Franklin Community Development (www.franklincommunitydevelopment.com) and Williamson County Homeless Alliance (www.wilcohomeless.com). All three organizations are located in Franklin, Tennessee.

Pastor Kevin believes one of the primary tasks of a pastor is to be the "conscience of the community." He is extremely active in the community and is respected as an advocate for the poor and marginalized. Pastor Kevin is also involved in prison ministry, especially Tennessee's death row, where his church has ordained one of the inmates and helped him start a church on death row called "The Church of Life." In addition to pastoring, Rev. Dr. Riggs taught sociology for fourteen years at Nashville State Community College. He has written three books: *Failing Like Jesus, Evangelism for the 21st Century,* and *Church Health.* Furthermore, Pastor Kevin has an active ministry in Honduras where he trains pastors and visits prisons. He is married to his high school sweetheart, Misty. Pastor Kevin is also an avid scuba diver. He and Misty live in Franklin.

Black Tulip: Have No Mercy IV

To my friend, Lois ~ much love, Kam

Black Tulip: Have No Mercy IV © Kam Ruble

ALL RIGHTS RESERVED

All names, characters and incidents, depicted in this book are totally the products of the author's imagination. Any resemblance to actual events, locales, organizations, or persons, living or dead, is entirely coincidental.

No part of this book may be produced in any form, by photocopying or by any electronic or mechanical means, including information storage or retrieval systems, without permission in writing from both the copyright owner and the publisher of this book, except for the minimum words needed for review.

ISBN: 978-0-9798087-2-2
Library of Congress Control Number: 2007938362
Published by Global Authors Publications

Filling the GAP in publishing

Edited by Barbara Sachs Sloan
Interior Design by Kathleen Walls
Cover Design by Kathleen Walls
Front Cover by Christine Patrick Jenkins

Printed in USA for Global Authors Publications

Black Tulip:
Have No Mercy IV

Kam Ruble

DEDICATION:

To my loving sisters, Brenda, Barbie 'Doll' and Mary.

AKNOWLEDGEMENT:

Bobby Ruble – for his expert law advice and editorial comments.
Brenda Stange – for her excellent editorial advice.
Barbara Sachs Sloan – for her excellence in editing.
Kathleen Walls – for her patience, understanding, and creative formatting.
Christine Patrick Jenkins – for her graphic art in creating a fabulous cover.

PROLOGUE

Psychiatrists, Psychologists, numerous other types of experts, specialists, and scientists alike have researched for years attempting to discover what drives a person over the edge to become a serial killer. Are they born that way? Or was there something in their lives that drove them to the breaking point? After several infamous serial killers were interviewed, along with a fair amount of professionally conducted studies on human behavior, there doesn't seem to be one set pattern for such violence. The conclusions had to simply be based on each of the separate individuals doing the killing. Without giving more fame to such treacherous individuals who have maliciously taken others lives in cold blood, here are some chilling quotes from a few of the unnamed convicted murderers.

"The first time I took a life, it made me feel superior. I was a bit frightened at first, but after that, killing came as easy as having my first cigarette in the morning. Just like the cigarette, murder became addictive. I didn't need a reason; I just got my highs that way."

"Voices told me it was the right thing to do. The voices said that I was chosen to be a promised one in heaven if I did away with certain offenders here on earth. I still hear those voices. Can't you hear them? They're telling me that you need to get me out of here as I still have a job to do. I can't stay locked up in prison. Don't you understand? Those people I assassinated were sinful. There are more evil people out there, running free, that I need to take care of. The voices talk to me and tell me what to do. That's why I had to kill. In the name of all that's holy, I did what was right. And, if you let me out, I will continue to kill because no one can stop the voices until I have completed my mission."

"I only killed prostitutes. So what's the big deal? Those so-called females walk the streets, turning tricks, and passing deadly disease. I had a couple of friends who got rolled by these dames. One of those friends died after contacting AIDS from one of those no-good broads. Nine out of ten times when a prostitute gets arrested, her pimp will have her back out working the street within hours. I even saw cops telling some prostitutes to move on out of the area. Big deal! So they move from one area to another. They give decent women and neighborhoods a bad name. The ultimate turning point was when one of those prostitutes got ahold of my son. Someone had to take the law into his own hands. I decided that someone had to be me. Besides, who's going to miss them? Well, maybe their pimp. But he can always get his hands on more female trash like that, so he's not out anything of importance. Those disgusting females seem to be a dime a dozen. I didn't even scrape the bottom of the barrel with the few I got rid of. Do I feel remorse? Ha! That's a joke! I only wish I would have done away with more of them before I got caught."

"I didn't kill anyone, but Tom, Teddy, Tobias and I know the truth. Big T did it to save us. I keep telling everyone that I'm innocent, but they still keep me locked up. When all of us were young and being molested by our father, Big T is the one who finally stood up for us. He killed our father. We stood by in silence and watched him. After Big T got rid of my father, it was easy for him to kill again — anyone who tried to hurt any of us. Big T was stronger than the rest of us were. Even if we would have wanted to, we couldn't have stopped him. And why should we? Big T kept us from harm. Sure, we know Big T also killed others who were child molesters. How do we know? He took us along to watch when he annihilated them. Problem is, Big T is dead now. Buried in my subconscious. He won't come out and admit that he's the guilty one. I can't blame him. After all, he saved our lives many times. Now it's time for me … us … to protect him. I can bring out Tom, Teddy or Tobias if you want to talk to them. But they will only tell you the same thing that I've just told you. I am innocent. Tom, Teddy and Tobias are also innocent. Big T is the one you want. But like I said, it's our turn to protect him."

"I don't consider myself a serial killer, so don't call me one. All I was doing was helping to clean up this filthy world we live in. If I didn't like your skin color, your nationality, your sexual preference, or your religion — then you're a dead man. Whites rule the earth! There are more supremacists out there just like me. We have devoted our lives to rid the earth of this trash. You may have me behind lock and key, but someone will always be there to take my place. You will never catch all of us."

"Why did I kill all of those people? It was time to even the score. I got tired of seeing the little people get run over by the big bullies of the world. I got tired of being dumped on. Those clowns thought they could keep getting away with walking all over people like me. But I showed them. It was time to even the score."

"They laughed at me. When I was little, the kids made fun of me because I was different. I couldn't help it that I was born a freak. As I got older, no one would accept me for what I had to offer. I was smart and creative, but no one would give me a job or the chance to prove myself. I just didn't fit anywhere. Why couldn't people look beyond my face and into my soul? Everywhere I went, people pointed and made fun of me. I was called a stupid freak more times than I care to mention. Well, I showed them, didn't I? Those smart, beautiful people are no longer around to laugh and call me names. I outsmarted them, didn't I?"

"It wasn't so much about a sex urge as it was about control. I needed those women to obey my every command. Murder was never on my mind when I raped the first girl, but she saw my face, so I had to do away with her. After that, I enjoyed having my victims look me in the face as I ordered them about, but I couldn't leave any witnesses. Those women had to be killed. I'm just sorry the last one survived."

"Everyone says I'm guilty, but I didn't commit those crimes. I was a good, law-obeying citizen. I had to be. You see my parents, who were always under the influence of liquor, abused me daily. If they weren't hitting or beating me, they were degrading me with their words. I was too afraid to turn against them, so a stranger came into my life to help me out. Like a true friend, he seemed to always turn up to protect my beliefs. They were his hands that destroyed the offenders. That stranger, it seems, became a part of my very being. He defended me when I couldn't stand up for myself. He is the one who killed those people, but no one will believe me. You see, they think I made it all up. Everyone thinks I'm crazy."

* * *

There are, without a doubt, murderers we detest with our very being because they took it upon themselves to take other human lives. Yet, there are a few murderers some say they have empathy for because of the circumstances that led up to them, the convicted, turning into killers. It doesn't make what they did right. Never! The victims are the ones we should mourn. However, there are times when we hear the background of a murderer or serial killer, that we stop for one second and say, If only someone could have seen the warning signs and helped him or her before it got that far. Do you feel a little empathy for that victim of circumstance? Few do; many do not.

 **CHAPTER ONE**

In the quiet countryside of Colorado, outside the hub of city life, twins, Jamie and Jessie, Jr., were born to Jessie Dole, Sr., and his wife Betty. As soon as the twins arrived home, Betty tossed their hospital gowns and receiving blankets in the trash. She immediately dressed Jamie in a pink gown and Jessie, Jr., in blue pajamas.

The twins were mirror images of one another when it came to facial features. Their personalities, however, were as different as night and day. From birth Jamie showed signs of being stronger-willed and physically more powerful than Jessie.

Because of Jamie's domineering ways, it became easy to convince Jessie to take the blame for anything and everything the cunning three-year old Jamie cared to conjure up. These antics consistently caused Jessie to get in trouble with their parents. Spineless Jessie was like putty in Jamie's hands. As small as the twins were, they knew better than to aggravate their father. Jessie, Sr., had a bad temper when he got riled. Keeping little Jessie in the virtual doghouse was not any great chore for Jamie since it was very clear their father had no use for his namesake. Mr. Dole felt that Jessie was weak like his mother. Mrs. Dole was aware Jamie was the chief instigator in all the mischief the twins would get into. However, having no will of her own, she never defended little Jessie.

For the most part, the twins had a happy life until they reached the age of three and a half. That was the time when Jessie, Sr., was severely injured on his job. He was no longer capable of working. Caused by his being unemployed and disabled, depression drove him to the bottle. As his drinking got worse, his temper frequently reared its ugly head against Betty and the twins. Unable to cope with her husband's persistent drinking and temper flare-ups, Betty started drinking, too. It was at this time both parents became physically and mentally abusive toward the twins.

When most of Mr. Dole's disability checks went for alcohol, it did not take long for the unpaid bills to start piling up. The man, who just years earlier was ecstatic about becoming a father, was now filled with hatred. He also became intolerant of having two small children underfoot all day long. And he was beginning to detest having to share what little disability income he was receiving to purchase groceries and clothes for two growing children.

One day, in his drunken stupor, Jessie, Sr., made a decision that would provide him and his wife more money.

"I think we need to get rid of one of the twins. One less mouth to feed around here. That's what we need."

Betty emptied her glass and poured herself another drink. Even drunk she could not believe the words that came out of her husband's mouth.

"You're not serious, are you?"

"Dead serious."

"Do you mean …," she swallowed hard, "to kill one of them?"

Shaking his head in disgust, he answered, "Of course not, you stupid woman. There are plenty of people out in the world that don't have kids of their own. I'm sure there's lots of them willing to pay big bucks for a kid like Jamie."

"Jamie? You would get rid of Jamie?"

"I'd get rid of them both if I thought I could get away with it," he growled. "But selling two kids might cause suspicion. I don't know who would care. But in case anyone from our past would happen around and stick their nose in our business, we could always explain one of the twins died. We'd never be able to explain how both of them died."

Mrs. Dole sat in silence. She had to carefully think through what her husband was suggesting before she opened her mouth again. Coming from an abusive family, she had been married to Mr. Dole since she quit school and ran away from home at age fifteen. She never saw or contacted her family again. If she were to take the twins and leave, she had no place to go. The Doles had been married for twelve years before she finally got pregnant. Having never worked a day in her life outside the home, she knew she could not support the children on her own. The only life she knew was taking care of her husband and now the children. As much as the thought of giving up one of the twins was distasteful to her, her husband was more important in her life.

After careful consideration, she approached her next question with caution. "Why have you chosen Jamie as the one to sell?"

"Besides the fact that Jessie carries my name, which means it would be pure stupidity to get rid of him, Jamie's the strongest of the two. As spineless as he is, we can get Jessie to do anything we tell him to do. As the kids get older, I can see we will get nothing but backtalk and rebellion from Jamie. Getting rid of Jamie will make life much easier and definitely quieter around here."

"So, you know Jamie was born with the devil inside --"

"I'm not stupid, woman," he blasted in fury. "But let's not talk about Jamie's wicked little ways or how stupid and weak Jessie is. We need to start getting our heads together and figure out how to sell Jamie. And we need to do it right away before those two brats get any older."

As luck would have it, it only took a few weeks before the Doles found the perfect couple willing to pay a small fortune for a small child and keep the Doles' horrendous secrets.

* * *

As the years went by, Jessie, Jr., learned to put Jamie out of his mind. The few times he brought up the subject of having another child around when he was very young, his mother was quick to respond. "That was a figment of your imagination."

Even in the home where Jamie grew up, the parents denied Jamie ever had a sibling. A brother by the name of Jessie was almost obliterated from Jamie's mind.

However, separated as they were physically, there was a mental bond neither realized until murder entered the twins' lives.

CHAPTER TWO

Forgive HIM, Father, for *HE* has sinned.
Because of the way you and Mother raised me in your abusive ways, I was too weak to stop HIM from killing you both.

I did my best to understand I deserved each beating with your belt, Father. Today I wear each and every scar as my badge of manhood. Your insistent yelling and cursing at me will forever rings in my ears. Until your demise, the two of you drove the stake of obedience into my head and pounded away at it almost every day of my life. A child, you said, was born into this world to obey without question and to be a slave to his parents. I served you the best I could, but now I have failed you. Because of my weakness, I had to stand by, helpless, and watch HIM destroy you.

On that terrible night when black storm clouds filled the sky, the deafening bolts of thunder shook the whole house. The vibration rattled every dish in the kitchen cupboards. As the electrical streaks of lightning thrashed across the atmosphere, lighting everything in its path, I lay there petrified in my bed. My fear was so overwhelming that I submerged my head under the blankets. I cowered there for protection. My entire body trembled. When I felt a presence in my room, I peered out from my covers. Even as the flashes of lightning illuminated my room, I couldn't see HIS face clearly. Yet, somehow, I knew HIM.

Like magic, I suddenly appeared in your bedroom. Both you and Mother were laying in your beds that were separated by that small table. As usual, the table was filled with your dirty glasses and empty whiskey bottles. Your room reeked with the obnoxious smell of liquor. However, that night was no different than any other night. You were both passed out. Dead to the world in your usual drunken stupor. Not even the tyrannical rage of the storm had awakened you.

Then I heard HIM. Even above the sounds of the storm, the beating of HIS heart was deafening. At that very moment I didn't know if HE was aware I was there, too. When I saw a butcher knife in HIS hand, I wanted to cry out. But my vocal chords froze. The sounds of the storm silenced the plunging of the blade. Completing HIS dreadful deed, HE dropped the knife to the floor. After planting instructions in my head, HE disappeared into the darkness as quickly as HE had entered.

As terrified as I was, I don't remember returning to my bed and falling asleep that night. But I must have. Come daybreak, I was wide-awake. I had to find out whether or not I had had a horrible nightmare. Or had I really witnessed your murders? It only took one quick look at the gruesome scene in your bedroom to tell me the truth I had dreaded. I felt as if my heart would pound out of my chest. Since it was all too real, I had to remember everything HE had instructed me to do. HE told me that within hours your bodies would be stiff from rigor mortis. At that point, your bodies would be hard to move. If I waited, the rigor mortis would reverse itself into full body relaxation. This would cause your bodies to become limp again and easier to move.

My wait seemed like a lifetime. But since it had stormed for days, the ground was far too wet for digging in the muddy soil. Even though I kept your bedroom door closed, the smell that reeked from your room was sickening. My only relief was getting out of the house to attend school. Each day when I returned home, I cleaned house — leaving your room untouched.

Imagine my surprise, Father, when I moved your favorite chair and found some loose boards under it. At first I was going to get a hammer and nails to secure the boards. But after second thoughts, I decided it would be better if I removed the loose boards. Then glued them, one by one, back in to place. That's when I discovered the metal box.

I got your set of keys from the kitchen cupboard, where you always kept them. On that key ring it wasn't difficult to find the right key that fit the small lock of the metal box. Imagine my amazement when I found all that money you and Mother had been hoarding. No wonder you always had money for liquor. There was so much money I really wondered if you had robbed a bank. How you got it, however, was not really my concern. All I really cared about was that the small fortune now belonged to me.

Sitting on the floor, I emptied the entire contents of the box. Several papers and a sealed envelope scattered about with the money. I found three documents I felt I might need. They were the deed to the house, the title to the car, and my birth certificate. When I discovered some information on my birth certificate had been scratched out with a black pen, it puzzled me. Right then, however, I wasn't going to worry about it.

There were no insurance papers or records of any bank accounts amongst the papers — although, I didn't find this very unusual. You were both too selfish to have insurance policies. If anything happened to you, you knew the financial burden would be on my shoulders. And in order to keep people from nosing into your financial status, having any type of bank records would be the last thing you would do. The rest of the papers, like your wedding certificate, were not important to me. I should have burned the papers I had no use for, but I decided to keep them.

As I reached out for the sealed envelope, something stopped me. It was as if I was afraid to find out the secret it held. After struggling with my thoughts of whether I should or shouldn't open it, I finally made my decision. The envelope would stay sealed. I already had enough guilt to bear. I certainly didn't need a skeleton from your past haunting me, too. I put the papers, the sealed envelope, and the money back into the metal box.

You never once placed Senior at the back of your name. Nor did you ever refer to me as Junior. And, as luck would have it, I remembered how much you and Mother were so surprised that my handwriting, especially my signature, was a replica of yours, Father. Since I was named after you, there would be no one to say any different than the fact that everything on paper was in my name.

Since you had the only keys to the car, the garage, and the shed, it only made sense for me to keep your key ring. Knowing your hiding place was as good as any place I might have thought of, I returned the box to its resting place. After replacing the boards, I put your chair back in place. As I did, a thought crossed my mind. To my knowledge, neither of you had any friends or relatives. At least if you did, you never spoke of them and I never met any of them. Just in case, however, I had to have a legitimate excuse for you two no longer being around.

Finally the storms stopped. When the sun had dried the earth from the rains, the time had come to clean your room. I buried you both in one hole along with the murder weapon and most of your belongings I knew could not be destroyed. I couldn't get the blood out of the mattresses. So I burned them along with all of your other bedding, clothes, and the rest of your personal belongings that could be turned into ash. I broke every one of your liquor bottles into small pieces and disposed of the broken glass.

After cleaning your room, your window was left open to air out the stench of liquor and death. At last, there wasn't a sign left of either of you. Other than my memories and the papers locked away in the metal box, you were both non-existent.

As time passed, my explanation of missing parents was tested. From the comments, those who had inquired about you appeared to be very pleased that you two had left the area — for good. Lucky for me, no one seemed to care that you're gone. So, you see, no one misses either of you. I had almost forgotten about your Social Security Disability checks until one came in the mail. Don't worry, Father, I took care of that too. I wrote "addressee unknown" on the envelope and returned it.

All that cash you and Mother had hidden from me really came in handy. I went to driving school and got my driver's license. I finally graduated high school and was able to pay my tuition for college — which, by the way, I will be graduating from in just a few short weeks from now. Other than the normal expenses for a college boy, I've been pretty frugal. Of course, it helped that the house and car were paid for before your untimely deaths. So even after all these years, there is still plenty of money left.

Remember that closet you and Mother used to lock me in? Well, I got rid of all the junk you had stored in there. Then I turned the closet into my own private room. That's where I keep my computer. I had two locks placed on the room's door. One is an outside lock to keep intruders out. An inside lock keeps me secure when I'm in there working.

For the most part, I still write by longhand, especially when I have private thoughts that I write in my journal. Other than college papers, I use my computer when I feel creative. Want to know the best part? In my little room HE can't get in. So HE doesn't know I have this machine. At least

— I don't think HE does.

Speaking of HIM again. After your deaths, a flower arrived. The card was addressed to me, but it didn't say who sent it. HE didn't fool me, though. I know it was from HIM. It took awhile, but I finally came up with HIS reasoning. Black represents death and tragedy. A single flower represents a person who is alone. The only meaning I could come up with for the tulip was the fact that the petals are separated — like our family. The black, single tulip was sent to me because your death made me an orphan.

The flower didn't last long, so I had an idea. I was fortunate the local nurseries carry the bulbs. So I hope you like the tulip I planted on your grave. Not that I'm particularly partial to black flowers of any kind, but this one reminds me of both you two and HIM. It's as though the joining of your bodies gave this flower life. Although I have a multitude of other flowers planted in the garden above you, the *Black Tulip* is the first one to bloom in the spring. When it does, it stands strong and unyielding. Just like HIM.

I now go to a place of worship and I read the Bible, Father. Something you and Mother never taught me. Since your deaths, I have gone from mourning you to hating you with a multitude of mixed emotions in between. Now I'm going through a new phase. Through faith, hopefully someday, I will learn to forgive myself. For now, I carry my burden of guilt on conscience-laden shoulders and ask that you forgive me. I get on my knees every night and ask God to forgive me. Your murder will forever bore a hole in my heart.

CHAPTER THREE

The New Year wasn't very old, and people seemed just as crazy as they did when the old year had ended in the promise of *Auld Lang Syne*. It seemed the entire twenty-four-man Detective Division of the Mt. Pride Police Department was engrossed in a rash of killings and a spree of robberies, sex crimes, and narcotics.

Lt. Detective Eddy Konklin was working on a double homicide. With all the other detectives working their own cases, Eddy knew he had to go this one alone until the captain returned. Although it had only been a short time since Konklin started on the case, the frustration of feeling he could not ask anyone to assist him was taking its toll.

There were only a few hairs left on the bald spot of the receding hairline, but Konklin had always managed to keep those hairs nicely combed. Now, however, from rubbing his head out of frustration, those few hairs seemed to stand on end and point in every which direction. He just knew he had more gray hairs than ever weaving through the rest of his once totally brown hair.

Just one look at him and one could tell from the bags under his eyes he had not gotten any sleep. Although he had been on the police force for a goodly amount of years, this detective had never before worked alone on a case. Even after his partner, Detective Joe Warner, had been promoted to captain, the two of them had still worked together to solve the homicide in the *Black Lily* case.

When Detective Anderson joined the unit, she and Konklin partnered for several years. However, that partnership was short lived. Although Konklin knew he was a capable detective, he secretly wished the captain would return to the precinct and help him out.

Some happy start to a New Year, he thought. *If I feel this lost when the crime just took place, how am I going to keep it together until Joe returns? Geez, why did I have to go and call him anyway? He's sure to think I can't handle things on my own. Come on, Eddy, and get that old confidence into gear. Joe put you in charge until his return. If he has that much faith in you, you can do it. Right! Who am I kidding?*

The lieutenant had never been a procrastinator and certainly never a daydreamer. However, from lack of proper rest, he was having a difficult time concentrating on his work. Leaning back in the office chair, resting his head on the chair's back, Konklin's eyes roamed across his small office. As he swiveled in the chair, he turned his back to the desk, facing the wall that normally sat at his back. When his eyes moved to his framed Mt. Pride Police Academy diploma that hung on the wall, he fixated on it.

Suddenly memories of the past, memories he had not thought about in years, came to the forefront. As if hypnotized, Konklin's mind drifted back in time to why he had changed his course in life and become a policeman.

All through school, because of a pleasing personality and wonderful sense of humor, Konklin always had a multitude of friends. Even though he was an excellent student, he was never considered to be a nerd by his peers. Although he was always very active and had a good physique, he never participated in school sports. His style was to just hang out with friends for pizza, beer, and a good time.

Having aspirations of going to college after high school graduation, he wanted to get a degree in business. Because of his dreams to one day own his own business, Konklin never allowed himself to get seriously involved with any particular female. However, during his senior year of high school, he allowed a young beauty to enter his life and change the course of his mindset.

Memories drifted through his head of the happy times when he finally fell in love, married the woman of his dreams, and found out his wife was expecting their baby. His decision to go to the police academy did not come until after the boating tragedy that had taken the life of his wife and unborn child. From that day on, he was determined to be a cop and put predators behind bars.

A ringing in the lieutenant's ears brought him back to reality. When he realized what the sound was, he blinked to clear his blurry eyes. Then he wiped away the tears that were sliding down his face. Turning back toward the desk, Konklin answered the desk phone. After the phone call, he realized he had more important things to do than sit around memorializing the past.

Taking a deep breath and exhaling with a dismal sigh, it was back to work. In his mind he went back to the crime scene of the homicide he was working on to make sure he had covered all the bases in directing the crime scene investigators as to his specific needs. Many of the technicians videotaped crime scenes. However, there were times when a photograph was best when looking for minute details that a video would not pick up.

As soon as the techs were finished with the crime scene, Konklin would need an immediate report on fingerprints and blood evidence from the crime lab. He would also need a pathology report from the medical examiner to ascertain the time of death and the exact cause of death. How the victims died appeared obvious. Nevertheless, Konklin's observation had to be proved. As proof, the courts required a pathologist's expert opinion.

He made a few phone calls to assist the investigation. He had just hung up the phone when there was a rapid knock on the office door. Before he could say, "Come in," the door opened. Konklin's eyes lit up. His round face beamed as he grinned from ear to ear.

"Well, I'll be. What in the name of sanity are you doing here?"

"Hey, is that any way to talk to your boss?" Warner joked as he entered the office and closed the door behind him. "You could at least wish me a happy New Year and offer me a seat."

"Yeah," Konklin grunted, "happy, happy." The lieutenant stood, reaching across the desk to shake hands with his captain. "Welcome back. Sit and take a load off. I didn't expect you back so soon."

Warner took a seat, draping his overcoat over his lap. "Heck, somebody has to keep an eye on you. I'm only gone a few days and you manage to get yourself involved in a double homicide. Can't you learn to stay out of mischief?"

"Very funny." Konklin sat back in his chair, propping his feet on the top of the desk. "I'm guessing you heard about the homicides on the national news?"

"Nope. Jeny told me."

Verbally, Konklin stated, "There was no need to rush back from Chicago." But he was thinking, *Thank God you're here.* "Didn't you have another week of training sessions?"

"Yeah. But when Jeny called, I had already shaken hands and bent elbows with everyone I cared to. Besides, spending New Year's Eve with some old friends was fun — just not the same without my better half. So, I --"

"Hold on, Joe. I'm a bit confused here. Are you telling me you went stag and left that lovely wife of yours home?"

"Not because I wanted to. That damned arthritis of hers started flaring up again. I was going to cancel the whole trip, but you know Jeny. She insisted I go."

"I'm sorry to hear that. Oh, I'm glad you went. I'm just sorry Jeny couldn't go along. Geez, if I'd have known that I would've called on her to see if she needed anything."

"As much as I appreciate that, Eddy, I didn't tell you as I knew Jeny just wanted to rest. Besides, Amandalee was there if she needed help." Warner shook his head in despair. "Wish one of those pills Jeny takes would work good enough for her to travel with me. Business trips, I don't mind. But not having her with me on pleasure trips is a real drag."

"I can imagine."

"Not to change the subject, Eddy, but you look terrible. Have you been sick or did you celebrate New Year's a little too much?"

"Damn, Joe, thanks for the compliment," he answered light-heartedly. "For your information, I didn't celebrate at all. In fact, I was zonked out before the New Year began. It's this case. It's got me bonkers. I can't seem to get my mind off it."

"Holy cow, Eddy. According to Jeny, it just happened yesterday morning."

"Yeah, but I haven't slept all night."

"You had better pull it together, chubby cheeks, or you'll be a basket case before we even get the case solved. You're too experienced to let one case ruin your health."

"You know me. I'm rather lost without a partner. Geez, I'm sorry you had to cut your trip short, Joe. I have to admit though, I'm sure glad you're back. I imagine Jeny knows you're back in town?"

Warner nodded. "Uh-huh. She picked me up from the airport. I hate to admit it, but since I have every confidence in you running things around here, I didn't rush to get here. I spent an hour at home with her before coming to the office."

"Oh, I see." Konklin let out a devilish laugh, moving his eyebrows up and down in a clown-like manner.

"No, way, you dirty old man! All we did was sit and talk. Besides," he smiled sheepishly, "put your evil mind at rest. It will take me longer than an hour to show my wife how much I really missed her."

"Bragger." Konklin laughed. "Since you still have your coat with you, I assume you haven't been to your office yet."

"Right. I wanted to check in with you first before I get buried in paperwork."

"Yeah, you do have quite a stack piling up on your desk."

"That figures. Hey, I've got some good news."

"Good. I could certainly use some about now."

"When I got in, there was a message waiting for me at the front desk. The new budget was approved. This will give our department the funds we need to hire another detective."

"That is great news."

"Yeah. I was a bit surprised Doogle finally okayed my budget. I've never been one of his favorite people."

"Hey, the chief loves you compared to what he thinks of me."

"He'll come around one of these days. You're a damn good detective. As long as I believe in you and your abilities, Ed Doogle can go pound sand up his nose." Konklin chuckled. "That comment wasn't meant to be humorous."

"It wasn't. I was just thinking of a great way to get on the good side of Doogle."

"Now what's on that evil mind of yours?"

"It's not evil. I was just thinking you should buy him a box of toothpicks."

"Very funny, chubby cheeks."

"I'm serious. Just think how many years it's been now since he quit smoking. Ever since then, he always has one of those toothpicks poking out of his mouth. I'm beginning to think he's as addicted to chewing on wood as he was to inhaling nicotine."

"That's healthier. At least we don't have him in the building any more. It was a glorious day when he moved out of our precinct and back to his downtown office."

"And how," Konklin agreed, rolling his eyes.

"I just wish he would retire. The older Doogle gets, the worse his temperament gets. Count your lucky stars that you don't have to deal with him as much as I do."

"Believe me, I do."

"Back to the vacant detective's chair. I'd like your input as to who you think should fill our vacancy from our pool of uniforms. As usual, I'd rather keep the promotion in our family instead of going to one of the other precincts for our candidate. Got any ideas?"

Konklin scratched his head as he thought about the choices. *Officer Ellison would have made a great detective. It's too bad his life was cut short because of a heart attack. Then, of course, his partner would have been next in line. But Finnley hung up his uniform after Ellison's death. So which of the uniforms ... Oh, yeah. With his superb record, he'd make a great detective.* Nodding, he finally replied. "De Mija would be an excellent candidate."

"De Mija?"

"Officer Leo De Mija. He's been a good cop with an excellent record ever since he came here from the academy. I knew we needed to hire another detective, eventually. So I've been keeping an eye on some of the uniforms. De Mija's performance record has been outstanding. Actually, he was my third choice. But you and I both know what happened to the first two good choices. Anyway, I even recommend that De Mija receive recognition for recently capturing a bank robber. I put the recommendation on your desk for approval."

"Which bank robbery?"

"The First National of Mt. Pride over on Morgan was hit the day you left. Didn't Jeny tell you about that, too?"

"No, she never mentioned it."

"Well, De Mija handled himself like a real pro. He followed everything by the book. Never jeopardized himself, his partner, or anyone else around the scene. Duncan said by the time he and Fratt got to the scene, De Mija had the robber cuffed and sitting in his patrol car."

"Were you on the scene?"

"No. I knew the Tag Team, Duncan and Fratt, could handle it. That's why I sent them."

"Good for you!"

"What's that suppose to mean?"

"You delegated an assignment, Eddy. I'm proud of you."

Delegating I'm good at. It's asking for help I have a problem with, Konklin thought before responding. "I delegated a lot of assignments while you were gone. But thanks for the compliment."

"Man, we've had a string of bank robberies over the past few months," Warner muttered under his breath.

"Are you speaking to me or just mumbling to yourself?"

"Just thinking out loud again. I just can't get over all the bank robberies we've had in this area."

"Times are hard. When unemployment goes up, a lot of good people turn into crooks in order to make ends meet. Not to mention the crooks already out there with their greedy fingers taking more than their share of a piece of the pie."

"Isn't that the truth?"

"So, what about Officer De Mija?"

"That's such an unusual name, you'd think I'd remember him."

"Bald head. Face full of facial hair."

"Oh, yes. Well, I'd like to see his employment files first. I'll also look over your recommendation for his commendation and get it forwarded to Roberts. Another good candidate would be Officer Kaufman. I'd like you to pull his records, too."

"Will do."

"It will sure be nice when all of our employees' files are stored on the computer."

"Says you. I still get frustrated using my computer. Give me a typewriter and good old hard copies any day," Konklin grumbled.

"You can't sit there and tell me you really want to go back to typewriters, carbon paper, and white-out for typing up your reports, can you?"

"Who says I can't?" Konklin said with a smile giving reason for Warner to chuckle.

"Good heavens, Eddy. We've been working with computers around here for a number of years now. One would think you wouldn't keep complaining about having to use them."

"Hey, I'm just an old fashioned guy with old fashioned ideas. What can I say?"

"You've just said it all," Warner quipped. "In all seriousness, you aren't as old fashioned as you claim to be. I've been around long enough to know you're always right on top of things."

"You know what? You're right. It just occurred to me I know something you obviously don't."

"I'll bite. What is it?"

"All of our records have been computerized. I was so busy complaining about computers, I forgot."

"When did this happen?"

"Several months ago. Obviously, you don't read all the memos I send you," Konklin teased. "So, do you want me to pull the hard copies, or do you want to look them up for yourself on your computer?"

"That depends. I definitely want to see employment reviews that have been signed by Capt. Roberts and anyone else in a supervising position over these officers."

"Not a problem. Those types of papers were scanned into the system. So you'll get the same info, signatures included, no matter which you choose to read."

"Then I'll look them up on my computer."

"Good. That'll save me time I can make better use of."

"So, tell me what you have so far on the double homicide."

"The CSIs were at the crime scene all day yesterday and last night. To my knowledge, since I haven't heard from them yet this morning, they're still there. I stuck around until after midnight. Then I came back here to get my notes together. Once I could decipher my own scribbling, I started entering the info on my computer."

"You mean you've been here all night?"

"You might say that."

"Why didn't you go lay down in the unit's crib or at least crap-out on my couch for a few hours?"

"I wouldn't have been able to sleep anyway. In all my years as a cop, I've never worked a double homicide before. Not like this. And that crime scene ... Damn, it was horrific."

"As you are aware, I've never worked one before, either. But I can't imagine there's too much difference between a single and a double homicide. Other than the number of bodies involved."

"Trust me. In this case, there's a huge difference. I've never seen such an atrocity before. In all my years on the force, it's the first time a bloody crime scene really got to me."

"That bad, huh?"

"Horrible, Joe. Just horrible."

"Who were the victims?"

"Mr. and Mrs. Brook. According to the ID's we found in the house, Pat Richard Brook was a twenty-eight-year-old male. Shelby Kay, his wife, was twenty-five. They resided over on Raider Ranch Drive. Pat worked for an insurance agency, and Shelby worked in the home doing some sort of computer work. The murders took place in their master bedroom. Let's see ...." Konklin paused. Placing his feet on the floor, he slid his chair closer to the desk. After clicking a few times on his computer mouse to refer to his notes, he continued. "Did I already tell you the victims' throats were slashed?"

"No. Good Lord! What a horrible way to die."

"I know."

"Jeny showed me the newspaper article, but it never mentioned the mode of death."

Konklin nodded. "The reporters swooped in like vultures before I could get in my car and get out of there. All I told them was that we were investigating a possible crime scene. And until we had more information, I would make no further statements. Geez, Joe, I never even mentioned double homicides. The news media made their own assumption there."

"Damn. I wish they wouldn't jump to conclusions before they're given the facts."

"Vince said it appeared as though the woman took a healthy blow to the back of her head. However, due to the small amount of hemorrhaging around the head wound, he surmised that wasn't the cause of death."

"So, on-the-scene assessment is that they both died from throat wounds?"

"Yes. Vince was guessing their main arteries were severed. The man's body was found in bed with a pillow over his face. On the floor just opposite the side of the male victim, the female was discovered with a pillow over her face as well. Colt took a liver probe of each victim. The time of death was around three A.M."

"What time were the vics discovered?"

"Just after seven."

"Just four hours after they were killed."

"Give or take a few minutes. We won't know any more until the medical examiner does his preliminary exam of the bodies."

"Heaven only knows when that will be, Eddy. Before I left town, the morgue's coolers were almost full of bodies."

"I haven't been over there lately. But I'm sure not too much has changed in the short time you were gone."

"Any ideas as to what hit the female in the head?"

"There was a lamp on the floor close to her body. Kevin found a trace of blood on it. We'll have to wait until the crime lab examines it before we know if that's what caused the wound to the back of her head. As for a murder weapon, we didn't find anything in the room that could have been used by the perp. However, we did discover a butcher knife in the kitchen sink. It tested for blood. Forensics will have to analyze it before we know whose DNA is on the knife."

"How far from the master bedroom is the kitchen?"

"Quite a distance. And I know what you're thinking, Joe. It hardly seems feasible that a perp would walk all the way from the bedroom to the kitchen just to put the murder weapon in the sink."

"Exactly. It doesn't make sense."

"I agree. However, to be on the safe side I told the techs to collect it as evidence."

"For sure, Eddy. I would have done the same thing. It just sounds a bit odd, unless the perp is some sort of weird neatnik. How did the perp get into the home, or do you know yet?"

"We discovered a broken window in one of the extra bedrooms. That's where I believe the perp made his entrance. It looked like something pretty heavy broke the window. When I saw a brick laying on the floor, I figured it was what the perp used."

"One would think a brick crashing through a window would have awakened somebody in the house."

"Under normal circumstances, I would agree. But there wasn't a whole lot of glass fragments laying about. Most of what we did find was stuck together with duct tape."

"Obviously to muffle the sound of glass breaking."

"That's what I think. The hole in the window wasn't very big, either. So I'm thinking the perp broke just enough of the glass to reach in, unlock the window, open it, and climb through."

"Is the window that accessible from the ground?"

"No. But out back, just under the window, sits a stack of bricks.

Whether they were there before the murders took place or the perp piled them there, we don't know."

"You think the perp stood on them to reach the window?"

"That's my guess. The perp has to be agile and on the lean side. Because that window is pretty narrow. I know my body wouldn't squeeze through it."

"That's not saying much."

Warner's humorous comment brought a smile to Konklin's face. "If you're trying to tell me I need to go on a diet, forget it. Kevin is about your size. Even he said he'd have difficulty getting through that narrow window. Until the crime lab comes up with anything vital, that's all I know about the perp. Lean and agile."

"Which could be one of millions of people."

"I'm well aware of that. But at least it tells me I can rule out anyone on the heavy side."

Laughing, Warner said, "That's a new one for the books."

"I have this theory. Shelby, the female vic, was either not yet asleep or she was a light sleeper. She heard a noise, opened her eyes and saw the perp. Before she could yell out, he hit her with the lamp, rendering her unconscious so he could murder Pat, the male vic."

"So, perp is in the room. Wife opens her eyes, sees him, and starts to react. The perp grabs the lamp and hits her on the head. The impact is so great that it knocks her out of her bed and to the floor. Unconscious for the moment, the wife is not a threat. So the perp slits the husband's throat and then does the wife in." Warner summed up Konklin's theory with a questionable look on his face.

"Well, that was one of my thoughts, but it could have gone down in other ways. If she woke up before her husband got murdered, the perp could have knocked her to the floor, covered her face with the pillow and slit her throat first. One, two, and it's over with, Joe. If he's quick and quiet, he could have done this without any disturbance to wake the husband.

"On the other hand, taking a lamp and knocking her unconscious before the husband was murdered might have caused enough noise to wake the husband. Then again, now that I think about it, how did the perp hit her from behind if she was looking at him?" Suddenly frustrated from his own words, he mumbled, "I don't know, Joe. I just don't know."

"Well, no sense dwelling on theories now. What else do you have?"

"Sorry, Joe. This case should be fresh in my memory but I'm too tired to remember everything."

Most detectives have experienced none to little sleep on certain cases. Konklin was no exception. However, Warner was worried Konklin's lack of sleep this time was obviously numbing his brain cells. Instead of airing his concern right then, Warner decided to sit in silence.

Referring back to his notes, Konklin scanned through them, then continued with his information. "Before I left the scene, the CSIs had almost completed their sweep of the master bedroom. Along with all the large items and trace evidence they picked up, they took their usual share of pictures and videos. The Brook home is a huge, ranch-style house. Doug and Kevin really had their work cut out for them."

"I'm happy to hear you have the head guru and his right-hand man processing the scene. They're both top-notch techs. Of course Colt is good, too, but all I've ever seen him do is check the liver temp and suggest the type of death. Then he leaves."

"Come on, Joe. The other CSIs are good at their jobs, too."

"Not as detailed as Rothchild and DuBois. They just seem to know exactly what you want before they're ever told."

"I'm sure it's only because they've been at their jobs a lot longer than the rest of the techs. However, I really do feel fortunate they're the ones that showed up to work on this case."

"Were there any prints outside the house?"

"Not that I know of yet."

"Was anything taken from the Brook home?"

"Not having an inventory of their household or personal items, I can't say for sure. But there didn't appear to be anything missing. Brook's billfold with money and his credit cards were still sitting on the bedside stand. The female's purse was sitting on a nearby vanity. I can't say for sure at this point. But everything seemed to be untouched. If this was intended on just being a burglary, I think the billfold and purse would have been rifled and the cash and credit cards would have been taken."

"How about driver's licenses or any other form of ID other than the credit cards? Today, with so many cases of ID theft, who knows what the perp could have been after?"

"Their licenses were there. That's how I ID'd them. Like I said, neither the billfold nor the purse seemed to be disturbed. Nothing appeared out of the ordinary like drawers opened and rifled through. Again, until I can get a family member or close friend to go through the home, I can't say for sure if anything was taken. To be honest, I think the perp went to the Brook home intending to murder them."

"Speaking of family and friends, have the next of kin been contacted yet?"

"Not yet. All I know is both Pat and Shelby's relatives live out of state."

"That should have been done before the homicides hit the news."

"I realize that, Joe. Under the circumstances, I had no other choice. You know, it would really be great if a person carried a 'next of kin' card around with them in their billfolds in case of emergencies."

"Some people do. Have you had a chance to question any of the decedents' neighbors?"

"Damn, Joe. I'm not a wizard. I can only do so much in one day."

"Easy, big guy. I realize that. However, you know as well as I do that spectators seem to come out of the woodwork when there are police cars stopped in the area. Just thought someone might have offered information to you or one of the officers on hand."

"Not this time. But for your information, I plan on canvassing the neighborhood today. Oh, I was able to question the babysitter for a few minutes before she fell to pieces. She's the one that told me the Brook couple doesn't have family in the area. She broke down before I could find out how to locate next of kin."

"What babysitter?"

"I guess I forgot to tell you the deceased couple have a little boy. He was asleep in his room when his parents were killed. Oddly enough, he was left unharmed. I have three different theories. The perp could have gotten scared off before he got to the kid's room. Or he didn't take the time to look around the house to see if it was occupied by anyone else. Or, as I said before, the perp entered the Brooks' home for the sole purpose of killing them and not harming the child."

"So where does the babysitter fit into this?"

"Since the female vic worked at home, she had a babysitter come in for a few hours each day to watch the son. The fifty-something-year-old babysitter, Kate Smither, is the one that found the bodies. It shook her up so badly, we had to call her doctor."

"That's terrible," Warner said with compassion. "When do you think she'll be up to answering questions?"

"I called earlier this morning to see how she was doing. Her doctor was there, so I spoke with him. He said as long as I didn't overdo my stay or upset her, he saw no harm in speaking with her. So, I set up a ten o'clock interview with her."

"Today?"

"Yes."

"Good. So what else have you got?"

"That's it for now. I'll get my preliminary report finished on the information I have so far. It'll be on your desk before I leave for home this evening."

"You did good, Eddy. I knew with you at the helm, this case was in competent hands. But I'm here because I thought you could use my help."

"You sure thought right."

"I can tell. Which uniforms were first on the scene after the bodies were discovered?"

"Officers De Mija and Ripley took the call since they just happened to be in the area."

"De Mija. The officer you think would make a good detective?"

"One and the same, Joe."

Warner had been leaning back in his chair in a semi-relaxed position. He leaned forward. Planting both elbows on the front of the lieutenant's desk, he cupped his hands together and rested his chin on them. "Off the record, Eddy, you really should have started the canvassing by now instead of sitting in your office working on your report. Why didn't you pull in one of the other detectives to help you on this case instead of trying to work it all by yourself — or worrying yourself sick that you might have to work it alone?"

"Reading my mind now are you?" Konklin quipped.

"I know you too well."

"Too bad Anderson isn't still around. Then I'd have a partner and we wouldn't be having this discussion."

"I'll give you that. You two made a great team. It's still hard to believe she's gone."

"Well, I hope that DWI driver that took her life is enjoying his stint behind bars. Anderson was one super lady and made a damn good detective."

"I miss her, too. But dwelling on the yesterdays is getting us nowhere. Now, answer my question."

"In case you haven't noticed, today is Saturday. What's more, this is only the beginning of the second day after the New Year. We don't have a full crew during the weekends. You know that. Not to mention the ones who took off for the long holiday weekend. The board's full. The detectives that are working have enough to keep up with. So there really wasn't anyone I could call on for assistance."

"Okay, big guy. You've proved your point."

"Shoot!" Konklin quickly rose from his chair. "I hadn't realized it was getting so late."

"What's up?"

"My appointment with the babysitter is in twenty minutes."

Latching onto his coat, Warner quickly got to his feet. "Okay, Eddy. Since you don't have a partner yet, I'll fill in. I'm coming with you."

"That's the best news I've heard in a long time. You driving?"

"Haven't I always?"

"Good. Then I'll call Kate from the car and let her know we're on our way."

"You'd better tell her I'm coming along so we don't overwhelm her."

Grabbing his overcoat from a hook on the back of the door, Konklin opened the door. "After you, boss."

"You trying to butter me up?"

"I was just being mannerly. At least I didn't say age before beauty."

Warner smiled. "Smart ass. Okay, let's go get some hot leads on your double homicide."

CHAPTER FOUR

It's been a long while time since I've written to you, Father. I apologize, but I've been very busy with my life.

I know you're not going to be real happy with me, but I've changed somewhat. No, I'm still not strong minded enough to chase away the demon. And I still can't tell anyone where you and Mother are or what happened to you. But I've changed my career path. I'm sure you and Mother wouldn't approve, but I'm happy. Want to know what else? I have a loving wife and a precious daughter.

It's so overwhelming to be loved by your own child. I discovered that children are not placed on this earth to be slaves to their parents or to any other adults. When I see those tiny, innocent creatures of God, all I can think of is that they need protection and guidance. Most of all, they need love. Not the kind of love you and Mother showed me by beating me every time I forgot to do something you asked. Or by yelling at me every time you talked to me. Children are humans, you know? They can be corrected in a gentle way and still mind their parents.

Do you know what else? I found out that most children from a loving family are allowed to eat at the same table and eat off the same set of dishes their parents use. My child will never have to get on the floor on all fours and have to eat garbage from a garbage bag as you and Mother made me do. But guess what? I forgive you both.

I've become quite the carpenter, too. One day, while cleaning the shed, I discovered you had quite an assortment of tools. Most of them were a bit rusty. But after a good scouring and sharpening those that needed it, I found I didn't have to purchase any new tools when I renovated the old homestead.

HE has come back again. I haven't seen HIM since that terrible night you and Mother left me. Once again, I couldn't stay completely out of HIS sight. So HE knows that I witnessed HIS brutal attacks. HE killed two more people. Only this time, Father, HE didn't use a butcher knife.

Now, another child has been orphaned. Separated from abusive parents. Oh, how caring HE is to be so protective of the innocent — those who cannot or are afraid to defend themselves.

Even though HE is a murderer, HE is truly a very intelligent man. So HE wouldn't leave a trace of evidence behind, HE concocted a head to toe uniform made from black plastic, leaf bags and black duct tape. To disguise HIS shoe prints, soles from a canvas pair were cut off; then glued to the bottom of a pair of HIS old shoes. HIS hands were covered with clear disposable gloves. HE's like a vigilante in black attire. At home, HE was able to burn the complete plastic body coverings so no one could ever trace the murders back to HIM.

I just knew HE felt that HE had committed the perfect crime for a second time. Just like you and Mother, no one would ever know but HIM and me. HE seems to be confident that I would never tell on HIM. As long as I continue to keep my mouth shut, I'm not afraid of HIM. In fact, I still admire HIM. HE is forceful where I am weak. HE stands bold where, most times, I cower. HE takes matters into HIS own hands where I stand by and watch. I hope someday to be strong and assertive like HE is.

I look in a mirror and what do I see? Someone standing boldly in place of me.

 CHAPTER FIVE

Once Warner and Konklin arrived at the home of Kate Smither, a young woman answered the door. Both detectives presented their identifications.

"Good morning, ma'am. I'm Lt. Konklin. This is Capt. Warner. We're from the MPPD Detective's Unit."

"Yes, we were expecting you," the woman stated as she took a step back. "Detectives, please come in."

The detectives stepped inside the house, allowing the woman to close the door.

Warner asked, "From the description I received, you're not Kate Smither, are you?"

Konklin bit his tongue. It was better to keep quiet than to embarrass his boss.

"No, I'm her daughter, Ellie." As she continued to talk, the detectives followed Ellie into the living room. "Please come in and make yourselves comfortable. I'll go get my mother." Hesitating, she said, "My mother has been in really bad shape, Detectives. Please take it easy on her."

After Warner and Konklin nodded in the affirmative, the woman left the room. Sitting on the couch next to Warner, Konklin began to quietly snicker.

"Hush, Eddy. What's so funny anyhow?" Warner asked, keeping his voice just above a whisper.

"You."

"Me? Why?"

"I told you I had already met Kate," Konklin whispered. "If you would've waited another second, Mister Common Sense would've told you that wasn't a fifty-plus year-old woman that answered the door. Geez, I don't know, Joe. Maybe you should get your eyes checked?"

"Very funny. I wasn't quite sure since you addressed her as ma'am, but I had to ask just to make sure. Remember you gave me her approximate age, not what she looked like. For all I knew, she could've had a face-lift by an excellent plastic surgeon. In our business you learn to never judge a book by its cover and never assume anything."

"You ought to know by now that I address most women as ma'am. No matter what their age," Konklin replied with a grin. "By the way, Kate prefers to be called by her first name."

"I rather assumed that after listening to you."

Their conversation quickly ended when the young lady returned. She had her arm around an older woman dressed in a robe and slippers. Both detectives stood as the two women entered the room.

"Please sit back down," Kate stated.

Ellie seated her mother in an overstuffed chair. She seated herself on the chair's arm. Warner and Konklin sat back on the couch. Konklin pulled a pad and pen from his pocket, ready to take notes.

"Mom, this is Lt. Konklin," Ellie said, gesturing as she spoke, "and this is Capt. Warner."

"Yes, Lt. Konklin and I met yesterday. Nice to meet you, Capt. Warner."

"It's nice to meet you, too. I'm just sorry it's not under the best circumstance."

"Me, too. lieutenant, I'm sorry you had to wait to talk to me. But yesterday I just fell apart when I found …." Getting choked up, she had to stop and take a deep breath before continuing. "It was such a dreadful sight."

"We'll try to make this as painless as possible, Kate. We would like to know how you came to discover the bodies at the Brook house," Konklin said.

"Oh my, I was hoping I wouldn't have to explain that again."

"You only gave me brief information yesterday before you collapsed. We realize how painful this is. But we need you to explain in more detail everything you can remember about yesterday morning."

"Well, the morning started out just like every other workday for me. I always arrived at their house at seven, just like clockwork, every morning from Monday through Saturday. No holidays, of course."

When Kate hesitated, Warner inquired, "How did you get into their house?"

"I have a key. Pat always left the house by six-thirty every morning. Just as soon as he was out of the drive, Shelby got busy right away on her computer work. Their little boy seems to have his own built-in time clock so he wakes up anytime between seven-fifteen and seven-thirty. At seven I would let myself in. Then let Shelby know I was there. I sat in the kitchen and drank a cup of coffee until their little one would wake up. Once he was awake, I bathed him, dressed him, fed him his breakfast, and then I played with him. Shelby would quit her computer work around eleven-thirty. Then we'd sit and talk for about twenty minutes before I would leave for home.

"I've worked for the Brooks since their little boy was born three years ago. Shelby never took any chances that an intruder might enter their house. So leaving the door unlocked for me to gain entrance was never an option. That's why she gave me a key to come in without her having to leave her work just to open the door for me. Besides, she couldn't hear a knock at the front door from her office. And ringing the doorbell would've disturbed the little one's sleep."

After wiping her nose with a tissue, Kate continued. "My daughter, here," she said, reaching up and patting Ellie's hand, "has done some nighttime babysitting for them on different occasions. She will agree with me, I'm sure, that they were a loving couple and they loved their child. I can't imagine …." She stopped talking as she fought back the tears. "I can't imagine what sick person would want to hurt those two beautiful children."

"On the morning in question," Konklin asked, "did you suspect anything was wrong when you entered the Brook house?"

"Well, yes and no. First of all, Pat's car was still sitting in the driveway. There has only been a few times that his car was there when I went to work. That was because he was sick with the flu. My first thought was that he had stayed home because he was sick. So it didn't set off any immediate alarms in my head. Normally, however, when he was home Shelby always made a point of calling me and letting me know before I left home on those mornings. She hadn't called me that morning. Then I thought maybe he was running late. On the other hand, in the three years I've worked for them, Pat was never late leaving the house."

"And that still didn't set off any alarms in your head?"

"Not really because another thought occurred to me. They were going to have a house full of company the day before for a New Year's Day celebration. So maybe Pat just overslept. Anyway, I unlocked the door and went inside. Shelby always kept her office door partially open when she worked. When I went to her office to let her know I was there, her door was wide open. It was kind of a given that if her office door was wide open that she needed to talk to me about something important before I started my day. When I looked in and saw she wasn't there and the computer wasn't on, I thought it very strange. Shelby was definitely a morning person, if you know what I mean?"

Almost in unison, both detectives nodded.

"Is that when you went to their bedroom?" Konklin asked.

"Not right away. I went immediately to the nursery. When I saw the little one was all right, I checked the kitchen. That's when I noticed that their morning coffee hadn't even been made. With no signs of either of them, that's when I headed straight to the master bedroom. On the way, I felt a cold draft come from one of the spare bedrooms. When I looked in, I saw an open window with broken glass shattered on the carpet. I also saw a brick laying there in the midst of the glass. A cold chill ran up my spine — and it wasn't from the cold air."

"I'm not familiar with the Brook house. Where is the child's room located in regards to the master bedroom?" Warner asked.

Konklin knew the answer to the question. However, since Warner was addressing his question to Kate, he kept quiet.

"The nursery is down at one end of the hall. The master bedroom is at the end of the hall on the opposite side of the house," Kate said, gesturing with her hands. "Two spare bedrooms, two bathrooms, Pat's study and a playroom separate them. Why? Is that important?"

"I was just curious why you hadn't felt the cold air from the broken window when you went to check on the child."

"Because I didn't go down the hall in that direction until after I had checked the kitchen."

"Now I understand. Please continue with what you did next."

"I hurried to the master bedroom. The door was partially open. I didn't want to just walk in their room, so I called out Shelby's name. When she didn't answer, I called out Pat's name. When he didn't answer either, I stepped inside the room and turned on the light. When I saw all that blood on the bed ...." Kate started whimpering and her hands began shaking.

"Mom, are you all right?" Ellie asked, putting her arm around her mother's shoulders.

"Yes, darling, I'm fine." She sniffed. Trying to compose herself, she said, "Be dear and get me a glass of water, please." Turning her attention back to Warner and Konklin, she apologized. "I'm sorry, Detectives. I don't think I will ever get over seeing --"

"We understand, Kate," Konklin interrupted. "We only have a few more questions for you. Then we'll be done for today."

"When did you discover Mrs. Brook's body?" Warner asked.

"Oh, I didn't. To tell the truth, I was so shook up when I saw all that blood on the bed that I ran out of the room to the nearest phone and immediately called 911. It wasn't until later, after the police arrived, that I overheard they found a male in bed and a female laying on the floor next to the bed and both were dead."

Konklin picked up the questioning again. "You told me previously that the Brooks didn't have any family in town. Do you know them well enough to verify that statement?"

"Yes. Both Pat and Shelby moved here to Colorado from Nebraska. That's where their families still live. Shelby always called me her surrogate mother."

As Ellie entered the room with a glass of water, she handed it to her mother and added to the part of the conversation she had overheard. "Shelby and I met at a computer class before she ever got pregnant." She seated herself back on the arm of her mother's chair. "We hit it off immediately and became as close as sisters. Mom kind of adopted her. Anyway, when the baby was born and Shelby wanted a morning Nanny, Mom volunteered for the job."

"Oh, it wasn't a job," Kate stated, reaching over and patting her daughter's arm. "Getting so close to Shelby and Pat ... well let's just say that their baby was like my own grandchild. What's going to happen to Jimmy now, Detectives?"

Turning to his boss, Konklin stated, "Jimmy's the son."

"Uh-huh," Warner acknowledged, nodding. From Konklin's expression, Warner knew he was expected to answer Kate's question. "I can't say for sure what will happen to Jimmy. In most cases like this, the nearest relative is contacted to come and take custody of the child. Of course, since the families live in another state, I imagine there will be some red tape they will have to go through first. However, that's not my expertise."

"That poor little tyke," Kate commented before taking a drink of water.

"A woman from child services contacted me just before you arrived. I gave her the name and phone number of Shelby's parents in Nebraska," Ellie stated.

Konklin spoke up. "That must have been Jill Maloy from Child Protective Services."

Thinking for a moment, Ellie finally nodded. "Yes, that was her name. Jill Maloy."

"I would have taken Jimmy, but I was hardly in any condition to take care of myself," Kate admitted. "And Ellie didn't feel she could handle caring for me and Jimmy at the same time. Poor Jimmy. He must think everyone familiar to him has abandoned him."

"I'm sure he'll be just fine," Warner comforted.

Once again, Konklin proceeded with the interview. "You said you knew how to locate Mrs. Brook's parents. We'd appreciate that information so we can notify them of their loss."

"Certainly," Ellie said.

"If you have the information on Mr. Brook's parents, too, we'd like that also."

"Sorry, I haven't the slightest idea how to contact Pat's family."

"Do either of you know anyone that held a grudge against either of the deceased?"

"Not at all," Kate answered. "They got along with their neighbors. I don't know much about Pat's fellow employees, but he never had a bad word to say about any of them. As for Shelby, anyone who knew her really liked her — as far as I know. They were both such pleasant people to be around. Wouldn't you say so, Ellie?"

"Yes, I agree with Mom. I knew almost everyone Shelby knew personally, and they all adored her. I didn't know all of Pat's co-workers. But the few I did know thought he was a top notch sort of guy."

When a look of disdain appeared on Ellie's face, Warner picked up on it. He did not know if it was because the interview was getting the best of her, or she was withholding information. "Ellie, are you all right?"

"I'm fine."

With Warner's first question answered, he did not hesitate to say, "If there's something you want to tell us, now's the time to do so."

"Not really."

"I can almost tell something is bothering you," Warner insisted.

"It really has nothing to do with your investigation. I was just remembering the times I could have strangled Pat with my own bare hands."

"Ellie!" Kate shrieked.

"I'm sorry, Mom. But it's true." Returning her attention to the detectives, Ellie said, "I wouldn't have seriously done it."

Both detectives were almost dumbfounded. Warner was quick to ask, "Why would you say such a thing?"

"I know that's terrible of me — especially since he's gone now. A person shouldn't speak ill of the dead. I'm sorry, but I loved Jimmy, too. It just broke my heart to see welts and bruises on that adorable baby."

"Are you telling us Mr. Brook was an abusive parent?" Konklin asked.

"I wasn't for sure until one day I questioned Shelby about it. She admitted Pat would get carried away when he spanked Jimmy. So, yes, Pat was an abusive parent. He was the cause of most of Jimmy's bruises. Shelby had been afraid to say anything in fear of Pat attacking her, too."

"So you just stood by and kept your mouth shut?"

"Shelby made me promise not to get the authorities involved. She was afraid Jimmy would be taken away from her. Since Shelby assured me she would find a way to deal with the problem, yes, I promised to keep my mouth shut. But I did warn her. If the harsh spankings continued and I noticed any more welts or bruising, I would go to the authorities."

"What was her response to your threat?"

"She said she would kill me first. And --"

"And, what, Ellie?" her mother asked, astonished.

"Well, I told her not if I killed her first."

"Merciful heavens. You two threatened each other? Why didn't you tell me this before?"

"Calm down, Mom. You have a sister. You know how sisters are? Arguments happen and you say things you don't really mean. Neither one of us were serious."

"When was this conversation?" Konklin asked.

"I can't remember for sure. But I know it was sometime just before New Year's Eve. Really, I don't know what difference this all makes now," Ellie said.

Before Konklin had a chance to speak, Warner stated, "Any information helps in an investigation. Since you were Jimmy's babysitter, Kate, I'm surprised you never mentioned the child being abused."

"Because I didn't think he was. If you've ever had children, Capt. Warner, then you'd know kids fall down, run into things, and bang themselves up all the time. Take Ellie, for example. This poor child was always sporting bruises from one thing or another. Right, Ellie?"

Waiting for an answer, Warner was reading Ellie's face: a look of shear hatred. His intuition was right the first time. But did he dare ask again? Before he had decided how to approach what she was thinking this time, he noticed Kate tightly squeezing Ellie's hand.

"Ellie," Kate said, "answer me. Tell the detectives how you were always bruising yourself while playing."

"Yes," Ellie finally said. "Even the kids at school teased me because I often had more major bruising and cuts than I had nice skin."

Warner quickly flashed back to the time his daughter was little.

Amandalee would get a few bruises, now and then. But never anything like Ellie had just explained. *She's probably just exaggerating*, Warner thought. So he dropped the subject and went back to the homicides. "Tell me, Ellie, where were you when the murders took place?"

"That depends. I don't even know for sure when they were killed."

In order not to give out too many specifics, Warner replied, "Somewhere between ten o'clock Thursday night and six-thirty Friday morning."

"Oh. Well, I was here with Mom. I had been to a party that day and came home around nine-thirty that evening. I was going to take a hot bath and go to bed. But Mom convinced me to stay up with her. So, I did. After we watched the ten o'clock news, we watched an excellent movie on the AMC channel. We love watching those old classics. I think the movie was over somewhere between eleven-thirty and midnight. Right, Mom?"

"That's correct. I remember the last thing I did before getting into bed was setting my alarm. The time was 11:56."

"You're sure about the time?"

"Yes, because I remember thinking how stupid I was to stay up so late when I had to get up so early the next morning."

"Did you go to bed at that time, Ellie?"

"No. After Mom went to bed, I got involved in another movie — which I shouldn't have. I was so tired I don't remember the name of it or what it was about. Sleep got the best of me."

"I can vouch for that, too, Capt. Warner. When I got up yesterday morning, I found her sleeping on the couch and the TV was still on. I knew she wasn't going to be too happy when she woke up."

"Why do you say that?"

"Because she was still dressed in her good clothes that she had worn to the party the day before."

"Mom. Please. I'm sure these detectives aren't interested in what I slept in."

"Are you employed, Ellie?"

"Not now," she answered, hanging her head in despair.

"It's okay, honey. We'll get through this together," Kate comforted. "Perhaps I should explain, Capt. Warner. My daughter worked for Shelby. They spent practically every weekday together in Shelby's office. And when Pat was away on business, Ellie stayed there overnight."

"I didn't know that. I'm sorry," Warner apologized. "Well, I don't have any more questions." Turning to his lieutenant, he said, "Do you?"

"Yes. Considering that fact that you both worked in the Brook home, is it safe to say you're familiar with their personal belongings?"

"I would more than Mom. Not only did I help out with their housecleaning, I always assisted Shelby during spring and fall cleaning. And that meant everything from washing windows to cleaning out closets. Why?"

"We need to know if anything was taken from the home. If you could accompany us to the crime scene to see if anything is missing, we would certainly appreciate your help."

"Sure, I can do that. Do you want me to go with you now?"

Leaving Ellie's question hanging in the lurch, Konklin turned toward Warner and quietly defended his reasoning. "I know it's still a crime scene. But I really would like to see if she can spot anything missing in the house. We certainly need to know whether or not we can rule out burglary."

Warner approved with a nod, adding, "You'll need to find out if the CSIs have completely processed the premises first."

"I'll call Doug right now and see how they're progressing,"

"Do you want to use my cell?" Warner offered.

"I've got mine."

After excusing himself, Konklin walked out the front door. Making the call in Kate and Ellie's presence was not an option in case he had to discuss any details of the homicides.

When he returned, he gave a positive nod to Warner, then turned to Ellie. "If it isn't too much trouble, we would appreciate you accompanying us now."

"Oh, Capt. Warner, Jimmy has his favorite blanket and a stuffed dog that he just has to have to go to sleep. I'm sure whoever has him right now would have less trouble getting him settled if he had those things. Could Ellie get those items from his nursery and give them to you to take to him?"

"I'm afraid not. Until we release the crime scene, everything stays in place."

"Oh, of course. I understand."

"This won't take too long, will it? I don't want to leave Mom alone any longer than I have to."

"Just time enough for you to look around their house," Konklin answered. "We'll have you back home in no time."

While Ellie was helping her mother back to her bedroom, the detectives walked out to the car. Warner got in the car to start it and warm it up, and Konklin stood beside the car waiting for Ellie.

When Ellie got to the car, she handed Konklin a slip of paper containing Shelby's parents' phone number and address.

The ride to the Brook house was silent. When they arrived, Rothchild was headed for the crime lab van with a bag full of physical evidence.

As Warner exited the car, Konklin turned to the back seat. "Please wait here a minute, Ellie."

"Sure."

Exiting the car, both detectives walked to the van to meet with Rothchild. The three men exchanged silent greetings with nods.

"We've got the young lady with us that I told you about over the phone, Doug," Konklin said. "Refresh me as to which rooms you have left in the house to process."

"Kevin is sweeping the kid's room, and I'm heading for the dining room," Rothchild responded. "Then we're going to check the outside, again, just as a precautionary measure."

"So all the other rooms are clear for us to go into?" Receiving an affirmative nod from Rothchild, Konklin said, "Okay. I want you guys to continue with your work to wrap this up. We'll do our best to stay out of your way."

"Doug, how about giving us a couple pair of protective gloves and booties?" Warner asked.

"You won't need booties, Joe, as long as you don't walk in the pool of blood in the master bedroom and stay out of the two rooms we haven't gone over yet. Hold on a sec and I'll get the gloves."

"Make that one pair," Konklin said. "I have a fresh pair in my coat pocket."

Warner waited while Konklin walked back to the car, opened the car door, and held out his hand to assist Ellie with getting out of the car. Then the three of them walked up the long sidewalk, ducked under the bright yellow tape marked with big black words '**CRIME SCENE DO NOT CROSS**,' and entered the house. Just inside, both detectives put on their disposable gloves.

Inside the Brook house there was an eerie feeling of Christmas past. Joe felt a chill rush up his spine, making his shoulders quiver. Decorative tree ornaments were scattered about the floor, obviously knocked off their original resting-places as the tree was starting to wither and lose its needles. Even the treetop angel was leaning to one side, barely holding on. Opened presents still sat nicely presented under the tree, laden with pine needles. The spirit of Christmas definitely did not fill the air. As Warner looked at the jovial smile on the face of the Santa that adorned the fireplace, he thought, *Santa, if you could only talk.*

"Ellie," Konklin instructed, "please don't touch anything. As a precaution, just in case you might be tempted to reach out subconsciously, maybe it would be better for you to keep your arms folded in front of you. We've already checked out most of the house for prints. But sometimes we have to come back and re-check certain things. There's no sense in you leaving any new prints around."

Nodding and folding her arms as suggested, she replied, "I understand."

As they walked from room to room, the two detectives opened every cupboard, closet door and drawer for Ellie to look inside and view their contents. Ellie could not stop her eyes from welling up when they entered the bedroom where her dear friends Pat and Shelby had been murdered. The sight of the blood on the carpet made her whole body quiver.

"I don't see one thing missing or out of place," Ellie stated when the search was almost over and they had returned to the living room. "Even their presents are intact. After presents were opened, Shelby liked to display Christmas gifts that way for all to see when they entered the house. She loved the holidays. So she never put presents away or took any of the decorations down until a good week after the New Year's celebration."

From the looks of the tree, she should have taken it down before New Year's. That is definitely a fire hazard, Warner thought as Ellie continued talking.

"See that bracelet?" She gestured with her elbow to a small box under the tree. "That's real 14 karat gold. I know because Mom and I bought it for her."

"Okay, I guess that rules out burglary as our motive," Konklin mumbled under his breath.

"Since you've been in this house before, Eddy, what's left? Or have we covered it all but the two rooms Rothchild mentioned?" Warner asked.

"That's it."

Speaking to Ellie, Warner asked, "Do you know if any valuables were kept in the dining room, like silver settings?"

"No. The only thing in there is a large dining room table with six matching chairs. It was the one room in the house they never used, so it wasn't completely furnished yet. Their goal for this year was to purchase a rather large china cabinet and other furniture items to make the room complete. The only china and silver they had is what I showed you in the kitchen and it was all there."

"Okay, we'll bypass the dining room. There's no reason we need to check Jimmy's room, either, as far as I can tell. I can't imagine they would keep any valuables in there."

"Yes, they do, Capt. Warner."

"They do? Like what?"

"Shelby started Jimmy a collection of stuffed animals that were covered in mink. Some of them are adorned with real jewels. Actually, she had started the collection for herself years ago but decided to give it to Jimmy when he was born. He wasn't allowed to play with any of the stuffed toys, of course, but he has a shelf full of them in his room. I know the collection has got to be worth a lot of money. Shelby said they had to take a special rider out on it on their insurance policy."

"Okay. Eddy, let's go to the child's room."

"It's this way." Warner and Ellie followed as Konklin led the way. He stopped when he got to the doorway of the nursery. "Kevin, is it okay to come in?"

"Hey, I'm glad you're here. Come in and take a look here in the crib," DuBois suggested.

Warner had Ellie wait in the hall while he went into the room with Konklin.

Pointing, Dubois asked, "What do you make of that?"

"A crib is definitely not a place to put a flower," Konklin stated.

"Have you photographed it yet?" Warner asked.

"Yes."

Warner summoned Ellie to join them. "Ellie, have you ever seen a flower in the baby's crib before?"

"Never. That doesn't belong there, either. Shelby would never allow something like that in the crib in fear of Jimmy choking on it."

"Either?" Konklin questioned. "Is there something else you're referring to?"

"Yes. That rattle and card there between the stuffed dog's front paws."

Dubois shook his head. "Sorry, I missed that."

"Lieutenant, who took the baby from his crib after the death of his parents?" Warner asked.

"I did. Then handed him over to Jill Maloy who was waiting in the hallway."

"And you didn't notice either the flower or the rattle at that time?"

"Quite frankly, no. To begin with, it was a dark, cloudy morning. The window blinds were all closed in here. I didn't want to frighten the little boy by turning the light on. The only light I had came from the hall. I could see well enough to pick up the child. But something like a black flower and brown dog were probably hidden by the darkness," Konklin explained in his defense. "And I never came back in this room until now."

Warner never responded. Instead he turned his attention to DuBois. "Get a couple of photos of this," he ordered, pointing to the tulip, rattle, and card. "Then give me a clear evidence bag." Focusing back on Ellie, he asked, "Are any of those expensive stuffed animals missing?"

"No, sir. They all seem to be there."

"Good. If you don't mind, I'll have you wait in the living room."

When DuBois finished taking pictures of the foreign items, he handed Warner a small plastic bag. After picking up the rattle and its attached note, Warner placed the items into the bag. The bag was then sealed with a piece of bright red evidence tape. On the outside of the bag Warner wrote his initials along with the date and time the item was taken into evidence. He left the tulip for the team to collect.

Normally, the CSIs would take evidence to the crime lab for further examination for fingerprints or any other pertinent information they could glean from it. However, Warner had his reasons for wanting to keep this one bag of evidence in his possession. After completing the normal chain of custody receipt for the CSI records, Warner stuck the evidence in coat pocket.

When DuBois left the room, Warner asked, "Eddy, do you have any other special instructions for the tech team while you're here?"

"No. But I do want to ask Doug a few questions before we leave."

"Okay, why don't you take care of it now? I'll call a uniform to take Ellie home."

"Sounds good. I'll meet you in the living room."

"Wait." Removing his gloves, he handed them to Konklin. "Here. You can deposit my gloves with yours in the tech's trash bag."

Konklin headed for the dining room. Warner went back to the living room.

"Well, Ellie, we certainly want to thank you for assisting us. If you don't mind, we'll have one of our officers take you home?"

"That's fine, sir, and you're very welcome."

* * *

As they waited for the car to warm up, Warner retrieved the evidence bag from his pocket and handed it to Konklin. "Here. Read what it says on the card."

Taking the bag, Konklin noticed there were printed words on the card. Pulling the plastic taut so he could make out the words, he commenced reading aloud. After handing the bag back to Warner, he said, "What do you suppose that gibberish means?"

"I don't know yet, other than the rattle and a black flower are strange calling cards for a perp to leave." Warner placed the bag back in his pocket.

"That flower, by the way, is a tulip."

"I know."

"The CSIs are trained to recognize anything and everything that might be evidence in a crime scene. I would like to know why Kevin didn't see the rattle as evidence?"

"Give me a break, Joe. Even in bright daylight, who's going to take special note of a rattle in a kid's room?"

"A rattle I might understand. But not with a card attached." Warner looked at the clock on the dashboard. "I hadn't realized the time. It's after one o'clock already. So, where to next?"

"Let's just go back to the precinct."

"What about starting the neighborhood canvassing?"

"My stomach's a bit unsettled right now, Joe. Maybe if I get something to eat I'll feel better."

"Do you want to stop somewhere for lunch?"

"Not today. I'll probably just get something from one of our snack machines."

Normally, Konklin would have been chattering away all the way back to the station. Instead, he sat perfectly quiet, lost in his own thoughts. Since Warner had a lot on his mind, too, he did not notice the silence.

Back at the precinct, Warner said, "After you eat, come to my office. I'll put on a fresh pot of coffee."

There was never a time Konklin did not enjoy having coffee with his boss. Plus, he and Warner had become personal friends away from work. This time it was different. Konklin almost dreaded responding, "Sure, Joe. I'll be there."

* * *

When Konklin entered the captain's office, Warner was fiddling with the evidence bag.

"That was fast. The coffee isn't even done yet."

Konklin loved to eat but not when he was depressed. He hadn't eaten at all but did not want his boss to know. "Yeah. Like I said, I was hungry."

"You know scarfing down your food always gives you indigestion. I love ya, chubby cheeks, but please don't have any of your foul gas attacks while you're in here," Warner teased.

"I won't," Konklin replied as he sat in a chair.

Warner had always been able to tease Konklin into everything from smiles to gut laughter. This time, however, Konklin remained somber and bore a hangdog look on his face.

"What's eating you, Eddy?"

"I feel terrible."

"You sick?"

"Sick at heart. I feel horrible about not seeing the tulip or the rattle in the child's crib."

"Your explanation made perfect sense."

"Well, I also feel badly that you're upset with Kevin. Hell, Joe, almost anyone would have overlooked a rattle in a child's crib. Even you and I didn't pay any attention to it until Ellie pointed it out."

"Come on now, Eddy. Quit taking everything I say so damn personal. You should know by now that I have a habit of thinking out loud. To be quite honest, after I made the statement in the car I've been thinking about it too. Just as you indicated earlier, a rattle doesn't seem out of place in a kid's bed. I apologize if I made you feel guilty about it. And I'll make it a point to apologize to Kevin. Feel better now?"

"I guess so."

"Good. Thank heavens that was all that was wrong with you."

"What does that mean?"

"I wasn't kidding a few seconds ago. I seriously thought when you said you were sick that you were going to start expelling nasty fumes again and stink me out of here," he joked. Finally getting Konklin to laugh, he said, "Okay, pal, that's better."

"What's your take on the rattle?"

"Well, I agree with Ellie. This isn't a good toy for a child to have. A little one could put it in his mouth and choke on it. I firmly believe, however, that the rattle, note, and tulip was placed there by our perp."

"His calling card."

"Yes."

"What do you suppose the meaning behind the black-colored tulip is?"

"I haven't the foggiest notion." Still holding the evidence bag, Warner said, "Let's go over these words again. Listen very carefully and see what crosses your mind." Once Warner had finished reading the verse, he asked, "Well, what's your thoughts?"

Hearing the last spurts and sputters of the coffeemaker, Konklin replied, "Let me think about it while I get us coffee."

Returning with two filled coffee cups, Konklin placed one in front of his captain and returned to his seat. "What I get out of that nonsense is don't yell at your kids, and don't spank them. Sort of like that old adage, 'spare the rod and spoil the child'."

"Exactly my thinking. It sounds like someone made up his own commandment for raising children. 'Beware of the snake that rattles' could have something to do with the attached rattle. Maybe even a double innuendo. On one hand, the rattle represents a child. On the other hand, it represents a rattlesnake that strikes with the intent to kill.

"Then he writes, 'He strikes with valid revenge for your unforgivable acts.' Maybe someone witnessed Pat abusing or mistreating his son, didn't like it, so he killed him? Since the wife was just as guilty for not stopping the abuse, he did her in, too. Does my theory make any sense?"

"Murder never makes sense, Joe. We both know that. However, it would certainly fit into what Ellie told us."

"Yes. And I found her comments most interesting, if not highly suspicious."

"Yeah. Wanting to choke Pat with her bare hands and then threaten to kill Shelby."

"Precisely. Whoever committed these murders had to be able to move swiftly. Ellie could certainly fill that bill. She makes for a good suspect."

"Not necessarily. Calling the authorities makes much more sense than killing someone."

"To us it does. Maybe Ellie just went there to kill the husband? If the wife woke up and recognized her and saw she had killed her husband, that's when Ellie decided to kill her, too. After all, she couldn't leave a witness alive to point the finger at her. Pat's murder would've been premeditated. Shelby's murder would've been an instant reaction by Ellie, making it a second-degree murder.

"There's something else we have to consider. Ellie's alibi stinks. The Smither house is only a block away from the Brook house. Hell, Ellie could have gone to the Brooks and committed the murders after her mom was asleep. She would have been back home and sound asleep way before her mother woke up."

"It's a cinch she tried to cover her ass by not remembering anything about the movie she supposedly watched."

"See. That's another good reason to consider her a prime suspect."

"Okay. Ellie goes at the top of my suspect list."

"Don't say that with so much enthusiasm," Warner quipped.

"I might not show it, but I am excited about having a suspect to investigate. A little, at least. It's just that I'm not as sure as you are about Ellie taking the life of someone she considered her sister."

"Wonder if the Smithers have flowers growing somewhere around their house?"

"What are you, nuts, Joe? It's too damn cold to grow flowers."

Warner laughed. "Not outside, chubby cheeks. There are such things as houseplants. A few years ago, Jeny grew some tulips in the house. They were very pretty too, I might add."

"Oh. But are you sure that was in January? I thought tulips were more of a springtime flower?"

"I don't know. But it's worth checking out."

"I'll add it to my list."

"So, are you ready to wear down the soles on your shoes?"

"I've thinking about that, Joe. Since tomorrow is Sunday, I really think I'll find more people at home. If you don't mind, I'll put off canvassing until then. Besides, I have some office work to catch up on."

"Sounds good to me. What time do you want to start tomorrow?"

"You don't have to go with me, Joe. Stay home and enjoy your family."

"What time?"

"Look, I know you don't get home from church until after ten. That's too late to get started."

"I'm sure God will forgive me just as he has done in the past. So I repeat, what time?"

"Dammit, Joe. You're relentless."

"I know."

"Oh, okay. We'll meet here around nine."

Warner drank the rest of his coffee; then got to his feet. "Well then, I'm going home for the rest of the day. Going to get something to eat and take a nap. Then I'm going to spend a nice evening with Jeny. And Amandalee, if she's home."

"That sounds wonderful. Especially the nap part."

"Don't work too late, and get some sleep tonight. That's an order. Those victims' families are depending on you to find the murderer of their loved ones. And you can't do that if you're not alert."

 **CHAPTER SIX**

Leo De Mija was a nice looking young man in a rugged sort of way. Everyone who knew him considered him a loner. His rangy appearance was very deceiving. Even though he was very strong at his six-foot-two-inch height and one-hundred-seventy-pound weight, he did not appear very muscular.

De Mija graduated from college with a bachelor's degree in education. But, due to changing factors in his life, he switched his career venue from a teacher to an officer of the law. He felt he could do more good in the world by wearing a uniform.

When the time came after taking the written exams (scoring in the top ten percent) and the oral interviews, De Mija was hired as a police trainee. Consequently, he attended the twelve-week police academy course where he excelled. Upon graduating from the academy, he was assigned to the Mt. Pride Police Department's 15th Precinct, Patrol Division. All reports from De Mija's supervisors rated him superior in all facets of police work.

De Mija's patrol partner, Officer David Ripley, was the direct opposite of De Mija. Barely hitting the five-foot-six-inch mark in height, he was built like a wrestler. With a very outgoing personality, Ripley loved to talk and joke around, and seemed to always have a smile on his face. He was single and loved playing the field.

The two had met at the academy, and both had been assigned to the 15th at the same time. When Ripley's first partner passed away, and De Mija's first partner retired, Ripley and De Mija became partners. After a few years of working together, they went from dayshift to graveyard shift: eleven o'clock at night until seven in the morning.

* * *

Out on their late night patrol, Officer De Mija was concentrating on his driving while listening as his partner yakked away.

"So when I looked over at her sitting there with some other girls, she was looking back directly at me. Then she gave me the old *come-on* look. I took my drink and strolled over to her table. Man, what a looker she was. I'm telling you, Leo, you should have seen those bedroom eyes of hers. Anyway, the table was pretty crowded with all these gals, so I asked this looker if she wanted to dance." Ripley broke into laughter and slammed his hand on the dash of the car. "Shit, Leo, when that woman stood up, I was mortified. Why, she must have been your height or taller in her bare feet. It was just my dumb luck that she was wearing three-inch heels on top of it."

"So, what did you do?"

"What could I do? I set my drink on their table and I had to dance with her. And of all the dumb luck, the music the group started playing was one of those slow, romantic ballads. My face rested on her bosom the whole time we danced."

"Well, from what you keep telling me, you're a boob man. So that shouldn't have been too difficult to take."

"Let me tell you, her boobs were nothing to write home about. I might as well have been dancing with a man. Damn, she held me so tight that I couldn't breath. I was so glad when that music was over. After I walked her back to her table, I left the bar immediately. Man, I'll never make that mistake again."

"Give me a break, Dave. You say that after each dumb experience you have with a woman."

"Ha, that's true. Oh well, it makes for a good laugh. Say, I keep forgetting to ask you. How's your stomach been tonight?"

"My stomach?"

"Yeah. When we got the call on that double homicide, you were in the can at the station with the cramps. Remember?"

"Oh, that. The cramps went about as fast as they came. I guess it was something I ate for dinner New Year's night."

"You were in that gas station's john for over an hour before the homicide call came over the radio. I banged on the door, yelling, but you didn't answer me right away. Man, you had me worried. It's a good thing we were close to the crime scene or we couldn't have given immediate response."

Changing the subject, De Mija stated, "I hear the head honcho of the detective's unit, Capt. Joe Warner, came back today."

"Yeah, I heard the same thing. You know both Warner and Konklin are sure nice guys to work with. I never had the opportunity of working with them before the Epstein case. Boy, that was certainly a case of *Have No Mercy*. That Epstein character deserved more time in lock-up than he got."

"I don't seem to remember that case."

"I'll tell you about it sometime."

"I've never had any dealings with Konklin until the double homicides. He seems to be a fun-loving sort of guy that likes to hear his mouth run."

"True. But he knows his job, and he's good at it. What do you think of Warner?"

"I've seen him around, but we've never been officially introduced. Scuttlebutt has it that Warner is pretty straight-laced, doesn't talk much, and has a dry sense of humor. Quite different than Konklin."

"You mean they are sort of like you and me, direct opposites?" Ripley laughed.

"You might say that."

"I'm curious, Leo. What did you have to get out of the trunk of the car the other night when you stopped at the gas station? All you said was that you had cramps and needed something out of the trunk. But you never explained what it was."

"What's with all the questions, Dave? I had a bad stomachache and got a bottle of antacids out of the trunk."

"I didn't know we kept any antacids in the trunk?"

"We don't, normally. I had indigestion all day. So I had been taking them pretty regular. Just in case I needed more of them, I brought the bottle with me and put it in the trunk before we went out on patrol that night."

"Obviously they didn't help."

"Well, I thought they were going to. But suddenly my chest started burning again and my stomach started cramping. When I pulled in the gas station to get them out of the trunk, my instincts told me to get to the can on the double. I didn't have time to stop and explain anything to you. When nature calls, there's no waiting." De Mija's irritation was beginning to show in his voice. "It was no big deal. Really, Dave, my diarrhea is not a conversation I care to share with you. Now, can we drop it?"

"Sure, but you don't have to bite my head off. Partners worry about each other, you know? One would've thought that you could've told me you weren't feeling so well that night before your cramps hit. I could have driven and let you relax in the passenger seat."

"At the time we started on patrol, I didn't have cramps. I just told you, they came on me unexpectedly. Now, please, change the subject."

Somewhat satisfied at his partner's explanation, Ripley gave in to his partner's suggestion. "So, how's the wife and kid doing?"

"Alianna's doing fine. She's talking about wanting another baby. But I don't know if I'm ready or not. My little Fayth is the apple of her daddy's eye. That little stinker could ask me for the moon and I'd move heaven and earth to get it for her. I can still remember the day she was born."

"So can I. You must have given away a cigar to every man, woman and child that crossed your path that day," Ripley joked.

De Mija was quick to defend his actions. "Give me a break, Dave. I never gave a cigar to a child."

"Ease up, Leo. I was only joking."

"That's nothing to joke about."

"It's just that you had a baby rattle tied to every one of those cigars you passed out the day Fayth was born. Shoot, I was beginning to think I had a kook for a partner."

"Yeah. Alianna thought I went a little over the top, too. But I thought it was a clever idea. I was so proud to finally become a father that I wanted everyone to have a remembrance of that day."

"It's a good thing we were on days back then. Or you might have missed Fayth coming into the world."

"Maybe … maybe not. I'm sure Capt. Roberts would have given me time off if I would've needed it."

"I doubt it. I have yet to see the good side of that man. Hey, remember the flack you got for slighting the detective's unit by not offering cigars to any of them?"

"You know as well as I do, Dave, by the time they got to the precinct that morning, you and I were already out on patrol."

"That's only because you were in such a hurry to spread your good news all over our patrol area." Ripley laughed. "You must have bought a gross of those rattles. Did you ever give them all away?"

"No. They're around the house. Somewhere. The cigars are all gone, though."

"What the heck are you saving the rattles for, another baby?"

"I don't know. It's like I said before. I don't think I'm ready to bring another baby into our lives. However, I think if and when the time comes, I'll probably do something different for the next child. I guess I keep those rattles because I'm a sentimentalist. I don't want to throw one thing away that is connected in any way, shape or form when it comes to my little Fayth. She's a real gift from heaven."

"Well, she's lucky to have two parents to raise her. When I think of that poor little boy whose parents got killed recently in that double homicide, it makes me sick to my stomach. Now he'll have to grow up never knowing the love from his mommy and daddy like you and Alianna give to your little girl. What a crying shame."

"Yeah, life is rough. On the other hand, some parents just don't deserve kids because they don't know how to treat them right. God works in strange ways. Maybe God had good reasons for taking the kid's parents? Who knows, maybe they weren't worthy of being parents?"

"That sounds dreadful and very callous, Leo. I seriously don't think you mean that."

"Of course I do. Stop and think about all of the child abuse cases going on in the world today. It sickens me to my very core as a human being."

"It does me too, Leo. But that doesn't mean that parents' lives should be taken by a slayer's hand. That's why we believe in our judicial system. Besides, those victims might have been perfect parents to their kid. We don't know."

"Speak for yourself, Dave. I believe in the uniform I wear and the job I do, but I have no faith in our judicial system. I didn't care much about a lot of things the mob or the vigilantes used to do. But you've gotta admit they took care of an offender the right way."

"You're kidding, I hope?"

"No, I'm dead serious. Think about it. Today we arrest the offenders for whatever the crime is, and we put them in jail. It seems like only a matter of hours and the clown walks because it's only fair in our judicial system that he or she gets out on bail until their trial. A certain percentage of those offenders skip bail. If we're lucky, the convicted offender gets locked up.

"Then we have another percentage of misfits that make plea-bargains for lighter sentences. Either way, they don't even stay behind bars long enough to pay for their crime. It irritates me that they get back on the street so soon. It's like giving them a free ticket to go out and commit another crime. A little slap on the wrists sure doesn't teach them anything. It's cost the taxpayers beau-coup money for the police force to get these bad guys off the streets. Then more money for their court costs. Every time a perp walks, it pisses me off."

As De Mija kept his eyes on the road, occasionally glancing about him, he continued airing his feelings toward American Justice. Ripley listened, keeping his eyes in motion, always watching for anything that looked suspicious.

"Speaking of taxpayers' money, those offenders in prison live better than we do. And we pay the bill. They eat better, have better libraries, and they have all the up-do-date exercise equipment to keep in shape. Most of them even have computers at their disposal. If I sat back and let you support me so I could have all of those things, what would you think of me?"

"I'd probably think of you as a freeloader. But to answer your question, I wouldn't support you."

"Exactly. Yet we, as taxpayers, are all supporting those thieves, murderers, and perverts that cops like you and I help take off the streets. I might not have liked the way I was raised, but I learned a long time ago that you don't get rewarded for doing wrong. No, I retract that statement. The reward for breaking the law should be strict and severe punishment just like I was taught growing up. The perps today have it made. No, don't tell me our judicial system works. Huh-uh. I'll take the mob way of dealing with offenders, any day."

"If that's how you truly believe, why are you wearing a uniform?"

Lost in his own thoughts, not wishing to discuss the issue any further, De Mija never answered.

 CHAPTER SEVEN

"Hey, Joe. You're here bright and early this morning," Konklin greeted, entering the captain's office. "Trying to get a head start on me?"

"Sort of. I wanted to go over your reports before we go out this morning. Coffee's hot. Help yourself."

After removing his overcoat and suit jacket, Konklin tossed them over a chair. "Geez, it's so cold out there this morning, it almost took my breath away. Do you need a refill?"

Handing his coffee mug across the desk, he responded, "I'd love one. I'm almost done here."

Quietly, Konklin returned to the desk with two coffee-filled mugs. He set Warner's cup within his reach, then sat in his favorite chair.

"Thanks. Well, I've finished reading all of your reports."

After taking a sip of coffee, Konklin moaned. "Umm."

"Was that moan because I finished the reports or for the coffee?" Warner asked, smiling.

"The coffee, of course." Konklin cupped his hands around the warm mug. "There's nothing like a hot cup of coffee to warm the cold body."

"At least we don't have any snow yet."

Konklin shivered. "It can stay away all winter as far as I'm concerned. Sometimes I wonder why I don't move to a warmer climate."

"Because you'd miss me. That's why?"

"Hardy, har, har. Well, did you find anything in my reports that you have questions about?"

"Not a thing. They're solid, detailed reports just like you always write."

"That's good to hear."

"I stopped by the ME's office this morning. Jerry was just opening shop."

"I think you've been here long enough to call him Saggy like the rest of us do."

"That's really an unusual name for a medical examiner. I'm guessing it comes from his last name Sagdorf?"

"Right. When I first came to the 15th, a few detectives were calling him Dorf. No one called him that to his face, but evidently he got wind of it." Konklin laughed. "He didn't care much for that kind of a handle, which I can't blame him. He sent out a memo to all the Mt. Pride precincts and informed everyone that he'd been called Saggy since he was in med school. And that's the name he preferred to be called. So from then on that's what everyone's been calling him. I'm surprised he hasn't said anything to you when you call him Jerry."

"Nope. He's never said a word. I don't blame him for not liking the name Dorf. If anyone called me Dorf," Warner chuckled, "they'd eat my knuckle sandwich. Anyway, Saggy said he had some information on your case."

"Great. Let's hear it."

"He confirmed what Colt told you. Both vics bled out from their jugular veins being severed. He was too busy to go into detail, but he did say the perp was left-handed."

"So we're looking for a southpaw?"

"Yes. Something else Saggy said puzzles me."

"What's that?"

"He doesn't think the wounds were made by a regular straight-edge weapon. Because of the entrance and exit wounds, he believes we're looking for a curved blade."

"Crap. That could be any number of things."

"Oh, really? Give me one example."

"How about an envelope opener?"

"Straight-edged."

"Maybe in your eyes. A sickle?"

"That's much too large to cut a throat. Hell, that would take off a person's head."

"Okay, how about a … a … oh, I don't know, Joe. But there has to be something that's sharp and curved that can be used as a murder weapon. If the perp found it, then so can we."

"Well, at least we can rule out straight-edged knives and razors."

"A thought just struck me. In all the years I've been here, I never knew Saggy worked on Sundays."

"Funny, I said the same thing to him. He only works Sundays when he's overbooked." Warner chuckled.

"Overbooked? That's a strange way of saying he's backlogged."

"That was his word. Not mine. Eddy, before we go any further on this case, let's get something straight. I kind of took over your case when I got back and I want to apologize."

"I don't think you did. No apology necessary. However, as far as I'm concerned, that's what you're supposed to do."

"No, it isn't — unless, of course, you weren't doing your job. As your captain, I have the right to oversee all cases the detectives work on. And I can get involved on occasion. However, since you're doing a good job on this case, you're still the lead. As I told you yesterday, I'll continue to work with you but only until we get you a new partner. Understood?"

"Geez, Joe, I don't mind you taking the helm. Really." Konklin took a few hefty gulps of coffee, then got to his feet. "Hate to break up our gab session, but we've got work to do."

* * *

It took most of the day, but Warner and Konklin managed to find most of the Brooks' neighbors at home. The detectives asked basic questions about seeing or hearing anything strange or unusual in the neighborhood the night of the murders, especially around the Brook house. They also inquired as to the character of the Brooks.

The negative responses to anything out of the ordinary in the night or early morning hours in question didn't give them anything to go on. The Brooks were considered wonderful neighbors: friendly and helpful. And they both appeared to be stern but excellent parents.

Back in the car, Warner said, "Well, the canvassing wasn't very fruitful as far as the case is concerned."

"You can say that again. Why don't we call it a day?"

"I agree. What's on the agenda tomorrow?"

"An interview with Pat Brook's employer. I have an appointment scheduled in his office at nine o'clock."

 **CHAPTER EIGHT**

On Monday morning, Warner and Konklin walked into the offices of the Abcon Family Life Insurance Company where the deceased, Pat Brook, had been employed.

Stopping at the receptionist's desk, Konklin stated, "Detectives Warner and Konklin to see Mr. Abcon. I believe we're expected."

"Yes," the young lady replied. "One moment please." From her desk phone, she contacted her boss. "Mr. Abcon, the two detectives you were expecting have arrived. Certainly." After hanging up the phone and getting to her feet, she said, "Come with me, Detectives. I'll take you to Mr. Abcon's office."

They followed the young lady through the large outer office, as Warner took in the surroundings. It amazed him that almost everyone in the room was dressed in dark colors. This was not exceptionally unusual for winter dress, but he found it unusual that there was not one bit of color. Drab browns and blacks seemed to tell him these people were in mourning for their departed co-worker.

As they passed by an empty desk, he noted it was covered with of an assortment of single-stemmed flowers. A large black bow was tied around the desk's chair. Now it was more than obvious to Warner that his suspicions were right. The entire office was in bereavement over losing a fellow employee.

A gray-haired, distinguished looking man dressed in a black suit greeted Warner and Konklin. " Good morning, Detectives." Hand outstretched, he introduced himself. "I'm Fredrick G. Abcon, the owner and president of this company. Please step into my office and make yourselves comfortable."

After thanking his receptionist, Mr. Abcon closed his office door. Once the detectives had taken seats in the two chairs directly in front of his desk, Mr. Abcon sat in his large, executive desk chair.

"Which one of you is Lt. Konklin?"

"I am."

Not giving Konklin a chance to introduce him, Warner quickly stated, "I'm Capt. Warner."

"I'm sorry it has to be under such dire circumstances, Detectives. Nevertheless, I am pleased to meet both of you."

Konklin began the interview. "We don't want to take up too much of your time, Mr. Abcon. But we would like some information on your former employee, Pat Brook."

"Yes, so you stated in your phone call. Well, there's not much I can tell you. Pat was here for about six years and was responsible for selling a big share of our insurance policies. He was a good employee. Always prompt."

"How did he get along with his fellow employees?"

"Excellent. We all loved Pat around here. He was personable, dependable, and always in a good mood. Yes, I can honestly say we all thought very highly of Pat." Shaking his head, Mr. Abcon picked up a pencil and started playing with it. "I just can't believe what happened. It seems one is no longer safe in the confines of their own home any more. Anyway, I don't know what more I can tell you."

"Can you think of anyone Mr. Brook had dealings with that might have had a beef with him or a grudge against him?"

"Not one person comes to mind. According to the feedback I get from our clients, they only had praise for Pat. I got more compliments about his pleasing personality and congenial manner than I did for anyone else on my sales staff. In fact, clients would call and specifically ask for Pat."

"Did Mr. Brook work on a salary or on a commission basis?" Warner asked.

"All my sales staff are paid a basic salary. They are also paid a commission each month based on the number of policies they sell. Why is that important?"

"If he was your top policy writer, he obviously got paid a bigger commission. That would tend to make a co-worker jealous, wouldn't you say?"

Dropping the pencil on his desk, Mr. Abcon asked, "What are you suggesting? Just because he made more money, one of his co-workers killed him in a jealous rage?"

"I didn't say that. I was only speculating that such a situation might make others envious of him," Warner stated.

"Well, I hate to disagree with your speculation, Capt. Warner, but you're way off-base. Pat would pass on his leads many times to the other insurance reps. He shared with them. And I know they appreciated it. No, there was absolutely no jealousy toward Pat Brook amongst any of my employees.

"As a matter of fact, that reminds me of something. Last year, when Pat celebrated his five-year tenure with us, the office crew and the sales personnel all chipped in to send him and his wife on a weekend skiing trip. One of the ladies in my office even took on the task of babysitting free for their youngster that weekend. Each and every employee in my office signed the congratulatory card. Now, no one gives you such a wonderful present if they are jealous of you or have an intense dislike for you."

Just because someone signs a card or gives a donation for a gift of a trip doesn't necessarily mean they aren't covering their tracks for future plans, Warner thought.

"I can give you another example of the camaraderie around here. When anyone in the office was in need of a helping hand, especially financially, Pat was the first one to offer his services and reach into his pocket. I hope you catch the person that did kill those two beautiful people. But I'll stake my reputation on the fact that you won't find their murderer amongst my employees."

Satisfied Pat Brook had no enemies among the insurance company's staff, both detectives thanked Mr. Abcon for his time. Outside, as they walked toward their car, they chatted.

"That was certainly a dead-end, huh, Joe?"

"It looks like it."

"Well, we're back to square one when it comes to motive or suspect. Except for Ellie Smither."

"Even though she's got motive and opportunity, Joe, we have no evidence that places her at the crime scene."

"Not yet, you mean?"

"True. All we can do is to wait for the info from the ME and the crime lab."

"Do you have any indication as to how long that will take?"

"Nope. We just have to wait in line."

"Well, let's figure out how to get to the front of the line, Eddy. So, what's next on your 'to-do' list for today?"

"I'd like to swing by the Brook house and check out Shelby's office," Konklin replied. "Hopefully, she'll have a list of her clients recorded somewhere in her paperwork or on her computer. They're the next group of people I think we should check out."

* * *

After close to a week of telephone calls, Konklin felt as though his ears were going to fall off. During that time, Warner kept busy with his normal tasks as chief of detectives.

Reaching for his phone, Konklin made an inner-office call. "Are you busy?"

"I'm always busy. What's up?"

"Thought I'd come to your office since we haven't had a chance to talk since Monday."

"My door's open."

* * *

Flopping into a chair, it was obvious Konklin was frustrated. "Banging into all these brick walls is giving me a headache," he complained, rubbing the top of his head.

"There's not much up there now, big guy. If you keep rubbing your head like that, those last few hairs will disappear like the rest of it." Warner laughed.

After a grunting chuckle, Konklin asked, "Why do you suppose we get bald on top first? I mean, why can't we keep the hair on top and start getting bald from the neck up?" Getting a very strange look from Warner, who could not keep from laughing at the absurdity of his questions, Konklin got back to business. "I called every last name on Shelby Brook's contract list. A week of nothing but phone calls — and not one single lead.

Everyone I talked to spoke highly of both victims."

"So both were extremely well-liked by everyone they came in contact with? Sounds like Ozzie and Harriet."

"Sure does. I didn't think there were such perfect people around. Geez, I hope I have at least half that amount of admirable comments about me when I go."

"Dreamer," Warner said with a laugh. Konklin gave him a smirk. "Just kidding, big guy. Just kidding. Seriously, the Brooks couldn't have been a perfect family. Not after what Ellie Smither told us."

"But she's the only one that had anything bad to say about them."

"I doubt if Pat Brook ever let his temper show around anyone other than his wife and kid. That's why everyone else is speaking so highly of them."

"That's probably true. Don't you get tired, at times, listening to all the homicides on the national news? I just don't understand what this world is coming to, Joe."

"I don't know what's happening today either. But I have my own theory."

"Let's hear it."

"Nah, you'd just laugh at me like Jeny does."

"I might, and I might not. Give," Konklin persisted.

"Well, if you believe in the Bible, like I do, we all came from Adam and Eve. Therefore, we are all related in one way or another. I believe Noah and his wife were somehow related to Adam and Eve. So even the big flood didn't wipe away the family genes. It just stands to reason, in my way of thinking, that eventually our world ends up with a lot of crazies."

"How do you come to that conclusion, Joe?"

"They always say that first cousins shouldn't marry. If they do, however, they definitely should never have children. If they have children — and I've never looked up the statistics — but my guess is most of those children end up with some form of a mental problem. I tell you, Eddy, it's going to hit every one of our generations. Someday, all the sane people will be dead and the insane will rule the world."

"I'd say we have a few of those insane types running our world right now." Konklin chuckled.

"Isn't that the truth?"

While stretching, Konklin checked the time. Getting to his feet, he remarked, "It's after six. Time to close up my office and head for home. There's not too much I can do around here since we don't have any reports yet. So, I don't plan on working this weekend."

"Good for you. Who's on call this weekend?"

"Yours truly." Konklin chuckled. When he got to the door, he stopped and turned. "Where does the time go, Joe? Did you ever stop to think how time disappears faster as you get older?"

"Not really. But, when I get to your age, chubby cheeks, I'll think about it."

"Yeah? Well don't look now but you're not too far behind me."

"Get out of here and go home, Eddy."

"Have a good weekend, my friend. Give Jeny and Amandalee my love. I'll see you on Monday."

"I will. Let's pray we get a lead on our perp. I hate the thought of murderer walking the streets thinking he committed the perfect crime."

CHAPTER NINE

At his desk, Konklin was deeply engrossed in reading an article in the morning newspaper. Out of the silence Warner walked into the office and yelled, "Hey, Eddy."

"Ah geez, Joe," Konklin rumbled, leaping about a foot off his chair. "Are you trying to give me heart failure?"

Laughing, Warner said, "No. But I bet you could use some toilet paper or a change of shorts right about now."

"Cut it out, Joe, or you'll be sorry. Remember, I know how to get even with you," Konklin joked back with a grunting laugh. "What's with the surprise visit and the outburst?"

"I've come up with a way to get to the front of the line. You've been around a lot longer than I have, which means you know more people than I do."

"What the heck are you talking about?"

"By people, I mean those we work with from to time like the crime lab techs."

"So?"

"So get on the horn and find out what's holding up our crime lab report."

"Geez, Joe, those techs are busy with other cases, too. They just can't drop everything to get our test results done. Most times it takes several months before we get any reports back. As captain, you aren't supposed to forget things like that."

"Don't be silly. Of course I haven't forgotten. But we've never had a double murder like this before. I just think the crime lab needs a bit of a nudge in our direction."

"You have a bad habit of asking me to use my influence, you know?"

"Come on, Eddy. You can't tell me you haven't done a favor or two for one of those lab techs."

"Well …." Konklin gave a sheepish look.

"See, I knew it. Well, big guy, can't you call in a marker? Maybe just a little one?"

"Okay. Close my door, sit down and I'll see what I can do." After dialing the lab's number, Konklin responded to the voice on the other end of the phone. "This is Lt. Detective Konklin from the 15th. Is Ben Mullins there? Sure, I'll hold." After a few seconds wait, Konklin said, "Ben, my man. This is Eddy over at the 15th. How are you? Yeah, it's been a while. I'm doing just great. How about you? Good. Good. Yes. Hey, you know better than to be listening to rumors. Ha! Ha!" Konklin let out a grunting laugh. "Yes, it's true. Oh? Well speak for yourself.

"Say, Ben, who's working on the evidence from my precinct? Yes, the double homicide. You don't say. Well, good buddy, do you have a report for us yet? I realize that, Ben. If you can do some maneuvering to move us to the top of the list, we'd sure appreciate it." As Konklin listened, he began to laugh again. "Yes. Yes, I'm on the case. Who am I working the case with? My boss and head of the detective's unit here, Capt. Warner. Why? No. Let's just say we needed it yesterday. Does that answer your question?"

Looking at Warner and giving him a wink, Konklin continued his attempt at persuasion. "Look, Ben, if you know anything about Warner, you know he is a very impatient man. Come on, I know you're swamped. You know I hate to remind you, but you still owe me a couple. You bet I am. Really? Yeah, that's great. No, we won't call it even. Oh, yeah? What about that blonde? Okay, Ben, I really appreciate it. Thanks. Yeah, you too."

Hanging up the phone, he gestured thumbs up. "Okay, Joe, he'll have the report delivered by nine tomorrow morning."

Warner puckered up and smacked his lips together, gesturing a kiss for Konklin. "I love ya, chubby cheeks."

"Get out." Konklin laughed.

"A blonde, huh?"

"Someday we'll have a few beers together, Joe, and I'll tell you all about it."

As soon as Warner left his office, Konklin rushed out of the precinct to make an unscheduled visit. In hopes the crime lab's report included some valuable fingerprints, he needed two more sets of prints to be compared to prints discovered at the crime scene: Kate and Ellie Smither.

"I would have had plenty of time to get their prints to the lab if Joe hadn't been so persistent. Now I can only hope I get them there before Ben completes his analysis and writes up his report," Konklin mumbled as he drove to the Smithers' house.

* * *

"I knew I shouldn't have said anything."

"Hush, Ellie. Lt. Konklin, why do you need our fingerprints?" Kate asked.

Ellie didn't give Konklin a chance to answer. "You know why as well as I do, Mom. The police think I'm a suspect and you're probably my accomplice. Right, Detective?"

Many detectives let a person know from the get-go that he or she is a suspect in a crime. Not Lt. Konklin. As far as he was concerned, the time for accusations is after there is more concrete evidence against that person. Konklin had also seen too many suspects flee the area once they were confronted.

So, Konklin lied when he answered, "No, Ellie, you aren't suspects.

Since you both stated you have been in the Brooks' house almost on a daily basis, we know your prints will be in the house. But we need them to compare with other prints so we can eliminate yours."

Convinced they were not suspects in the Brook murders, Kate and Ellie allowed the detective to take their fingerprints. After documenting the prints, Konklin rushed the information to the crime lab.

* * *

The following morning, Warner was at the front desk when Konklin walked in. "Morning, Eddy."

"Good morning, Joe. Brrr." His whole body shivered. "Have I ever told you how much I hate this cold weather?"

"Unfortunately, several times," Warner joked, grinning.

"Where's the Desk Sergeant?"

"Gleason's in the back checking on something for me."

"Any of the other detectives in yet?"

"Not that I know of, but I haven't been upstairs yet."

"Well, guess I'll go on up and get our community coffeepot started."

"One of the detectives should be in shortly. Let them do it."

"Can't wait. Need a hot cup to warm up and the sooner the better."

"Then make a pot in my office. I have a few things to do first, but I'll be there shortly."

"I'm wise to you, Joe Warner. You just want me to make your coffee for you."

"Darn, am I that transparent?" Warner laughed.

"Sometimes."

"Seriously, I need to talk to you before the day gets into full bloom around here."

* * *

When Warner got to his office, his favorite mug filled with fresh coffee was sitting on his desk. Konklin was not there. After getting situated for his morning business, Konklin walked in the door, coffee mug in hand.

"It must have been morning constitutional time," Warner remarked.

"Aw, come on, Joe." Konklin took a seat. "Do you have to tease me about my bodily functions all the time?"

"Sure I do, big guy. You couldn't stand to be around me if I was a mean old banty rooster."

Both had a good laugh to start off their morning.

"Were you able to get in contact with Shelby's parents?"

"Yes. The telephone is a terrible way to hear your daughter has just been murdered. After answering all the questions I felt they needed to know at this point, I told them I would keep them informed when we caught the perpetrator."

"That's news no parent ever wants to hear by phone or in person, Eddy."

"I gave them Jill Maloy's number so they can make arrangements to pick up Jimmy. Thank heavens Jill hadn't contacted them before I did. I'm sure I would have never heard the end of it."

"So what about Pat's parents? Have you been able to contact them yet?"

"Actually, Shelby's father, Mr. Peterson, said he knows them very well. He asked if he could be the one to tell them. I don't envy him the task, but I naturally said he could."

"That was nice of him to offer."

"Yeah. I left my name and number in case any of them could think of anyone who may have had a grudge against either of their kids. Right off hand they couldn't think of anyone but said they'd ask Pat's parents."

"Good."

"Oh, and guess what I found out yesterday? It's going to knock your socks off."

"It's too early for guessing games, Eddy. What's up?"

"About an hour after to speaking to Shelby's parents, I get this phone call. The female ID's herself as Sylvia Lufton, Shelby's sister. Said she had just spoken with her father about Shelby's murder. Her father asked her if she knew anyone who might have had a vendetta against Shelby or Pat." Konklin stopped to take a drink of coffee.

"Don't leave me hanging, Eddy. Where are you going with this?"

"Seems Sylvia was in town just a few weeks before the murders. While here, she stayed with Shelby because Pat was out of town. She happened to walk in on a scene that sickened her. The point is, Shelby and Ellie were lovers."

"What!"

"I told you the news would knock your socks off. Sylvia said she told her sister she needed to get her head on straight. Either she admit she's a lesbian and divorce Pat, which meant the possibility of losing her son. Or she stop the affair."

"Damn, Eddy, do you realize what this means? This is even a better motive for murder than protecting an abusive child. Shelby couldn't afford to lose her son. So, she told Ellie the affair was over. Ellie probably responded in fury, threatening to kill her. And, kill Pat, too, just to get even. I just knew something was troubling Ellie — when we interviewed her— by her facial expressions. She was probably thinking up the story she told us instead of revealing herself by admitting the truth."

"Your theory is convincing me more and more that Ellie could be our perp."

"What's on your mind for a follow-up?"

"I plan on digging into Ellie's background."

"Good plan, Eddy."

"After we get the crime lab's report, I'm going back to see Kate."

"Why?"

"I want to look around her house for black tulips."

"Without a warrant you know you can't do that."

"I'm not going in to search the place," Konklin defended. "But I'll think of some way to get Kate to show me around her house."

"Good luck. So, what else is on your calendar for the week?"

As the detectives talked, they had gone through a pot of coffee and were starting on the second pot. Before they had realized it, almost two hours had gone by.

Warner looked at his watch, comparing the time to the clock on the wall. "It's exactly nine A.M. Where in the hell is that lab report?"

"Patience, Joe. Geez, for a man who keeps telling me not to worry about things, you're worse than a child waiting for daybreak on Christmas morning."

"When someone says the report will be delivered at nine A.M., I expect them to keep their word."

"Ben is always a few minutes late. He's a bit of a slow mover. So, how was your weekend?"

The men made small talk as the seconds ticked by: 9:01, 9:02, 9:03, 9:04, 9:05. When it got to 9:15, Warner's disappointment was even more inflated. "Fifteen minutes late. This is ridiculous. What do you suppose the friggin' hang-up is? That report should've been --"

He was interrupted by the knock at the door by a female uniformed officer. Moving from his chair, Konklin opened the door.

Handing Konklin a large manila envelope, the officer said, "This was delivered at the front desk for you, Detective Konklin."

"Just what we've been waiting for. Thank you."

"Sorry for the delay. But when you didn't answer your office door, I had to ask around to find out if you had come in yet."

Overhearing the conversation, Warner got up and opened his blinds to the outer office. *Really stupid, Joe. How's anyone to know you're in your office with the blinds closed and the door shut?*

"No apology necessary." After signing a receipt of delivery, Konklin thanked the officer and closed the door. He walked over to the desk and handed Warner the envelope. "Here. You can have the pleasure." Then he returned to his chair.

After opening the envelope, Warner emptied the contents on his desk. The items included the lab report, the evidence bag with the rattle and card inside, and several photographs of the crime scene.

Konklin sat squirming in his seat in anticipation of the report revealing some red-hot leads in the case.

Tossing the envelope aside, Warner picked up the report. "I'm not going to read this to you, word for word."

"Not unless you want to bore me to death," Konklin joked. "I know how detailed those reports can be. So, just break it down for me."

"The note was written on medium-weight, white card stock, two and one-half inches wide by approximately three inches long. Conclusion, it's half of a three-by-five index card that was cut in half. From the uneven edge on one side of the card, they concluded the card was hand-cut with scissors. No prints were found on the card.

"From the impression around the small hole in the card where the ribbon is threaded, it was made by a single hole-punch. Due to the print type, the note was printed from a computer using a bubble-jet printer.

"It seems the miniature rattle is a decoration, not a child's toy. Made of pink and white plastic with a pink satin ribbon, the item was made in Japan. No prints were found on either the rattle or the ribbon."

Looking up from the report, Warner complained, "Oh, that's just great. It sounds like this rattle is a dime a dozen. One can probably be purchased at any superstore, card store, or any store that sells party decorations, baby items, or kid's party favors. And I won't even venture to guess how many stores sell office supplies and printers."

"As usual, we've got our work cut out for us. What else does it say?"

"The blood found on the lamp was nominal but enough for DNA analysis. Forensics lifted some hair and skin particles from the lamp. The DNA proved positive to the ME's sample from the female victim, Shelby Brook. All the other blood found in the room where the bodies were discovered positively matched the DNA of both Pat and Shelby Brook.

"Several prints were found on the lamp. Comparison proved conclusive the prints belonged to Pat Brook, Shelby Brook and Ellie Smither. Hot damn, Eddy. Did you hear that? That places Ellie at the scene of the crime."

"Yes, it does. To me, however, that's not conclusive evidence that Ellie killed the Brooks. Her prints would naturally be found in a house she worked in, babysat and slept in from time to time, and helped clean?"

"And obviously had an affair in."

"True. I'm still not convinced, though. This is only circumstantial evidence you're basing her guilt on."

"Are you telling me you're ruling her out?"

Konklin grinned. "No. Just disagreeing with you."

"You're entitled."

"Anything about the brick?"

"I'm getting to that. The brick they confiscated from the bedroom floor garnished no prints. The tape found on the window glass was your ordinary black duct tape. No prints there either.

"They lifted several fingerprints throughout the house. Most belonged to Pat and Shelby Brook. Several were identified as belonging to Kate and Ellie Smither. Several were identified as a child's print. Some they couldn't identify. But after running the unidentified prints through the national data base, there were no matches."

"None of the unidentified prints would belong to our perp. If he went to such great effort not to leave prints on his calling card or the lamp, he certainly wouldn't be stupid enough to leave prints all over the house," Konklin stated.

"I'm guessing the other prints belonged to the Brooks' New Year's Day party guests."

"That sounds reasonable. And the child's prints have to belong to Jimmy."

"I'd say that's a given.

"The traces of glass on the brick were too minute to render it the item that broke the window."

"So the brick was placed there in an attempt to fool us?"

"It appears so. Looks like we'll still be looking for a murder weapon, too. The traces of blood found on the knife in the kitchen sink proved to be animal blood. The DNA belonged to a bovine. Damn."

"After what Saggy reported, I thought we both had already ruled out knives."

"Just straight-edged knives, Eddy. For all we know, there's still a curved-shape knife out there we aren't aware of.

"Blood analysis proved the only blood at the scene belonged to Pat and Shelby Brook. The trace evidence they found in the room, especially on the pillows and bedding, belonged to the victims. And, last but not least, no evidence was found around the exterior of the home. So, that's basically it. What do you think?"

"That the perp is smart."

"Smart, yes. But we've got to be smarter. It seems this perpetrator doesn't like to see children get abused. He knows how to use a computer. And he likes to shop for party favors."

"And, he thinks he's a poet," Konklin chimed in. "You know, we always assume a perp is a male."

"True. But in this case, the calling card backs us up." Picking up the card, Warner chose a few words to reference. "'He's viewed. He strikes.'"

"Couldn't that just be a trick to throw us off like the brick? After all, you're the one that's trying to convince me Ellie Smither is our number one suspect."

"Damn, Eddy. I love it when you're right. However, I'm beginning to think this perp has a huge, twisted ego. He wants us to know he's a male."

"But a woman would be more apt to protect a child from an unkindly parent than a man would. Call it a mother's instinct to protect the children in this world."

"Shelby certainly didn't protect her son. However, the term figuratively speaking comes to mind. So, until we can prove otherwise, let's keep referring to the perpetrator in the male gender. It's less confusing."

"Maybe there's more than one perp? Two could attack a couple faster than one person could. Right?"

"That's another possibility. It gives us something to think about, that's for sure. Okay, it's time to call in assistance. Since we don't have time to send out a memo, I'll leave it to you to spread the word. Inform the unit there will be a meeting in the conference room today at three. Anyone who is available needs to be there, especially those in the homicide division.

The board didn't look too full this morning, but things could have changed since we arrived. We'll just have to wait and see how many detectives show up."

"Are you sure you want to wait until three, Joe?"

"Affirmative. I have lots of work to get caught up on."

"I thought you were caught up?"

"That's a laugh. You know as well as I do how much paperwork is generated around here each day. And lucky me, I get the privilege as captain to read it all. No wonder most captains stay in their office all day. All it takes is one day out on a case and you're three days behind in your office work," Warner complained in a pleasing manner.

* * *

Konklin just reached the top of the steps when he spotted Warner heading for the conference room. "Joe. Wait up."

Stopping, Warner's head turned toward Konklin's voice. "Glad you made it back in time. The meeting starts in ten minutes."

"I know." Konklin parked his rear on the edge of the nearest desk.

"Were you able to go through Kate's house without raising any suspicion?"

"You bet. With a bit of charm and lots of flattery."

"That figures. What exactly did you say?"

"I don't remember the exact words I used. But I started out by mentioning how lovely her house was. Then asked if I could get the grand tour. She was more than happy to oblige."

"Any black tulips?"

"Much to my surprise, yes."

"Serious?"

"Serious. Kate had three pots of them sitting in one of her kitchen windows. I mentioned to her how unusual they were. Then I asked her where she got them. She told me she had discovered them in a garden catalogue a few years back. So, she ordered some of the bulbs. And has been growing them ever since."

"Damn, you never cease to amaze me, Eddy. Let's get to the conference room. We can discuss more about this later."

* * *

Standing on a small stage behind a podium, Warner looked over the small group he would be addressing. He was proud of his whole division. Even though he could pull any one of them from his pool to place on any kind of assignment, he knew which detective excelled in which investigative capacity. Every one of his detective staff was well trained in all aspects of crimes. Some detectives were just a little more detailed than others.

The small group, including Konklin, whom he had called together today, was the cream of the crop when it came to homicide investigative work. With a double homicide to solve, he needed the best.

Black Tulip: Have No Mercy IV

As the detectives talked to one another, Konklin approached the front of the podium. "Looks like a pretty good turn out, Joe. Are you ready to start?"

Warner nodded.

Facing the room, Konklin addressed the group in a loud voice. "Let's quiet down, you clowns. We don't want Cap to ruin his vocal cords yelling above your chatter."

A few snickers were heard. Then silence. Konklin returned to his chair at the front table.

Warner brought the meeting to order. "I'd like to start by thanking you all for showing up. This is a better turnout than I expected.

"I know you're all aware, due to the loss of Detective Anderson, we've had an opening for another detective in the homicide division. We're supposed to run on a twenty-five-man crew. So I'm anxious to fill that empty chair. It's surprising how much extra work you have with one person missing. But I do appreciate all of you carrying the extra load without complaint.

"Eventually, I want to give this cop the same basic, all around training that every detective in this unit has had. The good news is, we finally got our new budget approved to allow us the added expense of a new detective. I guess the brass finally got tired of my ugly mug every time I showed up to complain how short-handed we were," he quipped.

"It's about time, Cap," Anthony commented from the back of the room. "Some of us were beginning to think the big boys used our money on the renovation of the downtown headquarters."

Warner chuckled. "Believe me, I was beginning to think the same thing. Fortunately, that wasn't the case. It seems the powers that run the finances took our detective allocation to spend on the officer unit here at the 15th. To be fair, let's just say they borrowed the money from us. Capt. Roberts needed more uniforms on the street, so I hold no animosity.

"Anyway, we have it back. Now we can move forward. I have a couple of good prospects in mind. As soon as I make my final decision, I will let you all know. I'm sure you ladies will get the word out but --" Warner had to wait until the interruptive laughter quieted down. Then he continued. "I'll be sending around a memo in regards to this matter, so those not in attendance today will be informed.

"Now, the lieutenant needs help on the double homicide he's working on. Until further notice, I will be working directly with him on this case. I brought you here today because we need to form our team. Since I haven't had a chance to completely read all of the updated reports on my desk, I'll need you leads to brief me when I call on you.

"Arjay, how are you and Kieyell doing on that mugging over on Moon Street?"

"We brought our alleged mugger in about an hour ago, Cap," Mayfield responded. "He's locked up awaiting arraignment. As soon as we get our report typed up and printed out, we're free for another assignment."

"Okay. Tony, how are you and Mike situated?"

DelGinny shook his head. "We've got Anthony and Brubaker working with us, Cap. So our case is still an ongoing investigation. But we're stalled and need your advice."

"Then stay put. We'll talk after the meeting. By the way, where is Mike?"

"An emergency came up, Cap. Holms apologized for not being able to make it to the meeting."

"What kind of an emergency?"

"His little boy was rushed to the hospital after falling on the ice. I told him I'd cover for him."

"Well, let's hope the little monkey will be all right. Brenda, how's it going with you and J.B.?"

"We're available, Cap. Our last case is all wrapped up," Ferndale replied.

"How about the paperwork?"

"Completed. After the meeting, our report will be on your desk."

"Good. Arnie, what's on yours and Eric's plate?"

"Nothing at present. I'm free, but remember I'm still working solo," Hathaway stated.

"Oh, that's right. Eric is still out on sick leave."

"Yes, Cap."

"Not a problem. You'll just have to work twice as hard," Warner quipped.

Hathaway smiled.

"Mitch and Dirk. I know you two don't normally work homicides, and I'm happy to see you here. But I thought I saw your names still on the board. Did you close your case already?"

"Sorry, Cap. No," Smith apologized. "We're still all tied up."

"Why are you here then? Or do you need some help, too?"

"No." Smith looked at his partner for help. "Dirk, you're the one that told me we needed to be here. So, why are we?"

"We heard you were holding a meeting, Cap. So," Jones shrugged, "here we are."

"Then get your Smith and Jones butts out of here and get back to your case," Warner commanded, giving a wink. As the two detectives hurried out the door, Warner continued. "Okay. Ferndale, Brown and Hathaway, you three will be working on this case until further notice. We need a few more on this team. So the rest of you, after you close your cases let the lieutenant know you're available to join us."

In a jovial manner, Roitstein asked, "What about us, Cap? Or are you giving me and Arjay a vacation because we're such a special team?"

Mayfield promptly took off his old, slouch hat and hit Roitstein over the head with it.

Warner could not believe he had forgotten about Mayfield and Roitstein's availability. Faint chuckling scattered about the room as Warner replied, "Special team? Somebody bring in the cleaning crew. The crap is getting a bit too deep in here." Using hand gestures, Warner got the group to settle down. "Kieyell, as soon as I have your report on my desk, we definitely want you and Arjay on this task force."

"You got us, Cap."

Turning his attention to Konklin, Warner stated, "Lieutenant, the floor is yours."

Warner stood to one side as Konklin took the podium.

Holding up a clear plastic evidence bag Konklin proceeded. "This is a rattle. But it's a decorative item. Not a baby's toy. We believe this was purposely left at the crime scene by our perp. When you came in, each of you were given a packet regarding this case. The CSIs were good enough to make a blow-up of the photo. I had several copies made. So there should be one in each packet along with pertinent information concerning it. If you don't have any of the info I will be talking about, please let me know at the end of the meeting. I'll see that you get copies.

"Brenda, J.B., your first assignment will be to check any type of store, large or small, that carries this exact item. I don't need to give you a list of the types of stores that might carry this item. I'm sure your common sense will dictate where to look." Konklin stopped to clear his throat. "For all of you joining this task force, this is going to take a lot of footwork. So be prepared. Those of you with flat feet, I suggest you stock up on the Epson Salts."

"Can we put that on our expense report, Lieu?" Roitstein asked, covering his head in anticipation of his partner hitting him again with the hat.

"Sure, right along with your new Lamborghini."

Roitstein's response, "Don't I wish," could barely be heard above the laughter.

"Back to the rattle. Start your search first in our precinct area. Then work out from there. Make sure you speak to the managers of each store you go to. Show them the picture so they know exactly what we're looking for. A good store manager knows his or her merchandise. However, if the managers can't help you, ask to speak to the merchandise buyers. This might not give us immediate help, but in the long run, our efforts should pay off.

"You'll notice the rattle is attached to a small business-like card. This card is a little wider in size and made of cheaper stock paper than a normal business card. This is believed to be a plain white, three-by-five index card that has been cut in half. Unless we get nowhere with other leads, the card will be the last item we check out. I'm only bringing it to your attention now because of the printing on it.

"Even though we have the blown-up photos, I noticed the printing on the card is difficult to read. I'll read it out loud to give you an idea as to this perp's frame of mind." After reading the information on the card, Konklin continued with his briefing. "Forensics tested the ink and print on the card. The print came from a bubble-jet printer. For now, Arnie, this will be your assignment. I'm certain Eric will help you when he gets back. From what I hear around the unit, you two are computer nerds. So this should be right up your alley. From every store you visit, we'll want a list of customer's names that have purchased bubble-jet printers. Other than credit card receipts, let's just hope there are such records. The same goes for you, too, Brenda and J.B."

All three officers nodded in acceptance.

"We have one suspect in this case. Ellie Smither. Arjay, I want you and Kieyell to dig into her past. I want to know everything about her from the day she was born. Stop by my office after the meeting and I'll fill you in on what I know about her so far.

"Okay, bear with me. As I know most of you are aware of what went down on this case, some of this will be repetitive of what you've already heard. Here's what we have to date." Konklin proceeded to inform the detectives of the who, what, where, when, and how of the case. As he spoke, some of the detectives took notes.

"As soon as we can get done following these leads, or we get more help, we need to start checking out the high schools and the one college in the area. We'll be looking for a student or past student who is or has taken courses in creative writing. It goes without saying that our perp could be new in town or a transient. Right now, however, we feel our best bet is to check out our long-time residents first.

"We'll also need the local home and garden nurseries and floral shops checked out. In particular, we're looking for names of those who have purchased black tulips, either in bulb form or as a fresh-cut flower.

"The captain and I will be busy checking into the backgrounds of every Tom, Dick, and Harriet of every unsavory character that has had a criminal record and resides in our area. Or one we can connect to being in our area at the time the homicides were committed. However, we'll be doing this in-house — for the most part. So any time you have any questions, need help or have anything of importance to report, you'll most likely find us in our respective offices. If we're not either place, call me on my cell phone.

"I don't need to stress how important it is that we get on this right away. Hopefully, this is an isolated case — the perp having a vendetta against the victims. If not, we need to catch this murdering snake before he strikes again. Any questions so far?"

Ferndale's motherly nature came forward. "How old is the child?"

"Twenty-three months. Any other questions?" Since there were only negative responses, Konklin said, "Okay, I'll turn the podium back over to our captain."

Warner stepped forward. "I really don't have much more to add other than let's get this murdering bastard behind bars where he belongs. Now, let's get back to work. This meeting is adjourned."

 CHAPTER TEN

"Hey, Dave, I'm starved. What do you say we stop at Chantilly Lace and get something to eat?" De Mija asked.

"Why don't we just go over to the Starlite Donut Shop?"

"No, I'm hungrier than that. I was thinking how good a big juicy hamburger, fries, and a hot cup of coffee sounds."

"It's not like you to eat that much so early in the morning, Leo."

"So I happen to be starving right now. What's the big deal?" De Mija snapped.

"Nothing. But you don't have to bite my head off."

Pulling in front of the all-night diner, De Mija put the car in park. As Ripley started to exit, he noticed his partner wasn't moving. "Hey, aren't you going to turn the car off and come in?"

"No. I don't feel like getting into one of Molly's long-winded conversations."

Molly was a good old gal. She always wore a scarf tied around her short bleached-blond hair with a bow at the top. The scarf not only adorned her hair, but it was the perfect place to keep the pencil she always carried for taking customers' orders. To fit in with the decor of the diner, all waitresses were adorned in a poodle skirt, tight-fitting sweater, bobby sox, and saddle shoes. With fond memories of days gone by, Molly loved dressing in the clothes she once wore back in her old school days.

De Mija swore Molly wore so much make-up he could scrape at least five layers of it off her face before ever seeing her skin. She wasn't at all attractive and not too swift in the brain department, but she had a good heart. Her boss purposely put her on the late-night-to-early-morning shift because of her smile, her gift of gab — which kept sleepy customers awake — and her boundless energy that magically rubbed off on most everyone she came in contact with. As dependable as the day was long, Molly was always there to greet the moonlight customers with her great personality and her favorite tune, *Good Golly, Miss Molly,* playing on the jukebox. She drove De Mija crazy, so he preferred to stay away from her.

Reaching for his billfold, De Mija pulled out a ten-dollar bill. "Here, Dave. Get our food for take-out, and we can eat in the car."

Taking the money, Ripley went into the diner.

The owner of the diner had named Chantilly Lace Cafe in remembrance of the man who made the song famous: Big Bopper. For any customer walking into the place, the immediate feeling was a step back in time. The gray-and-pink marbleized counter extended in an L-shape for much of the length of the room. The counter was lined with charcoal gray leather-like stools that sat on shiny silver, metal pedestals. Matching the decor were the metal-based, pink-and-gray-flecked Formica tables with a mixture of charcoal gray and pink leather-like chairs. Everything was pulled together nicely with the pale pink walls and the gray-speck tiled floor.

Fifties memorabilia decorated the cafe's walls. The jukebox that sat over in a corner of the room was filled with fifties rock-n-roll music. The sounds of the music generally filled the air, drowning out the chattering and laughter of the customers.

Open 24-hours a day, the diner was a popular place, specializing in extra large malts and milk shakes; and giant-sized, mouth-watering hamburgers, french fries, and deep-fried onion rings served in a plastic basket.

David found an empty stool and seated himself. Crazy about a man in uniform, especially policeman, it didn't take long for Molly to rush over to serve him. "Well, hi, Officer Dave," Molly greeted him from behind the counter. "Coffee?"

"No, thank you, Molly. Not right now."

"Where's your sidekick, Officer Leo?"

"Waiting in the car. I see the place is still jumping," Ripley stated, looking around the room packed with late-night customers.

"Always. The nightowls love us." Molly laughed. "We haven't seen you around here for breakfast in a long time."

"Yes, it's been a while. To be honest, we generally only stop for a quick donut and a cup of coffee any more. But my partner seems to have a real hunger pain tonight."

Ripley was in a hurry, but he didn't want to be rude as Molly continued to talk. "I'm talking about breakfast, Officer Dave. You and Officer Leo used to come in here around five-thirty or six in the morning for breakfast before you went to work. How come you're here at this time of the morning?"

"We got put on the graveyard shift, Molly. Say, I'm kind of in a hurry because we're on duty. Can I get a couple of orders to go?"

"Okay, what'll you have?" Pulling her order pad from her apron pocket and her pencil out of its resting place in her scarf, she was ready to write down his order.

"Two hamburgers, two orders of fries, and two black coffees to go."

"Everything on those burgers?"

Remembering his partner's sudden stomach cramps the night of the double homicide, he wasn't sure what to order on De Mija's hamburger. *Onions might not be such a good idea?* "Look, Molly, go ahead and put our order in. I'll be right back."

Ripley hurried outside, but the patrol car was gone. He ran to the middle of the street and looked one way, then turned and looked in the opposite direction. The black and white was nowhere in sight. Going back into the diner, he told Molly to put everything on both hamburgers and he would be right back. Right now he was more intent on finding out where De Mija went. Once again, he went out in search of his partner and their patrol car. Extremely worried, Ripley finally called De Mija on his shoulder radio.

"Leo, this is Dave. Where the hell are you?"

"Chasing down a suspect, Dave," De Mija's breathless voice responded. "Can't talk right now. Hang loose. I'll be back shortly."

Disgusted, Ripley went back into the diner and waited. Even after Molly delivered the take-out order in two small, white paper bags, he still sat and waited. Finally, he spotted the patrol car from the diner's window. Bags in hand, Ripley rushed to the car.

Handing De Mija one of the bags, Ripley said, "Here. This stuff is probably cold by now."

"Not too cold, I hope?"

"I got your burger with everything on it."

"Good. We can both suffer from onion breath and gas attacks."

"Very funny. So, what the hell is going on?"

As they began to eat, De Mija explained. "I was sitting here waiting for you when I saw this suspicious character coming out between those buildings over there." He pointed to an area just past the diner. "I yelled at him to stop, but he took off running. So I threw this baby into drive and chased him."

"Did you catch him?"

"Does a bird have feathers?" De Mija sarcastically remarked. "It seems he was just a guy that lives around here. He said when I yelled at him, he didn't hear me say I was a cop. All he heard was the word stop. He thought he was going to get mugged, so he started running."

"Well, the dumb ass. Didn't he hear your siren or see the flashing lights?"

"I didn't turn them on. I only chased him in the car for about a block. When he cut in between some houses, I got out and chased him on foot."

No wonder I didn't hear the siren. With food in his mouth, Ripley commented, "That's funny. I looked up and down the street and I didn't see our car."

"Partner, I don't know what you did or didn't see. But this car was parked just up the street about a block away. Maybe something marred your view from here?"

"Yeah, maybe?" Ripley replied, still doubting his partner's explanation. "You were gone for a good forty minutes, Leo. If it was only a block from here, what took you so long?"

"I told you. After I parked the car, I had to chase the sucker on foot. Once I caught him and frisked him, I had to find out for sure that he wasn't up to no good. Then, since I felt badly about scaring the poor innocent guy to death, I took him back to his place."

"I thought you said he lived around here?"

"He does. Not too far behind the diner. I guess he was taking a short cut when I spotted him. Hey, what difference does it make? You sound like you're putting me through the third degree here with all your questions. I don't have to answer to you when it comes to doing my job."

"Don't get snide with me, Leo. You know the regs as well as I do. You don't just take off on a wild goose chase and leave your partner stranded. If a Super had come by and seen what happened, we would've both been fired or put on suspension. I don't know about you, but I can't afford the monetary loss of either."

"Forget regulations and supervisors." De Mija smirked. "Come on, partner. I'm sure if the circumstances were reversed, you would have done the same thing."

"No, I wouldn't. And let's get it straight right now. I value our friendship. But if you pull a stunt like that again, I'll write you up. So get that superior look off your face. As I said, I can't afford to lose my job. Now, if you want another partner, see the shift commander. It's okay with me."

"I'm sorry, Dave. I'll try not to do that again. And, no, I don't want another partner. No one else would put up with me." De Mija chuckled, trying to make light of the situation. Taking his last drink of coffee, he stuffed all the paper waste into the bag.

"Better dig your napkin back out, Leo. You still have ketchup on your beard."

"Thanks." Napkin in hand, De Mija stretched his neck in order to view his beard in the rearview mirror. Once the ketchup was wiped off and the soiled napkin was returned to the bag, he asked, "Are you ready to roll?"

"Give me your bag and I'll toss these in the trash first."

Just as Ripley got back into the car, they heard a radio dispatch. "Zone 4?"

Ripley was quick to respond. "Zone 4."

"Unknown trouble at 10301 Del Ray Drive. Child crying. Neighbor reports no response from anyone in the house. Respond Code 3."

"10-4, responding Code 3."

Seat belts fastened, De Mija hit the lights and siren and tore away from the curb.

"I wonder what this is all about," Ripley questioned

"The parents are probably dead to the world after a night out of too much partying," De Mija complained. "Kids don't cry long enough or loud enough to disturb neighbors unless they're being beaten or neglected. Parents like that don't deserve kids."

* * *

Warner was shaken from a sound sleep by the ringing of the telephone. Reaching out into the darkness, he found the phone and answered it. "Hello. What?" Warner quickly perked up. After turning on the bedside lamp, he sat on the side of the bed. "Where? Yes. Get the CSIs over there on the double. And call Lt. Konklin … Oh." Making use of the pen and pad of paper he always kept on the nightstand, he said, "Give me that address again. Got it."

Quickly hanging up the telephone, Warner rushed to his closet.

Jeny rolled over and barely lifted her eyelids. After rolling her tongue over her lips to moisten them, she asked, "What's going on, Joe?"

"Another homicide," he replied, dressing as rapidly as he could.

"Oh, honey, that's terrible. But why did you get the call?"

"Go back to sleep, princess. We'll talk later when I come back to shower and change."

"What time is it?"

"4:35."

Sitting up and draping her legs over the edge of the bed, she asked, "Don't you want me to fix you some coffee?"

"No, I'll grab a cup later."

"Okay. But you stay warm and be careful."

After dressing, Warner walked over to the Jeny's side of the bed and kissed her. "I love you, princess."

"I love you too, my prince."

Even after twenty-plus years of marriage, the Warners were still madly in love with each other. She worshiped the ground he walked on. He would lie down and die for her. Jeny had gained more than a few extra pounds since the day they got married. But that did not change his love for her. Mushy or not, they were devoted to each other.

* * *

There were already two patrol cars blocking off the street from both entrances by the time Warner arrived at the scene. Their blue and red flashing lights lit up the neighborhood. Another patrol car was parked on the street directly in front of the house. The area around the house had already been sealed off with bright yellow tape.

Warner could see numerous people looking out of their respective windows, curious as to what all the excitement was about. The bolder curiosity seekers were standing out on their lawns with coats and blankets over their bedclothes. *Fools,* he thought. *Don't they know it's freezing cold outside?*

Inside the house, the sound of a crying baby filled the air. Met by a policeman, Warner flashed his badge and identified himself.

"Yes, sir. I know who you are."

"Officer Ripley, isn't it?

"The one and only." Ripley smiled.

"Has Lt. Konklin arrived yet?"

"No, sir. I've been stationed here at the front door for some now and I haven't seen him."

Dammit, Eddy. You live closer to here than I do. Where in the hell are you?

"Something wrong, Capt. Warner?"

"Are any of the CSIs here?"

"No one is here yet. You're the first to show up, other than the other uniforms."

"Great," Warner sarcastically commented. "Who turned on the lights in here?"

"I did because it was so dark here. I lit up most of the rooms after we checked the house to make sure no one else was around. But don't worry, sir. I did everything by the book. After we secured the residence and called for assistance, I put on a pair of disposable gloves."

"That's certainly good to hear. I'm assuming you were the first unit to respond?"

"That's right. My partner and I were only a couple of blocks away when the call came over the radio. We responded immediately."

"What time was that?"

"We received the call at 4:16. We were here within a couple of minutes. I called dispatch at four-thirty."

With the distressful sounds of the baby's cries, Warner asked, "Did anyone check to see if that poor child is all right?"

"Affirmative. My partner is better about handling babies than I am since he has one of his own. He said the baby was in good shape, other than a wet diaper and maybe hungry. Once we called in for assistance, my partner went back to the nursery. He's been trying to hush the baby but, as you can tell, he doesn't seem to be doing so good."

"Did you contact Child Protective Services?"

Ripley nodded. "They're on the way."

"Good. How did you make entry?"

"As soon as we arrived, we tried to get a response from inside the house. When no one answered the door, my partner made a forced entry. After we ascertained the baby was okay, we looked around for anyone else in the house. That's when we discovered the bodies. From --"

"Bodies? Plural?" A chill ran up Warner's spine.

"Yes. Two."

"But you didn't report a double homicide?"

"Not in those words, I didn't, sir. I could have sworn I told dispatch we had two bodies, though. But right now, I wouldn't swear to it."

"Okay, we won't worry about it at the present time. After you discovered the bodies, what did you do?"

"One look at the bodies and the pools of blood revealed they were both beyond any help we could give. We called dispatch, informed them what we had here and requested immediate assistance. While my partner waited outside the baby's room, a couple of the other officers and I secured the outside perimeter while waiting for assistance to arrive."

"Thanks, Ripley. I'll keep tabs on the door. You get your partner in here."

* * *

When Officer Ripley returned with his partner, he made the introductions.

"Thanks, Ripley. Now I'd like a few words alone with your partner. Go outside and keep an eye out for Lt. Konklin and the CSIs."

Once Ripley exited the house, Warner turned his full attention to De Mija. "Officer Ripley tells me you've been minding that crying infant?"

"Yes, sir. But short of picking him up, I can't seem to quiet the poor thing. Initially, I went into the room to see if there was any blood on the baby or the bedding. At that time, I also checked to see of the baby needed a diaper change. After Dave and I made the gruesome discovery and secured the interior, I went back to the nursery. Afraid of further contaminating the room more than I had previously, I've been standing in the doorway. My attempt at quieting the child by speaking softly to him has failed. I'm afraid my voice has only frightened the little guy more."

"It's a little boy?"

"I don't know, sir. It's just a figure of speech. It could be a little girl for all I know."

"Didn't you just say you checked the diaper?"

"I did. But I barely touched it. I could tell right away it was pretty well saturated. I never looked inside his diaper," De Mija explained. "A rep from CPS should be here soon to get the little one."

"So Officer Ripley has informed me. Is the baby in a crib?"

"Yes."

"When you were in the kid's room, did you notice anything unusual in the crib?"

"No, sir. But I didn't really look. I was more concerned about the baby. Besides, it's pretty dark in there."

Warner continued with his third-degree type questioning. "Then how could you check the baby for blood without a light on?" Even though Warner knew that was about the dumbest question he had ever asked, the words had flowed out of mouth before he could stop them.

"With my flashlight, Capt. Warner," De Mija replied with a bit of sarcasm.

"I knew that," Warner quipped, attempting to cover his blunder. "Just keeping you on your toes."

De Mija did not find Warner's comment a bit amusing. "When my partner was turning on lights, I asked him not to turn on the one in the nursery. I was afraid it might startle the baby more. Did I do something wrong?"

"No. Just trying to get some information before the CSIs arrive. I'd like to hear your version of what took place this evening from the time you took the call."

After listening to the officer's explanation, it was clear to Warner that De Mija had nothing more to add to what Ripley had already told him.

Warner turned as DuBois, Rothchild, and a third man walked in the front door. "Hey, it's about time you guys got here. Who's your buddy?" Warner asked as he greeted the men.

"Alex Davis, our new recruit," Rothchild replied. "We brought him along to get some field experience."

After a quick introduction to the new tech, Warner turned back to the officer. "Officer De Mija, show us where you discovered the bodies." As Warner and the crime scene techs followed De Mija, Warner asked, "Where we headed?"

"One of the bedrooms. I believe it's the master bedroom. One of the bodies is in the bed and the other one --"

"Let me guess. It's on the floor on the opposite side of the bed?"

"Why, yes. That's right."

At the bedroom entrance, Warner let his experienced eyes survey the scene. From the doorway, he could clearly see the shape of a body under the bed covers. Since there was a pillow covering the face, he could not tell if the victim on the bed was male or female. But he had his hunches. "Officer, did either you or your partner touch anything in the room?"

"Just the light switch. But Dave was wearing gloves at the time."

"Right. Do you sing?"

Since Warner's question came out of left field, De Mija was taken aback. "Do I sing?"

"Yes. Do you sing?"

"I sing in church, but I --"

"That's good enough. Go back to the doorway of the baby's room and try singing to him."

"I'll do my best."

Turning to the CSIs who had been patiently standing by, Warner said, "I was hoping Colt might show up by now. Well, we're not going to wait any longer. Give me a set of booties and some gloves, and we'll go in and get to work."

* * *

Inside the room, Warner shook his head at the grim scene. Since Konklin had not yet arrived, Warner carefully looked around, searching for clues. As he did, he issued the techs special instructions other than what they normally did when they processed a crime scene. After locating identifications of the victims, Warner stepped back close to the doorway allowing the techs to do their work.

A petite man with his black hair standing on end squeezed between Warner and the doorframe as he entered the room. "What have we got?"

"Hey, Vince. Do you ever comb your hair?"

Colt let out his goofy laugh. "Sometimes. So, what's happening?"

"Two bodies — both with pillows covering their faces. One's in bed and the other is on the floor on the other side. According to the ID's I found, I'm guessing we have one male and one female. That's all I can tell you right now. As soon as the techs get some pictures of the way they are now, you can do your thing."

"Looks and sounds exactly like the scene I covered just a couple of weeks ago. Ten bucks says there are two slashed throats under the pillows."

"No bets, Vince. I'm afraid I agree with you. Even though I wasn't there, I've heard all about the other scene. Every gruesome detail."

When the pillows were removed from the decedents, Rothchild said, "Here you go, Vince. One male vic on the bed and one female vic on the floor."

Colt nodded. "Yep, just as I thought." He left Warner's side and walked to the bed.

The grisly scene was more than Davis could endure. Holding one hand tightly over his mouth and the other clenched to his stomach, Davis tore past Colt, nearly knocking him down. Warner barely got out of the way as the inexperienced tech rushed passed him and down the hall.

"Well, so much for our new assistant." DuBois laughed. "His face was as green as his experience."

Warner ignored the men's chatter since he knew they meant no disrespect to the victims. He was well aware if many detectives, uniformed officers and crime scene techs did not make small talk and find humor in something, their jobs would become too overwhelming.

"Man, I'd rather be in here than outside where he's probably heaving his guts out," Rothchild joked back. "When you called Alex to accompany us, didn't you warn him not to eat breakfast since this was his first homicide?"

DuBois diabolically responded, "No one ever warned me. Initiation's a bitch."

Shaking his head and laughing, Rothchild replied, "Man, you're just plain cruel."

"In all seriousness, Doug, I did tell Alex not to eat. He informed me that he's Mister Macho Man and can handle anything. I guess anything didn't include a bloody scene like this?"

"You can't do this job and wear your heart on your shirtsleeve. Or let the site of blood and guts bother you. Shoot, I'd be a basket case if I let this kind of thing get to me. If Alex isn't tough enough to handle it, he's in the wrong occupation."

"Come on, Doug. You know as well as I do that this still bothers both of us."

"The tragedy of it all still gets to me, but not the gore. How did you react on your first assignment?"

DuBois laughed. "To be honest, the same as Alex. How about you?"

"My body literally froze on my first bloody assignment," Rothchild admitted, putting his camera back into his evidence case. "One of the head techs at the time had to nudge me back into reality."

"As much as I feel for Alex, I hope he gets back here soon. He's not going to learn anything with his head between his knees."

Listening to the techs' conversation as he did a routine examination of the first body, Colt added his point of view. "If you want to train a new tech, send them to the morgue. If they can handle watching Saggy perform an autopsy, then you'll know if he's going to make it in the field."

DuBois laughed. "That sounds like winning advice, Vince. How about it, Doug?"

"I'll have to think about that one."

Warner turned when he felt a tap on his shoulder. "Morning, Eddy." He took a step backward, allowing Konklin to enter the room.

"I'm glad you didn't say *good* morning," Konklin quipped. He leaned against a wall to put on his booties.

"Need some gloves?"

"Nope." Konklin pulled a pair from one of his pockets. "Got some."

"I should've known. Since I got here before you did, I gave the techs their instructions."

"Good. Officer Ripley told me they found two bodies." Looking at the bed, he said, "Where's the other one?"

"I'll give you two guesses."

Konklin swallowed hard. "Female on the floor on the other side?"

Warner nodded.

"Pillows?"

"Yeah. They've already been placed in evidence bags."

"Damn! This is like déjà vu."

"I rather figured as much."

"When dispatch called me this morning, I could have sworn they said this was a homicide. Not a double."

"They told me the same thing. Although, Officer Ripley isn't sure what he called in."

"Do we know who the vics are yet?"

"Yes. The male is twenty-four-year-old Richard Ainsworth Atkin. The female is Beth Ann Atkin, age twenty-three. Both the man's wallet and the woman's purse had credit cards, their driver's licenses and between them about a hundred and thirty dollars. I guess we can rule out burglary."

"Are there any other children in the house besides the crying infant?"

"No, just the one. I haven't checked him out yet. Officer De Mija is keeping a watch on the little one."

"That's good." As Colt removed the liver probe from the male's body, Konklin asked, "Vince, what's the verdict?"

"My educated guess — his main artery was severed. No self-defense wounds. According to his liver temp, I'm guessing he died between midnight and four this morning."

"Close to the same time as the Brook couple," Konklin stated. "The bed doesn't appear to be messed up other than the bedspread. With no signs of a struggle, looks like the perp caught the male sleeping."

When Colt started toward the female's body, Warner and Konklin followed.

Looking at the body, Konklin stated, "She was slain the same way."

"I'm afraid so," Colt said. After taking her liver temp, he reported,

"Her TOD is the same as the male's."

Konklin started looking around the floor.

"If you're looking for a murder weapon," Warner said, "I've already --"

"No. I'm looking for something that would have been used to hit her in the head."

Colt spoke up. "No need for that. She doesn't appear to have any head wounds."

"Then why is she on the floor?" Konklin asked.

"That's a good question," Warner responded.

"Beats me," Colt said.

"I don't know how you feel, Joe, but I believe we have a serial killer on the loose."

"Or a copycat. Let's wait and see what the lab comes up with before we jump to any conclusions. We can't do anymore in here, Eddy. Let's step out in the hall. I have a bone to pick with you."

Just before exiting the room, they removed their gloves and booties, placing them into an empty evidence bag.

Not caring for the others to overhear his conversation, Warner dropped his voice level. "I understand dispatch called you before they contacted me."

Taking the cue from his captain, Konklin kept his voice just above a whisper. "That's because they know I'm the lead on the case, Joe. I told them to make sure they called you."

"They did, and I know you're the lead detective. That's not my point."

"Then what is?"

"What took you so long getting here?"

"Sorry, Joe. My stupid car wouldn't start again this morning. I had to get a black and white to pick me up."

"I don't know why you insist on driving that old piece of crap. I've told you many times to take your department-assigned car home at nights. Then you won't have to worry about transportation."

"Never done it before and never will," Konklin firmly replied.

"Dammit, Eddy, other detectives take their assigned cars home. Quit being so damn stubborn. Besides, when you get an emergency call like this one, you need to be here ASAP."

"Sounds like somebody didn't have his morning coffee yet."

Frustrated, Warner grunted. "Sometimes, you're impossible."

"Capt. Warner," Ripley summoned from the far end of the hallway, "sorry for the interruption. But the attendants from the morgue are here to pick up the bodies."

"Tell them they'll have to wait outside until the CSIs are through with them."

"Let's go to the kid's room and see if we have a calling card," Konklin suggested.

"Wait. Are you carrying around extra hand and shoe coverings in your pockets?"

"No."

Warner stepped to the bedroom doorway. Addressing the CSIs, he asked, "One of you guys have a couple extra sets of booties and gloves on you, or do I need to get them from your van?"

"I do," DuBois replied. Retrieving new hand and foot coverings from his investigative case, he handed them to Warner.

As Warner handed a pair of each to Konklin, he said, "I wish CPS would get the lead out and get here to pick up the baby."

Heading toward the room where the crying was coming from, they saw Officer De Mija standing just outside the door. He was quietly singing a lullaby to the baby.

Warner got his attention. "You've got a good voice."

"Thank you, Capt. Warner. But I'm afraid not good enough. I've done my best to sooth this little one into calm, but it hasn't seemed to help."

"Thanks," Warner said. "We'll take over now. You can go back out front with your partner."

"Should we turn the light on in there?" Konklin asked, covering his shoes and hands. "I don't think we can scare the baby any more than he is already."

"True."

When the detectives entered the room, Konklin found a light switch and flipped it to the on position. This illuminated a table lamp close to the crib. The child was lying face down, knees under his stomach with his little bottom stuck up in the air. In a matter of seconds, the detectives zoomed in on a stuffed white rabbit in the corner of the crib. Resting on the rabbit's head was a single, black flower. The rabbit's paws held a small rattle with a card attached.

In unison both detectives stated, "Same calling card."

"You know, Joe, I'm sure that neither of those items were leaked to the news media."

"I know. At least now we can rule out copycat homicides," Warner stated with confidence.

"Maybe. We can't forget that we've got our team out there showing every store manager they come in contact with the picture of the rattle."

"I don't think the detectives are telling anyone that the rattle is connected to the homicides we're investigating. They're all too diligent to leak that kind of information. No, Eddy, I'm afraid your earlier conclusion is correct. We're dealing with a serial killer."

After a brief pause, Konklin said, "I'll get one of the techs in here to take some pictures."

Just as Konklin was turning away from the crib, a woman's voice came from the hall. "Pardon me, Detectives."

As she stood in the hallway light, Konklin recognized the woman in her navy blue coat and matching low-heeled shoes. The woman had a couple of baby blankets draped across her arm. "Hi, Jill."

"Good morning, Eddy."

"Joe, this is Jill Maloy from CPS. She picked up the Brooks' tot. Jill, this is Capt. Joe Warner."

Extending her hand, Maloy said, "Nice to meet you, Captain."

Making a point to show his gloved hand, Warner replied, "Joe's fine. Forgive me for not shaking hands, but it's a pleasure to meet you, too. Eddy, if you'll stay here and keep Miss --"

"Jill will do," she stated.

"Okay, Jill. Eddy, keep Jill company and I'll go get Kevin. Excuse me, Jill."

"Certainly. So, Eddy, do we have a boy or a girl?"

"I don't know," Konklin admitted. "Since he's dressed in blue, I guess we can assume he's a boy."

"Well, if you want to hand him to me, I'll get him out of here and see if I can't calm the poor little thing."

"We need to get a couple of pictures first," he informed her. "Joe will be right back with one of the CSIs."

"While we're waiting, have you tried patting the baby on his back? Sometimes that will calm them down."

"No." Konklin turned back to the crib and did as Maloy suggested. The baby went from screaming cries to uncontrollable sobs. "Hey, it works. That's okay, little fella. Everything's going to be okay," he comforted.

When Warner and DuBois entered the room, Warner smiled. "I should have known. The man with the magic touch."

"This wasn't my idea, Joe. It was Jill's."

"Well, step back and let Kevin get his pictures."

Once the pictures were taken, Warner followed the same procedure as he had at the Brooks' home. After signing the chain of custody form, he placed the evidence bag into his pocket.

Konklin leaned over the side of the crib. He gently turned the baby over. After lifting the child's nightshirt and checking to make sure the child had no wounds of any kind, he wrapped the tot in the blankets Maloy had given him. "The baby doesn't appear to be harmed in anyway, Joe. But the poor thing sure needs a diaper change. This one could float a battleship."

"I'm not surprised."

"Come on, little one," Konklin softly spoke as he finished wrapping up the child. "You're going for a ride."

As soon as he picked up the little bundle, the baby uttered, "Dada," between short breaths of insistent sobbing.

"Well, I'll be," Konklin stated with delight. "This little tyke just needed to be picked up and held." Carefully, he carried the bundle back to the doorway and handed the baby to the CPS representative. "Here you go."

Warner smiled. Never before had he witnessed Konklin picking up a child. He was quite taken as to the gentle way Konklin handled the baby. *He'd make a great father*, Warner thought.

Quickly, Warner turned his attention to Maloy. "According to the information I received, the baby has been crying for well over an hour before I got on the scene." Checking his watch, he shook his head. "Heavens, that can't be healthy for any kid to cry that long."

"That's what I call a good set of lungs." Konklin chuckled.

Loosening the blankets and taking a quick look in the baby's diaper area, Maloy stated, "Well, we'll get her wet diaper changed, give her bottle, and see if that doesn't calm her down."

"So, he's a she?" Konklin stated, surprised. "Well, she's a cute one."

Maloy left with the baby. Warner and Konklin walked to an area in the front hall.

"I've never had reason to meet anyone from CPS until now. In person, that is," Warner admitted. "I've had a few conversations with them over the telephone. However, the name Jill Maloy doesn't ring a bell."

"From what I understand, she's been there a few years. I only just met her at the Brooks' house. She's seems to be good with kids and dedicated to her job."

"I noticed you don't do so badly with kids yourself, Eddy. Hey, maybe she's single?" Warner teased, elbowing Konklin. "You should check it out."

"Geez, Joe, I'm no prize package, but she's not even pretty. Maybe if she'd wear her hair different than in an old maid's bun and put on some lipstick. Then she might be all right in a pinch. It's funny, but I'd swear she had on the exact same clothes when she picked up the Brooks's kid."

"It was a winter coat, Eddy. Not everyone owns more than one, you know? And wearing matching shoes just means she likes to coordinate her colors." Warner laughed. "You know, from someone who isn't interested, that's quite an observation, Mister All-Gray Two-Suit Man."

"Well, it's for sure you're not very observant. For your information, I have three suits and one of them is brown."

"Oh, yeah. I forgot about the brown one. Well, if nothing else, I have to say you have a sort of *je ne sais quoi* about you."

"I don't even know what that means, Joe. But I'm sure it's another insult."

"On the contrary, Eddy. That was a compliment."

"I'll bet. Say, are there any broken windows in the house?"

"You're wondering how the perp got in?"

"Uh-huh."

"I haven't checked yet, but ...." Warner stopped talking when he spotted Rothchild walking toward them, CSI kit in hand. "Are you guys through in the bedroom?"

"Almost. Kevin's going to finish up in there. I'm going to check on Alex. Then I'll be back in to check the backdoor area."

"Why the backdoor?"

"When we arrived, one of the uniforms told me to check it out. Evidently, while walking around the outside of the house he noticed the door was partially open. Could be how the perp made entrance. Didn't anyone tell you?"

"Which officer did you speak with?"

"Sorry Joe. I don't remember."

"Okay, Doug, you go check on Alex, and we'll meet you at the backdoor. Oh, did this officer tell you where the backdoor was located?"

Already walking away, Rothchild answered over his shoulder in a raised voice. "In the kitchen." He pointed. "That way."

"Guess that answers my question, huh, Joe?"

"Guess so."

As the detectives continued talking, they made their way through the house to the kitchen.

"Officer Ripley told me he and his partner were first on the scene."

"That's right. Funny neither of them mentioned the broken door. Especially since I questioned them both."

"Maybe they're the ones who broke in the backdoor to make a speedy entrance?"

"No. Officer De Mija made a forced entry through the front door."

"Why didn't they just come through the back way since the door was already open?"

"Maybe they didn't want to contaminate the area? Who knows? Whatever the reason, you can bet I'm going to find out."

"On the other hand, Joe, with that little gal screaming her lungs out, they might not have taken the time to check the outside perimeter before making entry."

"That doesn't fly. They both said they secured the house after they found the bodies. Which means they went from room to room, making sure no one else was in the house."

"I know what it means, Joe."

"I know. Just talking out loud, again."

"Well, here's the kitchen and there's the door." Konklin slipped. Grabbing hold of a countertop to keep from falling, he warned, "Watch your step, Joe. The floor's slippery with these booties on."

"I will. You okay?"

"Yeah. Just going to take smaller steps in here." Since the door was still ajar, Konklin opened it all the way. "The way this is jimmied, it does look like the perp made entry from here."

"This is a pretty flimsy lock. It wouldn't have taken much effort to break in, that's for sure."

"I agree, Joe. From the looks of the marks, the perp might have used a crowbar or a screwdriver."

When Rothchild joined them, Warner asked, "How's the new guy?"

"Doin' okay. I sent him to the bedroom to start carrying evidence bags out to the van. So, what do you think about the door being the perpetrator's entrance?"

"It sure looks like it," Warner responded. "Go ahead and get some photos of both the door and the frame and dust for prints."

"And take a chunk of wood from the frame back to the lab with you," Konklin added. "I'd like to know what type of tool the perp used to jimmy the door."

The detectives moved away from the door, watching as Rothchild took pertinent photos.

"I don't understand why more people don't get home alarms, Joe. It certainly would keep a lot of burglaries from happening."

"And more people from getting killed in their homes."

"Isn't that the truth? So, what did the card say?"

"I didn't read it yet." Taking the small bag from his jacket pocket, Warner read the card, silently. Then he handed it to Konklin. "Here. It's the same wretched poem. And it looks to me like the same type of rattle attached, too."

Taking the small bag, Konklin remarked, "Geez, Joe, why do you always keep evidence in your pockets?"

"Force of habit to keep my hands free."

"Stop joking around, Joe. I'm worried about some defense attorney making an issue of it. You know as well as I do that only the CSIs are supposed to keep --"

"You worry too much, Eddy. You saw me sign the chain of custody."

"Yes, but I remember that detective on the infamous Simpson case. In court, the defense attorney's made quite an ordeal about the evidence he had carried around in the trunk of his car."

"There's a huge difference. The evidence I have has been recorded by a CSI and it's sealed in that evidence bag you're holding."

"Just want to make sure we cover our backends. When we catch this perp, I want him convicted. Not slip through our justice system because of some stupid technicality on our part."

"Give me credit for being a better detective than that."

"Of course I do, Joe. You might be the captain, but as lead detective on this case my ass is on the line, too."

After a brief examination of the item through the bag, Konklin handed it back to Warner.

"I sure wish it would snow."

"What on earth for?" Konklin questioned.

"Then maybe our perp would leave a footprint or two."

Scratching his head, Konklin was bewildered. "I don't understand. How does this vicious animal get in and out of these houses without leaving any footprints around? Snow or no snow, one would think he would leave something. So far, we don't even have so much as a fingerprint."

"I know. Let's just hope he slipped up this time and the techs find us a good lead."

"But what about the moisture on the bottom of the shoes? Wouldn't that leave a print on the inside of the house where it's warm?"

"One would think so. Well, no sense in us sticking around here any longer. I'm going home to shower and change."

"Go ahead, Joe. I'm going to stick around a while."

"Why? You can't do any more hanging around here."

"I know, but I want to. You go on now and I'll meet you back at the office later."

Konklin stuck around the crime scene to take another look around. Even though he knew the CSIs were very thorough in doing their jobs, he had hopes he might discover something — anything that might have been overlooked.

One double homicide was horrific. But now with a second double murder just two weeks after the first, Konklin felt like a pressure cooker ready to explode.

CHAPTER ELEVEN

When Konklin finally got to the precinct, he joined Warner in his office. "I got the name of the male victim's parents. I thought they should be paid a call and told about their son and daughter-in-law before they hear it from the news media."

"What about the parents of the female?"

"We don't have her maiden name yet. I'm hoping the man's parents can enlighten us. If not, we'll check with the Bureau of Statistics for assistance."

"Have the techs completed the house sweep?"

"Yes. Thankfully it wasn't as big as the Brooks' house was. Anyway, I'm headed over to talk to the neighbor that phoned in the distressed baby call early this morning. Then I want to interview some of the other neighbors. Hopefully, someone saw something that might help us."

"That's what I call thinking positive, Eddy. Considering our last neighborhood canvass didn't give us anything."

"Well, we can always hope for the best. Want'a go with me?"

"You bet. Say, did you get something to eat when you went home?"

"No. I was in a rush to get cleaned up and get back here. I just grabbed a quick cup of microwave coffee."

"Yuck." Rising from his chair, Warner hiked up his pants and felt to make sure his fly was zipped.

Konklin laughed. "Got a problem?"

"Nope. Just checking. I got dressed in such a hurry I forgot to check whether or not I was showing more than I should be. Jeny was in a sound sleep when I went home to clean up, so I let her sleep. She generally checks me each day to make sure I'm put together right." Getting his coat he asked, "How about you and me grab a bite to eat when we get through with the interviews?"

"Sounds good, but I don't know how long this will take. Won't it ruin one of Jeny's delicious dinners having such a late lunch?"

"Never. And if that was a hint to get your butt invited to dinner tonight, think again."

"Can't blame a guy for trying." Konklin laughed. "Come on, Joe. You do the driving and I'll do the navigating."

"What else is new?"

* * *

On the way to their first interview, Warner said, "I have to apologize to you, Eddy."

"Again? What on earth for this time?"

"I should have waited around at the crime scene and given you a ride home. I'm not very good in the mechanical department, but I might have been able to help you get your car started."

"Oh, that. Nah, that was okay. I got a ride. Fortunately the auto club had the old booger running when I got home, so it got me to work."

"Park the damn thing this time and start using your assigned car," Warner ordered in a friendly tone.

"Yes, sir, Captain, sir," Konklin remarked, tucking in his chin and saluting as if he was in the armed forces. "I believe you made that point quite clear earlier this morning."

"Just wanted to make sure you remembered."

Once they reached the home of Mr. and Mrs. Dalton Atkin, the detectives went inside and gave them the tragic news about their son, Richard, and daughter-in-law, Beth Ann. Breaking into tears, Mrs. Dalton turned to her husband for comfort. As he held his wife, Mr. Dalton got all the information he could from the detectives. With the sad details of the deaths out of the way, Konklin then informed the grieving parents how to get in touch with Jill Maloy concerning their granddaughter.

According to Mr. Atkin, Beth Ann's parents lived in a small town approximately thirty minutes from Mt. Pride. Since the Atkins knew how to contact them, Konklin got their address and telephone number. He explained a detective would be sent to Beth Ann's parents' home to inform them of the tragic news.

Back in the car, the detectives headed to their next destination.

"I think this is the worst part of our job. I just hate having to inform anyone that a loved one's life has been snuffed out. Especially by the hands of another human being."

"I agree. It's heart-wrenching."

"Just think about that poor baby girl having to grow up without her parents. She sure was a little cutie pie."

"You were pretty good with her, Eddy. You should've had one or two kids of your own. Why haven't you ever remarried?"

"Hey, Joe, you missed our turn. Turn left at the next street," Konklin pointed, "and we'll swing back. These streets are all goofy in here. None of them run straight. How in the world did you make it to the crime scene this morning, and in the dark no less, without getting lost?"

"Probably because my adrenaline was flowing at record-breaking speed knowing I had to get to the scene as soon as possible. Now, quit trying to change the subject. That's a bad habit of yours."

"They say in time the pain of losing a loved one gets easier. That may be true for some people but not for me. Besides, I've never met another woman that could measure up to my first wife."

"I'm sorry to hear that, Eddy. I've never been in your position, but life goes on. If you stop comparing other females to your deceased wife, maybe you'll be able to find someone to share your life with."

"Why are you always trying to marry me off?" Konklin forced a laugh since the subject of bringing up his past was tugging at his heart.

"Because I think you have a lot to offer. I think --"

"This is Del Rio Street," Konklin interrupted. "Turn left."

"Where are you taking me? I thought we were going to interview a next door neighbor."

"Well, he's a neighbor, but he doesn't live next door. The male that reported the baby crying lives directly behind the Atkin house."

"Did you call first to see if he was going to be home?"

"Yes. Here it is. Stop here. I called from my cell on the way to the office. He said he would be home all day."

As Warner parked the car, he asked, "What's his name?"

"Lee Topple."

"Okay, let's go."

"Wait, Joe. I've got something to say first."

"Look, if it's about your love life --"

"No. It's about this case."

"Spill it."

"Will you please," he emphasized, "take over the lead on this case?"

"Eddy --"

"Please don't say no, Joe. Hear me out. When I have to start working with one of the other detectives, I'll take the lead. But working with you is different. Now don't get the wrong idea because I'm really not shirking my responsibilities here. It's just that it's rather difficult for me to stay on top of everything plus handle all the details with the team we have working with us. And it's for damn sure I'm not going to ask you to handle the little stuff. At any rate, this is no longer just a case of tragic homicides. We're chasing a cold-blooded serial killer."

"Okay, you've proved your point. Now, let's go."

* * *

A short, muscular man dressed in gray sweats answered the door. Showing his badge, Joe greeted him. "Good morning. I'm Capt. Warner of the Mt. Pride Police Department. This is Lt. Konklin. Are you Lee Topple?"

"Yes, of course. I've been expecting you. Please, come in."

Once they were seated in the living room, Warner commenced with the interview. "May I call you Lee?"

"Certainly."

"Okay. Lee, would you tell us what led up to your 911 phone call early this morning."

"I'm a health nut. I believe in eating the right foods, getting the proper sleep, and faithfully exercising every day. In fact, I was just working out when you rang the bell." Patting his abdomen as he inhaled and flexed to show off his body beautiful, he boasted, "I've never put alcohol, nicotine, steroids, or any drugs in this body. Pretty good shape for a sixty-eight-year-old man, don't you think?"

Feeling a little envious, Konklin tried to hide his amazement at the man's age.

Warner nodded and smiled. "That's wonderful, Lee. However, I'd like to get back to your 911 call."

"Of course. Well, I'm in bed by seven every night. I get up around three every morning, rain or shine, summer or winter. I have my protein shake, dress in my sweats, then jog around the neighborhood. I call it my daily constitutional as it wakes up my whole body after a good eight hours sleep. When I started out this morning, I thought I heard a baby crying from that house behind me. See, their backyard ...." Getting to his feet, he said, "If you'll come with me, I'll show you what I'm talking about."

Lee guided the detectives to a large exercise room in the back of the house where there was a doublewide set of sliding glass doors. Pointing out the back of the house across the way, he said, "See there? That's the back of the people's house. As you can see, we have an adjoining alley. That's where I start my run at three-thirty sharp every morning, like clockwork. So from out there, that's where I thought I heard a baby crying. I stopped to listen. My ears told me it was coming from that house. I got to thinking. A baby crying in the middle of the night isn't too unusual. So I went about my own business, jogging around the neighborhood.

"When I returned home from my run, I still heard that baby crying. I generally time myself so I would say I was gone for a good forty minutes. That would have been around 4:10. Now, it appeared strange to me that the baby would still be crying for that length of time and not be attended to. It also bothered me that I didn't see a light on in the house where the baby's cries were coming from.

"My sister has five kids, and I know she never let one of them cry past ten minutes when they were little. She always said you don't dare pick up a baby when it first starts whining or it'll get spoiled too fast. You know, one little whimper and they've got mommy or daddy jumping to their aid," he added, laughing. "But more than ten minutes is way too long. Anyway, I suddenly get this horrible thought that either these people are in a dead sleep and need to be woke up to tend to their little one, or they left the poor thing home alone. Well, Detectives, there's no sense in us standing in here while we talk. Let's go back to the living room."

The detectives gave each other a weird look behind Lee's back as they followed him back to the living room. Warner wanted so badly to echo the words of the infamous Joe Friday from the television show, *Dragnet*, "Just the facts, sir." But he knew he didn't dare. Back in the living room, the conversation continued.

"Now, where was I? Oh. Since I was coming from the alley, it was only natural to go to their backdoor first. I noticed the door was slightly open so I practically laid on the doorbell. When no one came to the door, I ran to the front door. Once again, I rang and rang the doorbell and pounded on he door. Still no response. Since I always carry my cell phone with me, I finally called 911. And, like someone once said, that's all she wrote."

"Did you hear any other strange noises around that house before or during the time you heard the baby crying?"

"If you mean from inside my house, no. This neighborhood is super quiet at night. Lucky for me, we don't even have any barking dogs around here. Nothing worse than dogs that bark at every strange noise. I'm a light sleeper, so if there were any unusual noises from outside, I probably would have heard them. On the other hand, I might not have heard a noise over by their house. As you probably noticed, there's a lot of property between the back of their house to the back of mine. I'll hear a car if it goes down the alley, or if someone clangs a garbage can lid. But I didn't hear anything last night or early this morning. It wasn't until I was outside in the alley that I heard that poor baby crying its lungs out."

"Did you see anyone in the area while you were out jogging?" Warner continued questioning.

"Not a soul."

"Okay, you said you noticed the back door was slightly open?"

"That's right. But I didn't want to open it and go in. The last thing on my mind was to enter a person's home without an invitation. Heck, a man could get himself shot that way. By the way, I saw the two large body bags as they were taken out of the house. How did those people die?"

"We're not at liberty to give you any details right now, Lee."

"The only reason I asked is for my own personal well-being. It's not like I'm afraid of anything, you understand. But if there's a murderer on the loose, I was wondering if I should put off my early morning jogging until you catch the killer? The morning news said this is the second double homicide in a matter of weeks. That's scary as hell."

"I don't think you have anything to worry about, Lee. But it's always better to be safe than sorry. Just use your own good judgment."

As Warner got to his feet and headed toward the door, Konklin followed.

"We appreciate your time, Lee. You've been very helpful."

"Sure. I'll do anything I can to help."

Warner took a business card from his billfold and handed it to Lee. "If you remember anything else about early this morning, please let us know."

"I will."

"Lee, you wouldn't by any chance have a disposable glass or paper cup, would you?"

Konklin tried not to appear too curious as to the captain's strange question.

"I always keep those throw-away plastic glasses in the house. Why?"

"My throat feels terribly dry. If you don't mind, I'd like to take a glass of water with me."

"Of course I don't mind. I'll be right back.

As Lee left the room, Warner was amazed that Konklin stood there completely silent. Within a short time, Lee returned with a plastic glass of water and handed it to Warner.

* * *

On the driver's side of the car, Warner quickly emptied the water in the street. Once he got into the car, he pretended to drink all of the non-existing water from the glass just in case Topple was watching from his house. Konklin was holding open a plastic bag. Warner placed the glass in the bag.

"How did you know?" Warner asked with a smile as he started the car.

"At first I didn't. Then it dawned on me that you wanted his prints."

"Just in case we need them. It was the only way I could think of right at the moment without tipping him off."

"Smart move." After closing the bag, Konklin wrote all the pertinent information on it. Then placed the sealed bag on the seat next to him. "Geez and double geez! What a physique for a man in his sixties," Konklin commented, patting his own round stomach as they drove off. "And you thought I had the gift of gab. Man, I didn't think that guy would ever shut up."

"Tell you what, big guy. I'll never complain about your talking, ever again."

"I'll remind you of that. What do you think of this guy?"

"I'd say he makes a possible suspect, Eddy. What do you think?"

"You mean for both doubles?"

"Uh-huh."

"Well, he's strong — which means he could easily slit a throat with one quick sweep. He's lean — which means he could fit through the narrow window at the Brook house. He lives in the vicinity of all the victims — which means he would easily access their houses. And he likes to jog at ungodly hours when no one else is up and around. All that adds up to opportunity, Joe."

"When we get back to the office, run his name through the National Crime Information Center."

"If NCIC doesn't have any info on him, do you want me to take the drinking cup to the lab to lift his prints?"

"You bet. Once they have them, ask them to run the prints through our local and state databases for a match. If they don't find anything, have them run the prints through the FBI's national database. Maybe we'll get lucky."

"That would be a switch."

* * *

After moving the car and parking in front of the Atkin house, Warner and Konklin made their way on foot around the neighborhood. Everyone they found at home, as they went from house to house, was asked the same questions. Had they heard anything suspicious outside in the middle of the night? Had they seen anything out of the ordinary around the victim's house? Were any suspicious vehicles driving around the neighborhood? Had they noticed any strangers in the neighborhood or anyone lurking around that looked suspicious or didn't belong in the neighborhood? What type neighbors were the Atkins? How did they treat their little girl?

Back in the car, Warner showed his frustration. "Once again, no one hears or sees anything. Damn!"

"That's what they all said, Joe. It didn't appear like any of them were hiding anything or were afraid to speak up, either. At least that's my take."

"The only thing we found out this morning is that both Atkins had a tendency to yell a lot at their little girl. What was here name again? I forgot what her grandparents told us."

"Reba."

"Right. Reba."

"Since she has red hair, I wonder if they named her after the attractive country singer, Reba McIntyre?"

"I don't know. But with the kid's set of lungs, she certainly has a good start on a singing career of her own."

"Since I've never had any kids, Joe, answer me a question. How can a twenty-one-month-old child do enough harm to get yelled at all the time?"

"Kids can be a handful. And at that age they're into everything out of curiosity. Some parents just don't have the patience to deal with little ones not understanding the word *no*."

"As far as I'm concerned, mental abuse is just as bad as physical abuse."

"According to the calling cards, it's obvious the perp thinks so, too. I wonder if that's the association between the four victims."

"Not to mention they live in the same area of town, Joe.

"I've been thinking. I'll drop that drinking cup off at the crime lab to save you a trip. Besides, I want to stop in and talk to Saggy."

"Sounds good to me, but not until after lunch. In case you didn't hear my stomach talking, it's saying 'feed me.'"

"Heaven help me, now his stomach talks. As long as it's talking food and not a gas attack, I guess it's all right."

"Very funny."

"My stomach doesn't talk but I'm a bit on the hungry side myself. How about a --"

"Sounds good to me," Konklin butted in, letting out a chuckle.

* * *

After dropping Konklin off at the precinct, Warner headed for the MPPD Crime Lab. Once there, he went straight to the morgue.

Not expecting to see such a repulsive sight, Warner spouted, "Holy cat crap, Saggy. That's enough to make a grown man toss his cookies."

As his bulging green eyes peered over his half-frame, granny-glasses,

Sagdorf smiled. Red ooze surrounded his mouth and colored some of the hairs of his snow-white beard. "Hi, Joe." Holding his half a sandwich in the air, he offered, "I've got plenty if you're hungry."

"Fortunately, I just ate. I guess I'll have to take a rain check. I hope you have a napkin."

The ME walked over to his desk, pulled a tissue from a tissue box and wiped off his mouth. "Did I get it?"

"No. You have some on your beard, too. I hate to hurt your feelings, Saggy, but that's truly disgusting."

"Sorry, Joe. My wife makes the best doggone meatball and ketchup sandwiches. This has been my lunch for almost ten years now. Don't knock it until you've tried it."

"That's not what I mean, you wiry, white-haired, old mongrel you," Warner teased. "You eating that sandwich with a bloody body laying on your lab table is enough to gag a maggot. No darn wonder no one likes to come to the morgue to talk to you."

"So, the guys finally got you, huh, Joe?"

"Got me?"

"Sure." Sagdorf laughed. "All of the other guys stay clear of the here unless they know I'm not eating. In reality, none of them show up unexpectedly. They call first."

"Uh-huh. I understand what you're saying. Thanks for the tip off, Saggy."

After taking another bite of his sandwich, Sagdorf apparently felt like venting. Unfortunately for Warner, he came for some valuable information on the latest double homicide. So, he had to bide his time, patiently listening.

"You wouldn't believe how many people from the brass down to the cadets have weak stomachs. If any of those strong macho men come in here, like you just did, they end up emptying their stomach contents. Jeepers creepers, I don't know how any of them handle bloody crime scenes." Sagdorf laughed. "That's one for the books, right Joe?"

"Even we strong men have our limits."

Rolling his eyes, Sagdorf shook his head. "So, what can I do for you, Joe?"

"I know you're swamped and you only just received the bodies this morning, but --"

"But, you want to know if I've had a chance to do a preliminary exam on the latest victims yet?"

"Yes."

"As a matter of fact, that's why I'm so late eating my lunch."

"You're the best, Saggy. What can you give me?"

Sagdorf placed the rest of his sandwich on the desk. "I've already completed my prelim on the female, so she's in the cooler. The male's still on the slab waiting to get rinsed off. Come have a look." The two walked over to the lab table. "They have almost the same MO as the Brook couple. Their offender was left-handed from the looks of the entrance and exit wounds on their necks."

"Do you have time to tell me how you make that determination?"

"Turn and face me and I'll demonstrate. I'm right handed. So if I had a sharp weapon in my hand, intending to slit your throat, I would attack with full force into the right side. According to the wounds on both victims, the offender plunged the weapon into the neck before slicing. So, the entrance wound is deeper. Now, as the weapon slides across the neck, exiting the left side, the wound isn't as deep. If I were left-handed, it would work the direct opposite. Understand?"

"Yeah, I do."

"The murder weapon was a sharp instrument, but not a straight edge like a knife or a razor. The weapon's blade couldn't have been very long. Even though they were fatal, the cuts weren't very deep — except, like I said, at the point of entrance. Of course, if pushed hard enough, only the tip of the weapon would have done enough damage to cut the jugular. In this case, the jugulars on both victims were completely severed. Their wounds definitely show curved lacerations to the throat."

"Curved? That's what you said about the Brooks' wounds."

"I told you this was almost the same MO, Joe."

"Do you have any idea as to what would make a curved wound?"

"I can't help you out there. All I can tell you is that it wasn't a straight edge that made these wounds. From the tearing at both the entrance and the exit of the skin," Sagdorf said, pointing to the victim's severed neck, "it almost looks like some sort of a hooked or curved weapon was used."

"Anything else?"

"Yes, as a matter of fact, but for me, not you."

"Anything, Saggy. What do you need?"

"How about giving me the names and ages of the victims. Even though I'm pretty good at guessing the ages of the bodies I get in here, I'd rather be exact. I was supposed to be given this information this morning, but I haven't received it yet."

"I'll have Eddy get it to you. What's the ETD on the victims?"

"Didn't Vince tell you?"

"Yes. And I know he's good at his job, Saggy. I just need you to confirm his findings."

"From the liver temp Vince reported, the estimated time of death was around three o'clock this morning."

"That confirms the timeline Lee Topple gave us," Warner mumbled.

"What's that, Joe?"

"Just voicing my thoughts out loud. It's a bad habit of mine."

Sagdorf laughed. "Jeepers creepers. I thought I was the only one that did that."

"You can't fool me, Saggy. You've been an ME too long. You don't talk to yourself, you talk to the corpses," Warner teased.

"You could say I have a captive audience that don't talk back."

Slapping Sagdorf on the back, Warner said, "You're quite the character. Look, I've got to get back to the precinct. I appreciate the time and the info. I'll have Eddy get the victims' info to you first thing in the morning."

"Stop in any time, Joe."

"Get me your prelim report in writing as soon as you can."

"You know I will."

As Warner started to walk out the door, he turned back. "I almost forgot. You mentioned in your autopsy report on Shelby Brook that she didn't die from her head wound. I'm not questioning your expertise, but how did you come to that conclusion?"

"A person doesn't bleed from another wound after they're dead. So, she had to have been hit first. Since the hemorrhaging was slight, she had to have been killed directly after the blow to the head."

"Just like the Brook female, we found the latest female vic laying on the floor next to the bed. But there wasn't anything lying on the floor that might have knocked her out before she was killed. And Vince said he found no head wounds."

"She does have a blunt force injury to the back of her head. There was no hemorrhaging, just a good-sized mark on her scalp hidden by her hair. By mark I mean, I could tell someone whacked her a good one. Often times, a person has to be dead for a while before any bruising shows up. Vince wouldn't have noticed the mark in his initial exam. I didn't notice it either until I washed her down before examining her."

"Why wouldn't there have been any hemorrhaging?"

"She probably wasn't hit hard enough to break the skin or render her unconscious, but hard enough to knock her down. Come with me."

Warner followed Sagdorf to the steel vault of drawers that held the morgue's bodies. He opened the huge, metal drawer that contained the body of Beth Ann Atkin. Sagdorf positioned her so Warner could see the back of her head.

"What happened to her hair?"

"I had to shave that area for a closer look at the mark on her scalp." Pointing, the ME said, "See this mark? This is called a pattern injury. If you can find a weapon that matches this pattern, you'll find out what she was struck with."

"Any ideas would be helpful."

"Sorry, Joe. That's your job. All I can tell you is that it was a blunt, flat instrument."

"Any signs of sexual abuse? Or, any trace evidence under her nails we can use for DNA?"

"Just like the first female, Joe. No signs of sexual abuse and her nails were clean. Everything will be in my report."

"Thanks, Saggy."

* * *

Back at the precinct, Warner went straight to his lieutenant's office.

"Great minds think alike."

"Oh, yeah?" Warner asked, taking a seat.

"I was just about to head your way to see if you were back from the morgue."

Warner was in one of his typical moods to pull Konklin's chain. Looking serious, he said, "Thanks for not warning me, Eddy. Here I thought we were friends."

"Not warning you about what?"

"Don't play dumb with me, chubby cheeks. You know damn well what I'm talking about."

"I swear, Joe. Give me a clue."

"Saggy happened to be eating when I walked in the morgue."

Konklin broke into laughter. "Was he eating one of his favorite sandwiches while standing over a bloody stiff?"

"You're darn lucky things like that don't make me sick." Warner laughed. "I owe you big time."

"Hey, you can't blame me. How was I to know he'd be eating a late lunch?"

"Maybe not. But in all the time I've been at this precinct, you could have warned me to call him first before going over there. I'm surprised none of the other guys ever said anything to me."

Still laughing, Konklin admitted, "I'm not. Everyone knows you're a good sport, Joe."

"You mean this was a conspiracy?"

"You might say that."

"Well, you're all on my list."

Wiping the tears from his eyes, Konklin got serious. "I don't imagine Saggy had anything for us yet?"

"Surprisingly, he did."

"He did?"

"Yes, that's why he was eating a late lunch. He's already completed the prelim on Beth Ann. And was ready to start on Richard's."

"And?"

"He says the throat wounds are exactly the same as they were on the first double homicides. Our perp is a southpaw. The murder weapon is sharp, short bladed and curved. Here's something that will surprise you — I know it did me. Saggy discovered a rather large mark on Beth Ann's head. He said it was due to a blunt instrument."

"Wonder why Vince never told us that when he did his prelim at the scene?"

"Because he didn't notice it. Saggy said he almost missed it."

"That certainly explains why Beth Ann was on the floor just like we found …." Konklin paused as a quick flash of the crime scene swept through his mind. "Something's not right here, Joe. What was Beth Ann hit with? There wasn't any sort of object laying on the floor but shoes from both vics. I know because I searched the floor for --"

"I know you did. A heavy shoe can give quite a wallop."

"Did you look closely at the shoes?"

"Truthfully, I never saw any shoes on the floor. Just a couple pair of house shoes."

"Exactly. They were both nothing more than soft-soled slippers. Neither one of them could have hit hard enough to knock someone down, let alone leave a welt on the head."

"Sorry, Eddy. I disagree. If one was holding the slipper in his hand, a good whack could leave a mark. And a strong person could hit with such force he could knock the person off their feet."

"That makes sense. So, should we go back to the scene and look for an object the perp used?"

"Let's think about this for a minute, Eddy. If this perp is in a hurry, and working in the dark of night, he wouldn't take time to replace such an object."

"Yeah. He'd leave it laying around like the lamp at the Brook scene. He could've been prepared this time and carried something in with him. Not everyone has a lamp next to their bed. The Atkins didn't."

"Yes, I noticed that."

"It might have even been the same tool he used to break into the house. If it was something like a crowbar, that would give a nasty blow to the head."

"I'm no expert, but I would think a crowbar would have drawn blood. Hell, he could have used a flashlight to hit her with. Look, have the CSIs go back to the scene. This time, have them move the furniture in the bedroom. Just in case something rolled and landed out of the normal view."

"Will do. But I'll almost bet they've already done that. You know how thorough they are?"

"I do. But no harm in double checking."

"Did Saggy have anything else of importance?"

"No. But I did ask him about the weapon. He didn't have any ideas as to what it could be."

"I remember he mentioned a curved or hooked weapon in his report on the Brooks. I've been racking my brain since our last discussion about the murder weapon. The only thing that popped in my head was a grapefruit knife. I haven't seen one in years, but I think it's curved."

"I think it is, too, but it's also serrated. No, we're looking for a straight edge that's curved on the end. Oh, before I forget, Saggy needs the basic info on the Atkins. I told him you would get it to him in the morning."

"Will do."

"Have you got anything new for me on your end?"

"Yeah. We ran Lee Topple's name through the NCIC database. No criminal record. No warrants. And not so much as a parking ticket."

"He's still a suspect."

"I know. I plan on canvassing his neighbors first thing tomorrow morning."

* * *

The captain's office door was open. Konklin stepped into the office as he rapped on the glass-paned door. "Got a minute?"

"Good morning. So, how did it go?"

"It seems this Topple character is another one of those good guys, according to everyone I spoke with this morning. He keeps to himself. But when he's out and around, the neighbors say he couldn't be friendlier. I'm still going to wait until we get a report on his prints. And I'll do some digging to see if I can connect him to the Brooks and the Atkins, other than living in the same area. But as far as I'm concerned, I really don't see him as a suspect."

"Have a seat."

"Don't have time. I want to check with the techs to see if they found anything at the crime scene that could have been used as a blow to Beth Ann's head."

"Did you get the info to Saggy?"

"Of course. See you later."

CHAPTER TWELVE

Father, *HE* is out of control!

HE has taken two more lives, and I just know HE will continue to do so. There doesn't seem to be any way to stop HIM. I don't know what to do. I feel comfort from HIM yet in a sense I still fear HIM. I'm almost positive HE won't harm my wife and child. But I can tell from the devil look in HIS eyes HE wouldn't hesitate to destroy me at the blink of an eye.

I've never before got a good look at HIM until recently. We finally met face to face. That mask HE wears doesn't fool me. I know who HE is. Since then, I see HIM quite often. I'm a bit puzzled, though. HE acts as though HE doesn't know who I am. It's as if HE looks right through me.

I want so badly to tell someone, other than you. But, Father, who would believe me? I know far too much about HIM. So, no matter whom I would talk to would only put the blame on me. The courts would *Have No Mercy*. I don't want to pay the penalty for HIS actions. Yet, I am so ashamed that I cowardly stand by without saying a word to stop HIM.

I am acquainted with a variety of people now, and many are in law enforcement. Although I don't consider any of them as my close friends, maybe I should take the chance and take one of them into my confidence? No, I dare not take the chance. Acquaintances are great to have, but friends are too nosey. If I let anyone get too close to me, they will only start asking questions. I don't care to answer nosey questions about my private life. Even my wife knows better than to question me about my own personal and private affairs. She only knows what I care to have her know. It's better that way.

God help me, Father. I'm alone in this disease of turmoil. I won't give up until there's a cure. Either I will become strong and gain control, or HE will continue to be mightier than I am and win. In the end, I'm afraid, only one of us will survive.

Many times I feel as if I'm losing control of my own thoughts. I don't know whether I am only having terrible nightmares, or I am actually witnessing these tragic events. This is so incredibly surreal. There are times when I feel like I'm really losing my mind. If I am truly witnessing everything, and it's not my imagination, I don't look forward to the day I have to match wits with HIM. Until then, my head continues to spin in this turbulence HE has brought into my life. I feel as if I'm in a deep canyon with no way out.

Twisted, turned, hurled into space, No direction in which to go;
Empty, cold, needless pace, My heartfelt pain wears the devil's face.

CHAPTER THIRTEEN

Unfortunately, alcoholics also raised Jamie. While the Doles were drowning their waking hours in cheap booze and beer, hoarding the excessive amount of money they had received from the sale of Jamie, the wealthy Vernons fell into their drunken stupors drinking expensive liquors and wines. Just like the Doles, the Vernons kept to themselves; lived in a secluded area in a modest house; and did not believe in banks. The only difference between the Doles and the Vernons were their financial situations.

Using their wealth, the Vernons were able to purchase a fake birth certificate for Jamie. They also drew up new wills making Jamie their sole heir to all their worldly possessions.

Just six months after purchasing Jamie, the Vernons decided a child, especially an impish one, did not fit into their lifestyle. They tried to return the child and get back their money. Mr. Dole adamantly refused. Consequently, the Vernons began hating the day they had ever met the Doles and taken on the responsibility as parents.

Stuck with a child they no longer wanted, the Vernons took their hatred out on Jamie. Instead of finding Jamie a good home, they decided the child would become their slave. This was the beginning of Jamie's life going from bad to worse. It did not take long for the mischievousness to be beaten out of the once strong-minded, strong-willed child.

Jamie's only outlet from demanding, abusive parents came when it was time to start school. At the age of ten, Jamie was put to work cleaning bathrooms in private homes after school and on weekends. The Vernons certainly didn't need the extra money. Their reasoning was selfish. The longer they could keep Jamie away from home, the better they liked it.

While Jamie was still in high school, the Vernons died a tragic death. Because they had allowed liquor and hatred to dominate their lives, neither had thought about changing their wills. After their deaths, Jamie was delighted at no longer having to scrub toilets for other people. There was one exception: The Johannsens. This was a wonderful older couple from Sweden. Since they had always treated Jamie with love and respect, cleaning toilets for them brought joy to the teenager's lonely life.

Remaining in the family home and keeping up with schoolwork, Jamie kept working for the Johannsens. Just to stay longer in their company, Jamie began helping out with other chores around the Johannsen house.

Having no children of their own, the Johannsens came to love Jamie as their own flesh and blood. It was not long before they had Jamie calling them Mamah and Pappy.

One day, after Jamie had just finished vacuuming the living room carpet, Mamah called out in her Swedish accent, "Jamie. My darling, come to the kitchen and have a cold drink with us."

"I want to put the vacuum away first."

"Nonsense," she insisted. "A pretty thing like you needs to take a break now and then."

"But --"

"I'll have no buts now, Jamie. Come, sit and relax with Pappy and me."

Obedient, Jamie entered the kitchen.

"Come, sit, my darling," Mamah said with a smile. "I just made some fresh lemonade."

"Yah, and it's mighty tasty, too," Pappy added as he took a sip of the lemon nectar from his glass. "Mamah knows just the right secret for making good lemonade." He laughed joyfully. "It's called a good husband who doesn't mind squeezing one hundred fresh lemons."

Wrinkling her brow, Mamah joked back. "Pappy, it wasn't one hundred lemons. Shame on you for teasing with your exaggerations. One of these days, your nose is going to grow as long as *Pinocchio's*."

Enjoying the playfulness between the Johannsens, Jamie took a seat at the table. Mamah filled a glass and placed it on the table. "There you be, Jamie. You know, the real secret is no ice," she stated. "You have to make the lemonade the night before you plan to drink it. Then you refrigerate it overnight. If you put ice in it, it just waters it down and ruins the taste. You taste it, Jamie. Then you tell me if it's to your liking."

Jamie drank several big gulps. "That's the best lemonade I've ever tasted."

When Jamie's pleasing smile suddenly turned solemn, Pappy asked, "What's the matter, child? Is the lemonade too sour for your taste buds?"

"No, it's fine. I'm sorry I told you a lie just then, Mamah. I'm ashamed of myself. I've actually never tasted lemonade before."

Pappy looked up at Mamah, who was still standing next to Jamie's chair. They both started laughing.

Wrapping her arms around Jamie in a big hug, Mamah stated, "That's wonderful. If this is your first taste of this fine drink, then it is the best you've ever tasted. So that's no lie. Right?"

Nodding, Jamie agreed.

Mamah took her place at the table, sitting next to Pappy and opposite Jamie. "My darling girl, there is a lot we don't know about you. We don't want to pry, but don't you think it's time you tell Pappy and me about your life?"

"You know all there is to know. I live alone because my ... uh ... parents are dead, and I attend school."

"But that's all we know. You were always a happy child around us. But did you have a happy home life as well?" When Jamie did not answer, Mamah sensed something was wrong. "You know, Jamie, from the very first day I answered a knock at our door and found this little urchin standing there asking for a job, my heart went out to you. Pappy and I hired you because we felt sorry for you. Our thinking was that you came from a poor family and needed the money to help put food on the table. It didn't take long for us to fall in love with you. Right, Pappy?"

"Right you are, Mamah."

"You don't have to tell us anything about your home life, if you don't want to. But don't you ever feel ashamed or embarrassed to tell Pappy and me any thing. Right, Pappy?"

"Yah, Mamah is right there. You had better listen to her."

"If I confide in you, I'm afraid you will never want to speak to me again," Jamie stated, looking directly into Mamah's eyes.

"Nonsense," she replied. Stretching out her hands across the table, she placed one hand on Pappy's and the other one on Jamie's hand. "We may not be blood kin to you, but we are like family. Considering we have no other family here in America, you are really all we have. And now with your parents gone, I think we are all you have. If you can't trust us enough to confide in us, then we have no love and respect for each other."

"Once again, Mamah is right, Jamie. We don't want to push you. But if there is something you want to get off your chest, then speak up. Whatever it is, we can work through it together."

Jamie squeezed Mamah's hand. "You won't go crazy on me or have a heart attack or nothing like that, will you?"

Mamah gave a warm smile. "My darling, if you've lived as long as Pappy and I have, and been through as much as we have in our lives, nothing would shock you anymore. Now, what do you want to tell us?"

"There's something very personal about me ... I just don't know how to tell you."

"Very personal? Are you a lesbian?"

"Good grief, Mamah. What a thing to ask her."

"Hush, Pappy. I know what goes on in this world. Well, Jamie, are you? Because if you are, that makes no difference to Pappy and me. We'd love ya just the same."

"No, Mamah, I'm not a lesbian. But I'm really a ... I mean, I'm not a ...." Jamie paused and took a big gulp of lemonade before continuing. "There's no other way to say this. I'm a he."

Looking puzzled, Mamah turned to her husband. "What does this mean, Pappy?"

"I thought you was so up on what's going on in the world, Mamah? Open up your brain. Jamie is saying he is a boy. Not a girl."

Turning back to Jamie, she stated, "Oh, how lovely." Suddenly she was elated. "Pappy, we have a son now. Isn't that wonderful?"

Even though he was a bit puzzled, Pappy nodded.

"I understand now why you are so strong," Mamah stated." But why do you pretend to be a female?"

"When I was very, very young I was led to believe I was a girl. My parents never dressed me in anything but dresses and kept my hair long and in braids. Neither of my parents ever undressed in front of me. But one day, when I was around five, I was in the bathroom brushing my teeth. My father was totally wiped out from too much wine as he stumbled into the bathroom. I don't even think he even realized I was there watching as he urinated in the stool."

"You mean you saw his fishing pole and recognized you had the same extension, only smaller?"

"Mamah!" Pappy shrieked in embarrassment. "Watch what you say, please."

Without taking her eyes off Jamie, Mamah defended her comment. "Well, Pappy, I call 'em as I see 'em. It seems that extension of the male anatomy most men are so proud of is what they use to catch a woman in today's times."

"Mamah, please," Pappy pleaded. "Where do you hear such nonsense?"

"Please yourself, Pappy. I read the newspapers and the magazines just as well as you do."

Shaking his head, Pappy mumbled, "I must be reading different ones than you do."

Turning her attention back to Jamie, she said, "You poor darling boy. That must have been a horrible shock?"

"If you hadn't ever seen a boy or a girl's … um …." Pappy paused. Not being able to find the right words, he was embarrassed to ask what he was thinking.

"Go on, Pappy," Mamah urged. "Finish what you was saying."

"I will. I will. I want to know how … well … before you seen your father's … you know what, how did you know the difference?"

Mamah grinned. "It's called a penis, Pappy. Surely you're not so old as to have forgotten the name of it?"

Pappy's face turned fire engine red. He looked at Jamie. "Leave it to Mamah."

"Hush now, Pappy. Let Jamie answer your question."

"I didn't. Not then. I found out when I was seven. Out on the playground, one day, I remember a girl telling some of us that mommies and daddies were different down there. Since I was young and naive, I asked how they were different. When she answered me, that's when I knew for sure I was boy."

"When you found out, did you question your parents as to why they were treating you as a girl?"

"No, Mamah. I didn't dare. You had to know my parents to understand. Questioning their authority or reasoning was just not something I dared to do."

"How in the world did you get by in school when it came time to go to the bathroom? And didn't you ever have physical education where you had to undress or take showers with the other girls?"

"Girls' bathrooms have what they call stalls, Pappy. And each stall has a door for privacy. Fortunately, I was never required to take physical education. So I was able to keep my manliness well hidden."

"I know I wasn't born and raised here in America. But I kind of thought Jamie was a strange name for a girl," Pappy said.

"At one time, I did too. But when I started high school, I found out it can be a girl's or a boy's name."

"You poor baby," Mamah sympathized. "I just can't imagine what you've gone through all your life."

"That's not all."

"There's more?" Pappy questioned.

"Yes and no. You see, somewhere in the depths of my memory, I seem to remember a sibling."

"Older? Younger? Brother? Sister?"

"Mamah, slow down and give the poor boy a chance to speak," Pappy scolded.

"That's okay, Pappy. The truth is, Mamah, I don't know since it's such a vague memory."

"You must at least remember if you took baths together?"

Pappy shook his head. "Mamah, what in heaven's name does a bath have to do with anything?"

"Because they would be naked together. Then Jamie would remember if it was a brother or a sister."

"No. I always took my baths alone. Actually, I'm not sure if it is really something I remember or not."

"And I suppose because of your parents being they way they were, you couldn't ask them?"

"Well, I did ask, once, Mamah. I was told I had an overactive imagination."

"Since your parents are deceased now, why haven't you changed back to what you really are?" Pappy asked.

"I sort of have. That's why I keep my hair short now and wear jeans instead of dresses."

When Pappy started to laugh, he quickly covered his mouth and pretended to cough. His fake attempt did not get past Mamah.

"Pappy, shame on you. What Jamie is telling us is nothing to laugh at."

"Forgive me, Jamie. I'm not laughing at that. I just realized why your voice changed. At the time, I thought it very strange for a girl. But now I understand."

"I don't mind you laughing, Pappy. It is rather funny, now. But back then, it was sheer horror for me."

"You're lucky you don't have a beard yet," Pappy stated, rubbing his chin.

"If you look close, I do have some pretty dark facial hairs starting to grow. But if I shave, I'll get whiskers."

"I don't see that as a problem, Jamie. Lots of women have dark facial hair."

"Oh, Pappy, you're right. Oh, I just thought of the perfect solution,"

Mamah said. "Get your face waxed. I read about it all the time in the magazines."

"Waxed?"

"Yes, Jamie. I'll tell you all about it later after you've finished answering Pappy's question."

"I thought I did."

"No, you was explaining why you haven't already turned into the boy that you are. Pappy's tickle-bone changed the subject."

"Well, I can't completely change until I graduate from high school. The kids at school know me as a girl. I want to go to college though. And when I do, I plan on enrolling as a male. That is, I hope I can."

"I mean no disrespect for the dead, Jamie. But your parents must have been pretty stupid if they thought you would never find out something so important as to what your gender is."

"Pappy, they must have had their reasons for believing the way they did. Right, Jamie?"

"If they did, I never figured it out. All I know is, they told me that they bought me through the black market when I was very young. Even my birth certificate is fake." Mamah covered her mouth as she let out a sigh. "Obviously they couldn't have children of their own. And because they were very wealthy, they paid big bucks for me. Since they didn't want to get in trouble with anyone if the truth was discovered, they kept almost everything about me a secret. I guess after so many years, they honestly believed I would never question the truth."

"Well," Pappy stated with a nod, "after what you have told us of those two, that would make sense. Liquor has a way of eating up one's brain and ruining the good sense God gave them."

"You don't know how rough it's been all my life, hiding my true gender. What's worse, I've never been able to have a girlfriend."

"How awful for you or anyone to have to live with such a lie," Pappy consoled.

"So, darling boy, did the Vernons ever adopt you?"

"They couldn't without getting in trouble with the law. No, I'm not legally a Vernon."

Pappy scratched his head in bewilderment. "Then how are you able to stay in their home since their deaths? I'm surprised someone — like a blood relative or even the government — didn't step in and put you out on the street. Or don't you live there any more?"

"Yes, that's where I live. After their deaths, I hired an attorney, showed him my birth certificate, signed some legal documents, and that was that. Today, everything the Vernons owned is legally mine."

"Either he was a very stupid attorney or your birth certificate looks very real," Pappy stated.

Jamie smiled. "A little of both."

"So if the fake one looks that real, maybe you can get yourself another one that says you were born a male child."

"I've already been trying to find out who can do that for me, Pappy. I want to get my driver's license soon. From what I understand, I'll have to show my birth certificate as proof of my age. I'm sure gender won't make a difference. But I'd rather their records show me as a male, not a female."

"Jamie, who are your real parents? Or do you know?"

"Yes. I know. When the attorney needed the deed to the property and the car title to legally change everything over into my name, I had to go through the family papers. The information I unearthed ate into my very soul. I finally knew who my real parents were. The rest of the paperwork only justified my convictions and verified that I was truly a black-market-child."

"But in a good way, wasn't it nice to find out who they are?"

"Not really, Mamah. The vital information I discovered only brought about loathing and disgust for my birth parents."

"Don't be foolish like the Vernons were, Jamie. Hate is a terrible disease that will eat you up inside. Now, no one says you have to like these people. But why not open your heart and at least find them. Maybe they have a good excuse for what they did? You'll never know until you find them and ask. Can't you do that to at least satisfy your own mind?"

"I don't know yet, Pappy. Part of me says I might have more family out there and I would like to be a part of their lives. But another part of me says there's no reason to find people who sold me like some piece of meat in a supermarket. Right now, I can't even imagine any parent having a good excuse for doing such a thing."

Pappy shook his head. "Well, son, when you are ready to find out, you know that me and Mamah will do everything we can to help you."

"Thanks, Pappy. I really appreciate the offer."

* * *

Through a bit of research, Jamie found out where his real family lived. It surprised him when he found out they resided in the same part of town as he did. For years he had grown up just a few miles away from his birth parents and never knew it. However, as the anger brewed within him, he vowed he would never meet them face-to-face until the time was right — after a planned encounter. First, he had to be positive that none of his birth family would ever recognize him.

In his junior year of college, he lost the two people closest to him. Mamah became very ill with a flu virus and eventually passed on from an acute case of pneumonia. Pappy soon followed due to a severe stroke. They left the young man — they had loved as a son — their modest country home and a large amount of money. The Johannsens took all of Jamie's secrets with them to their graves.

Even though there were happier memories for him in the Johannsen house, he sold it and continued living in the Vernon house. He opened modest checking and savings accounts, but kept the majority of his money hidden in his house.

CHAPTER FOURTEEN

Mayfield, Roitstein, Ferndale, and Brown were pounding the pavement, both by car and on foot, accumulating information about the rattle. Detective Hathaway was knee-deep in his search for bubble-jet printers. Mayfield and Roitstein were still in the field trying to locate background information about Ellie Smither.

Arriving at the precinct around six forty-five A.M., Warner stopped to talk to the Desk Sergeant. "Officer De Mija gets off duty in fifteen minutes, doesn't he?"

"Normally. Sometimes the guys don't check in until after seven, depending on if they've just been on patrol or they're working a call."

"Well, when he comes in, see that he comes to my office before he leaves for the day."

"Certainly, Capt. Warner."

* * *

While Warner was reading a report, getting updated on a home burglary case some of his other detectives were working on, he looked up when he heard a knock on the door. "Come in," he yelled, as he continued working.

As the door opened, Warner looked up. De Mija was standing in the doorway dressed in full policeman's uniform. He was clutching his hat between his forearm and his side. "You wanted to see me, sir?"

"Officer De Mija. Come on in." Warner closed the folder he was working on and set it to the side of his desk. "Shut the door behind you and take a seat."

Doing as asked, De Mija felt a bit uneasy as he sat in a chair close to Warner's desk. Sitting erect with both feet planted on the floor, De Mija placed his hat on his lap.

"Relax. You look like a kid that just got called into the principal's office for getting into trouble."

"That's rather how I feel, sir."

"Would you like a cup of coffee?"

De Mija was used to sitting as if at attention. The only time he allowed himself to relax was in his own home. However, he could feel the strain of tension as his jaws clenched, making it rather difficult to speak. He hadn't a clue as to why he was called to the chief of detective's office unless it had something to do with the homicides. He wondered where he had messed up. "No. Thank you, sir."

"You know, I've never seen you with your hat off before. I never would have guessed you as bald since you have so much facial hair. If you don't mind my asking, are you prematurely bald or do you have to shave your head every day?"

"I keep it shaved."

The short, direct answer gave Warner the clue to drop the subject. "I've been going over your personnel records and I must say they are very impressive. You have worn your uniform proudly. And that commendation you received for a good collar is like the cherry on the whipped cream."

"Yes, sir. Thank you, sir."

"Well, Leo, tell me a little about yourself."

"Like what?"

"Well, I know you attended the academy here in Mt. Pride. And Capt. Roberts hired you right after graduation. You appear to love your work, and your captain has nothing but good things to say about you. On the personal side, I know you're married and have one child. How am I doing?" Warner smiled.

"I can't vouch for what my captain relayed to you. But the rest of it is all true."

"Do you have any hobbies?"

"When I get time."

"So, tell me about them," Warner continued, attempting to force the officer into talking more about himself.

"I enjoy growing flowers."

"Then I'll bet you can hardly wait for spring to arrive?"

"Not necessarily. I have a hothouse on my property. Although I do a lot of outside gardening when the weather is nice."

"That's interesting. What else do you like to do?"

"Write. Someday, I hope to be a published author."

"Really? What do you like to write?"

"Although I enjoy creative writing of all sorts, I would really like to write romance novels. My wife says I'm a romantic at heart. She feels I would do good at that sort of thing."

Warner was intrigued by De Mija's unusual hobbies. *Such versatility*, he thought. "I envy anyone who can write. So, is there anything else you enjoy away from work?"

"Taking my little girl to the park or the zoo. I also take her to the flea markets with me. I guess you might say that my daughter is my greatest hobby. I'm what one would call a doting father."

"A real family man. That's good."

"My wife and child are my life, outside of my job. Kids need a lot of attention and understanding, and that's what I give to my little girl."

"I certainly understand that. My wife and I have a daughter. Don't blink because they grow up before you know it." Receiving nothing but silence from De Mija, Warner said, "You know, my wife likes to go to those flea markets. Do you look for anything in particular? Or, like my wife, do you just go to look at everything?"

"I collect knives of all sizes and shapes. So I'm always looking for a piece to add to my collection."

"That's rather a dangerous collection with a child around, isn't it?"

"Not if you use common sense. I keep them locked up in my display cabinet."

"Do you have other family in Mt. Pride?"

"No. My parents have been gone for sometime now. My wife is from out of state, so there's just the three of us here in Mt. Pride. That's really all the family I need."

"What are your aspirations, Leo?"

"I'd like to be a police captain, someday. Or an instructor at the academy."

Throughout the conversation, Warner could feel the uneasiness the officer was obviously feeling. He felt it was time to get to the reason behind the meeting. "Those are great aspirations. Tell me, have you ever thought about becoming a detective?"

"Certainly. I love investigative work. Especially when it gets the bad guys off the streets."

"All of the detectives around here are quite versatile. Although some of them are more qualified to work in one particular division, they work on all cases when need be. We have an opening for a detective. I would like to promote you to that position. Of course that means hanging up the uniform. What do you think?"

"I think that would be swell, sir."

"Is that a yes?"

"Yes. That's a definite yes." De Mija breathed a sigh of relief.

"Okay. I've already discussed this with your captain and the chief. So they are aware to get a replacement for you, assuming you would accept this position. There's a new group of graduates that came out of the academy recently. So we have a few extras above normal manpower requirements. Capt. Roberts doesn't seem to think he'll have a problem filling your vacancy on patrol."

"When would I start?"

"First thing tomorrow morning. Is that okay with you?"

"Sounds good. That will give me plenty of time to turn in my revolver and badge, and clean out my locker."

"Actually, I'm holding a meeting ...," Warner stopped to look at his watch, then continued, "in a little over an hour from now. I'm sure you know some of the detectives. But I'd like to introduce you as our newest member to the unit. I know you've been on patrol all night, but would you mind sticking around?"

"Not at all. Might I ask what the meeting's about?"

"Of course. We're working on a serial case that I will start you on first thing tomorrow morning. So I want you to be well informed."

"Do you mean the Atkin homicides?"

"Yes, but it also ties in with the dual homicides back at the start of the year."

"The Brook murders?"

Warner hesitated momentarily. He then said, "Oh, that's right. Lt. Konklin told me you and Officer Ripley were also the first uniforms on the Brook scene."

De Mija nodded.

"That's good. At least you'll start off with some knowledge of the two cases."

"But I didn't know you considered them a serial case. Does that mean you suspect one person killed both couples?"

"That's our theory. Okay, as soon as the meeting is over, you can be on your way. Then you can report to me first thing in the morning."

"You just tell me what time and I'll be here."

"Unless a special investigation requires night duty or you're on call, your workdays will begin at seven A.M. sharp. I'm sure after working the graveyard shift it will take a while for you to get used to your new work schedule. I'd advise you to get a good night's sleep tonight."

"I won't have any problem, sir. I haven't been on the night shift that long. It will be great to get back on days again."

"Good. I'll contact personnel and let them know to switch you from your uniform pay to detective pay, and issue you the detective's essentials. When you report to my office in the morning, we'll go over your wage difference. Then I'll put you to work." Standing and extending his hand, Warner stated, "Well, Leo, welcome to the detective's unit. I know you're going to be an excellent contributor to our unit."

De Mija immediately got to his feet. After placing his hat under his arm, he shook hands with Warner. "Thank you, sir. I promise I'll do everything to live up to your expectations of me."

"As much as I appreciate it, please drop the *sir*. It makes me feel like an old man."

"Then what do I call you?"

Laughing, Warner responded, "Captain or Cap will do. On rare occasions, I even answer to Joe. But that's after you've been around for a while. Any questions?"

"Yes. Where's your meeting being held this morning?"

"In the conference room. When you come back upstairs, just ask any of the detectives to show you the way. You'll find everyone in the unit most accommodating. Feel free to bring a cup of coffee or a cold drink with you. We might seem a little relaxed around here, but we get the job done. So unless you have any other questions, I'll see you at nine."

Just as De Mija was leaving Warner's office, Konklin caught the door before it closed. "Good morning, Joe. May I come in?"

"Of course. I see you brought your mug with you."

"Always. As ugly as it is, it seems to be attached to my head," Konklin quipped.

Warner chuckled. "Just for that, I won't ask if you want some of my good coffee," he teased, walking to the coffeemaker to fill his cup.

"That's okay. Mine is already full."

Returning to his chair, Warner made a gagging noise. "That mud from the coffee room isn't anywhere near what I call coffee."

"Well, we aren't all privileged to have our own coffeemakers."

"Nothing stopping you from putting one in your office."

"I know, but for me it would be more of a nuisance than a convenience. Besides, I don't know where I'd put one in my small closet of an office."

"I guess that's true. For crying out loud, Eddy, park your chubby cheeks in a chair. You know you make me nervous when you stand there like you're ready to run out the door if someone yells fire."

Grinning, Konklin took a seat. "So, what did you say to Leo? He always wears such a serious face, I couldn't help but notice he was smiling."

"I offered him the detective position and he accepted. That reminds me, I need to call Roberts and Doogle and inform them. Sit tight for a few minutes."

Konklin enjoyed his coffee while he listened to Warner's conversation.

"Chief, this is Joe over at the 15th. Well, sir, it looks like you will need that uniform replacement. Yes, he accepted it. Uh-huh. Yes. I know, I know. Hey, give me a break," Warner forced a laugh, giving Konklin a forlorn look. "It's Lee's own fault for highly recommending the kid. Just think of all the fun he'll have in training a new rookie. Yes, I'll call Lee and tell him. I just wanted to make sure you knew first.

"What? You want me to do it? But, I have a meeting at nine. Probably no more than an hour. Okay. Yes, I understand. Okay, chief, I'll talk to you later." Hanging up the receiver, Warner shook his head.

"Why the look, Joe?"

"Ed is a real pain-in-the-butt for one thing. He just informed me I have to speak to the press."

"Naturally. He can blame you if anything is leaked to the press that shouldn't be. Doogle only speaks to the press when a case is solved so he can take all the glory."

After Warner had spoken with Capt. Lee Roberts, head of the Uniform Division of the 15th Precinct, he said, "So, Eddy, we've got our man."

"That's great. We sure can use the extra help, especially on this serial case."

"I need to talk to Ed again later about our budget allocation. I want a window put in your office."

"That's not necessary, Joe."

"Don't you ever feel like you're caged in there?"

"Sometimes."

"Well, I'm not really giving you a choice. When you're in there working with your door closed, the rest of us would like to know."

"Geez, do I get window blinds, too, like you have?"

"Only if you promise to keep them open."

"Gee, thanks. Then I'll feel like I'm back in the fish bowl."

"You can't fool me, big guy. I know you miss sharing this office with me. Besides, don't worry about it yet. I have to get it ok'd first."

"Well, lots of luck. I know the red tape you have to go through to get anything done around here. Even the top brass has to wait for months before a requisition is taken into consideration by our city fathers."

"They've already informed me my new budget was approved. So they can't back down. Besides, look at all the money I saved the taxpayers by working a double load. That's two jobs for the price of one."

"Yeah, but you're lucky they didn't reverse it on you."

"How could they?"

"If you can do your captain's job and still do everyday investigative work, they could have taken advantage of that and never let you budget for the extra man."

"Very true, Eddy, with one huge exception. We are supposed to be manned with twenty-five detectives in our unit. That's the rule."

"Well, if anybody can do it, my money's on you. I have to sign my name in blood just to get office supplies. What's your secret?"

"It's called never taking no for an answer."

"So, are you ready for the press?"

"Hell, no. Oh, I just had a thought that will help me out. Sorry, Eddy, but I've got to shoo you out of here."

Konklin got to his feet. "No problem. I'll see you at the meeting."

* * *

In the conference room, Warner brought the meeting to order. "Leo, will you step forward, please."

Warner waited until De Mija came forward from the back of the room and stood beside him at the podium. "I want you to meet Detective Leo De Mija. He has agreed to join forces with our illustrious group." After a brief clapping of hands, he added, "I expect you to make him feel right at home and give him plenty of work to keep him busy. That is, after the lieutenant gets through with him." Warner had to stop again while he waited for the laughter to subside. "Okay, Leo, if you'll stay here, I'd like you to meet your new co-workers.

"Since you're all here this morning, I thought it would be a great opportunity for Leo to get to know the group he'll be working with. It always helps to recognize a face. When I call your name, stand up. After I've completed each five-man division, you may then take your seats.

"Homicide Division: Arjay Mayfield, Kieyell Roitstein, Brenda Ferndale, Joe (J.B.) Brown. Thank you, Detectives."

"Hey, Cap," Holms called out, "you need to recount your fingers. That's only four."

When the laughter broke out, Warner said, "Quiet down, ladies. Look, I've always enjoyed the lightheartedness that goes along with the seriousness in any of our meetings. But in one hour, I have to go outside and meet with the press. So if you'll all refrain from any more outbursts, I would certainly appreciate it.

"Okay, let's continue. Crimes Against Persons Division: Robert (Bobby) Anthony, Bryce Brubaker, Antonio (Tony) DelGinny, Michael (Mike) Holms, Mathew (Matt) Rayfelt. Thank you."

"Fraud Division: Austin Ridell, Arnold (Arnie) Hathaway, Eric Lennon, Mitchell (Mitch) Smith, Dirk Jones. Thank you."

"Robbery Division: Jesse (Jess) Duncan, George (Scooby) Fratt, Alex Landall, Gregory (Greg) Simpson, J.D. Lerner. Thank you."

"Narcotics Division: Justin Baker, Michael (Mickey) Chung, Deric Zeal, Art Lewkowski, and, last but not least, Lester (Les) Ballard. Thank you."

"I'd like to add here, it's great to see a full attendance today. Okay, Leo, you can return to your seat now."

Walking back to his seat, De Mija got the usual waves, pats, and handshakes, along with the verbal welcoming cant.

"Now, we all know how important partners are when you're out in the field. A detective needs to depend on his partner as much as he did when he was in uniform. In the right, or should I say in the wrong situation, if you can't depend on your partner, you're dead. No one knows that better than the man who's got years of experience up on all of you. That's this balding fella with the gray streaks running through what hair he has left, sitting in the front row. Lt. Konklin."

As the group broke into loud snickering, Konklin's voice rang above the joyful sounds. "Geez, give Cap a podium and he thinks he's a standup comedian."

"Darn straight," Warner admitted with a smile. "How many captains have you known that gave you free entertainment during working hours?"

"Every one of them," Konklin joked back. "Or so they thought."

The snickers burst into laughter.

"Okay, I concede. Calm down. Calm down," Warner said, gesturing with both hands for everyone to quiet down. "Anyway, the lieutenant feels that it would be wrong to split up any of you partners. He's asked that our new recruit, Leo, be his partner on this case. So, Mike, I hope that finally answers your question. That is, if you can add four plus one?"

In response, Holms gave a half-hearted salute.

"Now, I've heard the scuttlebutt that's been going around ever since I've been made captain. And no wisecracks that it took me so many years to hear the rumors you all pass around. Believe me, I was well aware of your ladies' gossip. I just chose to ignore it until now. Let's get the record straight, right now. No, I do not show favoritism because I've been working with the lieutenant again.

"As some of you are aware, I came in as his partner when I first came to this precinct many years ago. We were just at the beginning stages of an important homicide case when your last captain retired. I was asked to fill his position. Lt. Konklin and I continued as partners until the case was solved and placed into the 'closed file.'

"Then a high-priority case landed in our laps. Those of you who were around then should remember when the mayor of Mt. Pride disappeared which ended up being a huge homicide case. It wasn't until we had solved that case and placed it into the 'closed files' that Detective Anderson became Lt. Konklin's partner, freeing me to do my job. Unfortunately, Anderson lost her life to a drunk driver several months ago. This left the lieutenant without a partner once again.

"Because of the brass dragging their feet in approving my allocation, as I mentioned in our last meeting, and making the decision to promote Leo, we've been shorthanded. Even though I've been working closely with the lieutenant on this new and ongoing homicide investigation, he is actually the lead on this case.

"Also, for the record, I will continue to be an active captain. I didn't become a detective to sit behind a desk all day. Maybe a few years down the road I'll have to do that. But not right now. So any of you, at any given time, can expect me to show up on one of your assignments to help out. Another thing you might remember. Lt. Konklin is my right-hand man. So, from time to time, we will be working on cases together.

"I hope that settles the questions in everyone's mind about me showing partiality around here. Personally, I think it's a damn shame I have to stand up here and defend myself. Now, hopefully, you little old ladies will stop your gossiping and use your long noses for investigative work."

Leaving the group somewhat speechless, Warner left the podium and walked over to where Konklin was seated. Leaning over and speaking softly, he asked, "Do you want to take over here?"

"Not yet, Joe. Why don't you go ahead and get everyone's report. I can hold the next meeting."

"I see you're wearing your brown suit today."

"What's that supposed to mean?"

"You were wearing one of your gray suits the other day when we had a certain conversation. I think you left that self confidence at home with that suit."

"Please, Joe. I promise I'll hold the next meeting. I'm just not prepared right now."

"Hey, Cap," one of the detectives yelled, "didn't your mother ever teach you it isn't polite to whisper to someone in front of company?"

As the group chuckled, Warner looked up and nodded in agreement, both to Konklin's words and to the detective's comment. Wearing a big smile, Warner walked back to the podium. "The answer to your question, Detective, is yes. But you're not company," Warner teased back.

Putting a more somber look on his face, Warner got back to the business at hand. "Since we're dealing with a really demented serial killer on this case, the lieutenant has given a name to this case file: *Black Tulip*."

As Warner took a breath, Landall blurted out, "Damn, I hope you're not serious."

"I wasn't aware we had to okay the name with you first, Alex. What's your objection?"

"It's just not original, that's all. Years ago, I remember you telling us about the *Black Rosebud* case one of your detective buddies was involved with. Shortly after, you gave the name *Black Lily* to the mayor's case. And now you want to name this new one the *Black Tulip* case. Hell, before you know it," Duncan complained, "the rest of the units will be laughing at us. We'll be known as the *Pansy Unit*: delicate and feminine."

Keeping his poise intact, Warner responded, "If any of you agree with Alex, raise your hands." After looking around the room, he said, "None of you. Since you're outnumbered, Alex, kindly put a zipper on it. If you have any further objections, I suggest you take them up with me or the lieutenant. Later.

"Back to what I was saying. Those of you already on our special task force are aware that a *Black Tulip* is part of the perp's calling card. We don't know what this flower signifies to the perp. Hopefully, when we catch him he'll enlighten us. However, that's not the only reason the lieutenant chose the name. In case you don't know, our illustrious lieutenant likes to read murder mysteries. In so doing, he remembered reading a story where the *Black Tulip* symbolized multiple homicides. I agreed with him that the name was fitting. So, from now on that's how we'll refer to this case.

"Brenda, since you and J.B. were put in charge of locating the rattle, why don't you tell us what you've found out so far." Warner crossed his arms, leaned on the podium and rested on his elbows.

Detective Ferndale took the floor next to her chair. Standing with her feet spread about a foot apart for balance, she dropped her arms behind her back and clutched her hands together. "First off, I want to apologize. We didn't get in until late yesterday. So I'll brief you on that part. I'm sure you've been reading our other daily reports, so there's no need to give a run-down on them. That is, with all the paperwork and forms we have to complete for you each day, I hope you're reading them, Cap?"

"Yes, I've been reading them. However, for our new detective's benefit, and for those who weren't at our first meeting, I'd like you to briefly explain from the beginning."

"Sure, Cap. First off, J.B. and I have Bobby and Bry working with us. We are trying to locate all the stores in the area that sell the small rattle found at the two homes of the murder victims. First we went through the phone book to locate all the stores that handled baby items, children's items and specialty party items. We made our list to include every store from specialty to superstores, department stores to drugstores, and children's stores to party favor stores. Then we contacted the local phone company to see if there were any new listings, not in the phone book, for the same kinds of stores.

"After making up a long list of store names and addresses, we divided our list into sections. I, for one, never realized before that there were so many shopping centers and strip malls in our area. Of course it was just our luck that every department store and superstore in the area carry one form or another of the small party favor we're looking for.

"Now, we did as Lieu suggested and just focused on our part of the city for now. The four of us each took a section of our east-side area and started going from store to store, talking to the store mangers and some of the buyers. Due to the fact that we had a lot of ground to cover, we couldn't call ahead to make appointments. We just had to take our chances that we could get in touch with the person we needed to talk to at the larger stores. But let me assure you, none, so far, have been missed.

"With the stores we've already covered, we've narrowed our list down to forty stores. Each of these forty stores either has the same rattle on their shelf, as we speak, or has had it in the past three years. Meaning, of course, that some stores have discontinued the item because it wasn't a good retail item. The six stores who have discontinued the item have promised to go over their back records to see if there is anything that ticks a memory of any individual or any company in particular that had purchased this item in bulk or an overly unusual amount. However, from all of the managers and buyers we spoke with so far, not one of them remembers any special orders or anything that seemed out of the ordinary.

"Even though we've made a dent in our extensive list, we still have a lot of ground to cover. After our meeting today, the four of us will hit the streets again and continue our search. Incidentally, I purchased one of the store's products to show you how it's packaged." Bringing her arms forward and breaking her stance, Ferndale picked up a small cellophane package that sat on the table next to her.

Since this was De Mija's first meeting as a detective, he did not pay too much attention to what Ferndale held in her hand. He sat quietly at the back of the room taking notes.

"As you can see," she held the small cellophane package up in front of her, "a consumer can purchase this package which contains five small rattles for twenty-nine cents. I'll get this to the Lieu when I'm through." After a nod of acceptance from Warner, Ferndale placed the package back on her desk.

Picking up her notepad, she continued giving her verbal report. "I received a phone call from one of the department store buyers when I got to my desk this morning. She's a lady we had already interviewed. She gave me the name of the New York distributor of this item." Reading from her notes, she stated, "It's an import business called Myron's Miniatures. They import all kinds of party favors from China. Then sell to retailers at wholesale prices all over the United States. The lady buyer informed me that, to her knowledge, this importer is the only distributor in the states that sells this particular packaged rattle.

"When we're through here, before I head back out on the streets, I'll get on the horn to this import company and see what I can find out from them. Well, that's about it for now." Ferndale laid her notebook on the table and sat back in her chair.

Straightening up and moving his shoulders around to work out the kinks, Warner nodded and smiled to let the detectives know he was pleased with the report. "If any of you encounter any problems with any of these managers or buyers, don't hesitate to let the lieutenant know. We'll find cause to subpoena their books."

"I don't think that will do us any good, Cap," Ferndale responded. "They go by item and code numbers. We wouldn't have the slightest idea what we're looking for even if we did look at their records. The exception, of course, are their customer files. They would give us names and addresses."

"Well, if you do encounter any problems, I would strongly suggest to them that you can subpoena their books if you don't get an instant response. You'd be amazed how just the hint of a subpoena will suddenly refresh people's minds and how they miraculously find time to help in a police investigation."

"Shame on you, Cap," Brown uttered with a chuckle. "You aren't trying to tell us that we should intimidate or threaten these people, are you?"

"I don't believe either of those two verbs came out of my mouth, J.B." Warner laughed. "But, whatever works. Arnie, let's hear your report."

Hathaway stayed seated in his chair. "I've had a list that's large enough to choke a horse, Cap. I'll bet every office in Mt. Pride has computers and printers. After discussing it with the Lieu, I limited my list to begin with to the same types of stores that would sell the small rattle. And I've stayed just in our east-side area. We figured the same person would probably have access to both the rattle and a computer printer in the same area of work.

"Basically, I have pretty much of the same list as Ferndale's team have been using. My problem has been that most companies aren't as apt to give me an employees' list as they are to give out stock or order information.

"When I bring an employee list back to the office, I enter each name into my computer. I figure as we add to the suspect list, we will be able to cross-reference the names against each list. Hopefully, we'll find a match. I have about one hundred stores yet to cover. If I don't get anywhere with my current list of stores, I'll expand my search to the business offices in the area. That's it, Cap, except to say I'm happy to have Eric back so he can help me."

"Okay, everyone, for Leo's benefit let me refresh you on what we've got so far." Warner took a moment to shuffle through the papers on the podium in front of him. When he found what he was looking for, he began speaking again, going over details to keep the team updated.

As Warner spoke, De Mija felt a tremendous wave of sheer panic rumble through his body. *Settle down. There's not going to be any difference between being a uniform and being a detective. It's just a new group of fellow workers. Just keep your distance, as you always have, and your personal life will remain untouched.*

"Whoever this person is," Warner continued, "or whatever the gender, this perp obviously stakes out his victim's house and is aware of their daily schedule. Then, we believe, he hides in the darkness of the night before making entrance. The one obstacle this perp seems to be encountering is the female victim in each case. It's very obvious that the women have either been startled awake or only partially asleep as the perp has subdued them both with a bash to the back of their heads. Once this animal has committed his heinous crime with minimal struggle, he then exits the crime scene the same way he made entrance. Okay, Eddy and Leo ...." Warner stopped and called out, "Detective De Mija."

Dropping his pen on this pad of paper and quickly standing, De Mija replied. "Yes, sir."

Smiling, Warner stated, "Sit, Detective. You looked like you were in a trance back there. Do you have any questions so far?"

"No, sir."

"Okay. As I was saying, Eddy and Leo are going to start hitting dry cleaners first thing tomorrow morning. This perp had to be too close to his victims when he killed them not to have blood spatter on him. According to our medical examiner, he would have blood sprayed everywhere when he cut the jugular vein. Chances are he wore clothes he could either wash or readily dispose of. But we don't want to leave any avenues unturned.

"It beats me, with that much blood, how the mutt got out of the rooms without tracking all over the place. The CSIs seem to feel the blood smudges on the bedspread at the first crime scene and the top comforter on the second crime scene answers this question. It appears that the bottoms of these two items were used to wipe blood off something — perhaps the murder weapon, or the perp's clothes and or skin. Until we get a report on the DNA, we won't know if the blood evidence belongs solely to the victims. If the lab finds a foreign DNA on the bloodstained bedding, I'm hoping we'll have a lead on our perp.

"We've got the CBI Crime Lab involved to assist us. They are trying to find out what sort of weapon our assailant used. And what kind of a tool was used to break the window at the Brook house and jimmy the door at the Atkin house. We also sent them the rattles and the calling cards for further testing since our lab didn't find any prints on any of them. Using the CBI's more sophisticated equipment, we're hopeful they'll find something on at least one of these items that will help us.

"One last thing. I was informed before I came here that the press will be waiting outside for me to make a statement. Which, I already mentioned to you earlier. As usual, they'll be vultures waiting to pick my bones. If any of you leave the precinct within the next hour, make sure you use the backdoor. That's not to say someone from the news media won't be out back and ready to get a statement from you. Just remember to say nothing. If they persist, just refer them to me or to Chief Doogle.

"Above all, don't discuss this case with anyone. The general public knows nothing about this perp's calling card. We would like to ward off any copy-cat killers out there that get thrills out of taking over the limelight, or think they can get away with murder and blame the real perp for the crime they commit. Unfortunately, we are still in the newest area of this large city of ours. So we aren't privileged to have snitches. As always, keep your eyes and ears open and your mouths shut. That reminds me. Brenda, what excuse is your group giving for checking on this rattle?"

"We've been telling the people that we're chasing down a dope ring. Insinuating, of course, that the drugs are being smuggled into the United States inside the rattles they're selling or have already sold to their customers. We rather suggest that they could be accessories in this drug ring we're pursuing."

"No wonder you're getting full cooperation." Warner laughed. "Great cover. What about you, Arnie?"

"My excuse sounds lame compared to Ferndale's."

"That's okay. Let's hear it."

"I tell them that the governor of Colorado has received some poison pen letters and we've traced them back as coming from here in Mt. Pride. I also tell them the letters have been entered into a computer and printed out on a bubble-jet printer. Helping to locate that special printer will help lead us to the arrest of our perp."

"That's not so lame. In fact, both excuses are very inventive. You're all using your heads. That's what I like to hear."

"Cap, do we know for sure that this snake is left-handed?" Brubaker asked.

"Affirmative, Bryce. Okay, Arjay, how are you and Kieyell doing on your investigation?"

"This one's a real hair puller, Cap," Mayfield answered from his chair. "We were able to trace Ellie back all the way to her first day of school. But that's where any information on her ends. We can't find any medical records on her and no birth certificate. According to the Department of Vital Statistics, we located Kate Smither's marriage license and her husband's death certificate. By the way, Mr. Smither died in a car accident just six months ago.

"Nowhere are there any records showing Kate gave birth to any children. And there's nothing on record that she and her husband ever adopted Ellie. We were able to locate some of Ellie's teachers when she attended school. We just wanted to find out what kind of student Ellie was. The few we spoke to said she was a very intelligent kid and a loner. One teacher mentioned how she always felt sorry for Ellie. Evidently, Ellie always came to school looking like she had been used as a punching bag.

"I won't go into anymore details now, Cap. Kieyell and I haven't given up, though. We're going to go through some old files and see if any kids were missing or kidnapped around the time Ellie would have been a tot. Hopefully, we'll find something of importance. That's it."

"Wait, Arjay. Did this teacher you talked with say if she ever asked Ellie why she always looked beat up? Did she ever ask or suspect Ellie was being abused at home?"

"She asked. Says Ellie and her mother claimed Ellie was a klutz and kept running into things or falling down all the time. But the teacher also told me she found this very strange. Seems Ellie never had those kinds of accidents while attending school."

"Very interesting. As for finding out who Ellie's real parents are, if it's not the Smithers, you might check on family members. Sometimes a girl gets pregnant and doesn't want to keep the baby. And, instead of placing the infant up for adoption, a family member will raise the child as their own."

"Good thought, Cap. We'll do that."

"Okay, have I covered everything?"

"What about the murder weapon, Joe?" Konklin reminded.

"Oh, yes. We're looking for a straight-edged tool or instrument that's curved on the end. I hate to be so vague, but as yet we haven't the slightest idea what this could be. As I said, we've enlisted assistance from the CBI to help in this matter. But, if any of you can come up with any ideas, or see anything while you're out and about that might resemble such an item, please don't hesitate to inform the lieutenant. Anyone else have anything to add?" A short glance around the room told Warner there were no more questions or remarks.

* * *

Standing at the podium outside the precinct, Warner addressed the news media. "Good morning, members of the press. As some of you already know, I am Capt. Joe Warner, Chief of the Detective's Unit here at the MPPD 15th Precinct. When I've concluded with my briefing, I will try to answer as many questions as time allows.

"We have had two double homicides here in our east-side area of town. The first were Mr. and Mrs. Pat Brook. The second were Mr. and Mrs. Richard Atkin. Both couples were slain at approximately three o'clock in the morning. Each couple had one child. Fortunately, however, both children were left unharmed by the assailant.

"To save time, I have had a data sheet printed up for you. Officer Sooner, standing to my left," Warner acknowledged him with a hand gesture, "has this printed information to hand out to you when this press conference is over. This data sheet will give you pertinent details such as complete names of the victims, ages and homicide dates.

"Right now we have several leads we are following up on, but we have no prime suspects in either of the cases. Lt. Detective Eddy Konklin is the lead in this case. However, we have several detectives working on both of these double homicides. That's about it for now," he concluded.

Within seconds, Warner was flooded with questions.

"Capt. Warner, were the victims in the first homicides associated with the second victims?"

"No. Through our investigation so far, they didn't even know each other."

"Is there any similarity between the first murders and the second ones?"

"Yes. But I'm not at liberty to release those details right now."

"Where are the victims' children, Capt. Warner?"

"They were immediately placed in the care of Child Protective Services. To my understanding both, subsequently, have been picked up by family members."

"Capt. Warner --" one reporter belted out.

Cutting off the first reporter, another reporter hollered, "Capt. Warner, do you --"

"Wait. Please. I'll get to you one at a time," Warner stated, trying to get some order to the mass confusion of questions. Pointing he stated, "Yes, Jane."

"I've heard two different stories. One that the victims were shot, and the other was that they were stabbed. Which story is correct?"

"I won't comment on how the homicides were committed at this time."

"What was the murder weapon?"

"I believe I just answered that question," Warner replied, being as evasive as possible.

"You mean the department doesn't know what kind of a murder weapon was used?"

"Let's just say that if I tell you what the murder weapon is, you'll know how these people were killed. I prefer not to give you any more information until we've done further investigation into these homicides. Now, that's all the time we have. Thank you for coming."

"Capt. Warner. Do you think we have a serial killer on the loose?"

"Why don't you have any suspects yet, Capt. Warner?"

As the crowd of reporters continued yelling more questions, Warner retreated back into the building.

"Sometimes those people can be a lot of help and do a lot of good. And sometimes they're a pain in my neck," he complained loudly, heading up the steps to the second floor.

CHAPTER FIFTEEN

Warner had his short meeting with De Mija about the new pay raise, which included a sizeable annual clothing allowance for civilian attire. Then he sent De Mija to Konklin's office for assignment.

By mid-morning, Konklin and his new partner began their search of dry-cleaning establishments that might have received any clothes with suspicious bloodstains on them.

Toward the end of the day, when Konklin and De Mija returned to the precinct, Konklin popped his head into the captain's office. "Just checking in, Joe."

"Any good news?"

"Not a thing. Leo and I covered a lot of ground, but nothing to report."

"Damn. We need a break soon and get this lunatic locked up."

* * *

The rest of the week seemed to fly by with hurricane force. Even though everyone was diligently occupied as they searched for clues, they were no closer to finding their serial killer.

While Konklin and De Mija were still canvassing the dry-cleaning establishments, Konklin was desperately trying to bond with his new, temporary partner.

"You know, Leo, you sure don't talk much. Trying to get you into a conversation is like trying to wipe a bear's ass."

"Sorry, lieutenant. I'm just not the gabby type."

"Look, this is the beginning of our fourth day of working together. What do you say you start calling me Lieu."

"I don't mind. But I haven't been with the unit very long. So are you sure it's appropriate."

"It is perfectly permissible."

"If that's what you want, then it's fine with me."

"You know, I've met a lot of people throughout the years in different walks of life. I think the uniforms and the detectives are the only co-workers who are called, primarily, by their last names. Did you ever notice that?"

"I don't think I paid much attention to it."

"Yeah. Take a listen at the office sometime. It's Holms this or DelGinny that. Hell, what am I talking about? Sometimes I'm just as guilty as the next one," Konklin rambled on. "Well, Leo, do you miss driving the black and white yet?"

"Sort of."

"Geez, Leo, talk to me. I'm working my backend off here trying to make friendly conversation. And you give me all of three or four words in return."

"Like I said, I'm not much of a talker."

* * *

"Got a minute?"

"Always, Eddy. Come on in and have a seat. So, how did things go today?"

"More boulders in the road."

"I'm sorry to hear that. So, how's the new partner working out?"

"That's what I want to talk to you about, Joe. I don't know that I'm going to like working with Leo."

"Why? Isn't he responsive to the training?"

"Oh, that's not it. Leo's a quick learner and very serious about his work."

"Then what's the problem?"

"The man doesn't talk. I keep trying to strike up conversations with him. But he gives me a straight simple statement back. Then says nothing more. It's really boring to work with someone who doesn't want to converse. I feel like a proverbial magpie talking to myself most of the time. Also, the kid never cracks a smile. I'd swear, if I didn't know better, his face was made out of plaster."

Breaking into hearty laughter, Warner replied, "Is that all? With your gift of gab you probably don't give the poor guy a chance to respond with more than a couple of words."

"That's not true, Joe. I like to talk to pass the time, but I don't monopolize conversations. You know that better than anyone. And why doesn't the guy smile? I know he can because I saw him smile the day you promoted him. Geez, he's too serious. You know me? I'm serious about my work. But I enjoy a good sense of humor to break up the monotony of all the death and corruption in our profession."

"Come on, big guy, give him some time to warm up and get used to you and his new job. At least give it thirty days. If by then you're still unhappy working with him, we'll figure out something else. Okay?"

"Okay, Joe. But I'm telling you, I don't think we're going to make it as temporary partners."

When Konklin headed for the door, Warner stated, "Don't go away mad, big guy."

"I'm not. In case you haven't noticed, it's Friday again and quitting time."

"Are you working tomorrow?"

"You bet. There are tons of dry-cleaning establishments open on Saturdays."

"You know I can't authorize overtime yet, Eddy."

"No problem. It's just me, anyway. I don't mind the extra hours with no pay."

"So you didn't ask Leo to go with you?"

"Nah. I told him I'd see him on Monday."

* * *

Early Monday morning, as they walked to the parking lot, De Mija asked, "Would you like me to drive today?"

"No, thank you."

As they drove out of the precinct's parking lot, De Mija said, "You know, Lieu, I always drove the patrol car when David Ripley and I were partners. So I really don't mind driving."

"It's funny, but I drove all the time with my partners before Joe joined the department. Then when he came in as my partner … well, he took over. All that time that Joe drove, I sat in your seat and hated it. So I'm glad to be back in the driver's seat. I rather enjoy it. But, I'll make you a deal. The day I don't feel like driving, I'll turn the keys over to you. Deal?"

"If you say so."

"Are you originally from Mt. Pride?"

"Yes."

"Ever traveled around, like on vacations?"

"Sort of."

"Good for you. Sometimes I wish I'd have taken the time to do some traveling. So where did you go?"

"It was only once, so I don't remember."

"That's strange. Why not?"

"I was very young."

"Do your parents live in town?"

"Mother and Father are both deceased."

"Geez, I'm sorry. So I hear you're married and have a kid?"

"Yes."

"Tell me about your wife."

"You're certainly persistent, Lieu," De Mija stated. "I don't suppose you're going to let up until I tell you something about my personal life, are you?"

"Hey, the man can actually say more than a few words," Konklin joked. "Keep going, Leo. You're on a roll."

"My wife's name is Alianna. I call her Ali for short. Right after I got in uniform, she was the first speeder I stopped and ticketed. A few nights later I stopped at a restaurant to have dinner and ran into her again. I guess it was fate. The restaurant was crowded. We were both alone. So I asked her to join me for dinner. She had moved here to Mt. Pride just a few months before I met her. We started dating, fell in love, and got married. She worked for the local phone company until the doctor told her we were going to be parents. Today, Ali loves staying home being a housewife and mother to our little Fayth."

"How does your wife feel about your new position as a detective?"

"Very happy. But then, she always loved me in uniform, too. She's a good cop's wife — very supportive and proud of me. Of course, I wouldn't have it any other way. You can't be in this business and have a whiny wife or one who doesn't accept the fact that you face danger every day when you go to work. She's kind of an introvert, like me. Likes to keep to herself." De Mija stopped talking and continued to look straight ahead out the windshield.

"Don't stop now, Leo. Tell me about your little one."

"My sweet Fayth is a little over two and as cute as a bug's ear."

"Well, there's a proud daddy."

"Yeah. My wife thinks I spoil the kid, but I don't think so. Sure I give in to her cute ways, but she still minds me. I don't have to spank her or scold her. If she's doing something I don't approve of, I just talk to her very quietly. But she knows I mean business. Sometimes all I have to do is to look at her and frown, and she gets my message. I don't go for these parents who mistreat their kids with all that yelling and hitting."

"I don't believe in mistreating them either," Konklin stated. "But a good swat on my bottom never hurt me when I was growing up." *Finally, I found the right button to push. If I can just keep him talking about his family, maybe I can eventually get him into other conversations. It's about time. I couldn't stand the thought of having to work with someone I can't talk to.* "Didn't you get a backend swat or two when you were younger?"

"That's a joke. I had a father who liked to use his belt. And a mother who used whatever was handy. That is, if she didn't have a willow switch close by. I thought I was a pretty good kid — obedient to their every wish. But it was obvious they didn't think so."

"What did you do to make them think otherwise? I mean, no little boy is innocent when it comes to monkey business. I know," Konklin chuckled, "having been a little monkey myself when I was younger."

"Let's just say they felt they had their reasons for being abusive and drop it at that."

"Is that one of the reasons you became a cop, to stop child abuse?"

"You might say that. While still in high school, I had plans of going college in hopes of becoming an English teacher or a novelist. I excelled in creative writing. But something happened in my life …." De Mija stopped talking.

Konklin's inquisitive side leaped forward. "What was that?"

"Let's just say something inside me reached out and told me to change my path in life. A policeman's uniform kept popping up in my mind. So, that's the profession I ended up choosing. Taking child offenders off the street, however, gives me great satisfaction."

Changing the subject, Konklin asked, "What kind of creative writing do you do?"

"All kinds. I started writing poetry when I was around eleven, I guess. As I got older, I liked making up stories. You know, fantasizing. Those fantasies helped me escape the real world when it was unbearable for me. I was pretty good in English in both school and college, especially when we had to write short stories, book reports and essays. You know a person can really lose themselves and their problems when they write."

"I can certainly understand wanting to escape into a fantasy world. Geez, growing up sucks. I wouldn't be a kid again for all the furs in Russia. Have you given that all up or do you still write?"

"I write whenever time permits. Someday, I want to write ...." Suddenly, De Mija yelled, "Watch out!"

As De Mija braced himself with his arms outstretched and his hands flat against the dashboard, Konklin slammed on the brakes, bringing the car to a jolted stop. De Mija flew forward, then abruptly back against the seat back. As Konklin bounced from the steering wheel to the back of his seat, his hands were still tightly gripping the steering wheel.

"Geez! Did you see that? That son-of-a-bird-brain woman pulled right out in front of us. And look at her. She just keeps driving like nothing happened. For two cents I'd chase her down and give her a ticket. We're darn lucky there was no one behind us. Are you all right, Leo?"

"I'm fine. Are you?"

"A little shook up, but I'm okay. I just hope we don't both end up with whiplash. We could have hit that lame-brain woman if you wouldn't have warned me."

"I hate to tell you, Lieu, but I believe that driver had the right-away."

"You're kidding, aren't you? Did I run a stop sign?" Konklin asked, as he started driving again.

"No, there was no stop sign. But you did have a yield sign."

"I didn't see it. Well, sorry about that, Leo. I guess I shouldn't be upset with that other driver if I'm the one at fault." *Geez, it's just not like me to miss road signs.*

Since no one had gotten hurt, the driving incident that occurred that day was never reported. However, Konklin refused to let De Mija take over the driver's seat. Instead, Konklin watched more closely at highway and street signs while he was busy talking and driving at the same time.

Konklin and De Mija had eventually visited every dry-cleaning establishment in Mt. Pride's east-side area. After questioning each and every dry-cleaning establishment's owners and employees, they had no good news to report to Warner. Their lead for possible bloodstained clothes was hopeless.

All they could do now was to wait until the rest of the task force had concluded their canvassing in regards to the rattle and bubble-jet printer. In the meantime, Konklin continued with De Mija's training: teaching him the ropes of office policies.

* * *

Detectives DelGinny, Holms, Anthony, and Brubaker paid Warner a visit.

"We need help, Cap," DelGinny stated, shaking his head.

"I thought you caught your perp?"

"We think we did. But the DA said we don't have enough evidence to prosecute the female we picked up."

"Gall darn it," Holms interjected. "After finally capturing her, now the DA's talking about letting her walk."

Familiar with the case, Warner stated, "Let's see. One, you have the murder weapon." As he spoke, he was gesturing with his hands, as if to be counting with his fingers.

"Yes, the .38," DelGinny answered since he was the lead on the case.

"Yeah, a .38," Holms mimicked.

Oh, great. Mutt and Jeff are at it again. That drives me crazy every time Holms has to repeat what DelGinny says. "Two, you have motive."

"Yes. Three witnesses who will testify in court that she blatantly threatened to kill the victim if he didn't stay away from other women."

"Three witnesses," Homes repeated.

"And three, you have opportunity. You can place her at the scene, can't you?"

"Affirmative, Cap. A female eyewitness saw our suspect running out of the victim's apartment not two minutes after hearing a gunshot."

"Yeah, not two minutes after the gunshot."

DelGinny turned to Holmes. "You're doing it again. Just let me tell it. Okay?"

"Okay," Holms agreed.

"So what's the DA's problem?" Warner asked, relaxing his hands on the desk.

"Our suspect's prints weren't on the gun that killed the guy. Also, her attorney claims she has an alibi for the time the victim was killed and claims our eyewitness is lying."

After listening to the majority of the briefing, Warner asked, "Have you checked to see if the eyewitness has a criminal background or a vendetta against your suspect?"

"No. We had no reason to."

"Why not?"

"Just from conversations and questioning different people in the area. They all said the eyewitness is a wholesome, clean-cut, keep-your-nose clean sort of gal. She has a good job, supports a son, and keeps to herself. We saw no reason to check her out any further."

"Okay, let me make some suggestions. Do some digging into the background of your eyewitness. Maybe there's more to her than meets the eye?"

"Okay, Cap," DelGinny agreed. "But what about the female suspect we have waiting in one of our interview rooms? She could walk and take a hike out of town before we get any more evidence to hold her on."

"Have you officially arrested her?"

"No. We just told her she was picked up for questioning."

"So, she hasn't asked for an attorney yet?"

"Nope."

"Is someone from the DA's office still around?"

"No, Cap."

"Well, I suggest you cut her loose and apologize for any inconvenience you may have caused her. That should throw her off track. Hopefully, she won't plan on running if she is guilty. If you get further evidence against her — something the DA's office can sink their teeth into — then you can get a warrant and officially arrest her."

"Man, I know that dame's guilty. I hate to put her back out on the streets," DelGinny complained.

"Yeah, she's guilty, all right," Holms chimed in.

"Sorry, Detectives, but that's the breaks in our business and you all know it. I don't like it anymore than you do. But if the DA won't prosecute with the circumstantial evidence you have now, you have no other choice."

CHAPTER SIXTEEN

De Mija was absolutely fascinated by the variety of items in the children's shop called Tot's Territory. He had discovered the store even before he had ever gotten married and considered having children. All the bedroom furniture, clothes, toys, and gifts purchased for his daughter, he had bought at this store.

Cartoon characters covered the wallpaper that lined the shelved walls of toys. Mobiles of every shape and form hung from the ceiling. On display in one area of the store was a complete nursery done in white furniture. It had everything from the cradle to the pale-yellow-and-light-green-striped canopy crib. Covering the crib's mattress was a pale yellow quilt, accented by a light green satin pillow.

A soft, furry white bunny with a large light green bow sat in the middle of the crib, just begging to be picked up and cuddled. A carousel night lamp sat on the eight-drawer chest. When the lamp was turned on, a myriad of circus animals slowly turned around the lamp, as flickers of light sparkled off the walls and *Brahms Lullaby* softly played from the enclosed music box. Because the lamp was so soothing to babies and tots alike, this was one of the store's hottest sellers. The display was completed with a rocking horse, a changing table, and everything imaginable that a baby's nursery would need.

Next to the nursery display was a child's room magnificently set up to capture the buyer's attention. In another part of the store there were clothes from infant size 0 to size 4 in toddlers. There were shelves and shelves of toys scattered throughout the store. Caring so much for the little people, as storeowner Jessie Dole called them, he didn't sell any toy that was harmful to children. Directly in the middle of the store was a sitting area for parents and a play area for the little people. Parents could place their child or children inside the fenced-in section and know they were safe and happy at play while the parents did their shopping.

Always finding exactly what they wanted in this unique shop, Mr. and Mrs. De Mija took their daughter shopping. With Easter just a few days less than a month away, they wanted to buy Fayth a new dress. Since De Mija had done so much business at the store, he had become well-acquainted with Dole.

Alianna was occupied looking at the dresses and bonnets in her daughter's size. Holding Fayth as he stood next to the front counter, Leo was conversing with Jessie.

"So when I bought the crib from you, you told me that she could probably sleep in it until the age of four or five."

"That's true. Your little girl is still very tiny, Leo. She should get another three years out of that crib."

"I know you're right, but she's scaring me. When I see her bending over the side I'm afraid she's going to fall out on her head and really injure herself. I think I would prefer putting her in a youth bed with side rails. She'll be able to crawl out of bed, but at least there's less risk of her getting hurt."

"When you're ready to change, come in and go through my catalog. I can get you anything in there for a good price."

"That's good to hear."

"Your little Faith reminds me so much of my little Mary: natural curly hair and big brown eyes."

With a deadpan look, Leo ran his hand over his bald head and said, "Faith got her curly hair from me."

Before Jessie could comment, Alianna walked up to Leo with two frilly dresses: one in each hand. "Look at these. Aren't they just precious? I can't decide whether I like the pink ruffled chiffon or this cute little white cotton."

"You're not putting white on Fayth at her age. White dresses on females are for confirmations and weddings. I think the pink will be just fine for Easter Services."

"Pretty," Fayth said, reaching out toward the pink dress.

"Hear that? Even our daughter agrees with me. Get the pink one."

Alianna never disagreed with her husband, especially when they were out in public. Since Leo's word was law in their household, she took the white dress back to the clothes rack.

"You're a religious person aren't you, Leo?" Jessie asked.

"Yes."

"Somehow I knew that. So am I. My wife and I read the Good Book every night before dinner."

"We do the same in our house. If more people believed in God and his teachings, we'd have less crime. By the way, thanks for calling my wife yesterday and letting her know your spring stock came in."

"No problem. I remember how disappointed you were last year."

"That's true. By the time we got in here, your selection was already down to nothing. Neither Ali nor I were too happy about that."

While De Mija and Dole continued to talk, another couple with one small child entered the store. The father was carrying the little boy. They immediately headed over to the shelves of stuffed animals.

"Excuse me, Leo."

"Sure."

Dole walked over to the customers. "Good day, folks. May I help you find something?"

The woman answered. "We're just looking for now. Thank you."

"Okay. But if you need help, just let me know." Not wanting to appear over-zealous, Jessie took a couple of steps back. He watched and waited just in case he could be of some assistance.

The boy sat in his father's arms, seeming perfectly content without so much as a wiggle.

De Mija watched from a short distance away. *Now there's an old grump for a man with a young one*, he thought. *He looks like he would have rather taken a beating than take his lovely wife and child shopping. Some men just don't know how lucky they are having a nice family like he has. Doing things together as a family is what life's all about.*

"If you would like to put your child in the play area while you shop," Jessie suggested, pointing to the colorful fenced-off section, "please feel free to do so."

Looking toward the play area, the woman said, "Oh, what a great idea to have in a children's store. Look, Al."

Her husband took a quick glance and grunted. "My kid's fine where he is. If he wants to play, we can take him home. Just get what you need, Deb, and let's go," he tartly stated. "I've got better things to do than to hang around here all night."

Jessie stepped closer to the man. Gently tickling under the little boy's chin with his finger, Jessie made the little one smile. Jessie smiled back. "What a precious little boy. How old is he?"

"Greg is three," Debra answered.

As quick as one could say bounce the ball, the three year old had reached out and grabbed a small stuffed frog from the shelf his father was standing next to. Al's immediate reaction was to grab the frog from his little boy's hand. He threw the toy back on the shelf. Then he harshly slapped his son's hand. "Shame on you! You don't touch! Bad, bad boy! Daddy's ashamed of you," the father loudly scolded.

"It's quite all right," Jessie stated, changing his warming smile to a disdainful frown. "There's no harm done."

"I'll correct my child *my* way, and thank you to keep out of it," he bellowed. "If he thinks he can get away with it this time, he'll do it again."

Observing from where he was still standing by the counter, De Mija seethed inside. He hated witnessing a grown person striking an innocent child.

When Al hit his son's tiny hand again, the child started crying. De Mija stepped forward as the man was still ranting, "You know better than to touch anything --"

"That's enough," Leo stated in an authoritative voice. "I believe you've gotten your point across to your son. There's no need to keep striking him."

"Mind your own business," Al bitterly stated, throwing eye-daggers at Leo.

Hearing the argument from across the store and recognizing her husband's voice, Alianna came rushing to Leo's side. Since he was still holding his daughter, Leo kept a safe distance in case the verbal disagreement turned physical. Yet, he was close enough so Al knew he was a threat.

Fayth wasn't the least bit frightened by her daddy's gruff voice. But Alianna felt the need to place her hand on her daughter's back and pat it in a calming way.

"It is my business," Leo continued, "when a grown man abuses a child."

"I'm not abusing him," Al scoffed back. "I don't know who you think you are, but this is my child. And I darn well have the right to correct him the way I see fit."

"Correcting him is one thing, but yelling and hitting are uncalled for. As a matter of fact, striking him that hard is against the law and falls under the heading of child abuse."

Al sneered. "What are you, a cop or something?"

Not giving the man the satisfaction of knowing what his occupation was, Leo replied, "Let's just say I'm a concerned citizen. But if you strike that child like that again, I'll see that justice is done."

Before anything else was said, Jessie took a hold of Leo's arm. "Look, why don't you take Fayth over to the play area? You two grown men don't need to be yelling at each other in front of these children." As Leo started to open his mouth, Jessie quickly said with a little more force, "Please. I'll take care of these people in my own way."

Pulling his arm away, Leo replied, "Out of respect that this is your place of business, I'll do that. But you, sir," Leo said, looking directly at the man, "had better not lay another hand on your son while I'm around, or you'll pay for it."

Begrudgingly, Leo walked away with Alianna at his side. "Are you through shopping yet?"

"I found a couple of other cute outfits. I just can't decide which one to get."

"What was the matter with the pink dress you showed me?"

"It was cute. But when I hung the white one back on the rack, I found two more precious dresses. Both of them are yellow. Why don't you come over to the clothes section with me?"

"No. You go and get what you want. I'll take Fayth to the play area."

Back in the stuffed animal section, Dole stood by hoping he wouldn't lose a sale.

"Come on, Deb," Al raged. "Let's get out of here. I'm tired, the kid's tired, and I just want to go home."

The child had quit crying but was still sobbing as he held his hurt hand wrapped in his other tiny hand.

Trying to appease his customers, Jessie apologized. "I'm terribly sorry this turned into such a ruckus. But honestly, the child didn't hurt a thing. This shop is made with children in mind. In fact, I welcome them to touch and pick up the toys."

Looking at her husband, Debra said, "Al, we've been to three other stores already. I want to go home, too. But we need to get that birthday present for your nephew."

"Well, get it and let's get out of here. I knew we should have left this brat home with a babysitter," he complained.

"Perhaps if you give me some idea as to what you're looking for, ma'am," Jessie offered, "I can help you."

"Yes. I'd like one of these soft stuffed animals. But the boy we're buying for is crazy about lizards and dinosaurs. All I see here is --"

"Pardon me for interrupting. But if you'll follow me, I have a large selection of both of those items on the other aisle." Jessie continued talking as the couple followed him to the next aisle. "I have green ones, blue ones, yellow ones, and brown ones. I have small ones, medium-sized ones, and large ones." Once he got to the next aisle, he pointed out his selection of colorful, soft and cuddly reptiles and dinosaurs.

Debra quickly looked through the vast array before making her choice. "This will do nicely," she said, handing a large blue-and-orange dinosaur to Jessie. "His bedroom has these exact same colors in it. I just know he'll be pleased with this selection. Don't you think so, Al?"

"Fine," he mumbled.

"Do you gift wrap?"

"No, ma'am. But I have a great selection of wrapping paper, ribbons, and decorations over by my checkout counter. Perhaps you can find something that pleases you so you can wrap the gift yourself. If you want to go over there and look, I'll go get a box to put this dinosaur in."

Taking the stuffed animal with him, Dole headed for the back room. When he came back into the main store area, the couple was waiting by the counter with wrapping paper and ribbon.

"Will that be all for you today?"

"Yes," Al said. "How much do we owe you?"

Jessie rang up the items on his register. "Your total comes to $23.45."

To free her husband's hands, Debra took her son. Reaching into his back pocket, Al pulled out his billfold. Realizing he did not have enough cash, he handed Jessie a credit card.

Jessie looked at the name and expiration date. Turning the card over, he checked to see that it had been signed. Then he wrote up a charge slip and processed it. Handing back the card, he said, "Thank you, Mr. Carney."

With no verbal response, Al returned his credit card to his billfold.

"My, you certainly have a large assortment of children's items in here," Debra commented.

"Yes, I do. I like to be well-supplied for one-stop shopping when it comes to the little people." Placing the credit card receipt at the front of his customer and furnishing a pen, Jessie said, "Here you go, Mr. Carney."

As Al signed the receipt, Jessie bagged the customers' items then set the bag on the counter. After handing Al his copy of the signed receipt, Jessie placed the store's copy to the side of his register.

"Do you folks live in this area?" Jessie inquired.

"Close enough. We live over on East Nettles --"

Debra was rudely interrupted when her husband elbowed her in the ribs, ordering, "That's enough, Debra Jean."

Dole continued about his business, ignoring the fact that their conversation was abruptly cut short. Reaching back under the counter, he pulled out a small stuffed rabbit and started to hand it to the child.

"What's that for?"

"I give a small gift to all the children that visit my store."

"We don't want any of your handouts. Come on, Deb. Let's go."

Disappointed that the man rejected his gift to the child, Jessie bid them farewell by saying, "Thank you for shopping in my store. Please come back again."

Al grabbed the bag off the counter and turned to leave.

"We will be back," Debra offered in a low voice, smiling. "Thank you."

As the couple exited the store, Dole placed the stuffed rabbit on his counter. He got his pen off the counter where Al Carney had left it and picked up the charge slip. For future reference, he made a note of the street where Debra said they lived. Then he placed the charge slip back to the side of his register. After putting his pen in its place, he went back to the stuffed animal section to straighten up the shelves.

De Mija picked up his daughter and walked over to the counter. He blatantly picked up the departed customer's credit card receipt from Dole's register shelf and looked at it. He made a mental note: *Allen Carney. East Nettles.* After putting the receipt back where he got it from, he thought, *Somebody needs to teach you a lesson, Allen Carney, before you destroy your child's life. And you, too, Debra, for not defending your son. I have no tolerance for parents like you.*

CHAPTER SEVENTEEN

Every night after closing and chores were done, it was the same ritual for Dole. All outside doors were double-checked to make sure they were locked. Store lights used during business hours were turned off, leaving only the nightlights to cast a soft glow in the showroom. He turned on one nightlight in the back room, then cut off the rest of the overhead lighting. Once this was all accomplished, he took the store's receipts to the back room, locking the door to the front of the store behind him.

Remaining in the back room, he removed the brightly colored smock, decorated with an assortment of children's toys, he wore as a uniform during store hours. The smock was tossed into a laundry bag. This night was no different from any other night. When Dole felt confident he was free of outside harm, he unlocked his office door, went inside, and turned on a light. Closing the door, he locked himself inside the room. After taking his seat at the desk, he opened the zippered envelope that housed the day's register receipts and pulled out his charge slips. Thumbing through them, he separated the special charges that he had made notes on, such as the street name where Allen and Debra Carney lived. Once he had started his computer, he recorded his income and completed other tedious office work for the store.

Financial work done, he unlocked his desk. Way in the back of one of the side drawers, Dole kept his daily journal. Turning to the last page of his notes, he began his new entry. Never wanting to take problems home to his wife, Dole found keeping a journal was most comforting to say exactly what was on his mind. Before his parents died, he felt they did nothing but complain about everything. Once he was on his own, he vowed never to burden a loved one with such petty grievances. All of his secrets from the nadir to the apex, Dole faithfully recorded in his private journal.

* * *

As he drove home, taking care to watch where he was going, Dole took in all the new construction that was taking place. New homes and small strip malls seem to be going up everywhere. Continuing along the familiar route, he got lost in his thoughts. *Give them a couple of more years and those contractors will have new homes and a shopping center built in my front yard. We won't be alone out in the country much longer. They'll turn our quiet haven into a noisy suburban area.*

When Dole arrived home, his wife had the table set and dinner was on the stove. His little girl was sitting quietly in her highchair next to the table. After giving Mary a peck on the forehead, he walked over to the stove where Barb was preoccupied and gave her a kiss on the cheek.

"How are my two favorite girls this evening?"

"Hi, Jessie. We're both just fine, especially now that you're home."

"Dinner sure smells good," Jessie stated after taking a big whiff of the delightful aroma of fried chicken.

"Wash up and I'll get dinner on the table."

As asked, Jessie headed for the bathroom. Returning to the kitchen, Bible in hand, he sat down beside his daughter. As he waited for his wife, Jessie tickled and teased Mary, making her giggle. When Barb finally settled in at the table, they joined hands. Heads bent and eyes closed, Jessie gave the blessing. After a reading from the Bible, Jessie and Barb chatted as the three of them ate.

"So what are your plans for this evening?" Barb asked.

"I've got things to do in the yard and the shed."

"I wish you would wait until the days get warmer and longer. I'm so afraid you're going to catch your death one of these days."

"Barb, we've talked about this before. I'm used to working outside no matter what the temps are, day or night. Now, subject closed."

"I'm sorry. I didn't mean to nag. It's just that, well, I just wish you wouldn't work out there tonight."

"Why? Is there something you want me to do?"

"If you can? Our little pumpkin here tried her hand in artwork today in the bathroom. I'm sure you noticed it when you went in to wash up."

"Uh-huh. Why didn't you clean it up?"

"I'm sorry, Jessie, but I tried. Cleaning solutions certainly didn't help. The more I scrubbed, the more it smeared."

"First thing tomorrow morning, I'm taking those boxes of crayons off the store's shelves. The distributor's going to get a piece of my mind, too." Barb knew better than to interrupt when her husband was speaking. All she could do was wait for an opening to explain. "Those crayons are supposed to be water soluble. Oh, that's not going to sit well with any of my customers, either. They'll think I lied to them."

When Jessie paused to take a drink of milk, Barb had her chance. "Calm down, dear. You're jumping too conclusions. Obviously, you didn't take a good look at the floor."

"Well, I didn't get down on my hands and knees and inspect it, if that's what you mean."

"Mary didn't use crayons on the floor. The stinker got into my cosmetics. That coloring is a mixture of lipstick, eye-shadow, face cream and nail polish."

Jessie let out a sigh of relief. "For my customers' sake, I'm glad to hear that. But no wonder you couldn't remove the stain from the floor tiles. The nail polish probably glued the rest of your make-up to them."

"I know. I was lucky it all came off Mary's delicate skin."

"Daddy, Mary make pretty," Mary said, smiling proudly.

Jessie laughed. "It sounds like it, you little monkey."

"I feel so badly, Jessie. Is there anything we can do?"

"The best thing, I guess, is for me to cut out the damaged area and replace it. I laid that floor before we got married. But I'm sure I still have some tiles stored away in the shed."

"Is that stuff hard to cut? Because the stain is really an odd shape."

He smiled. "No, dear. You don't replace tiles that way. I'll just take up all the squares that have stains on them and replace them with new tiles. However, if I need to cut any of them, I have a tile cutter."

"I'm sorry you have to go to all that trouble. I was in here baking a pie and thought Mary was asleep in her crib."

"Whoa!" Jessie said, turning to Mary. "You crawled out of your crib?"

"Uh-huh. Mary big girl," she boasted.

"If Mary's a big girl, then she stays in her crib when Mommy and Daddy put her in there. Okay?"

"Okay," she said, shaking her head no.

Barb laughed. "One of these days she'll know the difference between nodding her head for yes and shaking it for no. So, Jessie, how soon do you think you can get to the tiles?"

"Right after dinner. When I'm finished in the bathroom, I'll get my work done in the shed. Since I have a lot to do, it'll probably be late before I get done. So don't wait up."

"What about your yard work?"

"I'll try to get up early and get it done before I leave."

"Working late. Getting up early. That hardly gives you enough time to sleep. Really, Jessie, just repairing the bathroom floor should be enough for tonight. What's so important outside that it can't wait until you get home tomorrow?"

"It just won't, Barb. If you'll get up around six in the morning and fix coffee for me, I would appreciate it. And if Mary happens to wake up, don't let her come outside. I'll have a fire going in the trash pit. And you know how I hate having to worry about her falling into that thing and getting burned."

"Of course. That reminds me. I've got a lot of old clothes I want to give to the church bazaar. Will you bring me one of those big plastic bags from the shed when you come back in?"

"Sure."

"How was business today?"

"Good. Remember me speaking of Leo De Mija?"

"Sure I do. He's the customer you said you had so much in common with?"

"Yes. I still can't get over the connection I feel with him each time he comes into my store. He's so much like me, Barb, that it's not even funny. Leo does have an irritating habit, though."

"What's that?"

"He's always wearing sunglasses. He even had them on this evening when he and his wife were in shopping."

"Maybe he has eye problems?"

"Could be. I just know it bugs me. I like looking at a person's eyes when I speak to them."

"Where does he live?"

"You know, I've never asked."

"Do they have any children?"

"Yes. One little girl."

"Oh, just like us. What's the wife like?"

"She's petite, brown hair, brown eyes …." He paused for moment then added, "She reminds me a lot of you."

"That's nice. It's too bad you don't like to invite people over to the house, or I'd suggest you ask them over sometime."

"Talking to Leo in the store is one thing. But I don't care to get super-chummy with him. Besides, he's made comments about how much of a loner he is, like me. So I don't think he would accept an invitation anyway."

"I just thought, since you two hit it off that --"

"Why the persistence? You don't like company anymore than I do."

"True. I was just offering to bend a little in case you have changed your mind."

"Well, I haven't. You and Mary are all the company I need."

"So, you said Leo and his wife were in your store today?"

"Yes, just before closing. Leo showed a different side of himself tonight. He got into an argument with one of my other customers."

"Well, that's not like you at all, Jessie. You're definitely not the arguing type. So how can you say the two of you are so much alike?"

"Trust me, Barb. We are. I handled the situation a little differently than Leo did. But I was just as irritated as he was."

"What situation?"

"A father was reprimanding his child for taking a toy off a shelf without permission. When the father proceeded to continually strike his son's tiny hand with adult force, that's when Leo became outraged. You know how I feel about abused children?"

"I certainly do."

"Believe me. It was all I could do to keep from slugging this man myself. However, when Leo stepped in and I realized yelling at the father was senseless, I interceded. Even though I could feel Leo's rage inside me, I knew there was a better way to teach that cruel father a lesson."

Barb nodded. "By treating the man with respect. Then, hopefully, he will learn to treat his child with respect. Right?"

Jessie had no comment.

CHAPTER EIGHTEEN

As Leo sat at the desk in his home office, the small light in the room cast the shadow of his hand as he wrote himself a 'to-do' list. He had been slowly renovating his house ever since he and Alianna had gotten married. Working on the police force did not exactly give him extra money to hire a contractor. He had to rely on his own inexperienced abilities. Even though he had plenty of money hidden a way, over and above his new pay raise as a detective, he preferred to only spend it a little at a time. If he lived beyond his means, someone might eventually start asking questions.

In the middle of his writing, there came a knock at his office door. Leo chose to ignore it. There was a second knock. This time, however, he heard his wife's voice from the other side of the door. "Leo, you're wanted on the telephone."

Aggravated by the intrusion, he threw his pen on the desk. After unlocking and opening the door, he said, "Would you please take a message, Ali? You know I don't like being bothered when I'm busy in my office."

"I know, Leo, but I thought this phone call was --"

"Nothing is that important that it can't wait," Leo interrupted. "Take a message. Whoever it is, I'll call them back. Okay?"

"Sure, Leo. I'm sorry I bothered you."

After completing his office work, Leo locked up his office and went to the kitchen. Alianna was sitting at the table sewing a button on one of his shirts. Fayth was in her highchair.

Leo laughed. "Look at that messy face. Is that cookie good?"

"Nummy cookie."

"It must be. You have it all over you. Mommy is going to have to put you in the tub when you're through."

"Tell Daddy a cookie just doesn't taste good unless you can dunk it in milk and make a mess. That's called pure enjoyment."

Far too busy enjoying her treat, Fayth ignored her mother's comment.

Leo sat in a kitchen chair and placed his notes on the table. "Well, Ali, I should be able to start on the living room real soon."

"Oh, Leo, that would be wonderful. I can hardly wait to use the new slipcovers I made."

"I'll paint the walls first. Then get the woodwork sanded and varnished. And, I have a big surprise for you."

"Tell me. Tell me," she begged with excitement.

"When I'm through in the living room, we can replace this old kitchen linoleum."

"Really?" she squealed with delight. "I'd love that."

"I thought you would be pleased. You can pick out any color you want. But, please, make sure you get something that doesn't show the soil. Fayth is still young and accidents happen. We'll want something that's near childproof."

Alianna laughed. "I don't think there is such a thing."

"I s'pose not."

"Leo, you know I've never asked about our financial situation. But are you sure we can afford redoing the living room and a kitchen flooring? Because if not, I can wait."

"We're not going to go overboard, Ali. I'm going to be doing all the work. All we need to spend is money for the supplies."

"What about the kitchen floor? Won't you need to hire someone to install it?"

"Definitely, not. I helped lay this one many years ago. All I'll need is a notched trowel, an L-shaped ruler, a linoleum cutter, and a hand roller. I have all those tools Father left me. So our only expense will be the linoleum and the glue."

"Which will be costly enough."

"Don't you worry your pretty little head about the money. Oh, who called earlier?"

Dropping her head down as if ashamed, Alianna apologized. "I'm sorry, Leo. I thought it was someone important. But it was only an insurance salesman calling."

"That figures. There are only a few rules I have in this house, Ali, and you know it. One of the most important rules is that I'm not to be bothered when I'm in my office. It's the only chance I have to get my thoughts together and clear my head."

Lifting her heard, she looked her husband in the face. "I know. But what if there's an emergency and they need you at work? With your new job, you told me they could call you on a case anytime. I would think that would be important enough to bother you?"

"If my work ever calls, they will tell you who they are. Then, and only then, will I accept a phone call. Now, let's not have any more discussion about it. I think our little pumpkin is ready for her bath," he added, looking over at his precious Fayth. "Are you ready for your bath, pumpkin?"

"Yes, bath," she uttered with her milk and chocolate cookie smile.

"Well, if Mommy will draw your tub water and get you all cleaned up, Daddy will read you a story and tuck you into bed."

"No bed, Daddy. Fayth want bath."

"Yes." He laughed. "You'll get your bath. Then you have to go to bed."

Getting up from her chair, Alianna walked behind Fayth and kissed her on the back of her head. Then she walked behind where Leo was sitting. Bending over, she cuddled her arms around his neck. Kissing him on the ear, she spoke softly and lovingly. "Have you thought any more about us having another baby?"

"I've thought about it. Honestly, I still don't think we're ready yet."

"Why not, Leo?" Her voice was filled with disappointment.

"The main reason is this house and the expense to finish fixing it up. And we just don't have enough room for another baby right now. Someday — when I can add on to the house — then we'll talk about another baby."

"Now, don't get angry at me for asking. But didn't you tell me once we had a savings account? Or is that what you're using for all the renovation?"

"I've been keeping the bills paid and renovating this house on my salary, Ali. It took most of our bank savings for you to get pregnant with Fayth. There just hasn't been any extra money to start building our savings again."

Pulling her arms back from Leo's neck, she stood erect. Alianna walked to the sink and got a damp washcloth. "I've already checked with Dr. Layman, and he says we have excellent credit with him. Since we paid in full for the first procedure, he will accept payments if we decide to increase our family. Also, I think two children's beds or twin beds would fit in Fayth's room just fine."

While Alianna took the washcloth over to her daughter, Leo attempted to defend his rationality.

"Be reasonable, Ali. Let's give it another year or two before we make the decision to bring another child into this world. That will give us enough time to have the house completely finished, including the extra room, and all the expenses paid for. It will also give us time to put away some more savings. I'd rather stay out of debt if it's at all possible.

"And you're wrong about the space in Faith's room. Unless we move some of her other furniture out of there, two cribs will not fit. She's going to need a bigger bed soon. But just like the cribs, twin beds won't fit, either. Now, bunk beds would. However, Fayth is not going to be sleeping on a top bunk until she is closer to six or seven years old."

Finished wiping a good share of the cookie off Fayth's face and hands, Alianna placed the soiled washcloth in the sink. Disappointment was written all over her face as she turned back to her husband. "You're right, Leo. I guess I wanted another child so badly that I just wasn't using common sense."

"I'm glad you see it my way."

* * *

After Fayth was tucked into bed, Leo joined his wife in the living room. "Anything worth watching on TV tonight?"

"I haven't really been paying attention."

"You're not still upset with me about this baby business, are you?"

"No. I told you I understand."

"Then what's bothering you?"

"I was just thinking about what happened earlier this evening. Do you think it was wise to argue with that man in Jessie's store? You know how other people raise their children is really not your concern."

"Of course it's my concern." Leo fumed. "You know I have no tolerance when it comes to parents' abusing their children, especially in front of me. I couldn't just stand by and watch that poor little boy being hurt like that by a bully of a father."

"I know you're right. But maybe you could handle a situation like that differently next time. It isn't good for you to raise your voice in disgust in front of the children. You know that argument had to be upsetting to Fayth, not to mention that poor child that was already traumatized by his father's actions. I, for one, was happy when Jessie got you to calm down and let him deal with his customer in his own way."

"As far as upsetting the children, I understand where you're coming from. Maybe confronting parents like that is the wrong way to handle it. I'll use another method to teach them a lesson when a child isn't eyewitness to my wrath."

"That's right, dear. You might not wear a uniform anymore, but you are still a policeman. There must be other ways to handle parents like that."

"There certainly are."

CHAPTER NINETEEN

Since Konklin's office door was partially open, Warner rapped on the doorframe. "May I join you?"

"Of course." Konklin left his desk chair and walked around the desk. After picking up several bulky manila folders from the one and only extra chair in his office, he said, "Have a seat." As he walked back to his chair, he complained. "Sorry for the mess. I just don't have enough room in here for all the files I'm accumulating in this case."

"I certainly understand that." Warner made himself comfortable. The mail he was carrying, he placed on his lap. "How was your weekend?"

"Believe it or not, I went for a walk in the park yesterday. The air was still a little brisk, but it was delightful to get out of my apartment for a while and enjoy the sunshine. Lately, my mind has been on my deceased wife. So it was good to get out and try to shake some of the cobwebs out of my brain."

"Is there anything you want to talk about?"

"You mean about Sheri?" Warner nodded. "No. I just think it's my age, Joe. I've been feeling a little melancholy lately." Konklin took a deep breath. "You and Jeny would have liked my Sheri."

"I'm sure we would have. You know, I'm rather ashamed of myself. We've been friends for a number of years now. Yet, I've never asked about her family — only your immediate family."

"That's understandable. Why would you be interested in a family of someone you never met?"

"But I am interested, Eddy. Once you were married, they became your family, too. Are any of her family members living in the area?"

"Not any more. Since Sheri's been gone, two of her brothers and both parents are deceased. The rest of her siblings and their kids are spread all over the country now."

"So you don't really have any family here in Mt. Pride, your own or by marriage?" Warner asked totally concerned for his friend.

"Nope, not a one."

"Have you kept in contact with any of them?"

"You know, I've lived in Mt. Pride all my life. They know my name. If they ever wanted my phone number, all they had to do was call information. I've had the same phone number for years. I think for the short time Sheri and I were married, her family never really got to know me — or cared to. So if they don't care to keep in touch, why should I bother? Say, let's get off this subject before I break down into a jabbering idiot. How about you? Did you do anything exciting over the weekend?"

"I'm almost ashamed to tell you."

"Come on, Joe, don't be that way. I dearly loved my wife and my beautiful memories of her, but she's gone. As you once told me, life goes on. So don't go feeling sorry for me. I couldn't stand it. Besides, you know you're the closest thing I have to a family now. I always enjoy hearing about your home life. If I didn't, I wouldn't ask."

Warner smiled and nodded. He certainly understood where his buddy was coming from. After all, he had come to love Konklin as a brother. "Jeny and I had a wonderful weekend. Mandy went to stay with a girlfriend, so we had the whole house all to ourselves. I chased my wife all over the house." Raising his eyebrows, he chuckled. "I even caught her a few times, too."

"No! Stop!" Konklin laughed. "That's more information than I need to know."

"I'm kidding, Eddy. But it was great to be alone for a while. We locked all the doors, kept the blinds closed, and didn't bother getting dressed for the two whole wonderful days."

"Weren't you afraid Amandalee might come home unexpectedly?"

"Nope. She knows better. That reminds me. Mandy will be moving out in a few weeks."

"Why? I thought you enjoyed having her live at home?"

"Hey, she's an assistant district attorney now. It's about time she started living on her own and paying her own bills. I'm happy she's moving."

"Who do you think you're talking to, Joe? I know better. She's been Daddy's little girl ever since I've known you. It will break your heart when she moves."

"Well, maybe at first. But Jeny and I discussed it. It's time to let our little bird leave the nest. So, enough talk about our personal lives. If I remember correctly, I gave you thirty days to try and work with Leo. Those thirty days have come and gone. Since you haven't said a word, how's it going?"

"Please don't say, 'I told you so,' but it's working out. He still doesn't talk too much, but I get him to open up now and then. Recently, I even got a laugh out of that starched face of his which finally broke the ice."

"Don't get too big-headed. If he laughed at one of your dumb jokes, he was probably only placating you," Warner teased.

"Nope. We stopped for lunch at that new place called The Cookbook. Both of us ordered liver and onions. About an hour later, we're driving down the street and he lets out one of the loudest gas bombs I ever heard roar out of someone's behind. I mean it wasn't one of those little tootin' tadpoles. It was a full-blown frog. For a split second, I thought he ripped his pants." Konklin began laughing. "I got the giggles so bad I could hardly see to drive from the tears in my eyes. Well, then I started ripping them off. The more I laughed, the more I frogged. Leo got to laughing and started doing the same thing. It was hilarious. I swear onions work on him the same way they do on me. When we got back to the station, I had to use a whole can of air-freshener to get the rotten smells out of the car." Konklin was heehawing so hard he had to hold his sides from pain.

"I hope you got it all out of your system. From the way you're laughing now, you'll kill me in this small office if you let loose."

Wiping the tears from his eyes, Konklin settled down. "I'm sorry, Joe. But you had to be there to find the humor in it."

"I'm glad I wasn't."

"Enough of the small talk. What's going on today?"

From the mail on his lap, Warner picked up the top envelope and proceeded to open it. "The mail was being delivered as I came in. So I waited for the desk sergeant to sort it. I received this letter from the CBI Crime Lab. I'm sure it has to do with our serial case."

"Geez, I hope it's good news. We need a break. The longer these homicides go unsolved, the colder our case gets."

After scanning over the letter, Warner smiled. "Well, that's more than we knew before."

"What is, Joe? What does it say?"

"They couldn't specifically identify the murder weapon. But from the information and photos Saggy sent them, they're sure it is either a carton opener or a tile cutter."

"Either of those would have to be pretty old tools, wouldn't they?"

"Why?"

"Because most people today use those razor blades that slide in and out of a metal or heavy plastic holder. They're similar to the Stanley knife. At any rate, I think they're the same type of tool. Of course, I'm not positive. But, if I'm right, it certainly wouldn't have a curved blade."

"True. A razor would definitely make a straight cut. However, I'm going to disagree with you about the tools being one and the same. Since the CBI Crime Lab mentions both of them, I think we need to search for both types of tools."

Konklin nodded. "Is that all they have for us?"

Warner referred back to the report. "They found a small particle of wood in the blood samples from Beth Ann Atkin. They state that there could be three explanations for this. One, if she were killed on a hardwood floor. Two, the murder weapon had a wood handle. Three, it was a small piece of debris that might have fallen off the slayer's person."

"We know for a fact that the bedroom floor was carpeted where we found Beth Ann's body. That means we can rule out the wood floor."

"Ruling out one out of two isn't bad. From the wood samples we sent them from the Atkin house, they determined the marks were made by a crowbar. Well, that's not much. But at least we have something to go on."

"I wonder if they compared that small sliver of a wood sample to the wood off the frame of the backdoor?"

"That's a very good question, Eddy. I'll leave it to you to find out."

"A curved blade and a possible wooden handle. Damn if that doesn't sound like the carton openers we used to use."

"Oh, it sure does. But I haven't seen one in years. Hell, I don't even know if you can purchase them any more."

"I don't either, but it sure fits the bill."

"So you're thinking the old style wood handle is what the perp's using?"

"Think about it, Joe. As clever as he is, he would certainly know a tool like that would be harder for us to trace."

"And the particle of wood found in Debra's blood could have come from the handle of such a tool?"

"It's a possibility, Joe."

"You could be right. However, we can't rule out the aspect that the particle of wood, as the CBI states, fell off the perp's clothes or body. Hmm, maybe we're looking for a carpenter?"

"Or a handyman. Heck, anyone engaged in home improvement around his own house could own one of those wooden-handled tools or have a sliver of wood on their clothing."

"You know, you might have just hit upon something."

"Here's another thought. If the CBI Lab thinks a crowbar made the jimmy marks on the backdoor of the Atkin house, maybe that's what the snake used to hit Beth Ann in the head."

"That would make sense, too. Especially since there was nothing found at the crime scene that indicated such a blow. Well, I guess you and Leo need to start hitting the hardware stores."

"Yeah, and every home improvement center and one-stop super stores. There's no way Leo and I can cover them all."

"Ferndale's group should be completing their rattle search by now. If so, there's four more detectives to help out."

"Great. I'll check with her." Konklin's face lit up. "Oh, I just had a thought."

"Enlighten me."

"I'm going to call Sue down at records. I'll bet if there's still one of those old-type carton openers around the main office, she would know. If I can get it, or a picture of it, I'll have something to refer to when we hit the stores."

"Eddy, barnstorming with you always pays off. That's why you're my main man," Warner complimented.

"Cut it out, Joe. You're making me blush."

"That will be the day. Listen, it would be a good idea to gather a list of local carpenters in the area. Then cross check them against the NCIC."

"Good idea. Say, anything in that report about the blood evidence found on the bedding at both crime scenes?"

Scanning the report, Warner finally said, "Yes, but it's bad news. Seems the DNA tested positive for the victims only." Picking up his mail, Warner got to his feet. "I've got an appointment with the chief. I'll probably be out of my office for a couple of hours. So, I'll catch you later. Happy hunting."

The desk phone rang. Before Konklin answered it, he said, "Hang on a minute, Joe. I need to ask you one quick question."

"Sure. But make it snappy."

The captain stood by dumbfounded as he listened to the lieutenant's part of the telephone conversation. When Konklin hung up, he rushed to his feet.

"That didn't sound good, Eddy. Another double?"

"Another double," Konklin echoed. "Just when we thought our snake had gone underground. Up pops his ugly head."

"Let's go. Get Leo and you two can ride with me. You can tell me where we're going in the car."

"It's too early. Leo isn't due in for a good thirty minutes yet. We can't wait."

"Then call him from the car. Let's move."

As Warner drove, Konklin navigated and explained what he had been told on the telephone.

"That's all I can tell you, Joe. Excuse my French, but son-of-a --"

"Don't say it. I know where we're going now, so why don't you try reaching Leo again?"

"Yeah. I want to call Sue, too."

* * *

"Unless they didn't bring the van, looks like the CSIs aren't here yet," Warner observed.

"No ME's van, either."

"I've got gloves and booties in the trunk. Do you need any?"

"Believer it or not, yes."

"Okay, let's get them and go in."

As they exited the car, a man ran up to them. "Are you from the police department?" He asked in sheer panic.

Warner allowed Konklin to handle the situation while he stood by.

"We're from the detective's unit. I'm Lieutenant Konklin. May I help you?"

"Yes. The officers won't let me in the house. If something has happened to my daughter and son-in-law, I have a right to know what."

"Your name, sir?"

"Doug Cook. Can you tell me what happened in there?"

"Calm down, Mr. Cook. Let us go in and see what happened. Then we'll let you know."

"I'm the one who called the police."

Konklin's wheels started turning. "Are you saying you've already been in the house?"

"No."

"Then how do you know something happened in there?"

"I'm not stupid."

"I didn't mean to imply that. I would just like to know why you called the police."

"My wife and I took the two grandsons on a Friday night stay-over. Al and Debby — that's my daughter and her husband — were supposed to pick them up by noon on Saturday. We called and called and called. But they never answered their phone. Yesterday, I came over and banged on their door. Still no answer. This morning I called Al's place of employment. When I found out he hadn't showed up for work, I came here again. This time, I walked around the house. I was going to start banging on the back door. When I discovered a broken window, I called 911."

Konklin pulled out his small notebook and pen from his pocket to make notes. "You said the couple's names are Al and Debbie?"

"It's really Debra Jean and Allen."

"What's their last name?"

"Carney."

"Okay, Mr. Cook. Would you like to sit in our car while you wait?"

"No. I'm too upset to sit. I'll wait right here. You will come out and tell me what's going on, won't you?"

"Yes, sir."

Warner waited until the man had walked away from his car before he opened the trunk. He quickly retrieved the disposable garb and stuck it in his pocket.

As the detectives headed toward the house, Warner said, "I hope Leo is on his way."

"Likewise. He should have gotten my phone message by now. I can't imagine why he's not answering his cell or my page."

"Me either. He knows his pager is to stay on. And if not, he needs to call and check in with you."

As they entered the house, Konklin's first comments were directed to the police officer guarding the door. After showing his badge and introducing himself, he said, "I don't believe we've met."

"That's because I'm new on the force, lieutenant. I'm Officer Chriss Hanson."

"Officer Hanson, this is Capt. Warner." Warner nodded. "Tell us what happened here."

"Dispatch called for a possible Residential Burglary. My partner and I took the call. While we were securing the house — making sure the perpetrator wasn't still on the premises — we discovered the bodies. The victims are --"

"Don't tell me," Konklin interrupted. "Two bodies in the bedroom — one on the bed and one on the floor. Both in a pool of blood with pillows over their faces. Right?"

Hanson nodded. "Affirmative, sir." Before either Konklin or Warner had a chance to ask any questions, she added, "There's a broken window at the mid-section to the backside of the house. It looks like the intruder gained entrance there. When you're ready, I'll show you the area."

Officer Hanson proceeded to explain the procedures she and her partner had followed to determine if there was any life left in the bodies.

Almost apologetic, she told how she removed the blood-laden pillows from the victims' faces to identify the genders. This was her first call to a murder case. Neither Warner nor Konklin were happy with the situation but decided now was not the time for a rulebook lecture.

At the conclusion of her verbal report, Warner replied, "Show us the scene."

Once they reached the room, Hanson headed back to the front door. Konklin walked just to the threshold of the bedroom door and stopped. Warner stood behind him, peering over Konklin's shoulder. The male victim was lying in the blood-drenched bed. The bloody pillow was on the bed next to him.

"Look familiar, Joe?"

"All too familiar."

"You know," a deep voice resounded from behind the detectives, "we're going to have to stop meeting this way or someone might get suspicious."

Recognizing the voice, neither detective bothered to turn.

"Rothchild, you're not my type," Konklin replied in jest.

"Like he's mine?" Warner quipped.

As both detectives turned, Rothchild and DuBois greeted them.

"Where's your new sidekick?" Warner inquired.

Rothchild answered. "Alex is coming."

"He's getting some equipment out of the van," DuBois offered.

"Glad to hear he's hanging in there." Warner laughed.

As Warner and Konklin stepped aside, Konklin said, "The female rookie cop removed the pillows."

"Was she wearing gloves?" Rothchild asked, as he and DuBois entered the bedroom.

"I doubt it, Doug," Konklin replied. "But we'll find out later."

As the two detectives followed Rothchild to the bedside of the male victim, DuBois walked over to where the female was lying on the floor.

"We've got blood droplets over here on the carpet," DuBois announced. "They seem to trail from the female's body to," he motioned with his head, "that door over there."

Just then, Davis entered the room. "What do you want me to do first, Doug?"

"Help Kevin."

"Kevin, do you want me to bring my kit over?"

DuBois finished taking another picture of the female victim before he responded. "You bet." Resting the camera on his shoulder, he pointed to a door. "Check both sides of that door for prints and blood. Then you can collect samples of one of the blood droplets here on the carpet."

"When you're through with the door," Konklin said, "leave it open."

Once Davis had finished dusting and swabbing, Konklin followed Warner to the door's entrance.

Warner looked inside the room. "It's a bathroom."

Looking at the threshold between the bedroom carpet and the bathroom vinyl, Konklin commented, "The blood trail ends here at the door. What do you make of that?"

"That our snake got wounded this time." Warner turned on the bathroom light. "Looks like he came to the bathroom to grab a towel or something to stop the blood from dripping. Then quickly left the scene."

"There's not one speck of blood in here," Konklin said after carefully looking about the room. "If he was dripping blood when he came in here to get a towel or whatever, why isn't there blood on the floor here in the bathroom."

"Maybe he cleaned up after himself and the blood residue isn't visible to the naked eye. The CSIs can use some of their magic tricks from their lab kit and let us know. We should have the drains checked also — just in case our perp rinsed off before leaving the scene."

"From the looks of the matching towel sets hung about, it doesn't appear that anything is mussed up, missing or out-of-place in here, Joe. Unless … maybe the woman was in here, and he hit her when she exited the bathroom? That could be her blood that dripped from here to where she's now laying?"

"It could have gone down that way. When the perp came in, he noticed the woman was in the bathroom. He kills the man. Then waits behind the door to knock her out."

"Exactly."

"Let's go check the female before we make any more presumptions."

Walking back into the bedroom, Konklin asked, "Kevin, are you through getting shots of the female?"

"For now, lieutenant," DuBois responded. "Did you two take a good look at her face?"

Next to the body, both detectives stooped to get a better look. "Geez, Joe, it looks like our snake almost got caught again by the wife."

"Looks as though she was bludgeoned until she was knocked out cold or she died that way."

"Then why slit her throat?"

"Either to throw us off or to make sure she was dead."

"I guess that's where the term overkill comes from?"

"I would say so. Where in the hell is Vince?"

"He's on vacation this week," Rothchild responded. "I called Saggy. He should be here soon."

"No wonder he said he felt so special." DuBois laughed. "I called him, too."

"Well, I'm not waiting," Konklin stated. "I want to see the back of her head."

"Looking for head trauma?" Warner asked.

"Yes." Konklin did a quick check for a head wound. "There's signs of blood on the head and a bloodstain on the carpet underneath where her head came to rest. Get some shots of this, Kevin."

After taking the necessary pictures, DuBois said, "Got it."

"Lay her back down, Eddy. We'll let Saggy deal with it. Did you notice that white phone on the other side of her?"

"Yeah. It's got blood on it too. Kevin, did you get photos of the phone over here."

"Already done."

"Thanks." Konklin stood erect. "Sorry, Joe. The old knees can only stoop for so long."

As Warner stood, he said, "Old knees, hell. You're just out of shape."

"I'd rather blame it on age," Konklin quipped.

"If the perp caught the female vic coming out of the bathroom, he could have used the phone to beat her with." Warner watched in disbelief as Konklin suddenly got back down on the floor — only this time on all fours. "Why in the world are you down there now, Watson?"

"Because, Sherlock, I wanted to see if your theory holds water."

"By looking under the bed?"

"I just wanted to see how long the phone cord was. I thought if it was short it would rule out your theory."

"Right. A short cord wouldn't reach that far. Very good deduction, Watson. So, what's the verdict?"

"We can't rule it out. Although the cord is short, it's unplugged from the wall." Konklin returned to his feet. "Something still isn't right. Doesn't it seem strange that the cord is still laying intact under the bed and not out in this area?"

"Yeah, that is strange. It looks more like someone just pulled the cord from the wall to disconnect it."

"So, if he didn't use the phone, what did he use?"

"Well, both lamps on the bed tables are in place. Of course, we could go back to the same theory we used in the Atkin murders."

"The perp used a crowbar to break in — then used it to hit her with?"

"Uh-huh. Well, let's go see if the perp left his calling card."

"Yeah. I'm curious about that, too. Especially since their children weren't in the house when they were murdered.

CHAPTER TWENTY

At the chief's office, Warner was getting more than perturbed defending his division of detectives. "Give me a break, Ed. I have a team of detectives working on this case, plus me. Yelling at me doesn't accomplish a damn thing." *You old fool, let up,* he thought. *Eddy was right. I should have brought the chief a box of toothpicks as a gift. In a way, I wish he'd go back to smoking. Who am I kidding? I think he was born an old grouch.*

Ed Doogle was close to retirement, but he still made no bones about who was boss. He loved his job and the authoritative position that came with it. "You don't understand, Joe. This particular case is murder on me. No pun intended. I can't believe your division has nothing after all this time."

"You know as well as I do, there's a lot involved with finding one person we can connect to the leads we have."

"A rattle and a printer? Really, Joe," Doogle stated with sarcasm. "You can't tell me you and your task force have only been working on just those two leads?"

Warner did his best to keep his temper below the boiling point. "No. All the cleaning establishments have been checked out for information concerning bloody clothes. We've questioned every ex-con and public offender in our area. Unfortunately for us, all of their alibis checked out. We're collecting student names from all the high schools, the junior college, and any other establishment that offers creative writing in our area."

"So, you're still keeping the investigation primarily in your area of town?"

"For now, yes. The homicides have been within just blocks of each other. I firmly believe the perp does not reside out of our precinct area."

"What else?"

"As soon as I get more manpower, we can start checking florists and nurseries for *Black Tulip* customers. And, just before we got the call this morning on these last homicides, I received a letter from the CBI's Crime Lab. They gave us some idea as to what type murder weapon we need to be looking for. With all the places in town that sell tools, that will be another lengthy, pavement pounding canvass. As if that's not enough, we also plan on checking out construction companies and carpenters in our area. As each list of names is gathered, they are input into one of our computers. If we happen to come up with the same name in two or more categories, we may have something tangible to go on. All I can tell you right now is that we're doing the best we can under the circumstances."

"Not too long ago, you told me you had a prime suspect. Why didn't you ever arrest her?"

"Oh, Ellie Smither. We have opportunity and motive, but the DA's office said that isn't enough. We need solid evidence that she's the one committing these crimes. So far, we haven't been able to find any. The perp is too smart. He or she hasn't left so much as a partial print in any of the first two houses. We won't know about the crime scene this morning until we get the results back from the crime lab."

"Okay, Joe. But we've got to get this public enemy off the streets. A killer on the loose is one thing, but a serial killer is scaring the dog britches off me. Every parent with a small child has been calling my office in panic since the last homicide. And heaven help me, the phones will be ringing off the hook as soon as word gets out about today's tragedy."

"I'm well aware of that, Ed. I get the same phone calls. It's like I told you earlier. We need your help. I figure if we can frighten the perp enough with extra patrol units on the streets, we can keep this deranged murderer underground until we can get a good lead on him — and some good, hardcore evidence. Lee is perfectly willing to get more of his uniforms out there patrolling the residential areas at night. However, this means double shifts for his men. Without your consent, Lee's hands are tied."

"Okay, if you and Lee think it will help deter another homicide, I'll okay the overtime."

"We do or I wouldn't ask."

"I'll contact Lee and tell him to start rescheduling his men immediately."

"And you'll authorize the overtime pay?"

"Of course. Is there anything else?"

"Yes. I need authorized overtime for my unit, too. With this third double homicide, I'm going to need the crew to work as many hours as possible."

"Why don't you just ask me for my eyeteeth, Joe?"

"Because I have my own."

Ignoring Warner's trite sense of humor, Doogle begrudgingly agreed. "Okay, I'll authorize it. But you had better find this creep and get him locked in a cage — ASAP."

CHAPTER TWENTY-ONE

"From the look on your face, I won't even ask how it went with Doogle."

"Just the usual hot air, Eddy. However, he did agree to authorize the extra overtime to get more uniforms out on the street. And for our unit to work the extra hours we need to get this case solved."

"Wow. I'm impressed. Say, speaking of uniforms, when did the precinct get the new female officer?"

"You mean Hanson?"

"Yeah, I've never seen her before this morning. Have you?"

"No. I've only heard about her. She's De Mija's uniform replacement and Ripley's new patrol partner."

"That Ripley's one lucky SOB. This new one's some looker. And what a body." Konklin smiled, as his eyebrows danced up and down.

"Sorry, Eddy, old man. She's too young for you."

"Maybe. But no harm in looking."

"No. But take my advice. Stay away from a woman who wears long pants."

"What? Why would you say that?"

"Because she will want to continue to wear the pants in the family. They're very domineering females."

When Konklin figured out Warner was only joshing with him, he said, "Geez, Joe. You'd think after all this time I wouldn't fall for your stupid remarks."

"Sorry, chubby cheeks. But sometimes you're so easy to get the best of."

"Well, if you're finished giving me a bad time, what are you going to do about her behavior this morning?"

"You mean removing the pillows?"

"Yeah."

"I'm going to call Roberts and suggest he reprimand her. Then he should put her on desk duty for a while and make sure she restudies the manual. Officer Hanson may be attractive, but I don't think she's ready to be on the streets. It almost makes me wonder if she didn't just squeeze through the academy with her bare teeth."

"She was definitely in the wrong. However, I have to blame Ripley, too. He's an experienced cop."

"I agree. Ripley should have stopped her immediately."

"Switching gears, I've been thinking about the Atkin homicides. We never did find the blunt object that was used to hit Beth Ann in the head."

"Are we back to your crowbar theory, again?"

"I am."

"Even though it's a good theory, Eddy, I can't believe someone who's in a hurry to kill would want to drag along something that heavy and that could slow him down."

"A crowbar wouldn't slow the perp down if he felt he needed it. Let's say the perp used a crowbar to break the window of the first house. He left the crowbar outside and entered. When he was confronted by a waking female he panicked. He grabbed the lamp to knock her to the floor. Now, knowing this could possibly happen again, he went in prepared the next time. After using the crowbar to break in the backdoor, he carried the crowbar in the house with him. He used it on the second victim. That would be much faster than looking for a something in the room to hit her with. Are you with me so far?"

"Keep going."

"Now he's well aware he can't kill two people in the same bed without awakening one of them. His best bet is to kill the male first since the male would probably put up more of a struggle than the female. However, he still has to keep the female from getting away or calling for help. So, once again, he breaks a window with the crowbar to enter, and uses it to knock out female victim number three. I'm also thinking she put up a fight more than the first two female vics. That's why he hit her so many times."

"You're getting too good, Eddy. Shoot, I'd better watch my back or you'll be working to take my job."

"Not in my wildest dreams."

"I see Leo hasn't showed up yet. Have you heard from him?"

"Nope."

"This is not acceptable, Eddy. You need to talk to him."

"Me?"

"Yes, you."

* * *

A knock at this office door prompted Konklin to yell, "Come in."

"May I talk to you?"

"Certainly." Noticing the bandage-wrapped hand De Mija was sporting, Konklin asked, "What happened?"

"Nothing much. I just had a little accident with one of the knives in my collection. I'll be fine."

"Geez, it must be pretty bad, Leo. Your whole right hand is wrapped. Will you be able to take any notes when we go out today?"

"Sure I will. I'm left handed. Or haven't you noticed?"

"No. Guess that sounds pretty lame coming from a veteran detective and your so-called partner on top of it? But I never paid any attention. Close the door and take a seat. I have a bone to pick with you."

"What's up?"

"Do you realize what time it is?"

"Of course. That's why I came to talk to you."

The lieutenant leaned back in his chair. "Look, Leo, I don't expect to know your every move when you're off duty. But if you're going to be out of pocket, at least have the common courtesy to let me know. Let's say I got called to a shootout in the middle of the night. Geez, the first thing I'd do would be to call you to be there to back me up. Do you understand what I'm saying?"

"If there was a shootout, I doubt you'd be called. The uniforms would be handling it, wouldn't they?"

Konklin could not figure out if the rookie detective was being sarcastic or making a serious comment. He decided to give De Mija the benefit of the doubt. "Not always. I guess that was a bad example so I'll get straight to the point. This morning, I called your home. When no one answered, I left a message on your machine. I tried to call you on your cell. No answer. I also tried to page you. The whole reason for issuing that pager to you was so the department or I could contact you in an emergency."

"I'm sorry about that, Lieu. What was so urgent?"

"Suppose you let me ask the questions. Where have you been?"

"In an emergency room having my hand stitched up. I guess in all the pain I was in, all I could think about was having my wife grab our little girl and rush me to get medical attention. I'm sorry I forgot my pager and cell phone at home. And I'm sorry I didn't check in with you first," he retorted.

"You're a trained cop, Leo. If you would have had an emergency when you were expected to be out on patrol, would you have checked in with your unit?"

"Well, yes. But --"

"No buts about it. So tell me, when --"

"Wait, Lieu. Why are you asking me questions like you're cross-examining me?"

"We were called to another double homicide this morning and I needed you there. That's why."

"Oh. I'm sorry to hear that. Will you please hear my side of this before we go any further?"

"Enlighten me because I'm about one inch away from the end of my fuse."

"This all started when my little girl woke us screaming from a stomachache. I believe that was around four-thirty this morning. Ali didn't feel too well herself before we went to bed. So I told her to go back to sleep and I got up with Fayth. I was sitting on the couch with my little girl, watching TV, when she finally quit fussing and went to sleep. I put her back in her crib, but by that time I was wide-awake.

"So I did what I normally do when I can't go back to sleep. I started cleaning some of my knives from my collection while watching television. I guess I was paying more attention to the TV than I was the knife I had in my hand. It slipped and cut me good. The cut was so severe, I was afraid to drive. I had to wake both Ali and Fayth so my wife could rush me for immediate medical assistance. Once there, it seemed like we waited forever to get help. I was beginning to think I was going to bleed to death before I ever got to see a doctor.

"Anyway, we didn't get back home until around nine this morning. Ali put Fayth to bed and she went back to bed. Then, I'm sorry to say, I fell asleep on the couch. It must have been the pain pill I was given in the emergency room that knocked me out. When I woke up, I hurriedly dressed and got here as soon as I could."

"Okay, Leo. I'll give you a pass, this time," Konklin conceded. "But if something like this ever happens again, I'll have to write you up on report. Got it?"

"Sure. Are we cool now?"

"Yes. By the way, I hope your daughter's feeling better."

"I'm sure she is. She was still sleeping sound when I left."

"Good."

"So, tell me what happened this morning."

"Another married couple lost their lives. It has a similar MO to the first two cases."

"Similar?"

"Yes. The only difference this time was that we believe the woman was bludgeoned to death first. We won't know for sure until we get Saggy's prelim report."

"That's horrible. Did they have a kid, too?"

"Two young boys. Fortunately, they weren't in the house at the time."

"Two? That's a shame. Any evidence this time?"

"In one of the boys rooms we found the same calling card as the last two houses: the printed message attached to the rattle and a single *Black Tulip*. We can't figure out why the items were left only in the one boy's room. Unless the perp wasn't aware the couple had two children."

"Evidently not."

"We also found some blood droplets on the carpet. Other than that, we'll have to wait until we get a prelim from the crime lab."

"Blood droplets?"

"Uh-huh. They probably belong to the female vic since, like I said, it looked like she was bludgeoned to death."

"What is this rattle about, anyway?"

Flabbergasted, Konklin said, "What? Haven't you ever seen the small rattle the perp leaves at the crime scenes?"

"Can't say that I have. Not the real thing, anyway. I have one of the pictures in my file, but it just looks like any other baby rattle to me. And you have to admit, the blown-up photo is a bit distorted."

Konklin was more than slightly disturbed. Here he had a detective working with him on an important serial murder and the detective had little knowledge of pertinent evidence in the case. "So a picture is all you've seen?"

"True."

"Well, the perp's rattles are locked up in the evidence room. Brenda purchased a package of the rattles back in late January. That package is probably floating around here somewhere, but I don't have time to run it down right now. Wait. As I recall, you were at that meeting when she brought the packaged items and showed them to everyone."

"Are you talking about the day I got my promotion?"

"Exactly. So how did you miss seeing the real thing?"

"I was too busy taking notes that day, I guess. Also, if you recall, I sat at the back of the room. When Detective Ferndale was showing her exhibit, she had her back to me. Like I told you, I've only seen the picture. By the way, how are the Salt and Pepper team doing in their search?"

Konklin started chuckling.

"What's so funny?"

"Salt and Pepper. I swear, you detectives come up with the strangest handles."

"Hey, I didn't give them that handle. Some of the other detectives told me. In fact, they seem to have handles for all the partners that work together."

"I've only known about Mayfield and Roitstein who the detectives refer to as the Bowery Boys. Good grief, do they have a name for us, too?"

"Do you really want to know?"

Prepared for anything, Konklin commented, "I asked, didn't I?"

"They call us the Comedy Team."

"The Comedy Team? Where did they come up with that?"

"Holms told me it's because you're always jovial and like to laugh a lot. And I'm your straight man, never cracking a smile."

"Well, I'll be jiggered. That's a good one."

Somewhat surprised, De Mija asked, "That doesn't offend you?"

"Geez, no. I think it's kind of neat. Makes me feel like they think we're part of the group and not outsiders. I always felt my age set me apart from the rest of the group. But now I know they really do accept me. I think that's great. Anyway, let's get back to this recent homicide." Instead of going into details, the lieutenant briefed De Mija on the latest crime scene.

"I don't know if I would agree with your crowbar theory, Lieu. The perp could have used a glasscutter on the windows. Then used it to cut the victims' throats."

"No, that doesn't fit either scenario. A glasscutter would have made clean cuts, not shatter the glass like we found in two different houses. Also, a glasscutter wouldn't match the cutting edge of the murder weapon."

"Oh, right. We're looking for some sort of curved instrument or tool. I still can't figure out what that could be."

"According to a report Joe received earlier this morning from the CBI Crime Lab, we now have more of an idea as to what we're looking for."

"Really? What is it?"

"A carton opener or a tile cutter."

"How can that be? Both tools are straight-edged razors you place in a holder."

"Maybe today. But back in my day, they were totally different."

"What was the estimated time of death?"

"We don't know yet. That reminds me. There's something I've been meaning to ask you."

"What?"

"When you and Ripley arrived on the scene at the Atkin house, why did you make entrance by breaking in the front door?"

"How else was I to get in?"

"The back door was open." When De Mija didn't reply, Konklin asked, "Something the matter?"

"Huh? Oh, no. I had to think back to that night. Truthfully, I don't remember Dave and I even checking the perimeter of the house. There was a baby in distress so we didn't want to waste time getting inside. It wasn't until after we had secured the house, found out the baby was okay, and discovered the bodies that I found out about the back door. Now, I may be wrong on that. But I'm sure Dave wrote a report up on it. So you can check with him."

"I don't need to. Your word is good enough."

"Any ID's on the latest victims yet?"

"Yes. I have them written down in my notepad. Tell you what. Let's discuss this new case later. Right now, I need you to get busy."

"Doing what?"

"I want you to start making a list of all the hardware, home improvement, and any other stores that sell hand tools. I'm going to lunch. When I get back, we'll start looking for that tool."

* * *

"Turn left at the next corner."

"You know, Leo, in all my years as a detective, this is the worst case I've ever had the displeasure of working on. Can you imagine wanting to kill parents for correcting their children when they do something wrong?"

"Do you really believe that's the motive behind all of these murders?"

"If you take to heart the meaning of the perp's poem, then yes. It sounds so sinister. But what other explanation could there be?"

"I don't know for sure. But I think there must be more to it."

"Like what?"

"It's one thing to correct a child. But it's quite another thing to be abusive toward a child. We took our daughter shopping this past Friday when I got off work. Ali wanted to get Fayth a new outfit for Easter Sunday services. We took her to this place called Tot's Territory. This store has everything for kids from party favors to kids' furniture. I highly recommend that place."

Konklin grinned. "I don't have children. So cut the sales pitch."

"It does sound that way, doesn't it? I just think the store is the greatest, that's all. And the owner goes out of his way to please his customers."

Konklin was enjoying the fact that De Mija was finally talking to him like real partners do. He tried to keep up with the flow, but in his mind he wondered, *What does any of this have to do with a motive for murder?* "So, did you find something cute for your daughter to wear on Easter?"

De Mija was watching for street signs. Also, it was a natural instinct as a trained officer to scope the surroundings while patrolling the streets. After their near accident, De Mija could not tell if the lieutenant was as diligent, or just driving and talking. So, he felt he had to watch out for both of them.

"Did you hear me, Leo?"

"Yes. And we did find a cute dress for Fayth. Anyway, on this particular evening …." De Mija continued talking until he had told Konklin the whole story. "Just for my own knowledge and future reference, I got the man's name and the street he lives on. Oh, and get this. The mother just stood by and didn't say a word. She didn't even try to comfort the child. The only thing she seemed to care about was buying some stuffed toy for a relative. Man, I couldn't just stand by and watch. I really let that man have it verbally with both barrels."

"Calm down, Leo. It appears that you're still upset with that man."

"Let's just say the Carney couple got what was coming to them. Parents have got to realize that kids are human beings. That Carney guy --"

"Wait, Leo!" Konklin quickly interrupted as he focused his attention on De Mija and not on his driving. "What was that name you just said?"

"It was … WATCH OUT!"

CHAPTER TWENTY-TWO

At the hospital, Warner rushed to the nurse's station in the emergency room area. "I'm Capt. Joe Warner from the MPPD, 15th Precinct," he said to a nurse standing behind the desk. "I received word that two of my detectives have been brought in from the scene of a traffic accident."

"What are their names?"

"Eddy Konklin and Leo De Mija."

After checking over her list of current arrivals, she replied, "Yes, they're both here."

"How are they?"

"I'm sorry, sir. I can't give you any information. If you would like to have a seat in our waiting area --"

"No, I don't want to sit." Warner did not mean to be rude, but he was filled with concern. "Who can tell me how they are?"

"Excuse me! Excuse me!" A panicky voice cried out as a woman ran up next to where Warner was standing. "Please, nurse, someone called me and said my husband was brought here. Can you help me?"

"I'm sorry, ma'am," Warner stated, "but I'm trying to find out about my --"

"No, I'm sorry," she interrupted in hysteria. "My husband was in a car accident and I need to know if he's all right."

"Go ahead, nurse," Warner said, trying to show that he was still a gentleman. "Give the lady her information. Then you can help me."

"Thank you," the woman stated.

"What's his name?" The nurse asked.

"Leo. Leo De Mija."

Warner turned and looked at the woman. "You're Leo's wife?"

"Yes. Who are you?"

"I'm Capt. Warner, your husband's boss. I'm here to find out about your husband and my lieutenant."

"Well," the nurse stated, "if you'll both please take a seat, I'll have one of the attending physicians talk to you just as soon as possible."

Warner took hold of Alianna's arm. "I think we'd best do as the nurse suggests." Turning and walking toward the chairs, he said, "Your name is Alianna, isn't it?"

"Yes. Oh, I'm sorry for forgetting my manners. My mind is just too preoccupied worrying about Leo."

"I understand perfectly. Let's sit here."

As they each took a seat, Alianna sniffled. "I would have been here sooner, but I had to find someone to watch my little girl. We don't socialize, and we live a mile away from the closest neighbor. So it was real difficult finding someone to help me out. May I ask you a question, Capt. Warner?"

"Certainly. And considering the circumstances you can call me Joe for now."

"Okay, Joe. What have you heard about the accident?"

"From the random report I received, it appears they collided with a semi. I heard the driver of our department's car was critical and the passenger was injured. I'm afraid I don't know any other details right now."

"Oh, dear God," she cried, grabbing at Warner's hand. "Was Leo driving?"

"I'm not positive, but I believe Lt. Konklin was the driver."

"Why do you think that?"

"Because he's been driving ever since the two of them teamed up. I'm just assuming that hasn't changed."

"Leo hasn't told me very much about his new job. But I know he always drove when he was out on patrol. He hates being a passenger. Even with his hurt hand, I knew Leo could still drive today because he had to drive to work. I think you're just trying to make me feel better," she sobbed, wiping the tears from her face with the back of her hand. "I don't know what Fayth and I will do if we lose him. He's our life."

Warner held her hand and tried to comfort her. "Let's not jump to the wrong conclusions until we hear from a doctor. You mentioned Leo's hand. What happened?"

Alianna was preoccupied in her own thoughts. When she didn't answer, Warner just let the conversation drop. The two of them waited patiently for word on both Konklin's and De Mija's prognosis. It seemed like an eternity.

Finally, a young man in a green uniform approached them. "Are you Mrs. De Mija?"

Looking up at the man, Alianna answered, "Yes."

"I'm Dr. Riteweiller."

"Do you have information about my husband? May I see him?"

"Your husband will be out as soon as they finish cleaning him up."

"You mean he's all right?" Delighted to hear the good news, she got to her feet.

Warner also got up from his chair and stood next to Alianna, listening to the doctor's report on De Mija.

"Your husband had a severe gash in his head which took ten stitches. Although he says he doesn't really remember, he thinks he hit his head on the car's dashboard. He was complaining his right shoulder hurt, so we took some x-rays. Actually we took several x-rays of various parts of his body. Everything looks good. He says he was the passenger in the car. So I imagine he bruised the shoulder pretty good when he obviously hit the side of the door on impact.

"He broke open his previous stitches to his right hand. So we sewed that wound back up again. Other than a few aches and pains, and his complaint of a minor headache, he appears to be in pretty good shape. He should be as good as new in a few days. I wrote him out a prescription for pain relief. Make sure he gets it filled and takes the pills as needed. Your husband doesn't appear to have more than a minor concussion. But if you notice any critical changes in his behavior, call your personal physician immediately."

"What kind of changes?"

"Pardon me for butting in, doctor," Warner said. "But if you're worried about a concussion, shouldn't you keep him overnight for observation?"

"I strongly recommended to Mr. De Mija that we admit him for the night. But he isn't willing to go along with my suggestion. Since he guaranteed me that he would get plenty of bed rest, and someone would be there to monitor him for the next 48 hours, I agreed he could go home."

"I'll be right there with him," Alianna said. Frowning, she asked, "Forgive my medical stupidity, but what exactly is the difference between a minor and a major concussion."

"A minor concussion is a sharp blow to the head that gives one a pretty good headache. Within a short period of time, the headache will decrease and the patient will be just fine. A major concussion can lead to lasting physical or psychological problems. The patient will experience depression, abnormal irritability, and even paralysis."

Dr. Riteweiller continued to tell Alianna what symptoms to watch for. He also reassured her that, in his professional opinion, she had nothing to be alarmed about. Then he suggested, "If he's on the mend, which I'm sure he will be, just make sure he sees his own personal physician in a week as a follow-up. He'll probably be inactive for a while. Other than that, your husband should be as good as new in no time."

"Oh, that's wonderful news," she uttered in relief.

"Mr. De Mija told me he's on the police force."

"Yes. He's a detective in my unit," Warner offered.

"Well, I'd give him about two weeks' recovery period. His physician will tell him when he's well enough to start working again."

"We have our protocol, too. Once his physician releases him, our physician will have to examine him. If his health is okay, he'll be able to come back to work."

"Well, that's not my concern. For now, I just want him to take the proper time to heal."

"No problem there. He can take as much time as he needs to recuperate."

"Will he have any scars after he heals?" Alianna asked.

"I don't profess to be an expert artist like his plastic surgeon evidently was," Dr. Riteweiller said with a smile. "I'm sure he'll have a small scar, but it won't be too noticeable."

"Plastic surgeon?" Alianna asked with a questionable look.

"Why, yes. From the x-rays, your husband obviously underwent quite extensive facial reconstruction some years ago. I assumed you knew."

"No, I didn't."

"What about the driver of the car Leo was in, doctor?" Warner asked.

"Dr. Adams is attending the other accident victim. I'm sure he'll be with you as soon as he can."

"Can't you tell me anything about him?" Warner persisted.

"No. I'm sorry."

"Look," Alianna exclaimed, "it's Leo."

As a nurse pushed De Mija's wheelchair into the waiting room, Alianna ran to her husband's side and gave him a kiss on the cheek.

Dr. Riteweiller walked away.

As Warner headed in De Mija's direction, a female approached him. She was wearing the same type of green uniform Dr. Riteweiller wore. "I'm Dr. Adams. The station nurse told me you were waiting to talk to me."

"Are you Eddy Konklin's attending physician?"

"I am."

"I'm Capt. Warner of the MPPD. Eddy Konklin is one of my detectives. I want to find out about his condition?"

"Do you know how to get in touch with any of the members of Mr. Konklin's family?"

Warner's chin dropped as he thought the worst. "You mean … he … he didn't make it?"

"I didn't say that, Capt. Warner."

"Thank God. Well, Eddy doesn't have any family members in the area. They all live out of state. I'm not only his boss but I'm his closest friend."

While Warner was speaking with Dr. Adams, he noticed a couple of his detectives enter the waiting room. They stopped to chat with De Mija who was still sitting in the wheelchair with Alianna by his side.

"Without his consent, I really need to talk to Mr. Konklin's next of kin," Dr. Adams stated.

"Then ask *him*. He'll tell you I'm the one that's supposed to be contacted in case of an emergency."

"I can't ask him, but I'll take your word for it. I'm sorry, but your friend is in critical condition. His heart stopped while we were working on him. We had to resuscitate him. The best that I can tell you is to leave your name at the front office. We'll notify you if there is any change in his condition. The next forty-eight hours are going to be very crucial."

"May I see him?"

"Say, your first name isn't by any chance Joe, is it?"

"Yes. Why? Has Eddy been calling for me?"

"He's been in and out of consciousness since he was brought in by the EMTs, but he's been calling out the name Joe. Okay, I'll take you in but only for a minute."

Walking in De Mija's direction as he followed behind Dr. Adams, Warner hesitated for a moment to acknowledge the other detectives. Dr. Adams waited.

"Help him to their car and follow them home. I'm sure Mrs. De Mija could use the help getting him in the house. I appreciate you fellas showing up, but there's nothing you can do here." As he gently patted De Mija on the back, he said, "Stay home. Take as long as you need to mend. When you feel up to it, call me and let me know exactly what happened." As he touched Alianna's arm, he added, "Take good care of our boy."

Alianna nodded, smiling.

De Mija said, "Thanks, Cap. Is Lieu going to be okay?"

"I don't know. I guess he's in the hands of God and the doctors now." Turning, he said, "Okay, doctor. Let's go see my friend."

In the emergency room, Warner had expected to see the worst. He thought he had prepared himself. But the sight of his lieutenant brought his heart to his throat. Every part of Konklin's body was covered with cuts, bruises and blood. He was connected to a heart monitor, an IV, a catheter and oxygen. His legs were in temporary splints to keep him from moving them, causing further damage to broken bones. There was an attending nurse standing at his bedside, gently wiping the blood from Konklin's face. His bloodstained torn clothes were laying in a pile on the floor.

"We just finished suturing all the severe gashes, so we haven't had a chance to finish cleaning him up yet," Dr. Adams softly stated, watching the blood drain from Warner's face. "You don't have a weak stomach, do you?"

Warner could not speak; he could only shake his head. He had seen people in worse condition, but he never knew them as he did Konklin. He walked as close to the bed as he could possibly get. Shaking from emotion, he carefully reached out and touched Konklin's hand. "Eddy, it's me. Joe," he said as his voice crackled from the lump in his throat. After he cleared his throat, he continued to try and get Konklin to respond. "Hey, big guy, can you hear me?"

Konklin's eyelids fluttered. Then slowly, he opened them. "Joe," he said in a broken whisper.

Leaning in closer in order to hear him, Warner replied, "Yes, I'm here, Eddy."

"I know … it's … it's Leo --"

"I'm sorry, but he's out again," the attending nurse stated.

Taking Warner's arm, Dr. Adams walked him back out into the hall. "It's better that he rests now. You can come back tomorrow and we'll let you know how he's doing."

"Please be honest with me, doctor. How are his chances?"

"Prognosis isn't good. But he'll get the best care possible. When we've finished cleaning him up and setting his broken bones, your friend will be moved to ICU. There he will have round-the-clock attention until he is out of the woods."

"Then there is hope?"

"There's always hope."

"He called me Joe. Then he called me Leo. Why did he know me at first then mistake me for his partner?"

"He's suffering from a severe concussion which will make his mind fuzzy."

Oh, dear God! After what Dr. Riteweiller just explained to Alianna about a major concussion, Eddy could live and still have severe problems. "Thank you, doctor. I'll be back first thing in the morning. Oh, and about leaving my phone number with the front office. Wouldn't it be better if I leave it here at the emergency room desk?"

"I'm afraid not. ICU is in a different part of the hospital. Once our patients are admitted, we no longer have information on them in this area."

"You mean you will no longer be his doctor?"

"No. I'm just the emergency room attending physician. Mr. Konklin's personal physician will be called to take over the case."

"Do you know who that is?"

"Yes. He was able to tell us in one of his conscious moments."

* * *

At home, Joe sat at the dinner table moving food around his plate with a fork.

Worried, Jeny said, "Come on, Joe. You've got to eat something."

"I'm just not hungry. I think I'll just have another cup of coffee. Can I get you a refill?"

"No, thank you."

Amandalee got to her feet before Joe had a chance to move. "I'll get it, Dad. You sit still."

When Amandalee returned from the kitchen, she placed Joe's cup on the table.

"Thanks, Mandy."

"You're welcome, as always." As she sat back at the table, she commented, "I overheard you talking on the phone before dinner about Eddy's accident."

"I did too," Jeny confessed. "Do you want to talk about it, Joe?"

"I apologize to both of you. I guess I'm so worried about Eddy, I can't think straight. The call was from the officer who was the first to arrive at the accident scene. He was just filling me in with what he knew." After taking a drink of his coffee, Joe continued. "Eddy and Leo hit head-on with a semi-truck. The driver of the semi was conscious enough at the scene to tell the officer that he had lost control of his rig, started to jack-knife, and ended up crossing the median into the oncoming traffic. You have to understand that the accident happened over on Snelling."

"Wow, Dad. That's one of the steepest hills around, other than actually driving up into the mountains."

"I know. Anyway, the semi driver said he tried to swerve back into his lane, but the oncoming car, meaning Eddy's, was too close. He thinks Eddy's car tried to swerve out of the way. But it all happened so fast, he wasn't real sure. The officer did confirm that Eddy was driving the car. They had to pry him out with the Jaws of Life. I guess that would explain why Eddy took the worst beating, and Leo got off with less body damage. Of course I won't know anymore until I can speak with either Leo or Eddy."

"Why didn't the officer question Detective De Mija at the scene of the accident?" Amandalee asked. "Wasn't he conscious?"

"He was apparently conscious when the officer got to the scene. But he passed out within seconds after the paramedics arrived."

"How's the driver of the semi?" Jeny asked.

"I didn't ask about the severity of his injuries, but I do know he'll be in the hospital for a while. There will be an investigation into why he lost control that caused the accident. I hope for his sake that it was the truck's fault and not the driver's. Incidentally, I don't recall if I told you when I got home, but I left my number at the hospital in case there's any change in Eddy's condition." Resting his elbows on the table, Joe rested his face in his hands. "Oh my, Eddy has just got to pull through this," he sighed as the tears welled from his eyes. "I'm sorry for breaking down like this."

Jeny got up from her chair and walked to the back of Joe's chair. She wrapped her chubby arms around his strong shoulders. After a gentle kiss, she rested her face on the top of his head.

Amandalee reached over and placed her loving hand on Joe's hand. "Eddy will make it, Dad. He will."

"We both know how much Eddy means to you, Joe. We love him too. So you go ahead and let it all out," Jeny comforted.

* * *

The following morning, bright and early, Warner showed up at the hospital. The emergency room staff sent him to the front desk. As he walked to the front of the hospital, he chastised himself for not remembering Konklin was to be moved to the ICU unit.

From the front desk, he was sent to the third floor. At the nurse's station, he asked, "What room is Eddy Konklin in?"

"Are you a relative," the nurse inquired.

"No. But I'm the closest thing he's got. I was told I could visit him this morning."

Checking her patient files, she said, "Sorry, sir. But you'll have to speak to Dr. Richards. I'll have him paged."

"Who's Dr. Richards?"

"There are a few chairs over there by the elevator, sir. I'm sure the doctor won't be very long."

Warner heard the page over the loud speaker. Too wound up to sit, he paced the hospital's corridor near the nurse's station. After a fifteen-minute wait, the nurse motioned for him to approach the desk.

"Yes."

"Dr. Richards just stepped in the back room. He'll be right with you."

Before Warner could thank her, a man in a white smock appeared and asked, "Are you Capt. Warner?"

"Yes."

"I'm Dr. Richards, Eddy's personal physician."

"Nice to meet you, doctor. How's my friend doing this morning?"

"I'm afraid he has fallen into a coma."

Warner's heart plummeted. "My God. When did this happen?"

"Late last night."

"I left my name and phone number with the hospital's front office. I don't understand why no one called me."

"I really don't know."

"Now what? Will Eddy come out of the coma?"

"Only time will tell right now. We're keeping him in ICU and will continue to monitor his vitals."

"The MPPD has excellent insurance. If Eddy needs anything, and I mean anything, I want to make sure he gets it."

"I can assure you, he's getting the best of care. However, we do need someone to go to the insurance office to give them Eddy's insurance information. Perhaps you could do that for him?"

"I know the name of the company, but not Eddy's ID number. If I could get the card out of his wallet, I can take it to the insurance office."

"You'll have to ask the head nurse what they did with Eddy's personal belongings when they brought him up from the emergency unit. Now, before you go in to see Eddy, I need to ask you an important question."

"Ask."

"Eddy and I have become well-acquainted in the past few years since he's been my patient. However, I don't believe we ever discussed him being an organ donor or having a Living Will. Now, according to his driver's license, we found out that he is a donor. But we still don't know if he has a Living Will. Do you know?"

"I don't have the remotest idea. I do, however, know his attorney, Dan Ruffle. So I'll find out for you."

"We'll need that information as soon as possible." Dr. Richards reached into his pocket and pulled out his business card, which he handed to Warner. "If there is a Living Will, both the hospital and I will need a copy of it. Either way, call or have his attorney call me and let me know."

Taking the card, Warner placed it into the upper pocket of his suit coat. "I don't want you to pull the plug on Eddy unless it's ninety-nine percent hopeless."

"I'm sorry, Capt. Warner. Unless you have the authority, you can't make that decision for him."

Feeling hopelessly powerless, Warner had to respect the system. "I'll find out about that Living Will as soon as I leave here today. Anything else?"

"Not for now. Thank you."

"Now may I see him?"

"Of course. I don't really know much about detective work. But have you ever seen anyone in a coma before?"

"No."

As they started walking, the doctor briefly explained, "Coma patients appear to be in a very soothing sleep. Some say they can hear everything that goes on around them. So if you are one of those believers, you're welcome to speak to him." Stopping at a door, he said, "Here we are. Oh, a few of his co-workers showed up here last night. Other than next of kin, we don't really welcome visitors to the ICU unit."

"I'll make sure to tell them. Thank you."

Patting Warner on the back, he said, "We're doing everything we can for him. If you know any prayers, I'd certainly say them."

Warner's knees were shaking as he walked into his friend's room. Hesitating momentarily, he took a deep breath. Then he walked to the side of the bed. Wringing his hands together, Warner tried desperately to compose himself. He couldn't allow his hands to shake or his voice to crack. Konklin might sense he was not going to get well. His friend had to feel and hear strength, truth, and optimism from him. With the greatest of care, Warner slowly lifted Konklin's limp hand and encased it in his own.

"Hey, chubby cheeks. It's me, Joe. You know you'd better get well real fast because I can't solve this *Black Tulip* case without you. The rest of the unit needs you, too. And what about your new partner, Leo? He's still green and needs you to show him how to become a top-notch detective. Just like you. Come on, Eddy, fight. Fight with everything that's in you. I need you to get better, big guy. I know you can do it." Warner fought back tears. "I know this probably sounds pretty lame, but I love you, big guy. Of course, if you ever tell anyone I said that when you wake up, I'll deny it." As hard as it was to have a sense of humor at a moment like this, he knew if his friend and co-worker could hear him that laughter more than sadness would bring him around. After carefully putting Konklin's hand back down on the bed, Warner said, "I … I have to go to the office now. But I'll be back later. See you soon, pal."

* * *

At work, Warner felt as if a dark cloud was hanging over the entire precinct. Everyone, including himself, seemed to choke on the words *good morning*. It was Saturday, but Warner had work to do. He went straight to his office. The very first thing he did was to contact Dan Ruffle and give him the sad news about Konklin. There was no Living Will. As Konklin's attorney, Ruffle promised to call the doctor and the hospital and pass on the information.

After his conversation with Ruffle, Warner made an in-house call. "Jess."

"Yes, Cap," Duncan replied.

"We're expecting a full crew today."

"I know."

"As the detectives start arriving, I need you to pass the word. No one leaves to go out on assignment until I give the word. Tell everyone to stay at their desks. As soon as everyone is in and accounted for, with the exception of Lt. Konklin and Detective De Mija, let me know."

"Will do, Cap. Anything else?"

"That's all"

After making a pot of coffee, Warner tried to bury himself in paperwork. It was no use. He found it hard to concentrate. After closing his inner-office window blinds, he filled his mug with fresh coffee. Sipping the coffee, he paced the floor until Duncan called. Everyone was present and waiting.

After refreshing his coffee, Warner went to the front office. He walked to a spot where he knew everyone could see and hear him. As he stood, half in a daze, the quiet was deafening. Warner placed his cup on the nearest desk. He stood for a second and looked over the solemn faces of his detectives.

"I can tell you've all heard about the terrible auto accident. The good news is Leo went home yesterday with limited injuries. If all goes well in his healing process, he'll probably be back at work in a couple of weeks.

"The bad news is, Eddy wasn't so lucky. He had severe head trauma and suffered extreme bodily injuries. His heart stopped yesterday, but they were able to revive him. I stopped by the hospital this morning and his personal physician informed me that he had fallen into a coma late last night. Now, I don't know if any of you believe in the power of prayer. But if you do, please say a prayer for him.

"Before I forget, his physician informed me a few of you tried to visit Eddy last evening. As you found out, and I want the rest of you to know, no one is allowed to visit a patient in ICU unless you are the next of kin. Since he has no family around …." Warner paused, trying to think of what to say. Nothing came to mind that felt appropriate. So he said, "For lack of a better explanation, I'm filling in. But I promise, I will keep you all informed."

After a moment to gather his thoughts, he continued. "As for work, we will carry on as usual. I want the team that's working on the *Black Tulip* case to come to my office a soon as I'm done here. The rest of you who have vital cases of your own can go on about your work. Since we are severely short-handed now with both Eddy and Leo out of commission, I'll need even more help on Eddy's case. I know I'm repeating myself, but please report to me as soon as the cases you're working on are wrapped up.

"Oh, one more thing. It's not very often that I ask all of you to give up your weekends to work. I just want you to know how much I appreciate it. From here on until this case is solved, we are all going to be working long hours, six days a week. We will only work a skeleton crew on Sundays. Make sure you tell your families. I know I generally do the scheduling. But, under the circumstances, I'm going to ask each of you to work out a schedule with your partners and the other divisions. We don't have that many beds in the crib, so you'll have to schedule resting periods accordingly. You will all be compensated for the extra hours. Now, I need two volunteers for food service." As hands rose, Warner said, "Mickey and Derek, you get the honor."

"What do you want us to do?" Chung asked.

"I want donuts, rolls and coffee in the morning. Sandwiches and soft drinks at lunch, and whatever everyone wants for dinners."

"For the whole unit?"

"For everyone who's working at the time, yes. All I ask is that you all be reasonable. I'd better not see any steak or lobster and definitely no alcoholic drinks," Warner stated, forcing a smile. "Mickey, you and Derek come to my office after my meeting with the *Black Tulip* task force. Or, if you get called out on the case you're working, make sure you see me before leaving this evening. Anyone have any questions?"

"Yes," Lewkowski replied. "When do we start this new work schedule?"

"I know it's short notice, Art, but I'd like you all to start immediately. Sometime during today and tomorrow, I'm sure you can all find time to plan your schedules and go home to inform your families. So on Monday, we'll go ahead in full force. Anything else? No. Then that's it. Get to work and have a good day. Above all, stay safe."

* * *

Inside Warner's office, he informed the small group of detectives about the Carney murders. Opening his window blinds, he continued talking. "So, we believe there is a self-proclaimed child protector out there that deems himself judge and jury against parents he feels are offenders towards their children. I'm sure I'm repeating myself, but this is only speculation at this point. It goes without saying that we hope our hunch is wrong. Okay, that just about sums it up.

"I believe you all know me by now. I've always tried to keep a cool head and my wits about me. Even in the worst situations. However, I have to be honest. As much as you and all the rest of the unit mean to me, I'm much closer to Eddy. As all of you are aware, an unexplainable friendship happens between partners. Don't any of you get the wrong idea. That still doesn't mean I show him favoritism when it comes to work. Anyway, I'm sure you'll understand that my brain is just a bit foggy. With your help I'll be back on top of things shortly. So, if you'll bear with me, I need a quick refresher course. This will be much easier than me trying to concentrate on your reports right now. "Brenda, bring me quickly up to par how you and J.B. are sitting."

"We've completed our list of stores Myron's Miniatures Import Company supplied us with. We still don't know any more now than we did when we started our search. However, all the pertinent store managers and product buyers that we spoke with have our number in case they come up with any new information that can assist us. From the lists we have been able to collect, all names have been input on Arnie's computer."

"Arnie, how are you and Eric doing?"

"We've completed our assignments, too."

"For both the bubble-jet printers and the tulip? All customers' names are on the computer."

"Good to hear. Arjay, I know you and Kieyell haven't been able to find out any more on Ellie Smither. Correct?"

"Correct, Cap. But we're still looking. If we don't come up with anything soon, I suggest we subpoena Kate Smither for her daughter's birth certificate."

"That will be our last resort. Switching gears here, the lieutenant asked the whole unit to be on the lookout for a tool with a sharp, curved or hooked blade. Have any of you been looking for the tile cutter or the carton opener?"

As the team looked at one another, shaking heads and shrugging shoulders, Brown said, "We've more or less kept our eyes open for such a tool, Cap. But --"

"I'm sorry, J.B., but let me stop you for a moment. Make yourself a note to call over to the lot where Eddy's car was taken." Warner continued talking as he shuffled papers on his desk until he found what he was looking for. Picking up a pink incoming call slip, he reached out across his desk with it. "Here's the phone number." Brown got up from his chair and took the note, then returned to his seat. "I received that message last night that all items in the car were ready to be picked up there. Hopefully, Eddy's notes are among the belongings. If so, add his info to your report. If not, we'll have to start his and Leo's search from scratch."

Brown had not the slightest idea what the captain was talking about. However, he nodded in agreement.

Ferndale, on the other hand, was not afraid to ask. "If Lieu had any information, I would think Leo would know about it. Either J.B. or I could call him and ask."

"No. As serious as this case is, I don't think Leo will be of much assistance right now. Wait, I just remembered something important." Warner picked up his phone and dialed the front desk. "Warner here. Did Lt. Konklin receive a phone message or a courier package yet from the main station downtown? He did? Yes, if you could do that I would appreciate it. Yes, I'm in my office. Oh, until further notice, please see that I get all of Lt. Konklin's messages and mail. Yes, for Detective De Mija, also. Thank you." Hanging up the phone, Warner said, "Hopefully, we'll have a look at a tool that could be what we're looking for as the murder weapon."

"How's that, Cap?"

"Eddy's the one that had the idea about this tool, but it may not be on the market today. He had a hunch that there may be one still being used at headquarters, downtown. Yesterday, he asked a friend of his in records to scout around for said tool. And, if she found it, to send it over."

"Sorry, Cap. But if nobody else will ask, I will," Mayfield stated. "What in the devil are you talking about?"

Warner tapped his forehead. He had forgotten that he and Konklin had only discussed this tool idea yesterday morning. What with the homicides and the auto accident, the rest of the team did not know about the tool Konklin and De Mija had been out searching for. Before Warner had a chance to start explaining, there was a rap at his door. Recognizing the face, he motioned for the officer to enter.

"Good morning, Officer Carson. I see the desk sergeant has you running errands again."

"Not really," she said, giving Warner a warm smile. "He just happened to catch me before I walked out the door. Here." She handed Warner a small package along with a form. "I'm told you need to sign this release that you're taking responsibility for this delivery."

Warner looked at the box. In big bold letters for the return address, it read: PROPERTY OF MT. PRIDE POLICE DEPARTMENT, MAIN HEADQUARTERS, DEPARTMENT OF MAINTENANCE. After scanning over the form, he understood why he was requested to sign it. "Seems this is an important package that needs to be taken care of and returned when we're through with it. I guess this way, if it gets lost, it's my skin," Warner said with a bit of a chuckle. He signed the form, and Officer Carson exited his office.

Warner opened the box. He took out the tool and a note that was enclosed with it. Laughing, he read the note out loud to his associates. "'Eddy, I looked in every nook and cranny I could get into searching for this thing. By the end of the day, I had everyone I could talk to helping me in my search. Not the young ones, of course, as they wouldn't have the slightest idea what I was looking for. I guess that ages us! Anyway, just when I was about to give up and go home, I made one last attempt and cornered our good old handyman. Bless his heart. He had this locked away in his old tool room. Not only does this belong to his department, but I promised, faithfully, to personally hand it back to him. So don't you go and lose it.' It's signed Sue. Then she added a postscript. 'P.S. I'll expect a nice dinner for this one.'

"Well, here it is," Warner said, holding up the tool. "Any of you ever seen one of these before?"

Everyone but Mayfield shook their heads. "I have, Cap. My Father owned a grocery store when I was growing up. We used to have a couple of those around to open cardboard boxes when we received shipments."

"Great, Arjay. Do you know the proper name for it?"

"Nope. We just called it a box opener."

"That's great," Warner responded, somewhat displeased. "That's what Eddy said. Well, from the looks of it, it could very well be used as a murder weapon." It took a while, but Warner was finally pulling himself together as the meeting continued. He was a good cop and couldn't afford to carry his emotions around on his shirtsleeves.

"As I was going to tell you before this package was delivered, we received the CBI lab report in yesterday morning's mail. They concurred with Saggy's report that the victims' throats had been cut with a curved-edge blade that narrows to a point. They also found a small particle of wood in one of the victim's blood samples. After telling the group the three possible explanations the lab had given for the particle of wood, he added, "So, we immediately eliminated a wood floor. It was Eddy's idea that we look for a tool that would fit both the blade type and a wood handle, such as the one I'm holding."

"I'm guessing, Cap," Ferndale offered, "but I got this idea from what Arjay just told us about working in a grocery store. If we can no longer find this tool in the retail stores, maybe we should check out the older grocery stores? Maybe there are some around who still use this sort of tool instead of the newer razor blade versions they sell today. By the way, today they call the new ones box cutters, I think."

"I'll issue orders in a minute, Brenda. But I'll take your suggestion into consideration. Besides, I just told you Eddy's take on the CBI report, not mine. They also suggested that the particle of wood could have fallen off the murderer's person."

"You mean it may have been on his clothes or body from the get go?"

"Right, Kieyell. With this theory, Eddy and I also discussed that we could be looking for a carpenter or a handyman. Now we have to add grocery stores to our list."

"What about buildings that have their own maintenance departments?" Brown asked.

"Cheese and crackers! Instead of narrowing down our leads, they appear to be getting more extensive," Warner admitted. "Eddy was going to have Leo develop a list of carpenters in our area. The accident rather put the skids on that."

"I can do it," Ferndale offered.

"The assignment's yours, Brenda. However, before you begin, check out Leo's computer. He might already have the list — or at least started one. And we also need to get those items from Eddy's car picked up. It could be that Eddy and Leo had the list with them before the accident. J.B., as soon as you get those items, bring them directly to me. "Warner placed the tool toward the front of his desk. "Arnie, take this and get a good snapshot of it. Then get about ten copies. When you do, we'll lock this baby up for safekeeping. Like the photo of the rattle, the ones of this tool will show the people you talk to exactly what we're looking for. Oh, and do me a favor, will you? Make sure the copies are clear. The ones we have of the rattle were far too fuzzy."

"Sure, Cap. I'll make sure they're good copies," Hathaway said.

"Eric, I want you to check out a car from the auto pool. For now, I want you and Arnie to work separately in search for this tool."

"Cap, will you call down to authorize me to take out a car?"

"Affirmative. Any questions about your assignments for now? Yes, Brenda."

"If we have a complete list — between the items J.B. brings back and what I find on Leo's computer — do you want me and J.B. to canvass separately, too?"

"Definitely. Oh, okay. I'll call down and authorize one of you to take out another car from the auto pool. That's it," Warner concluded.

* * *

When the *Black Tulip* case team dispersed, Detectives Chung and Zeal entered the office per Warner's request.

"Have a seat, fellas. I'll be right with you." After he made a few phone calls, Warner said, "Okay, we're all set up. Dunkin Donuts will have seven-dozen of a variety of breakfast rolls and donuts ready for you to pick up each morning by seven A.M. Louie's Deli will deliver a variety of sandwiches and condiments around noon. As you heard, I ordered ham, pastrami, roast beef, and chicken salad sandwiches with a variety of cheeses on the side. Two sandwiches each should be enough to tide everyone over until dinner. When the food arrives, it will be your responsibility to sign for it and set it up in the coffee room. Keep all receipts for my records. As for dinners, I'm not going to have you taking special orders and driving all over town to appease everyone. One restaurant or drive-thru each night is the only run you need to make. Make up some sort of a menu. By that I mean, have pizza and salads one night, chicken and all the trimmings one night, etcetera. Do either of you have a wholesale grocer's ID card?"

"I have a Sam's Club card," Zeal answered.

"Good. Which one of you is going to be responsible for paying and collecting my receipts?"

"I will."

Warner retrieved his billfold from his back pocket and pulled out a credit card. "Here you go, Mickey. I'm not a wealthy man, so use it within reason. On the other hand, we don't want anyone starving to death."

Taking the plastic card, Chung asked, "Why are you footing the bill, Cap?"

"It was bad enough getting Doogle to agree to overtime. I didn't want to push my luck asking for food allocation, too. However, I don't want anyone but you two knowing I'm footing this bill. Got it?"

"Yes, Cap," Chung replied.

"You've got our word," Zeal stated.

"Good. Okay, my gold MasterCard will cover for the dinners and at Sam's. Derek, that's where your ID will come in handy. You two can get cases of sodas and whatever else you need from there for the unit. Make sure you keep your out-of-pocket receipts separate than mine. I'll reimburse you at the end of each week. That won't put either of you in a financial bind, will it?" When both detectives gave him the negative shake of their heads, he said, "Good."

"Anything else, Cap?"

"Nope. That's it. Will one of you please tell Tony to bring his team in now?"

* * *

Upon request, DelGinny, Holms, Anthony, and Brubaker entered the captain's office. Once the door was closed and the men had taken their seats, Warner asked, "So, Tony, what's happening?"

"In a nutshell, Cap, it all boils down to the DA being right. After further and more comprehensive investigation, due to your suggestions, we found the correct suspect. You should have the completed reports on your desk later this morning."

"Brief me."

"Our eyewitness, Della Smither, was the real perp. After being confronted with the evidence, she confessed, and --"

Warner shook his head as if to clear water out of his ears after a swan dive into a swimming pool. "Wait. Wait. Wait. What was that name again?"

"Della Smither."

Warner looked between the slats of his window blinds. "Good, they're still here. Eric, go out and bring Arjay and Kieyell in here."

As Lennon left the room, DelGinny asked, "What's up, Cap?"

"Your suspect. I'm hoping she can help us on --" Warner was cut short when Lennon entered the room with Mayfield and Roitstein. "Arjay, how many people with the last name of Smither did you locate in the phone book and through the phone company's new listings?"

"Ten," Mayfield answered.

"Among those ten, were you able to contact each of them?"

"Yes."

"Did you ever come across the name Della Smither?"

Mayfield shook his head and looked to Roitstein for confirmation. Roitstein answered. "No, Cap. That name doesn't ring a bell."

Warner then turned to DelGinny. "Tony, do you recall if your perp had a land phone or a cell phone in her name?"

"As a matter of fact, she doesn't have either. I remember because when we thought she was still the witness, we asked her how she made the 911 call. She told us she had to use the pay phone in the hall. What's this all about, Cap?"

"Arjay and Kieyell have been searching for background information on a suspect in the *Black Tulip* case. Her name happens to be Ellie Smither. They can't find any connection between her and her parents. Right, Arjay?"

"Right. We've not been able to find any birth records on her. And no record that her mother, Kate, gave birth to her or that the Smithers adopted her. Cap, are you thinking we should question this Della Smither?"

"You bet I am, Arjay. If nothing else, it's worth a try. If she doesn't know anything about Ellie — no harm, no foul."

"Where is this Della Smither?"

DelGinny said, "In lock up."

"Arjay, you and Kieyell go talk to her. The rest of you are now officially on the *Black Tulip* special task force. Since your case is closed, go out and report to Brenda. She'll fill you in on your assignments. If any of you need extra cars, just have the auto pool contact me for authorization."

* * *

"Well, one mystery is solved," Mayfield stated.

"Finally," Roitstein added.

"So, tell me what you found out."

"Well, Cap, Della and Ellie are sisters. Due to drug addiction, their birth parents lost custody of them when they were very young. At that time, both girls were placed into foster care. Somewhere along the line, their papers were either lost or destroyed when the girls were split up to live in different households."

"That doesn't make any sense," Warner said. "How did they both end up with the same last name Smither?"

"The Smithers were the original foster parents both girls went to live with. The two girls were never adopted, but they carried the Smither name. Kate Smither fell in love with the baby, Ellie, but didn't want the older child, Della. So she sent Della to live with another couple."

"But Della kept the Smither name?"

"Right."

"Do Della and Ellie keep in contact with each other?"

"Della said she tried. But Kate warned her to stay away and to keep her mouth shut."

"Keep her mouth shut?"

"Yes. Ellie was never told she had an older sister or that the Smithers weren't her birth parents. Also, the Kate didn't want to get in trouble with the law for keeping Ellie as her own child, or for giving Della to another family without the courts knowing. Kate told Della that it would devastate Ellie should she ever find out the truth. So, unless she wanted to take on the responsibility of ruining her sister's life, Della would keep her mouth shut. Della agreed and stayed away."

"Kate Smither is a real winner. I smell a case for the DA's office," Warner stated.

"Cap, do you think the psyche of murderer could run in the family?" Roitstein asked.

"I don't follow you, Kieyell."

"Both girls are from drug-addicted birth parents. That screws them up to begin with if the mother was on drugs when the kids were conceived. Della ends up going off the deep end and murders a man for rejecting her advances. So maybe Ellie has gone off the deep end, too?"

"I can't answer that. That's something you would have to ask a qualified expert."

CHAPTER TWENTY-THREE

Being a chief of detectives didn't just involve the responsibility to keep on top of all the caseloads that the detectives were bogged down with, or to be there for advice. A certain amount of work scheduling was also involved. The captain had to also see that weekends, holidays and emergencies were covered at all times. Although he had asked the unit to do their own scheduling during the *Black Tulip* case, there were a few changes he felt obligated to make.

Since Warner had a few men in his unit that practiced Judaism, he knew Passover was a highly religious celebration that lasted a week. According to his calendar, Passover would start at sundown on a weekday in April. Unless the detectives wanted to take vacation over these high holy days, Warner could not give them the full week off from work. But, he did issue a memo stating all those detectives that followed the Jewish faith would be able to leave work by noon on the day Passover started. Furthermore, they would have the following day off. His decision to send out the memo did not come without consequences.

When his desk phone rang the following morning after the memo was sent, Warner could almost sense who was on the other end of the call. "Capt. Warner."

"Joe, this is your chief."

"Good morning, Ed. What can I do for you this morning?"

"If I wasn't afraid it would cause more problems, I'd call you downtown to my office," he stated in disgust.

"What seems to be the problem?"

"A saw a copy of your recent memo allowing certain detectives to be off for a religious holiday," he grumbled.

"I'm allowing a few of my men to leave work early and have an extra day to celebrate their religious day with their families, if that's what you're referring to. I didn't know there was a law in the rulebook that says I couldn't do that."

"Well, I got hit with a complaint when I first walked in the door this morning. You can't be showing favoritism for one special group of people. When you do that, the whole rest of the precinct gets up in arms. Then it spreads like a disease. Before you know it, I'll have all the precincts down my neck wanting the same privileges."

Warner was highly upset. He really disliked arguing with his boss, but he certainly was not going to stand by and get chastised for something that did not break any rules or regulations of the department.

As he listened to Doogle rattle away, Warner thought, *So, I've got a rat in my group. I'll just bet I know who it is.* "Now wait a minute, Ed. Most everyone leaves work early for Christmas Eve and has Christmas Day off because it's a Christian holiday — whether other non-Christians like it or not. During that time, do you want to know who always volunteers to be on call should an emergency happen? My small group of Jewish detectives, that's who. Shoot, we've been giving our Latin Americans time off for their Cinco de Mayo, and our Afro-Americans for their Kwanzaa celebration. Also, we --"

"Stop. I get the picture," Doogle blatantly interrupted. "You can't compare a national holiday with numerous other religious holidays."

"Ed, I do most everything by the book. But I'm going to disagree with you on this one. I've got a great bunch of detectives here," *with the exception of one complaining rat*, "and as long as they do their job, I plan on keeping it that way. Leaving work a little early or taking a day off while others cover their jobs won't hurt anyone. Now, may I ask who the whiner was who bent your ear and saw to it that you received my memo?"

"You know I can't tell you that, Joe."

"Never mind, you don't have to." *I know exactly who the big mouth is.* As much as Warner did not want to aggravate Doogle any further, he had to stand up for what he believed in. "That reminds me, Ed. I hear by the scuttlebutt that you're allowing a couple of uniforms to go home early on Good Friday. Is that true?"

"They're both devout Roman Catholics and have to be at special church services with their families."

"Oh, I see. So that means they should have special privileges like having time off, right? It seems to me that you've got two different sets of values, Ed," Warner bit the bullet, as he proceeded with, "or are you a bit prejudiced?"

There was nothing but complete silence on the other end of the telephone for at least ten seconds. Finally the chief spoke. "Look, Joe, it's obvious there's a little bit of unrest with your crew. Get it straightened out," he ordered.

You've got your nerve. "Sure, chief, whatever's right."

Warner set the receiver back on the phone's cradle. He debated how to handle the one detective in his unit who loved to stir up trouble. While he was pondering what to do, his phone rang again. "Capt. Warner."

"Cap, it's Detective De Mija."

"Leo, how are you feeling?"

"Very stiff, and my head is pounding."

"The accident only happened a few days ago. Give yourself a chance to heal."

"Trust me, Cap, Alianna is taking good care of me."

"I'm sure she is."

"I thought I had better call and let you know about the accident while it is still fresh in my head."

"That's good, Leo. I'm anxious to hear your side of it."

"Well, Lieu was driving us to our third hardware store on our list for the day. We were talking about one thing and another, passing the time. We were headed south up that steep incline on Snelling. I have this tendency to watch everything around me, especially if I'm a passenger in the car. So, while I was also watching for the street we wanted to turn on, I noticed this semi heading towards us. He was in his own lane at the time so I didn't really pay too much attention right then. I turned away. But when I looked back, I saw his trailer starting to jack-knife. As I saw the semi swerve toward us, I yelled at Lieu. But it was too late. It happened so fast. It was like the world exploded. I can still hear the sounds of metal smashing against metal.

"The next thing I knew, I was out on the ground. It seemed like a struggle, but when I got to my feet, I was a little dazed. I realized we'd had an accident and I must have been thrown out of the car. I spotted the wreck and ran to it to see where Lieu was. He was jammed inside the wrecked car. I tried, Cap, but I couldn't get him out. The worst part was that I couldn't get him to respond when I talked to him. I really thought he was dead. Shortly thereafter, the uniforms and the EMTs showed up. I was so concerned about Lieu that I didn't even know my head was bleeding until someone made me lay down on the gurney. I really couldn't tell you if it was a uniform or a paramedic that asked me what had happened. I assume I lost consciousness at that point. Next thing I knew, I woke up in the hospital."

"That seems to coincide with the story the driver of the semi told the officer at the scene. Your information helps me complete my report."

"How's Lieu doing, Cap? Do you think he will pull through?"

"I certainly hope so. We're all pulling for him. It goes without saying that we're all happy you came out of the accident with just a few minor injuries."

"What happened to the driver of the semi?"

"He'll be in the hospital a couple of days longer. He suffered a severe whiplash and a few other minor problems. When he's released, he'll be enjoying the comfort of one of our plush cement cells."

"Why?"

"According to his statement at the scene, he lost control of his vehicle when the brakes failed. He forgot to mention the fact that speed was a big factor."

"Oh, he was driving over the speed limit, huh? No wonder he came on us so fast."

"Well, yes, he was speeding. But he was also high on speed."

"You've got to be kidding?"

"I wish I were. The officers that arrived first on the scene suspected drugs or alcohol from the dilation of his eyes and his rapid speech. Of course, a bad accident — such as it was — could have caused those effects. However, just to play it safe, the officers requested a blood test at the hospital. The test confirmed their suspicions. If I have any say about it, it will be a cold day in Hades before he gets behind the wheel of a big rig or any other vehicle again. I just hope the state doesn't have to prosecute him for vehicular homicide."

"You mean if Lieu doesn't make it?"

"I don't even want to go there. Look, you take care of yourself, Leo. I appreciate your phone call."

"Okay, Cap. See ya in a few weeks, God willing."

"When you do, be prepared. Almost everyone's been put on a 24/7 work schedule until we catch the serial killer."

"I'll remember that, Cap. Bye for now."

"Bye."

Warner pushed one of the buttons on his phone to get another outside line. He called the hospital to inquire about Konklin. There was still no change in his condition. After he was through, he pushed the inline button and dialed an extension to one of the desks in the outer office. As if there wasn't enough to do, it was time to deal with the department's troublemaker.

Alex Landall was a thorn in everyone's side when it came to office protocol. He had the biggest mouth and always seemed to cry the loudest if he felt someone got more privileges than he did. Ever since Warner had been captain, he had had more than his share of Landall's complaints.

Landall complained because his desk was not next to a window. When a computer was placed on his partner's desk, Landall complained that he should be the one with the computer as he was on the force longer. So Warner had the computer moved to Landall's desk. When Landall found out that having the computer at his desk meant he had to complete the reports for him and his partner, Landall whined again.

When a detective that generally worked in the Crimes Against Persons Division was allowed to go to the hospital to see his first baby being born, Landall threw a fit. Warner quieted him down by telling him that he, too, could have time off when his first baby was born. Being a confirmed bachelor, Landall had no comeback.

Most of the detectives would walk around ten desks in order to avoid going past Landall's desk if he were sitting there. Others grinned and turned a deaf ear when he started complaining. The only thing he had going for him — he was a good detective when it came to his work.

Oftentimes, Warner thought about getting rid of him, but he opted not to. This time, however, was the last straw. Warner was under a lot of pressure with a serial killer still lurking in their area, and his lieutenant's life was hanging on the edge of life. He was in no mood to mollycoddle Detective Alex Landall.

"Landall's desk."

"Alex, come to my office."

"Now?"

"*Now*," Warner demanded, practically yelling in Landall's ear. *Jerk. When did he think I meant, next week?*

Before Detective Landall could even get to the office door, Warner's phone rang. "Capt. Warner."

The voice on the other end of the phone sounded breathless and had a ring of terror in it. "Cap, Duncan here."

"Jess, what's up?"

"A robbery gone bad. We've got four perps inside the Pinnacle Bank over on Oak and Davenport Road. They've got at least fourteen hostages that we know of inside. From the sound of the gunshots, they're armed with automatic weapons and handguns. Black and whites are here, and SWAT is on the way. Fratt's down."

"On my way. I'll catch you on the car radio so you can fill me in."

Slamming the phone down, Warner jumped to his feet, grabbed his coat, and ran out the door. He practically knocked Landall down as he rushed out of his office. "Sorry, Alex. We have an emergency."

"What's up, Cap?"

"I'm on my way to a hostage situation at the Pinnacle Bank at Oak and Davenport Road. Get Greg and you two get over there, ASAP."

With that, Warner rushed through the large office, down the stairs, and out to the parking lot. As fast as he could, he grabbed his bulletproof vest out of the trunk of his car, put it on, and then took off. On his way to the bank, he informed the FBI as to what was taking place.

Within minutes, Warner was at the scene. He pulled up behind some patrol units and ducked as he got out of his car. Keeping his head down, he ran to where Police Captain Lee Roberts and some of his officers were crouched behind a police car. Roberts, a twenty-five-year police veteran, was holding a megaphone. Looking over at the bank, Warner spotted Detective Fratt lying on the sidewalk in front of the building. The tension in the air was thick as everyone's adrenaline pumped at rapid speeds.

"I'm sorry, Warner. We can't get your man out of there. It's too risky," Roberts said as he kept his eyes on the bank.

"Is he alive?"

"We can't say for sure. But he hasn't moved since we've been here."

"Other than Fratt, have any other men been injured?"

"Negative, as far as we know. Did you call the FBI?"

"Affirmative. They should be here shortly."

Roberts filled Warner in on everything he knew about the bank robbery and the hostages.

Landall and Simpson arrived. Keeping their heads low, they made their way to where Warner was using a squad car as a shield. "Where do you want us, Cap?" Landall asked.

"Where's your car?"

"About three cars over."

"Okay. Get yourselves in a safe position behind your car where you can observe Fratt. We don't know if he's hurt or just laying still. We'll just have to wait and see. But keep your eyes on him and your guns ready. Stay safe. Now, get a move on it."

Within minutes, FBI Agent Doug Shield arrived on the scene along with Sgt. Leon Franklin, the hostage negotiator. Warner had worked with both men before, so no introductions were necessary. And, under the circumstances, no greetings were exchanged.

"What do we know so far?" Shield asked Warner.

"We have four bad guys with automatic weapons. They're holding, to the best of our knowledge, fourteen hostages. Nine bank employees and five customers."

Franklin asked, "How many perps?"

"We don't know yet?"

"Then how did you get the hostage count?"

"A female employee was hiding under her desk. Somehow she reached the phone on top of her desk and managed to call 911. She gave the operator the information about the robbery taking place, how many people were in the bank, and broke the numbers down. When the operator started to question her further, she thought she heard the sound of gunshots. The phone went dead. There's a good possibility they killed the caller."

"Who's that up front on the pavement?" Shield asked.

"That's Detective Fratt, one of my men. Detective Duncan said he and Fratt were just two blocks away when the call came from dispatch. They arrived before a black and white got here. Fratt was going to take a look in the front door and Duncan went to the back. Duncan said he heard a spray of gunshots. The next thing he heard over his radio from one of the uniforms who had arrived on the scene was that Fratt was down."

Warner proceeded to explain that no one knew for sure if Fratt was injured or not. As they were talking, a woman's voice rang out from behind them. "Oh, my God!" She hysterically yelled. "My husband's in there. My husband's in that bank."

As Warner, Shield and Franklin turned to see where the voice was coming from, they spotted a woman running toward them. Roberts had also seen her.

Quickly turning to his closest uniformed officer, Roberts yelled, "Get that woman out of here and out of the line of fire."

Turning back toward the bank, Franklin inquired, "Roberts, have they made any demands yet?"

"The norm. A million in cash. A vehicle to take them out of here. And an airplane fueled and ready to fly them out of the country."

"Well, let's see if I can make contact."

Shield asked, "Is SWAT in position in case negotiations fail?"

"In position and ready to go," Warner replied.

Taking his cell phone from his pocket, Franklin dialed the bank's number and let it ring. While he patiently waited, he squatted down, leaning his back against the patrol car that was shielding them. The phone rang six times before it was answered.

"Yeah," said the deep voice of a male on the other end of the phone line.

"My name is Sgt. Leon Franklin. I want to speak to the person in charge."

"You'll talk to me or nobody," the man stated in a matter-of-fact tone.

"I'd like to know what I can do for you."

"You already know what you can do for me, pig. You'd better do it real soon, or the hostages won't like it. Got it?"

Calmly Franklin asked, "Do you have a name so I can at least know who I'm speaking to?"

"We call ourselves the Zebra Gang. That's all you need to know. Hey, pig, we're starved in here. Get us some burgers, fries, and cold beers. And hurry it up," the man demanded with rage, "or we start shooting."

"Calm down. We'll get enough for you and the hostages."

"Wrong! The hostages don't need to eat."

Shield had to think fast. It was imperative he received a confirmation on the amount of people inside. "Use your head, man. If the hostages are busy eating, they're less apt to cause you any problems while you and the rest of your group eat." Without giving the man a chance to respond, Shield quickly added, "Let's see, that's fourteen hostages and two of you, right?" Shield knew a gang had to be more than two people. But he thought voicing a lower number would throw the man off guard enough to tell him the correct amount of perpetrators inside the bank. He was right.

"Don't try and cheat my guys and I on the food, pig. There's four of us and thirteen hostages."

"No one's trying to cheat you. I thought there were fourteen hostages?"

"One of them ain't hungry no more."

Franklin heard a roar of laughter coming from the other end of the phone. "Where's the other hostage?"

"Hey, pig, you figure it out. Now get our food or a few more of these hostages might lose their appetites, too. For every thirty minutes you make us wait, another hostage can take their last breath — hungry. Got it?"

"Okay, the food will be here shortly. Unfortunately we can't get you any beer. You'll have to settle for cold sodas."

"I said, we want cold beer," the man demanded.

"If you know the area, then you know there isn't a liquor store within forty-five minutes from here. Look, when you get out of there, you can have all the beer you want. Right now you've put me on a time schedule. There's no way to get there and back in less than ninety minutes."

"Use your siren and step on the gas."

"Be reasonable. Listen, the time limit you've put me on won't allow us to argue over beer or sodas."

"Okay, pig, cold sodas. But get a move on it. The clock is ticking away. And tell your buddies to get the lead out. We're not going to wait forever for our money and a car to take us to the jet."

Immediately following the man's last comment, Franklin got disconnected. "Shield."

"Yeah."

"There's four perps. All males, from what I gather. There were fourteen hostages. But he practically told me they have already killed one. That's probably the gunshots heard by the 911 operator. We only have thirty minutes to get food and drinks in there before another hostage is killed. These guys are nutcases. I got them to accept cold sodas in place of cold beers. But other than that, I don't know whether or not I can reason with them. Best get SWAT ready to make a forced entry."

All the law officers were highly concerned that another senseless death could soon take place. Franklin got the word out to get the requested food delivered to the scene. It was a life and death emergency.

Lt. George Michaels, the head of SWAT, was briefed and informed that Shield would give them a green light at entry. The green light meant using deadly force when entry was made. They would toss Flash Bangs and then enter and find a target. It would be dangerous for the hostages, but safer than the systematic murders that the Zebra Gang had threatened if their demands were not met.

Someone yelled, "Food's here."

Franklin immediately got back on the phone to inform the Zebra Gang that the food was on the way. In turn, Franklin was given orders as how the food was to be delivered.

"Hey, pig, you in a uniform?"

"No. I'm wearing a business suit."

"Then I want you to deliver the food. I don't want to see any uniforms coming at us flashing their guns. Or we'll shoot them on sight. Got it?"

"I'll get the food to you, but I want all women and children out the door first."

"No deal, pig. Get the food in here now or we shoot another hostage. You diggin' what I'm sayin'?"

"Yes, I understand. But I'll need help. There's a lot of food here."

"What are you, a weakling? Come alone or no deal. Remember, your time is almost up."

"Okay. Okay. I'll be carrying plastic bags full of food and drinks."

"Don't pull any funny business. Keep your hands out in front of you so we can see them," the perp demanded. Abruptly, the call disconnected.

"What's going on?" Shield asked.

"They want me to deliver their food."

"Not a good idea."

"I agree with Shield," Warner said.

"You know I'm trained for this, so I don't mind."

"What exactly did they ask for?" Shield asked.

"They don't want any uniforms approaching or they start shooting. I told him I was wearing a business suit." As Franklin spoke, he was reorganizing the food and cans of sodas so the weight was evenly disbursed from the five bags into three. When Warner saw what he was doing, he pitched in to speed up the process. "You're the only other one here that's wearing a suit, Warner. I'm certainly not going to ask you to chance going in."

"But if they get trigger-happy with you, we lose our negotiator,"

Warner said.

"I agree," Shield stated. "We can't afford to lose our negotiator. But we don't want to lose you either, Warner."

"You won't lose either one of us. They've never seen your face, Franklin, so I have an idea. Hold on a second."

As much as he was a thorn in Warner's side, he knew Landall was also dressed in a suit. He called Landall over and instructed, "Take these bags of food over and set them down just inside the door of the bank."

"You got it, Cap. I can carry my gun hidden behind one of the bags. Maybe I can --"

"No! Put your hands through the handles so the bags drape over your arms. Keep your hands where they can see them. If they don't see both hands, they'll shoot first and ask questions later. Just set the food down and back out of there. No gun and no stupid heroics, Landall. Understand? If not, I'll get someone else to do it."

"Yes, Cap. I understand." Landall picked up the bags with one hand. "These are heavy. I hope the bottoms don't fall out before I get there," he complained.

"They'll hold. Another thing, Landall, see if you can find out if Fratt is hurt. If so, find out how badly he is injured and can he get out of there without further injury. Walk slow and talk fast."

"I know what to do. I don't need your fatherly directions. One would think you're talking to a rookie."

Warner did not have time to argue with his detective. Not with the clock ticking. Hopefully, he had made the right decision in getting Landall to do the job. Even though bank robberies were Landall's expertise, Warner could only hope that the big mouth, whining detective would do the right thing. Warner turned to Franklin with a comment. In the short time it took for Warner to turn his back, Landall had taken his gun out of its holster and tucked it in his belt. When Warner turned his attention back to Landall, he watched the detective slowly cross the street and head toward the front of the bank. "Dammit, Alex. I told you to walk slow, not creep," Warner mumbled in disgust. "By the time you get there, are thirty minutes will be up."

Overhearing him, Shield said, "He's doing fine, Warner. I'd rather he move like a turtle than rush over like a gazelle."

As Landall neared Fratt, he quietly called, "Hey, Scooby."

Barely squinting so it would appear his eyes were still shut, Fratt softly said, "Alex, is that your ugly voice?"

"Who else? You okay?"

"I'm fine. I'm not even hit. Just waiting for the chance to get the hell out of here."

"You have three kids, right?"

"You know I do."

"Well, having loved ones at home is something I don't have. Make sure you kiss them all for me." Slowly edging toward the door and still keeping his voice down, Landall said, "Hang tight, Scooby. I'll help you in a minute. I have a plan."

"Don't do anything stupid, Alex. I think the perps think I'm dead. I'm sure I'll be okay here until this whole thing is over."

"You sound like our boss, always treating me like I can't think for myself. Shut up and listen! Get ready to run when you hear shots."

Fratt was in no position to yell out for help or stop Landall from following through with whatever plan he had in mind. All he could do was pray Landall would not jeopardize his own life or anyone else's in the process.

Holding his hands out in front of him so the bags covered the gun in his belt, Landall neared the door. He could now see one of the bad guys, wearing a ski mask, standing just inside the bank's glass door. As Landall opened the door with his left hand, the man in the ski mask took a step backward. Slowly, Landall stepped inside. Then he bent over as if to place the bags of food on the floor.

From outside, Warner watched Landall's movements with binoculars. What happened next, made Warner as angry as he was compassionate for a fellow detective. He witnessed Landall suddenly dropping the bags. Then, in the wink of an eye, Landall extended his arm in a combat crouch. He began firing at the man who stood in front of him. Landall struck the mutt in the chest, knocking him to the floor.

"NO!" Warner yelled as he spotted another perpetrator on Landall's left. It was obvious to Warner that Landall saw him, too, as he turned to fire. One bullet took Landall to his knees. The mutt's other bullets hit Landall in the stomach and upper chest before he went down. Warner yelled, "Landall's down."

Within seconds, Franklin's cell phone rang. "Yes!" He answered in haste.

"Your pig was very stupid. Now he's not only stupid, he's dead. Now get this straight because I won't repeat myself and I won't answer the phone again. One of my men is dead because of you pigs. So here are my final words. Meet our demands within the hour or we kill one hostage every ten minutes that you make us wait. So long, jerks."

When the line disconnected, Franklin briefed Shield and Warner. Shield was ready to give SWAT the green light. While the shooting had been going on, Fratt managed to crawl to safety and was now back behind the car with Warner.

"Thank God you're all right, Fratt." Worried about Landall, Warner shot questions like bullets from a revolver. "We're you able to see anything from your position? Do you think they killed Landall, or is he just wounded? Maybe playing possum like you evidently did?"

Fratt shook his head. "I'm sorry, Cap. I opened my eyes just as I saw bullets stitch his midsection like a sewing machine. Then I ran like the blazes. There's no doubt in my mind. He's dead. It's funny, but, as he was walking by, he asked me about my children. Then he told me to kiss them for him. I'll probably never know for sure, but I think — in his weird way of thinking — he thought he was saving my life."

Warner did not like Landall even a little bit, and he was upset that Landall did not follow orders. However, Landall was still a cop and no one kills a cop and gets away with it. It was time to even the score.

Well, with Landall's death, I won't have to make the decision to fire him or demote him. For his sake, I'm glad there wasn't time to mar his record as a good detective, Warner thought. *So, Mister Crybaby, you didn't follow orders but you gave your life to save a fellow officer. May God bless your soul.* Warner turned to Shield. "Let's take those bastards down."

"Lt. Michaels, this is FBI Agent Doug Shield. Maneuver your team into position for entry. When you're in position, let me know and I'll give you the okay. Just remember this is a green-light mission. Be very careful of the hostages."

"10-4, Agent Shield."

Within seconds, Michaels informed Shield that he and his team were ready. Shield responded with two words, "Do it!"

Those outside waiting could partially see the bright flashes and feel the concussions of the Flash Bangs. Warner held his breath as he heard short bursts of gunfire. Then, it was all over. Warner did not take a decent breath until he heard the voice over Shield's radio.

"Agent Shield, Michaels here. All secure. We have six dead: one female and five males."

"The hostages?"

"Thirteen accounted for. They're all pretty shaken but no physical wounds."

"That's good news. What about the perps?"

"We removed ski masks off of four male gunmen: two Caucasians and two Afro-Americans."

"I guess that's why they called themselves the Zebra Gang?" Shield replied. "Are we clear for entry?"

"Clear."

* * *

No reason was ever found for the incident, other than it being a bank robbery gone terribly wrong.

Landall was a loner with a capital L. He had no family or anyone listed on his records to call in case of an emergency. As Warner went over the detective's employee file, he felt a bit of emptiness for the man. "Not so much as one close friend or neighbor to call. No loving family to mourn you. How sad. No wonder you had such a bad attitude, Landall."

A few days later on St. Patrick's Day, Detective Alex Benjamin Landall was laid to rest. Even though Landall was not well-liked by most who knew him, he was given a hero's funeral. Over one thousand policeman in full dress from around the state and surrounding states attended to pay their respects to a fellow officer: another fallen hero killed in the line of duty.

Warner almost felt guilty for disliking Landall's personality when he was alive. Yet, as he stood by the graveside with a lump in his throat, he said, "Rest in peace, Landall."

CHAPTER TWENTY-FOUR

On the following day after paying his respects at Landall's funeral, Warner received reports on the Carney murders. He opened the medical examiner's autopsy report first and started reading parts of it.

"Allen Charles, male Caucasian, 30, and Debra Jean, female Caucasian, 22. Male victim bled to death when a sharp weapon with a curved blade cut his jugular vein. Female was bludgeoned with several strikes to the face and one to the back of her head with a heavy weapon. Her throat had also been cut. Due to the shortness of time-span between the time she was beaten and when her jugular vein was cut, it is hard to determine which incident was the cause of death."

Before he even finished reading, Warner put the report aside and opened the preliminary report from the crime lab. After scanning just a few statements, he shook his head. "Well, it's not what I'm looking for, but at least it's something. Let's see now, the blood droplets on the floor did not come from either of the victims. Blood droplets tested O Negative. Blood splotches found on the telephone matched the deceased female. However, the telephone had no hair or skin evidence on it." *I guess that rules out the theory that the snake beat her with the phone. Maybe Eddy's theory is right about the use of a crowbar.*

"The only skin and hair particles found at the crime scene belonged to both victims. Fingerprints lifted from the scene belonged to the victims. A minute fragment of clear latex material was found next to the female's body, origin unknown. White calling card and rattle same as … Damn! Just two lonely clues after six horrific homicides. That's definitely not good news. Let's see. Further information will follow after a more thorough examination of evidence. As if I didn't know. Come on techs, I needed this follow-up yesterday." Warner threw the report on his desk. The time had come to call for expert assistance.

In all of the United States there were only fifty profilers. Two of them were located in the State of Colorado. Sergeant Kym Davies, who worked out of the Denver area, was one of these two. She had an astounding record for the past seven years for her accuracy in helping the police catch their perpetrators. Even though she was a small frame of a woman, her brisk walk made others take long strides or short quick steps to keep up with her. Her speech is quite the opposite: slow and deliberate.

Davies was very detailed and extremely methodical in her work. Many of her peers deemed her to be a psychic, as her profiles were mostly dead-on accurate. Her description of a perpetrator covered almost everything but the perpetrator's name. Warner had never worked with Davies before, but he knew her from several seminars they had both attended. With the serial case at a near standstill for clues, Warner was in dire need of Davies's keen sense, sharp eye, and ability to put herself in the perpetrator's mind. No matter how late it was, Warner needed to speak with her immediately. After looking up her home phone number, Warner made the call.

"Kym Davies."

"Kym. Joe Warner from the MPPD."

"Well, if it isn't the illustrious captain from the 15th. How are you, Joe?"

"I have a splitting headache from beating my head against a cement block barricade."

"I can believe it with the case you're up against. Mt. Pride has been all over the newspapers down here in Denver. To tell you the truth, I expected you to call way before now."

"Maybe I should have, but I thought we'd be further along than we are. Unfortunately, we're getting nowhere in identifying and stopping this snake. It's like walking around in a circle with one foot nailed to the ground."

"The news reports have been pretty generalized."

Warner laughed. "On purpose."

"I understand. Copycat killers are too frequent when they get too much information. What do you have so far?"

"Little physical evidence, I'm afraid. Blood type of our perp, I assume, since the blood drops at the last scene didn't match the victims. The crime lab also has a fragment of some latex material. This snake only strikes in the early morning hours when most people are asleep. All the vics so far have had small children. We have an idea as to what the murder weapon could be. Oh, and at each scene our perp has left an unusual calling card. That's all we've got for now."

"Okay, send me copies of all your reports and your crime scene photos. As soon as I get the information, I'll get right on it. I'm working on a couple of other cases right now, but I can fit you into my schedule."

"Thanks, Kym. I'll get everything together and get it couriered to your office first thing in the morning."

"Your unit has certainly had more than its share of tragedies this month. I understand your lieutenant is out of commission, due to a serious accident. And, you've lost one of your detectives in a bank robbery."

"What do you have, a hot line to one of my detectives?" He joked.

"Close. Computers are great for getting news as soon as it happens practically everywhere in the world."

"That's true."

"So, I'm assuming my computer canary was right about you losing a detective?"

"Yes, Landall was a great loss to the unit. I have to admit that he wasn't one of my favorite people, but he did his job. As for Lt. Konklin, he's alive, but that's about all I can say."

"I'm sorry to hear that, Joe."

"All we can do is stay positive. Listen, I won't keep you, Kym. And I do apologize for bothering you at home."

"Anytime, Joe."

"You should have everything on this case first thing tomorrow morning. If you have any questions, don't hesitate to call me."

"Will do. I'll be talking to you soon."

"Thanks, Kym."

* * *

Warner had one of his detectives make copies of everything on the *Black Tulip* case and ready the packet to be sent to Davies. Then he sat back, mulling over the crime lab's preliminary report. Like an ocean wave crashing against a rock-laden shoreline, two ideas hit him in the head. Waiting for more reports would not do. He needed answers, now. Warner called the local lab.

"This is Capt. Warner from the 15th. Is …," he quickly looked to see who signed the report he had received, "is John Atchison there? May I speak with him? Yes. Thank you." As he waited impatiently, he fiddled with his pencil. "John, this is Capt. Warner. Yes, just this morning. That's why I'm calling. No, no, there's no problem with your report. I just have a couple of questions. Okay. Concerning that small piece of latex found at the crime scene, was it checked out for prints? That small, huh? Well, I was thinking it could have come from a disposable glove. What do you think? Oh you did? I see. That's great. Yes I do.

"My second question is about the blood evidence found on the carpet. Is type O Negative a pretty normal blood type? Hey, that's why you're the lab technician, not me," Warner quipped. "That rare, huh? I see. No, nothing more. Thanks, John, you've been a big help. Yes, please do. Yes, you too. Thanks again."

Not waiting for a dial tone, he punched another button on his phone and called the medical examiner. "Saggy, this is Joe Warner. Well, I need a quick lesson in blood analysis." He laughed. "First of all, what was the blood type of the last victims in the *Black Tulip* case? Yes, Carney. Okay, I'll hold. Yes. Yes. Type A Positive. Would the blood type of their children be the same, or could they possibly have a child with type O Negative? Uh-huh. Uh-huh. Yes, I just found that out. It certainly does. Yes, from the crime lab's report on blood evidence taken at the scene. I'll bet my eyeteeth that blood type O Negative belongs to our snake. I agree. Okay, that's all I needed, Saggy. Thanks."

At last Warner had a break. He wrote down some notes so he would be sure to inform the rest of the team what he had found out. Not only could the rare blood type be of great help in tracking down the perpetrator, but also the latex might be of great significance. The crime lab had sent the minute piece of latex to the CBI Crime Lab for further, more-detailed analysis. For the first time since the first double homicides had occurred, Warner felt elated. Finally he could take a step forward on the case instead of two steps backward.

CHAPTER TWENTY-FIVE

Speaking in a loud voice to get the captain's attention, Ferndale said, "Cap, wait up."

With a quick turn of his head, Warner saw the detective walking toward him. "Good morning, Brenda. What's up?"

"We've got some information for you. How's your schedule?"

"Give me ten minutes. Then come on in."

* * *

Detectives Ferndale, Brown, Hathaway, Lennon, Mayfield, Roitstein, DelGinny, Holms, Anthony, and Brubaker filed into Warner's office. Making themselves comfortable, eight of the detectives filled every available seat, including the arms of the leather sofa. With no place else to sit, Holms sat on the floor. Lennon leaned against a wall.

"Damn, Brenda, when you said we, I didn't realize you were bringing the whole motley crew with you."

"Hey, Cap, you didn't think we'd pass up a chance to come sit in your plush office again, did you?" Brown remarked.

"At least you brought your own filled coffee cups with you," Warner said. "Actually, I'm glad you're all here. When I picked up this morning's mail, I received a large manila envelope from the CBI Crime Lab."

"Aren't you going to open it?" Hathaway asked.

"After you all tell me what new info you have."

Ferndale gave a very detailed and comprehensive report on their findings about the rattle, the bubble-jet printers, the small white cards, and the carton opener. She concluded with information on creative writers. "It seems there were several students for the past ten years who excelled in creative writing. Thankfully, I guess, many of them have moved away from the Mt. Pride area. I checked out the names of those that are still here in the city and living over here on the east-side of town. None of them have any felony arrests or any warrants."

"Are all of the names in the computer now?" Warner asked.

"Yes. In all the hundreds of names we started with, we came up with a good fifty names that matched at least two of the lists. We'll check out those fifty, and that should help dwindle the list down even more."

"Here's a funny one for you, Cap," Brubaker interjected. "Our own Detective De Mija is on our list of creative writers."

"That makes sense," Warner said. "Leo told me he liked creative writing. What else do you have, Brenda?"

"If you don't mind, I'd rather wait until after you open your CBI envelope. I can't speak for everyone else, but curiosity has the best of me."

"I think she speaks for the rest of us, too, Cap," DelGinny said, receiving nods from the other detectives. "We'd all like to hear if there is any good news to help us on this case."

"Okay." Warner pulled the large brown envelope from his pile of mail and opened it. After reading in silence, he said, "Wow. Those techs must have put a rush on that particle of latex our lab sent them. They didn't find any prints, but they confirm my suspicions. It did come from a latex glove." Reading a little further into the report, he added, "Here's more good news. Damn, I wish our crime lab had the technology and equipment that the CBI has."

"Don't keep us in suspense, Cap. What did they find?" Mayfield asked.

"They discovered a trace of blood on the latex and were able to test the blood. Bingo! It matches the blood evidence taken from the carpet at the Carney crime scene." Warner was delighted with the good news. He placed the report on his desk. "Now, if we can just figure out a way to get blood samples from those fifty people you've thinned the lists down to, we might be able to narrow this search down even more. Okay, team, let's move on. Brenda, when we first started this task force, Eddy and I gave you a list of felons living in our area. Have you had time to check them out yet?"

"Yes."

"What kind of crimes did they commit?"

Referring to her notes, she stated, "All for attempted murder. And all out on parole."

"Are any of them in good enough shape to climb through windows and murder two victims within a matter of seconds?"

"Give me a minute, Cap, and let me look over the information I have here." For a short period of time, everyone in the room sat quietly. Ferndale finally said, "Here's what we have. Four are either wheelchair-bound or limited to their activities due to health problems."

"Eliminate them immediately, Brenda. The physicians in the big houses pretty well know if a prisoner is really physically incapable or not. I'll take their word for it and assume we don't have to follow-up on their whereabouts for the nights of our homicides."

"Okay. Two of the parolees weighed about two hundred pounds when they got out of prison, and one is a dwarf."

"Hold on a minute. Have all of these parolees been out since our serial killer has been on a rampage?"

"All but one has been out since last December. One got paroled around the first of November. So, the answer is affirmative."

"Okay, continue."

"What about the last three?" Ferndale asked.

"Unless he stood on someone's shoulders to reach the windows, I would rule out the dwarf. As for the hefty ones, they could've lost a lot of weight since they've been out. So they're worth checking out."

"Okay. Well, the last five could be of the weight and height that would have easily reached the windows and gotten through them," Ferndale surmised. "However, two of them were shooters. The other three attacked their victims with knives."

"Is there anything in their records that show any of them do any kind of creative writing, mainly poetry?" Warner asked.

Ferndale shook her head. "No, Cap, I'm sorry. I just got their names, addresses, height, weight, and copies of their rap sheets."

"But they are definitely residing in our area of Mt. Pride?"

"Yes."

"Then check them out. If they don't look like they fit the bill, just tell them you're checking to see that they've been keeping their scheduled appointments with their parole officers. If they do look like the type of perp we're looking for, check their alibis for the dates of the homicides."

Warner thought about his next move as he took a drink of coffee. While he was contemplating giving out assignments, he turned toward the inner-office window and noticed a familiar face. "Well, team, it looks like help has arrived. Here comes someone I'd like you all to meet." Warner went to the door and opened it. Stepping out into the main office, he greeted the female with a welcoming handshake. "Kym, you're just in time to meet most of the team I've got working on this serial case. Come on in."

As Davies preceded Warner into the office, everyone got to their feet. Warner made the introductions. Offering Davies his seat, Duncan sat on the floor next to Holms.

"I didn't mean to interrupt your meeting, Joe," Davies stated.

"Not at all, Kym," Warner replied, going back to his desk chair. "It's good you're here so the group can answer any questions you may have in regards to this case."

"I have a question," Anthony stated.

Before Warner could say anything, Davies smiled and said, "Certainly. What would you like to know?"

"I've read a lot of information on profiling, but I've never worked with a profiler before. So I'm rather interested in hearing about how you help solve cases."

"That's a great question. To begin with, I received my profiling training at the FBI Academy. Profilers are known for picking up things that detectives working on a case may have overlooked. Sometimes a detective may look right at some small piece of evidence and not realize its significance, which is only human. Every detail, no matter how minute, has to be reevaluated, or looked at from a different angle.

"Often times, detectives might be too close to a case, where a profiler can take a fresh look as an outsider. Of even greater value to an investigation, profilers can almost get into the head of the perp. We are highly trained in determining the perpetrator's personality, background, occupation, living habits, why the perp kills, and if the perp would strike again. In other words, we analyze behavior clues."

Once Sergeant Davies had answered all the questions, she flipped the coin. Asking questions of her own, Davies had to be sure she had all the facts straight before she would even attempt to give out the wrong information on the perp. At the conclusion of her visit, she headed back to the Denver office to commence working on her profile for the case.

Warner continued where the meeting had left off. "Hopefully, Kym will be able to give us everything on this snake but his name. Let's see. Brenda, what did we narrow the parolee list down to?"

"Seven. Two shooters. Three who stabbed their victims. And the two heavy men who could have lost weight."

"Okay, divide them up. Brenda, you and J.B. take four. Tony and Mike, take the other three. Watch your backs. "Bobby and Bryce, you two check out the list of creative writers. Arnie and Eric, double crosscheck the input data. Not that I don't trust you, Brenda. I just think two more sets of eyes might catch a name you overlooked."

"I understand," Ferndale said.

"Have any of you come up with any new info on the tool yet?"

"Not yet," Mayfield replied. "So far all we can find is the new-style tile cutter."

"And the same for the carton opener," Roitstein added.

"Cap."

"Tony."

"It's only a suggestion, but I think we're going about this all wrong. I think we should be looking at some of the older hardware stores first. In my opinion, they would be more apt to carry the older-type tools like we're looking for. These newer home improvement centers and department stores cater more to the most popular, state-of-the-art tools."

"I agree," Bobby said. "Many of the young carpenters I've spoken with don't even know what I'm talking about. On the other hand, the older carpenters know exactly what I'm talking about when I show them the copy of the tool. It's just that they don't use them anymore in their craft."

Warner nodded. "Good points, both of you. Agreeing with you, I think that Marshall Square would be a place to put at the top of your list. I don't shop for tools, but I do know that is the oldest part of the east-side. Lots of mom-and-dad-owned stores over there. Okay, Kieyell, your up. Tell the group what we discovered about our prime suspect."

"Sure, Cap."

After Roitstein brought the team up-to-date on the information about Ellie Smither, Warner asked, "Does anyone have anything else?"

Looking very serious, Brown said, "I do."

"What is it?"

"When you asked for volunteers to take care of the food service while we work on this case, several hands went in the air."

"Your point?"

"I was just wondering why you selected Chung and Zeal of all people to be getting us food?"

Warner was puzzled. Brown was dark-skinned, so he knew he was not prejudiced. "I'm afraid you've caught me off guard, J.B. What seems to be the problem with me selecting Mickey and Derek for the food service?"

After several chuckles in the room, Brown said, "Obviously you don't know their handle is Fatal Weapons. Hell, they might poison us."

"Very funny." Warner grinned. "Okay. Other than the assignments I have already given you, I want the rest of you to keep looking for the tool when your out and about. If any of you finds one, buy it and bring it to me. That's it, team. Let's get back to work."

As the group rose from their seats to leave, Mayfield asked, "Say, Cap, when's Leo due back?"

His question got everyone's attention. They all waited for the captain's response. "I don't keep in contact with him. I wanted to give him a chance to recuperate. However …," Warner checked the calendar on his desk, scanning the days since the car accident, "the accident occurred exactly two weeks ago today. So," he said looking back up to Mayfield, "it should be any day now."

"That's good news. You know I never complain, but we sure could use his help."

"Hey," Anthony commented, slapping Mayfield on the back, "just think how lucky we are. There hasn't been another showing of our vicious viper since the accident happened."

"That's true." Mayfield laughed. "As long as that snake stays in his hole, we can play catch up."

"I know how rough it is around here pulling some of you out of your own departments to work on this case. But I haven't had a chance to even consider my next candidate to fill Landall's chair. Until then, you detectives will just have to keep pulling double weight to keep up."

"I can handle double weight," Brubaker chuckled, patting his stomach.

Grasping Brubaker about the neck, Anthony pulled him out the door, saying, "He meant double duty, you dumb bunny."

"And they wonder why they're called Frick and Frack?" Roitstein commented with a grunting laugh, as he and the rest of the team filed out of Warner's office.

* * *

Come Monday morning, Warner had a surprise waiting for him at the precinct. When he reached the top of the stairs he saw De Mija sitting at his desk. Warner headed directly toward him.

"Well, speak of the devil. Welcome back, Leo."

"Thanks, Cap, but what's with the devil?"

"Oh, the team was just asking last Friday when you might be returning. I see your hand is still heavily bandaged."

"Yeah, for a while yet."

"So how are you feeling?"

"Other than a few headaches from this," De Mija answered, gesturing toward the scar on his forehead, "much better, thank you." Taking note that the captain looked as if he was feeling sympathy pains viewing the scar, De Mija reported, "It's fine, Cap. It really feels better than it looks. They just took the stitches out Saturday."

"I assume the staff physician gave you the proper release to return to duty?"

"Yes, sir. I was given the green light. He said for you to call him if you had any questions."

"I'll do that."

As Warner started toward his office, De Mija said, "Wait, Cap. What do you want me to do today?"

"Just hang tight. I'll let you know."

After Warner called and confirmed that De Mija was fit to be back at his job, he called the detective into his office. "Have a seat, Leo."

"I assume everything checked out?"

"Yes. The doctor said your head and hand are both healing nicely. I have two problems, however. I can't send you out alone because you aren't experienced enough. And, even if you were, you can't drive with one hand inaccessible as it is. You can't type, so computer work is out. With the right hand completely bandaged like that, I can't even give you any deskwork that requires writing."

"Sure you can, Cap. My writing hand is perfect."

Tilting his head and raising his eyebrows with a bit of surprise, Warner asked, "You mean you're left-handed?"

"I sure am. You act as shocked as the Lieu did when I told him. I guess I must be the only southpaw in the unit."

"You are. Well, hey, if you can still write and answer the telephone, that's good news."

"Is there anything new on the homicides I was working on?"

"We have Profiler Kym Davies working with us on the case. I'll have Brenda bring you up to date. Okay, you can go back out to your desk. I'll get some things together to keep you occupied for the next few days."

Rising to his feet, De Mija asked, "Have you been to hospital to see the Lieu lately?"

"Every day that's humanly possible."

"I've called the hospital every day to check on his status. But I haven't gone to see him yet. Just as soon as he comes out of his coma, I want to do that."

"It's a good thing you didn't try to go see him. He isn't allowed any visitors as long as he's in ICU. But I can tell you when I was there earlier this morning there was no change."

* * *

At the closing of the day, Ferndale asked her partner to meet her for a drink at a specified local pub. It wasn't the usual hangout where many of the detectives liked to spend their time for a few beers after work. Ferndale needed to go someplace where no one would disturb them. She had already seated herself in a booth and ordered two beers before Brown got there.

Once he entered and she spotted him, she motioned to him. Brown joined her in the booth, sitting directly opposite her.

"I've got two drafts coming," she said. "I hope that's okay?"

"Great." Pulling out a package of cigarettes from his jacket pocket, he asked, "You don't mind do you?"

"Of course I don't, J.B. It's your funeral," she said, smiling.

Brown lit up a cigarette. Exhaling the smoke, he asked, "So what's with all the secrecy, Brenda?"

"I have a problem and need your advice."

"If you just needed advice, we still could have met at the unit's favorite watering hole."

"No. You're …." Ferndale stopped talking when the waitress approached their table and served them their glasses of beer. Once the waitress was out of earshot, Ferndale continued. "You're my partner, J.B. I trust you."

"Okay, Brenda. What's going on?"

"Cap had me go over the *Black Tulip* case file with De Mija today."

"I know. So what's the problem?"

"When it came to showing him the package of rattles, he said something interesting." She wiped the condensation from the outside of her glass as she spoke. Brown sat quietly listening as he drank his beer and smoked his cigarette. "De Mija took the package out of my hand, obviously not listening to what I was saying at that moment.

"Then he asked me where I got the rattles. I told him that's what I was explaining. Repeating myself, I told him it was a sample of what the perp had been leaving at the crime scenes. He laughed and said it was a small world. When I asked him what he meant, he said he had purchased that same rattle a few years earlier. Seems he purchased a whole lot of them when he became a father. He tied them to cigars he had passed out for the joyous celebration."

Brown snapped his fingers. "That's it."

"That's what?"

"That's why that rattle looked so familiar to me. A few years back, I remember one of the uniforms told me a fellow officer was a new father. He showed me the cute cigar rattle thing the guy was handing out. Being a smoker, I kidded the uniform and told him the new father was being a bit selfish by not sharing his joy and handing out a few cigars to the detective's unit."

"Was that new father, per chance, Leo De Mija?"

"The one and the same, I found out later. Of course I didn't know him at the time."

After a moment or two, Ferndale said, "So?"

"So?" He echoed back. "So what?'

"So don't you think that's all too weird?"

"No. He's right, Brenda. It is a small world. I'm sure it was nothing more than a coincidence."

"Is it just a coincidence, too, that his name came up on our creative writer's list?"

"Probably. If you recall, even the captain said he knew De Mija loves to write. There's a good reason right there to stop insinuating that De Mija could be a suspect. If the captain isn't worried about him, then you shouldn't be either."

"That was before the rattle incident. I think this is more than a coincidence. Furthermore, I think Cap should know."

Brown shook his head and set his glass on the table. "Wait, Brenda. You'll be going into dangerous territory if you do that."

"You mean crossing the imaginary barrier?"

"You got it."

"But we're talking about a serial killer here, J.B. If we swore to uphold the law when we entered into this profession, doesn't that mean turning our backs on that stupid barrier? Even if the killer is one of our own, aren't we obligated to catch him?"

"Look, Brenda, you're only guessing here. You have no other facts that say De Mija is the perp we're looking for. Two stupid parallels don't justify pointing the figure at him. Unless you have solid proof, you could ruin the man's career with your suspicions. You're a good detective, Brenda. You know the difference between circumstantial and hard evidence."

With a somber look, Ferndale shook her head in disagreement. "I'll bet if I told Cap my suspicions, he might agree with me."

"Don't do it. If you're wrong, you'll be haunted and chastised by the rest of the unit until you quit or disappear," he warned.

"You're the last person I ever thought would threaten me, J.B.," she retorted.

"Calm down. I'm not threatening you. I'm just telling you how it is. I don't care how secretive it is. If you confide in Warner, someone is bound to get wind of the fact it was you who started it. Look, Brenda, you said you wanted my advice. My advice is, let's keep this conversation between you and me. You're my partner, and I support you in every way. So, here's the deal. We'll wait and see if De Mija's name pops up somewhere else of importance in this case. If it does, then I would have to say that would be more than coincidental. In the meantime, we'll keep our eyes and ears open."

"I don't know. What if --"

"No what ifs," Brown insisted. "Put the idea of De Mija being the snake on the back burner for now. If and when the time comes that there are more facts to back up your suspicions, I promise you I will help turn up the fire under him."

CHAPTER TWENTY-SIX

The next few weeks came and went. All the people from the team's first list of possible suspects were questioned as to their whereabouts on the dates the homicides had taken place. Most had legitimate alibis. Those who did not were asked to submit to a blood test. Some agreed with no problem; others refused on the grounds that it was against their civil rights. The people who did have blood drawn and tested proved to no longer be suspects. It was the same for the creative writers: some cooperated, some refused. All parolees were checked out and not only did their blood results release them from suspicion, but they also had valid alibis.

Spring had peeked its nose into winter's backdoor; then immediately went back undercover. The days remained cold and damp.

There had been a wet, unyielding snowfall on Easter Sunday. The morning after, Joe got up earlier than his usual time to clear his snow-laden driveway. Jeny was preparing a hot breakfast and a fresh pot of coffee.

"Boy, it's a good thing the temperatures aren't still in the freezing range," Joe remarked, removing his boots at the backdoor. "The snow should melt fast, hopefully. But it sure is wet and heavy."

"And a lot of it," Jeny offered, as she helped him remove his heavy jacket. "The moisture will be great for our lawn."

"Thanks, honey." He rubbed his hands together to warm them. "Umm, what do you have cooking that smells so good?"

After hanging Joe's coat on a hook by the back door, Jeny returned to her cooking. "We had some leftover ham from yesterday's big dinner. So, my prince, I'm fixing you ham and eggs. Sound good?"

"Delicious. How soon before it's ready?"

"Two minutes. So you'll have to get dressed for work after you eat," she answered in her usual pleasant manner.

Looking at the clock on the wall, Joe realized it was still very early. "That's fine with me."

After washing his hands, Joe sat at the table. Jeny placed the food on the table, poured the coffee, and joined him.

"If the streets are decent, I'm going to go see Eddy today." Jeny had her mouth full, so she just nodded. "I feel badly that I haven't been to the hospital since last Thursday."

"Now don't go getting down on yourself, Joe. We both know you didn't go yesterday because it was Easter. You told me you couldn't go last Friday because they were removing Eddy's casts."

"That didn't take all day. I got so busy at the office, I couldn't take time to go see him after they had finished with him. Then we had church services Friday night, so I had to get straight home after work."

"And don't forget we had relatives from out of town on Saturday."

Shivering, he remarked, "Ooh, don't remind me."

Jeny frowned. "Shame on you, Joe Warner."

"I can't help it if I think my cousin — the first class nerd from Idiots Ville and a freeloader on top of it — bores the tar out of me. I was extremely happy when they left."

"I know, Joe. You must have told me that ten times already," Jeny commented, smirking.

"Well, my goodness, they got here at eight o'clock in the morning and didn't leave until eight that night. I thought for sure they were waiting for an invitation to sleep overnight."

"They might have had you not mentioned — twenty times or more — that he might get arrested."

Laughing, Joe had to grab his napkin so he did not spew food all over. "Could you believe that, Jeny? When he told me they had left their dog outside in the backyard, I just couldn't resist telling him it was against the law to leave an animal unattended that long. 'Really, Joe?' he says. I had a devil of a time keeping a straight face."

"I know." Jeny, too, was laughing so hard she could hardly eat. "One would think that anyone who owns a large dog like a St. Bernard, has a doghouse for it, left the animal sufficient food and water, made sure the dog is fenced in, and had the neighbors keeping an eye on it, would have known you were just pulling his leg."

"Nope, not him. Well, his wife was just as gullible."

Jeny looked at the clock. "I hate to break up this lovely conversation, Joe. But I believe you need to get going."

* * *

It was the start of a good day for Warner. Or so he thought. As he walked into the precinct, the desk sergeant handed him an important phone message. Reaching in his pocket for his cell phone, Warner immediately called the number written on the message slip. After two rings, he heard, "Dr. Richards."

"Doctor, this is Joe Warner. I just got your message. Is it Eddy?"

"Capt. Warner, your friend regained consciousness about ten minutes ago. When I left my message, I gave you my cell phone number as I'm on my way to the hospital as we speak."

"I'll be there as soon as I can."

"No rush. I want to give him a good going over first."

"No problem, doctor. I'll meet you there."

* * *

At the hospital, Warner stopped by the nurse's station close to Konklin's room. Since Dr. Richards was occupied, examining Konklin, Warner was asked to wait until the doctor could speak with him. Warner paced the floor like an expectant father. Out of nervousness, he kept checking his watch. After a good hour, Dr. Richards and a female joined him.

"Capt. Warner, I apologize for keeping you waiting. The examination took longer than I thought. This is Melody Abrams. Melody is a therapist, specializes in working with recovering head trauma patients. I've been conferring with her since Eddy went into his coma, just in case he came to and suffered any side affects from his head injuries."

Offering his hand, Warner said, "It's nice to meet you, Miss --"

"It's quite all right for you to call me Melody. And it's a pleasure to meet you, Capt. Warner."

"If were going to dispense with formalities, why don't you both call me Joe?"

Abrams nodded acceptance with a smile.

"Either Miles or Doc will do for me," Dr. Richards said, showing a gentle smile.

"Okay, Miles, what's the good word?"

"Eddy's awake, but he doesn't remember the accident."

"Does he remember anything else?"

"He knows his name, address, and telephone number. He knows he's a detective and works at the 15th precinct. He also knows the name of the current President of the United States. He doesn't know the date. However, that would only be natural. Those are the only questions I asked him."

"That sounds good," Warner replied.

"It's promising, Joe. But head trauma cases are very deluding. Please remember he's been in a coma for quite a few weeks. Now, when I take you in to see him, I'd like you to ask him a few questions while we observe. Don't say anything to upset him. We'll talk again when you're through with your visit."

Concerned, Warner asked, "What are you afraid of, or more exact, what are you looking for?"

"I'm not going to speculate. Why don't we wait until we go in there and find out what his responses are to your questions."

"What kind of questions do you want me to ask him?"

"If he's working on something in particular, ask him something you would both know the answer to."

"Is he aware he's been a coma?"

"That was my first clue that we were facing a problem. When I joked about him sleeping through March wrapped up in his plaster cocoon, he gave me a bewildered look. So I explained to him that he had been in an accident and had been in a coma. His first question was what kind of an accident. Even after I told him, he still didn't remember."

"How is he doing physically?"

"He's stable and his heart rate data looks good. We won't take him off the monitors for a couple more days. As I've told you before, he has no internal damage which is a miracle in itself."

"Not too long after Eddy's accident you told me you didn't know if he would ever walk again. Do you still think that way?"

"I can't answer that question yet. The casts are all off and, according to the x-rays, his bones healed nicely. Unfortunately he isn't a young man, nor was he in the best physical condition before the accident. So he'll be wearing a few braces for a while. There's still a possibility after extensive physical therapy that we can get him up on his feet again. Fortunately he had no damage to his spine. So there's always hope of full physical recovery. A lot of it depends on how hard Eddy is willing to work at walking again."

As Warner had stood silently, listening to Dr. Richards speak, vivid pictures thrashed about in his head as to how Konklin had looked after his accident. In the emergency room, Konklin was nothing but a mass of mangled flesh drenched in blood. For weeks both of his legs were in white plaster casts from the tip of his toes to the trunk of his body. His left arm was in a cast with only the tips of his fingers showing. And there was a brace around his neck.

The stitches that went from his left eyebrow up and across his forehead into his skull were dark in color. All of Konklin's face was swollen and bruised with black, blue, and muted shades of red — as if someone had used his face for a punching bag. He had to lie on his hospital bed in an awkward position with his head up as both legs hung in overhead slings. He had wires and tubes connecting him to numerous machines.

Only recently had Konklin's face taken shape again; the bruising had disappeared and the swelling had gone down. His stitches had been removed, but the dark scarring was unmistakable.

Warner was brought back from his thoughts when he heard Dr. Richards say, "Eddy's in a lot of pain. I'm going to give him something — but not yet. I want him lucid when you speak to him. So we'll make your visit short. Why don't we go in now? Like I said, we'll continue our conversation after your visit."

Warner, Dr. Richards, and Abrams entered Konklin's room and walked to opposite sides of the bed — Warner on one side, and the doctor and therapist on the other. When Konklin smiled, Warner immediately looked across the bed at Dr. Richards. Dr. Richards gave Warner a slight shake of his head. This head movement indicated to Warner to not say anything about what he was observing.

"Hey, is that you, Joe?" Eddy warbled with a lisp.

Looking back down at his friend, Warner replied, "Yes, it's me, big guy. How ya doin'?"

"I sure hurt a lot, Joe. Miles says I was in an accident. But I don't remember. Can you tell me what happened?"

Warner knew Konklin had already been told about the accident. With the look of help in his eyes, he looked to the doctor for assistance. With a signal nod, Dr. Richards gave him the *go ahead* sign.

"You were driving your car when a semi hit you head on," Warner explained. "You're lucky to be alive."

"Where was I going?"

"You were out on an investigation."

"Investigation?" Konklin thought for a minute. "Oh, that Epstein guy in the *Have No Mercy* case. Now I remember." Not knowing how to respond, Warner just nodded. "Have you and the wife found a house to buy yet?"

"Yes, Eddy. We found a lovely home."

"Geez, that's great. I can hardly wait to see it. You know, Joe, you keep talking about Jeny's home cooking. I can hardly wait for that dinner invite you keep promising."

"Just as soon as you're out of here, I promise you, Jeny and I will have you over for your favorite meal."

"That sure sounds good, Joe. Say, how's Amandalee doing in school?"

"Wonderful, as always. Is there anything I can do for you, Eddy?"

"Well, from the looks of me, I don't guess there's too much you can do right now," Konklin joked. As he laughed, he groaned. "Oh, that hurts. I sure hope I don't have to cough or sneeze while I'm wearing this new set of body armor."

"No, I don't guess so." Warner smiled. "But if you think those braces are bad, you should have seen the white plaster babies they had you garbed in."

"Yeah, that's what Miles told me. He said I slept through March. How long have I been here, Joe?"

"From the looks of all that iron, my guess is not long enough."

"I should have known you wouldn't give me a straight answer," Konklin quipped. "Well, I don't know how long I've been in this bed, but I want to get up and they won't let me."

"Don't be so cantankerous. You listen to your doctor so you can heal faster. Look, I've got to get back to work, Eddy. I'll be back tomorrow. You get some rest and don't flirt with any cute nurses. Remember, they can run faster than you can."

Starting to laugh again, Konklin complained. "Oh, that's not fair, Joe. As my partner, you're supposed to be kinder to me. Don't make me laugh anymore. It hurts too much."

"Hey, they say laughter is good medicine for what ails you. I'll see you later."

* * *

Outside in the corridor, Dr. Richards asked Warner, "Why didn't you ask him questions like I asked you to do?"

"I didn't have to. We closed the case he was talking about several years ago. And he's been to my house numerous times to enjoy my wife's cooking. Amandalee is my daughter, and she's a district attorney's assistant. And I'm no longer his partner. I'm his captain. I don't understand what's going on."

Abrams explained. "We're not positive at this point, but I'm afraid your friend Eddy is probably suffering from Post Traumatic Amnesia. In the medical field, we call it PTA."

"What exactly does that mean?"

"Presently, memories are scrambled in his brain. Since he's not aware of it, Eddy doesn't know how to sort things out."

"I'm still not following you, Melody."

"He's obviously only finding and pulling out bits and pieces of his memory from his subconscious. These can be memories from both his past and his present."

"Right now, it sounds like more memories of the past. Is this a temporary or a permanent situation?"

"At this point, Joe, it's really hard to say."

"Is this PTA caused from the severe concussion he suffered from the accident?"

"There's no question about that."

"Melody, after your observation earlier and just now, what's your decision?" Miles asked.

Perplexed, Warner asked, "Decision? What decision?"

"To take Eddy on as a patient, Joe. Miles, the answer is, yes. I'll be more than happy to work with Eddy."

Dr. Richards excused himself, allowing Warner and Abrams to continue their discussion with regard to Konklin.

"Exactly what do you do to help him get his memory back in the right order, if you don't mind my asking?"

"I'll have to teach him many things, like a child that is first learning word association. I'll start by word and picture association. Then we'll go from there."

"Is there anything I can do to help?"

"Sure. Bring in some of Eddy's co-workers, since I understand from Miles that he doesn't have any relatives or close friends in town other than your. If he doesn't recognize them at first, don't be alarmed. Just introduce Eddy to them as people you want him to meet. Never tell Eddy that he should already know them. We don't want to confuse his mind any further by having him realize, just yet, that he doesn't remember. Hopefully he'll start recognizing familiar faces, like he knows your face and who you are."

"I can do that. As a matter of fact, I think the first person I want to bring here is his partner, Detective Leo De Mija. Leo was also in the car the day of the accident."

"That sounds like an excellent start," Abrams agreed.

"When should I do this?"

"Since Miles went to order a pain reliever for Eddy, let's give him a good twenty-four hours of rest. Tomorrow morning would be a good time to start."

"We'll be here."

* * *

As soon as Warner got back to the precinct, he summoned De Mija to his office.

Feeling more at ease now in the captain's presence, De Mija sat in a chair in a relaxed position. "What's up, Cap?"

"I thought you would like to know that Eddy regained consciousness this morning."

"That's great news, Cap. Have you been able to talk to him yet?"

"Yes, I just came from there."

"How is he?"

"Under the circumstances, I guess as well as can be expected. He seems to be suffering from something called PTA."

"What in the name of glory is that?"

"It's a form of amnesia. I wanted you to be the first to know because I need your help."

"Anything, Cap, just ask."

"I want to take you over to see Eddy tomorrow morning."

"Sure. But why do you want to take me? I can go on my own."

"I want to take you because I want to see if he recognizes you."

"Don't you think he will?"

"I don't know, but I want to find out. I'll pick you up at your house. Then one of the detectives can give you a ride home after work."

"Uh … no. That won't be necessary, Cap. Since I can drive, I'd just as soon meet you here in the morning."

"That's fine with me."

"Anything else?"

"No, that's it for now. I'll make the announcement to the unit later."

De Mija got to his feet. "I almost forgot. I'd stay away from Chief Doogle today if I were you."

"Why's that?"

"From what I understand, after weeks of getting everything coordinated, he's pretty upset that he had to cancel yesterday's MPPD's annual Easter Day egg hunt. The crew says he's really in a bad mood."

"Oh, that's right. With all that snow, it certainly would have been canceled. I don't have little ones, so I don't pay too much attention to gatherings like that. Cheese and crackers! Now, I suppose, we'll all be eating hardboiled eggs for a week," Warner jested. "Boy, this will be one time I'm happy that Eddy isn't around."

"Excuse me?"

"Hardboiled eggs end up as a gas explosion that smells worse than sewer gas after Eddy eats one of those things." He laughed. "You know, frogs?"

"Oh." De Mija forced a laugh. "I see Lieu told you about the day we ate liver and onions?"

Still laughing, Warner said, "Yes. He's an excellent detective but a real character."

"The man has a real good sense of humor, that's for sure. Well, I'll go back to my desk now and get busy."

* * *

As soon as De Mija got to work the following morning, he and Warner left for the hospital. They had to wait until the nurse had finished spoon-feeding broth to Konklin. As they waited, Warner told his detective what to expect when he saw the lieutenant. He asked him to please not say anything to Konklin unless Warner gave him the okay sign by the nod of his head.

"From what I understand, Leo, Eddy's illness is an extremely delicate situation. We don't want to cause any more trauma."

"I understand, Cap. Maybe I shouldn't go in there at all?"

"Negative. I need you to go in there with me."

"Okay, wait a minute. I've never heard of the PTA other than in my school days. I believe that used to stand for Parent Teacher's Association," Leo said, almost cracking a smile. "All that malarkey you told me yesterday and just now, you were setting me up. I just realized that you're pulling my leg because April Fool's is just a few days away. Man, Cap, you almost had me."

For a moment, Warner was dumbfounded De Mija thought this was all a joke. Suddenly, realization hit him that he was known around the office for being somewhat of a chain-puller. "I completely understand your skepticism, Leo. But I can assure you this is no joke. I realize I tease a lot, but I wouldn't joke about the lieutenant's condition. I've never heard of Post Traumatic Amnesia, or PTA as it's called, before either. No, I'm sorry to say, this is very real."

De Mija felt a sharp pain shoot up through his shoulders. "I'm sorry, Cap. I --"

"No apology necessary."

"When we go in there, what do I call him?"

"For now, I think you should call him Eddy. If he recognizes you, then you can call him Lieu, like you normally do."

Konklin's nurse appeared in the doorway and motioned for them to enter. As soon as they did, they walked to his bedside.

"Good morning, big guy. How are you doing today?"

"Same as yesterday, Joe. Who's your friend?"

"This is Leo De Mija, Eddy. He's one of our new detectives."

"Hey, that's great. For some strange reason he looks familiar to me."

"Yes, Eddy, you've met him before. Do you remember?"

After concentrating on De Mija's face, he replied, "I seem to recall you in some sort of uniform. Oh, were you my mailman?"

Without thinking, De Mija remarked, "No. I was a uniform."

"What's a uniform, Joe?" Eddy inquired, frowning.

"A cop, Eddy. We were all in uniforms before we became detectives."

"Oh, yeah. It's been so many years ago, I almost forgot. So, young man, how do you like being a detective?"

De Mija stood in silence until the captain gave him a nonchalant nod.

"I like it just fine."

"Who's your partner?"

Warner jumped in before De Mija had a chance to answer. "He doesn't have a partner yet, Eddy. He's still in training."

"Oh, you really are new. Say, Joe, how do you like your big office by now?"

"It's great, Eddy. Just great."

"Do you miss me sharing it with you?"

"I sure do."

Konklin pulled his sheet up to look under it.

"Got a problem there, big guy?"

Letting the sheet fall back on his body, Konklin complained, "It's the darnedest thing, Joe. For some reason I feel like I'm supposed to be looking for something important. But I can't figure out why or what I'm looking for."

"Whatever it is, I don't think you'll find it under your bedding," Warner quipped. "Anyway, I wouldn't worry about it for now. All you need to be thinking about is getting well and out of this bed. We miss you at work."

"Yeah. It's nice to know the unit finally accepts me." He yawned. "Sorry about that. I can't remember sleeping so much before in my whole life and still being tired. I think it's the medicine they keep giving me."

"I'm sure it is, Eddy. We don't want to wear you out. So we're going to go now."

"But you only just got here."

"I know, but duty calls."

"Okay, Joe. Thanks for stopping by. It was a real pleasure to meet you, young man."

"For me, too," De Mija responded.

In the hall and out of Konklin's hearing range, Warner said, "That's so sad. It literally breaks my heart."

"I certainly understand that, Cap. I'm not as close to him as you are. But that is even tough for me to take."

"Something Eddy said kind of threw me for a loop."

"What?"

"For years, Eddy has always felt the unit never accepted him. Of course it was all in his mind. But now, for some reason, he thinks everything with them is okay."

"I think that's because of something I told him before the accident."

"What's that?"

"I told him the rest of the unit refers to us as the Comedy Team. He thought that was a great compliment."

"Finally, something got through to him that the rest of the crew likes and respects him. No matter how corny, I think that's great."

"Why doesn't he remember me as a detective, Cap?"

"It's that form of amnesia I told you about. I wish he had some relatives. They could certainly be of some help right now."

"I don't quite understand this PTA problem. Why does he remember some things and not others?"

"I'll explain on the way back to the precinct."

CHAPTER TWENTY-SEVEN

When they returned to the 15th, Warner had a special delivery envelope waiting for him at the front desk. It was from Kym Davies.

"That looks important, Cap," De Mija commented.

"I hope so. Go on up and get to work. I'll talk to you later."

After taking a few minutes to speak with Desk Sergeant Russ Gleason, Warner went upstairs to his office. At his desk, he loosened his tie, then opened the envelope. It was Davies's report. As he silently read through the six pages of theories and clarifications, Warner highlighted words, phrases, and sentences to summarize the details.

Once he finished, Warner went back over the report and verbally repeated the highlighted areas. "Possibly had two sets of abusive parents: birth parents and those who raised him. Sees victims' faces as parents' faces. Stabbing (or cutting throats) is a very personal vendetta. Beaten down (both mentally and physically) since childhood. Probably killed both sets of parents, which started his murdering spree. Religious. Prose on card his Commandment. Self-proclaimed savior of children. Sees himself in each child he frees. Rattle is gift to children. Flower represents freedom of innocence (the child). Black represents death of abuse (the parents). Organized. Hygiene important — wears body cover to keep blood off him. Dedicated worker. Loner (no close friends). Well respected. Wears type of uniform for work. Secretive. Packrat of sorts. Excels in studies and employment. Has feminine side — creative writing and gardening. Married. Probably no more than one child. Subconscious rules planning and killing mode. Pillows used to muffle screams so they do not bring him back to reality. Does not remember he committed the heinous crimes — but remembers every detail as if he had watched a movie. Probably still lives in home he was raised in. Money hidden away. Idea of how to murder came from his collection. Smart not to use weapon that could be traced back to him. Not a schizophrenic but has two faces."

Tossing the report aside, Warner looked at the time. After checking to see there was nothing pressing to keep him around the office for an hour or so, he went to the hospital to pay his daily respects to his lieutenant.

CHAPTER TWENTY-EIGHT

Finally the snow was melting. Even though the sun showed its glowing face, it was a cinch that it certainly did not cast any light on the multiple homicides that were tied to one particular deranged murderer. The fear in each Mt. Pride family's home with small children was intensifying, even though there had not been another double homicide in well over a month,.

In spite of the profile report, the serial murder case was running cold. Many times it takes years for murders to be solved; many cases go unsolved. But Warner was stubborn. This particular snake had first shown its fangs of destruction just a matter of months earlier. So Warner was not even close to quitting his investigation.

Just when Warner thought perhaps the snake had crawled into a hole and gone underground, he struck again with his poisonous venom. To Warner's amazement, De Mija was already at the scene when he arrived.

"Good heavens, Leo. How did you get here so fast?"

"I was lucky, Cap, and hit all the green lights," De Mija said, halfway joking.

Well, a jovial comment with a real smile. I guess I was right from the beginning? This kid just needed a chance to feel comfortable working with us, Warner thought.

"I was just talking with my old partner. You remember Dave Ripley, don't you?"

"Certainly." Warner greeted Ripley with a nod. "So, Leo, do you think you've asked all the right questions?"

"Questions? Uh … no. I thought I should wait and have Dave, here, report to you. I've been on the other side of this coin, Cap. But this is my first time working from this side as a detective. I didn't want to screw up."

"Understandable." Focusing his attention on Officer Ripley, Warner inquired, "Who called this in?"

"The oldest daughter of the victims. She --"

Without thinking, De Mija blurted out, "What?"

Warner did a quick take, looking at De Mija and frowning. "Why the outburst?"

"I'm sorry, Cap. I was just imagining what was coming next."

"Meaning?"

"I guess my mind was outguessing Dave's next comment that the daughter wasn't home at the time, came home and found the bodies. I have moments when my mouth runs without permission. Really, Cap, I apologize."

Shaking his head, Warner turned back to Ripley. "Please, continue."

"Leo's right. The girl had been out on an overnight babysitting job and didn't arrive back home until six o'clock this morning. She said --"

Interrupting, Warner asked, "How many kids?"

"Two daughters."

"How old is this oldest girl you're talking about?"

"I didn't ask her, but my guess is fifteen or sixteen. Does that make a difference?"

"Not really. It's just if she's of school age, I can't imagine her babysitting and coming home at six in the morning. Well, that's not important right now. Continue, officer."

"She said she always checks in with her parents to let them know she's home safe. When she went to their bedroom, she discovered their bodies."

"That poor kid. So, our perp is changing a bit of his MO."

De Mija's ears perked up. "How's that?"

"He's defending older children now, or so he thinks."

"Not necessarily," Ripley stated. "I said the oldest daughter made the distress call. The victims other daughter is a toddler."

"Oh," Warner replied. "Where are the kids?"

"The oldest daughter is sitting in the living room holding her baby sister. Officer Hanson is in there with them."

Dammit! Hanson has no business still being out on patrol. Warner hid his anger. "Hanson hasn't touched anything, has she?"

"No, sir. Capt. Roberts read her the riot act after her last boner of removing pillows from the vics. If I'd have been watching her that never would have happened."

Warner dropped the issue and got back to the here and now. "How did you get in?"

"The oldest daughter was waiting at the door when we arrived. The poor kid was beside herself. And before you ask, Capt. Warner, we didn't call CPS yet."

"Why not?"

"The oldest girl keeps asking to call her granny. I figured since she was doing a pretty good job handling her little sister that we'd wait until you got here. If you want me to, I'll call them now."

"No. Hold off until I can talk to her."

"Both my partner and I checked the bodies, but there were absolutely no signs of life. Rigor had already started to set in. And, no, we didn't touch the bodies. We could just tell from looking at them that there was no hope of life in either of them."

The men stood and talked as they waited for the CSIs to arrive.

"It looks like our perp isn't discriminating against any one color," De Mija stated.

"What does that comment mean?" Warner asked.

"This family is black where the others have been Caucasian."

"Have you been in there to see the victims?"

"No, Cap. I saw the children."

"Oh. Well, this is your first experience at a crime scene."

"No, it isn't. If you recall, Dave and I were at the first two scenes."

"As uniformed officers. But you didn't see any of the vics after the pillows were removed. If it's as bad as the last three this perp has left us, I hope you have a strong constitution."

"While in uniform, I've dealt with knifings and shooting before, Cap. I'll be fine."

"Look, I've called in Detective Ferndale to take over for me today. Since you're green at this, she'll have much more patience than I'll have in showing you the ropes. Plus, I have an appointment I have to keep so I won't be here for very long."

"Okay," De Mija remarked without question.

"Officer Ripley, you wait here. Leo, show me where the girls are." As De Mija led the way to the living room, Warner explained, "We always question both officers at a scene like this."

"I know, Cap."

Warner grinned. "Of course you do. Well, I'll let you get Officer Hanson's info to see if she has anything more to offer than Ripley did."

"Alone?"

"Yes, alone. All you have to do is listen. If you think of any pertinent questions, like you were asked when you stood in her position, then ask. Take notes so you don't forget anything."

Stopping at the living room doorway, Warner turned his eyes to the sounds of the sobbing. He saw a young girl sitting in a large recliner rocker, holding her sister as she rocked back and forth. The little girl was asleep in her arms. Officer Hanson was kneeling down beside the chair with her hand on the oldest girl's knee. When she saw the detectives, she stood and walked over to them.

"Hanson, step out in the hall and give Detective De Mija your rundown."

"Okay, Capt. Warner."

Hanson and De Mija disappeared out of the captain's hearing distance. Warner walked over to the children and squatted in front of the chair.

"Hello, young lady. My name is Capt. Warner."

The girl said nothing. She kept on rocking as she stared into space.

"What's your name, honey?"

Trying to control her sobbing, she answered, "Rosy."

"That's a pretty name, Rosy. What's your little sister's name?"

"Starla Belle."

"My, that's a pretty name, too. I must say it's one I've never heard of before."

"She was born on Christmas."

"Oh, I see. And I'll bet you were born in the spring when roses bloom?"

"Yes."

"How old are the two of you?"

"Starla Belle is three and a half and I'm sixteen," she said after a hefty sniffle.

"Do you go to school?"

"No. I graduated a few weeks ago."

"Congratulations, Rosy. That's a mighty fine achievement for a young lady of sixteen."

"Thank you."

"Look, honey, do you have someone we can call to come after you and your little sister?"

Nodding her head, she stated, "Yes, my granny. I told those police officers, but they wouldn't let me call her. Can I call her now?"

"Does Granny live close to here?"

"Yes," she sobbed.

"Do you think she's home?"

"Granny's always home. She never goes anywhere unless me and Mama takes her."

"Well, Rosy," Warner said, patting her knee, "if you'll wait a few more minutes we'll drive you both to your granny's house."

"Okay."

"I need to ask you if you were in your sister's room after you found …." Warner was quick to pause, not wanting to say something to upset the young girl any further. "Where was your sister when you got home?"

"She was asleep in her bedroom."

"Other than picking her up and bringing her in here, did you touch anything in her room?"

"Yes. I put the side of the crib down. I picked her up and got her blanket."

"Thank you, Rosy. I'll be back real soon."

De Mija and Hanson had already returned to the front entrance by the time Warner got there. Simultaneously, the front door opened and in walked Ferndale. Brown entered right behind her, followed by the tech team of Rothchild and DuBois.

"Whoa! Don't look now but your shadow is following you," Warner quipped.

Everyone broke into a quiet laughter.

"Ah, hell, Joe," Rothchild stated. "Kevin lives in my footsteps."

"Not you, you moth-eaten old crow," Warner said in jest. "I know you don't show up any place without Kevin to hold your hand. I was talking about my detectives."

"Whoops. Sorry." Rothchild laughed. "Show us the way and we'll get out of here."

"I haven't seen the room yet."

"You must be slipping."

"Well, I didn't think the victims were going anywhere," Warner quipped back. "Hey, where's Davis?"

"Hopefully, he's on his way."

"One of the uniforms will show you where to go, Doug. We'll join you shortly."

As Ripley led the CSIs to the scene of the crime, Warner focused his attention back on his detectives. "So, why are both of you here?"

Ferndale explained, "I asked J.B. to join me, Cap. I wouldn't want to mess up and overlook something important while teaching Leo the ropes. I know I'm a good detective. But a teacher, I'm not."

"Finding the minute things we detectives overlook is the techs' job. However, I am glad you're here, J.B. Leo should get a lot of good training today with both of you on board. I'm sorry to ask you to take over, but it's imperative that I take my wife to the doctor this morning."

"We sure don't mind covering for you, Cap. What do we have, another dual?" Brown asked.

"Unfortunately, yes. Since the officers followed everything by the book, and both victims were deceased, I figured there was no need for me to go in and start looking around. Then explain everything to you before I left. There are two children here. When I leave, I'm going to take them to their grandmother's house."

"Pardon me for interrupting, Cap. But as long as both Brenda and J.B. are here, and you have an appointment to keep, why don't I do that for you," De Mija suggested.

"When you were in uniform, Leo, did you ever have to break the bad news to a family member that one of their own had just been murdered?"

"Yes, sir, a few times."

"How are you going to learn the ropes here if you don't stick around?"

"Look, Cap," Ferndale spoke up before De Mija could answer, "I have an idea. If this was just another homicide, I would say let Leo stay here and learn. But since this is the serial killer we've been chasing, maybe it's not the best time to be investigating and teaching him at the same time. Besides, I have J.B. here, and as you said, the techs --"

"Okay, windy, catch a breath." Warner laughed, holding up his hands, "I'll concede. The two of you can take over. Leo, you take the kids. I'll be in the office later today if anyone needs me. But if it's an emergency, you --"

"Can reach me on my cell," Ferndale and Brown chimed in, ending with a chuckle.

"Okay, I'm out of here."

* * *

After Warner and De Mija left the house, Officers Hanson and Ripley stepped outside for a bit of fresh air and conversation. After a lull in their conversation, Ripley broke the silence.

"Say, Chriss, let me ask you something. Strictly off the record."

"Look, Dave, if you're going to ask me out again, the answer is still no."

"No, that's not it," he said in all sincerity. "I know you're still considered a rookie, but if you thought you knew a bad cop, and he was your partner, would you turn him in?"

"What have you done?" Hanson shouted, giving him a devastating look of disappointment.

"Nothing. I haven't done a thing. And keep your voice down. I'm just asking a simple question, that's all."

"Well, give me some more information first."

"Like what? I just want a simple answer. Would you or would you not turn this person in?"

"There is no simple answer. If it was a minor law-breaker the cop committed, maybe he, generally speaking of course, could be talked to and he could change his ways. But, if this cop knowingly broke a major law, then yes. Who are we talking about, Dave?"

"I don't want to say right now."

"Well, it doesn't take a rocket scientist to guess you're talking about Detective Leo De Mija."

Ripley eyes widened. "Why would you say that?"

"It's a cinch it's not me. From everything you've talked about since we've been together, you've only had two other partners. And, according to you, your first partner is no longer around. So common sense tells me it's De Mija. Now give. What's up?"

"Okay, Chriss. It is Leo. My problem is I don't know if he's done anything or not. It's just that everything I hear about what's happened, all fingers point to him. I don't want to say anything to anyone because if he isn't guilty, my suspicions and big mouth could ruin him. I would be getting him into quicksand for no reason."

"On the other hand, if you don't say anything — and he is guilty of whatever you're talking about — then you'll have withheld vital information."

"Yeah, I know. It's been driving me crazy as to what to do."

"I think the best thing for you to do is to search your soul and remember the reason you're wearing that uniform."

CHAPTER TWENTY-NINE

Officer Ripley had not slept well in months. His mind was too preoccupied, wondering what to do. Finally making his decision, Ripley headed for the downtown headquarters immediately after his shift was over on Monday morning. As he walked toward the chief's office, he noticed Doogle was about to unlock his door.

"Chief," Ripley said, loud and clear.

Doogle turned his head toward the voice. "Well, Good Monday morning, Officer …."

"Dave Ripley from the 15th."

"Right. Right. Well, Officer Ripley, what brings you across town so early?" Doogle asked, unlocking and opening his door.

"I'm sorry to bother you, chief, but I really have a dilemma and I need your advice."

As Doogle turned on the lights then walked inside his office, Ripley followed. Doogle never responded to Ripley's comment. He placed his briefcase on the desk. Then he took the newspaper he had carried in under his arm and tossed it on his credenza. Removing his uniform jacket, Doogle finally spoke. "Look, Ripley, if you've got a work problem, you need to take it up with your superior, not me."

"No, chief, it's nothing like that. It's, in a sense, work-related, but … well, sir, may I explain what the problem is all about?"

It was not until Doogle had hung his jacket on a hanger at the back of his office door, then sat behind his desk, that he responded. "Okay, Ripley, but it had better be good. Sit down and tell me what's on your mind."

Out of habit, Doogle opened his desk drawer, took out a toothpick, and placed it in his mouth. Ripley took a few steps back to the door and looked out in both directions to see if anyone was around. He stepped back in, closed the door, and took a seat near the chief's desk.

"By the way you were peering in the hallway, you act like your visit is a military secret."

"Chief, this is so highly confidential that I don't want anyone to know about our conversation."

Biting down on his toothpick, as he played with it in his mouth, Doogle asked, "Why?"

Ripley tilted his head back and looked toward the ceiling. He ran his tongue over the roof of his mouth. He was in the hot seat now to either tell what he knew or to make up a wild story for his reason for being there, then get the heck out of there. However, lies were not in his make-up. He had to tell the chief what was eating away at him. "This has to do with the serial killings that I've been involved with since January," he stated, now looking straight at Doogle.

"Oh, and what would you know about these homicides that the rest of us don't know?"

"Nothing, really, but there are too many things that don't add up."

Doogle leaned back and got a cocky look on his face as he smirked. "Really? Like what?"

"I can tell right off that you're not going to believe a word I'm going to tell you. So why don't we drop it. Forget I was even here." Upset, he got up to leave.

"Hold on now. If you know something about this case, why didn't you go to Capt. Warner? He's the chief of detectives at your precinct. Furthermore, while his lieutenant is laid up, he's also the lead on this serial case."

"Because I can't afford to be seen in Capt. Warner's office, especially if I'm wrong."

"Okay, Ripley. I can tell you've got something really heavy to unload. Sit back down and tell me about it. I'm a born skeptic, so you'll have to forgive me. Plus fighting this tobacco monkey is still stressing me out. You know, everyone lies to you about kicking the nicotine habit. It's been several years now, and I still want a damn cigarette."

With more important things on his mind, Ripley was not really interested in Doogle's personal problems. However, as not to offend the chief, he felt obligated to reply. "I don't know, sir. I've never smoked."

"And lucky you are about that, Ripley. Bet you didn't know that I was in the U.S. Marine Corp and served time in Viet Nam, did you?"

"Yes, sir, I did."

"Well, I'll bet what you didn't know is that we got rations our government sent us. Guess what else we got, outside of that lousy mess they called food?" Ripley, like ever other employee who worked for the MPPD, had already heard Doogle's rant. However, before he could get a word out, the chief continued with his on-going complaint. "Cigarettes, my dear boy. Our government sent us cigarettes. I didn't smoke before Viet Nam, but I sure came back a smoker. Our government got me hooked. Then they had the guts to tell me I had to quit. They could give us those cigarettes free, but do you think they'd pay for anything that would help Vets like me kick this habit? No sir! Will they authorize our insurance companies to help pay for these aids to help us quit smoking? No way! We put our lives on the line, they sent us cigarettes for whatever their reason was, and now they won't even accept responsibility for getting us hooked."

Not knowing how else to respond, Ripley simply said, "I'm sorry, sir."

Doogle threw the toothpick in the wastebasket and got fresh one out of his desk drawer. "Well, Ripley, now that I've gotten that off my chest, it's your turn. Begin at the beginning."

"As you are well aware, Leo De Mija and I were patrol partners before he got promoted to detective."

"Yes."

"Well, in the early morning hours of January 9, De Mija and I were on the last leg of our graveyard shift. Around five A.M., if I remember correctly — my report should be in file to verify the time — De Mija pulled into a gas station and parked out front of the main door. He said he had to go to the bathroom."

"That's not so unusual."

"No, I didn't think so at the time either. But the door to the men's john was on the side of the building where he could have parked just outside the door."

"Sitting in a patrol car, as you well know, can be very tiring. Maybe he wanted the exercise and fresh air?"

"Maybe," Ripley said, disappointed that the chief was making his situation even harder than it already was. "After getting something out of the trunk of our patrol car, he disappears around the corner of the building. Then he's gone for well over an hour."

"Ripley, there is no --"

"Please, chief, hear me out before you say anymore."

Now even more disgusted, Doogle threw his second chewed-up piece of wood in the wastebasket and got another one out of the drawer. He placed the fresh toothpick in his mouth and bit down. "This better be good. I've got a lot more pressing issues to take care of this morning than to hear your complaints about a partner taking longer in the john than you think he needs to take."

Ignoring Doogle's comment, Ripley continued. "While I'm sitting in the patrol car waiting for him, we get this call about the double homicides over on Raider Ranch Drive. I ran out of the car, around to the side of the building, and pounded on the door. De Mija didn't answer. I pounded again, only this time I yelled at him. He still didn't answer. I ran back to the car to call in that we couldn't respond when I see De Mija walking toward the car. Opening my window, I yelled at him to hurry as we had a homicide to check out. As he jumped in and drove off, I called in that we were responding to the scene. De Mija was always in pretty good shape. So I found it puzzling that he was breathing hard, as if he had run a ten-mile race."

"Did you ask him about his heavy breathing?"

"Not at that time. I was too busy watching where we were headed, and my mind was on the homicide call. At a later date, when I asked him about that morning, he just said he his breathing was abnormal because he had had the cramps. Now if you ask me, that's the most ridiculous thing I ever heard of. But I couldn't question his answer as he immediately changed the subject. Now, in the early morning hours of January 16, De Mija decided he was hungry." Ripley went on to give a detailed explanation of De Mija's disappearing act and his reasoning behind it.

Getting impatient, Doogle said, "So far, I don't understand what your concern is. How does De Mija's bathroom habits and sudden appetite have anything to do with a serial murder case?"

"There's more."

"Okay, carry on."

Ripley picked up where he had left off. "When we got to the scene, De Mija said he would take the backdoor and I was to take the front. I rang the doorbell and pounded on the door, yelling, 'Police. Open up.' Before I knew it, De Mija opened the front door and let me in. He claims he pounded on the backdoor and when he got no response, he broke in. Later, however, he changed his story and told me the backdoor was unlocked so he walked in. But he tells me not to tell anyone how he really entered the house. Then he asks me to cover his ass and say he broke in through the front door when I'm questioned about us making entrance. Like an idiot, I did. But, chief, he wasn't anywhere near the front door. I was. According to the way we were trained, the perp could have still been in the house. If De Mija was going to enter through the backdoor alone, he should have let me know. Right?"

"That's correct."

"So, what do you think?"

"You're actually coming in here complaining about something De Mija did, but you're putting your own head in the noose. If you lied for him, then that's something you'll have to live with. However, since no laws were broken, I'd say drop it."

"No. That's not my point. Why did we just happen to be in the same areas as both double homicides? Why was De Mija conveniently out of my sight not too long before we received both dispatch calls? There's just too many questions. Do you think he might be involved in these homicides?"

"I think you either have a grudge against De Mija or you're letting your imagination run away with you, Ripley. That's what I think. Or maybe you're jealous that he got promoted to detective and you didn't."

"No, that's not how it is," Ripley protested. "Why would a man come back after sitting for forty or fifty minutes on the can and be out of breath? It would make more sense if he were constipated and spent the time straining."

"Grunting can make a man breathe a little harder," Doogle joked.

"Sorry, Chief, I'm not in the mood for joking around right now. Besides, he told me he had the cramps from diarrhea."

"Okay, Ripley, do you have any more to tell me?"

"Not that I can think of right now."

"Well, to satisfy your suspicions, I'll talk to Capt. Warner. Okay?"

"As long as De Mija doesn't know I've said anything, that's fine." Ripley got to his feet and walked to the door. Then he turned. "You know, I would really like you to prove me wrong." After opening the door, Ripley once again peered into the hallway. When he saw it was safe, he rushed away from the chief's office.

Doogle called the 15th.

"Capt. Warner."

"Joe. This is the chief. I need you to come down to my office on the double."

"Certainly, Ed." *Now what?* "What's going on?"

"I'll explain when you get here. Oh, and don't tell any of your men where you're going."

* * *

Generally, Doogle was a no-nonsense chief. However, he was almost laughing as he conveyed Ripley's suspicions to Warner. Warner listened attentively as thoughts rolled around in his head.

When Doogle had finished, Warner asked, "If this is such a big joke to you, why did you call me here?"

"So you'd be aware of Ripley's suspicions. And to nip it in the bud before rumors get started."

"You know, Ed, I could take this story of Officer Ripley's a bit farther."

"Oh, come on, Joe. You don't seriously think this story holds water, do you?"

"Of course not. I just want to tell you how easy it is to turn coincidence into suspicions. You see, I was in Eddy's office when he received the call on the third double homicides. Since it was too early for De Mija to be at work yet, Eddy tried to contact him from the car on the way to the scene. There was absolutely no response. I told Eddy he had to talk to our new detective and clue him in as to his obligations as a detective.

"From what I understand, De Mija showed up that morning with his hand all wrapped up in bandages. It seems he had cut himself with a knife from his knife collection. Now, I didn't see him that morning, so I'm only going by hearsay. Oddly enough, that morning at the crime scene we found blood droplets on the carpet in the victim's bedroom."

"Right. And if I remember correctly, that blood didn't match either of the victim's blood types," Doogle stated, now starting to understand Ripley's suspicions. "You're saying the blood could have come from De Mija?"

"No, Ed, that's not what I mean. Anyway, at this last scene, De Mija was there before I arrived. I know for a fact that after dispatch was notified, I was the first detective called to the scene. How did De Mija beat me there, unless he was already in the area and heard the call come over the radio? To make matters even worse, De Mija fits a lot of aspects in the profile that Kym Davies submitted."

"Sounds more like you're building a case against Officer De Mija, not defending him."

"You're taking this all wrong, Ed. I was just trying to show you how easy it is to be in the wrong place at the wrong time and end up having people pointing fingers at you. There's no way I'm going to believe one of our own is a serial killer." Shaking his head, Warner added, "No, it's just a series of coincidences. I'm sure."

"Coincidences or not, Joe. You've got to check him out."

Begrudgingly, Warner admitted, "Yeah, I know."

"Well, do it quietly. I don't want Internal Affairs getting involved until you have positive proof that De Mija is involved in these homicides."

"You don't have to warn me, Ed. I don't like IA nosing around any more than you do."

* * *

Warner gave De Mija a few errands to run, therefore keeping him occupied and out of the main office. As soon as De Mija left, Warner called Ferndale, Brown, Mayfield, and Roitstein to his office. They all took a seat with the exception of Mayfield.

"Is this about the serial killer, Cap?" Mayfield asked, keeping his hand on the doorknob.

"Yes."

"But Leo just left. Do you want me to try and catch him?"

"No, Arjay. If I wanted him in here, I wouldn't have sent him away from the precinct. Now take a seat. Brenda, I'll listen to your information about these last homicides, but first I have another very important problem to handle." Warner sat back in the chair and bit at his lower lip. "You have all been working with Leo since Eddy's been laid up. Have any of you noticed anything, let's say, peculiar about him?"

Everyone shrugged their shoulders and shook their heads except Ferndale. She dropped her sight so she would not have to look at her captain. Warner picked up on it.

"Come on, Brenda, what have you noticed?"

"Nothing really."

"Brenda, you're a good detective, but you're a lousy liar. Something's on your mind. Trust me, if it's about Leo, I need to know."

"I don't know exactly what you mean by peculiar."

"Okay, let me rephrase that question. Have you noticed anything suspicious about Leo?"

Out of the corner of her eye from where she was sitting, she could see Brown. He gave her a *go-ahead* look with his eyes.

"Okay, Cap, but it's nothing that I've seen him do."

"What is it then?"

"His name came up on our suspect lists."

"Lists, as in plural?"

"Yes, Cap."

"What was the first one?"

"Creative writing."

"We've already discussed that at an earlier meeting, so that's old news. What else?"

"He was surprised when I showed him the package of rattles. He told me had purchased the same rattle a few years ago when his daughter was born."

"So his name also came up on the rattle purchase list?"

"No, Cap, it didn't. Either a store didn't have his name recorded, didn't admit to knowing him, or didn't remember Leo had made the purchase from them."

"So what you have is his word that he had purchased the same type rattle a few years prior?"

"Yes, sir."

"So his name has actually only shown up on one list, not two?"

"That's true, but --"

In order to validate his partner's comments, Brown interrupted her. "You know, Cap, now that Leo is being discussed, did you ever notice that he is left-handed?"

"Yes," Warner abruptly replied. He could not figure out if he was irritated because fellow officers were throwing around even more suspicions about one of their own, or extremely outraged because De Mija could actually be the snake they were chasing. He did not want to condemn any man, especially one of his detectives, on wild suspicions and accusations. "Does anyone else have anything to offer?" Getting a negative response, Warner asked, "Which one of you gets along the best with Leo?"

Three heads turned toward Brown. "Leo's kind of a loner, Cap. I think Lieu probably got along with him better than any of us do. Since Lieu's been out of commission, I guess I'm next in line."

A stick of dynamite exploded in Warner's head. Slamming his hands flat on the desk, he declared, "That's it! That's what Eddy was trying to tell me. He didn't think I was Leo, he was trying to tell me it *is* Leo."

"Clue us in, Cap. What are you talking about?" Roitstein asked.

"Listen, without raising any suspicion, J.B., I want you to get close to Leo. Start paling around with him. I'm going to assign you and Leo to be partners for the next two weeks. This reasoning is twofold. You'll get to know him better in a one-on-one situation. I can't think of a better way to do that than to be sitting in a car together for eight hours a day while you're out on assignment. Also, you can keep your eyes on him. I don't want him out of your sight for five minutes — even if you have to follow him to the bathroom. Got it?"

"Yes. But the team is way understaffed now. If you pull me off --"

"You are, in actuality, still working the *Black Tulip* case by getting close to our now number one suspect."

"Oh," Brown replied, a bit fuzzy as to Warner's reasoning.

"Brenda, I want you to do a background check on Leo. I want to know how he was raised, where he was raised, everything you can find on his parents, if he has any relatives, and anything you can get on him. When you've got everything we need to know about him — that will either clear him or build a case against him — report to me pronto. Okay?"

"Got it, Cap."

"Arjay and Kieyell, I'm sure you're aware Leo hasn't been put on the new schedule yet for this serial case. I was going to, but decided to wait until his bandages are removed. That means, of course, that he goes home at normal hours. Quite unlike the rest of you. So, I want Leo under a 24/7 surveillance until further notice. That is, of course, other than the times that J.B. is with him. I also want his house staked out. Any questions?"

"I do," Ferndale said. "What's going on, Cap? Do you think Leo is involved somehow with this case, or do you think he's our perp?"

"Yes and yes. We received an inside tip that Leo might be the serial killer we're chasing." Warner received looks from anger to disbelief. "What's with the faces? You've all been sitting here while all the accusations have been made against Leo. Now you act like you're surprised."

"I think we're just overwhelmed that it really could be Leo," Roitstein commented.

"I know. I know. It puts a sour taste in my mouth to even say that one of our own could be our snake. At this point, he is only a suspect. But under no circumstances do I want him to know we suspect him. If it were anyone else, we would immediately pick him up bring him in for extensive questioning. However, since he is one of ours, I want to give him the benefit of the doubt until our suspicions are proven or dismissed. If any of the other detectives ask what job you're working on, lie through your teeth. But make it convincing. There's no sense in starting unqualified rumors."

"Why don't we just be honest and tell them we're still working on the serial case, especially since the perp struck again two days ago?" Brown suggested.

"That suggestion will work as long as you follow this rule of thumb: If Leo comes to any of you with any questions about this case, send him to me."

"There's another thing I just thought of, Cap," Roitstein said. "Do you know how Leo said he cut his hand back around the time of the third double homicides?"

Warner nodded. "Yes, I heard from the rumor mill that he cut it while cleaning a knife from his collection. I never had any need to doubt the rumor. So it was never checked out."

"Damn, I didn't even know he had a knife collection," Ferndale said. "Since most of the killings have been by slitting the victims' throats, that's yet another strike against him. Don't you think, Cap?"

"I'm afraid I have to agree with you."

"What about DNA, Cap? Can't we get a sample of his blood?" Mayfield asked.

"I will, eventually. At the risk of repeating myself, I don't want to tip him off that he is a suspect. I want him checked out *first*. However, in your investigation, Brenda, you can check all the hospitals in the area. Find out if Leo was in the emergency room at one of them on the night in question. If he was, get the exact time he arrived and when he left."

"You're talking about the morning of the third killings?"

"Yes."

"A task force against one of our own," Mayfield said, shaking his head. "I knew there were dirty cops around. But I never dreamed that I'd be working with one, or involved with flushing one out."

"None of us did, Arjay. None of us did. If Leo is our perp, we'll throw the book at him so fast he won't know what hit him," Warner stated. "If he's in the clear and this is all some crazy theory, we will all breathe better. Again, I can't stress enough to keep this under your hats. Until we get some positive evidence against Leo, we don't need Internal Affairs butting in to our investigation. Okay, get to work."

"What about my report on the last homicides?" Ferndale asked, waving her papers in the air.

"Leave your report on my desk. I'll go over it. If I have any questions, I'll let you know."

CHAPTER THIRTY

Father, *HE*'s out of control again. I want HIM to stop. Make HIM stop, please, Father. I beg of you. You and Mother created HIM and now, somehow, you've got to destroy HIM before HE kills again. This last time before HE struck, I tried with all my power to stop HIM. But HE was too forceful. I wanted to be like HIM, strong and powerful. But, now, I no longer wish to be like any part of HIM. I have a wonderful life with a loving wife and child, but HE comes in and disrupts everything. No, my little family doesn't even know that HE exists. And I hope HE never shows HIS ugly face when they are around.

The nightmares of what I've seen, what HE has done, tear me to pieces. The dreams are so real that I wake up wounded and bleeding. Yes, I believe they are nightmares because when I see HIM it is generally in the middle of the night. It's as if I have been floating in space or walking in my sleep. When I wake up, HE's gone. Sometimes I think my face is on HIS body. It's almost like I am the one that is committing these treacherous crimes.

I think I'm losing my mind at times. Since I've been married, my wife and I have shared your old room together. Now, I've had to move out of the bedroom because of these violent dreams. I'm afraid I'll hurt my wife. We moved my little one in with my wife; I moved to my old bedroom. Alone again. HE's destroying my life!

It is 3:00 a.m. in the morning. I couldn't sleep because I had this terrible feeling come over me. I felt as if I knew HE would appear tonight. I've never felt this gut warning before. I thought if I stayed awake, I could keep him from appearing again. I have my door locked, but I know there are no barriers strong enough to keep HIM away from me. I … No! Stop! I feel his presence trying to take over. HE's too overpowering …

What a weakling Jessie turned out to be. Yes, it's me. I bet you thought you were rid of me. Sorry to disappoint you.

The time has come for me to tell you what I truly think of you. Father. You, too, Mother. Mother and Father. Ha! That's a joke. I hate you! I hate you both. You and you alone are responsible for creating this overwhelming hate that burns like the fires of hell inside me. I hope the two of you burn in hell through all eternity. Do I cry for you? Never! Do I have remorse for what I did or am doing? Never! You never wanted me in your lives. I don't need to know the reasons behind what you did or why you did it. I already know. It's because both of you are evil.

Quit trying to fool me by placing yourselves in front of me disguised as other people. I know it is really you two under those human masks. You can't fool me. I'm smarter than you are. Why can't you just stay buried under the flower garden? I know why. Because you're both as evil today as you were the day you died. You work for the devil, and he allows you to come back and taunt me. Well, I'll keep fighting. What's more, I'll win.

I'll kill and keep killing until I've defeated you once and for all.

CHAPTER THIRTY-ONE

According to the doctor, Konklin was healing much better, physically, than expected. He had been transferred to a care unit in the hospital and put on a regular daily schedule of rigorous physical therapy. A nurse had just wheeled him back to his room in a wheelchair just as Warner arrived for a visit.

"Hey, Eddy, out for a spin I see."

"Yeah, in a convertible with mag wheels and a good-looking woman as my chauffeur."

With Warner's assistance, the blushing nurse helped Konklin to an overstuffed chair. Once he was made comfortable, the nurse left the room. Warner pulled up a chair, then sat facing his friend.

"So, big guy, what's the good word from your therapists."

"Which one?"

"Well, let's start with the physical therapist since you just got back from there."

"My prognosis isn't good as far as my physical condition is concerned, Joe. I was told I may never walk again." Warner tried to keep a smile on his face, but Konklin saw through it. "Oh, don't give me the sad eyes, Joe. You know I'm a tough cookie. I'm going to beat this rap."

Warner patted him on the arm. "That's the spirit. So what progress have you made with the PTA?"

"Not much there either, I'm afraid. Melody still comes to see me once a day. But I can't see where any of the sessions are doing any good. I feel like an idiot."

"Why do you say that?"

"They make me play these stupid word, picture, and noise games. Geez, Joe, what am I supposed to be remembering anyhow?"

"I can't tell you because …." Warner stopped talking when he noticed Konklin's attention was drawn away from him.

From behind him, Warner heard, "Go ahead and give him a clue."

Warner turned and smiled. "Hello, Melody," he greeted, getting to his feet.

"Good morning, Joe. Hi, Eddy. How's my favorite patient today?"

"Better now that you and Joe are both here."

"Are you ready for our session?"

"Not really. Joe just got here."

"That's okay, Eddy. I should leave anyway."

"No, Joe, please stay," Abrams insisted. "You might be able to help while you're here."

"I'll try. What do you want me to do?"

"Give him some clues. So far none of the word associations I've given him have brought back any of Eddy's recent memories. Perhaps if you could tell him something without going into details, it might tick a familiar incident."

"Come on, you two," Konklin rebelled, smiling. "I'm right here. Not in the next room. Talk to me."

"So you are, big guy. Does the term abusive parents ring a bell?"

Konklin dropped his sight to the floor. The tile was white with a spattering of gray flecks. When he spotted a tiny fleck design that reminded him of a snowflake, he fixed his eyes on it. While Konklin appeared to be in deep thought, Warner pulled up another chair for Abrams. They both sat down.

Breaking the silence, Warner asked, "Anything come to mind?"

"Nothing," he admitted, looking back at Warner. "Give me something else."

"Victims with cut throats."

Since staring at the floor had not helped, this time Konklin closed his eyes. After a few seconds, he opened his eyes. "Again, nothing, Joe. But I remember wearing a policeman's uniform."

"That's a good sign," Abrams remarked.

"Can you give me something else?"

Before Warner could answer, Abrams interceded. "No. I think that's enough for now, Eddy."

"Okay. But I'll think about what you told me, Joe. If I come up with anything, I'll let you know."

"Look, I've already taken up enough of Melody's valuable time. So I'll be on my way." Warner stood and put his chair back in place. Then he walked back to Konklin's chair. "You keep working at getting well, both physically and mentally, chubby cheeks. I'll be back to see you tomorrow."

Abrams stood. "Eddy, if you'll excuse me for a minute, I want to speak with Joe in the hall."

"If it's about me, I think I ought to hear."

"No, it's not about you. I'll be right back."

Abrams brought Warner up to date on Konklin's progress. Even though he was improving, the progess was slow.

"That's good news for Eddy, but I really needed his memory back now. I'm working on a new aspect of this case that I'm almost sure he has vital information on. Look, Melody, I'm sorry. That sounded rather callous. It didn't come out the way I meant. I'm totally pleased that you're optimistic about Eddy regaining his memory."

"Don't worry. I understand what you meant. From what I've seen, Eddy doesn't have a better friend than you've been. Now I really must get back in there."

"Thanks, Melody. I appreciate you being candid with me."

CHAPTER THIRTY-TWO

Sitting in the passenger seat while De Mija drove the department's car, Brown started digging into De Mija's mind. "So Leo, since we're going to be working together for a while, why don't you tell me about yourself."

"There's not much to tell. I'm married and have one daughter."

"Hey, that's great. I have three sons. Boy are they a handful. What one doesn't think of getting into, the other one does. Many times, it's just plain 'monkey see, monkey do' nonsense. I bet you don't have that problem with just one little girl?"

"No."

"I have to give my boys a swat on the seat, now and then, to make them mind," Brown stated, trying his best to lure De Mija into a leading conversation. "Do you believe in spankings?"

"No. I believe children are just small adults and should be treated as such. As a grownup, I wouldn't want to be spanked or yelled at. Would you?"

"Spanked, no. But I've been yelled at a time or two. However, children are children, not grownups. I believe children need to mind. A good old-fashioned spanking never hurt anyone. I'm talking about a spanking, of course, not a beating. There is a big difference."

Keeping his eyes on his driving, De Mija remarked, "Not in my book. I don't go for either. In fact, it infuriates me to see a child spanked. Just hearing about it makes the hair on the back of my neck stand up."

"Do your parents like to spoil your daughter like my parents do?"

"My parents aren't around."

"Do they live out of town?"

"They're both deceased. Say, what are we supposed to be looking for, anyway? All Cap said was that we had patrol duty for the next few weeks. I don't understand why we're not working on finding that serial killer."

"Cap is waiting for the Crime Lab report on the last homicide, for one thing. You should know by now that those reports can take weeks sometimes. There's nothing else we can do but wait. In the meantime, we have to earn our pay." He laughed. "I guess Lieu never got a chance to tell you that we all take our turns going out on patrol. Sometimes we're lucky and spot something suspicious. We've stopped a lot of fights before they've gotten blown out of proportion this way.

"One day," Brown laughed, "Brenda and I pulled up to a stop sign and we were approached by a car thief. It was a beautiful warm day. Not hot enough for the air conditioner, so we had our windows open. This perp stuck a gun to Brenda's head and demanded that the two of us get out. Well, let me tell you, he picked the wrong car to highjack. Brenda got out of the car.

When she did, she blocked his view from watching me. I jumped out of the passenger side, drew my gun, and aimed for his hand. *Boom!* With one clear shot, I hit his hand and the gun dropped. You should have seen the look on that's guy's face." Still laughing, Brown added, "It was worth a million."

"Weren't you afraid he could have shot Brenda in the head?"

"Oh, no. I'm a good shot but not foolish. He had already moved the gun away from her head when she exited the car." Just as smooth as ice, Brown slid back to digging into De Mija's personal life. "So, where do you live, Leo? Do you live close to the precinct?"

"Nope. We live farther out of the city, closer to the mountains."

"That must be quite a drive to work and back, not to mention the heavy traffic."

"Not really. I'm still on the east side. And I know all the back roads. Even short cuts most drivers aren't aware of. I can be anywhere on this side of town within a matter of minutes."

"Boy, I envy you. We can't even see the mountains from where we live. Do you have a good view of them from where you live?"

"Yes."

Brown continued to pry. "No neighbors to block your view, huh?"

"Nope. We're really out in the country. Houses in my area are set pretty far apart from one another."

"But you do know your neighbors, right?"

"Only by sight. The wife and I don't socialize."

"Oh, that's a real shame, Leo. You're missing out on the great suburban life. Sometimes we have backyard barbecues and get-togethers with our neighbors. Of course it's not like it used to be back in the fifties. Those were the days."

"You don't appear to be that old, J.B.'

"Me?" Brown let out a hearty laugh. "I'm not. My parents always talk about how great the fifties were. According to my mom, back then it was nothing to block off a street so the whole neighborhood could have a grand time together. That's when most mothers didn't work and families did things together. We always make time for our boys." Realizing he was rambling, Brown got back to his questioning. "Well, if you don't have parents around, and don't socialize with your neighbors, who sits for your daughter when you and your wife want to go out for an evening?"

"There's never any need for a sitter. The both of us like to stay home. As I said, we don't socialize. So we don't have too many friends. And we don't have any relatives in Mt. Pride. If we go out on my time off, we always take my little girl with us."

"Where do you go when you take your daughter with you?"

"You know, I think you're a little too nosey for your own good. Why don't we skip the small talk about my private life and just keep a lookout for whatever we're supposed to be watching for," De Mija stated with a biting tongue.

"Sure, Leo, whatever you say. I was just trying to be friendly and make small talk."

    Brown did not dare write anything down or De Mija might have gotten suspicious. He had to make a mental note of everything De Mija said so he could report back to Joe.

CHAPTER THIRTY-THREE

A few days later, much to Warner's disappointment, the chief summoned Warner to his office for distressing news.

"Dammit, Ed. You can't retire Eddy. That will kill him," Warner objected loudly.

"I'm sorry, Joe. I have no other choice. According to the reports, that you just verified, Konklin may never walk again. And who knows when his mind will straighten out. I just have no other recourse. You've got to face facts that he isn't fit to carry a badge any longer."

Shaking his head, Warner rose from the chair he was seated in, and walked over to look out Chief Doogle's window. As he watched the traffic, and people walking along the sidewalks, his eyes welled with tears. *I can't believe that Eddy will never be able to walk, or never work as a detective again. I know what his doctor and the therapists say. But I know Eddy. He is strong-willed.*

Warner stood there for a few moments, fluttering his eyelids. He did not want the chief to see his tearful eyes. Confident his eyes were clear, he turned back toward the chief. "Ed, let's be reasonable here. It hasn't even been two months yet since Eddy's accident. Don't you think we could give him a little more time to heal?"

"It will be two months the day after tomorrow if you want to split hairs."

"Put yourself in his place, Ed. How would you feel if the force gave up on you?"

"You're working on a serial killer case. And you're already shorthanded, especially with Konklin in the hospital. You're better off to get him off the payroll so you can hire another detective. Which reminds me, you still haven't filled Landall's position."

"Hiring *ten* more detectives on this case wouldn't even help us right now," Warner bitterly stated. "Please, Ed, give Eddy at least thirty more days. Then if his reports are still negative, I'll concede."

Doogle leaned back and rocked in his chair. As he moved his toothpick about in his mouth, he debated between what was right for the department and what was fair to Konklin.

"Look, Ed, I took some pictures of the *Black Tulip* case over to the hospital yesterday. The woman that's working with Eddy is going to start showing them to him. Hopefully they will bring about some good results. I believe all of my men are worth fighting for, but especially Eddy. His experience is priceless to our unit."

"Okay, Joe, you've got until the first of July. No longer. If he hasn't shown any improvement by then, I have to retire him with a pension for getting injured on the job. That's my final word."

Not at all happy with Doogle's final decision, Warner could only hope that Konklin would recover in time to keep his job. "That's not thirty days, but you're the boss."

"That's right. I am. So, what have you been doing about replacing Landall?"

"Each time I get a spare moment, I've been checking records on your uniforms. So far I've come up with three good candidates."

"Who are they?"

"Keep in mind, I still believe in promoting from my own precinct."

"I understand."

"I've narrowed it down to Officers Ripley, Sooner and Kaufman."

"All three are excellent officers, Joe. As much as I hate to lose any of them, I would say Kaufman has the best nose for detective work. He's also been on the force a lot longer than the other two have. I was surprised you overlooked him when you promoted De Mija."

"Well, credit where credit is due, chief. If you recall, Al Kaufman was a leading contender, right along with Leo De Mija. Even though Eddy gave me his admirable input, you, too, couldn't say enough good things about Leo."

Doogle felt a tinge of guilt. A feeling he found very distasteful. "Wait a minute, Joe. I didn't know De Mija was a dirty cop when I recommended him."

"Hell, Eddy and I didn't either. Look, don't get your shorts in a bind, Ed. I take full responsibility for Leo's promotion from uniform to detective. I'm just saying, I want a little more time before I make my final decision as to who I want working in my department."

* * *

When he got back to his office, Warner called the hospital to speak to Abrams.

"Hi, Joe. I'm glad you called. Eddy was asking for you today."

"I haven't had time to stop in and see him yet. I'm calling to find out how your session with him went today."

"I showed him the picture you gave me of the baby rattle. He stared off into the distance and said he heard a baby crying. But he can't remember why. The other pictures didn't mean anything to him."

"Remembering a baby crying should be a good sign, Melody. That would fit into one of the homicides he was working on?"

"That's good to hear. Maybe there's more progress than I realized."

"So, what happens next?"

"I'll take the same pictures back in there tomorrow. I'm also going to take along some tapes with baby cries."

"Right now, anything is worth a shot. Okay, Melody, I'll check back with you tomorrow. Thank you."

"Wait, Joe. Are you going to be able to visit Eddy today?"

"Definitely. But it won't be for an hour or so."

"I'm at the nurses' station by his room. Before I leave, I'll pop in and tell him to expect you. I know he'll be pleased."

As soon as Joe hung up the phone, he looked in his card file for Dr. Richards' phone number. He was fortunate to get the busy doctor on the phone without too long a wait.

"Dr. Richards."

"Hello, Miles. This is Joe Warner."

"What can I do for you today, Joe?"

"Your honest opinion as to Eddy's recovery?"

"Well, you're in luck. I was just going over my latest reports. I had a serious of x-rays taken, and it looks like his bones have healed much better than I anticipated. Because of his age, I was a little worried. But now he shows promise of complete recovery."

Warner gasped. "That's wonderful news. How's his physical therapy going?"

"Obviously you haven't spoken with Eddy today?"

"No, I haven't. I just got off the phone with Melody, but she didn't say anything. What happened?"

"I spoke with his physical therapist earlier. Seems Eddy was capable of standing today with the support of crutches. Getting to his feet is a real achievement."

Not being able to contain his joy, Warner excitedly asked, "Does that mean he'll be able to walk again?"

"I've told you before, I'm very optimistic that he will — in time. However, don't get your hopes up as far as work is concerned. If and when he does walk, I don't see Eddy going back to work for quite some time yet."

"Yes, I understand. As much as I'd like to have him back to work, his health is more important to me. I won't keep you any longer. Thank you for the good news. Good bye."

"Anytime, Joe. Bye for now."

Disconnecting his phone call, Warner immediately made another call.

"Chief Doogle."

"Ed, this is Joe. Look, I just spoke with Eddy's physician. He told me that Eddy stood on his own today."

"Well, Joe, that is good news. However --"

"Wait, Ed, he also said Eddy needs a lot more therapy before he walks again. But he's hopeful he *will* walk. With this good news, I wanted to ask if you would extend your deadline. I just can't stress it enough that Eddy's been too good a detective to just put him out to pasture."

"Joe, you've got better things to do with your time right now, I assume, than to be worrying about the lieutenant. Let's get to the beginning of July. Then we'll go from there. Now, if there's nothing else, I have a meeting to attend."

With that, the chief hung up the phone. Warner sat there holding the receiver, as thoughts whirled around in his head.

He's right. I do have better things to do. I just can't help worring about Eddy. Ed, you old geezer, you don't abandon a friend when he's down and out. I'm not about to give up on my friend and co-worker. I don't care what you say.

Warner finally laid the receiver in its cradle. As hard as he tried reading some of the reports stacked on the desk, he couldn't concentrate. Looking at the clock he decided to go visit his friend.

* * *

A mile-wide grin adorned Konklin's face when Warner walked into his room. "Hi Joe. Boy, am I ever glad to see you. I thought you forgot about me today."

"Not a chance, Eddy. I just got too busy at the office."

"I've got some great news." He beamed with delight.

"Well, lay it on me, big guy."

"I stood today. Isn't that the greatest?"

"That *is* the greatest, Eddy. It's the best news I've had in a long time. So, when do you take your first steps?"

"We're going to try tomorrow. Down in the physical therapy room they have this little walk with guardrails on both sides."

"That's wonderful. Say, what exactly do they do for you — or to you — down in therapy?"

"Ah, you don't want to hear about all that boring stuff."

"Sure I do, Eddy. I'm curious."

"Well, they put this machine on me that sends out little electrical shocks to stimulate my muscles. Then they use this other funny machine that has heat in it."

"What kind of machines are they?"

"Oh, come on, Joe. I don't ask what they are. I just know they're supposed to help me, so I don't ask questions."

"For crying out loud, Eddy. Do you take a pill the nurse brings you without asking the name of it or what it's for?"

"Of course. I figure they know what they're giving me. So why bother?"

Warner laughed. "You're too much. So then what do they do?"

"Well, my therapist spends quite a while on bending and working with my injured limbs. Then he makes me lift some weights. Sometimes I can hardly bear the pain. Look," he said, bending his arm and wiggling his fingers, "I'm beginning to use my arm and hand again. It's a little sore, but it sure feels good to know the broken bones are all back together. At lunch today, I held a fork in my hand for the first time since I've been here. "

"Great. That ugly mug of yours looks a lot better, too." Konklin suddenly clammed up, put his chin down, and looked away from Warner. "Hey, Eddy, did I say something wrong?"

"I looked in a mirror for the first time today. Why didn't you tell me some of my front teeth were knocked out?"

Speechless, Warner thought, *Damn. I was talking about his scruffy whiskers being gone. I didn't realize he didn't know about his teeth.*

"What's the matter, Joe?" Konklin asked, turning back for an answer. "Lost your tongue? There's no cat in here."

"I'm sorry, Eddy. I guess I thought you already knew. How could you not know?"

"For many good reasons. Look around the room. There's no mirror in here."

Glancing around, he asked, "I guess not. But isn't there one in the bathroom?"

"Yes. But when you have to be lifted from your wheelchair to the can, you really don't feel like asking a nurse to hold you up in front of a mirror."

"When I mentioned you looking better, I was referring to the beard you'd been growing. It's obvious you're now clean-shaven. So what about when you shaved today, or the times you've brushed your teeth? Don't you look in the mirror then?"

"When you're right-handed and your right hand is out of commission, and the left hand doesn't work so well either, you can't do too much for yourself. The nurses and their aides have been taking care of me like I was a baby. Today was the first time I could even feed myself, Joe. No way am I ready to hold a razor in my hand — straight-edged or electric."

Warner did not know if he was asking so many questions because he was curious, or to satisfy his own guilty conscious for not saying anything about the missing teeth. "How about your tongue? Moving it about in your mouth ... well, wouldn't that have been your first clue?"

"Sure it would, to someone in their right mind. One of the nurses made a comment to me a few days ago about my teeth. But at the time I thought they must have been that way for a long time. I figured it was just something else I didn't remember. I guess everyone else around here was too embarrassed to say anything. Today, after one of the aides shaved me, he held up a hand-mirror for me. As soon as I opened my mouth, I remembered that I used to have all of my teeth. Let me tell you, Joe, it was quite a shock."

"That's good news, Eddy."

"What?"

"Oh, I didn't mean it that way. I mean it's good news that you remembered something that important. Did you tell Melody?"

"No," Eddy grunted.

"I think you should. To tell you the truth, I was more worried about your total health, not just your teeth. It didn't even cross my mind to say anything to you. But, hey, the dentists have great technology today. They can fix you up so well, no one will ever be able to tell the fake from the real teeth once they're finished with you. Do you have a dentist?"

"Yes."

"Why don't you call and ask him to stop by and take a look at your teeth. He can explain what he can do for you. If not, I'm sure he can recommend a good --"

"Geez, Joe, dentists don't make house calls," Konklin interrupted with a laugh, quickly covering his mouth.

"I think, under the circumstances, one would. If your dentist won't, you just let me know. I'll find one that will. And put your hand down. I've looked at your ugly mug for a long time now. A few missing ivories just adds personality to it," he joked. "Besides, you were getting too serious there. I love to hear you laugh again. So, let's get back to your physical therapy. Is that all that goes on when you're there?"

"Other than a long soak in the Jacuzzi and a good rub down, that's about it. What do you want to know all this stuff for anyway?"

"I was thinking about moving you to our house when you get out of here. Amandalee said she would help me with you, but I wanted to know everything your therapy consisted of."

"No way. I mean, that's awfully nice of you to offer, but I wouldn't want to impose. You and Amandalee have your hands full already, especially when you need to help Jeny. That reminds me, how's Amandalee doing on her job?"

"You remember she's working?"

"Sure I do. She's an ADA. Why? Oh, is that something I had forgotten?"

"Yes, it is, Eddy. But that's another good sign. Do you remember anything else?"

"Something tells me your daughter was supposed to move into her own apartment. Right?"

"Right."

"Then that's another reason for me not to impose on you. Poor Jeny would be the one stuck caring for me. I won't have it."

"Okay, we'll discuss that later. What else do you remember?"

"I keep hearing a baby cry. Then when I stop to concentrate on why, I see a small child looking at me calling me dada. But that can't be, Joe. I've never had any children of my own."

"We've been working on a case that involves children, Eddy. That's why you're remembering those things."

"But the Epsteins don't have any children. Neither do the Lains. You know, I just can't remember if we're calling it the Epstein case or the *Have No Mercy* case?"

Warner took it upon himself to say more than he probably should have. But he had to take a chance that he might help his friend, not cause a setback. "It doesn't make any difference. We closed that case years ago. We've been working on a new case since January."

"What? Geez, Joe, why wouldn't I remember something as important as that?"

"According to Melody, it's all part of your mental process."

"Did we ever catch the perp on the case I remember?"

"Yes."

Suddenly Konklin burst out with, "The ocean was involved. Right? I see something about an ocean."

"Right. What else do you remember about that case?"

"That's all. Sorry."

"Do you remember how to use a computer?"

"Did I ever learn?"

"You bet, and you were getting pretty good at it. When you get your ticket out of here, I'm going to see to that you have a computer at home. I suggested the idea to Miles. He agrees it will help strengthen the movement of your hands. And, it may also help your memory."

"I don't know how it can help me if I don't even remember how to use one."

"Well, we won't worry about that right now. Listen, I've got to skat. I'll be back tomorrow, as usual."

"Give Jeny and Amandalee my love."

"I sure will, Eddy. That reminds me, they want to come up and visit you. Since you're feeling much better, do you mind?"

"Geez, Joe, of course I don't mind. I'd love to see them. Besides, they're much prettier to look at than you are. Just warn them first about my missing teeth." Konklin quickly turned his joyfulness to sobriety. "Speaking of pretty, I'm worried about Sheri. She hasn't been up to see me. I hope nothing's happened to her. You know she's carrying our first child, Joe. Would you mind terribly if I asked you to check on her for me?"

Not knowing exactly what to say or how to react to the request, Warner was once again without words. He wished that Abrams would magically appear to help him out. If he told Konklin the truth, it might bring about more depression. That was exactly what Abrams had warned him against doing. On the other hand, how could Konklin move forward in his memories unless he knew the truth of the past? Warner made a decision he hoped would not come back and haunt him. "Eddy, Sheri won't be coming to see you. Sheri's … well, she's been deceased for years. She was killed in a terrible accident."

Eddy slumped into the pillows that lined the bed from his head to his back. He tried to get his mind clear with the visual picture Warner had just painted for him. Unfortunately, the images were far too fuzzy for him to make any sense of them. Highly depressed and ready to give up, something flashed through his brain. "Geez, I should have remembered that. Sheri was killed in a boating accident many years ago, wasn't she?"

"Yes, Eddy, she was."

"Thanks for reminding me, Joe. Here I've been worried sick as to why she hasn't so much as called me. My mind just keeps playing tricks on me and I get all confused."

"Are you okay with hearing such bad news?"

Konklin reached over and patted Warner's hand. "Of course I am. I won't lie to you. It's hard to grasp such a disappointment. But I'm glad you told me the truth. Maybe if everyone would start telling me the truth, instead of treating me like a two-year old, I'd remember more."

"Take it easy, big guy. Your mental healing is just like your walking. Take it one step at a time."

CHAPTER THIRTY-FOUR

Warner was amazed at how well the work scheduling was going. Putting their heads together, the detectives worked it out so everyone had a chance to go home, spend time with their families, and sleep in their own beds — at least once in a while. The schedule also cut down on overtime pay. No one had to say a word. But the unit just knew their captain was footing the food bill. So any way they could help keep extra costs at a minimum, they did.

To keep other expenses from rising, even the detectives' wives were helping. Several took it upon themselves to keep the bedding in the unit's sleep-room laundered. Others would pitch in by bringing the unit an occasional homemade meal.

When Warner called the special task force (those engaged to check into De Mija's life) into his office, Detective Roitstein did not attend. It was his shift to keep a watchful eye on De Mija.

"It's been a while since you've started your background search and surveillance on Leo. I don't mean to show any prejudice against you *guys*. But I want to hear from Brenda, first."

"Ladies first, again," Del Ginny jibed.

"Look, Tony, when I'm at work, I'm a cop — same as you. Got it?"

"Hold it. Let's stop the BS."

"Sorry, Cap. But I've just about had it with the snide remarks just because I'm a female."

After Del Ginny apologized, Warner said, "Okay, Brenda. Let's hear it."

"I don't have any good news, Cap. As of right now, I'm at a dead end."

Jumping the gun, Warner said, "So that's it? Nothing?"

"Not really. But I'm not sure any of the information I've collected is going to help us."

"Every little thing we find out about Leo is important. So, what did you learn about him?"

"Before he entered the police academy, Leo attended college here in Mt. Pride."

"Which we already knew from his employee records," Warner stated.

"Right. The college administration office showed me Leo's personal files. This gave me his date of birth, where he was born, his address, where he graduated high school, and the names of his parents. From there, I checked with vital statistics. There is absolutely nothing on record for a Leo De Mija. It's like he was dropped from outer space and mysteriously appeared one day here in Mt. Pride," she said, shrugging.

"You're telling me Leo got into college with falsified records?"

"At this point, that's how it looks. But here's what's strange. Leo did give his correct residential address on his college records. It's the same house he still resides in today. The deed to Leo's house is in his name, and he's owned it since before he even started college."

"His house is bought and paid for?"

"That's right."

"What kind of a job did Leo have before or while attending college?"

"As far as I can determine, he didn't work."

"That can only add up to one simple explanation. Leo came from a family with money. Who did he purchase the house from?"

"The previous owner was Alex Vernon."

"Have you checked him out yet? Maybe he can offer some info on Leo."

"Not yet, Cap. But he's on the top of my list."

"When you checked vital statistics, did you check his marriage certificate?"

"Yes. He was married right after he joined the force."

"And he was married under the name Leo De Mija?"

"Yes, Cap."

"Anything else?"

"Not right now."

"J.B., what have you been able to find out?"

"Leo lives out in the country, close to the mountains. He has no close neighbors. According to him, he has no relatives in the area. And, he has no close friends."

"He wasn't even close to his ex-partner, Officer Ripley?"

"Not according to Leo," Brown replied.

"I find that difficult to understand. What a lonely life that must be. Continue."

"I found out he's a loving and devoted husband and father. Most of all, he hates — with a red-hot passion — parents who abuse their kids. I mean, Cap, this man is adamant when you even bring up the subject of spanking or yelling at kids. I tried to get more info out of him. But several times he just flat out told me to mind my own business."

"Were you able to find out anything about his parents?"

"Yeah. Leo told me, in one of his better moods, that his parents had decided to do some traveling. One day on their trip there was a terrible thunderstorm. The rain was beating down so hard it evidently marred their vision. They drove off a cliff and the car caught on fire. Leo said their bodies were badly burned by the time help finally arrived. They were pronounced dead at the scene. He said with what little remains were left, he had them both cremated and their ashes were scattered in the area where they had died. That's all I have, Cap."

"Did you verify the accident?"

Shaking his head, Brown explained, "The only info I got out of Leo was that the accident happened while he was still in high school. When I asked him where it happened, he immediately changed the subject. It was like he told me more than he had planned on, so he clammed up. I wouldn't even know where to begin to look. The accident could have happened in any state, and any year for the past --"

"Okay, J.B.," Warner interrupted. "I understand. Is that it?"

"Yes, sir."

"Arjay, do you have anything to report on the stake-out?"

"Leo's very boring," Mayfield stated. The group laughed, nodding in agreement. "When he leaves for work in the morning, he comes straight here. After work, he goes straight home. In the evenings, he stays home — with the exception of taking his car to the station to fill up with gas. On the weekends, I've followed him to a couple of flea markets, rummage sales, pawnshops, the zoo, the park, and to the grocery store. Most times his wife accompanied him, but he always had his daughter with him. I have nothing on him out of the ordinary."

With a slight hand motion, Ferndale caught the captain's attention.

"Yes."

"I just thought of a couple more things, Cap."

"Go ahead."

"Do you realize that the printers we have in the other room are the same bubble-jet printers you had Arnie and Eric checking out?"

Raising an eyebrow, Warner stated, "No, I didn't. Whoa, wait a minute. If I understand the point you're making, Leo wasn't even a detective back in January. He wouldn't have had access to these printers at that time."

Brown spoke up. "I hate to differ with you, Cap. But he could have very easily. He was a uniform working the graveyard shift at that time. It wouldn't have been out of place for him to be around the precinct during hours that our office wasn't in full operation. He could have sneaked up to our floor when no one was around. No one, not even the desk sergeant downstairs, can see us come and go unless we purposely stop by the front desk. Man, it would have been easy for him to get up here, print out what he needed, and then leave, unnoticed. Add to that fact that he was computer-literate even then — one, two, three, he's home free."

"We shouldn't forget either," Mayfield added, "that Leo says he's got a computer setup at home. He could have a bubble-jet printer there, too."

"Since we don't know for sure what kind of printer he has at home, let's rule that out for the moment. However, as you just stated, J.B., Leo had the opportunity to use one of our department's computers and its printer for making up the calling card. Leo also had a window of opportunity to have committed these crimes. That brings us back to the night the Carney murders occurred. Brenda. Did you check out Leo's alibi for that night?"

"Yes. I checked all the major hospitals in our area. Not one of them had a record for Leo during the hours in question."

"There goes one vital alibi out the window. Well, gang, none of this does us much good right now. All I can say is keep digging."

CHAPTER THIRTY-FIVE

Stepping inside Warner's office, Ferndale asked, "Got an hour to spare? I've got some intriguing news."

"For an hour, it better be worth it," Warner quipped. "Come on in and have a seat."

"I think it is." Carrying a manila folder full of papers, Ferndale sat in the closest chair to the captain's desk.

As she opened the folder, Warner's eyes widened. "Those papers aren't for me to sign, I hope?"

"No. These are all my notes on the information I want to tell you about."

"Good news, I hope?"

"Well, if it gives Leo a motive for murder, I'd say so."

"Hot damn, Brenda. What did you find out?"

"Do you want the info in detail or brief form?"

"Details. I want to hear it all."

"Okay, after digging through records and interviewing a lot of people, here's what I found out about Alex Vernon." Ferndale went on to explain everything she had discovered about the Vernons.

When she completed her verbal report, Warner asked, "So what ever happened to them?"

"According to one of the locals in the area of De Mija's house, Mr. and Mrs. Vernon moved out of state. They haven't been heard of since. But here's where it really gets crazy. According to vital statistics, Mrs. Vernon never gave birth to a child — not even a stillborn."

"What did they do, adopt?"

"No. And you're not going to believe this. I finally found a contact, Dick Smythe, in a rest home. He had worked with Alex Vernon years ago. And here's what he told me …."

"*Black Market*!" Warner raged.

"That's right, Cap."

"That's not only illegal as hell but disgusting. Who were the birth parents that would even do such a thing?"

"I have no clue. That's just one of those dead ends I keep running into."

"What about the kid?"

"As far as the neighbors know, she left town shortly after high school graduation."

"Other than Leo purchasing the Vernon's house, how are the two of them connected?"

"I couldn't find any other connection. But here's my theory. Maybe

Leo knew the Vernons before they left town. If so, he could have been witness to the way the Vernons treated the child they took in. If so, that could have started his hatred for what he believes to be abusive parents."

"You might have something there, Brenda. I don't think the Vernons are any longer our concern. However, I would still like to know how Leo managed with no income to purchase a home."

"Oh, but he was receiving an income. I don't know what his pay was, but here's what I found out …."

When Ferndale was finished feeding Warner all the information she had gathered together, Warner said, "Brenda, if I weren't a married man, I could kiss you." Ferndale grinned. "Get the crew rounded up, on the double. We need to get this ball rolling downhill."

* * *

Ferndale explained her discoveries to the rest of the detectives. Then Warner took over the meeting.

"Remember now, Brenda's last statements are just her theory. It may or may not be the motive behind these homicides. However, I think we have enough circumstantial evidence to forge ahead. We'll need a couple of search warrants. Hopefully we'll find the murder weapon in Leo's possession." Warner checked the time. "It's getting late, but hang tight." Warner made an important telephone call. As he hung up the phone, he nodded and smiled at the detectives.

"Good news, right Cap?" Mayfield asked.

"Yes. The judge wasn't too happy that I bothered him at home, but he will issue the warrants we need." Warner reached into his desk file drawer and pulled out two Search Warrant Affidavits. As he filled in the required information, he continued talking. "Arjay, you and Brenda take these affidavits over to Judge Nidstrom's residence and pick up the warrants. I'll attach a Post-it note with his address. As you all heard, I asked for the second search warrant for Leo's car."

"If Leo went home, Cap, the one warrant should suffice," Brown said.

"Right. But his car will be here in the parking lot," Warner said, as he continued writing.

Even though his comment did not make any sense at the time, no one said a word. They knew their captain would eventually explain what he meant.

Holding up the completed forms in outstretched hand, Warner said, "Here, Arjay. Take these and stand by."

Mayfield walked to the desk and took the paperwork. He then stood by the door, waiting for further instructions.

Picking up the phone, Warner made another call.

"Yes, cap."

"How did you know it was me calling?"

"Simple. On my cell phone --"

"Never mind. You can explain it to me another time. What's your location?"

"I'm about two hundred feet from Leo's house. He pulled into his drive about an hour ago."

"I'm going to call him back to the office on the pretense that I need him to help on this case. Hopefully he'll cooperate and come in. Keep out of sight, but follow him back. If he gets suspicious and bolts, I want you on his tail so we don't lose him. Let him see you by the time you get to the parking lot here. If he questions you, tell him you were called in, too. I'll be waiting for you when you get here. Oh, in case I'm not in my office, I'll have my cell phone with me. So call me on it if you need to contact me."

"10-4," Roitstein replied.

Warner hung up the telephone.

"Now we understand why you said Leo's car will be here, Cap. You had us all confused there for a minute. Detectives we are. Mind readers we're not," Brown teased.

"Sorry. Guess the gears in my head were turning so fast I didn't explain what I had on my mind. Calling Leo back into the office will give you plenty of time to search his residence. In the interim, I hope to get some questions answered. To be perfectly honest, I'd rather arrest Leo than play these stupid games. But I need a lot more to go on first. By the way, Leo mentioned to me once that he had a hothouse on his property. Don't quote me, but I think that's the same as a greenhouse. When you check it out, see if he's growing any tulips in there." Warner rubbed his tired eyes.

"Black ones, right, Cap?" Brown asked, smiling.

"As if you had to ask," Warner quipped. "Okay, you all know what's happening now. Brenda, keep an eye on my office window. When I give you two the *go* sign, take a car and follow Arjay to the judge's house. When you get the search warrant for the house and grounds, Arjay, go straight to Leo's place. J.B. will meet you there. I'll get Bobby and Bryce over there to assist you two."

"But they don't know we suspect Leo as our perp, do they?"

"No, J.B. But it's about time the whole unit knows what's going on around here. Besides, it certainly won't remain a secret once Leo shows up and I take him into an interrogation room. Brenda, once you get the search warrant for the car, head on back here. I'll have you check out Leo's car while I'm questioning him. I'll send Tony and Mike down to help you. When you're through, come on up to the main office and stand by. If Kieyell contacts me that Leo got wise and starts running, I'll be sure to let you all know. So, everyone, keep your lines open." Warner's stomach gurgled. "It must be dinner time," he remarked with a smile. "Okay, let's move it."

As the detectives filed out of the office, so did Warner. He stopped at Anthony's desk and briefly explained where he wanted Anthony and Brubaker to go and why. They were to wait until Warner gave them the high sign when it was time for them to leave. Then Warner stopped by Del

Ginny's desk where he and Holms were working on some computer data. After a brief explanation to them, Warner told them to wait in the office until De Mija returned. That would be their cue to go down to the parking area to assist Ferndale.

Rayfelt's desk was Warner's last stop in the outside office. Once he explained what was going down, Warner said, "Since you're in charge of the electronic equipment around here, make sure the camera is turned on in interrogation room two, Matt. I also want a detective in the room with me when I question Leo. Hang tight because it may be you."

"No problem, Cap. I'll go right now and make sure the camera's running. We just had it serviced not too long ago. So I know the audio and video are working in top order."

CHAPTER THIRTY-SIX

Back in his office, Warner called De Mija. Having spent so much time on patrol with Brown, De Mija was pleased to be called back to the office to work on the serial homicides.

After the phone call, Warner rapped on his window and gave Ferndale the *thumbs-up* signal. He watched as Detectives Mayfield, Brown, Anthony, and Brubaker played *follow the leader* as they shadowed Ferndale down the steps and out of site.

Then he called Doogle to inform him as to what was taking place. Warner was relieved the chief was behind his actions.

Next was an in-house call to the downstairs officer on duty. Warner knew if De Mija were to get hostile and create a physical disturbance, he and the remaining detectives on duty were capable of handling him. But having another backup was simply taking extra precautionary measures.

Phone calls completed, Warner relaxed, wondering if he had covered all his bases. When his stomach gurgled and grumbled with intensity, he knew he had forgotten one very important telephone call.

"Warner residence."

"Hi, princess."

"Hi, Joe. I gather something came up at the office?"

"Yeah. I'm sorry, honey, but I won't be home until much later this evening."

"I understand. I'll keep your dinner in the oven."

"What did you fix?" Warner asked, feeling the twangs of hunger.

"Not much, just pork chops, baked potatoes, creamed --"

"Stop, you're torturing me." He laughed. "I'm starved, and it sounds delicious."

"Amandalee is here, Joe. Do you want me to fix you a plate and have her bring it up to you?"

"No, princess, but I appreciate the offer."

"You must have something important going on."

"I'll tell you about it later. Right now, I've got to go. I love you."

"I love you, too, Joe. I'll see you when you get here. Bye."

"Bye, honey."

Warner sat back, deep in thought. *Since Eddy seems to be beating all odds in his physical healing, why can't the same be happening with his mental healing? Why can't he at least remember this case we're involved in? When he came out of the coma, his first words to me were, 'Joe, I know it's Leo.' If I only knew for sure what that meant. Did Leo tip his hat in something he said to Eddy just before the accident? Well, sitting here speculating on what Eddy did or didn't mean doesn't get me anywhere. I just have to face it. With or without Eddy's confirmation, I have to believe I'm making the right choice in believing Leo is our snake. It's times like this that I wish I had just remained a detective and said no to being the captain.*

As he slowly swiveled his executive-style desk chair, Warner sat staring out his inner-office window. While most detectives were busy at their desks working on their computers, doing paperwork, or talking on their telephones, others were conversing in small groups.

Before long, Warner spotted De Mija at the top of the steps. Roitstein was a few steps behind him.

When Warner walked out of his office, he greeted De Mija. "Leo, I'm happy you got here so fast." Looking passed De Mija, he noticed Roitstein giving him a *come-hither* motion with his head.

"Well, Cap, you said you needed my help," De Mija responded. "So I figured it was important enough to get back here on the double."

"I really appreciate it, Leo. Since my desk is a mess, I'm going to hold this small meeting in interview room two." Warner pretended to just notice Roitstein. "Kieyell, I'm glad you're back. Hang tight a minute. I want to talk to you."

Then Warner motioned for Rayfelt to join him. "Matt, you and Leo go on into room two. I'll be there shortly." Warner made small talk with Roitstein until he was sure De Mija was out of earshot. "What's up, Kieyell?"

"Did you want me to go down and check out Leo's car?"

"Negative. Brenda should be back any time now with a search warrant to do just that. I'd prefer you come into the room with me for extra backup. Well, here she is now," Warner said, noticing Ferndale bouncing up the steps."

As Ferndale approached Warner and Roitstein, she said, "Is he here?"

"Yes. He's in room two with Matt, waiting for me."

"It just dawned on me. I don't know what Leo's personal car looks like," Ferndale admitted with a smile.

"I do. I'll search the car while you go in with Cap," Roitstein offered.

"Sounds good. But take Tony and Mike with you, Kieyell. I've already told them they'll be helping to search Leo's car. If you see anything suspicious, no matter how minute it seems, get one of the crime scene techs over here to assist you."

"Do Tony and Mike know Leo is our suspect?"

"I briefed them. But I'm sure they'll still have all kinds of questions. Feel free to answer them while you're sweeping the car."

"Got it, Cap."

"Okay, then. Let's do it."

Ferndale followed the captain into the interrogation room, closing the door behind her. De Mija was sitting on the edge of the table, his feet propped on the seat of a vacant chair. Rayfelt was standing close to him, leaning on a chairback. While Ferndale took a seat at the table, Warner walked over to De Mija. After Warner verbally stated the date, time, and all those in attendance, he read De Mija the Miranda. Bewildered, De Mija waived his rights to an attorney. Warner also informed him that everything in the room was being audio and video taped. Still not understanding what was going on, De Mija had no problem with being recorded.

"Leo De Mija, stand and very slowly take your gun out of your holster. Hand it over to Detective Rayfelt," Warner ordered.

"Why? What's going on here?"

"Just do as I say, and we won't have any trouble."

De Mija got to his feet as he removed his gun from the shoulder holster. Instead of handing it to Rayfelt, he placed the gun on the table. Rayfelt picked up the gun and took a step back to wait for further instructions.

"What the devil is going on?"

"You'll find out soon enough." It was a well-known fact that many detectives carried a second weapon hidden on their person in case they needed it for backup. Warner was not taking any chances. "Do you have any other weapons on you?"

"No."

"Then you won't mind if Detective Ferndale frisks you?"

"I'm assuming I don't have a choice in the matter? But if you insist, I'd rather have a man do it. No offense, Brenda."

"No offense taken."

Agreeing to De Mija's request, Warner looked over at Rayfelt to give him the *go ahead* sign. Rayfelt handed De Mija's gun to the captain. De Mija raised his arms in the air.

"He's clean, Cap," Rayfelt said after patting down De Mija.

"Good. Here, take this gun out of here. Put it on my office desk." As Rayfelt left the room, Warner ordered, "Take a chair, Leo."

Reluctantly, De Mija sat down. Before Warner started his interrogation, he thought back to the times he and Konklin had played *good cop-bad cop* with their suspects. That had always worked in the past. Even though Ferndale was an excellent detective, Warner knew De Mija was far too smart for the *good cop-bad cop* routine. Instead, he had to play the tough guy, putting his suspect in the hot seat in hopes of getting De Mija to talk.

"For months you've had the wool pulled over our eyes. Not anymore."

"Honestly, you've got me buffaloed here. I don't have the slightest idea what you're talking about."

"Oh, I hate when skunks like you think they can hide behind a badge and want to play games. Okay, where were you on the night of March 12?"

Rayfelt returned to the room then stood quietly, leaning against a wall.

De Mija looked down at the table trying to remember what he had been doing on the night in question. At that moment, nothing came to mind. "That was three months ago. Right off hand, I don't remember. Why?"

"I'll refresh your memory. The night you injured your hand."

"Oh. That was the night I was at home cleaning one of my knives from my collection. Why?"

"It's hard for me to imagine an owner of a knife collection being careless. How did it happen?"

"Simple. I was paying more attention to TV than I was to what I was doing. The polishing cloth slipped as I was running it over the blade, and I sliced my hand."

Warner took a pen from his pocket and handed it to De Mija. "Show me how you clean the blades of your knife?"

"I don't have a hankie or anything I can use as a cleaning cloth."

"Improvise." After a brief demonstration, Warner said, "Just as I thought. You are holding the pen in your right hand and polishing with your left hand. So how did you manage to cut your right hand if the blade was pointing toward your left hand?"

De Mija looked down at his hands. "Force of habit, Capt. Warner. Normally, I do hold the knives in my left hand and polish with my right hand. Since my right hand has been bandaged for so long now, it's just natural that I baby it. Holding an object in my sore hand is much easier, right now, then moving it back and forth to demonstrate how I polish a blade."

This arrogant piece of crap has an answer for everything, Warner thought before asking, "Who took care of the wound?"

"I went to the emergency room at the twenty-four-hour clinic in my area. I don't understand. I already explained my accident to the lieutenant after it happened. Are you going to tell me why I'm being questioned again about something that happened months ago?"

"What's the name of the clinic?" Warner persisted, taking the pen out of De Mija's hand.

"I don't remember."

"How convenient. Do you know the address of this clinic?"

"It's on East Mountain Road, between Woodman and Collins."

Warner moved his eyes from De Mija to Ferndale. This was Ferndale's cue to leave the room and check out De Mija's alibi. With both hands on the back of a chair, Warner leaned forward. He looked De Mija square in the face. "You know, there's nothing I hate worse than a dirty cop. And you're about as dirty as they come, Leo. You've got innocent blood on your hands and I'm going to prove it."

"Cap --"

"Don't Cap me. You've lost that privilege. From here on out, my name is Capt. Warner to you," he stated with authority.

"Am I under arrest for something, *Capt. Warner?*" De Mija asked with belligerence.

"Should you be?"

"You know I'm not some scumbag you picked up off the street. I know my rights."

"I'm happy to hear that. Since you know the rules and regulations of the law, then you should know you waived your rights after I read you the Miranda. If you don't remember, I can have Detective Rayfelt --"

"That won't be necessary. I know what I said."

"I hear you think that parents who correct their children are abusive parents in your book. They make you angry by spanking or scolding their kids. You get so angry, in fact, you spit fire when you hear about or witness such deeds. Maybe even get angry enough to kill the abusers. Right, Leo?"

Not giving De Mija a chance to answer, Warner kept pounding away for the next hour.

Finally, De Mija spoke up, raising his voice above Warner's insistent questions, statements, and accusations. "Enough. Get to the point, Capt. Warner. I haven't the faintest notion where you're going with this. Again I ask you, are you arresting me? If so, I'd like to know what the charge is."

"Hopefully, it will be for Murder One for eight homicides, De Mija."

De Mija smirked, giving Warner a hateful look. "Man, if you think I'm your snake, you're barking up the wrong tree."

"Am I? We'll see about that."

"This interview is over, Capt. Warner. I want to call my lawyer."

Ferndale opened the door and motioned for Warner to join her outside the room.

"Keep an eye on him, Detective Rayfelt. I'll be right back."

De Mija stood. "I'm leaving."

"Sit down, Leo," Warner ordered. "You're not going anywhere."

"You have no right keeping me here."

"I have every right. Now, if you don't sit down, I'll put you in lock up. Got it?"

Stepping into the hall and closing the door behind him, Warner could still hear De Mija yelling, "You can't do this, Warner. I have my rights. Do you hear me? I want to call my attorney."

Seething inside, Warner asked, "Well, Brenda, was he telling the truth?"

"Yes, he was. I'm sorry it took so long, but Leo gave us the wrong street information. The clinic is on Collins between Woodman and Mountain Road West. The operator had a dickens of a time trying to find it for me."

"Bottom line."

"The nurse at the clinic wouldn't verify the time or any other pertinent information over the phone. I'm going over there. I figure if I show up in person and show her my badge, she'll tell me what we want to know."

"You'll probably need a court order to confiscate the records."

"That won't be necessary, Cap. The nurse said she would be more than willing to cooperate. She just wants to make sure she wasn't receiving a prank phone call. Like she said, anyone can make a phone call and say they are an officer of the law in order to get personal information about a patient. I don't blame her for being cautious."

"Did you get the exact street address of the clinic?"

"Here it is." She held out a slip of paper and offered it to him.

"Hold on a sec." Warner opened the interview room door and asked Rayfelt to step outside. He had Ferndale give Rayfelt the clinic's address, explained what he needed, then sent Rayfelt on his way. "Brenda, keep an eye on Leo through the observation window. I've got to make a few quick phone calls. Then I'll be back."

"You don't think Leo will try and leave?"

"I've alerted Officer Fishbach to assist us. I'll ask him to come up and guard the door until I return."

"Have you arrested Leo?"

"Not officially. But we'll let him cool his heels in there for a while."

Warner went back to his office. Removing De Mija's gun from his desktop, he locked it in a drawer. He made an in-house phone call downstairs to Fishbach and asked him to come up to the detective's unit. Fishbach was to guard against any attempt De Mija would make to leave the interview room or the building.

Then Warner made an outside telephone call.

"Yes, Cap."

"Damn, Arjay. One of these days you guys are going to have to teach me how you know who's calling you. Anyway, have you got anything for me yet?"

"We've almost completed our search of the house. The only thing we discovered so far is that Leo does have a bubble-jet printer. Oh, and it appears Leo is doing some renovations inside the house."

"And that takes tools. I'm keeping my fingers crossed you find the murder weapon amongst his tools."

"We do, too."

"So how long before the sweep of the house is complete?"

"I'm not sure, Cap. But we left Bobby there to finish up. The rest of us are now in the garage."

"Then I don't suppose you've checked out the greenhouse yet?"

"Briefly. Since it's out by the garage, I took a quick tour. The De Mija's have several black tulips growing in there."

"Hot damn."

"I thought you'd be pleased."

"What else?"

"So far in the garage we've found box after box of that tiny rattle. It's the same kind of rattle that the snake has been leaving at the crime scenes."

"Make sure you bring a box of them with you. Can you give me an approximate timeline yet?"

"We're going to be here for hours, Cap. You can't believe the boxes and crates full of stuff that we have to sift through. If you can send us some more help, we might be able to get done faster."

Warner looked out his inner-office window. "It's a good thing we have so many detectives working on overtime. Will Mitch and Dirk do?"

"You bet."

"Okay, hold on and I'll transfer you through to Mitch's desk. You can give him the address. Listen, keep at it and let me know the minute you find the weapon."

"How's it going there, Cap? I don't suppose Leo has confessed, has he?"

"Ha! That's a laugh. No, he's playing hardball. Okay, Arjay, hold on for the transfer."

After Warner connected Mayfield to Smith's desk, he called Hathaway. "Arnie, have you and Eric finished the input of all the *Black Tulip* case files so I can bring them up on my computer? I'm in a hurry and hate like hell to have to go through the mounds of paperwork right now dealing with this case."

"It's all been recorded, Cap."

"Thanks."

On his computer, Warner scanned the files until he found the information he needed. Debra Chow was one of the district attorney's deputies, and also the attorney that would be prosecuting the case. Once, h had briefly met with her once discuss the case. But now it was time to get her official reaction to DeMija's arrest. Although Warner had not worked with this ADA before, they were already on a first-name basis. It was well after business hours, so he dialed her home number.

"Hello," Chow answered in a perky voice.

"Debra, this is Joe Warner."

"Yes, Joe."

"I apologize for bothering you at home, but this is important. I'm about to make an official arrest on the serial murder case."

"That's wonderful news. Hold on and let me get a pad and pen." Warner waited until he again heard her voice. "Okay, I'm back. What's the suspects name?"

"Leo De Mija."

"For some reason that name sounds familiar."

"He's one of my detectives that's been working on the *Black Tulip* investigation."

"A cop! You're not kidding, are you?"

"I wish I was, Debra."

Once she got over the initial shock, she commented, "I'm sorry to hear that. Well does Leo De Mija have a middle name or initial?"

"If he does, it's not in his personnel files."

"Okay. What evidence do you have against him?"

"Right now we only have motive and opportunity."

"Any tangible evidence?"

"Do you recall the information about the perp's calling card?"

"I don't have my file on the case at home with me. But I believe part of it was a small white card with a poem written on it and a small rattle attached. There was also a tulip — a black one, I believe. Am I correct?"

"On the money. We can connect De Mija to that rattle, and to a bubble-jet printer we believe was used to write the poem. He also grows black tulips in his backyard greenhouse."

"That's still not proof of anything, Joe. What else have you got on him?"

"De Mija has a background in creative writing, he's a handyman of sorts, and he's left-handed."

"Wait, Joe. What does being a handyman have to do with this case?"

"He may be in possession of a certain tool we've been searching for, Debra. At this point, we're only assuming of course, that a handyman would make use of this type of a tool. And this tool could be our murder weapon."

"Oh, you're speaking of the carton opener or tile cutter you told me about at our first meeting?"

"One and the same."

"So you don't have the murder weapon yet?"

"Negative. As we speak, the suspect's residence and car are being searched. Hopefully, the murder weapon and other incriminating evidence will be found. As for motive, we firmly believe he despises all parents who he thinks are abusive to their children."

"Believing something won't stand up in court."

"I know. I'm just hoping he'll crack under pressure."

"You mentioned opportunity. Can you place him at the scene of the crimes?"

"I'd say within spitting distance," Warner said with a laugh.

"I'll take that as a yes. Any eyewitnesses come forward yet?"

"Only one who can place him near the scenes at the time two of the homicides took place."

"Is this witness credible?"

"Definitely. It's another officer. He was De Mija's patrol partner before we promoted De Mija to detective."

"Excellent. I must say, though, I'm a bit skeptical since you haven't mentioned any hard evidence that places him at any of the scenes."

"Believe me, we'll get the hard evidence you need before going to court."

"That would be great, but don't get me wrong. I think we've got enough circumstantial evidence to prosecute this case. I would, however, feel better if you had already found the murder weapon in the suspect's possession. We don't want to get shot down in court, nor risk a lawsuit against us if your suspect proves to be innocent."

"I understand, Debra. But I firmly believe the man I have is guilty. If I let him go, this snake might slither away and disappear under a log."

"Is his attorney there?"

"Not yet."

"Joe, you did read him his rights, didn't you. You're not jeopardizing this case by --"

"Hold on, Debra. I've been doing everything by the book. So, yes, I did read him his rights. De Mija didn't ask for an attorney until after he got tired answering my questions. That's when I stopped. Everything is on video to verify it. I'll let him make his one phone call as soon as I get back in there and officially place him into custody."

"It's not that I doubted you, Joe. Often times just one little slip-up can throw even the best cases out of court on a technicality."

"I understand your concern."

"Well, if his attorney gives you any problems, don't hesitate to call me back."

"I won't, and I will."

"Okay. I've got everything I need for right now. Keep in touch."

After his telephone conversation ended, Warner called Roitstein. "What the hell is taking you guys so long? Have you found anything of value in Leo's car yet?"

Roitstein laughed. "Negative. If you look up, Cap, I'm almost at your office door."

Warner looked out his window. There was Roitstein's smiling face looking back at him.

"Well, get off the phone, you joker, and get in here."

Roitstein was still laughing as he entered the captain's office.

"I'm glad someone finds this whole ugly situation funny."

"Sorry, Cap. But we still need to keep our sense of humor."

"I seem to have lost mine at the present. So the car's clean, huh?"

"Not just clean, but c-l-e-a-n. The only time I've seen a car that clean is at a new car lot. Has Arjay reported in yet?"

"I just spoke with him minutes ago. No murder weapon yet, but I still have high hopes." Warner got to his feet. "I'm going in now to make this official and slap some cuffs on our dirty cop. Get a personal property form and a large brown envelope and meet me in the interrogation room."

Warner stopped by the observatory window where Ferndale was watching De Mija. "What's he been doing?" He asked, looking through the window.

"Nothing, Cap. Just sitting there and staring this way. He knows someone is here watching him."

"Of course he does. As soon as Kieyell brings the paperwork, you get the honors of completing the form and getting his signature on it. I'll take his badge."

"Why me?"

"Come on, Ferndale. If you mean, *why you* because you're a woman, you know better."

"That's exactly what I mean. After De Mija's crack about not wanting a woman to pat him down — then you allowing Matt to do it — I don't know what to think."

Shaking his head, Warner rolled his eyes. "Here's how it is, Brenda. If De Mija were a perfect stranger, you could have and would have done the pat down. However, since De Mija has been a co-worker of yours, I honored his request. On the other hand, if I had had a female in there, and she had requested another female to frisk her, I would have also honored that request. So, are we on the same page?"

"Here's what you asked for," Roitstein said as he approached Warner from behind.

Warner turned around. "Good. Give them to Ferndale." Turning back to Ferndale, he asked, "Are we okay on this?"

Ferndale smiled and nodded. She took the forms and large envelope from Roitstein. "May I borrow your pen, Cap?"

Smiling back, Warner handed her the pen from his pocket. "Okay, you two, let's go."

Stopping at the door of the interrogation room, Warner spoke to the officer. "I assume you have cuffs on you?"

"I do," Officer Fishbach replied. "Do we need them?"

"Yes. I want our suspect cuffed in case he decides to put up a fight."

"You just lead the way, Capt. Warner."

As they walked in the door, De Mija looked over at them. "Fishbach, what are you doing here?"

Ferndale sat at the table across from their suspect.

As Warner and Fishbach approached De Mija, Warner said, "Leo De Mija, stand up. You are under arrest for the charge of First Degree Murder. Cuff him, officer."

Officer Fishbach joined himself and the suspect together with a set of handcuffs.

De Mija raged, "Are you going to let me call my attorney or not?"

"Calm down. You can make your phone call just as soon as we're through here."

Warner emptied De Mija's pockets. As the items were placed on the table, Ferndale made a list of them and placed them in the large manila envelope — all but De Mija's detective badge, which Warner held on to. After the envelope was sealed, Ferndale had De Mija sign the form listing his personal items. As the official arresting officer, Warner signed the form, too.

"Detective Roitstein, please assist Officer Fishbach in escorting De Mija to a telephone. Then you two can take him to lock up. Thank you for your assistance, Fishbach."

"Always happy to assist."

"Are you hungry, De Mija?" Warner asked.

De Mija's eyes bore holes through Warner. "One thing you don't know about me, Capt. Warner. I'm a survivor."

"Is that a yes or a no?"

"Keep your food for someone who needs it."

"Fine with me. Take him away, officer."

"Any special orders, sir?" Fishbach asked.

"I'd like to say, lock him up and throw away the key. But I know better. Just treat him like you do any other perp."

Warner took De Mija's badge back to his office and locked it up in the same drawer as he had placed De Mija's gun earlier that evening.

"Cap, there's some hot roast beef dinners and all the trimmings still in the coffee room," Ferndale stated, standing in Warner's doorway. "Can I bring you something?"

"No thanks, Brenda. It sounds good. But my wife has dinner warming in the oven for me when I get home."

"Don't you think you should go home then? You look exhausted."

Warner smiled. "No more tired than the rest of you."

"But we can catch our z's in the crib."

"Well, as soon as Matt gets back with that clinic info on Leo's alibi, and when the task team returns from Leo's house — then I'll go home."

"I don't mean to step out of line, Cap, but you already have Leo in custody. He's not going anywhere. Any of the information the guys bring back can wait until morning."

"You know what, Brenda? You're absolutely correct. Now, go on and get out of here and enjoy your dinner."

Warner turned off his office lights, closed the door, and headed for home. He was content he had the serial murderer behind bars.

CHAPTER THIRTY-SEVEN

"Good morning, Detectives," Warner greeted the pair waiting for him. "From the smiles on your faces, can I assume you have good news for me?"

"You can, and we do," Mayfield replied.

"Great, come on in."

Mayfield and Brown entered Warner's office. They placed three large plastic bags on the floor in front of Warner's desk before sitting.

"Did you have to bring your garbage with you?" Warner joked.

"This so-called garbage is actually bags of treasures," Brown said, smiling.

"We found everything we need, Cap."

"Oh, but the key question is, Arjay, did you find the murder weapon?"

"I believe so. Show him, J.B."

Brown opened one of the bags and pulled out a clear plastic evidence bag with a tool enclosed. He handed it to Warner.

"Hot damn! This is the carton opener we've been looking for. What else do you have in your bags of goodies?"

"We have a few rattles; some white, unlined index cards; a box of disposable gloves; and a journal," Mayfield responded.

"Actually, we have a large box of journals still out in the car. We found them in the garage along with box after box of black garbage bags," Brown said.

"What's in that journal? Did he keep a record of the murders he committed?"

"I don't know, Cap. We found it taped under the top of Leo's desk in his home office. I thought it might bear important information. But I didn't take time to read its contents. It may or may not be of value in this case, but I didn't want to take the chance in it disappearing."

"Good thinking." Warner stared at the tool as he spoke. "Did Leo's wife give you any trouble?"

"We scared her to death when we got there," Brown said. "But she didn't give us any heat. She just sat in a chair holding her little girl. And she kept repeating Leo has nothing to hide because he isn't guilty of anything."

"One of the doors in the house was locked. Mrs. De Mija told us that was Leo's private office and only he had the key. We had to break in."

"Is that where you found this tool?"

"Actually, no. It was found in his garage." Mayfield smiled. " Bryce was looking around, not watching where he was going --"

"And he was tired," Brown added in Officer Brubaker's defense.

"Yes, we were all dead on our feet," Mayfield commented. "Anyway, Bryce tripped over a stack of wood. As the logs went rolling everywhere, they uncovered that little beauty you're holding, Cap."

"Sometimes it pays to be a stumblebum." Warner laughed. "Where are Bryce and Bobby?"

"I sent them home to clean up. J.B. and I decided we'd get this evidence to you then we'll run home and clean up. We can be back in an hour, if that's okay?"

"Here they come," Brown said, viewing Anthony and Brubaker through Warner's window. "Do you need them in here?"

"No. That's not necessary. Where's the journal?"

Mayfield looked in one bag, while Brown checked another. Going through the third bag, Mayfield chuckled. "You might know it would be in the last one we checked. Here it is."

"Thanks, Arjay." As Warner took the journal, he handed the evidence bag to Mayfield. "Here. Take this tool over to the crime lab. If our luck holds, they'll find blood traces of at least one of our vics, and Leo's prints on it."

"Will do."

"Did either of you make a list of the items in those bags?"

"We sure did." Mayfield reached in his pocket, pulled out some folded papers, and placed them on the captain's desk. "Here's the list of everything we took."

"Give it to J.B. I'm keeping the journal until I have time to look it over." After completing the Chain of Custody Form, Warner handed it to Brown. "Okay, you two take this form, your list, and the bags. Lock them up in the evidence locker. Arjay, don't forget to ask the lab to put a rush on analyzing that tool. Then you two can go home and freshen up."

"Is Leo in lockup?" Brown asked as he picked up two of the bags.

"Yes. He's been there all night. I don't know who he has for an attorney, but the guy didn't show up last night when De Mija called him," Warner explained. "At least he wasn't here before I left."

"Ouch! I'd fast be getting me another attorney."

"I agree with J.B. Problem is, suspects don't get their choice of public defenders."

"Leo isn't using a public defender. He has is own attorney. We still haven't found out where his money --" He was interrupted by the ringing of his desk phone. "Capt. Warner. Certainly, send him up." Hanging up the phone, Warner said, "That was the desk sergeant. Leo's attorney is here. Okay, out of here you two. There's still a lot of work to do. We want to make sure that we've left no rock unturned so we have an air-tight case against Leo."

As the two detectives, an older, gray-haired man, dressed in a three-piece business suit approached Warner's door. Motioning for him to enter, Warner got to his feet and stood behind his desk.

Entering the office, the husky-voiced man asked, "I assume you're Capt. Warner?"

"That's what they tell me." From the look on the man's face, Warner's humor went over like vinegar in ice cream. "I understand you're Leo De Mija's attorney?"

"I am." Carlton approached Warner's desk. "My name is Carlton G. Wentworth."

"Please," Warner said, gesturing with his hand, "have a seat."

"No, thank you. I'm only here to ask you a few questions. Then I need to confer with my client."

"Suit yourself. But if you don't mind, I'll be seated." Sitting back in his chair, Warner asked, "What do you want to know?"

"On what grounds have you arrested my client?"

"We have enough evidence to show that your client is the suspected perpetrator of eight homicides."

"What evidence?" Carlton rumbled.

"You'll have to discuss that with the district attorney's office."

"I see I'm not going to fair well asking you anything more. So I won't take up anymore of your time. I'd like to speak to my client now."

"I'm sure after waiting all night for you to show up, he'll be grateful to see you," Warner mumbled under his breath.

"What's that?"

"Nothing, sir. Nothing." Warner looked into the front office. Not seeing Ferndale, he made an in-house phone call.

"Roitstein."

"Kieyell, find Detective Ferndale and send her to my office. Then get De Mija out of lockup and put him in interview room two."

"Right away, Cap."

* * *

A few days after his arrest, to Warner's dismay, De Mija was no longer locked up behind the steel bars of the law. Instead, the liberal bars of justice had set him free.

According to the medical examiner, the blade of the tool found on De Mija's property matched the marks found on the victims' neck wounds. The ME had sent the tool to the CBI for further examination.

Although the crime lab had found traces of blood on the tool, the blood type did not match any of the victims. Demanding his rights, De Mija refused to submit to a blood test. For reasons Warner could not figure out, De Mija's fingerprints were not found on the tool. Not at all satisfied with the CBI report, Warner asked that the tool be sent to the FBI Crime Lab for more conclusive information.

Even though De Mija was the number one suspect, his attorney was very persuasive in court. The judge appeared to be in the defendant's corner through the whole arraignment procedure.

"Miss Chow, until such time as you get your official report back from the FBI Crime Lab, I see no reason for the prosecution to pursue this issue. I'm overruling your request for a blood test from the defendant at this time," Judge Roland announced. "Now, with regard to releasing the defendant on bail --"

Standing from his chair, Carlton pleaded De Mija's case. "Permission to address the court, Your Honor."

"What is it, Mr. Wentworth?"

"Before you rule on the bond issue, please hear me out."

"Very well. Let's hear it."

"Your Honor, I respectfully disagree with Miss Chow. Leo De Mija has no past record of any criminal activity. When he was an officer in uniform there wasn't a mark on his excellent work record. Furthermore, Mr. De Mija also received a commendation from the chief of police. Again, because he was such an outstanding police officer, he was promoted to detective. My client has no intentions of leaving town, Your Honor. In fact, he has every intention of staying in town to go to court, prove his innocence, and clear his good name."

"I strongly object to this man being released on bond," Chow protested, jumping to her feet. "Your Honor, the defendant wasn't arrested for some minor crime. He is the suspect in a series of heinous crimes. We are talking about a serial killer here. And may I remind Your Honor, with all due respect, that the murder weapon was discovered on the suspect's property."

"I object, Your Honor," Carlton bellowed with contempt. "Miss Chow does not know for a fact that blood from any of the victims' was discovered on the tool in question. Nor were Mr. De Mija's prints found on the *so-called* murder weapon. The tool Miss Chow is referring to could have been planted on the defendant's property to make him look guilty. Furthermore, I --"

Arguing, Chow raised her voice over Carlton's. "Your Honor, --"

Pounding his gavel, the judge raised his voice above the disputing attorneys. "Both of you, be quiet and sit down. Now, Miss Chow, Mr. Wentworth, this is not the time to debate this case. This is only a bond hearing. I've heard enough to make my decision. Due to Mr. De Mija's excellent record in law enforcement, and the fact that he has no previous criminal record, be it so ordered that I am releasing this man on a $500,000 bond. See the bailiff."

CHAPTER THIRTY-EIGHT

De Mija had only been out of jail for a few days when Mt. Pride was plagued with another double homicide. Warner received the telephone call at six o'clock in the morning. He was informed the male victim was still alive. The officers at the scene had already called the emergency medical team for immediate assistance.

Warner awakened his wife. "Jeny, honey, I need your help."

Seldom did her husband ever wake her with such distress in his voice. Jeny sat up in bed as if lightning had struck her. "What's the matter?"

Warner had dialed a call on his cell phone. "Here. Get Doug Rothchild on the phone. Then tell him to hold. If he's not there yet, get the lab to page him for me." When Jeny took the cell phone, he made another call on the land phone directly to Mayfield's desk at the precinct. "Arjay. This is Warner. Listen, I don't have time for small talk. I want Leo De Mija picked up, immediately. There's been two more homicides. I know. I know." Jeny nudged her husband, nodding and pointing to the phone. His other contact was on the line. Holding up one finger, he gave Jeny the *wait* sign as he continued his conversation. "Have a cruiser go along for backup in case Leo causes any problems. Is Brenda at her desk? Good. Put her on. Brenda, hold on a second."

Still holding the phone up to his right ear, he took the cell phone from Jeny and held it up to his left ear. After briefly explaining the reason for his phone call, Warner said, "Thanks, Doug. I'll see you there." Switching to the other phone, he explained the same information to Ferndale as he had just told Rothchild. Warner concluded with, "Yes, I want you and J.B. to cover it. I'll be out the door in ten minutes. Meet you there."

While thanking Jeny for her assistance, Warner threw on some jeans and a shirt. After kissing his wife goodbye, he headed out the door.

* * *

The EMTs were already at the crime scene. As he covered his hands with protective gloves, Warner had an officer inside the house show him the way to the bedroom where the victims were found. Just as Warner was about to enter the room, three EMTs filed past him.

"Wait," Warner said, grabbing the arm of the last EMT to leave the room. "How's the patient?"

Somber-faced, the woman shook her head.

"He's gone?"

"Yes. We don't know what kept him holding on as long as he did, sir?"

"How did he?"

"It looked to us like there was a struggle. And the assailant only got half the job done before he killed the female and fled. The man was clenching a sheet to his throat when we got here."

"That must have been what kept him alive long enough to call for help. Was he able to say anything?"

The EMT shrugged her shoulders. "He did, but I don't know if I heard him correctly."

"What do you think he said?"

"He barely got out the word, 'noem.'"

"What was that?" Warner asked to be sure he had heard correctly.

"Noem. At least that's what it sounded like."

"I've never heard that word before."

"I asked the team working with me, and they never heard of the word either."

Wrinkling his brow, Warner said, "Maybe it's a foreign word. Well, I'll try and figure that out later."

"You might be right about it being a foreign word. The deceased appears to be of Asian decent."

Warner thanked the EMT and sent her on her way.

After Ferndale, Brown, and the CSIs showed up, Warner left and went home to shower and get ready for the office.

* * *

While he was having a quick cup of coffee, Warner received a telephone call.

"What do you mean he's not home, Arjay? Are his wife and child gone too? Put out an APB on him, ASAP," he ordered before slamming down the receiver.

Rushing to the kitchen, his wife asked, "What's with all the yelling, Joe?"

"I'm sorry, princess. Leo De Mija skipped bail."

"Oh, no. From everything you've told me, you really believe he's the serial killer, don't you?"

"I do, and this proves it. I will never understand our justice system. Letting a suspected serial killer out on bond just doesn't make any sense, Jeny. That stupid judge gave Leo free rein to kill again, right under our noses." Giving his wife a peck on the cheek, he said, "I've got to go, honey. I want to stop in and see Eddy before I get to the office."

"It's not even visiting hours yet."

"I've got pull," he said with a grin. "I'll call you later."

* * *

Warner arrived just as Konklin's food tray was being delivered.

"Hey, Joe. Did you come to have breakfast with me?"

"No. I don't have an appetite, especially for hospital food."

"This is the care center, remember? They serve better food in here than the hospital did. I get wet scrambled eggs instead of dry ones." Konklin laughed.

"Yuck! How do they expect you to get well enough to go home eating that kind of chow?"

"Eating, my dear fellow, has nothing to do with my walking out of this place on my own two feet. Besides, you know me, Joe. I can eat just about anything." After taking a drink of coffee, he asked, "What's going on? Why are you here so early this morning?"

Without even thinking, Warner blurted out, "We had another double homicide." Realizing what he had said, Warner almost bit his tongue.

"Geez, Joe, how many does that make now?"

"Wait. Do you remember the homicides?"

"Huh? Oh, I said that didn't I? Yes and no, Joe. I remember something about a serial killer. Is that possible?"

"Yes, big guy, that's possible. What else do you remember?"

After thinking about it, Warner shook his head. "Nothing, Joe. I'm sorry."

"Okay, pal. Well, you keep trying."

"Guess what, Joe?

"What?"

"I got off of the crutches yesterday, and now I can walk with two canes."

"You're kidding?"

"Not about walking I'm not. Miles and my physical therapist say I can go home soon. Of course I need to find a way to get back and forth to therapy. But isn't that wonderful news?"

"It tops any I've heard in a while, Eddy. You just let me know as soon as they release you. You're going home with me."

"Nonsense, Joe. We've already discussed this, and your home is not an option."

"Like I'm going to listen to you." Warner laughed. "Jeny has the spare room all ready, and Amandalee is looking forward to working out with you."

"Jeny also has her own physical problems. And your daughter has her own apartment. That's putting both of them --"

Ignoring his friend's concerns, Warner explained, "You're going to be very comfortable at our house. Between the three of us, we will see that you get back and forth to therapy. Jeny's used to cooking and cleaning for three. So you won't be any extra problem for her. As for Mandy, she will move back — temporarily, of course — to help out for the time you're there. I had some of the guys help me move your computer from the office to our spare room. Like we've discussed before, it will be great physical therapy for your hands getting those fingers flexible again."

"I think I've asked you this before, Joe. Do I know how to operate one of those things?"

"Look, if you don't remember right away, don't worry about it. I still have some of those *how-to* books around the house. If not, I'll help you when I can and so will Mandy.

"Geez, Joe. I hope you're not getting in trouble because of me. Did you get the chief's permission to move the department's property?"

"Not exactly."

"Come on, Joe. I don't want you sticking your head in a noose on my account."

"You let me worry about my neck. All I care about right now is getting you back into shape as soon as possible."

Konklin's eyes filled with tears. "You're being too good to me, Joe. I don't want to be an imposition."

"You just keep up the good work on getting well. I need you back at the office."

"You don't have to kid me. I know I don't have a job anymore. The chief called me."

Warner was stunned. "Ed called you? What did he say?"

"Well, he didn't come right out and say it, but in so many words he asked me how I would feel about an early retirement. Don't look so down, Joe. I knew it was going to happen. I've been in here too long. And I don't have my full mental faculties or the complete use of my legs yet. What good would I be as a detective in this condition?"

"What's wrong with desk work? I could still use you as my right-hand man, especially to keep up on the paperwork and computer work for me."

"I'm not sure I want to go back to the unit as a glorified secretary. Even for you."

"No ones asking you to be a secretary. I need my assistant back."

"I don't know, Joe. I really don't know."

"Well, you think about it. In the meantime, I'll have a talk with Ed. I've been staying away from him these past few days. But now I'll make it a point to pay him a visit."

"Don't make any more waves on my account. I appreciate all you've done and all you're doing, but --"

"But nothing. You just concentrate on walking, and I'll worry about your job. Say, what does Melody say about you going home?"

"Oh, I forgot to tell you. I still have to see her once a day, Monday through Friday. But she'll come to my apartment --"

"My house."

"Okay, *your house* for the sessions."

"Great. Before you leave here, I'll make sure she has my address. Well, pal, I need to take off. Enjoy your raw eggs," Warner joked as he walked out the door.

* * *

"Aren't you on the wrong side of town this morning, Joe?"

"You've heard, I take it, that we had another double homicide?"

Doogle grumbled. "I heard. Not a pleasant way to get woke up out of a sound sleep. Did you pick up De Mija?"

"No. He's skipped bail. I've got an APB out for his arrest. That's not why I'm here, Ed."

"What else could possibly be on your mind?"

Warner walked to the chair that sat in front of the chief's desk. He wrapped his fingers over the chairback. "It's Eddy. He informed me that you called him yesterday."

"So I did."

"But in the conversation we had recently, you promised to wait until the first of July."

"I didn't promise anything, Joe."

Warner's fingers tightened his grasp on the chair. "Did he tell you he's walking on canes now and soon to be walking on his own?"

"No, as a matter of fact, he didn't. But what difference does that make, Joe? He won't be any good to you or the department in the condition he's in."

"He'll make an excellent desk man until he's moving freely about again. If he was older, I could see having him hang it all up. But he's not."

"According to his personnel files, Konklin is fifty-three."

Biting the old familiar bullet, Warner said, "I seem to remember your sixtieth celebration back in --"

"Okay. So I'm a lot older than he is. The difference is I'm in great physical condition. Konklin's not. That rather sums it all up, doesn't it?"

"Not from where I stand." Determined to win Doogle over, Warner continued to defend his lieutenant. "Eddy has been a good cop with an excellent record for too many years for you just to toss him out to pasture like some old workhorse you can't use anymore. He has a lot of good years left in him, Ed. I just don't understand why you can't give the man a break."

"Okay, Joe, have it your way. I'm tired of arguing about it. You're right. If you think you can get the proper work out of him, then so be it."

Warner's heart was pounding. "You're serious? I mean, one minute you're fighting me. Then, suddenly, you make a three-sixty."

"I said okay, didn't I?"

"I just want to make sure you're not going to change your mind again."

"No, that's my final word on it. Now get out of here and go catch that dirty cop that's giving this whole MPPD a bad name. The commissioner has really been on my ... well, you know what."

"Thanks, Ed. You won't be sorry."

"I had damn well better not be."

* * *

Feeling as good as one could feel on such a gruesome morning, Warner went to the office with a smile on his face. As soon as he sat at his desk, he called Konklin. "Well, chubby cheeks, have you finished that disgusting breakfast yet?"

"Sure, Joe. Believe it or not, it was really tasty."

"Oh, yeah? Well let me tell you something, Mister Cast Iron Stomach. If you can eat that food and think it's tasty, I don't ever want to hear a complaint from you when you have to eat my cooking."

"That's fair. Did you forget something when you were here earlier?"

"No. I couldn't wait to tell you the good news. I just got through having my talk with the chief. As soon as you are capable of coming back to work, you have a desk job." Not hearing anything but the sound of silence on the other end of the phone, he asked, "Eddy, are you still there?"

"Yes, Joe, I'm here. I was just running the pros and cons of returning to work as an invalid."

"You're not an invalid. Look, the desk job won't be permanent, if that's what you're really worried about. Once you get back in shape, you'll be put on regular duties again."

"Okay, Joe. I'll take your word for it."

"You had better. Okay, buddy, I'll see you tomorrow."

"Yeah. And, Joe, thanks for sticking behind me. I've never had a friend like you before. I want you to know that I really appreciate you."

"Oh, for crying in a bucket, Eddy. Don't get all mushy on me. My mascara will run."

Konklin laughed. "Maybe you should think about buying some of that waterproof stuff?"

"Hey, the old sense of humor is coming back. It's music to my ears, chubby cheeks."

"Yeah. Music. See ya around, Joe."

"Sure, buddy. See ya around."

CHAPTER THIRTY-NINE

"Good morning. Wentworth, Attorney at Law Office."
"This is Capt. Warner of the MPPD. May I speak to Mr. Wentworth, please?"

"One moment, please."

"Thank you."

It did not take long for Warner to hear, "Well, Captain, what can I do for you today?"

"Have you seen or heard from your client, Leo De Mija?"

"Not recently. Why?"

"It appears he has skipped bail," Warner emphatically stated.

"On the contrary, Captain. Detective De Mija was given permission to go visit his out-of-state in-laws over the weekend to help celebrate their wedding anniversary."

"Who in the devil would give a man out on bail for a murder rap permission to leave town?" Warner ranted as his temper surfaced.

"Judge Rolando."

"You're a fool, Carlton."

"I don't appreciate name calling, Captain."

"I just meant that you should chose your clients more wisely. Are you aware we had another double homicide and there's an APB out for De Mija?"

"No, I wasn't aware of either. However, I am very confident Detective De Mija will be able to verify his whereabouts."

"Where do his in-laws live?"

"Someplace in Kansas."

Warner was even more infuriated. "That's all you can give me is someplace in Kansas?"

"If you are bringing Detective De Mija in for questioning when he returns, I suggest you notify me immediately. Under no circumstances will you be allowed to question my client without me being present."

"You don't have to tell me the law, Carlton. Furthermore, I suggest you quit calling your client Detective De Mija. The department has suspended him and he has been stripped of his firearm and badge."

"Look, Capt. Warner, I really don't care for your tone of voice. When my client gets back to town, I'm sure he can verify his whereabouts with a valid alibi."

"Oh, I'll just bet he can."

Warner hardly ever lost his cool in any situation. However, he was outraged that De Mija was capable of committing another homicide thanks to some liberal judge. Disgusted, Warner slammed down the phone.

"Stupid, stupid, stupid!" He voiced, loudly. "We've got people locked up for less crimes while the system lets a serial killer move about the country like he doesn't have a care in the world. What in blue blazes is our world coming to?"

* * *

Pacing his office, Warner was on pins and needles waiting to get word that De Mija was back in town. That is, if he were coming back. Attempting to get every detail straight in his mind, he was suddenly struck with doubts about De Mija's guilt.

Talking to the walls, Warner verbalized his thoughts. "Even though Ripley questioned De Mija's lengthy absence on the nights the first two homicides had taken place, he had to admit De Mija returned in the same clean condition. Not one spec of blood on him. Although Ripley stated De Mija was breathing hard on both occasions, Doogle could be right. Under both circumstances, a person would be short of breath.

"De Mija's explanation about cutting his hand with a knife from his collection checked out. So his alibi for the night of the third homicides was valid.

"Now, if De Mija is our man, and Davies is right about our perp wearing a covering of some sort, what would that be? It couldn't be anything made of plastic or vinyl, as blood would have dripped all over the place. There were no bloodstained clothes found anywhere on De Mija's property. But that just brings me back to what did the perp wear and how did he dispose of the bloodstained clothes or covering?"

Although this was still a puzzle to Warner, he had to go back to all the evidence against De Mija. Another factor stared him straight in the face: the recent homicides. Since no inventory was taken of the remaining items, particularly the small rattles, left in De Mija's garage, he would have had easy access to them. And the perp's calling card had never been released to the press. So the general public had no knowledge of the rattles, just those involved in the investigation and the serial killer. All fingers still pointed to De Mija.

Then, as if someone had hauled off and hit him in the head like one of those, "you should have had a *V-8*" commercials, Warner went back to his desk. Although he had already skimmed through De Mija's journal, mostly checking out entries for dates around the times the homicides had taken place, he had never read the entire thing. Since nothing he had read at the time showed any evidence of De Mija's being a murderer, the ledger had been locked in his desk.

Taking the journal from his desk drawer, Warner started on page one.

Several days later, after many hours of reading, Warner was ecstatic. He thought he had finally found the missing link to opportunity and evidence: motive.

 CHAPTER FORTY

Warner was just opening the blinds on his office door, when he spotted Roitstein headed his direction. Opening the door, he asked, "Any news on De Mija, yet?"

"They just brought him in downstairs. Where do you want him?"

"In prison serving life without the possibility of parole."

"That sounds good to me, too."

"Bring him up and put the snake in one of the interview rooms, Kieyell. And don't let him out of your sight. I'll call his lawyer."

"Okay, Cap."

Looking beyond Roitstein, Warner recognized the man walking in their direction. "Looks like someone beat me to it. His mouthpiece is here already. Go get De Mija."

"Where's my client?" Wentworth demanded.

"On his way up. How did you know we picked him up?"

"His wife called me. Which room will he be in?"

"Whichever room my detective puts him in. When you see your client come up the steps, you can follow him." Hearing his desk phone ring, Warner said, "If you'll excuse me, I've got a phone to answer." Closing the door in the attorney's face, he rushed to answer the phone. "Capt. Warner."

"Joe, this is Saggy."

"Yes, Saggy. Do you have that preliminary report for me on the last homicide victims?"

"It's ready. You can have one of your detectives pick it up or I can courier it over to you."

"Fast work, Saggy. I appreciate it. Look, I've got De Mija waiting to be questioned as we speak. Is there any new information you can give me over the phone?"

"Certainly. I found some skin and blood scrapings under the male's fingernails. It looks like he clawed his assailant good, as the skin and blood samples don't match either of the victim's DNA. I checked the blood sample against the blood droplet samples taken from the Carney scene They're a match."

"You mean that rare type, O Negative?"

"Yes. I would really need your suspect's blood to compare to the tests I've already run. It's vital, Joe, because it can either cinch your case or, perhaps, set the man free."

"According to the court's ruling, my hands are tied. You would think, if De Mija is as innocent as he says he is, that he would gladly submit to the test. Wait, Saggy, I don't know why I didn't think of this before. We can get his medical records from the department's physician."

"You won't have any luck there, Joe. I already tried. It seems De Mija has never had to give a blood sample. So they don't have his blood type on record."

"Not even with our new regulations requiring the test?"

"Sorry. Somehow he slipped through the cracks."

"That figures. Nothing about this case has been easy. Okay, I'll do my best, Saggy. Anything else?"

"Yes. I also found a piece of black plastic that was clutched in the male victim's fist. According to the CSIs, there was nothing in that room that remotely resembled black plastic. I can only assume it had to be something taken from your perp when he attacked the victim. I found some brown hairs on the plastic that can be tested for DNA. I thought you might want to send this evidence to the CBI Lab in Denver for analysis since their equipment is far superior to what I have to work with. I'll bet one of my meatball-and-ketchup sandwiches that the hairs will match the blood DNA analysis I have in my report."

"That's one bet I hope you don't lose. Besides, I'd hate like hell to take one of those lip-smacking sandwiches away from you." Warner chuckled.

"Like I said, Joe. Don't knock it till you try it. So, how do you want to get my written report?"

"I'll have one of my detectives pick it up. Got to rush now and contact the ADA. Thanks, Saggy."

Warner's call to the DA's office proved fruitless. Due to the vast amount of court cases, according to the secretary, no legal assistance was available. Even though he knew someone from the district attorney's office should be present to question De Mija, Warner could not take the risk of De Mija being on the loose again. He would have to proceed on his own.

* * *

In the outer office, Warner glanced around. The only detective that did not appear to be busy was Duncan. So Duncan was sent to pick up the items from the ME. When Warner spotted Roitstein standing outside one of the interview rooms, he approached the detective. "Why are you out here?"

"The attorney wanted to confer with his client in private."

"How long have they been in there alone?"

"Ever since I brought Leo upstairs."

"That's long enough. Come on."

When Warner and Roitstein entered the interview room, Wentworth was sitting at the table next to De Mija. Warner and Roitstein took seats at the opposite side of the table.

"I hope someone from the DA's office shows up soon. We'd like to get this over with so my client can be on his way."

"We don't need a rep from the DA's office to get this interview underway," Warner responded.

Looking over at his client, Wentworth reiterated what he had told De Mija before the detectives had entered the room. "Just remember what I told you, Leo. You don't have to answer any questions or offer any information."

"I'm sure you're aware, De Mija, that we found two cases of rattles stored in your garage?"

"I already know that. So what?"

"They just happen to be the same type of small rattles that our snake has left at every double homicide. Don't you find that a bit of a coincidence?"

"Yes, as a matter of fact I do. But we already went over all of this when I was arrested the first time."

"So humor me and tell me again."

"I bought those decorations before my daughter was born since we knew we were going to have a girl. You can ask any of the uniforms I worked with because I tied them around all the cigars I passed out the day my little Fayth came into the world."

"I find it interesting that all the time you worked on this serial case you never once mentioned that you had the same kind of rattle in your possession."

"At first, I had only seen a picture of the rattle you're referring to. I never put two and two together as them being one and the same. It wasn't until much later that I finally saw the real sample. At that time, I told Detective Ferndale it looked just like the ones I had. She never commented on what I told her. So I never thought any more about it."

"Right. You also happen to be a creative writer. I suppose that's just another coincidence in regards to our perp?"

"Listen, Capt. Warner, you knew that piece of information on the day you promoted me. I've never kept my writing a secret."

"Uh-huh. And now we have two coincidences, right, De Mija?" Not receiving an answer, Warner continued. "Now that I'm on a roll, explain to me why you would need to have so many boxes of disposable gloves stored in your garage."

Wentworth cut in before De Mija could answer. "Leo, you don't need to answer that. Save your defense until we get to court."

"It's all right, Carlton," De Mija said, keeping his focus on Warner. "I'd just as soon clear up a few of these matters now. Maybe then the good captain here will see that the DA doesn't have a case against me. To answer your question, Captain, I don't like getting my hands dirty. I use those gloves around the house and in the yard. Since I go through so many of them, they're cheaper to buy in large quantities. That's certainly not a crime."

"Haven't you ever heard of work gloves like most people wear for yard work?'

"Of course I have. I find them too cumbersome."

Right. You wouldn't be able to hold on to a murder weapon as well with cumbersome gloves as you can wearing latex gloves, Warner thought. *Well, I better not go there. I'll leave that up to Debra when she prosecutes this poor excuse for a human being.* "Tell me about your childhood."

"Capt. Warner --"

De Mija quickly rested his hand on his attorney's arm. "Carlton, it's okay. I really don't mind Capt. Warner prying into my background. I have nothing to hide. Both of my parents were alcoholics, but I had a good childhood."

That's the first time he's ever mentioned alcoholic parents. The shithead knows I read his ledger. Well, let's see what else I can get out of him. "Most alcoholics make lousy parents. Were your parents abusive?"

"I don't have to answer that."

"I believe you just did. Where are your parents now?"

"They died in a car crash. I ... I don't wish to discuss them."

"How did they really die, De Mija? Better yet, where are they buried?"

De Mija froze, gritting his teeth. Placing his elbows on the table, he placed his face in his hands.

Warner kept at him, hoping De Mija would crack. "I understand that you got permission to leave town for a week to go to Kansas. Is that where you really went?"

In a comforting way, Wentworth placed his hand on De Mija's back. "You don't have to continue, Leo."

Sitting erect, De Mija said, "I'm okay. Yes, Captain, I really went to Kansas. I took my family to go visit my in-laws."

"When did you leave town? I want the day and the time."

"We left the day after I bonded out. I called Carlton for permission to leave the state. After he called me back with a go ahead, I guess we left somewhere around three that afternoon."

"I can verify that Leo called me. After I got Judge Roland's permission for Leo to travel, I called him back with the information."

Ignoring Wentworth's verification of De Mija's statement, Warner continued pounding away at his suspect. "Did you drive?"

"Of course."

"Where in Kansas do your in-laws live?"

"See here, Capt. Warner, that is really none of your business. Enough is enough," Wentworth highly objected.

"Look, Mr. Wentworth, I need to know if De Mija was close enough to sneak back into town and commit the last homicides. I have every right to question him about where he was when the last homicides took place."

"And I say, when you're asking about where his family lives, he doesn't have to answer those questions," Wentworth reiterated. "At the rate of repeating myself, he doesn't have to answer *any* of your questions."

De Mija sat in silence almost in defiance of Warner.

"I would like to question your in-laws, De Mija, just to be sure you were there. If they can give you a *bona fide* alibi, it will clear you in this last case. I would think clearing your name would be important enough to tell me."

"My in-laws may be able to help me out later in court. But they can't do me any good right now."

"And why's that?"

"They left on a European cruise yesterday."

"Oh, how convenient," Warner commented, slamming his hand on the table. "I'm sure it's no surprise to you that we checked out your work background."

"So? Like I said earlier, I have nothing to hide."

"Really? I'm sure it won't surprise you to learn that we didn't just arrest you and then forget about you, De Mija. We've done some serious digging into your past. For example, you were able to pay for your college education and purchase your own home. Yet none of the part-time jobs you had at the time could have paid for such a heavy expense. I find that very interesting." All the time Warner was talking, De Mija sat expressionless. "Also, you've had facial reconstruction for no apparent reason that we can find. That's another vast expense for a young man on a small income. You may be trying to hide from someone by having plastic surgery, but your fingerprints don't lie. They haven't yet proved that you are who you say you are. That's something we haven't figured out yet. But we will. Who were the Johannsens?"

De Mija felt a chill run up his spine. Had all the dark secrets of his past been discovered?

"Come on, De Mija, I'm waiting," Warner insisted.

"They were people I worked for." De Mija turned to his attorney. "The Johannsens have nothing to do with this case the captain is trying to hang on me. Can't you object or something?"

"I keep telling you, Leo, you don't have to answer these questions. You can stop at any time."

"And, for the most part, he's right, De Mija. But if you don't, how are you going to convince me that my inclinations about you are wrong?"

"Okay, Captain," De Mija conceded. "I had no friends when I was growing up. My parents, my school and my cleaning jobs were all I had for years. When my parents died, they left me with some money. The inheritance from them paid for a portion of my college education.

"After the loss of my parents, I started doing a lot of work around the house and yard for the Johannsens. They never had any children. So they came to consider me like one of their own. I thought the world of them, too. When they passed on, they left me their house and a small inheritance. Since I already owned a house, I sold the Johannsen place. Part of the money for that sale is how I completed my college education and paid for my living expenses. If you want, I'll give you the attorney that handled my inheritance. Now, can we go on and leave the Johannsens out of this?"

"I would appreciate that attorney's information. But I'd also like to know what you did with the rest of the inheritance."

"The rest?"

"Yes. You just said you used part of it for college and living expenses. What did you do with the other part?"

"Not that it's any of your business, but I used some of it for my plastic surgery. I put the rest away in a safe place."

That makes sense why the bank records didn't show an unusual amount of money in either his checking or his savings account. "Any reason for not keeping your extra money in the bank for safe keeping?"

"That's my business."

"Let's get back to what's under that bush you wear on your face. Why did you have your face reconstructed? Is there something or someone from your past that you're afraid of?"

"I'm not afraid of anyone or anything, Capt. Warner. It just so happens I had a bad accident and really messed up my face. I didn't want to walk around the rest of my life looking like I belonged in freak sideshow."

"What kind of an accident?"

"One day, while I was working for the Johannsens, I was burning some trash. I hadn't realized it, but they had thrown a half-empty can of charcoal lighter fluid into the barrel of papers I was burning. It exploded and I ended up with some severe facial damage. Naturally they insisted on paying for having my face reconstructed. Not having insurance on myself, I agreed to let them pay for it. They died before I could get the surgery done. I'm sure that's one of the reasons they left me enough money to cover the surgical expenses. I really don't see where you're going with this. All I wanted was to look like a human being again instead of some monster that the fire had turned me into."

"How long ago did you have this plastic surgery?"

"That's none of your business."

"Where was this surgery performed?"

"In a hospital."

Smart ass. "Here in the United States?" When De Mija did not answer, Warner said, "Fine. Give me the name of the surgeon and how to locate him, and I'll change the subject."

Once again, Wentworth objected. "That's enough. This line of questioning is uncalled for. I suggest you change the subject immediately because we certainly are not obligated to give you information that is not pertinent to the charges you have against my client."

Certainly not because of the attorney's objection, but Warner decided to drop the subject. He would not pursue it again until he could confer with Debra Chow and find out the legal aspects in obtaining the vital information he needed from De Mija.

All the time Warner had been sitting across the table from De Mija, he was taking a good look at his suspect's face — what he could see of it. There was not a scratch or claw mark on it. Since Sagdorf had not mentioned any hairs found under the last male victim's fingernails, Warner could only assume the scratches were located on some other part of De Mija's body — like his arms. However, he could not see De Mija's arms as he was wearing a long-sleeved shirt.

Coming up with an idea, Warner excused himself and Roitstein, momentarily, and they left the room.

To save on energy when the 15th Precinct was built, electrical heat was installed. For comfort and convenience, each room had its own thermostat control. The thermostats for each of the individual interview rooms were installed in the hall.

"Kieyell, run and get me a Band-Aid."

"What do you have in mind, Cap?"

"Just be prepared for a steam bath. Now, hurry. I need that Band-Aid before we go back in there."

Warner turned up the heat as high as it would go. When Roitstein returned, Warner stuck the Band-Aid in his pocket. Both detectives returned to the interview room and retook their seats.

Now Warner had to wait for his opportunity to see if his hunch was right. Not wanting to ask De Mija any more pertinent information, Warner stalled for time by striking up a cordial conversation. "So, De Mija, have you heard that the lieutenant's healing nicely from the accident?"

"No, but I'm happy to hear it. Lieu's a good guy."

"One of the best. He's regaining his memory, too. Does that surprise you or worry you in any way?"

"Now what does that supposed to mean?"

"Nothing in particular. I just know you two were getting pretty close before the accident."

Warner could feel the perspiration building up under his arms. He removed his suit coat and hung it over the back of a chair. Then he rolled up his shirtsleeves. Roitstein followed suit. Wentworth loosened his tie and unbuttoned the neck of his shirt.

"Why is it getting so hot in here?" De Mija asked.

"Sorry about that. It seems the thermostat is on the blink lately."

"Can't we move somewhere else where it is cooler?" Wentworth asked.

"No." Warner had to quickly think up an excuse. "Every interview room is the same. From what I understand, the malfunction has something to do with the cheap brand of thermostats that were installed in this building. We've got a repairman coming in tomorrow to fix them. But, until then, we just have to put up with either freezing to death or dying of heat."

"Then let's end this interview so we can get out of here," Wentworth suggested.

Before Warner could comment, he noticed De Mija starting to roll up the shirtsleeve of his right arm. Taking a good look at his arm, Warner did not notice anything out of the ordinary. However, his plan was working. To stall for more time, Warner said, "Just give me a few more minutes. I'm rolling around a few thoughts in my head as to what questions I have left."

"Can't you at least open a window?" Wentworth complained.

"Are you kidding? If those windows opened, we'd have every

perpetrator that comes in here trying to escape."

"Well, hurry it up then before we all suffocate in here."

When De Mija rolled up the sleeve on his left arm, Warner immediately noticed long, scabbed-over scratches. He reached across the table and grabbed De Mija's arm.

"Hey," De Mija yelled.

"You look like you got into a recent dog fight. What happened to your arm?"

"It wasn't a fight, but it was a dog. These scratches came from my in-law's dog."

"I'll just bet they did."

As Warner let go of De Mija's arm, he purposely scratched one of the scabs with his fingernail. Just as he had hoped would happen, a scab tore loose from De Mija's skin and begin to bleed.

Feeling the pain, De Mija complained, "Now look what you've done. I'm bleeding."

Reaching into his pocket and pulling out a clean handkerchief, Warner handed it to De Mija. "Oh, I'm sorry. I certainly didn't mean to do that. Press my handkerchief against it to stop the bleeding, and I'll go get you a bandage."

Clutching the handkerchief to his arm, De Mija said, "A bandage isn't necessary. I'll be fine."

Heading for the door, Warner was insistent. "Nonsense. I feel badly that happened. The least I can do is to get you a Band-Aid so you don't bleed all over your clothes."

Warner exited the room with a serious look on his face that quickly turned into a wide grin when he stepped into the hallway. What he had just accomplished could possibly help to convict De Mija.

When he reentered the room, Warner exchanged the Band-Aid from his pocket for the return of the handkerchief. He was quick to roll up the soiled handkerchief and stick it in his pants pocket. Removing his suit coat from the back of a chair, he said, "Well, this interview is over. Oh, and in case I didn't mention it, Mr. Wentworth, under Judge M.E. Nidstrom's orders, bail has been rescinded. Your client is going back to jail and that's where he is to stay until his trial."

De Mija sat silent with his head erect, looking straight ahead at the wall.

However, his attorney was outraged. Jumping to his feet, Wentworth's legs hit the bottom of his chair. The chair fell backward and hit the floor with a loud crash. "You do *not* have the right to lock Leo up again!"

"Take it up with Judge Nidstrom. Detective Roitstein, cuff De Mija and escort him back to a cell."

When Warner stepped back into the hall, he felt like dancing the jig. As far as he was concerned, the *Black Tulip* case was closed. The only thing left was the court trial. With all the evidence against De Mija, Warner was confident De Mija would never walk free again.

 CHAPTER FORTY-ONE

During the first week in July, just like Warner had hoped for, Konklin was back at his desk. His teeth had been replaced, but his face still bore a few nasty scars. He still walked with a limp, but he only needed the use of a cane. So he wouldn't get bored sitting around all day and feeling useless, Warner kept his word. Konklin was kept busy with computer tasks and paperwork.

It only took a few days after the lieutenant's return for Warner to get back into his previous routine of visiting with Konklin. He had missed their barnstorming sessions and friendly conversations to break up the monotony of the day.

"So you seem to be quite an expert on the computer now, Eddy."

"You were right. Much of what I had already learned came back to me. And I certainly had plenty of time to learn new stuff on the darn thing thanks to your daughter. "I keep forgetting to ask. Did the chief ever find out you took the computer home for me?"

Placing his finger over his closed lips, Warner made the *shh* sound. "That's our little secret."

"Yeah, me, you, and the guys that helped move it to your house and back." Eddy laughed.

"I'm ashamed to admit it, Eddy. But ever since Landall left us, God Bless his soul, and De Mija is out of here, I discovered this whole unit is very protective of their captain and their lieutenant. We truly have a great group of detectives now. It's amazing how stupid they can become when necessary."

"That sounds reassuring enough for me. You know, Joe, there are still some factors in the serial case that I can't recall."

"Aw, don't worry about it. Ever since we've had Leo in jail awaiting trial, we haven't had any more double homicides. He was our snake, all right."

"No, I still think you're wrong, Joe. My guts tell me that you have the wrong person locked up."

"I hate to tell you, but I believe your intuitions are off base this time. Give it up. The case is closed."

"I can't give it up. There's just something that keeps coming back in my mind. Problem is, it's still too fuzzy to get a handle on. All I can tell you is that it has something to do with Leo."

"I think I know what it is, Eddy."

"Geez, Joe, now you're playing mind reader again. Okay, Mister ESP, tell me what you think it is."

"The day of your accident, I came to see you in the emergency room.

You called me Joe. Then you immediately said, 'I know it's Leo.'"

"I know it's Leo what?"

"I thought at the time, because of your severe head trauma, that you were confused. First you thought it was me. Then you thought I was Leo. Then, much later, I got to thinking about it. I figured you found out something about Leo that day of the accident and you were trying to tell me. It could have been something very incriminating against him."

Without warning, words about De Mija flew out of Konklin's mouth. "Oh, you mean that argument he had with Carney a few days before the Carneys were murdered?"

"What?" Joe shouted. "You remember? Is that it?"

"Geez, Joe, quit yelling. I don't know why, but that just came to me."

"So you remember Leo telling you he had an argument with Carney?"

"Yes. He said he and his wife were shopping at some kid's store. Carney and his wife and kid entered the same store. For some reason Carney got very angry at his son. Then he said something else, Joe, but I can't remember exactly what it was."

"Take your time, Eddy. You're doing just fine."

Rubbing his forehead, Konklin remarked, "Geez, I'm not sure. I think it was something like Carney paying for what he did. Oh, I don't know for sure. It's still so much of a blur."

"You did fine, Eddy. Just fine. That's all I needed to hear from you anyway. You have just proven to me, along with the stack of evidence, that Leo truly is our serial killer."

"Hold on, Joe. I still don't think that's true. There's got to be more to that conversation that was important to me at the time. I just can't put my finger on it."

"Take it easy, big guy. It's no longer important to remember the rest of the conversation. Testifying in court to what you just told me will be more than sufficient evidence against the bastard."

"I might not know him very well, but I think I know him better than most of the detectives around here. I don't think he's a murderer," Eddy insisted.

"I'm sorry to disillusion you, Eddy, but he's our man. Leo fit the profile. He had motive. And he definitely had opportunity. Also, I might add, we have the murder weapon. But, hey, don't think about it any more for right now. Remember what Melody said, you shouldn't force yourself to remember things."

"I try not to, but it isn't easy."

"Well, as usual, all good things must come to an end. I've got to get back to my office. It's really great to have you back in the present, if you know what I mean."

"Sure I do, Joe. Maybe, soon, all of my memory will be restored."

With Warner's exit, Konklin went back to his deskwork. However, he could not concentrate. He hobbled with his cane in one hand and his coffee mug in the other and went to the coffee room. Suddenly, Konklin's mind went into a tailspin. Flashes of memories started flooding his mind. Leaving his mug sitting next to the coffeemaker, he went back out to the front office. As he stopped to look around, he noticed Hathaway was sitting at his desk working on the computer. He headed for Hathaway's desk.

"Arnie, may I bother you for a few minutes?"

"Sure, Lieu. What can I do for you?"

"I need your lists that you and the serial killer task force team accumulated. You do still have them, don't you?"

"Which lists?"

"How many were there?"

"Creative writers, handyman, carpenters, hardware stores, department stores --"

"Stop," Eddy interrupted. "How about all of them?"

"Yes, I have them. To tell you the truth, I haven't had time to copy them from my computer to a disk yet." Hathaway, along with all the other detectives, was aware that the lieutenant still had huge lapses in his memory. They were informed, however, to give him as much information as he needed to help him close those memory gaps. "Lieu, you do know that case is closed and we have De Mija locked up, don't you?"

"Yes, I'm aware of that fact. I just have some loose threads of my own that I need to tie up. Is everything in the 'closed case' files?"

"Not yet."

"Then I'd like you make a disk copy of those lists and all files pertaining to that case for me to use on my computer."

"That's not necessary, Lieu. All the info is in an inner-office file on your computer."

"You mean any detective in the unit can read it?"

"Ever since the whole unit got involved on the case, the captain made all the info available. Is there a problem?"

"No. No problem. I just thought going over the records might help refresh my memory."

Konklin hobbled back to his mug and filled it with coffee. Then he returned to his office. After bringing up the *Black Tulip* case files on his computer, he began scanning through the reports.

For some reason he felt the rattle was a clue to something missing in his memory about De Mija. Straining his eyes to view the vast amount of names on the monitor, he carefully scanned all the lists. When he came across the name of a business that rang a bell, and the name of the owner, Konklin wrote down the address. He phoned Detective Hathaway's desk.

"Hathaway."

"Arnie, this is the Lieu. Are you free to drive me someplace?"

"When?"

"Immediately."

"I'm sorry, Lieu, but that's one thing I can't do unless you can wait until later this afternoon. I have a witness coming in --"

"Never mind. Is Brenda around?"

"Sure."

"Put her on the phone."

Within seconds, Konklin heard, "You wanted to speak to me, Lieu?"

"This is personal business, Brenda, but I need a favor."

"Shoot."

"I just found out an old friend of mine has a new baby in the family. The store where I want to get the gift will be closed when I get off work. Are you free to take me?"

"No problem. When do you want to go?"

"Right away."

"I can do that."

"Great. Since I have to ride the elevator, I'll meet you downstairs in five minutes."

Once he had informed the captain that he would be out of the office for a short time, Konklin had Ferndale take him to Tot's Territory. As they drove, Konklin planned in his mind to introduce himself but not as an officer of the law. He was afraid the store's owner would clam up and not give him the information he was seeking.

Ferndale waited in the car while Konklin went inside the shop. Looking around, Konklin did not see anyone. He limped over to the counter where the cash register sat. Still seeing no one about, he hollered. "Hello. Is anyone here?"

Dole came walking out of the back room with a box and a tool in his hands. He placed them on his counter. "Sorry, sir. I got busy unpacking some new merchandise and didn't hear anyone come in. May I help you?"

Within seconds, Konklin's eyes picked up on three very important factors. For the moment, he let a couple of them slide by. Extending his hand, he said, "I'm Eddy Konklin. Are you the owner of this wonderful establishment?"

"Yes, I am, Mr. Konklin." Shaking hands with Konklin, he said, "Jessie Dole. What can I do for you?"

"Say, I like that thingy you're wearing. What do you call a shirt like that?"

"Thank you. It's called a smock. My wife makes them for me. It's kind of a uniform I wear around here for the kids. They love naming all the toys and animals in the pattern."

"Cute idea. Listen, I don't mean to pry, but those are some nasty looking scratches on your arm. What happened?" Getting a look of bewilderment from Dole, Konklin backpedaled. "I'm only asking because I was in a car accident a few months back. I still carry these scars on my face." Since the scars were obvious, Konklin felt no need to specifically point them out. "It looks like you had quite an accident, too. I was wondering if those scabs on your arm will turn into scars."

"I'm not a doctor, so I don't know."

"Yeah, I guess that was kind of a stupid question to ask." *Really stupid.* "May I ask what happened?"

"I got these from my rose bush. I'm generally pretty cautious when I prune or deadhead them. But this time, a few thorns got me good. They were pretty deep scratches at the time. So they're just taking their own good time to heal."

"Well, at least you can cover them up with shirtsleeves if you want. There's no way I can cover mine."

"What does your doctor say about your scarring?"

"He says at my age I'll probably be scarred for life. Doesn't that bother you to have people see that arm? I mean, it looks really ...." Konklin paused for a moment. After the strange look Dole was giving him, he felt he had better try to give a believable explanation for his comments. "I'm sorry. That is really none of my business. I guess I'm still looking for a little hope that the doctor is wrong and these darn things will eventually disappear."

"That's quite all right. You just threw me a curve for a moment. Not too many people walk up to you and start asking about your impurities, no matter how obvious they are and how bad they look."

Laughing, Konklin agreed. "You're right. I guess I would have been a little dumbfounded, too, if someone had done that to me. I guess I should practice a little more finesse? So, you mentioned you grow roses. I like roses. Actually, I love all flowers. Too bad I never had a green thumb, or I would have a garden full of all types and colors — especially tulips. Do you only grow roses?"

"No. I have a lovely garden with a variety of flowers. Mr. Konklin, forgive me for being impolite. But unless I can help you with something, I have work to do."

"I'm so sorry. I was just enjoying the conversation. Do you by any chance know Leo De Mija?"

"Leo? Certainly I know him. He was a very good customer of mine. He's been all over the news, recently. What a shame. You know it's funny, but I didn't know he was a policeman until I saw him on TV."

"Was Allen Carney your customer, too?"

"He was only in here once. But I guess you would call him customer since he made a purchase at that time. Leo and his wife were here then, too. I was shocked to find out Mr. and Mrs. Carney were one of the couples Leo is accused of murdering. And they were killed soon after shopping in here. What's really weird, all those people were my customers."

"You mean all of the murder victims?"

"I sure do."

"Interesting. Would you by any chance remember any sort of incident that occurred in your store between De Mija and any of the murdered victims?"

"Yes. Yes." Dole nodded. "I remember it too well. Leo was very upset that Mr. Carney was scolding and hitting his son over some stupid stuffed animal the child wanted to hold."

"Did De Mija ever make any verbal threats toward Carney in your presence?"

"Yes."

"How about any of the others?"

"No, not to their faces like he did to Mr. Carney. Leo and I discussed some of the other, now-deceased, customers when they weren't around listening."

"What were you discussing?"

"How badly some parents treated their children."

"I take it you don't care for parents correcting their children in public?"

"In public or behind closed doors. Yelling and slapping kids around is abusive. Wait a minute. Are you a reporter or some type of investigator?"

"I'm just here as De Mija's friend."

"But not a close friend, I assume, since you refer to him by his last name."

Like the flick of a switch, Dole's comment triggered another of Konklin's memories. Using last names was not one of his normal traits. He had to quickly think up a good excuse for calling a so-called friend by his last name. "Oh, that?" Konklin laughed. "That comes from my old military days calling everyone by their last names."

"I see. I was never in the military so I didn't know that's how soldiers referred to one another. You know, I would have never dreamed that Leo was the serial killer. Anymore than I am. May I ask why you're asking me all of these questions about him?"

"I believe Leo is innocent of the charges against him. As a friend, I'm trying to prove it. Leo had mentioned your name to me several times. I thought you might be able to clear him of unwarranted charges against him."

"I don't know how I could help. We aren't bosom buddies or anything like that. He's frequented my store quite often in the past. So we became friendly on a conversational basis only. We were both amazed as to how much the two of us were similar in our personalities, our beliefs, are childhood ….Well, I'm sure that's not what you're seeking to find out, is it?"

"Not really. But it would certainly help if you can remember the conversation that day between Leo and Mr. Carney."

"Well, I don't believe Leo really threatened him — at least not around me. But he did say Mr. Carney would answer to him if the child was abused again in his presence."

"That's not what I really wanted to hear," Konklin said, feeling really depressed about the answer he received. "I had hopes that you could help Leo. I see I was wrong."

"I'm sorry."

"Well, I appreciate your time." Konklin turned to the side so he could view the main part of the store yet not have his back to Dole. "I've heard some wonderful things from Leo about your store. You seem to have everything in here that a child would need or want. I'm impressed."

"Thank you. If you'd like to look around, please feel free to do so. Do you have any little ones of your own?"

"No, I wasn't that lucky. However, I'll do as you suggest and look around. Maybe I'll get some ideas for gifts. Every once in a while one of my co-workers' wives has a baby. This seems like it would be the ideal place to get that special baby gift."

Konklin took a few minutes to walk through the store. Spying something of interest, he called for Dole's assistance. Konklin purposely placed both hands on his cane as if he were leaning heavily on it for support. Then he let out a few groans, as if to be in pain.

"Mr. Konklin, are you all right?"

"Oh, I just overdid it." Konklin forced a laugh. "The doctor says I should only be on my feet for five or ten minutes at a time. I guess I'm such a stubborn old fool that I was trying to prove him wrong. I'm afraid I've overdone it. Anyway, I called you over because I would like a package of those." Konklin pointed out a small cellophane package. As Dole picked up the item, Konklin pulled some money out of his pocket. "Here. If you'll be so kind as to put my purchase in a bag, I'll just wait right here."

Taking the money, Dole suggested, "It's a small item. If you would prefer not to carry a bag, you can put it in your pocket."

"Uh, no. I hate to sound like a cheapskate, but I use plastic shopping bags for waste-can liners at home. I'm on a fixed income, so it saves me money. You do have plastic carrying bags, don't you?"

"Yes, of course. I only made the suggestion to make it easier on you since you're walking with a cane. I generally use my small paper sacks for items of this size. But if you want a plastic bag, I'll be more than happy to accommodate you. I'll be right back."

Returning to Konklin with his purchase, receipt and change, Dole asked, "May I do anything else for you today?"

"No, Jessie. You have done quite a lot for me already. Thank you."

* * *

Konklin went back to the car where Ferndale was waiting.

"Well, Lieu, did you get what you came for?"

"I was lucky, Brenda. It was bargain day." He chuckled. "So I got a lot for my money."

"But you only have one bag, and it doesn't look to full to me. If the rest is still in the store, I can certainly go in and get it for you."

"Nope. I've got my little treasure right here," he replied, patting the bag.

"Okay, Leiu, if you say so. Where to now?"

"Take me back to the precinct."

* * *

When Warner spotted Konklin heading his direction, he quickly opened the office door. "Come in."

"Geez, Joe, I can open a door by myself," he grumbled. After being seated, he placed the bag on his lap and leaned the cane against the front of the captain's desk.

As Warner sat on the front of his desk, close to Konklin, he quipped, "Okay, so you're not an invalid. You know, with all the weight you've lost, chubby cheeks just doesn't fit you anymore. I guess I should start calling you gimpy."

"You do and you'll wear my cane as a decoration around your neck."

"That's better than up my --"

"You're right there." Konklin laughed. "You know what, Joe? When you first came to this precinct, there was hardly a foul word that came out of your mouth. Throughout the years, things have changed."

"Are you saying a swear a lot? Because if you are, I don't know if you're serious or not behind that laughter."

"Of course I'm serious. But haven't you noticed that I've done the same since you've known me?"

"Okay, is that good or bad?"

"I don't know what it is. I was only making an observation. Maybe as we get older, tougher, or it's just the business we're in. But there has definitely been a change in our language."

"Change is good," Warner joked.

"I want to be serious for a minute, Joe."

"Sure. What's on your mind?"

"I think you've got the wrong person in jail."

Putting his hand up to stop Konklin in his tracks, Warner objected. "Now wait, Eddy. You're not going to defend Leo again, are you?"

"Yes. But I'm remembering more and more. Hear me out before you cut me off at the knees. One bum leg is enough."

"Very funny. Ha. Ha. Okay, I'm listening."

"I remembered the name of the store that Leo was shopping in when he had a verbal confrontation with Allen Carney. Brenda took me there and I spoke with the owner, Jessie Dole."

"So that was your important errand?"

"Yes. Anyway, Leo had told me once that he and Jessie had become friendly and were on a first-name basis. In their friendly conversations, Leo also told me that Jessie thinks that kids are the most precious treasures that God gives to parents. In other words, he has the same philosophy that Leo has about child abuse. He hates all child offenders. Jessie, himself, admitted that he and Leo were alike in many respects. Now, I only went to Jessie's place with a few questions in mind. But I got a lot more than I bargained for."

"Like what?"

"Jessie has a number of scratches across his left arm. He informed me they were scratches he had received from a rose bush. Also, when he came out of his back room, he was carrying an old-fashioned carton opener, just like the murder weapon in the *Black Tulip* case. The tool had discoloration all over the handle that could be bloodstains. Another important thing I noticed is that he had a nasty scar on his right hand, like he had cut himself pretty severely at one time from something very sharp. And get this. Jessie is left-handed. Are you following me so far?"

"Not really, Eddy, but keep talking."

"While I was looking around this Tot's Territory children's store, I noticed that Jessie carries packages of a certain tiny rattle. The same rattle the snake used with his calling card. He had several of them over on his gift-wrap counter. So, what do you think?"

"What do you mean, what do I think?"

"Come on, Joe. Don't shoot me down here. I think this information is a matter of great importance. Don't you think this guy ought to be checked out?"

Smiling, Warner replied, "On what grounds, Eddy? Just because he knows Leo, dislikes abusive parents, has scratches on his arm, is a southpaw, and carries the same type of rattle in his store? None of that gives us a reason to check him out. Cheese and crackers, Eddy. What are you thinking?"

"Look, Joe, you and I both know that nothing is as it seems when it comes to our work. I just think that a background check on Jessie Dole would be the right thing to do. If he checks out okay, then fine. No harm done. It's just too much of a coincidence about everything that I observed today."

"Eddy, the case is closed already."

"Not until the verdict comes down. Plus, you forgot about the most important factor and that's the carton opener I saw Jessie carrying. I might not remember everything, but I do remember how hard it was going to be finding that out-dated tool."

"Okay, Eddy, we'll check him out. You are really something, big guy. First you don't even want to work with Leo. Now you'll go to all ends to prove he's innocent."

"Every man is innocent until proven guilty, right Joe?" Using his cane for leverage as he got to his feet, the bag fell on the floor.

Warner was quick to retrieve it and handed it back to him. "What's in your bag?"

"Just a small item that interested me. So, we will check out Jessie Dole, right?"

"I'll get a couple of the guys on it right away, Eddy."

"I want to help."

"I'll do you one better. You handle it. Check the board and see who isn't busy working on a case, and get some help. Let me know what you find out, if anything. Oh, let's try and keep this investigation of yours under the collar. No sense in having the chief get wind of it."

Walking toward the door, Konklin remarked, "Thanks for the vote of confidence."

As Konklin left the office, Warner closed the door, beaming. *Doesn't that beat all? Eddy didn't hesitate for one second when I told him to handle the Dole investigation. He walked out of here with more confidence than I've ever seen in him. That's one part of his personality I'm glad Eddy can't remember — and hope he doesn't.*

In the outer office, Konklin went to the case board. Getting the information he needed, he hobbled over to Mayfield's desk.

Mayfield looked up with a smile. "Hey, Lieu. Are you bumming or just getting some exercise?"

Konklin smiled back. He did not have any wise comeback, so he simply stated his business. "Other than Batman and Robin, the Bowery Boys are the only other names not on the board."

Mayfield burst into laughter. "Damn it's good to have you back, Lieu. We've missed your jolly sense of humor around this place. So, what can I do you for?"

"Keep the roar down to a whisper, Arjay. This is all on the QT. I need some quick and quiet investigative work done."

"And you don't want the Batman and Robin team because ...."

"As good detectives as both J.D. and Justin are, I prefer you two because you've worked on the *Black Tulip* case almost since it started back in January."

"I'm almost sure that case is closed, Lieu."

"Officially, yes. Unofficially, no. Interested?"

"Of course."

"Then get Kieyell and come to my office on the double."

"We'll be right in."

"Each of you bring a legal pad with you because I want you to take some notes."

By the time Konklin reached his office door, Mayfield and Roitstein were already right behind him.

"Come on in, guys, and close the door." As Konklin sat behind his desk, he apologized. "Geez, I'm sorry one of you has to stand. But there's no room in here for more than that one chair."

Since both detectives had been in the lieutenant's office many times in the past, they realized that was just another tiny hole in Konklin's memory. As Mayfield sat in the chair, Roitstein was quick to reply, "That's okay, Lieu. I don't mind standing."

Getting settled, Konklin hung his cane on the arm of the desk chair. He then placed his package on the desk in front of him. "Okay, I'm officially forming a small task team. That will only be the three of us. We're going to check out an individual who I think might be the real perp in the serial killer case."

Giving the lieutenant a look of disapproval, Roitstein replied, "Pardon me for being outspoken, Lieu. But we've already got Leo by the short hairs."

"Of course we do. But I want to check out all other possibilities.

Remember, I wasn't around here as all the evidence was building up against Leo. I've got a line on someone that also fits the profile as our snake."

"Isn't the case officially closed?" Kieyell asked.

"That's what everyone keeps telling me. But, like I told your partner, officially, yes. Unofficially, we've got Joe's approval to check out my suspect. On the other hand, we have to keep a lid on it. Joe is going out on a limb for us, and I don't want him to get in trouble."

"Okay, with me," Roitstein said.

"Count me in," Mayfield stated. "Who is he and what do you want us to do?"

"Arjay, I want a complete background check on a man named Jessie Dole. He's the owner of a business called Tot's Territory. It's a children's store. I want the same information on him that the team collected on Leo."

"Hey, Arjay," Roitstein said, patting his partner on the back. "Doesn't that name Jessie Dole ring a bell?"

"No. Why? Should it?"

"I don't know. It just ticks something in my brain, but I can't quite put my finger on it."

"If you remember, tell me," Konklin said. "It may be important." Picking up the bag, Konklin held it in outstretched hand across his desk. "Here, Arjay, pass this to Kieyell." As the bag got passed, Konklin added, "Don't touch the contents inside. I want this taken immediately over to the crime lab for prints. I purposely had Dole pick up the enclosed package and place it in the bag. The package inside might have other prints on it as it could have been touched by dozens of Dole's customers. But I hope not. When you get to the crime lab, ask for Ben Mullins. I'll call ahead and tell him you're on your way. As soon as we get those prints back from the lab, I want you to check them out against the *National Crime Information Center*. If --"

"Excuse me for interrupting you, Lieu. I believe we can dispense with the NCIC and save us some time."

"How's that, Kieyell?"

"Sergeant Kym Davies, the profiler that worked on the case, said that the perp wouldn't have a past record. She based her findings on the age factor of the perp. I didn't read the report, but I remember Cap briefing us after it came in."

"Okay, scratch the NCIC for now. We'll keep it in mind if we decide to check out those files later. Now, Ben should get those prints back here by tomorrow." Konklin stopped talking when he saw Mayfield lift his forefinger as if to get his attention. "Is there a problem?"

"Sort of. We never got any prints of the perp from any of the crime scenes. So what are you going to compare Dole's prints to?"

"This is just a precautionary measure, in case we do need them, Arjay. Any other questions?"

"No."

"Kieyell, hurry back here from the lab. While Arjay's busy with his end of this investigation, I want you to help me double-check some computer information."

"Since the case is already in the closed file, how do you want me to list this on the board?" Mayfield asked.

"Rats! Hold on a minute." Konklin phoned Warner.

"Capt. Warner."

"Joe. Would Doogle be upset if I had a couple of our detectives help me regain some of the missing pieces of my memory?"

"He probably would on company time."

"But this would be work-related. Not personal."

"Hold on and I'll find out." Placing Konklin on hold, Warner made an outside call. After receiving his answer, he reconnected with Konklin. "As long as there are no pressing cases, especially in the homicide division, then it's okay by Doogle."

"Thanks, Joe." Hanging up the phone, Konklin grinned. "Well, here's your answer, Arjay. Write down Konklin on the board under your and Kieyell's names. Everyone knows I still need help with my memory, so this should satisfy most of the other detectives' curiosity. For those super-insistent ones, just send them to me. Well, the day is half over and we're racing against time. So, let's get busy."

As soon as the two detectives left his office, Konklin called his friend at the crime lab and explained what he needed.

"I can't get those prints for you for at least two or three weeks," Mullins reported.

"Come on, Ben, this is a matter of life and death. I need them by tomorrow morning at the latest."

"You're asking the impossible, you know. What's the big rush, Eddy?"

"I want to make sure Leo De Mija gets a fair shake. Those prints could help my investigation."

"Fair shake, hell," the lab tech remarked with bitterness. "I have no use for a dirty cop, especially a murdering one. Hey, wait. I already have De Mija's prints in the record files. Why do you need them lifted from the package of rattles you're sending over?"

"Those aren't his prints on the package, Ben. They belong to a man by the name of Jessie Dole. I don't have time to sit and explain everything. Do I get the prints tomorrow, or do I let that blonde know how to contact you?"

"Boy, talk about playing dirty. That's pretty close to being blackmail, Eddy." He laughed. "Okay, you win. We're swamped over here, so I'll have to stay a lot later than normal. You'll get your prints by one o'clock tomorrow afternoon."

"Geez, my hearing must have gotten screwed up when I had my accident. I could have sworn you said by nine tomorrow morning. Thanks, Ben. I knew you'd see things my way." Konklin chuckled.

"Just remember, you owe me one, Eddy. That blonde business should be dead and buried by now."

"I'll try to remember that in the future, Ben. Bye."

* * *

When Roitstein returned to the lieutenant's office, Konklin had already made two printouts of the lists from the serial case files. "Here," Konklin said handing one set of the printouts to Roitstein. "None of these damn lists were in alphabetical order. Geez. One of these days, I'm going to have to teach you computer whiz kids how to use your machines." He let out a grunting chuckle. "Have a seat, Kieyell, and I'll tell you what we're going to do."

Rearranging paperwork, Konklin cleared some space on his desk so he and Roitstein could work without all the clutter.

"You recognize these lists, don't you?"

"Sure I do."

"Good. We're looking for the name Jessie Dole. Since four eyes are better than two, I figure it's better that we both look through these lists of names. Each time you find this guy's name ...." Konklin paused and opened his top desk drawer. Getting out two highlighter pens, he handed one to Roitstein. "Highlight it. Then we'll go back and compare notes."

"I hate to tell you, Lieu, but we've already cross-checked these lists. That's one of the reasons we suspected Leo because his name came up on a couple of them."

"Well, then, I guess I'm running uphill backwards. Did you find any other names that came up on two or more lists?"

"Offhand, I don't remember. But it should be in one of the reports on file."

"I've only scanned the surface of the file. It will take hours to read every report to find that information. Geez, it would really save a lot of time if I knew that answer. Other than the reports, who would know?"

"If anyone would remember, it would be Brenda. See, Arnie and Eric did all the input. But Brenda is the one that crosschecked all the names." When Konklin reached for his phone, Roitstein asked, "What are you doing?"

"I'm going to call Brenda."

"That's what I thought. She's not at her desk."

"That's just great."

"Not a problem, Lieu. I can reach her on her cell."

"Geez, why didn't I think of that?" As Roitstein removed his cell phone from his belt and started to key-in Brenda's number, Konklin stopped him. "Wait. Maybe that's not such a good idea, Kieyell. I know Brenda is trustworthy. But I really don't want to involve any other detective in this investigation right now."

"We've already got it covered."

"How do you figure?"

"Since helping you regain parts of your memory is the new case on the board, Brenda won't suspect a thing."

As Konklin nodded, Roitstein proceeded to depress the remaining digits of Ferndale's cell number.

"Detective Ferndale speaking."

"Brenda, Kieyell here."

"What's up?"

"Can you talk for a minute?"

"Sure. I'm just out running an errand for the captain. What's up?"

"I need to pick your brain regarding the *Black Tulip* case."

"Why, are we reopening the case?"

"Oh, hell, no. I'm trying to help our lieutenant regain some of his memories concerning our old case files. Also, since he wasn't around for some of that particular case, I was just filling him in on the evidence we gathered."

"That's great. How can I help?"

"Other than Leo De Mija, do you remember who showed up on our lists more than once."

"Wow, Kieyell, you don't want much, do you?" She laughed. "Hmm, let me think a minute. Oh, now I remember. There were only two that I know of. But you just said you didn't want Leo's name."

"So, who was the other one?"

"Someone by the name of Doll. Da … De. Dell. No, that's not it. It wasn't a real unusual name. Something about the name reminded me of food. Or maybe it was the other way around. Hold on, Kieyell, I'm thinking."

"I'm not going anywhere."

"I think his last name reminded me of pineapple. Oh, that's it. The name was Dole. Jessie Dole."

"Good girl. Say, now I remember why that name rang a bell with me. His name came up on the computer list."

"Right. He has two computers, both with bubble-jet printers. One in his home and one in his place of business."

"What else do you remember about him?"

"His name also came up on the creative writing list." There was a brief moment of silence. Finally she responded, "Oh, he owns his own business and purchases a large amount of the rattles from the import house back East. He carries the small packages of rattles for retail in his store."

"Anything else?"

"No, Kieyell, that's all. If you recall, once we started after Leo, we no longer pursued anyone else."

"Vividly. Okay, Brenda, you've been a big help. See you when you get back."

Briefly, Roitstein recapped the information he had received from Ferndale. Konklin was elated.

"Jessie Dole, huh? We may be on to something, Kieyell, my boy.

Okay, I'll repeat what we have so far, and you play the devil's advocate. Since your hands move faster than mine, I'll let you take notes."

After going over a few of the lists, Roitstein asked, "If Leo had two cases of those tiny rattles sitting in his garage, how come none of the stores we visited had a record of him purchasing such a large order?"

Leaning over the desk was beginning to put a strain on Konklin's back. He sat back in his chair to relax. "Leo told me that he started visiting Dole's store long before he ever got married. It seems he wandered in there one day, just out of curiosity He and Dole became friendly. My guess is, Leo ordered the rattles from Dole before the De Mija baby was born."

"Then why didn't Dole tell us about the order when we questioned him?"

"Was he questioned?"

"Well, now that you mention it, I don't really know for sure. I thought we had checked out every store in the area that sold the rattles."

"Maybe Dole's store was overlooked, Kieyell? Or maybe he was questioned and lied because that would put him too close to the investigation? If he keeps his mouth shut, he doesn't get any more detectives snooping around."

"Any of those explanations could make sense."

"Here's two more factors for you, Kieyell." Konklin went on to explain Dole's scar and scratches. He ended with, "Even though I was around when Leo cut his hand, it was bandaged when I saw it. So I never saw the wound, nor do I know if he bears a scar."

"He does." Roitstein put the papers and highlighter on the lieutenant's desk. Placing his right hand flat on the desk, he used his left index finger as a pointer. "Right about here," he said, moving the left finger across his right hand, "is where Leo's scar is."

"Damn, Kieyell. That's in the same area as Dole's. Do you know where the scratches on Leo's left arm were located?"

"Sure." Switching hands, Roitstein moved his right forefinger across an area on his left arm. "Right in this area."

"Again, same as Dole's."

"This is getting too weird, Lieu."

"I know. Now, according to the files, Chow and Cindy Lu Chiu King were the last victims. The dying man's last word to the EMT was noem — n-o-e-m."

"Right. When we found out they were of Chinese descent, some of us thought maybe the word was Chinese. But after researching the language, we couldn't find anything that helped us. Truthfully, none of us understood all the symbols that language is made up of."

"Okay, so let's stick to English. Could that possibly mean, 'know him'?"

Roitstein leaned back in his chair, bringing his left foot up to rest on his left thigh. "Know him," he repeated.

"While you're thinking, here's why I came up with it. Each one of the victims had small children. It only stands to reason why each one of them shopped at Tot's Territory, since it's located in close proximity to where all of the homicides took place. Dole verified all the victims had been his customers. And, he had witnessed parents correcting their children in ways he didn't approve of. So it's only natural the victims recognized their assailant's face. That's how I came up with *know him*."

"It could possibly mean that. But if it did, Leo would also fit the bill."

"What do you mean?"

"We found out that he was pretty well-known in that area, too."

"Looks like I should have read more of the case file. So, what's the connection?"

"That's the area he and Ripley used to patrol when Leo was still in uniform. I guess you would call that another coincidence."

"I guess." Kieyell laughed. "Well, let's get back to some facts. The FBI Crime Lab reported that the piece of black plastic found in the last victim's clutched fist could have been a part of a garbage bag."

Puzzled, Roitstein wrinkled his brow. "I didn't know the FBI reports were back yet to confirm those findings."

"They're not," Konklin replied, flashing his devilish grin. "I'm only guessing since I don't know of anything else that's made out of black plastic. Oh, ding-a-ling." Konklin's eyes widened. "A bell just went off in my head."

"Give."

"No wonder we couldn't find any clothes at the cleaners with bloodstains. If our snake covered his body with black plastic garbage bags, he would naturally keep his own clothes clean. That way he wouldn't leave any DNA behind. Not to mention how disposable the bags would be after the killings. Add the piece of latex found at one of the crime scenes and you've got latex gloves covering the perp's hands."

"Could be, but I think you're grasping at straws. The gloves I can understand. But it would take a really creative mind to figure out a way to cover your complete body with garbage bags."

"Creative mind, indeed. Let me ask you something, Kieyell. If your neck was in the noose, and you knew you were innocent, wouldn't you rather have someone like me fighting in your corner? Or would you prefer the whole force turn their backs on you and not try to prove your innocence?"

"There's no question that I'd like to have someone like you trying to prove me innocent."

"So grasping at straws, no matter how far-fetched, would be within the realm of possibly saving an innocent man. Especially a man who is one of us."

"Definitely."

"You agree that Dole is a good suspect?"

"With everything you've told me so far, he sounds as good as Leo does for a suspect. So what do we do next?"

"We need to wait for Arjay's report. I can't go to Joe until I have all the details. Also, if everything checks out the way I think it will, then we'll have enough to get a search warrant for Dole's store."

"That reminds me, Lieu. You're going to need a sample of Dole's blood."

"True. So?"

"So, lots of luck. Since the court ruled in Leo's favor, Cap had to trick Leo to get some of his blood for testing."

"I know. And there's no way I can get a court order to get Dole's blood tested until I have more proof against him. Well, until I can think of something as clever as Joe did, we won't worry about it for right now."

"Okay. Well, unless you have anything further for me to do in here, why don't I give Arjay a hand?"

"Good idea, Kieyell. Boy, it's amazing how much footwork these computers save us. One click on-line and you can practically find out everything you want to know about someone without ever leaving the office."

"True. On the other hand, I blame this freedom of information era for the rash of stolen identities that are plaguing this country. If our government would outlaw anyone from posting, giving away, or charging for personal information on *any* individual, it would sure make our jobs much easier."

"You're right there, Kieyell. We could spend less time searching for ID thieves. And more time on other crimes."

* * *

The following morning, as promised, Mullins had the set of prints delivered to Konklin's office. Regardless of what the profiler had stated in her report, Konklin decided to have the prints checked out with the NCIC. Roitstein followed through with the lieutenant's orders. To Konklin's dismay, Jessie Dole had no previous arrests or records.

* * *

As the days progressed into weeks, Mayfield and Roitstein were still accumulating important information on Dole. All Konklin could do was wait.

CHAPTER FORTY-TWO

Most felons who are arrested and put behind bars have to wait — many times as long as two years — before they ever get their day in court. De Mija was one of the fortunate ones. He had not even spent a total of six weeks in lock-up and his trial date was already scheduled for the second of August. Many felt this was because of the public's outcry that De Mija had been a policeman and they wanted swift justice.

Warner was pleased with the upcoming court date. He was ready to have De Mija proven guilty and locked up for life.

On the other hand, the usual jovial Konklin was vexed. Court was going to convene in five days. Konklin felt like a time bomb waiting to go off. He had not received enough evidence yet to take to Warner or the district attorney's office to get De Mija's case either postponed or have all charges against him dropped. So far, everything he had on Dole, no matter how it looked, was only circumstantial.

Early one morning, as Konklin sat at his computer writing up some reports for Warner, there was a knock at his door. "Come in," he bellowed. As his door opened, Mayfield and Roitstein stepped inside. Happy to see them, he said, "Well, fellas, it's after seven A.M. I figured you two would be out and about already."

"No need to," Mayfield said.

"Why not?"

Mayfield made himself comfortable in the spare chair and placed his file of notes on a portion of Konklin's desk. After closing the door, Roitstein leaned against it.

"We've got lots of information for you."

"Say again. You have information for me?" Konklin was teasing, of course, and the detectives knew it.

Mayfield laughed. "This is so weird, Lieu. In the book of life, one would swear Dole's background was taken from the same pages as De Mija's."

"He's right, Lieu," Roitstein chimed in. "Wait until you hear the low-down."

"Well, let's hear it."

Picking up his legal pad of notes to refer to, Mayfield began. "Dole's parents disappeared just before he graduated high school. While in school and the first few years of college, he held down odd cleaning jobs. However, he had money to keep his bills paid, afford him college fees, and start his own business. Dole is married and has one daughter. The strange thing about his marriage is the fact he was married on the exact same day as the De Mijas. And both Dole's and De Mija's daughters were born on the same day.

"Dole excelled in school, especially in creative writing. As far as personal friendships, he has none. He's a loner, just like De Mija. Again, like De Mija, Dole still lives in the house he was raised in. The house and property set pretty much in a secluded area, so neighbors are at least a quarter-mile away. So, Lieu, what do you think so far? Don't these two guys' lives sound alike?"

"Although it's all very interesting, Arjay, none of it is essential. Don't you have anything I can really sink my teeth into?"

"Kieyell, why don't you fill Lieu in on what you found out while I take a breather and get a cup of coffee."

"Hey, that coffee sounds like a great idea." Konklin picked up his empty coffee mug and handed it to Mayfield. "I could sure use a cup myself."

"Sure." As Mayfield took the cup, one look at the interior made him cringe. "Ooh, don't you ever wash this thing?"

"Why? It just gets dirty again." Konklin laughed.

"Kieyell, can I get you a cup?"

"No, thanks. I've had my caffeine limit for the day."

"Okay, I'll be right back."

Roitstein moved away from the door so Mayfield could pass. The door was left ajar so Mayfield could return with two cups of coffee and easily enter. Moving to the back of the now-vacant chair, Roitstein proceeded with his verbal report.

"First off, I went to the library and checked out a fully illustrated book on flowers." When Konklin started snickering, Roitstein smiled. "This really does have to do with our investigation, Lieu. I promise."

"I'm sure it does. It just touched my funny bone. I'm sorry, Kieyell. Please go on."

"Taking the book with me, I took a drive out to Dole's place. From the back alley, with the assistance of my trusty binoculars, I could see a garden. It sits just behind the house. In the middle of the garden are several green plants. They looked like flowers that had lost their blooms. So, I checked the book to see what the stems of tulips looked like. I was able to determine those were tulips in his garden. Now, I don't know how you're going to find out if they have black blooms."

"Easy. Next time I see Dole, I'll ask him."

"Okay. Not too surprising with everything else they have in common, the Doles live in the same area as the De Mijas. Which, of course, you had already told us about. I must of knocked on twenty doors around Dole's house before I found someone who remembered his parents. Seems the parents were both alcoholics, very abusive, and ...."

Slamming his hand on the desk, Konklin startled Roitstein. "That's the kind of meat and potatoes I'm looking for, Kieyell. A background of abuse gives Dole the perfect motive for murder."

The conversation stopped when Mayfield entered with the two cups of coffee. He placed them both on the desk and reclaimed the vacant chair. Roitstein closed the door and, once again, leaned against it.

"Thanks, Arjay," Konklin said with a smile.

"No problem. Okay, where are we?"

After taking a cautious sip of his steaming hot coffee, Konklin responded, "Kieyell just told me about Dole's childhood abuse. Do you have anymore to add, other then what you two have already told me?" Both detectives shook their heads in response. "Well, hopefully we've got enough." Konklin picked up the phone and dialed.

"Capt. Warner."

"Joe. Eddy. Do you have time to hear the information we've gotten together to help prove Leo is either innocent or there is too much doubt to prosecute him?"

At first there was dead silence on the other end of the phone. Finally, Warner answered. "Sure, Eddy. Come on over."

Konklin hung up the phone and started gathering up his paperwork. "Okay, guys, head on over to the captain's office. I'll be there shortly."

Knowing the lieutenant's pride, both Mayfield and Roitstein were afraid to offer him any assistance. They left his office. With papers in one hand and his coffee mug in the other, Konklin followed.

When they entered the room, Warner was taken aback at what he was witnessing. "Hey, Eddy, where's your cane?"

No one was more surprised than Konklin as he looked at his hands. Neither he nor the other two detectives had even noticed that he had walked without assistance. "Geez, Joe, I walked over here without it. Isn't that great?"

"That's wonderful. But please, sit down before you overdo it."

When everyone was seated, Warner said. "You know, Eddy, I promised to hear you out with an open mind. However, you can't tell me that you've got enough evidence together in such a short amount of time that will prove Leo's innocence."

"Maybe not. But we sure have a lot to cause reasonable doubt of his guilt. All the heavy-duty legwork was done months ago. So we started with one simple question to Brenda. With her memory, the computer, and two great detectives to work with, we found out what we needed to know in record time."

"Okay, Eddy, let's hear what you've got."

Warner sat back, patiently and attentively, listening to all the information. When the three detectives concluded with their information, Warner was almost flabbergasted. But, not yet convinced. "You're right, De Mija and Dole are like two peas in a pod. However, it's not enough solid evidence."

"Come on, Joe. It's pretty much the same evidence as you have on Leo. Can't we at least pick Dole up for questioning? We can ask him about his whereabouts on the nights of the murders. Then we can check out his alibis. If that doesn't prove anything, I swear in the name of all that's holy,

I'll give up. I promise."

Warner was trying desperately to take into consideration that Konklin, in his present state of mind, was not the excellent detective he once was. He did not want to placate his lieutenant, but he did not want to offend or disillusion him either. He hated walking on eggshells. "Look, we don't have anything tangible to connect Dole with the homicides. You don't even know for a fact that he knew but only one of the victims. And that's because Dole and De Mija were both present when the Carney's were in his store."

"Like I told you from the get-go. Dole told me *all* the victims were his customers."

"There's a huge problem though, Eddy. From what you've told me, you never once bothered to tell Dole that you were an MPPD detective. None of your conversation with him will hold up in court."

"I don't think you give me enough credit for doing my job, Joe. I'm well aware I sneaked in the back door, so to speak, to get Dole to talk to me. But I knew if I could get enough circumstantial evidence on him, we could get a court order to confiscate his business records. If so, we should be able to find out for sure if any or all of the victims did patronize his store."

"Without good cause, we can't do that. It's too bad you don't have his blood sample. Now that would be something we could use since the rare blood type we were looking for is O Negative."

Slowly, Konklin rose to his feet. Turning to Roitstein and Mayfield, he winked. "Okay, Joe, you're right. I didn't have my thinking cap on. I'm sorry to have taken up your time. Come on guys, we still have a few days left. Let's go."

In the outer office, Konklin asked, "You guys up for a ride?"

"As long as you're not driving," Mayfield joked.

"Very funny, wise guy," Konklin retorted with a laugh. "Give me some time to put my coffee cup and papers in my office. I'll meet you two downstairs in the parking lot."

From the top drawer of his desk, Konklin took out a pencil and small notepad. The notepad was placed into his shirt pocket. Then he pulled a clean hanky from the back pocket of his pants and tucked it into his side pocket. Picking up his cane, with pencil in hand, Konklin walked out the door. On the way through the front office, he stopped at the pencil sharpener. After sharpening the lead to a lethal point, he carefully stuck the pencil into the pocket with the notepad.

* * *

At Tot's Territory, Konklin entered the store with pencil and notepad in one hand, cane in the other. Spotting Dole, Konklin smiled. "Hello, Jessie. Do you remember me? Eddy Konklin."

"Sure I do. How are you doing today?"

"Still toughing it out." Konklin laughed as he hobbled slowly toward

Dole. *Good, he's wearing one of his short-sleeved smocks again,* he thought.

Getting as close to Dole as he possibly could without being obnoxious, Konklin suddenly lost his balance. As his body lunged forward into Dole, his arms flew in the air and back down, like the speed of lightning when it strikes. As his hands grabbed out at Dole for assistance, his cane went clanking across the tiled floor, followed by the notepad and pencil.

"Hey, watch out," Dole yelled, trying to pull back from Konklin's body yet keeping him from falling to the floor. "Are you all right?"

Konklin allowed Dole to support him and help him to stand upright. Once Dole figured Konklin was balanced enough to stand on his own, Dole let go and retrieved Konklin's cane.

"Here you are. Gosh, I hope you're okay? You nearly scared the wits out of me."

Taking the cane with his left hand, Konklin leaned on it. He held his right hand up to his chest. "Thanks, Jessie. Yes, I think I'm okay. I just had a dizzy spell there for a moment."

Dole picked up the notepad and pencil. As he handed them back to Konklin, he said, "That's a pretty deadly weapon you have there."

"Yes. I like my pencils sharp," Konklin admitted, placing the notepad and pencil in his shirt pocket. "I was going to have you write down some items and prices for me. But now I'm not feeling so good."

"Do you want to sit down?"

"No. No. I'll be fine. Oh, my," Konklin stated, pointing to Dole's arm, "You're bleeding. How do you suppose that happened?"

Dole looked at his arm. "I think you got me with that weapon you call a pencil. When you lunged forward, it jammed into arm."

Konklin pulled the handkerchief out of his pocket. "I feel so bad, Jessie. Here, let me wipe off the blood that's dripping down your arm." As Dole started to take the handkerchief, Konklin pulled back. "Now come on. Let me help. You'll make me feel better since I'm the one that caused your wound." Dole conceded. "I hope you have something around to put on that, Jessie." Konklin said, pulling his hand away and clenching the bloodstained handkerchief.

"I have a first-aid kit in the back room."

"Why don't you go put something on your arm. Since I'm not feeling as well as I thought I was, I think I'd better come back another time."

"I'll be fine. But I think you need to get someplace and sit down."

"You're absolutely right there, Jessie. My car's just down the street."

"You don't mean you drive in that condition?"

Konklin chuckled. "No. I have a driver. Well, I'll see you soon."

"I hope you feel better," Dole called out as Konklin hobbled out the door.

"Oh, I'm going to feel much better in no time at all." Konklin chuckled to himself. He felt so exhilarated, he wanted to skip to the car where Mayfield and Roitstein were waiting around the corner from the store.

As Konklin got into the car, he let out a roar. "Yahoo, fellas. Turn on the siren and get me to the morgue, ASAP. I have a date with Saggy."

As fast as Mayfield drove, Konklin talked. He explained his riveting performance in the store. Mayfield and Roitstein had a good laugh.

"How in the world did you ever dream up such a scheme?" Roitstein asked.

"Easy. I just took a chapter out of our captain's book."

"I didn't know Cap had written a book."

Mayfield removed his hat and hit Roitstein in the head. "He didn't, screwball."

"Hey, Eddy just said he did," Roitstein complained with humor. "Keep your hands on the wheel, Arjay, before we have an accident. When Eddy asked you to rush him to the morgue, I think he meant while he was still alive."

"You've got that right," Konklin spouted from the backseat.

"So, Lieu what did you mean when you said Cap wrote a book?" Roitstein asked.

"I believe the report on his actions has been recorded for posterity. And soon, so will mine."

Puzzled, Roitstein asked, "I'm still confused."

"Lieu's talking about the way Cap got a blood sample from Leo," Mayfield explained.

"Oh. Now I get it."

"It's about time. You'll have to forgive my partner, Lieu. He's a great detective but sometimes a bit dense."

In retaliation, Roitstein switched rolls with his partner. Grabbing the slouched hat from Mayfield's head, he hit Mayfield across the arm. This, of course, gave all three of them a good laugh.

Not wanting to get their butts in a sling, Mayfield slowed down and turned the siren off a block from the lab where the ME was located.

Getting out of the car, Konklin asked, "You two coming in with me?"

"Have a heart, Lieu," Mayfield replied. "It's way past lunch time and we're starved."

"I should only be in there a few minutes. If you'll wait, I'll go have lunch with you." Suddenly, he got the most unusual look on his face.

"What's the matter, Lieu, are you sick?" Mayfield asked out of concern.

"No, and I hope I'm not going to be."

"Then what's the matter?"

"Lunch plus Saggy. The two of them don't mix in my book."

Mayfield and Roitstein roared with laugher.

"Good luck, Lieu. Hurry back."

Konklin headed straight to the Medical Examiner's office.

"Well, as I live and breathe," Sagdorf commented as the detective walked through the door.

"Hello, Saggy. Hey, I don't think I've ever seen you sitting at your desk. What, no corpse to work on today?"

"I just finished a stiff not twenty minutes ago. Just making some notes before I forget. I heard you were back, Eddy. Sorry I haven't had time to call and welcome your return."

"That's okay. I understand." Konklin held out his hand that held the soiled handkerchief. "I've got an urgent request."

Looking at the hand Konklin was extending, Sagdorf asked, "What happened? Did you cut yourself?"

"No. That's not my blood. I took it off a perp in a very important murder case, Saggy. I need it tested, yesterday. I need to know the blood type."

"I can do it for you maybe tomorrow."

"Oh, Saggy, you're breaking my heart. I said I needed it yesterday. It really is a matter of life or death."

"Well, if it's that important."

"It certainly is."

The ME checked the desk calendar where he kept his handwritten schedule. "I guess I can put that off for a while."

"So, you can fit me into today's schedule?"

"Actually, I was thinking right now. If you want to stick around?"

"You bet I do."

Rising from his chair, Sagdorf said, "Hold on to the hankie and follow me into my lab."

Konklin followed medical examiner into the laboratory. After covering his hands with latex gloves, Sagdorf took the handkerchief from Konklin's hand.

"There's disinfectant soap over there." Sagdorf motioned to the sink with his head. "You wash up, and I'll get busy."

After Konklin had thoroughly washed his hands, he called and let the detectives know their wait would be extended. Then he rested against a countertop and waited.

When Sagdorf's test was conclusive, he said, "Strange. I hardly ever see O Negative blood type. Now I've tested it twice just in the past few months."

Konklin stood erect. "Tell me that blood type again. I want to be sure I'm not hearing things."

"O Negative."

"Saggy, that's music to my ears. Tell me something, why didn't you test Leo De Mija's blood?"

"Since Joe wanted to make sure there wasn't a tinge of doubt, he had me send De Mija's blood sample to the CBI Lab."

"But you've never been wrong with any of your lab results, have you?"

"No, that's true. However, I have to admit, they have far better technology than I do. And their results in court hold more water than mine do. As a matter of fact, if this is so important to you, maybe you should consider sending this blood sample to them also."

"Maybe later, if it's needed. For now, your results are all I need."

"For my records, whose blood did I just test?"

"Jessie Dole. Now, if you can write me an official report that states your findings, I'll have one of the men pick it up tomorrow."

"After lunch, I hope?" Sagdorf strongly suggested, peering over his glasses.

"After lunch it is. You may have just saved a man's life. I'll let you get back to your office work. Thanks a million, Saggy."

Konklin rushed back to the car.

"That was the longest thirty minutes I've ever spent in my life," Roitstein quipped.

"Can I make it up to you if I give you the good news?"

"Throw in lunch and we'll forgive you," Mayfield teased.

"It's a deal. Let's go."

"Where to?"

"Anywhere that serves food and is air-conditioned," Konklin replied.

* * *

Konklin felt like the Pied Piper as he headed to Warner's office. He could see through the window that Warner was alone and sitting behind his desk. He rapped on the glass.

"It's open," Warner yelled.

"Capt. Warner, permission to enter, sir," Konklin clowned.

"You must have either had a few cocktails for lunch or you have some good news. Which is it?"

"Have you even known me to drink at lunch while I'm on duty?"

"Nope. But you can't blame me for asking." Warner smiled. "Come on in and sit."

As the three detectives stepped inside the office, Konklin said, "We don't have time to sit. I want you to know, Jessie Dole's blood is O Negative."

Warner's eyes widened. "What? How do you know that?"

"I won't take the time to tell you now. But Saggy's official report will be in your hands tomorrow afternoon. Now do I have your permission to bring Dole in as a suspect?"

Warner shook his head. "Cheese and crackers, Eddy. You are really putting yours and my butts on the line."

"Nope, just mine, Joe. I got it all figured out. Let's say I do this without your permission. Then the chief can't hold you responsible. And, when the time comes that he calls me on the carpet, I'll play loss of memory."

Warner had to laugh in spite of himself. "Eddy, you … what about your partners in crime that are standing behind you? How are you going to keep them out of trouble?"

"Easy. These detectives were just following orders. After all, I am the lieutenant."

When Konklin winked, Warner took the lead.

"All three of you get out of here," Warner demanded. "You have my final say on this issue and we never had this conversation. So what you do when you leave here is your responsibility."

"Yes, Capt. Warner." Konklin smiled with a twinkle in his eyes. "I don't understand. But, you're the boss." Konklin turned to Mayfield and Roitstein with a dejected look on his face. "Sorry, fellas, I thought I had the right evidence this time. Well, come on. We'll go back to my office and kick around a few more ideas. The captain's right. We have to do everything by the book."

The three men walked to Konklin's office. Once everyone was inside and the door was closed, Konklin's facial expression changed from anguish to euphoria. He tossed his cane on the desk and sat in his chair. "Okay. You two pick up Dole and bring him in."

Still standing, the bewildered Mayfield and Roitstein looked at each other. Then they both turned and looked at the lieutenant as if he had really gone off the deep end.

Somewhat stupefied, Mayfield asked, "Didn't you hear the captain?"

"I certainly did, Arjay. Didn't you hear me?"

Roitstein was also questioning the order. "Sir?"

"You are acting under my orders. Dole knows my face, and he's never seen either of you before. So I want you two to hurry back to his store and pick him up for questioning. I want him to account for the nights of the homicides. Go over your notes so you have the exact dates and times in question. Like I said before, once we get that info we can check it out. If he has valid alibis, then he's home free. If not, then I believe Joe will climb aboard our ship. When you get back, take him into room two. I'll be observing from the window of opportunity." Eddy chortled.

CHAPTER FORTY-THREE

Time had slipped away as Konklin busied himself with computer work. It seemed like no time at all when he heard a knock at his door. "Come in."

Opening the door, Mayfield stuck his head into the office. "Kieyell's taking Dole into the interview room now."

"Great."

"I assume the camera's on."

"Geez, Arjay. I spent a lot of time away from here. But what's your excuse?"

"For what?"

"While I was gone, Joe had a new camera installed. It runs 24/7. How come you don't know that?"

"Because I've been too busy to read inner-office memos, Lieu."

"Take the time so you know what's going on around here." Mayfield nodded. "Better get in there with Kieyell and Dole. I'll be at the two-way, shortly."

Before leaving, Mayfield held up crossed fingers. "Here's wishing us luck."

As fast as he could move, Konklin rushed to the observation room. As he listened and observed, it appeared to him that Dole was very cooperative. Once all of their questions had been answered, the two detectives came out of the room and joined Konklin.

"Well, I assume you heard everything," Mayfield asked.

"Yes. According to Dole, he was home every one of those nights, and his wife can verify it. Dole didn't make any telephone calls before he left the store, did he?"

"No."

"Arjay, get on over to his house and question Mrs. Dole."

"If she's a loyal spouse, you know her statements are going to agree with what Dole told us," Roitstein said. "She might lie — just like the Cap thinks Leo's wife is lying for him."

"We'll have to take that chance, Kieyell. Arjay, you can tell Mrs. Dole that we're investigating her husband. But don't mention that he's here. Now, if she comes straight out and asks you, then don't lie to her. Kieyell, go back in there and get into a friendly conversation with Dole. Maybe if he feels more comfortable with a one-on-one, he'll slip and give us something of value. I'll be back in my office waiting for your return, Arjay."

"Yeah, and make it snappy," Roitstein said. "I don't know how long I can keep a conversation going with Dole before he'll get suspicious."

"As gabby as you are, I doubt it," Mayfield teased.
"Okay, you two. Get to work."

* * *

In his office, Konklin paced back and forth. When his legs gave out on him, he sat and rested for a while. Then he got back up and paced some more. Two hours later, Mayfield returned.

"Anything?"

"Nothing. His alibis check out. Mrs. Dole says she's a light sleeper so she can hear her daughter if she wakes up. And she's positive she would have heard her husband leave his room and leave the house in the middle of the night."

"Backup. What's that part again about his room?"

"She says her husband started having terrible nightmares since the beginning of the year. So he moved to the kid's room and has been sleeping on the floor. In turn, the kid was moved into Mom's room. Dole's reasoning was because he was afraid of accidentally hurting his wife during one of his nightmares. So the move was for her safety."

"Arjay, just out of curiosity, did she give you any explanation as to where and when Dole got the scar on his hand or the scratches on his arm?"

"Well, yes. The times bothered me at first, but the answers sounded reasonable."

"What do you mean?"

"Her explanation was due to Dole's nightmares. She said one morning he woke up and had a terrible gash on the top of his right hand. The only thing they could figure out was that he had hit his hand against the corner of the crib as he tossed and turned. When I asked her if there was any blood on the bottom of the crib, she said, 'As strange as it sounds, we never found any.' Another night, Dole woke up from another horrific dream with the gouges on his arm. The only explanation they could come up with was that he actually clawed himself in his sleep."

"So, how does that bother you?"

"You're not going to believe this. Each morning he had awakened with blood on him, were the exact days that two of the homicides occurred."

"What? Something's not right here."

Mayfield's cell phone started playing *The Stout-Hearted Men* music. "Hold on, Lieu. It's Kieyell. Hey, what's up?"

"You and Lieu better get in here on the double."

"We're on our way."

Konklin and Mayfield rushed into the interview room. Dole was sitting in a chair as if he were in a trance.

"What happened?" Konklin asked, observing Dole.

"I don't know. We've been talking for some time now. Finally he asked me if he was a suspect in the murders we were asking him about. When I told him we were just asking questions, he clammed up. When I tried to get him to talk, it was like I wasn't even in the room," Roitstein explained. "Look at his eyes. They're all glassy and spooky looking."

"Arjay, get Cap in here on the double," Konklin ordered.

When Warner entered the room, his first response was, "What in the hell is going on?"

"We don't know, Joe. I think this guy is a mental case," Konklin replied. "He seems to have disappeared into la-la land."

"Arjay, Kieyell, move him to the floor so he doesn't fall off that chair. Then meet the lieutenant and me on the other side of the two-way."

As Warner and Konklin left the room, Warner called the EMTs and the department's psychiatrist."

Mayfield and Roitstein joined the captain and the lieutenant.

"Wasn't that strange, having him stand up so we could get him to the floor easier," Roitstein remarked to Mayfield.

"Yeah. Like he's awake and asleep all at the same time. He certainly gives me the creeps."

"Not so much as a body movement or a facial expression," Konklin stated, keeping his eyes on Dole. "It's as though he were a living corpse. What do you make of it, Joe?"

"Did anyone read *Silas Marner* by George Eliot?" Roitstein asked. "If I remember correctly, he went into trances. Maybe this Dole guy has the same problem?"

"I wouldn't venture to guess what his problem is. I was lucky to get ahold of Dr. Leams. He's on his way. What in the hell did you guys say to him, Eddy?"

"Give me a break, Joe. All Kieyell did was answer a question. Dole was fine up to that point."

"What was the question?"

"If he was a suspect for the serial homicides. Kieyell said no."

"Did he come in voluntarily?"

"Yes," Mayfield answered. Roitstein nodded in agreement.

* * *

When the EMTs arrived, Konklin took them into the interrogation room. Dole's vitals were checked. Conferring over a phone with a hospital physician, everyone seemed to be stumped as to Dole's ailment. The physician ordered the EMTs to take Dole to the hospital for a thorough examination.

As they were getting ready to place Dole on a stretcher, Dr. Leams arrived. He stopped the transport, taking full responsibility for Dole. Per Leams's instructions, Dole was seated in a chair facing the table. The EMTs were asked to stand by in the outer office in case they were needed. Konklin led Leams to the observation room where Warner, Mayfield, and Roitstein were waiting.

The four detectives briefed the doctor before he re-entered the room.

"Hello, Jessie. I'm Dr. Leams. How are you feeling today?"

For some unknown reason, Dole responded as if nothing was wrong. "A doctor? Why? Who's sick?"

"No one, Jessie. I just wanted to come in and speak with you. I understand you're being questioned in a serial murder case."

"Yes, for quite a long time now. I'm getting thirsty and tired. If they're through with me, I'd like to go home."

"Do you know what city you live in?"

"Of course. Mt. Pride. Why?"

"Do you know who you are?"

"That's a stupid question."

"Humor me," Leams said.

"My name is Jessie Dole."

"Good. Does it bother you that the detectives think you may be involved in several *homicides*?" Leams emphasized homicides as he looked directly into Dole's eyes. Dole's eyes started turning glassy again. Patting Dole on his knee, Dr. Leams said, "Stay with me, Jessie. Talk to me."

"I'd rather talk to Jamie."

"Who is Jamie?"

"She was real. I know she was real. But Father and Mother told me she was just a figment of my imagination. You believe me, don't you?"

"Okay, so Jamie was a real person. What happened to her?"

"She's in my head. HE killed her."

"Who is HE, Jessie?"

Jessie's head made sudden side-to-side movements, as he appeared to be checking out the room. "HE might be listening. I can't take the chance that HE will hear me."

"Who are you talking about?"

"I see every evil thing that HE does. HE makes me watch."

For the next hour that Dr. Leams got Dole to talk, none of the detectives could believe what they were listening to. When Dr. Leams finally left the interview room, he returned to the observatory window.

"I find this man most interesting. He says he sees what someone is doing, but he did not say anything about hearing voices. Many of the disturbed killers I have worked with often tell me the voices in their heads told them they had to kill. If you want my professional opinion, I believe this man has a lot of psychological problems."

"From what we've heard, I agree," Warner said. "What do you make of all this? Is the guy a psychopath?"

"I cannot honestly say, right off hand. It could be that he is a schizophrenic and has not brought out his other half to talk to me yet."

"That would be the HE that Dole was talking about?" Konklin asked.

"I cannot give you any answers at this point. I believe the best thing to do is to have him committed for clinical observation," Dr. Leams suggested.

"He admitted to being an eyewitness to every crime the serial killer committed," Warner said.

"He even gave you details that only the real murderer would have known," Konklin added.

"In your professional opinion, doctor, will he be able to stand trial?"

"My educated guess is to say yes. He does appear to have all of his faculties. I will let you know more after I have been able to observe him, test him, and ask him more questions. Right now, I want to get him to the hospital."

"We'll notify his wife," Warner said.

"I am assuming," Dr. Leams commented, "after what he said in there that you will be wanting this man under house arrest."

"That's an affirmative with a capital A," Warner admitted. "Is he coherent enough to understand the Miranda?"

"I will go in with you or whomever is placing him under arrest. I will be able to tell by his eyes if he is or is not understanding his rights."

"Lieutenant, would you like the honors."

"I certainly would, Captain."

"I will make sure Jessie Dole's room is well guarded, Detective Warner. And I will keep you posted on his physical and mental state. Don't hesitate to call me if you have any questions."

"I'll do that. Thank you, doctor."

* * *

After Dr. Leams and Dole were gone, the small task group followed Warner back to his office.

"Well, Dr. Watson, you outsmarted old Sherlock," Warner said. "I can't believe I was so wrong in believing in Leo's guilt."

"Hey, Joe, don't beat yourself up. All the evidence pointed to him. I would have been in your corner, too, if I hadn't gotten to personally know Leo."

"Well, you've proved one thing, Eddy. You're certainly worth your salt as a detective. I'm very proud that you proved to me that you could come back to work and do an excellent job. Just as you've done in the past. In fact, even stronger. I imagine the chief won't appreciate eating a little crow for breakfast in the morning." Warner laughed.

Mayfield and Roitstein, who had been sitting quietly by as Warner and Konklin conversed, broke into laugher.

"Hey," Warner said, "a noted response from your two conspirators. The Bowery Boys."

"I can't believe that Lieu was right about the perp's uniform to protect him from blood spatters," Roitstein stated. "Who'd have thought someone could have covered their whole body in black plastic garbage bags and black masking tape. Well, all but the latex gloves on his hands."

"I think I can speak for both of us, Cap. We've really enjoyed working with Lieu," Mayfield said, getting an approving nod from his partner.

"Yeah," Konklin agreed. "I've enjoyed working with them, too. As a matter of fact, all the detectives I have worked with since I've come back to work have been just swell."

"What's this?" Warner asked with a grin. "A change of heart about working with --"

"You don't have to say any more, Joe. I get your gist. Now we need to work on getting a search warrant for Dole's store and residence, getting a court order to confiscate his business records, and, most of all, getting Leo out of jail."

"Slow down, Eddy, or you'll burst a seam."

Warner made a call to the judge for the important documents they needed. Mayfield was sent to the judge's residence to pickup the official papers and return with them to the office.

Once Mayfield returned, Warner sent him and Roitstein, search warrant in hand, to Dole's store to pickup his business records, the carton opener, and whatever else might be used in evidence against Dole. Ferndale and Brown were called in, handed the other search warrant, and sent to Dole's house.

Then the prosecuting attorney was called.

After the third ring, Warner heard, "Hello."

"Good evening, Debra. This is Joe Warner."

"Good heavens, Joe. Don't you guys keep regular working hours?"

"As detectives, we're always working."

"You know I'm joking, of course? There are times I wonder why I decided to follow a law career with all the hours I put in."

"I can understand that. But neither of us would change our paths even if we could. Right?"

"Right. So, what can I do for you?"

"I need to get Leo De Mija released and the charges against him dropped."

"Have you been drinking, Joe?" she asked with a bit of witticism in her voice.

"Sorry to disillusion you, but alcohol has nothing to do with my request. I'm dead serious. We have the wrong man locked up."

Konklin sat by, wiggling in his chair. All he could hear was Warner's part of the conversation. But he was anxious to hear De Mija would soon be a free man.

"Oh, I see. You must have received the CBI report back and that wasn't the murder weapon you found in Leo De Mija's garage. Well, it's not important because we still --"

"Hold on a sec, Debra. I haven't received either the CBI report for the weapon or the FBI report confirming De Mija's blood type. But that doesn't matter now. I have a new suspect. Just over an hour ago, he confessed."

"You have someone who confessed to the murders, and you believe him?"

"Well, he didn't actually confess. He gave detail for detail of each of the murders. No one but the real perp would have known what he described. So, do I believe him? Yes, I'd say so."

"You sound a bit hesitant, Joe. What more is there that you're not telling me?"

"I had to bring our staff psychiatrist, Dr. Leams, in on the case. Our perp might be a schizophrenic."

"Oh, that's just great," Chow replied, not at all happy with the information. "His defense will be to plead insanity. He'll end up getting a few years of mental evaluation — and little psychiatric help — then walk. That's a real bummer."

"I understand how you feel. But my part of this investigation is almost over. How you try the case is your bailiwick. However, we have a lot of evidence against this man to assist you. So, are you going to drop the charges against Leo De Mija?"

"Man, you don't know how hard I've been working to build an airtight case against him. We had enough evidence against De Mija to hang him. Are you absolutely positive that De Mija is innocent?"

"How about ninety-nine percent sure? Will that do?"

"I guess it will have to. One thing, you haven't arrested your new suspect yet, have you?"

"Not officially. But he was read the Miranda"

"Good. You know you and I would both be read the riot act if you arrest a second suspect for the same Murder One charge while the first suspect is still in jail."

"I know. That's why I want to get DeMija out as quickly as possible. How soon can you make that happen?"

"Let's see. Tomorrow is Saturday. The courthouse will be open until noon. Okay, I'll get the paperwork for De Mija's release taken care of first thing in the morning. He should be released by noon or shortly thereafter."

"That's great."

"Boy, talk about cutting things close. A few more days and we would have had Leo already on trial for a crime he didn't commit."

"I know," Joe agreed. "But it's better we found out about his innocence now than later. I don't think I could have lived with myself if I helped put an innocent man away for life, or even worse, condemned him to death."

"It's not that I don't trust your judgment, Joe. But I've never come across something like this before. It's still hard to believe, with all the evidence against him, De Mija isn't guilty of these murders."

"If you were to hear the whole story my lieutenant told me about the coincidences involved concerning De Mija and our new suspect, you would."

"You'll have to make a point in telling me sometime. For my own knowledge, how did you mange to come up with this new suspect?"

"To tell you the truth, I didn't. Eddy Konklin is totally responsible. Eddy always believed in De Mija's innocence. And, while trying to prove it, he found the real perp."

"For Leo De Mija's sake, it's a good thing Eddy stuck to his convictions. Okay, hold on and let me get my legal pad and a ballpoint so I can get the info on this new suspect."

Once Warner had given the ADA all the information she needed to start criminal proceedings against Jessie Dole, he sat back and took a deep breath.

"So," Konklin said with baited breath, "when did she say Leo would be released?"

"Tomorrow, somewhere around noon. I think you should be there when Leo gets the good news. He should know it was you who saved his ass. I also think I owe the man my deepest apology."

"I'd love to be there, Joe, but I don't want to take any bows. I just want him to know that not all of us believed he was guilty."

"Well, I'm hoping he doesn't hold a grudge and that he'll let us reinstate him."

"Look, why don't you go home. I'll wait here for everyone to return, and call you later if anything new develops."

"I have a better idea, Eddy. Since you are the one who's still on the mend, why don't you go home? I'll wait."

"Well, geez. If you want to be stubborn, we'll both wait." Konklin laughed, knowing full well he could not leave even if he wanted to. "How about we make a fresh pot of coffee."

"That's the second best idea you've had today, Eddy."

* * *

When it got to be eleven P.M., Warner called both Mayfield and Ferndale, informing them that he and the lieutenant were calling it a night. Mayfield reported that he and Roitstein would soon be heading back to the office. They had found the tool in question, Dole's business records, and other items of interest. Ferndale and Brown had found some items of interest, but they were still searching. Warner instructed the detectives to lock up their findings in the evidence room when they returned to the precinct.

While Warner had been making his phone calls, Konklin had locked up his office. He was now waiting in the captain's office.

Getting up from his desk and stretching, Warner said, "Come on, big guy, let's go home. I called Jeny and she's got our dinner warming in the oven."

As the two men walked out of the office, Konklin said, "Since I can walk on my own now, I should be able to drive a car. I guess I'll be moving out of your house soon and going back to my place."

"We're going to miss having you there," Warner replied, putting his arm around Konklin's shoulders.

"Well, I have to look on the brighter side, Joe. As comfortable as your home is, it will be nice not to have to run to the bathroom every time I get gastritis."

"Oh, give me a break. If you don't think the gals and I haven't smelled those sneakers you've been letting loose, you're nuttier than a fruitcake," Joe teased, laughing.

"You're pulling my leg again."

"The heck I am. Why just this morning, Jeny mentioned that she wanted to repaint the living room. For some strange reason the walls have turned from off-white to crappy brown since you've been there."

Warner continued to harass his friend in a jovial manner as they headed for home. Konklin was in a super good mood because he had finally cleared Leo's name, and the real snake had been captured. Warner was feeling cheerful because he had his best friend back in good health. They both felt that all was right with the world.

Or was it?

CHAPTER FORTY-FOUR

Warner and Konklin were waiting for De Mija as he was released from jail. Giving Warner the cold shoulder, De Mija walked over and spoke to Konklin.

"My attorney informed me that you are responsible for getting the charges dropped against me," De Mija stated rather smugly.

"Well, I believed in you, Leo. But a few others helped me prove there was another perp in this case," Konklin replied with great humility.

"Leo," Warner said, extending his hand, "I'm happy to hear this all came out okay. Please understand that I was just doing my job. I hope there's no hard feelings."

As De Mija shook his hand, Warner flinched from the pain.

"Of course there are harsh feelings, Capt. Warner. You had *me*, a clean cop, locked up behind steel bars on suspicion of several homicides. It's a shame, as a fellow officer, that you didn't believe in my innocence."

Pulling his hand away from De Mija's grip, Warner said, "Look, Leo, all evidence pointed to you. Again, I apologize for the inconvenience. I'd like to reinstate you and give you your badge back."

"I don't think so," De Mija emphatically stated. "You have dirtied that badge along with my excellent law-enforcement record. As far as I'm concerned, Capt. Warner, you know where you can stick that badge and your apology."

"But Leo, won't you please understand," Konklin interceded, "that all of the evidence was stacked against you? Joe had no other choice but to suspect you."

"No, I don't understand, lieutenant. Now, if you two are quite through, I want to get out of here. The stench is overwhelming."

"Certainly. Keep in touch," Konklin said as he and Warner watched De Mija walk away.

"Man, that guy's got quite a solid handshake when he's hostile. I thought for a minute I was going to pull back a stub. Come on, Eddy, let's get out of here." Warner headed toward the door to exit the building.

Konklin followed a few steps behind him. "Slow down your pace, Joe. I'm doing pretty good, but you're walking too fast for me to keep up." Once Warner slowed down so the two could walk together, Konklin asked, "Did you notice anything strange about Leo?"

"Other than his bad attitude and solid iron-man handshake, no. Why?"

"He was more outspoken and very bold — quite different than I remember him when we worked together. How does a man go from an introvert to an extrovert in a matter of a six weeks in the slammer?"

"I guess jail time could change a lot of personalities from bad to worse, good to bad, or bad to good, Eddy. Let's just hope Leo's personality change is for the better. And he puts this episode of his life behind him."

"Yeah, I certainly hope so for his sake. Hey, I decided I'm going to move back to my place tomorrow."

"At breakfast this morning you said you were moving next weekend. What happened to change your mind so fast?"

"I was all set for next weekend until Jeny said you would be the chief cook and bottle washer for two nights next week while she helped Amandalee with some things." Konklin let out his usual jovial laugh.

"Like I told you before, big guy. My cooking is one heck of a lot better than those raw eggs they served you in the convalescent home. Besides, what do you suppose those things are that Jeny and Amandalee need to tend to?"

"I haven't a notion."

"They're going to be at your place cleaning and stocking your refrigerator with groceries. So when you go home you won't have much to do."

"That's not necessary, Joe."

"It isn't?" Joe laughed. "Obviously you didn't see the state you left your apartment in the day you had your accident. When I went over to get you some clothes, I was shocked. I thought you were neater than that."

"I'm a bachelor. Remember? I only clean if I know someone is coming over, which isn't often. Anyway, Jeny and Amandalee have enough to do. They don't need to be cleaning my apartment. Besides, it will be good for me, physically, to be moving about when I get home. I can't sit all day in the office — then sit when I get home — until the doctor says I'll no longer need therapy on this leg of mine. That reminds me, when can I start back on active duty?"

"We'll talk about it after the doctor gives you a final release."

"So, if I really have to stay another week, what do you say I take you out those two nights for dinner when the girls are gone?"

"And miss out on Joe Warner's hodgepodge delights? No way!"

"What do these delights consist of?"

"Let's just say Saggy would be more than pleased."

CHAPTER FORTY-FIVE

Tuesday morning, Warner had an out-of-town visitor. After a brief introduction between the two men, Warner asked, "So, Mr. Donahay, what can I do for the government today?"

"This is rather awkward, but I actually only wanted directions to an address I'm trying to locate."

Bewildered, Warner asked, "Directions? I don't think I understand."

"As I told you, Capt. Warner, I work with the Social Security Disability Department. I do investigative work, rather like you do. I came to Mt. Pride looking for an SSD recipient. Not being familiar with this area, I got lost. Believe me, even your wonderful city map didn't help me. Anyway, as I was driving around, I noticed your police station. So I stopped in for assistance. While I was explaining my dilemma to the officer at the desk downstairs, a Detective Ferndale was standing there and overheard our conversation."

"You'll have to excuse my ignorance here, Mr. Donahay. But I'm still in the dark as to why you wanted to see me."

"The last name of the party I'm looking for is Dole. When I mentioned that name to the officer, Detective Ferndale suggested I come up here and speak with you. To tell you the truth, I don't know why either."

"Oh, now I understand. We have a Jessie Dole in custody right now. Is that who you are looking for?"

"Why, yes."

"Is he in trouble with the government, too?"

"No, Mr. Dole isn't in any trouble with my department. However, I was able to find out that he still lives in his father's house. Jessie, Jr., that is. That's the address I'm trying to locate. I was hoping the young Dole could tell me the whereabouts of his father."

"His father? I believe he's deceased."

"I thought of the possibility that he was deceased, but I can't seem to find any death records for him. So that's what I need to find out for positive. Do you know where Mr. Dole, Sr., died or where he's buried?"

"That's a rather unusual request. Perhaps you could tell me why you're trying to find him?"

"For a period of two years, Mr. Dole's checks were returned with 'address unknown' written on the envelopes. This was several years ago, but I still need to check it out. If for a fact Mr. Dole is deceased, then I need to delete his name from our records."

The true investigative nose of a detective was coming forth in Warner's questions. "If this all happened years ago, why are you looking for him now?"

"The SSD has file upon file of people to investigate, Capt. Warner, and only a handful of investigators, such as myself. On top of that, papers do fall through the cracks and get lost or misfiled. I wasn't aware of this case until just a few days ago."

"I see. Well, Jessie Dole is, at present, in the hospital. I can't honestly tell you if he would be capable of answering your questions right now."

"We are speaking of Dole, Jr., correct?"

"My guess would be yes."

"Why is he in the hospital?"

"For clinical observation purposes. He appears to be coherent, but I don't know how he would react to questions about his past. I'll give you the name of the doctor who is in charge of his care. Dr. Leams would be a better judge of Jessie Dole's mental state than I am."

"Would you mind telling me why you know so much information about Jessie, Jr.?"

"Not at all. As I told you, Dole is in custody. He's a suspect in a serial killing case."

"My word. Maybe I don't want to go speak with this man if he's that dangerous."

"I wouldn't worry about him attacking you, Mr. Donahay. Dole only attacked abusive parents. Besides, there's a uniformed officer posted right outside his door at the hospital. If you decide to go see him and you're still apprehensive, just ask the officer to go in the room with you."

Warner jotted down Dr. Leams's name and phone number and handed it to Mr. Donahay.

"Thank you, Capt. Warner. I appreciate your valuable information. And I'm sorry to have troubled you."

"Not at all. It was my pleasure. If you don't get the answers you need from Jessie, come on back. I'll try to give you easy directions to his home. Maybe his wife can shed some light on your case."

"I don't think that will be necessary. I have another source to check out first if Jessie can't assist me."

# CONCLUSION

"This corner of your couch is beginning to feel like home," Eddy said after taking a healthy gulp of his Coors.
It should," Joe replied.
"Is this going to be a ritual after each case we solve, Joe?"
Relaxing in his favorite easy chair, Joe laughed. "I guess it should be. It does seem that we end up here having one or two drinks, talking over our last solved case, while Jeny's in the kitchen cooking up something special for our celebration dinner."
"I just hope you aren't celebrating too soon, Dad. Some of your cases have really taken a pretzel-twist at the end."
"Not this time, honey. That so-called pretzel already twisted when Eddy proved De Mija was innocent and Dole was guilty. This one has already ended with a slam-dunk. Our part is done, and the case is closed. It's all up to your colleague now."
Fluffing up an accent pillow, Amandalee approached Eddy. "Slide forward so I can put this pillow behind your back and make you more comfortable."
"I wish you would quit being such a fuss-budget with me."
"You know better than to argue with these two women around here, Eddy. You'd better do as she says or she won't leave you alone."
He leaned forward, allowing Amandalee to place the pillow behind him. Then she sat on the arm of the couch at the opposite end from where Eddy was sitting. "How does it feel to be back at work in full force, Eddy?"
"Since my doctor gave me a clean bill of health, and your father put me back into action, I feel wonderful. Even my heart specialist told me that the old ticker is in great shape. I know I'm repeating myself since I stayed here for so long, but you just can't imagine how difficult it was for me when I was physically and mentally incapacitated. Even though you were all there for me, no one can understand unless they went through the same thing."
"Well, Eddy, the remarkable thing is you made it through that tragedy with flying colors. That's quite an accomplishment for anyone at any age."
"Yes, amazing, isn't it, Joe? My doctor says he wants to write a journal about a man my age healing so remarkably from such a severe accident. Hey, maybe I'll become famous?"
"Heaven forbid. We have a hard time putting up with you now," Joe teased.
"Did you ever decide who is going to be your new partner?" Amandalee

asked after taking a drink of Pepsi.

"All of them. I found out when the chips were down, all the detectives are a great group to work with. I'm sure your father told you that we have two new detectives in the department?"

Looking at her father, she replied, "No, Dad, you didn't tell me. Who moved up from the uniforms?"

"I wanted Officer David Ripley, but he turned in his uniform. He claimed it was because of poor health, but I didn't buy it. I think some of the other uniforms found out he was the one who sparked the flame that made De Mija the suspect in our *Black Tulip* case. So they gave him a bad time. Ripley couldn't take the heat, so he quit. It really --"

"Holy cow, Dad. I just asked a simple question and you haven't even answered it," she said, smiling.

"Sorry. I promoted Al Kaufman and Sylvia Sooner."

Eddy began laughing.

"What's so funny, big guy?"

"Have you heard what Sooner's nickname is?"

"No."

"Stinky. Isn't that a funny handle for a cop — especially a female?"

"Oh, I don't know. There have been several times I was almost tempted to give you that nickname," he quipped.

"Me, too," Amandalee confessed while laughing.

"Come on, you two. It's not polite to pick on your guest."

Amandalee dashed over to give Eddy a hug. "In this house, you're not a guest. You're family, Eddy. That's why we can tease you. We love you, you know?"

"I love all of you, too, honey. Now go back and sit down before you have me in sentimental tears."

"Dad, I don't think I know either one of the two new detectives," Amandalee admitted. "Oh, wait. Isn't Kaufman the guy you wanted to promote last time instead of De Mija?"

"Yes."

"I remember you telling Mom and me about him. But I don't recall you ever mentioning Sooner."

"She's been around the precinct almost as long as Kaufman has," Eddy replied, adding to the conversation. "I've been training her. And let me tell you, she's one sharp lady."

"Umm!" Amandalee uttered, grinning. "Is she pretty, Eddy?"

"Geez, girl, you're as bad as your father." Eddy smiled, then took a drink of beer.

"Well, it's your fault for being such a good-looking, eligible bachelor."

"Oh, right, Joe," Eddy retorted. "Let's get back to the reason we're here tonight."

Amandalee kicked off her shoes and placed her feet on the cushion of the couch. "Oh, please do. I want to hear all the final details."

"Doesn't your mother need help in the kitchen?" Joe asked.

"No, she said she would yell if she did. Now quit stalling, and give."

"How come you don't know all the details? Don't you work with Debra Chow?" Eddy asked.

"Yes. But we've both been too busy to discuss each other's cases. So go ahead, Dad. Fill me in."

"Okay, okay. First of all, you know we cleared Ellie Smither?"

"Of course I do. Get to the part where you dropped Leo De Mija from your suspect list and started concentrating on Jessie Dole."

"Where do you want me start?"

"Well, did you ever hear from the Social Security Agent again?"

"Yes. When he couldn't get any valuable information out of Jessie Dole, he went in search of Jessie's twin."

Surprised with the information, Amandalee asked, "Twin? What twin?"

"I was as shocked as you are when I heard Jessie had a twin. After getting no help from Jessie, and not being able to locate Jamie Dole, Donahay returned to my office for assistance. Evidently, many years ago, Dole, Sr., applied for two more dependants on his SSD income. Since Jessie, Sr., had to list the dependents' birth dates, the information was kept in his file. Then we discovered our own information that verified Donahay's records. Do you remember when I told you that Ferndale and Brown found a strongbox in Dole's house with a large brown sealed envelope in it?"

"Vaguely," she admitted.

"In that envelope was a birth certificate for another child, Jamie Dole, born on the same date as Jessie Dole was born."

"Is Jamie a girl or a boy?"

"We didn't know at first. The baby's sex was blacked out on the birth certificate."

"That's strange."

"We thought so, too."

"So where is this twin?"

"Slow down, Mandy. Give me a chance to explain." Joe laughed.

"That's why she makes a good prosecuting attorney," Eddy said, throwing in his two cents worth with a laugh.

"Okay, Dad, I'm sorry. Go ahead and explain. I'll try to refrain from so many questions."

"After Donahay, Eddy and I compared notes — that's where Eddy stepped in." Turning his attention to Eddy, Joe said, "Okay, big guy, your turn."

"You see, Amandalee, I had come in contact with Jessie a couple of times before he was arrested. He became rather friendly toward me when he found out I was a friend of Leo's. Due to this fact, your dad and Dr. Leams thought maybe I could get some straight answers from Jessie. So, I went to the hospital to talk to him. Of course I found out more than I bargained for ...." Eddy paused to quench his thirst.

"Jessie proceeded to tell me, to his recollection, that his parents got rid of Jamie when they were very young. In the back of his mind, Jessie remembered Jamie, but he had no idea what had happened to his sibling. And, due to the abusive way his parents treated him, he was always afraid to ask. Then he went into some weird tangent about his twin being dead. Jessie kept saying, 'He killed her, but she still lives in silence.'"

"So, Jamie was, is a girl?" Eddy nodded. "Why did you say you got more than you bargained for?"

"When he was lucid again, Jessie told me that his parents were buried in his back yard under his garden. A little side note here. Jessie was growing black tulips over their grave. Anyway, Jessie claimed the person he sees in his dreams killed his parents with a butcher knife and instructed him to bury them. That's what cinched our murder case against Jessie. When the FBI report came back inconclusive on the carton opener, we still didn't have a murder weapon. We also had no eyewitness that could place Jessie in any of the crime scene neighborhoods. Just before that, the DA — your esteemed boss — felt they might not have enough physical or trace evidence to prosecute him. Once we got a court order, we exhumed the bodies. Or, I should say, the remains of the Doles. When we did, we also found the knife they were killed with. The prints on the knife matched Jessie's prints. Thankfully I had gotten his prints when I started my investigation of him. That was all your boss needed for the DA to have a rock-solid case against him."

"So, he won't be standing trial for the serial homicides, only for the murders of his parents?" Amandalee stated with a question in her voice.

"Sad but true," Eddy admitted.

"But what about the blood and skin evidence that was found in some of the victims' homes?"

"Well, Debra is still waiting for the CBI reports on the blood from the carpet, and the skin and blood tissue that was discovered under the one victim's fingernails. As soon as they get their comparative test of those samples and Jessie's DNA concluded, they will forward their results to her. The CBI is so backlogged with lab testing it isn't even funny. We were lucky to get such fast results on the two carton openers we sent them. So, until such time as those results are known, Debra Chow is basing her whole case against Dole on his parents' murders."

"Did you ever find out what really happened to his twin?"

Joe took over the conversation. "Yes and no. The sealed envelope we found at Dole's house also held information that makes us think the twin was sold on the black market. After searching through years of records, we discovered Jamie was never reported as a missing person and there were never any adoption papers on her. Nor did we ever find a death certificate for her. Since it was never really important to our case, we dropped the investigation as to Jamie Dole's whereabouts. For all we know, Jessie could have killed his sister and buried her."

"We also figure that's why he told me, 'He killed her, but she still lives in silence.' Oh, and we forgot to tell you about Jessie's journal. In his own hand, he confessed to murdering his parents."

"A handwritten confession? That's fantastic. Now I understand why it's a wrap on the case against him."

"Not quite," Joe stated.

"What? Why?"

"Dr. Leams brought in an expert witness from back east. This expert, Dr. Von Borch, specializes in the studies of twins raised in two separate homes. According to him, there is a remote possibility that one twin can experience the exact same thing that the other twin is actually going through. The doctor believes the journal entry Eddy is referring to was written when Jessie truly believed he became his twin."

Shaking her head, Amandalee said, "So, Dad, now you've really confused me. Does that help or hinder the so-called rock-solid case against him?"

"At first we were worried. Due to the good doctor's expert opinion we decided, unanimously, that his information wouldn't help Debra's case. In fact, Debra's hoping the journal won't even be brought up during the trial since it could be viewed as being in his favor once Von Borch testifies in court – helping to prove Jessie's innocence. It got a little hairy for a while when we thought Jessie might have an out. However, this was all before we found out about the grave in his backyard. Yes, we have a rock-solid case. And, yes, I know a jury will convict Jessie Dole for his parents' murders."

"Hey, Joe, I hate to butt in," Eddy said, "but it's getting mighty dry here."

Amandalee got to her feet. "I'll go get you another beer. But I don't think you or Dad should have any more booze."

"Mandy, that isn't nice," Joe reprimanded her in a nice way. "We've only had one drink each."

"Yeah," Eddy boastfully agreed. "We're allowed two, at least, since we're not on call tonight."

"Well, I have good reason." She laughed. "You two are full of it with this outlandish story you're feeding me. I can't believe I'm sitting here listening. Man, you really had me going there for a while."

Eddy replied, "You've lost me, Amandalee. Which part of the story don't you believe?"

"The part that one twin experiences what the other twin is going through."

"It's true," Eddy defended. "At least that's what Dr. Von Borch said. He believes one twin can actually hear, see, and feel what the other one does. If one twin is cut, the other one can bleed. The doctor's credentials on such studies are quite extraordinary."

"Eddy's right, honey. No one could make up something this crazy. Here," Joe said, holding out his glass. "How about a refill for your old dad?"

* * *

Once the men had their drinks, and Amandalee was again seated, she had a few more questions. "Okay, now that you've filled me in on the details about Jessie Dole, what about Leo De Mija?"

"What about him?"

"Well, Dad, you've left a gaping hole in my head. Did his alibis ever check out, and what happened with the FBI report on his blood sample?"

"Again I have to answer you with a yes and no. When we questioned De Mija's wife after his arrest, both Debra Chow and all of us working the case thought Mrs. De Mija was lying through her teeth when she backed up De Mija's alibis for the first two homicides. The night of the third homicide, De Mija was at an emergency clinic getting his cut hand tended to. Now, the nurse at the clinic vouched for De Mija being there. But she couldn't swear to the exact time.

"As for De Mija's in-laws, it appears they couldn't verify his alibi for the night of the last homicides because they had already left on their vacation. So, at the time, only De Mija's wife was his alibi. But as you well know, unless she wanted to, Mrs. De Mija did not have to testify. Then of course, thanks to Eddy, things took a huge turn. Since we picked up Dole, and De Mija was released, we never bothered probing any further into De Mija's alibis." Joe stopped to take a drink, then continued. "Again, because DeMija was exonerated, we never followed through with his DNA tests."

"But I thought you had already sent a sample of his blood to the FBI Crime Lab?"

"We did. When De Mija was no longer our suspect, I contacted the lab and left a message that we no longer needed the DNA report on him. Instead, we had Saggy send them a sample of Jessie's blood to test."

"I remember you telling me you never found the murder weapon. Right?"

"That's right, honey. Both of the tools we found, from De Mija and from Dole, fit the cuts on the victims' throats. However, as I told you, neither could be proved to be the murder weapon."

"Did you ever find out what kind of a weapon or tool was used to bludgeon the one victim to death?"

"Yes, it was a crowbar. Just like Eddy had guessed. The only problem there was that Jessie doesn't remember where the person in his — quote unquote, dreams — put it. And, to make matters worse, we never found it."

"You know," Eddy said, "Leo sure turned out to be one heck of a nice guy."

"Oh, you're still in contact with him?" Amandalee asked.

"No, not really. I was shopping at one of the strip malls a couple of nights ago, and ran into Mrs. Dole. I had met her when we brought her in for further questioning about her husband's so-called nightmares. After I asked her how she was holding up, she told me that Leo had contacted her."

Concerned as he always was for a perp's family member, Joe said, "You didn't tell me that. So, is Mrs. Dole doing all right?"

"Not really, Joe. She still maintains that her husband is innocent of everything. But what she told me really made me realize what kind of a compassionate person Leo is."

"How's that?"

"Right after Dole was arrested and booked for murder, and Leo was released, he telephoned Mrs. Dole. Leo wanted to see if there was anything he could do for her or her daughter before he and his family moved away from Mt. Pride."

"So, he left town in a big hurry, huh? I can't say as I blame him," Joe replied. "Getting out of Mt. Pride where your name has been dragged through the mud is probably the best thing for him to do. I sure feel badly about that."

When the telephone rang, Amandalee jumped to her feet to answer it. When she returned to the living room, she said, "Dad, that was Debra on the phone. She's on her way over here."

"Did she say why?"

"Only that she had something very important to talk to you about. She's coming directly from the office."

"Go tell Mom we have another dinner guest coming. Then set an extra place setting at the table."

"Sure, Dad."

"Joe, are you sure Jeny won't mind another guest?" Eddy asked.

"Come on, you know Jeny. She cooks enough food for an army and loves company."

Joe and Eddy chitchatted until Debra arrived. Amandalee brought her into the living room.

"Hi, Debra. Come on in and have a seat. Would you care for a cold drink?" Joe offered.

"Hi, Joe. Hi, Eddy. If you two are standing on my account, please sit down. Amandalee didn't tell me your were having a dinner party until about ten seconds ago. I feel terribly embarrassed about intruding."

"Don't give it a second thought," Joe said. "We're happy to have you join us. Amandalee is our drink hostess. What would you like? We have sodas, juices, beer, wine and hard alcohol."

Amandalee spoke up. "You're way off base, Dad." She smiled. "Debra drinks water."

"Oh, is that right? Well, we have seltzer water, tap water, ice water, fish tank water, dishwater, tub water, toilet water and bottled spring water. Which one would you prefer?"

"Dad! Don't mind him, Debra. Dad loves to pull people's chains. I'll go get you a bottled water. Have a seat and tell them why you're here."

"Yes, please sit down, Debra. I can't stand much longer." Eddy was teasing and serious at the same time.

"I'm sorry, Eddy," she said, taking a seat in an empty chair. "It's so seldom I've been treated like a lady, I had forgotten gentlemen don't sit until the woman does. I believe women's lib rather spoiled the good old-fashioned manners."

"Hear, hear," Eddy responded.

As Eddy and Joe returned to their seats, Joe asked, "I have a terrible feeling you're bringing us some bad news, Debra. What is it?"

"I don't even know where to begin."

"Try the beginning," Eddy said.

Amandalee entered the room, placing a glass of ice and a bottle of water on the table next to Debra.

"Thank you."

"You're welcome." Amandalee took her place back on the arm of the couch. "What did I miss?"

"Nothing. Debra was just about to tell us why she's here."

"Please don't take this wrong because I believe the whole unit at the 15th are excellent when it comes to investigative work. However, a private investigator isn't as restricted as to where he goes or who he talks to."

Joe asked, "You're telling us the DA hired a PI?"

"Well, with his permission, I did."

"So, did you find out anymore than we did?"

"Lots." Debra informed Joe, Eddy, and Amandalee of the long, drawn-out story about Jessie's twin, Jamie, and his life growing up, part of the time as a girl. "Furthermore, as identical twins, Jessie and Jamie don't have the same fingerprints. But, they do have the exact same DNA. I did a bit of research. The University of Minnesota's Center for Twin and Adoption Research, founded by Thomas J. Bouchard, Ph.D. is the largest, ongoing study of separated twins in the world. The information I read on their studies is absolutely fascinating. Now, before you ask, I've already confirmed the DNA information with Dr. Von Borch."

"Holy Mary, Mother …!" Joe blurted out. "We never got one set of the perp's prints from any of the crime scenes. Only DNA. So now what do we do?"

"Will the real perp please stand up?" Eddy muttered under his breath.

"What a terrible life to live having to pretend you're a girl when you're really a boy," Amandalee said.

"Well, did your PI ever find Jamie Dole?"

"No, Joe. But I'm sure I have. Have any of you put two and two together yet?" Debra asked.

"About?" Joe raised his eyebrows.

"Do any of you play around with anagrams?"

"I do," Amandalee said. "Why?"

"If we had time, I'd give you one to figure out. But I'll tell you since anagrams are a hobby of mine. I was playing around with Jamie Dole's name before I called to come over here this evening. Then, oops, there it was staring me in the face. Jamie Dole turns into Leo De Mija."

Joe pounded his fist on the arm of the chair. "No wonder Jessie and Leo are so much alike. All those coincidences make sense now."

"But, Debra, what about their looks?" Eddy asked. "We know Leo had constructive surgery, but he had to know Jessie was his twin."

"First off, Leo never had any accident. He had his face changed on purpose along with his name change. According to his plastic surgeon, since he had to pretend to be a girl most of his life, he wanted the change before entering college. That way no one would recognize and chastise him for being a girl all through school, then changing to a boy in college.

"Now to answer your question. I asked Von Borch and Leams the same question. According to both of them, Leo had to know Jessie was his twin. I believe he used that information to get away with the perfect crime. He knew full well his twin brother, Jessie, would be blamed for the murders. But he also knew no one could prove it beyond a shadow of a doubt without fingerprints left at any of the crime scenes."

"So, Jessie was actually seeing Leo or Jamie committing these crimes while he was sleeping, just as he said?"

"I don't understand the whole thing, but it is something like reading his twins thoughts."

Amandalee asked, "Like, telepathic?"

"It has to be more than telepathic," Joe said. "Because according to Jessie, in his mind he actually saw the murders being committed. And he had actual scars and claw marks that he bled from."

"Any other surprises for us, Debra?" Eddy asked.

"Well, just a bit of news I received late this afternoon. Leo took his family and moved out of the country."

While Debra filled her glass from the bottle of water, and took a drink, Joe said, "Eddy just told us he heard De Mija was moving away from Mt. Pride, but not out of the county."

"When did you find out all this information?" Eddy asked.

"About an hour before I called here. I knew Joe would want to hear this new information as soon as possible. I was delighted to hear you were here, too, Eddy."

"And you were right," Joe admitted. "Is there anything else to knock us off our pedestals?"

"Oh, I almost hate to tell you, Joe. I'm so sorry you feel that way."

"I'm half kidding and half serious. But please, Debra, lay it all on us. We're going to have to go back to the drawing board anyway to find out which of the twins is really the guilty party."

"Well, the PI went snooping around De Mija's property. Once again, I know your detectives are excellent investigators, Joe. But this PI is the best in his field. He found a carton opener — bloodstained on the handle and on the blade — and crowbar in, of all places, a drainpipe connected to the garage. And, after sifting through the ashes of the burn-pit by the garage, he discovered minute pieces of some black and clear type plastic materials. They will be sent to the FBI Crime Lab for testing. After what you discovered in your investigation, I think the particles will be proven to be pieces of black plastic bags and latex gloves."

"Told you, Dad," Amandalee said. "There's always one last twist to the pretzel in practically every case you and Eddy investigate."

"Joe, are you thinking what I'm thinking?"

"I certainly am, Eddy. Our real snake slithered out of our hands."

About the Author:

A published author of adult and children's books, and an award-winning poet, writing has been Kam's hobby since childhood. To date, Kam has had four full-length mystery novels published (one as a ghost writer) by Global Authors Publications; and three ebooks published by Blue Leaf Publishing. Paperbacks include: *Have No Mercy*; *Black Rosebud: Have No Mercy II*; *Black Lily: Have No Mercy III*; and *Stitchers and Bitchers*. E-books include: *The Dawg Who saved Christmas*; *Dawg Eyes still Top Dog*; and *Dawg catches Rat*.

Read the fantastic reviews and purchase copies of Kam's paperbacks on line at Amazon.com, GlobalAuthorsPublications.com and BarnesandNoble.com,. Or, go to your nearest Hastings Book and Video store. For purchase of Kam's e-books, go on line to BlueLeafPub.com and FictionWise.com.

WHAT'S NEW? Look for Kam's upcoming fully illustrated print work. Designed for the child who loves picture books, "Princess Annado Tandy's Versery-Rhymes" will take readers into a fantasyland. Illustrated by award-winning author, T.C. McMullen, "Annado" will be released in late 2007 through Global Authors Publications.

Also, look for Kam — and husband, Bobby's — non-fiction contribution in Dorothy Thompson's novel, *Romancing the Soul*.

Printed in the United States
141074LV00003B/33/A